P9-DYA-197

YOU AND THE LAW

Debra Goldentyer, J.D.
and
Visual Education Corporation
Princeton, New Jersey

South-Western Publishing Co.

Managing Editor: Robert E. Lewis
Production Editor: Joseph P. Powell III, Nancy Shockey
Associate Director/Design: Darren Wright
Associate Director/Photo Editing: Devore M. Nixon
Associate Photo Editor/Stylist: Linda Ellis
Marketing Manager: Donald H. Fox

Copyright © 1993

by SOUTH-WESTERN PUBLISHING CO.

Cincinnati, Ohio

ALL RIGHTS RESERVED

The text of this publication, or any part thereof, may not be reproduced or transmitted in any form or by any means, electronic or mechanical, including photocopying, recording, storage in an information retrieval system, or otherwise, without the prior written permission of the publisher.

ISBN: 0-538-61467-6

3 4 5 6 7 Ki 98 97 96 95

Printed in the United States of America

Library of Congress Cataloging-in-Publication Data

Goldentyer. Debra, 1960-
    You and the law / Debra Goldentyer and Visual Education
Corporation.
        p. cm.
    Includes index.
    ISBN 0-538-61467-6
    1. Law—United States—Popular works. I. Visual Education
Corporation. II. Title.
KF387.G64 1992
349.73—dc20
(347.3)   92-12063
                                                                         CIP
                                                                          AC

Contents

Introduction

You and the Law is an introduction to personal, practical law. This textbook is designed to prepare students to recognize and understand how the law works in their communities and throughout the country. It shows students how the law strives to promote fairness, equal justice, and individual rights so that they will understand the value of acting as responsible citizens. The aim of *You and the Law* is to give students a working knowledge of the law—to help them avoid legal problems and show them how to handle problems of this type if they occur.

One of the main purposes of law-related education and of this textbook is to provide students with an understanding of the legal system of the United States. The text discusses the protections the legal system affords its citizens and explains what the system expects from people. When a law is presented, it is discussed in connection with a case study illustrating how the law affected a particular individual. By studying the situations that arise when people become involved with the law, students understand the practical application of the legal process—how the law works in everyday life.

Legal issues that are of broad interest and concern, such as the rights of minorities and privacy issues such as abortion and random drug testing, are presented in an evenhanded, nonjudgmental way—offering teachers and students a forum for open and informed discussion.

You and the Law is meant to give students a working knowledge of practical, personal law. It should not, however, be used as a substitute for professional legal advice for specific legal problems.

Text Organization

You and the Law is divided into 6 units containing 19 chapters. Unit 1 explains constitutional law. Chapter 1 explains why laws are necessary and describes the different kinds of laws in the United States. The chapter focuses on the U.S. Constitution as the basis of all law in the United States. The chapter also briefly outlines the divisions of government, the lawmaking process, and the court system. Chapter 2 explains the basic freedoms and rights that are granted to every individual in the United States under the Constitution and discusses how the courts decide whether a law is constitutional. Chapter 3 explains the rights that are granted under the Constitution to individuals who become involved with the criminal justice system.

Unit 2 discusses criminal law. In chapter 4, students learn about the elements of a crime, about the different degrees of a crime, and about some of the main types of crimes. Chapter 5 discusses the steps of the procedure followed in the criminal justice system, as well as services available to crime victims. Chapter 6 discusses the special justice system that has been established to help children who require the help of the law. The rights of juveniles are also discussed.

Unit 3 explains two major areas of civil law: torts and contracts. Chapter 7 gives a brief explanation of the purpose of civil law and the procedures that are followed when two people have a dispute. Chapter 8 focuses on torts: the purpose and procedures of tort law and the rights and responsiblities of individuals when injury or damage occurs. Chapter 9 discusses the basics of contracts law: what a contract is, how it is formed, and how it is enforced. The chapter also discusses the rights and duties of the parties to a contract.

Unit 4 explores family law issues. Chapter 10 discusses the laws governing marriage and the rights and duties of couples before and during marriage. It also includes a discussion of the rights of unmarried partners under the law. Chapter 11 discusses the responsibilities that parents have to provide for their children. Adoption, innovative conception techniques that affect legal parenthood, and child abuse and child neglect are also discussed. Chapter 12 discusses separation and divorce, including the financial consequences and child custody issues. Chapter 13 discusses the legal implications of dying without a will, how to make a will, and how to make sure your wishes will be carried out if you become incompetent.

Unit 5 discusses several practical legal issues that affect people every day: as employees, as consumers, as home renters or homeowners, and as tax-payers. Chapter 14 discusses individual rights of employees as they apply for a job, while they are on the job, and when they leave a job. Chapter 15 explains the legal protections offered to consumers, what it means to buy on credit, the legal protections offered to borrowers and creditors, and the legal results of not paying back a loan. Chapter 16 explains the rights and duties of landlords and tenants and the process involved in buying a home. Also discussed in this chapter are housing programs for low-income people. Chapter 17 explains the legal right of government to collect taxes, along with the types of taxes that are collected and the way in which they are collected. The main focus of this chapter is the procedure for collecting individual income tax and the responsibilities and rights of income tax payers.

Unit 6 explains how to work within the legal system if you need a lawyer or have to go to court. Chapter 18 explains what a lawyer's role is, how to find one, and how to be sure to get the best representation from an attorney. The chapter also discusses alternatives to hiring a lawyer. Chapter 19 explains the procedures that are followed when a case goes to trial. Pretrial and trial procedures and rules and the roles of each person in the courtroom are discussed.

Learning Aids

You and the Law offers many features to help students understand each of the law-related concepts presented in the text.

- ■ *Objectives.* At the beginning of each chapter there is a list of the main ideas discussed in that chapter.
- ■ *Case Study.* Each chapter opens with a real court case that illustrates an important legal issue that is to be presented in the chapter.

- *Legal Terms.*   Many terms in the text are unique to the study of law or are used in a way that may be unfamiliar to students. All such terms are highlighted in bold print when they are defined in the text. They are defined again in the Glossary at the back of the book.
- *Review Questions.*   After every main head within the chapter, questions are asked to reinforce what students have learned in that section.
- *Chapter Review.*   At the end of each chapter, the main concepts from the chapter are summarized and ten of the legal terms are reviewed. In the sections called Applying the Law and Case Studies, students are asked questions about real and hypothetical cases. The purpose of these questions is to test the students' ability to relate a point of law or point of fact from the chapter to a practical situation.
- *Features.*   Three types of one-page features appear throughout the text, one in each chapter. The Viewpoints feature presents opposing sides of timely issues such as gun control, adoption record laws, and abortion. The Latest in the Law feature discusses the current status of state and federal law in regard to issues such as homelessness, parental leave, and the use of cameras in the courtroom. A third feature presents careers in the law.

Acknowledgments

Writing a book of this scope is an enormous task, one that I could not possibly have done alone. Many people contributed their time and talent to make this book possible. I'm grateful for their assistance and feel fortunate to have had the opportunity to work with them.

I'd like to give special thanks to the people who researched and wrote the chapters on areas of law I know little about. I am indebted to Katharine B. Soper, J.D., Ph.D., executive legal editor and author at the Institute of Continuing Legal Education, Ann Arbor, Michigan, for writing Chapter 10 (Marriage Issues) and Chapter 12 (Separation and Divorce). Katharine also cowrote Chapter 17 (Paying Taxes) with Gary Rogow, a certified public accountant and tax partner in the Ann Arbor firm of Rogow & Loney. I'd also like to thank Nancy Lasher, J.D., instructor of legal studies at Middlesex County College in New Jersey. She provided background research, outlines, and sources for ten chapters.

I'm grateful to Cindy Mooney for putting together the Student Workbook, the testing material, and the Teacher's Resource Book. In doing so, Cindy helped me make sure I'd said what I meant to say.

I am especially grateful to Susan Garver, Senior Project Director at Visual Education Corporation. She edited my words, helped me sort my thoughts, and held my hand when things got tough. Susan also wrote Chapter 1 (The Constitution and Lawmaking).

Finally, I want to thank my husband and partner, Mark Schaeffer, the only person who can understand my words and translate them into a language that other people can understand.

Debra Goldentyer, J.D.

Unit 1

The Constitution And The Law

Chapter 1

The Constitution and Lawmaking

Chapter Objectives When you have read this chapter, you should be able to:

- ■ Explain the need for laws.

- ■ Describe the different kinds of laws in the United States.

- ■ Explain the importance of the U.S. Constitution in American law.

- ■ Explain the legal responsibilities of the three branches of the federal government.

- ■ Explain legislative lawmaking at the federal, state, and local levels.

- ■ Discuss the federal and state court systems and the authority of the different courts.

Case Study

New Jersey v. T.L.O., 469 U.S. 325 (1985).

On March 7, 1980, a teacher in a New Jersey high school found two ninth graders smoking in a school lavatory. Because smoking was a violation of school rules, the teacher took the two girls to the principal's office. One girl admitted she had been smoking. The other girl, identified in court papers as T.L.O., denied it. (The girl's name wasn't used because she was a minor.) The assistant vice principal demanded to look through T.L.O.'s purse, where he found a pack of cigarettes. But that wasn't all he found.

As he was removing the cigarettes, the assistant vice principal noticed a pack of cigarette rolling papers. He knew that these papers are often used by people who smoke marijuana. He believed that he might find more evidence of drug use in T.L.O.'s purse, so he continued his search. Besides finding marijuana, he found empty plastic bags, a list of students who owed T.L.O. money, and other evidence that T.L.O. was selling drugs. The student was then charged by the police with delinquency under New Jersey state law.

In juvenile court, where T.L.O.'s case was tried, her lawyer argued that the evidence of drug dealing should not be admitted during the trial because it had been obtained illegally. The lawyer stated that T.L.O.'s rights had been violated under the Fourth Amendment to the U.S. Constitution. According to this amendment, or addition, to the Constitution, a person's property cannot be searched without a warrant (prior approval from a judge). The school officials did not have a warrant when they searched T.L.O.'s purse. But without the evidence found during that search, the prosecutor could not prove the state's case against T.L.O.

However, there are certain exceptions to the Fourth Amendment rule in which searches without a warrant are legal. The judge at the trial had to decide whether the search of T.L.O.'s purse was one of those exceptions. To do this, he had to decide whether the Fourth Amendment's freedom from unreasonable searches applies in a school situation. The judge ruled that school officials can search a student without a warrant if they have good reason to suspect the student of breaking school rules or of committing a crime. The judge found T.L.O. guilty.

In the United States, the party who loses has the right to ask a higher court to review a lower court's decision in the hope of having the decision overturned. T.L.O. and her lawyer did this, but the higher court agreed that the search was legal. T.L.O.'s lawyer then went to the state's highest court. There the decision of the two lower courts was reversed. The court said that the items from the purse should not have been used as evidence against T.L.O. because the search was unreasonable.

However, when it comes to questions involving the U.S. Constitution, state courts are not the final authority. The prosecutor who had lost in the appeal to New Jersey's highest court asked the U.S. Supreme Court to make the final determination in this case. The Supreme Court is the highest court in the United States.

As all courts do when a person's rights are in conflict with the law, the Supreme Court applied a balancing test. The Court weighed the rights of the student against the need of the school to keep order. The Court said that students have considerable rights under the Fourth Amendment. However, teachers could not keep order in schools if they had to obtain warrants before searching students who were causing trouble. After weighing these issues, the Supreme Court determined that the search was reasonable and therefore legal.

T.L.O. had a responsibility not to break the laws of her state by using and dealing drugs. The officials in her school and the law enforcement officials of the state had a responsibility not to violate T.L.O.'s rights as a citizen. These two concepts—the rights and responsibilities of citizens and government—are the foundation of the legal system in this country.

In this book you are going to learn a lot about practical, personal law in the United States. What happens if you are accused of breaking the law? What happens if someone takes you to court because of a personal disagreement? How does the system work? What is the best way to defend yourself or to get what you think is right? These are important questions, and a knowledge of the law will help you answer them.

First, however, this chapter will raise the following questions: What exactly is the law? Why does it exist? Who decides what it should say? To answer these questions, we have to look at our system of government because one of the duties of government is to make laws. We also have to look into human nature because ideas of and feelings about fairness and injustice, which lead to the making of laws, are deeply ingrained in all of us.

LAW IN OUR SOCIETY

Laws are rules that help communities maintain order and that protect the rights of individuals. These rules tell people what is right and wrong behavior. Ideas of right and wrong are based on the moral and ethical beliefs of the community. Because not everyone's idea of right and wrong is the same, the people of the community choose leaders who make the laws for the group. In our democratic form of government, the majority decides who will be chosen. It is the job of lawmakers to uphold the will of the majority while protecting the rights of the minority. Ideally, laws are fair to all people and clear enough to be understood by the average citizen. In reality, not all laws meet these requirements. That is why the government has built in safeguards. For instance, an unfair law can be overturned.

Illustration 1-1 Without laws, people could drive at any speed they wanted, which could be unsafe for everyone.

Laws are made at every level of community: local, state, and federal (national). Values and needs vary from community to community and from time period to time period. Therefore, laws are different in different communities and also change over time.

Why do we have laws? Why can't people decide for themselves how they should act? You can probably answer these questions yourself. If each person decided for himself or herself what was right and wrong behavior, there would be chaos. Without law, a customer could just take an item from a store without paying for it. People would be able to drive at any speed they wanted and on whichever side of the road they wanted. Government leaders could throw people in jail without cause. Banks and other lending institutions would be able to charge as much interest on a loan as they wanted. As you can see, we need laws for our protection. We also need laws to guide us in our actions.

Kinds of Laws

In your life, you will have to follow the laws of your local community, your state, and the nation. These laws have many sources and are enacted for many purposes. The sources of law include constitutions, statutes, court decisions, and administrative regulations. Laws are made for the purposes of handling disputes between individuals and of dealing with criminal activities.

Constitutional Law **Constitutions** are legal documents that explain the powers and limits of government and list the freedoms and rights of the people. The United States has a national constitution, and each state has a constitution that is modeled on the national one.

Statutory Law A law that is enacted by a legislative, or lawmaking, body is a **statute**. Our national lawmaking body is the U.S. Congress. Laws passed by Congress apply to the entire country. State legislatures enact state laws, and local legislative bodies, such as city councils, make local laws. Statutes can be changed or repealed if they are out of date or become unnecessary.

Court Decisions Starting in the eleventh century in England, the king or queen chose judges to resolve disputes between neighbors and to punish people who had done harm. From the judges' decisions, a series of rules based on general custom was developed. This body of law based on judges' decisions is called **common law**. Other judges then applied the rules to cases they were deciding, modifying the rules as they saw fit to reflect the changing values of people over time. To prevent too much uncertainty and unfairness, however, judgments made in earlier cases were written down. These cases established a **precedent**. It was accepted that unless the argument against doing so was very compelling, precedent should be followed.

Much law in the United States today is based on English common law. When there is no statute to cover a particular situation or when a law is not clear, the precedents established under common law are used by the courts to decide a case. In many cases, statutes are also based on common law.

Today the major role of judges is to interpret and apply existing statutes. Even though there are many laws on the books at both the federal and state levels, sometimes it's not clear which law applies in a particular case. When courts decide such cases, they examine the facts of the case before them and review precedents. Precedents show how previous similar cases were handled. Most of these cases are collected and published so that lawyers and judges can refer to them.

Administrative Law   Administrative law is made and enforced by government agencies. These agencies are set up by legislatures to execute, or carry out and enforce, laws that the legislatures have passed. Because of the work they do, the agencies are usually part of the executive branch of government. Once the agencies are set up, they issue rules and orders needed to carry out the statutes passed by lawmakers. These rules and regulations have the force of law.

At the federal level, these agencies are created by Congress. Top agency officials are appointed by the President, with the approval of the Senate. Some agencies are part of major departments within the executive branch. For example, the Internal Revenue Service (IRS), which is the federal tax collection agency, is part of the Department of the Treasury. The IRS carries out and enforces the federal tax laws passed by Congress.

Sometimes Congress sets up an independent agency to enforce laws it has passed. For example, Congress set up the Environmental Protection Agency in 1970 to enforce the federal antipollution laws.

State and local governments have also set up agencies to enforce and administer laws at those levels. For example, state agencies administer state laws relating to health care programs, public school attendance, and working conditions.

Civil and Criminal Laws   Laws differ not only in their origin but also in their purpose. The legal system includes both civil and criminal law. **Criminal law** defines crimes and spells out punishments of fines or imprisonment for violators. **Civil law** deals with issues not covered by criminal law, including marriage, divorce, business contracts, civil rights, and housing.

REVIEW QUESTIONS

1. Why do we need laws?
2. What are the four main sources of law in the United States?
3. What is common law, and what are its origins?

THE BASIS OF OUR LAWS: THE U.S. CONSTITUTION

The U.S. Constitution is the blueprint for organizing and running this country's government. It achieves a delicate balance between the need for the states to have a government strong enough to unite them and the states' wish that the national government not have too much power over them.

Safeguards have been built into the Constitution to make sure that limits are put on the government. Without these safeguards, leaders might pass laws that took away individual liberties or that imposed personal whims on the people. In this country the greatest protection against an overly powerful government is the fact that the source of all government power is the people. Through the Constitution, the people choose the government, and the government has only the powers the Constitution gives it. Other safeguards include dividing the government into parts so that no branch can become too powerful.

To understand why the United States has all these precautions within its government and lawmaking system, we must look back to the beginnings of the United States.

How the Constitution Was Written

When the American Revolution ended in 1783, the newly independent states had to decide how they would be governed. The links that had held the states together up to that point were weak. The national government that had been set up under the Articles of Confederation in 1777 did not have enough power to make the states follow the national laws. As a result, the states quarreled over money, boundaries, and other issues. However, they did not want to be controlled by an all-powerful central government, not even one that they created themselves. After all, they had only recently fought their way out from under England's oppressive rule. In May 1787, 12 of America's 13 states sent their most learned men to Philadelphia. (Rhode Island did not send any delegates.) The states gave these 55 men the task of planning a government that would unite the individual states into a stronger nation.

The delegates went to Philadelphia with very different ideas. They disagreed about how the new national government should be organized. For many weeks they argued and debated, sometimes bitterly. Small states worried about having equal representation with large states. Southern states worried about regulation of trade since they exported so much tobacco. They reached compromises on these issues. However, all the delegates were in agreement on one issue. They all felt strongly that the states must never again be subject to the personal wishes of a tyrant.

It took the delegates nearly four months to agree on the form the new government should take. None of the delegates—or framers, as they became known—were entirely happy with the constitution they drew up. After all, none of them had convinced the others that he was entirely right about how the new government should work. However, 39 of the framers signed the Constitution and sent it to Congress, which forwarded it to the state legislatures. Eleven of the 13 states had **ratified**, or approved, the Constitution by 1788. Thus, the government of the United States of America was established. (North Carolina and Rhode Island ratified in 1789 and 1790, respectively.) The document the framers produced is still the basis for all law in the United States.

Parts of the Constitution

The Constitution is divided into three parts: the preamble, the articles that made up the original Constitution, and the amendments that have been added since 1788. (The Constitution is reprinted in Appendix A.)

The Preamble   In the preamble, which is the introduction, the framers spelled out their goals, which were very ambitious. The primary concerns of the framers were to set up a system of cooperation among the states, establish justice and peace, promote the welfare of the people, secure liberty, and provide for the defense of the nation. Most important, the framers presented a concept essential to our democratic government: that the government was established by the consent of "we the People."

The Articles   In the first three of the Constitution's seven articles, or parts, the framers set up the three branches of the national government—the legislative, the executive, and the judicial—and defined their powers. Article IV spelled out the relationships of the states to one another and to the national government. Article V established rules for changing the Constitution. A very important statement in Article VI is that the Constitution, along with the laws of Congress and treaties with foreign countries, is "the supreme Law of the Land." Article VII described provisions for ratifying the Constitution.

The Amendments   Nowhere is the Constitution's role as the protector of people's rights more evident than in its **amendments**, or changes. The framers were wise enough to know that any plan for the new government, no matter how good, would need changes or additions over time. Article V makes this provision for amending the Constitution. There are four ways to propose and ratify an amendment, but only one way has been used extensively. Twenty-five of the 26 amendments have been proposed by a two-thirds vote in both houses of Congress and ratified by three fourths of the states.

The first ten amendments, known as the Bill of Rights, were added only three years after the original Constitution was ratified. Some states agreed to ratify the document only if these amendments were added. They guarantee basic personal liberties and protect individuals from the government. (We will discuss the Bill of Rights in Chapter 2.) The most recent amendment, ratified in 1971, extends the minimum voting age to 18. Before this amendment, the minimum voting age for federal elections and most state elections was 21.

Illustration 1-2   The Twenty-sixth Amendment to the Constitution, passed in 1971, allows people who are 18 or older to vote in federal and state elections.

The Supremacy Clause

Article VI of the Constitution provides for **federal supremacy**, which means that federal law is a higher authority than state law. The states agreed that they needed one uniform highest form of law—and that it would be the U.S. Constitution. No other form of law—federal or state—can contradict it. Directly below the Constitution are the laws and treaties passed by Congress. Below the U.S. Constitution and congressional laws is each state's constitution, followed by the state's statutes. Below state law are local laws.

REVIEW QUESTIONS

1. What is the basis of all the laws in the United States?
2. What are two safeguards that have been built into the Constitution?
3. Name the parts of the U.S. Constitution.
4. By what method have almost all the amendments been proposed and ratified?

THE LEGAL RESPONSIBILITIES OF THE BRANCHES OF GOVERNMENT

The Constitution determines the main divisions, or branches, of the federal government and defines the powers and responsibilities of each division. Together, the three branches form a national government that is strong enough to meet the needs of the states. At the same time, no one branch has the power to control the government as a whole. This **separation of powers** prevents any branch from having too much authority.

The Legislative Branch

The U.S. Congress is the legislative branch. It has the power to make laws that govern the nation as a whole. The job of the members of Congress is difficult. They must interpret the will of the people who elected them and pass laws that reflect the wishes of the majority. The two chambers, or houses, of Congress are the Senate and the House of Representatives. The power of Congress is divided between these two houses.

The Senate has 100 members—2 for each state, regardless of the state's size. The House of Representatives has 435 members. The number of members for each state is determined by the size of the state's population.

In addition to making laws, Congress has other law-related responsibilities. For example, it creates all federal courts below the Supreme Court. It also has the power to **impeach**, or accuse of misconduct, and remove from office not only federal judges but even the President.

The Executive Branch

Article II of the Constitution defines the executive branch of government. This branch consists of the President and Vice President of the United States. According to the Constitution, the main law-related duty of the President is to execute the nation's laws. That is, the President is responsible for enforcing and carrying out the laws of the country. This duty involves appointing federal judges. The President also recommends laws to Congress. Every year the President delivers a State of the Union message that serves as an agenda, or plan of action, for Congress.

The President has the power to grant **clemency**, or mercy, to people accused of federal crimes. The President also can issue **pardons**, which free individuals from punishment in federal criminal cases. For example, President Gerald Ford pardoned President Richard Nixon for any crimes Nixon might have committed during the Watergate scandal in the early 1970s.

As part of his function of executing the laws of the country, the President can issue executive orders. These orders have the force of law but do not need approval by Congress. Executive orders have been issued in many areas, including civil rights and economic issues. For example, in 1965 President Lyndon B. Johnson issued an executive order requiring firms winning federal contracts to set up programs for hiring more minorities. These orders cannot, of course, go against the Constitution or a statute. Any order that does can be overturned by the Supreme Court.

The Judicial Branch

Article III of the Constitution created the judicial branch of government. The judicial branch includes the Supreme Court and all other federal courts that Congress creates. This branch is responsible for interpreting and applying the laws of the United States. It resolves disagreements about laws, and it can overturn any law that conflicts with the U.S. Constitution.

The only court that the Constitution created directly is the U.S. Supreme Court. However, the Constitution gave Congress the power to create federal courts at lower levels. Using this power, Congress set up the federal court system when it adopted the Judiciary Act of 1789. Congress has created many additional courts and judgeships as the country has grown over the last two hundred years. We will discuss the court system in detail later in this chapter.

Checks and Balances

Each of the three branches of government is equal yet separate. To make sure that no branch becomes too powerful, the Constitution set up a system of **checks and balances**. This system gives each branch ways of influencing what the other branches do. For example, if Congress adopts a law that someone feels goes against the Constitution, that person can go to court to have the law overturned. Congress has the power to remove federal judges and the President from office, and it can propose amendments to the Constitution to overturn Supreme Court decisions. The President checks Congress with the power to **veto**—or reject—laws passed by Congress. Congress, however, may override the veto with a two-thirds vote in both houses. The President influences the court system by appointing federal judges, but the President's choices must be approved by the Senate. The system of checks and balances requires that the three branches work together.

REVIEW QUESTIONS

1. What are the three main divisions of the federal government?
2. What is the main law-related duty of each branch of government?
3. Who created the federal court system below the level of the Supreme Court?
4. Explain the system of checks and balances.

HOW LAWS ARE MADE

Statutes are passed by Congress at the federal level, by each state legislature at the state level, and by community governments at the local level.

How Congress Passes Laws

The congressional lawmaking process begins with an idea for a new law or a change in an existing law. This idea may come from members of Congress, citizens, the President, or any group that believes there is a need for such a law. A

Illustration 1-3 The federal lawmaking process begins with a member of Congress proposing the law in either the Senate or House of Representatives.

member of Congress will propose the law in the Senate or House of Representatives (whichever chamber he or she is a member of). The proposal, or bill, is sent to a committee for consideration. Many bills are "killed" in committee by simply being ignored, or pigeonholed. A bill that a committee wants to consider is studied and researched. In some cases public meetings are held so that people with a special interest in the bill can present their opinions. A bill approved by a committee is scheduled for a vote by all the members of that house.

The House and the Senate debate the merits of important bills before voting on them. During that time, any member of the House or Senate may propose an amendment to the bill being debated. A bill approved by one house of Congress then goes to the other house. There it must be approved by a committee, debated, and voted on.

The House and the Senate often pass different versions of the same bill. For example, a bill that is passed by the House and sent to the Senate may be altered during debate in the Senate. If neither body is willing to change its version, both bills are referred to a conference committee. This committee, which includes both Senators and members of the House of Representatives, irons out the differences between the two versions.

When both houses of Congress have approved the same version of a bill, it goes to the President. The President can sign the bill into law or veto it. If the President does neither, the bill becomes law automatically. If the President vetoes a bill, it does not become a law unless two thirds of the members of each house of Congress vote to override the veto.

Any citizen can influence the lawmaking process. One way to do this is to stay informed about political candidates and to vote for those whose views reflect your own. Even if you are too young to vote, you can write letters to your legislators and express your views on bills that may be coming up for a vote. Legislators pay attention to such letters because they know that they will win elections only as long as they follow the wishes of the people they represent.

State Lawmaking System

The U.S. Constitution assigns certain specific powers to the federal government and gives Congress the sole authority to pass laws needed to enforce those powers. For example, it certainly makes sense for Congress alone to have the power to do the following: regulate commerce (the traffic and sale of goods between states and with other countries); establish a postal system; coin, or make, and set the value of money; and declare war against other nations. If the states could exercise these powers individually, each state would end up acting as its own country, making its own money and its own foreign trade agreements.

However, according to the Tenth Amendment to the Constitution, state governments have all the powers not expressly given to the federal government and not forbidden to the states. For example, the Constitution does not authorize the federal government to create a national public school system or to make marriage and divorce laws. Therefore, each state has the power to make its own laws in these areas. In addition, some powers are concurrent, which means that both the federal and state governments have those powers. For example, both the federal and state governments can collect taxes and set up court and prison systems.

Each of the 50 states has a constitution that defines the state's government and its powers. The state constitutions resemble the U.S. Constitution, but most of them are longer and more detailed. All state constitutions provide for separation of powers among three branches of state government. In other words, your state has its own legislatures to enact state laws, its own courts to interpret them, and its own chief executive—the governor—to carry them out.

Different states have different laws. For example, in some states first cousins are not allowed to marry, but in other states they are. In many states the minimum age at which people can get a driver's license is 16. In other states the minimum age may be as young as 15 or as old as 19. State laws also differ in the punishments they set for crimes, in the kinds of taxes they collect, and in their license requirements for certain kinds of businesses. Each state government seeks to meet the unique needs of its citizens. Needs may differ depending on the location of the state, its climate, its industries, and its population.

Suppose that in a few years you get married in your home state and later move to another state. Will your new state recognize your marriage? Yes, it will. That is because the **Full Faith and Credit Clause** of the U.S. Constitution requires the states to honor each other's "public Acts, Records, and judicial Proceedings." This clause is part of Article IV.

As you read earlier in this chapter, state laws may not conflict with the U.S. Constitution or with federal statutes. Sometimes, though, the federal government may pass a law but leave the door open for the states to pass even stricter laws. For example, federal laws prohibit unfair job discrimination. (To discriminate is to classify or treat people differently.) States also may pass laws against such discrimination. If a state law is tougher in its regulation of the workplace than the federal law is, the state law will be in force in that particular state. State officials will enforce the law. In this situation, the goals of the federal law are being met or even exceeded, so the federal government is willing to leave control to the state.

Local Lawmaking

Besides the national and state governments, there is another level of government that affects everyone's daily life: local government. This is government at the municipal (town, borough, or city), township, and county levels. Local governments pass certain traffic laws and handle zoning laws as well as others. Laws at this level are called ordinances. Municipal courts help interpret these laws. The powers a local government has depend on the state in which the local government is located. Some states have more centralized control than others do. For example, most decisions about which textbooks are to be used in schools and what teachers' salaries should be are made at the local level in New Jersey. In North Carolina, however, these decisions are made at the state level.

Local ordinances must comply with any state law restrictions placed upon municipalities. Local laws may not infringe on the rights that citizens have under the constitution of their state or the U.S. Constitution.

REVIEW QUESTIONS

1. How is a law enacted by Congress?
2. How does Congress override the President's veto of a bill?
3. What can you do to influence the lawmaking process?
4. What is the Full Faith and Credit Clause of the U.S. Constitution?

THE COURT SYSTEM

As you just read, both the federal and state governments have the power to set up court systems. (Figure 1-1 shows the arrangement of federal and state courts.) These court systems are separate. It is decided by the Constitution and by statute what the **jurisdiction**, or authority to hear and decide cases, of each set of courts is. Some cases can be heard only in federal court or only in state court. In these instances jurisdiction is **exclusive** to one court. Sometimes courts have **concurrent**, or shared, **jurisdiction**; this means that a person may have a case heard in either federal or state court. (See Table 1-1.)

Another division of jurisdiction is that between original and appellate. Courts that hear a case first have **original jurisdiction**. Courts that hear a case on appeal from a lower court have **appellate jurisdiction**. As you read in the opening case, when T.L.O.'s lawyer did not agree with the decision of the juvenile court (the court of original jurisdiction), the lawyer was able to appeal the case to two higher New Jersey courts (courts having appellate jurisdiction).

Federal Courts

The main purpose of federal courts is to interpret and apply the U.S. Constitution and federal statutes. Federal courts, from the lowest to the highest, include district courts, courts of appeals, and the Supreme Court. The federal system also includes special courts that hear cases in specific areas of law.

District Courts   Congress created the system of district courts in the Judiciary Act of 1789. Today the 50 states are divided into 89 districts, with some larger states having more than one district. In addition, Puerto Rico and the District of Columbia have one district court each. Each district has its own court, which has at least two judges; some have many more.

The district courts have original jurisdiction in civil and criminal cases involving federal law. This means that most federal cases are heard at this level first. District courts are sometimes called trial courts. Cases at this trial level are decided by the presiding judge or panel of judges or by a jury. Like other federal judges, district court judges are appointed by the President. These appointments must be approved by the Senate. The judges are appointed for life as long as they practice "good Behaviour," in the words of the Constitution. Of course, they may retire or resign.

Figure 1-1 Federal and State Court Systems

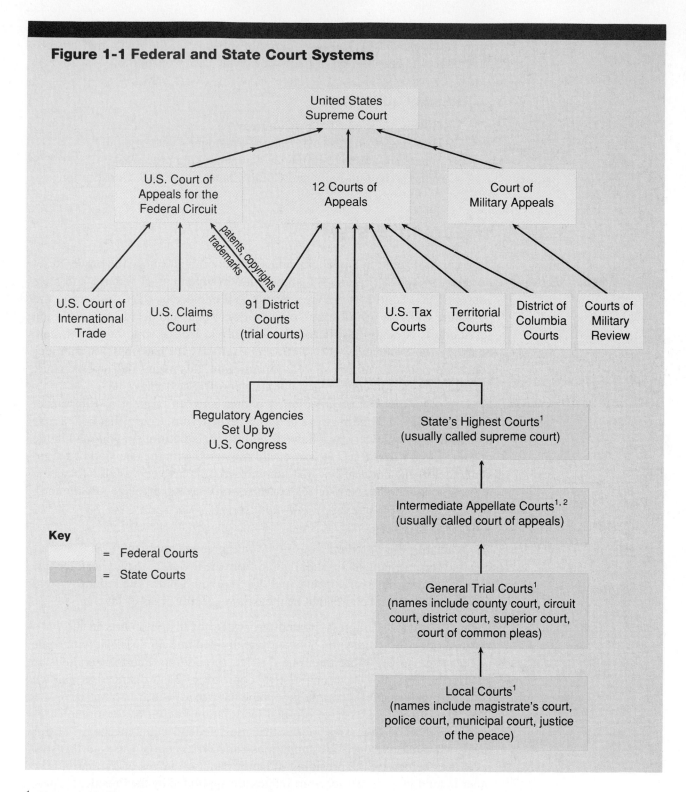

Key

　= Federal Courts

　= State Courts

[1.] Names vary from state to state.

[2.] Not all states have intermediate appellate courts.

Table 1-1 Exclusive and Concurrent Jurisdiction of Federal and State Courts

Federal	Shared	State
Cases involving	Cases involving	Cases involving
■ The U.S. government or one of its officials or agencies	■ A citizen of one state suing a citizen of another state (when the amount of money is under $10,000, state court; when the amount is at least $10,000, federal court)	■ A state and its own citizens
■ Interpretation of the Constitution		■ Violations of state laws or local laws
■ Violations of federal statutes or treaties		■ A citizen of one state suing another state
■ Actions on the high seas or shipping	■ Crimes that break both federal and state laws, such as kidnapping	■ Areas of federal jurisdiction if the parties in the case want it
■ Patents or copyrights		■ All cases not heard by federal courts
■ An ambassador or other official representative of a foreign government	■ Bankruptcy (only very few in state court)	
■ A state suing another state, a citizen of another state, a foreign government, or a citizen of a foreign government		
■ An American citizen suing a foreign government or one of its citizens		

Courts of Appeals   In 1891 Congress created the federal courts of appeals to hear appeals of district court rulings. Until that time the Supreme Court had been handling all those appeals, but it had become so overloaded that it was three years behind.

Today the United States is divided into 12 circuits, each with a court of appeals, including one in the District of Columbia. These courts have only appellate jurisdiction. That is, they hear only cases that have come from a lower court. Each appeals court hears cases from district courts that are in its circuit. (See Figure 1-2.)

Cases are appealed when either party in a case believes that the wrong procedure was followed by the lower-court judge or when new evidence comes to light. Appellate courts also review cases that involve constitutional issues. Lawyers present their arguments to the judges, usually a panel of three. The appellate judges review court records and listen to lawyers' arguments before making one of three decisions:

1. To let the original verdict, or decision, remain
2. To overturn the original court's decision
3. To send the case back to the lower court for a new trial

The appellate judges issue their opinions in writing. An **opinion** is an explanation of the legal issues in a case and the precedent on which the opinion is

Figure 1-2 Geographical Boundaries of U.S. Courts of Appeals and U.S. District Courts

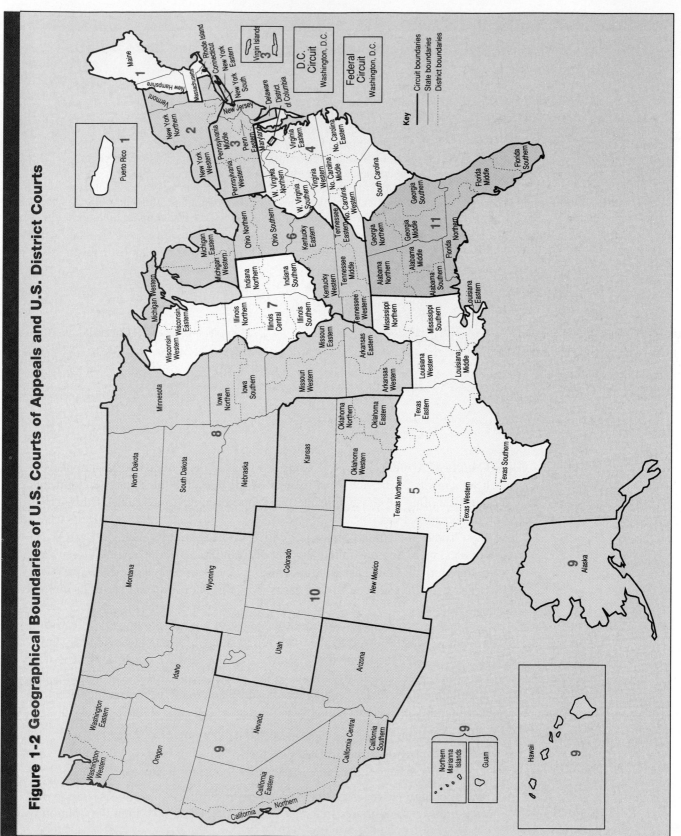

Source: Administrative Office of the United States Courts

based. The **majority opinion** is the explanation of the ruling. If the decision is not unanimous, a minority **dissenting opinion** may be presented. Sometimes concurring opinions are presented. In a **concurring opinion**, a judge agrees with the ruling but for different reasons, which are explained in the opinion. The rulings made in appellate courts are used as precedents in later cases that deal with the same issues.

One additional appeals court was created in 1982. The Court of Appeals for the Federal Circuit hears certain kinds of appeals from district courts throughout the country as well as appeals from some specialized courts.

Specialized Courts   In addition to district courts and appellate courts, the federal judiciary includes courts that handle only specialized cases. One of these is the Court of International Trade, which hears cases involving civil laws that apply to trade between the United States and other countries. Other specialized courts created by Congress are the Claims Court, the Tax Court, territorial courts, courts for the District of Columbia, and courts of military review. The special appeals court for military personnel is the Court of Military Appeals.

The U.S. Supreme Court   The highest federal court is the U.S. Supreme Court. The Supreme Court consists of a chief justice and eight associate justices, all of whom are appointed by the President with the approval of the Senate. One of the most recent appointees was David H. Souter. Nominated by President George Bush in 1990, Justice Souter was approved by the Senate by a vote of 90 to 9. Openings occur when a justice dies or decides to resign, as Justice William J. Brennan Jr. did in 1990 and as Justice Thurgood Marshall did in 1991.

The Supreme Court is the final court of appeal in all disputes involving federal statutes. The Court also handles final appeals on any federal *or* state action that involves a constitutional issue. Once the Supreme Court has made a ruling in a case, the case cannot be appealed further. The Supreme Court's power to examine the constitutionality of federal and state statutes and court decisions is called judicial review. This power will be discussed later in the chapter.

Remember, we mentioned that a system of checks and balances is in place so that no one arm of government can become too powerful. If Congress disagrees with a Supreme Court decision, it can propose a constitutional amendment that would, in effect, overturn the ruling.

The Court hears relatively few of the cases that are brought before it. Of the more than 5,000 cases sent to it every year, the Court gives only about 150 cases a full hearing and review. The Court's decision not to hear a case cannot be appealed.

Requests that the Supreme Court review a case may be presented by either party involved in the case in a lower court. Less frequently, a lower court may request that the Supreme Court review a point of law.

When the Court is in session—from October to June or July—it follows a certain procedure for deciding which cases to review and for making its rulings on those cases.

Illustration 1-4   Openings occur when a justice dies or decides to resign, as Justice Thurgood Marsall did in 1991.

1. All written petitions that are in order are put on a **docket**, or list.
2. Each justice looks at this docket to see which cases merit review. Once the justices have done this, a list of cases worthy of discussion and a vote is compiled.
3. During conferences, which are private, cases on the docket are approved for or denied a hearing.
4. Oral arguments for cases being heard are presented by lawyers for both sides. Written statements and records are presented to the Court ahead of time. The written arguments are called **briefs**. Lawyers for each side are given a half hour to speak, and justices may ask questions during that time.
5. More conferences are held to discuss oral arguments and to vote. A majority vote is needed to decide a case. Six justices must be present when a vote is taken. In such a case, at least four must agree.
6. Opinions are written and published. As in lower appellate courts, if the decision is not unanimous, dissenting opinions may be written in

addition to the majority opinion. Concurring opinions may also be written by justices.

One of the most important powers of the Supreme Court is that of **judicial review**. With this power, the Supreme Court can rule on whether a statute or other act of federal or state government conflicts with the U.S. Constitution. Any act of government that goes against the Constitution is called **unconstitutional** and can be declared "null and void." This means that it should not be obeyed or enforced.

Judicial review gives a great deal of power to the Supreme Court. It can overturn any statute or executive order that doesn't live up to the Constitution.

The way in which the Court has used this power has been disputed through the years, especially when it has been used to decide controversial or sensitive issues, such as abortion rights or discrimination. People don't always agree on how the Court reaches its conclusions in reviewing a law's constitutionality. There are three basic views on how the Court should make its decisions:

1. *The justices should use the literal meaning of the Constitution.* This is often difficult because the document is very short and so many of its statements are general. Not every situation is covered by the words of the Constitution.
2. *The justices should follow the intent of the framers of the Constitution.* It is difficult to get into the minds of the framers and know what they intended.
3. *The justices should use perspective.* Laws that are written for today reflect the values of society today, not necessarily the values of society two hundred years ago, when the Constitution was written. People who hold this view of judicial review believe the justices should consider today's values when deciding a case.

In practice, the justices try to use all three methods in making their decisions. They also review the precedents established by decisions in previous Supreme Court cases.

The Court, however, has infrequently gone against precedent and overruled one of its previous decisions. For one thing, conditions within the country and the views of its people change. In our democratic system of government, the views of the majority of people, who elect the President and members of Congress, are reflected in the type of person the President chooses and the Congress approves to be a Supreme Court justice.

When the views of the majority of justices on the Court change, the Court may look at a point of law differently. If the justices feel an error has been made, they will overturn a previous decision when a similar case comes before the Court. For instance, in 1941 the Court upheld a federal law that regulated child labor and set maximum hours and minimum wages for workers in companies that shipped goods outside the state. In this decision, the Court overturned its 1918 decision that the federal government has no right to regulate the child labor practices of such companies. In 1918 the Court felt that such regulations should stay in the hands of the states.

State Courts

All states have court systems that include several levels. Together, the 50 states have thousands of courts with jurisdiction only in cases involving state and local law. Judges may be elected or appointed, depending on the state or local area.

In general, state court systems mirror the federal court system. States have trial courts that are modeled after federal district courts. They also have appellate courts that hear cases on appeal from the trial courts.

Each state has one court that has the final word in interpreting the state constitution, just as the U.S. Supreme Court does with the U.S. Constitution. Sometimes cases that go to the state's highest court involve questions about the U.S. Constitution or a federal statute. The case *New Jersey v. T.L.O.*, which was presented at the beginning of this chapter, is an example. As you read in that case, a decision by the state's highest court may be reviewed by the U.S. Supreme Court.

The ultimate power of judicial review lies with the U.S. Supreme Court. However, most state courts can also rule on whether an act of state government or a state law conflicts with the U.S. Constitution or the state constitution.

States also have courts with narrower jurisdiction. For example, they have small claims courts that hear disputes about small amounts of money, juvenile courts that hear criminal charges against people below a certain age, and traffic courts that handle cases involving parking and traffic violations.

In addition, most cities and towns have local courts to handle minor cases that arise within their borders. These local courts are also part of the state court system.

States differ in the names they use for their courts. For example, New Jersey calls its highest court the supreme court, whereas the highest court in New York State is called the court of appeals. States refer to their trial courts by many names, including county court, court of common pleas, and circuit court.

REVIEW QUESTIONS

1. What are the three levels of federal courts? Which of these courts has original jurisdiction?
2. What three decisions may the judges in appellate courts make when they hear a case?
3. What is an opinion? Explain the three types of opinions appellate court judges may write.
4. What is the purpose of the U.S. Supreme Court's power of judicial review?

Viewpoints on the Supreme Court's Interpretation of the U.S. Constitution

It is the job of the Supreme Court to interpret the U.S. Constitution. The Court is asked to decide whether the actions of state and federal governments are constitutional. How should the Court make its decisions? Should the justices decide cases only on the basis of the words of the Constitution and on what they believe was the original intent of the framers? Or should they, as they apply the basic principles of the Constitution to the problems that emerge today, take into account the changes in public opinion that have occurred since the Constitution was written? These questions highlight two important views on constitutional interpretation: strict constructionism and judicial activism.

The Strict Constructionism Position

Strict constructionists believe that it is the job of the Supreme Court to enforce only the codes stated or clearly implied in the Constitution. Former Attorney General Edwin Meese III summarized this view by stating that federal judges should try "to resurrect the original meaning of constitutional provisions and statutes as the only reliable guide for judgment."

Strict constructionists, sometimes called advocates of judicial restraint, believe that if a government action is unfair or unwise, it is up to Congress or the state legislature to do something about it. These elected groups represent the people's wishes more directly than does the Supreme Court. Strict constructionists believe that when judges go beyond interpreting the actual words of the Constitution or the intent of the framers, they are imposing their own preferences on the people of the United States.

The Judicial Activism Position

Those who support judicial activism agree that it is important to consider the intentions of the framers. They believe, however, that enforcing these intentions is not enough. New issues never dreamed of by the framers—such as segregated schooling and the right to die—have emerged throughout the history of this country. In addition, standards of behavior as well as public values change over time. Judicial activists point out that when the Constitution was written, slavery was an accepted practice. As late as 1879 public executions were an accepted method of punishment for certain crimes. Today's Supreme Court justices cannot be expected to return to such values and beliefs in making their decisions.

Judicial activists believe that the basic principles on which our nation was founded—such as freedom and democracy—constitute a kind of "higher law." It is the activists' view that the Supreme Court must remain true to this higher law in interpreting the Constitution in modern American society.

The Supreme Court Today

The debate between these two groups will probably never be resolved, and it may not need to be. The makeup of the Court changes periodically from a majority of strict constructionists to a majority of judicial activists and back again. These swings help the Court maintain a balance somewhere close to the middle.

In addition, few justices can be placed unwaveringly in either camp. A justice may advocate strict constructionism at one time and judicial activism at another, depending on the circumstances of the case before the Court.

Chapter Review

Chapter Summary

- Laws serve two main purposes in society: to maintain order by providing rules that the community follows and to protect the rights of individuals.

- The four main sources of law are constitutions, statutes, court decisions, and government regulations.

- The two main purposes of law are to settle disputes between individuals and to punish people who commit crimes.

- The U.S. Constitution is the blueprint for organizing and running the national government. The Constitution is made up of the preamble, or introduction; the articles, or main parts; and the amendments, or additions.

- The highest form of law in the nation is the U.S. Constitution. Below it, in order of authority, are the laws of Congress, state constitutions, state statutes, and local statutes.

- The three branches of the national government are the legislative, the executive, and the judicial. The legislative branch—Congress—makes the national laws. The executive branch—the President—enforces and carries out those laws. The judicial branch—the courts—interprets and applies the laws.

- The Constitution set up the separation of powers and the system of checks and balances to make sure that no one branch of government becomes too powerful.

- The U.S. Congress, which is made up of two houses, is the national lawmaking body. Laws that are needed to carry out the powers reserved to the federal government can be passed only by Congress.

- States have constitutions and legislatures that resemble those of the federal government.

- According to the Tenth Amendment, any powers not given to the federal government and not forbidden to the states belong to the state governments. States can make their own laws in these matters.

- The Full Faith and Credit Clause of the U.S. Constitution requires states to honor each other's laws. No state law may contradict the U.S. Constitution or federal statutes. States may pass stricter laws than the federal government as long as those laws don't contradict the federal law.

- Both federal and state courts have courts of original jurisdiction (those that hear cases first) and courts of appellate jurisdiction (those that hear cases on appeal).

■ The U.S. Supreme Court is the highest federal court. It is the final court of appeal in all disputes involving federal law.

■ The power of judicial review gives courts the right to overturn any statute or other federal or state action that conflicts with the U.S. Constitution. The ultimate power of judicial review rests with the Supreme Court. State courts may also use this power to decide whether state laws go against the state constitution or the U.S. Constitution.

■ The state court system is set up like the federal system. Local courts are part of the state system.

Understanding Legal Terms

On a separate sheet of paper, match the terms below with the definitions that follow.

amendment	dissenting opinion
appellate jurisdiction	judicial review
checks and balances	majority opinion
common law	precedent
constitution	statute

1. Court decisions that are referred to when courts are making decisions in future similar cases
2. Written explanation given by an appellate court of its ruling in a case
3. System set up in the U.S. Constitution that gives each branch of the federal government the power to influence what the other branches do
4. Written explanation by an appellate court judge who disagrees with the decision of the majority of judges in a case
5. Change or addition to the U.S. Constitution
6. Body of law based on judges' decisions
7. Power of courts to rule whether a statute or act of government is unconstitutional
8. Power of courts to review cases appealed from a lower court
9. Law enacted by a legislative body
10. Legal document that explains the powers and limits of government and the rights of the people

Applying the Law

1. When Homer Winslow and his friend Alex Norberg are tossing a football in the park, the ball hits a jogger who is running by. The jogger's nose is broken as a result. The jogger takes the two boys to court to pay for his injury. Assuming that there is no statute on the books that explains the law in this case, how will the case be decided? Include in your answer who will decide the case and what type of law will be applied to reach the decision.

2. A federal judge, appointed by the President to the court for life, has been found guilty of tax fraud. By what power, set up in the Constitution, can Congress remove the judge from office?

3. Congress votes in favor of a bill and sends it to the President for approval. The President does not take any action. Can the bill still become law? Explain your answer.

4. Cindy Melnick and Albert South are legally married in Ohio according to that state's laws. They decide to move to Indiana. Will they need to remarry in their new home state? Explain your answer.

5. Joe was charged with stealing a car, and the trial court found him guilty. Since his trial, however, a witness has come forward who saw someone else steal the car. What can Joe's lawyer do in this situation?

6. In 1970 the Supreme Court ruled that Congress can lower the voting age only for federal elections, not for state and local ones. Congress disagreed with this decision. What, if anything, could Congress do to overturn this decision, since the Supreme Court is the final court of appeal?

Case Studies

1. Because of a tip given to the officials of a high school, the assistant principal called the police and asked them to search a high school student suspected of carrying a gun. The police did not get a warrant first but searched the student anyway. He was found to be concealing a gun and was arrested. The court determined that the search was legal. Using the reasoning of the Supreme Court in *New Jersey v. T.L.O.*, explain why the court found this search to be legal.

2. The Equal Rights Amendment (ERA) was proposed in and approved by Congress and sent to the states for ratification. The purpose of the amendment was to outlaw discrimination, or unfair and unequal treatment, on the basis of sex. A total of 35 of the 50 states ratified the amendment. Did the ERA become part of the U.S. Constitution? Explain your answer.

3. In the mid-1950s the Supreme Court made a ruling about school segregation. In this ruling the Court stated that having separate public schools for black and white students was unequal and therefore unconstitutional. Officials in one state, however, tried several things to get around this ruling. One step was to pass a law permitting children in racially mixed schools to ignore compulsory attendance laws. The state also adopted an amendment to its constitution which said that the Supreme Court decision should be opposed. Why, in 1958, did the Supreme Court declare the state law and the amendment to be unconstitutional? By what power was the Supreme Court able to make this decision about the state's actions?

Chapter 2

Constitutional Freedoms

Chapter Objectives

When you have read this chapter, you should be able to:

■ Identify at least four individual rights protected by the U.S. Constitution.

■ Explain how the courts decide whether a law is permissible under the Constitution.

■ Describe at least two ways in which the First Amendment protects us from government interference in religious practice.

■ Explain what is—and what is not—protected by the First Amendment guarantee of freedom of speech.

■ Explain when discrimination is permissible under the Constitution.

Case Study

West Virginia State Board of Education v. Barnette, 319 U.S. 624 (1943).

In the 1940s, as today, most American schools began each day with the pledge of allegiance to the flag. In classrooms all over the country, students were required to face the flag, place their hands over their hearts, and say: "I pledge allegiance to the flag of the United States of America and to the republic for which it stands,. . . ."

In many states this was not just a custom; it was the law. In West Virginia, for example, students who didn't stand and pledge allegiance were marked absent for the day and could be expelled. Their parents could be fined or sent to jail.

The Barnette family lived in West Virginia. Their religion, called Jehovah's Witnesses, taught them that they must never swear allegiance to anyone or anything other than God. Mr. and Mrs. Barnette wanted their children to attend public school, but they didn't want the children to be forced to violate their religious beliefs. In 1943 the dispute between the Barnettes and the West Virginia Board of Education ended up before the U.S. Supreme Court.

The Court listened to the Barnettes' story. It also listened to the West Virginia Board of Education. The board argued that the pledge was an important way to instill a sense of patriotism and good citizenship in young Americans. The Court's task was to balance the *right* of the Barnettes to practice their religion against the *interest* of West Virginia in encouraging good citizenship.

In considering this case, the Court turned to the highest law of the land: the U.S. Constitution. The Constitution guarantees all Americans the right to practice their religious beliefs. The Court also looked back at previous Supreme Court decisions dealing with freedom of religion. These past decisions stated that the right to religious freedom is so fundamental—so clearly important—that only the most compelling (extremely important) interests of the government may interfere with that right.

The Court agreed that good citizenship is a very important interest. It decided, however, that there are other ways to develop good citizenship that would not interfere with the Barnettes' religion. Therefore, the Court ruled that West Virginia's law had to be changed. The Barnette children had to be allowed to sit silently while their classmates pledged allegiance to the flag.

THE BILL OF RIGHTS

To understand the Barnettes' right, we must go back to the years following the American Revolution, when the newly independent states came together to form a single nation. Representatives of the states developed a constitution for the new United States of America. As you read in Chapter 1, a constitution is a document that describes a form of government and sets up a system for making laws.

The original Constitution described, in great detail, the duties and powers of the new national government. It said nearly nothing, however, about the rights and freedoms of American citizens.

Americans were outraged. They had just been freed from an oppressive British government that had denied some of their most basic liberties. It had prevented them from holding political meetings. It had told them what religion they were allowed to practice. It had even entered their homes without permission and jailed them without trial. The American people demanded a guarantee that any laws passed by their new government would not interfere with the basic rights of individuals.

Illustration 2-1   The rights of American colonists were often abused by the British rulers.

In response, the new U.S. Congress passed ten amendments, or additions, to the Constitution. These amendments formed a **Bill of Rights**—a list of basic rights that would be guaranteed to all American citizens. Among those rights are freedom of religion, freedom of speech, and freedom of the press. The Bill of Rights also guaranteed that people's property could not be taken away from them unfairly and that people accused of crimes would receive a fair trial.

Originally, the Bill of Rights protected the American people only from unreasonable laws passed by the federal government—not by the individual states. A later amendment, the Fourteenth Amendment, extended this protection. Today, no government, federal or state, may restrict the rights guaranteed by the U.S. Constitution without an extremely important reason.

While the Constitution offers protection from laws passed by any government or government agency (such as the school board in the opening case), it does not offer the same protection against private rules and regulations. It offers no protection, for example, from rules laid down by employers or by private clubs and institutions.

However, the Constitution is only one set of laws that protect our rights and freedoms. Congress has passed many civil rights acts over the years. **Civil rights acts** are laws that protect individuals from unequal or unfair treatment. These federal laws may extend to actions by government and by private individuals and companies. In addition, all states have passed their own bills of rights as part of their constitutions. As you'll see, both state and local governments have also passed equal protection laws and other laws that extend to private institutions. State and local laws often provide even greater protection than the federal government does.

Rights versus Interests: A Balancing Test

The Constitution guarantees all Americans certain fundamental, or basic, rights. Fundamental rights are extremely important in a free society. (Freedom of speech, for example, is a fundamental right in the United States.) Why, then, do federal, state, and local governments often pass laws that restrict individual freedoms? In some cases these laws are passed for the purpose of protecting citizens. For example, to prevent the spread of dangerous diseases, many states require children to have vaccinations before they enter school. To protect public safety, states make the sale and use of certain drugs (such as marijuana and cocaine) illegal. To preserve the beauty of neighborhoods, cities and towns forbid people to cover walls and buildings with graffiti.

All these laws represent important interests—needs or wants—of the government. In many cases, however, government interests conflict with the rights of individuals. A law requiring vaccinations, for example, goes against the belief of certain religions that medical treatment violates God's will. A law prohibiting the use of certain drugs interferes with people's freedom to do what they want with their own bodies. A law against graffiti restricts people's ability to express themselves as they please.

When a law conflicts with the rights of an individual, someone must settle the dispute. Under the American system of government, that task belongs to the courts. Courts settle conflicts like these by performing a **balancing test**: they weigh the interests of the government against the rights of the people.

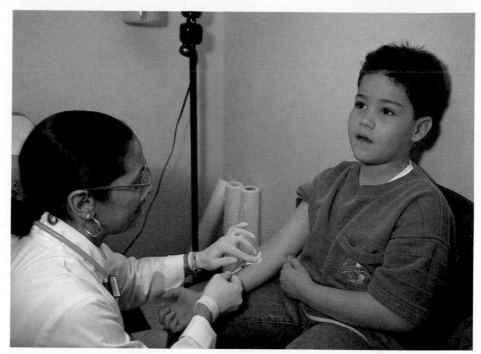

Illustration 2-2   In the case of vaccinations, the need for the government to protect public health must be balanced against the freedom of individuals to make their own decisions.

When a law interferes with a fundamental right guaranteed by the Constitution, the case may be brought before a state or federal court. Eventually, it may reach the Supreme Court for review. Like other courts, the Supreme Court listens to arguments from both sides and performs a balancing test. Sometimes the Supreme Court decides that the government's interest is more important than an individual's rights. (State governments clearly have the right to restrict drug use, for example.) At other times the Court decides that an individual's fundamental rights are more important than a particular law. In such a case the Court will declare the law unconstitutional because the law interferes with rights guaranteed in the Constitution. (This is what happened in the Barnettes' case.)

As you read through this chapter, put yourself in the Supreme Court's place—try to weigh the rights of the individual against the interests of the government. For each law you read about, ask yourself: What is the government interest that makes the law necessary? How important is that interest? What is the individual right that the law is interfering with? How important is that right? Are there other ways in which the government could satisfy its interest without interfering with a fundamental right?

REVIEW QUESTIONS

1. What is a constitution?
2. What is a bill of rights?
3. How does the Supreme Court decide whether a law is constitutional?

FREEDOM OF RELIGION

Our nation has always placed special emphasis on freedom of religion. Many of the earliest settlers to the New World came here to escape religious persecution. When the United States set up its federal government, Americans were eager to maintain a clear separation of church and state. They wanted to keep the government from interfering in their practice of religion, and they wanted to keep religious leaders from telling them how to run the government.

The first line of the First Amendment says that "Congress shall make no law respecting an establishment of religion, or prohibiting the free exercise thereof. . . ." This statement has two parts, or clauses. The **Establishment Clause** guarantees that Congress will not establish a national religion or pass laws that favor one religion over another. The **Free Exercise Clause** guarantees that Congress will not pass laws that restrict how we choose to practice religion.

Establishment of Religion

In 1958 the board of education in New Hyde Park, New York, made a rule that all school days had to start with a prayer: "Almighty God, we acknowledge our dependence upon Thee and we beg Thy blessings upon us, our parents, our teachers, and our country." Many parents were offended. They took the school board to court, claiming that this rule represented an unconstitutional establishment of religion. When the case eventually reached the Supreme Court, the parents' objections were upheld and the morning prayer was stopped.

The Establishment Clause of the First Amendment says that the government may not establish a state church or support one church or religion over another. This clause was designed to let Americans practice any religion—or no religion at all—without government involvement. As a result of the Establishment Clause, the government cannot require schools to hold morning prayers, Bible readings, or any type of religious service. No government money can be used to build churches.

Although the government may not directly aid or establish religion, the Supreme Court has allowed governments to support secular (nonreligious) programs even if those programs indirectly benefit religious institutions.

For example, many communities have two kinds of schools: public schools and parochial (religious) schools. Both kinds of schools teach basic skills such as math, English, and science, but parochial schools generally teach religion and Bible studies as well. The state pays for the math books used in public schools. Can it pay for the same math books if they're used in parochial schools?

Because education is such an important interest, the Supreme Court has held that state governments may help support general educational programs in parochial schools. For example, a school district, as a government body, may pay for secular materials such as math books. It may not, however, help a parochial school buy religious materials such as Bibles.

Free Exercise of Religion

This chapter began with the story of the Barnette children. The Barnettes' religious beliefs required that they pledge allegiance only to God, but the law required that they pledge allegiance to the American flag. The Supreme Court found the law to be an unconstitutional intrusion on the Barnettes' religious freedom.

Illustration 2-3   The freedom to practice one's religion is a fundamental right.

The Supreme Court has a history of upholding religious freedom even when the interests of government seem especially strong. In 1972, for example, a group of Wisconsin families objected to a state law requiring children to attend school until age 16. These families practiced the Amish religion, which demands complete separation from modern industrial society and from worldly influences. The families claimed that sending Amish teenagers to high school would teach them values contrary to their beliefs.

The Supreme Court recognized that the state of Wisconsin had a very strong interest in this case: For our society to function, every child must receive a basic education. The Court decided, however, that the religious rights of the Amish were even more important. The Court ruled that Amish families must be allowed to take their children out of school after the eighth grade.

Although the Supreme Court tries to protect freedom of religion as much as possible, sometimes it must decide in favor of the government's interest. In the nineteenth century, for example, members of the Mormon faith practiced polygamy. According to this belief, men are permitted to have several wives. However, a federal law said that polygamy is illegal. The Supreme Court decided that the federal law was necessary to preserve the traditional family structure. The Court ruled that the religious practice of polygamy could not be allowed.

The Court has also upheld restrictions on the freedom of religion in order to protect public health. At the beginning of the twentieth century, during a deadly outbreak of smallpox, the state of Massachusetts passed a law requiring all the state's residents to be vaccinated against the disease. A man named Henning Jacobson refused, saying that his religion, Seventh-Day Adventism, did not permit him to be vaccinated. The Supreme Court decided that the need for the law outweighed Jacobson's religious freedom because mandatory vaccinations would protect the health of the entire community.

Balancing the right to religious freedom against the government's interest in public health continues to be difficult. For example, some people practice religions that do not permit blood transfusions or surgical operations—even when these procedures may save a person's life. The Supreme Court has allowed adults to refuse lifesaving treatment on religious grounds. It has not, however, allowed parents to refuse treatment on behalf of their children. When religious beliefs would keep a child from getting medical care, the Court has decided that the government's interest in protecting children's health outweighs the parents' religious objections.

REVIEW QUESTIONS

1. Explain the two clauses of the First Amendment that set up the separation of church and state.
2. Describe one way in which a state government can offer financial support to a parochial school without interfering with the Establishment Clause of the First Amendment.
3. Name two state interests that, according to the Supreme Court, are important enough to outweigh an individual's freedom of religion.

FREEDOM OF EXPRESSION

Another very important protection in the Bill of Rights is the right to free expression. The First Amendment says that "Congress shall make no law . . . abridging the freedom of speech, or of the press. . . ."

Although the amendment mentions only speech and the press, the Supreme Court has interpreted it much more broadly. Today the First

Amendment allows us to express ourselves through nearly any medium imaginable—on radio, television, and computer networks, for example. It protects our right to wear T-shirts and buttons that express ideas. It protects our right to express ourselves without words by wearing armbands or marching silently. It even protects our right not to express ourselves at all.

Freedom of Speech

As with all fundamental rights, the right to freedom of speech may be restricted if it interferes with the rights or safety of others. If we were free to say whatever we wanted at any time, life would be difficult and even dangerous. Protesters would be free to march past your house, shouting, at three o'clock in the morning. Troublemakers would be free to yell "fire" in a crowded theater where there was no fire. Your classmates would be free to stand up in class and insult each other or their teachers.

To maintain a safe and orderly society, the government may make laws that restrict what we say (the *content* of the speech) and when, where, and how we say it (the *time, place,* and *manner* of the speech).

Content Restrictions   Despite the protection of the First Amendment, certain types of speech are harmful enough to be declared illegal. One of the most common types of harmful speech is defamation.

Defamation means telling lies that hurt someone. When the lies are spoken, the act is called **slander**. When the lies are written, the act is called **libel**. (Both kinds of defamation will be discussed in more detail in Chapter 8.)

For example, Lisa is envious of Roberto's grades in history. To get Roberto in trouble, she lies to his history teacher, saying that Roberto cheated on a test. In telling this lie, Lisa commits the crime of slander. Her right to lie is not protected by the First Amendment.

Obscenity is another form of illegal speech. **Obscenity** refers to words or pictures that portray sexual activities in an offensive manner. To be considered obscene, the words or pictures must meet three conditions established by the courts.

First, they must appeal to a purely sexual interest. Obscenity laws do not regulate speech that is simply violent or racist, no matter how offensive it may be.

Second, they must have no serious literary, artistic, political, or scientific value. For example, sexually explicit pictures in medical textbooks are not considered obscene because they are used for the worthwhile purpose of training doctors.

Third, they must depict sexual conduct in a way that the average person in the community would find offensive. The definition of obscenity therefore varies from place to place: words that one community considers obscene might not offend another community at all.

In 1990, for example, the state of Florida found certain lyrics sung by the rap group 2 Live Crew to be obscene. The group's concerts were banned, as was the sale of albums that included the objectionable songs. Other states did not find the songs obscene, and the albums remained available in those states.

Fighting words are another form of speech that is not protected by the First Amendment. **Fighting words** are words used to insult someone with the intention of starting a fight. The government's need to keep the peace outweighs an individual's right to provoke violence.

The final type of illegal speech considered here is **subversive speech**— speech that represents a danger to national security. The First Amendment doesn't include the right to give away national secrets, especially during a war.

Time, Place, and Manner Restrictions   In New York City, street musicians have traditionally performed in subway stations. During the 1980s some of them began using amplifiers and large speakers so that they could be heard at a greater distance. In 1990 two groups of people objected. Subway passengers complained that the amplified music was too loud and disturbing, and performers who worked without amps complained that they could not be heard over the noise. A federal court agreed that the rights of both groups of people were being intruded upon. The court banned amplification in the subways, saying that noise control is a reasonable restriction on free expression.

To preserve peace and safety, the government has the power to restrict the time, place, and manner of speech. For example, it can regulate how many protesters can march downtown in one afternoon, or it can ban marches from residential streets. It can prevent students from disrupting classes by making speeches in the hallway. These kinds of restrictions are entirely constitutional as long as they are reasonable and apply equally to everyone.

Symbolic Speech   Until the early 1960s laws in many states separated black people from white people. In Clinton, Louisiana, for example, the public library was reserved for whites only. Black citizens who wanted to read or take out a book had to use the bookmobile parked outside. One day in 1964 five young black men walked into the library, sat down, and refused to leave until they were arrested.

In 1970 a young man protested the U.S. involvement in the Vietnam War by taping a peace symbol to an American flag and flying it outside his window. In 1988, to protest the policies of President Ronald Reagan, another man set fire to an American flag.

What were these people doing? They were expressing their opinions through actions rather than words. The Supreme Court has held that nonverbal expression, known as **symbolic speech**, is entitled to protection under the First Amendment. The acts of symbolic speech described in the preceding paragraphs were all upheld by the Supreme Court, and laws preventing them were declared unconstitutional.

The Supreme Court has affirmed that students, even when they are on school property, are free to speak symbolically. In 1965 a group of Iowa high school students expressed their opposition to the Vietnam War by wearing black armbands to school. They did nothing to disrupt classes, but they were still suspended from school. When the case came before the Supreme Court, the Court said that this sort of demonstration must not be prohibited—that it could, in fact, be as important to a young person's education as formal classroom teaching. Students have the right to express themselves in school—by means of armbands, buttons, or other forms of speech—as long as they don't "materially and substantially disrupt the work and discipline of the school."

Of course, there are limitations on the right to symbolic speech. In 1966, for example, a student in Boston publicly burned his draft registration card to protest the Vietnam War. His action was found to be harmful and illegal because it interfered with the nation's need to maintain a military.

Freedom of the Press

Freedom of the press is closely related to freedom of speech. The First Amendment allows newspapers, magazines, and other news media to express themselves without government interference. Like freedom of speech, however, freedom of the press is subject to certain restrictions.

For example, a newspaper cannot make up stories and print them as facts. As you found out earlier in this chapter, printing deliberate lies about someone is called libel and is a crime.

The right to a free press is somewhat more limited for high school students than it is for adults. In a recent case the Supreme Court upheld the right of a school to censor an article in a student newspaper. The Court decided that the article—which discussed birth control, pregnancy, and sexual activity among teenagers—was inappropriate for some of the younger students at the school. Therefore, the Court ruled that the school's interest in protecting those students outweighed the newspaper's right to publish the article.

REVIEW QUESTIONS

1. Name three types of speech that are not protected by the First Amendment.
2. What is the difference between slander and libel?
3. What is symbolic speech? Give two examples.

OTHER RIGHTS AND FREEDOMS

Freedom of religion, freedom of speech, and freedom of the press are only a few of the rights guaranteed by the Constitution. The Constitution recognizes a number of other fundamental rights.

Freedom of Assembly

The First Amendment gives all Americans the right to assemble—to gather together in groups. This right covers not only social gatherings but also political gatherings, rallies, and demonstrations in which groups seek support for their points of view. Freedom of assembly proved to be very important during the 1960s, when black people all over the country marched in support of civil rights.

Illustration 2-4   In this country, people are permitted to gather and to express their views.

Governments may regulate the time and place of marches and demonstrations, but their regulations must treat all groups equally—even unpopular ones. In 1977, for example, the American Nazi party announced plans to march down the streets of Skokie, Illinois. Skokie is the home of many Jewish people who were persecuted by the Nazis during World War II. The people of Skokie demanded that the march be stopped, but the Supreme Court ruled that the town had to permit the march. The Court said that even American Nazis have a constitutional right to assemble and speak freely.

The First Amendment has also been interpreted to permit freedom of association—the right to join organized groups, including political parties, without interference by the government.

The Right to Travel

All Americans have the right to travel both within the country and abroad. In 1969, for example, Pennsylvania passed a law that withheld welfare payments from people who had lived in the state less than a year. The law was declared unconstitutional because it conflicted with the freedom to travel from state to state. In 1958 the federal government passed a law denying passports to Americans who belonged to the Communist party. This law was declared unconstitutional because it deprived Americans of their fundamental right to travel outside the country.

The Right to Vote

For over a hundred years the statement in the Declaration of Independence that "all men are created equal" applied only to white males over the age of 21. One of the most important rights of a citizen—the right to vote—was restricted to people of a certain sex, race, and age. Even the poor were prevented from voting because many states passed laws requiring each voter to pay a poll tax—a sum of money paid for the right to cast a ballot.

After the Civil War, a number of constitutional amendments granted voting rights to these excluded groups. The Fifteenth Amendment, passed in 1887, allowed black men to vote; the Nineteenth Amendment, passed in 1920, allowed women to vote; and the Twenty-sixth Amendment, passed in 1971, allowed everyone age 18 or older to vote. In 1964 the Twenty-fourth Amendment outlawed poll taxes. As a result of these amendments, adult Americans of all races and income levels now enjoy the right of **suffrage**—the right to vote.

Because suffrage is a fundamental right in a democracy, any restrictions on that right—such as laws requiring literacy tests, political knowledge tests, and English language tests—have consistently been declared unconstitutional.

The Right to Bear Arms

Is the right to own a gun protected by the Constitution? Some people feel that this right is as fundamental as free speech and freedom of religion. They say that right to gun ownership is protected by the Second Amendment, which says, "A well regulated Militia, being necessary to the security of a free State, the right of the people to keep and bear Arms, shall not be infringed."

Illustration 2-5   The Nineteenth Amendment, passed in 1920, allowed women to vote.

Other people, however, fear the rapid rise in gun ownership and the increasing number of murders reported every year. They want to pass strict laws controlling or even outlawing the use of guns by private citizens.

The Supreme Court has said that the Second Amendment is meant to protect the *state's* right to use guns to maintain the peace. The Court has not said that *individuals* have a right to do so. As a result, an increasing number of states have passed laws restricting the ownership of guns. Some states allow the sale of only certain kinds of guns; others require that gun owners acquire a license or register their guns with the police. Some require a waiting period for gun purchases so that the police will have time to check buyers for a possible criminal background. The Supreme Court has found none of these restrictions to be a violation of the Second Amendment right to bear arms.

The Right to Privacy

In 1965 a state law in Connecticut prohibited anyone, including married couples, from using contraceptives, or birth control devices. Estelle Griswold opened a birth control clinic in that state and counseled married couples on the use of birth control. She was convicted of violating Connecticut's law. The issue was brought before the Supreme Court. The Court overturned Griswold's conviction and struck down the ban on contraceptives, saying that it interfered with a married couple's right to family privacy.

The right to privacy is not explicitly mentioned in the Constitution, but a series of Supreme Court decisions have developed that right. The right to privacy now is generally held to be a right to engage in certain highly personal activities. These include marriage and having children as well as other activities relating to traditional family values. The Court has held that this is a fundamental right and that, as with any other fundamental right, the government may restrict the right to privacy only when there is a compelling reason to do so.

One of the most important events involving the right to privacy happened in 1973. That year, in a case called *Roe v. Wade*, the Supreme Court overturned a Texas law that banned all abortions within the state. The Court ruled that the law was an unconstitutional restriction of the right to privacy. That decision, and the idea of a right to privacy, has been a magnet for controversy ever since.

If a state can't outlaw abortion, can it regulate it? Since the *Roe v. Wade* decision, many states have passed laws that restrict women's access to abortion. Among them are laws that require a teenager to get parental consent before an abortion can be performed, that require a married woman to get her husband's consent, that require doctors to show women what a developing fetus looks like in the womb, and that deny government funds to poor women for the abortion procedure.

Every time such a law is passed, it is challenged in court almost immediately. The Supreme Court, as well as lower federal courts and state courts, is wrestling with some very difficult questions. Is an unborn fetus a "person" protected by the Bill of Rights? Does a woman's right to privacy extend to what she does with her own body? These issues have not yet been settled by the courts.

Even though the right to privacy now protects many very personal activities, such as getting married and having children, the Supreme Court has said that this right does not permit people to engage in all kinds of sexual activity. In 1986, for example, Michael Hardwick was arrested for violating a Georgia law that forbids homosexual behavior. The Court said that because homosexual activity is not related to childbearing or to choices within the family, it is not protected by the constitutional right to privacy.

The future of the right to privacy is uncertain. Because the right to privacy is not found in the text of the Constitution, it is possible that the Supreme Court will weaken or even eliminate this right.

In the meantime, many privacy-related questions are being considered by the courts. Should the government be allowed to give lie detector tests to prospective employees? Can government employees be forced to give urine or blood samples for drug testing? Should the government be permitted to use electronic surveillance devices to spy on American citizens? Should it be allowed to look at your telephone bills to find out whom you've called? When the courts are asked to weigh an individual's right to privacy against the government's need to protect public safety, the results are unpredictable.

REVIEW QUESTIONS

1. Why can't a city government stop marches or demonstrations by unpopular groups?
2. What is a poll tax? Is it constitutional?

3. According to the Supreme Court's interpretation of the Second Amendment, who has the right to use guns to protect the peace?
4. According to the Supreme Court, what broad fundamental right includes a woman's right to have an abortion?

EQUAL PROTECTION AND DUE PROCESS

Imagine a law that permitted men to work in bars at night but did not permit women to do so. Imagine a law that automatically allowed white citizens to vote but required black citizens to pass a test of reading ability first. Compare these laws to a law that allows driver's licenses to be granted only to people over age 16. What do these laws have in common?

All these laws *discriminate*. They classify or treat people differently on the basis of certain personal characteristics.

Discrimination is not always a bad thing. Most people would agree, for example, that the law restricting driver's licenses to people over 16 is a reasonable law. At the same time, most people would agree that discrimination on the basis of race or sex is almost never acceptable.

Equal Protection under the Fourteenth Amendment

The Fourteenth Amendment, passed in 1868, guarantees all Americans the "equal protection of the laws"; that is, it guarantees that no person or group will be discriminated against unfairly by a law. Along with the Thirteenth Amendment (which outlawed slavery) and the Fifteenth Amendment (which gave nonwhite citizens the right to vote), the Fourteenth Amendment was passed to end the unequal treatment of black Americans after the Civil War. Today the protection of the Fourteenth Amendment has been extended to other groups that may be discriminated against unfairly.

The Fourteenth Amendment doesn't require that the government treat all groups the same. It does require that if the government treats groups differently, it must have a valid reason for doing so. What constitutes a valid reason differs from case to case.

As you read earlier, any law that treats groups differently is subject to scrutiny, or review, by the courts. In deciding discrimination cases, the court may use different levels of scrutiny—ranging from strict to mild—to decide whether the discrimination is legal and constitutional. The level of scrutiny depends on whom the law discriminates against.

Strict Scrutiny   The highest level of scrutiny by a court is called **strict scrutiny**. Strict scrutiny is applied most often to laws that discriminate on the basis of race or national origin.

For a law to pass the test of strict scrutiny, it must satisfy a *compelling* (extremely important) government interest. In addition, discrimination against certain groups must be *necessary* to satisfy that interest. Very few laws that discriminate are able to pass this test.

For example, a law in San Francisco required people of Chinese descent to get a special permit to run a laundry. These permits were not required for laundry owners who were not Chinese.

When the Supreme Court was asked to judge the constitutionality of this law, it used the test of strict scrutiny. The Court asked: What state interest is this law intended to satisfy? Is it a compelling interest? Is discrimination based on national origin necessary to satisfy this interest? Because the Court saw no compelling reason to treat Chinese business owners differently from non-Chinese business owners, the law was declared unconstitutional.

Earlier in this chapter you read about racial discrimination in the town of Clinton, Louisiana. Only whites could use the library. Blacks had to use the bookmobile. This rule clearly discriminated on the basis of race. Like the San Francisco law, it was declared unconstitutional when the Court used the strict scrutiny test.

Imagine, however, that the town of Clinton had set up two separate—but equally good—libraries. If the town required whites to attend one library and blacks to attend the other, would that be considered discrimination? A case like this one came before the Supreme Court in 1954. At that time black children in Topeka, Kansas, went to schools for black children, and white children went to schools for white children. Linda Brown, a black girl, was not allowed to attend the elementary school near her home because it was for whites only. She had to walk 20 blocks each morning to reach an all-black school. Nevertheless, the Topeka board of education insisted that its system of separate schools was legal and fair. The schools taught the same subjects, and the quality of education was the same in both schools.

The Supreme Court decided that separate schools were, by definition, unequal. It ruled that all Topeka schools must be open to students of all races. Since then no public institution has been permitted to have different rules for different races—no matter how "equal" the rules are.

Over the past few decades the federal government and many state governments have passed **affirmative action laws**. These laws give special treatment to groups that have historically been discriminated against. They may require colleges to admit a certain number of black students, or they may require businesses to take positive steps toward hiring more minority employees. Although these laws discriminate on the basis of race, the courts have declared them to be constitutionally acceptable ways to overcome past discrimination.

Intermediate Scrutiny   The Supreme Court has found that some types of discrimination are less serious than discrimination based on race or national origin. These types of discrimination require a lower level of scrutiny, usually called the intermediate level. For a law to pass the **intermediate** level of **scrutiny**, it must satisfy an *important* (rather than compelling) government interest. In addition, discrimination against certain groups must be *substantially related* (rather than necessary) to that interest.

Intermediate scrutiny is applied most often to laws that set up different rules for men and women. For example, in Oklahoma in 1972, low-alcohol beer could legally be sold to women 18 and older but men had to be 21 and

Illustration 2-6   The Supreme Court has held that separate schools for black and white children do not pass the test of strict scrutiny.

over to buy it. In reviewing this law, the Supreme Court applied the intermediate level of scrutiny. The Court asked: What state interest is the law intended to satisfy? Is it an important interest? Is discrimination by sex substantially related to this interest?

The Court acknowledged that the state interest—keeping the road safe from drunk drivers—was an important one. It did not agree, however, that the gender of beer drinkers was substantially related to this interest. There was no evidence that young men drank more or caused more traffic accidents than young women did. Therefore, treating the sexes differently was unconstitutional.

Using the same test, however, courts have found that some instances of discrimination based on sex are constitutional. Laws that require separate boys' and girls' teams in contact sports and the law that requires only men to register for military service are permissible under the intermediate level of scrutiny. (They might not be permissible under strict scrutiny.)

Many people feel that discrimination based on sex should not be allowed in any circumstances. Some of these people have tried to establish a new constitutional amendment—the Equal Rights Amendment (ERA)—that would guarantee equal treatment of men and women.

Legislators have introduced this amendment several times since the turn of the century. Despite active pro-ERA campaigns, the proposed amendment has not passed, although it came very close in the 1980s. Some people felt the amendment was not necessary because other laws already protect women's equality. Others feared that the amendment would eliminate laws that were designed to protect women.

Reasonable Relationship Test   The lowest level of court scrutiny is the **reasonable relationship test**. This test is most often applied to laws that discriminate on the basis of age or wealth. For a law to pass the reasonable relationship test, it must satisfy a *reasonable* government interest. In addition, discriminating against certain groups must be a *reasonable* way of satisfying that interest.

In 1985 the city of Dallas, Texas, wanted to have places for young people to meet and socialize. It set up dance halls that were open only to teenagers between the ages of 14 and 18. A challenge came before the Supreme Court, saying that the law discriminated against people who were not in that age group. Using the reasonable relationship test, the Court decided that the government's interest—to protect younger teens from the influences of older teens and adults—was reasonable. It also decided that restricting admission to the dance halls was a reasonable way to meet that interest. The law, therefore, was constitutional.

In recent years the Supreme Court has held that the reasonable relationship test applies to discrimination based on sexual orientation. Laws that restrict the employment of homosexuals in the military and in other government posts have been declared constitutional because they are reasonably related to a reasonable government interest.

Other Equal Protection Laws

Remember, as you read earlier in this chapter, the Fourteenth Amendment applies only to discrimination by the federal and state governments. It offers almost no protection against discrimination in businesses, educational institutions, and social clubs.

To fill this gap, Congress has passed many civil rights acts that prohibit discrimination by private citizens and organizations. Some laws make it illegal to take race into account when selling a house or renting an apartment. Others do not allow owners of public places, such as hotels and movie theaters, to discriminate. The Equal Pay Act (1963), the Age Discrimination in Employment Act (1967, 1978), and many education-related acts have helped lessen discrimination based on race, age, sex, and national origin in schools and at work.

More recently, a great number of civil rights acts have focused on the needs of handicapped people. These laws have ensured that all children, regardless of mental or physical disabilities, receive an education. They have ensured that reasonable efforts are made to remove architectural barriers so that blind and wheelchair-bound people can move about freely. The most extensive of these laws, passed in 1990, is the Americans with Disabilities Act. It offers people with mental and physical disabilities—including people infected with the AIDS virus—the same job rights and access to public facilities that other Americans enjoy.

Illustration 2-7 Congress has passed civil rights acts to give people with disabilities equal access to public buildings.

Federal laws are not the only laws that protect our civil rights. Some state constitutions offer more protection than the Fourteenth Amendment does. Some states have passed their own equal rights amendments, prohibiting laws that treat men and women differently. Some cities have begun to prohibit discrimination based on sexual orientation. For example, San Francisco, California, has passed a "domestic partners" act. This law treats homosexual couples as families, giving them some of the rights heterosexual couples enjoy. These city ordinances are a small step toward affording some civil rights to homosexuals. You'll read more about the rights of nontraditional families in Chapter 10.

The Right to Due Process

Besides protecting our right to equal treatment, the Fourteenth Amendment forbids state governments to "deprive any person of life, liberty, or property, without due process of law." (The federal government is prohibited from this action by the Fifth Amendment.) **Due process** refers to a set of legal procedures that must be followed when the government is punishing or taking away the property of an individual. These procedures—whether in a civil or a criminal case—must be fair and reasonable. In 1971, for example, Deborah Fox and a number of other students got involved in a violent demonstration in their Columbus, Ohio, high school. They were immediately suspended from school for ten days.

The students challenged their suspension in court. They argued that the school (acting as a government body) had taken away their property (an education) and their liberty (the right to a good reputation) without due process of law. The Supreme Court agreed. It said that before students are suspended from school, they must have a fair chance to defend themselves. The school must notify students of the charges against them and give an explanation of the evidence. Students must then be allowed to tell their side of the story.

Due process means different things in different cases. In general, more serious situations require stricter forms of due process. For example, the Supreme Court noted that if Deborah Fox and her classmates had been suspended for more than ten days, they would have been entitled to other rights. For example, they would have had the right to call witnesses to describe what happened.

By limiting the rights of government to deprive a person of life, liberty, or property, the Fourteenth Amendment ensures that no person or group is treated unfairly by the legal system.

REVIEW QUESTIONS

1. What test does the Supreme Court use to determine the constitutionality of laws that discriminate by race? By sex? By age?
2. What are affirmative action laws? Are they constitutional?
3. Explain what is meant by due process.

Viewpoints on Abortion

Cheryl D. is 18 years old. In three months she will graduate from high school. She has been accepted by a college and plans to study nursing in the fall. Cheryl has just learned that she is six weeks pregnant. Now she must make one of the most difficult decisions of her life. Should she have the baby and give it up for adoption? Should she have the baby and keep it? Should she have an abortion?

The Antiabortion Position

Ever since the Supreme Court's 1973 ruling in *Roe v. Wade*, Cheryl and other women have had the right to obtain legal abortions. People who oppose abortion would like to change that. They want to outlaw abortion because they believe that abortion is murder. (Exceptions are made to allow abortion in the case of rape or incest or if the mother's life is in danger.) Opponents of abortion rights believe that human life begins at the moment of conception. They feel that during the entire time a woman is pregnant, the fetus should have the same legal rights that all people have. They believe that women who become pregnant have a moral obligation to give birth. Those who oppose abortion rights call themselves right-to-lifers or prolife advocates to identify themselves as defenders of the unborn.

Since 1973 the prolife activists have tried to have *Roe v. Wade* overturned. They have also worked hard to persuade their state legislators to pass strict laws regulating abortion to try to reduce the number of abortions being performed each year. Some prolife groups hold demonstrations at abortion clinics to try to persuade women who are seeking abortions to change their minds.

The Proabortion Position

People who favor legal abortion believe that a woman should have the right to decide what to do with her own body and that she should not be forced to carry and bear a child against her will. They argue that a woman's rights are greater than those of a fetus because a fetus has the potential to become a person but is not a person during its early stages of growth. They believe that fetuses gradually become human beings as they develop in the womb.

Many abortion advocates agree with the Court's ruling in *Roe v. Wade* that to deny women access to abortion is a violation of their constitutional right to privacy. Abortion advocates would give Cheryl the right to choose a legal abortion. These people call themselves prochoice advocates to emphasize their concern for the rights of the mother.

The prochoice movement believes that strict state abortion laws do not reduce the number of abortions that are performed but instead force women to have illegal, and possibly unsafe, abortions.

The Courts and Legislatures

The legal position on abortion is always changing. Some state legislatures have adopted very strict abortion laws in recent years. The Supreme Court has upheld some of these laws and overturned others. Utah passed a tough abortion law in 1990 that is certain to be challenged in court. Some lawyers argue that the Utah law will enable the state to prosecute women and their doctors for murder in abortion cases. In some states prochoice groups are pressuring their state legislatures to enact laws to preserve liberal abortion laws in case *Roe v. Wade* is overturned.

The abortion issue arouses deep feelings in people. Unlike other public issues, abortion seems to offer little room for compromise between the two sides. As a result, the abortion debate is destined to continue for many years in the living rooms, churches, streets, legislatures, and courts of the United States.

Chapter Review

Chapter Summary

■ The Bill of Rights and other amendments to the U.S. Constitution protect our fundamental rights and freedoms from unreasonable interference by state and federal laws.

■ When a law conflicts with an individual freedom, the Supreme Court uses a balancing test to decide whether the law is constitutional.

■ The Establishment Clause of the First Amendment prohibits the government from telling us what religion to practice or favoring one religion over others.

■ The right to freedom of religion includes the right to practice any religion in any way. Only the most compelling government interest can interfere with that right.

■ Our First Amendment freedoms of speech and of the press include the right to express ourselves in many ways or not to express ourselves at all.

■ Speech that is not protected by the First Amendment includes defamation, obscenity, fighting words, and subversive speech.

■ Freedom of speech can be restricted in time, place, and manner.

■ Other fundamental rights protected by the Constitution include freedom of assembly, freedom of association, the right to travel, the right to vote, and the right to bear arms.

■ The Supreme Court has determined that the Constitution protects a right to privacy. That right allows us to make certain choices about marriage and children, as well as about other activities relating to traditional family values, without government interference.

■ The Fourteenth Amendment guarantees our right to equal protection under the law.

■ Laws that discriminate on the basis of race or national origin are subject to strict scrutiny by the courts. Laws that discriminate on the basis of sex or other characteristics are subject to less strict review.

■ A number of civil rights laws passed by Congress protect individuals from discrimination on the basis of race, sex, age, national origin, religion, or handicap by both the government and private citizens or groups.

■ Some state and local laws may offer greater protection against discrimination than federal laws do.

■ The right to due process, which is guaranteed by the Fourteenth and Fifth amendments, ensures that the government will follow certain procedures before taking away an individual's life, liberty, or property.

Understanding Legal Terms

On a separate sheet of paper, match the terms below with the definitions that follow.

affirmative action laws	reasonable relationship test
Bill of Rights	slander
civil rights acts	strict scrutiny
due process	subversive speech
libel	symbolic speech

1. Laws that protect people from unfair or unequal treatment
2. Speech that represents a danger to national security
3. Laws that give special treatment to groups to overcome past discrimination
4. The basic rights listed in the first ten amendments to the Constitution
5. The highest level of scrutiny, or review, by a court
6. Written lies that hurt someone
7. Nonverbal expression
8. Spoken lies that hurt someone
9. The set of legal procedures that the government must follow when punishing or taking away the property of an individual
10. The lowest level of scrutiny, or review, by a court

Applying the Law

1. A New Jersey law provides that all children who live more than a mile from school be taken to school by bus. The law covers children who attend parochial schools as well as children who attend public schools. The buses are to be paid for by the state. Is this law constitutional? Why or why not?
2. New York State prisons have a rule that all new inmates must have their hair cut short so that identifying pictures can be taken. Inmate Brooks is a Rastafarian. His religion requires that he wear his hair long. Can the prison officials force Brooks to have his hair cut? Explain your answer.
3. A group of nurses went on strike against a Delaware city hospital. To draw attention to what they considered unfair treatment, they marched on the street outside the hospital with picket signs and protested loudly. City police arrested them because they were violating a law that prohibited loud demonstrations within 500 feet of a hospital. Is the law constitutional? Why or why not?
4. To protest the firing of a favorite teacher, a group of students in a Missouri high school had buttons printed saying "Administration unfair." Each morning they stood in the yard and refused to let other students into the school until they agreed to wear the buttons. Can the school administration stop this behavior? Why or why not?

5. A state is concerned that too many people are voting in state and local elections without understanding what they are voting for. The state passes a "voter competency" licensing test. Similar to a driver's license test, it requires state residents to answer questions about the electoral process in order to receive a license permitting them to vote. Is this law constitutional? Why or why not?

6. A Massachusetts state law requires that all police officers in the state retire when they reach age 50. The purpose of the law is to maintain police forces that are physically healthy and strong. Officer Murgia, a 50-year-old officer, challenges this law, saying he is as fit and healthy as any other person on the force. What test will the Supreme Court use to decide this case?

Case Studies

1. Adell Sherbert is a Seventh-Day Adventist. Her religion requires that she observe Saturday as a day of rest. She works at a mill in South Carolina. The mill fires her when she refuses to work a Saturday shift. After she is fired, she claims unemployment compensation money from the state. The state denies her unemployment pay because of its policy of excluding anyone who refuses available work without good cause. Ms. Sherbert says that for her to have accepted that available work, she would have had to violate her religious beliefs. Is the denial of unemployment compensation a violation of her freedom of religion? Explain your answer.

2. Every morning a California woman named Yetta Stromberg flew the national flag of the Soviet Union over the camp where she lived and worked. She did this, she said, to promote the adoption of the Soviet system of government in the United States. A California law prohibited the raising of such a flag as a "symbol of opposition to organized government." Ms. Stromberg was arrested. Was the law under which she was arrested a constitutional law? Explain your answer.

3. A federal law provides that the wives of men in the U.S. Air Force are dependents and therefore are entitled to benefits such as medical and dental care. Husbands of women in the Air Force are entitled to the same benefits only if they have no other income and are actually dependent on their wives. The reason for this law is economic and administrative convenience, as the Air Force has found that "wives in our society frequently are dependent upon their husbands, while husbands rarely are dependent upon their wives." Lieutenant Sharron Frontiero and her civilian husband, Joseph, claim that this law is unconstitutional. Is it? Why or why not?

Chapter 3

The Constitution and Fair Legal Procedure

Chapter Objectives

When you have read this chapter, you should be able to:

- Explain when law enforcement officers are permitted to make searches and seizures.

- Define the exclusionary rule and explain how it protects against illegal police action.

- Explain what the Miranda warnings are and why they are used.

- Name at least three pretrial rights that the U.S. Constitution guarantees to a person accused of a crime.

- Name at least three rights that the U.S. Constitution guarantees to a criminal defendant at a trial.

Case Study

Rochin v. California, 342 U.S. 165 (1952).

The Los Angeles County sheriff's office received information that Antonio Rochin was selling drugs. Early one morning in 1949 three deputies were sent to his house to investigate.

The deputies walked through Rochin's open front door, went upstairs, and forced open the door to the bedroom. Rochin and his wife were inside, still in bed. Looking around the room, the deputies noticed two small capsules that appeared to contain some sort of illegal drug.

When he realized what the deputies were looking at, Rochin grabbed the capsules and shoved them into his mouth. The deputies immediately jumped on him and hit him, trying to retrieve the capsules before he swallowed them. They were unsuccessful.

The deputies handcuffed Rochin and took him, against his will, to a hospital. A doctor pumped his stomach and retrieved the two capsules. They turned out to contain morphine.

At his criminal trial Antonio Rochin was found guilty of illegal possession of morphine. The chief evidence against him was the two capsules that had been pumped out of his stomach.

Rochin protested his conviction, saying that his treatment by the deputies had violated his constitutional rights. The Supreme Court agreed. It stated that obtaining evidence by breaking into a man's home, prying open his mouth, and forcibly pumping his stomach is conduct that "shocks the conscience" and "offends a proper sense of justice."

The Fifth and Fourteenth amendments say that no one may be punished "without due process of law." Although the Constitution doesn't define the phrase, the Court said that the way Rochin was treated was clearly not due process.

For these reasons, the Court held that the two morphine capsules had been obtained illegally. Therefore, the capsules could not be used as evidence in a trial against Antonio Rochin.

THE SCOPE OF RIGHTS IN THE CRIMINAL JUSTICE SYSTEM

It was important to the founders of our government that innocent people not be punished for crimes they hadn't committed. Therefore, the founders included in the Constitution and the Bill of Rights a number of protections for people who become caught up in the criminal justice system: those who are suspected of criminal activity, those who have been accused of crimes, and those on trial. Among these protections are the right to a speedy trial, the right to a jury, and the right to due process of law.

Convicting someone of a crime is a long process, of which the trial is only the last stage. Along the way there are many opportunities for mistreatment.

Imagine, for example, that the police suspect you of having committed a crime. Their first step might be to watch you for days or weeks, looking for signs of criminal behavior. Once they had enough information, they would **arrest** you (take you into custody) and accuse you of having broken a certain law. Before, during, and after the arrest, the police would collect evidence of your crime. The evidence might take many forms: illegal or stolen goods found in your home, information from witnesses, your fingerprints at the scene of the crime, or your comments while in police custody.

At the time you were arrested, you would be advised of your constitutional rights and told of the charges against you. Soon afterward you would appear in court. There a judge or jury would listen to the case against you and decide whether there was enough evidence to bring you to trial. (Once you were charged in court with the crime, you would be referred to as the **defendant**.)

You might have to wait a long time—months or even years—between this pretrial hearing and your trial. In most cases you wouldn't have to spend this time in jail. You would be allowed to go free in exchange for paying **bail**. Bail is a sum of money that you would deposit with the court. Later, when you showed up for your trial, the court would give the money back.

The bail system ensures that accused criminals will not attempt to run away before they are tried. The amount of bail is determined by a judge and varies from case to case. If you were accused of a serious crime, you might be required to pay thousands of dollars for bail. If you were accused of a minor crime, and you seemed trustworthy, you might be released without paying bail.

Finally, on a prearranged date, you would appear for trial. At the trial, the **prosecutor**—the government's lawyer who would be trying the case against you—might call witnesses who would present facts and evidence that indicated your guilt. You would then be allowed to answer the charges. The defense attorney representing you would present witnesses and evidence that demonstrated your innocence. Under the Constitution, you are guaranteed fair treatment at every stage of this process.

Over the years, some of these constitutional safeguards have become controversial. Many people feel that the Bill of Rights goes too far in protecting criminals and that it does not go far enough in protecting the rights of crime victims. The founders, however, did not intend to "protect criminals." Their aim was to make sure that people would not be *treated* as criminals unless they had been proved guilty at a fair trial.

Another area of controversy involving the rights of the accused stems from the general wording of the Constitution. It relies on ambiguous phrases, such as "due process of law," that are not defined anywhere in the document. As a result, the Constitution sometimes raises more questions than it answers. For example, how soon must a trial occur in order to be considered "speedy"? How much bail is "excessive"? Is the death penalty a "cruel and unusual" punishment?

The Supreme Court and the lower courts are responsible for answering these questions. As you read in Chapter 1, the courts interpret the Constitution; that is, they decide what the Constitution means in each specific case.

During the 1960s, the courts tended to interpret the Constitution loosely. In doing so, they expanded the rights of people accused of crimes. They decided, for example, that suspects must be told their constitutional rights at the time they are arrested—even though this requirement does not appear in the Constitution. In more recent years, courts have begun to move in the other direction. Their decisions have tended to reduce the rights of the accused.

As you read about your constitutionally protected rights, keep three points in mind. First, the Constitution controls only the conduct of the federal and state governments, including government agencies such as the police. It does not protect you from mistreatment by nongovernment agencies, such as private employers and store owners.

Second, if you are under a certain age (16 or 17 in most states), some of the rights discussed here may not apply to you. You'll find out more about the rights of juveniles in Chapter 6.

Third, as you found out in Chapter 2, the Constitution gives you a set of minimum rights that no legislature or court may take away. Laws and court decisions may, however, give you additional rights. For example, even though the Supreme Court has declared the death penalty legal, executions may not be permitted by your state's constitution. The Supreme Court requires that a jury in a state or federal court have no fewer than 6 members; many states require a minimum of 12 members.

This chapter will focus on what the Constitution says about criminal justice and how the Supreme Court has interpreted the Constitution. In Unit 2 we'll look at types of crimes and the specific steps in the criminal justice process for both adults and juveniles.

REVIEW QUESTIONS

1. Why does the Bill of Rights include so many protections for people accused of crimes?
2. What is bail?
3. When a statement in the Constitution is vague or unclear, who decides what the statement means?

SEARCHES AND SEIZURES

FBI agents had been watching Charles Katz for a few weeks. They suspected that he was involved in illegal gambling. They noticed that every day, at the same time, he went to a public phone booth and made some calls. Believing that the calls might be related to Katz's gambling, the agents placed a bugging device on the booth.

The next day, as usual, Katz came to the phone booth. He went inside, closed the glass door, and made a call. The FBI agents, with their listening device, heard every word of his conversation. They then arrested Katz for gambling. Later, at his trial, they used his phone conversation as evidence against him.

Katz objected to the use of his conversation as evidence. He said that when he had made the phone call, he had closed the door of the phone booth so that no one would hear what he was saying. By listening in on his private conversation, the FBI agents had conducted an unreasonable search in violation of the Fourth Amendment. The Supreme Court agreed with Katz, ruling that the phone conversation could not be used as evidence. To reach this conclusion, the Court had to balance the fundamental right of individuals to privacy against the community's need for effective law enforcement.

Police officers have the right, and the duty, to watch citizens whose actions seem suspicious. If they see signs of criminal activity, they need to collect evidence of that activity. To do so, they may *search* areas for evidence and clues, and they may *seize* any evidence they find. If they have good reason to believe that certain people are responsible for a crime, they may also "seize" those people—in other words, arrest them.

Naturally, the police could do their job much more efficiently if they had unlimited powers to search and seize. They would be better able to catch criminals if they could eavesdrop on our phone conversations, break into our homes without warning, or arrest anyone at any time. If the police had these powers, however, people's privacy and security would be put in danger. Therefore, the Fourth Amendment limits the power of law enforcement officers to interfere in people's lives. It protects the "right of the people to be secure . . . against unreasonable searches and seizures."

Searches and the Right to Privacy

In prohibiting unreasonable searches and seizures, the Fourth Amendment raises a difficult question: When does a search or seizure become unreasonable? In other words, what are the limits on our right to privacy?

According to the Supreme Court, the limits to privacy are different in different situations. They depend on how much privacy a reasonable person could *expect* to have under the circumstances. For example, if you're at home with your doors closed and your window shades drawn, you shouldn't expect anyone to be watching you. By contrast, if you're sitting on your front steps, you should expect that anyone—including the police—will be able to see what you're doing.

Illustration 3-1   Police are limited in their methods of collecting evidence.

Most examples are not so simple. Charles Katz, for instance, knew he could be seen inside a glass phone booth. Because he had closed the door, however, he reasonably expected that his conversation would not be overheard. For this reason, the Supreme Court ruled that his privacy had been invaded.

Over the years, the Supreme Court has made many equally difficult decisions about the limits of privacy. For example, the Court has ruled that officers who look into your home through an open window don't invade your privacy, while officers who look through a keyhole do. Searching a shed behind your house invades your privacy, but searching the trash can you put out on the street for collection does not. Searching a hotel room that you're staying in invades your privacy, but searching the same room after you've checked out does not.

The Supreme Court has ruled that law enforcement officers may use simple tools to help them see better. As long as these tools are used reasonably, this is not considered an invasion of privacy. For example, an officer in Washington, D.C., was looking for stolen car parts. Seeing that Harold Wright's garage door was slightly open, the officer peeked inside. It was dark inside the garage, so he turned on a flashlight. The flashlight revealed the stolen parts. Wright complained that the officer's use of a flashlight had invaded his privacy, but a court later decided that the search was legal.

Courts also permit the use of binoculars and telescopes—but, like flashlights, they must be used reasonably. Peter Kim lived in an apartment on an upper floor of a tall building in Hawaii. No other buildings nearby were as tall as his. He kept his curtains open, with the reasonable expectation that no'one would be able to see inside his apartment. In the course of investigating Kim, an FBI agent set up a telescope on the roof of a building a quarter mile away from Kim's. The telescope was so powerful that the agent could see the title of the magazine Kim was reading. A court later decided that the use of this telescope invaded Kim's privacy.

In general, courts have held that we cannot reasonably expect privacy when we are in a public place. Suppose Judy is walking down the street, smoking a marijuana cigarette. A police officer could legally arrest her for possession of drugs because her action is in plain view. Even if Judy were in a less visible location—for example, in a dark corner of a park at night—an officer could still arrest her without invading her privacy. Judy may expect not to be seen, but because she is in a public place, a court would not consider her expectation to be reasonable.

Law enforcement officers may make seizures based on sounds and smells as well as on sight. For example, courts have held that police officers may stand in hotel corridors and listen to conversations that take place in guests' rooms as long as they don't use special listening devices to do so. They may sniff for marijuana smoke under someone's door or use drug-sniffing dogs to detect illegal substances in someone's luggage.

The Supreme Court has ruled that wiretapping, bugging, and other kinds of electronic surveillance are invasions of privacy. It has made the same ruling for searches of the body, such as blood tests and urine tests.

In recent years, however, the federal government has become concerned about individuals whose drug use threatens public safety. Congress has passed several laws that make government employees subject to random drug tests. (These laws also apply to private employees, such as railroad workers, whose jobs affect the safety of large numbers of people.) Under these laws, an employee can be tested for drugs even if there is no reason to believe that he or she is using drugs. In this situation, the Supreme Court has said that the need to prevent drug use on the job outweighs the employees' right to privacy.

Warrants

Does a person's right to privacy mean that as long as an individual breaks the law behind closed doors or keeps evidence of a crime hidden, the police cannot reach him or her? No, law enforcement officers are allowed to conduct searches or seizures that invade someone's privacy as long as they obtain a warrant first. A **warrant**, as required by the Fourth Amendment, is a court order that authorizes a search or an arrest. A **search warrant** lists the items the officer is looking for and names the place where the officer intends to look for them. An **arrest warrant** names a person whom the officer intends to take into custody.

The warrant system is a compromise between the needs of law enforcement officers and the needs of private citizens. If the police were never allowed to invade our privacy, they would rarely be able to solve cases or capture criminals. If the police were allowed to invade our privacy whenever they wanted to, they would disrupt the lives of many innocent people. The warrant system allows these choices to be made individually, based on the circumstances of each case.

Illustration 3-2   Warrants are court orders that allow the police to conduct searches or make arrests.

To get a warrant, an officer must go to a neutral party—a judge. To obtain a search warrant, the officer must convince the judge that a crime has been committed and that a search or seizure of property is necessary. To obtain an arrest warrant, the officer must show that a particular person committed a crime. The officer must have more than a hunch or suspicion that something is wrong. He or she must have probable cause.

Probable cause is the reasonable belief that a crime has been committed or that a certain person has committed a crime. This belief may come from facts that are personally known to the officer, events the officer has witnessed, or information provided by a trustworthy source. If the judge believes that the officer has probable cause, he or she will issue a warrant.

A warrant does not give a police officer blanket permission to search anywhere and seize anything. It applies only to the items, places, or people named on the warrant. If the officer wants to conduct further searches or seizures, he or she must go back to the judge and obtain another warrant.

Search and Seizure without a Warrant

So far, we have discussed two general rules about searches and seizures. First, if law enforcement officers can carry out a search or seizure without invading anybody's privacy, they are free to do so. Second, if a search or seizure requires invading somebody's privacy (for example, if it involves entering a private home), the police must obtain a warrant first.

Of course, like most general rules, these rules have exceptions. At times, an arrest or a search and seizure of property that interferes with someone's right to privacy is permitted even without a warrant.

Warrantless Arrests   Many times the police make arrests without first getting a warrant. However, in such a situation they must have some evidence that the person has committed a crime. In other words, they must have probable cause.

For instance, when the police have witnessed a person committing a crime or have seen someone running from the scene of a crime, they can arrest that person immediately. Not all situations are so clear-cut, however. The police must sometimes make a decision about whether they have enough proof against a person to make a warrantless arrest. For instance, if the police see a person fitting the description of a robbery suspect, they may stop and question that person. If the person is wearing a watch stolen in the robbery, the police have probable cause to arrest that person.

Warrantless Searches   Police may make searches without a warrant in the following situations:

- *Preventing the loss of evidence.* Armando Schmerber smashed his car into a tree. He was taken to the hospital, where the police took a blood sample. The blood test revealed that the alcohol content in Schmerber's blood at the time of the accident was over the legal limit. The police arrested him for drunk driving. Schmerber objected to the use of the blood test in court, saying that his Fourth Amendment right to privacy had been violated. He claimed that the police should not have taken his blood without getting a warrant first. The police argued that getting a warrant takes at least a few hours. In that short time, the evidence—the alcohol in Armando's blood—would be gone. The Supreme Court ruled that in situations like this one—where the delay caused by getting a warrant would result in the loss of evidence—a warrant is not necessary.

- *Search incident to an arrest.* When an officer arrests someone, he or she is permitted to search the arrested person without getting a warrant. The officer may also search the immediate area in which the arrest takes place. These searches are considered necessary to protect the arresting officer, because the person under arrest may be hiding a weapon. A search beyond the immediate area, however, is not permitted without a warrant. (The officer may not, for example, search the arrested person's entire house.)

- *Hot pursuit.* Law enforcement officers don't need a warrant to conduct a search when they are in "hot pursuit" of a suspect. For example, if the police see someone run from the scene of a crime and enter a building, they may enter that building without a search warrant.

- *Emergencies.* Police may enter private homes without a warrant in emergencies, for example, if they hear a scream or smell smoke. In such situations, waiting to get a warrant might result in harm to innocent people.

- *Consent.* The police may search your private property without a warrant if you give your permission. Anyone else who has access to your

Illustration 3-3 A school principal may legally permit the search of a student's locker.

property may also give permission. A wife, for example, may legally permit the police to search her husband's dresser. Parents may legally permit the search of their child's room. A school principal may legally permit the search of a student's locker. There are exceptions, however. For example, a landlord cannot permit the search of a tenant's apartment, and a college official cannot permit the search of a student's dormitory room.

■ *Plain view.* If a law enforcement officer sees a suspicious item while he or she is in your home for another reason, that item is considered to be in plain view. Suppose you call the police to complain about a noisy neighbor. When a police officer comes into your living room to talk to you, he or she sees a bracelet that has been reported stolen. The officer may seize the bracelet, and arrest you, without a warrant.

■ *Border and airport searches.* At international borders police and customs officials may search cars, luggage, and people without a warrant. Officials may also search luggage at airports, even for domestic flights. The use of hand searches, x-rays, and various kinds of electronic screening is permitted without a warrant.

■ *Vehicle searches.* A private vehicle, such as a car or truck, is not given the same protection as a private home. If law enforcement officers have reason to believe that a car contains illegal items, they may search the car at any time without a warrant.

■ *Stop and frisk.* Suppose a law enforcement officer sees some people acting suspiciously. Even if the officer doesn't have probable cause to arrest those people, he or she is permitted to stop them and question them. For self-protection, the officer may also pat them down for weapons. This kind of search is called a **frisk**, and it does not require a warrant. A frisk is permitted only to search for weapons. While conducting a frisk, the officer may *not* look inside pockets or clothing in search of other items (such as drugs).

Keep in mind that these rules about searches and seizures apply only to law enforcement officers and federal agents. Depending on the state you live in, private citizens (such as parents or teachers) may fall under a different set of rules. Your parents may be allowed to search your bedroom, or school officials may be allowed to search your locker, without getting permission from anyone.

The Exclusionary Rule

For much of our country's history, the Fourth Amendment tended to be ignored. Police officers often conducted searches and seizures that most people would consider unreasonable. Citizens had the right to bring civil or criminal charges against officers who invaded their privacy, but they rarely did so. Few people wanted to anger the police, whose help they might need someday.

Around the beginning of the twentieth century, the Supreme Court came up with an effective way to enforce the Fourth Amendment. The Court ruled that if evidence is found or seized illegally, it cannot be used in court. This is called the **exclusionary rule**.

Suppose the police are investigating a murder. In response to a phoned-in tip, the police break into a suspect's home and find a knife. The knife has the suspect's fingerprints on it and is covered with the victim's blood.

Ordinarily, this knife could be used to prove that the suspect committed the murder. In this case, however, the police have obtained the knife illegally. They didn't have permission to enter the suspect's home, and they didn't take the time to get a warrant. Therefore, under the exclusionary rule, the knife cannot be used as evidence in court. If this is the only evidence against the suspect, he or she probably will not be convicted.

The exclusionary rule encourages law enforcement officers to obey the Fourth Amendment. They know that if they break the rules, any evidence they find illegally will be thrown out of court and their efforts will have accomplished nothing.

Many people have objected to the exclusionary rule because it sometimes prevents clearly guilty people from being convicted. Those who have committed serious crimes may be allowed to go free on what most people view as a technicality.

In recent years the Supreme Court has begun to make some exceptions to the exclusionary rule. One is the "good faith" exception: Suppose an officer goes through all the legal procedures necessary to obtain a warrant. The officer then uses the warrant to seize a piece of evidence. Later, he or she discovers that the warrant is invalid—perhaps because the judge made an error in filling it out. Because the officer acted in good faith—that is, because he or she didn't deliberately violate the Fourth Amendment—the evidence may still be used in court.

REVIEW QUESTIONS

1. Explain what is meant by the Fourth Amendment right to privacy.
2. What is a warrant? How does a police officer get one?
3. Describe four situations in which a police officer can invade a person's privacy without a warrant.
4. What is the exclusionary rule? How does it protect people against illegal searches and seizures?

AFTER THE ARREST

Imagine that you have been arrested and are in police custody. The police will try many ways to get evidence that can be presented at your trial. They may, for example, ask questions, take fingerprints, request blood samples, or ask for other identifying information. They may line you up with a group of other suspects and ask a witness to pick you out of the group. They may even try to persuade you to confess.

A confession can make the prosecutor's job much easier. If you willingly confess to having committed a crime, that confession can be used as evidence to convict you.

Not all confessions, however, are given willingly. In the past police officers sometimes used heavy-handed tactics to get confessions or information from people in their custody. Some officers made threats; others made false promises. Some tried to beat confessions out of people accused of a crime. One man in custody was told that his seriously ill wife would be taken from her bed and brought in for questioning if he didn't cooperate. Others have complained of being interrogated for 36 hours straight, being kept awake all night, or being held in solitary confinement until they confessed.

The Fifth and Sixth amendments protect people against mistreatment while in police custody. The Supreme Court has used these amendments to develop a set of rules about what the police can and cannot do to get information.

The Right to Remain Silent

The Fifth Amendment says, "No person . . . shall be compelled . . . to be a witness against himself." This amendment protects you against **self-incrimination**. It means, in other words, that no one can force you to say something that might link you with a crime. If you are being tried on criminal charges, you may refuse to speak at the trial.

The Fifth Amendment applies not only in the courtroom but at all times while you're in police custody. You are *never* required to answer police officers' questions or to respond to their statements, whether at the scene of the arrest, in the police car, or at the police station. Your decision to remain silent cannot be taken as a sign of guilt, and your silence cannot be used as evidence against you in court. If you choose to speak, however, anything you say *can* be used as evidence against you. For example, if the police start chatting with you, hoping that you'll say something incriminating in casual conversation, your comments may be used against you.

The Supreme Court has made some exceptions to the right to remain silent. For example, Billy Joe Wade, an accused bank robber, was asked to stand in a lineup with several other men to see if one of the bank employees could identify him. The employee said that she couldn't remember the robber's face but that she would recognize his voice if she heard it. The police asked each man in the line, including Wade, to repeat the words the robber had said. Wade refused on the grounds that he might incriminate himself by speaking.

In its ruling on the case, the Supreme Court disagreed with Wade. The Court said that giving a "voice sample" didn't constitute self-incrimination. In other cases, the Court has held that a person accused of a crime may be required to give a handwriting sample or a blood sample; to put on certain articles of clothing, hairpieces, or eyeglasses; or to submit to an x-ray examination. None of these activities are considered self-incrimination.

The Right to Counsel

The Sixth Amendment says, "In all criminal prosecutions, the accused shall enjoy the right . . . to have the assistance of counsel for his defence." In other words, from the moment you are arrested, you are entitled to have a lawyer defend you. Early in this century, the Supreme Court expanded its interpretation of the Sixth Amendment. The Court ruled that if you can't afford to hire a lawyer, the government must hire one for you.

Naturally, you can't expect to choose any lawyer you want and have the government pay the bills. Some states and counties employ full-time **public defenders**—lawyers who are assigned to help people with low incomes who have been accused of a crime. Other states and counties have a roster of private lawyers who are willing to do public defense work.

The Constitution doesn't say how poor you must be to qualify for a court-appointed lawyer. (The Supreme Court has never answered this question either.) In general, courts make a decision based on the individual circumstances of each case. For example, if you have no money but you own six cars, a court would probably ask you to sell one of your cars to pay for a lawyer. In contrast, if you have no money and only one car—and you need the car to get to work every day—the court would probably hire a lawyer for you.

In making its decision, the court looks only at your own resources, not at the resources of your friends or family. If you have a low income but have wealthy relatives, the court may still be obligated to hire a lawyer for you.

You are entitled to **waive**, or give up, any constitutional right. (For example, as you saw earlier in this chapter, you can waive your right to privacy by consenting to be searched.) You can, if you wish, waive your Sixth Amendment right to a lawyer by telling the judge that you choose to defend yourself in court. In most cases, however, the judge will try to discourage you from representing yourself. Though you may be innocent, you could easily be convicted because you don't understand the legal process well enough. If that happens, you won't be allowed to complain later that your trial was unfair because you didn't have a lawyer.

The Right to Due Process

In addition to these specific rights, the Constitution gives you an important general right: the right to "due process of law." This right is mentioned in both the Fifth and Fourteenth amendments. The Rochin case at the beginning of this chapter showed you one way in which the right to due process has been applied. The Supreme Court decided that by beating Antonio Rochin and pumping his stomach, the police had deprived Rochin of his right to due process.

Although the Constitution doesn't define the phrase, *due process* is generally understood to stand for a broad idea of fairness. The criminal justice system must apply the law fairly and equally to everyone, without cutting corners or taking shortcuts.

The Miranda Warnings

In the early 1960s Ernest Miranda was arrested on the charge of rape. The police followed their usual procedure: They took Miranda to the police station and into an interrogation room. Except for the two officers and Miranda himself, no one knows what happened in that room. When they came out, however, Miranda had signed a confession to the rape.

As a result of his confession, Miranda was convicted and sentenced to 20 years in prison. Afterward, he complained that he had been treated unfairly. He was not a lawyer, and so he knew nothing about his rights under the Fifth and Sixth amendments. No one had told him that whatever he said to the police could be repeated in court. No one had told him that he could have a lawyer with him in the interrogation room. As a result, he had been deprived of his right to due process.

His case went to the Supreme Court. The Court agreed that Miranda had been cheated of his constitutional rights. To make sure that the same thing would not happen in the future, the Court ruled that all suspects must have their rights explained to them at the time they are arrested. Since 1966, law enforcement officers have been required to say the following when they make an arrest:

You have the right to remain silent. Anything you say can be used against you in court. You have the right to consult a lawyer and to have a lawyer with you while you are being questioned. If you cannot afford a lawyer, one will be provided for you before any questioning begins.

Illustration 3-4 When the police are arresting a person, they must explain clearly to the suspect his or her rights and be sure the suspect understands those rights.

These statements have come to be called the **Miranda warnings**. Although officers do not have to repeat the exact words shown here, they do have to explain the suspect's rights clearly. They must also make sure that a person accused of a crime understands those rights and has no questions about them.

Earlier in this chapter you read about the exclusionary rule—the rule that prevents illegally obtained evidence from being used in court. The exclusionary rule applies to words said by the accused as well as to physical evidence. If a person accused of a crime makes a confession before hearing the Miranda warnings, that confession can't be used as evidence.

As you might expect, many people object to this use of the exclusionary rule. They do not believe that signed confessions should be kept out of court just because the Miranda warnings weren't read to the suspect. In recent years the Supreme Court has made some exceptions to the exclusionary rule.

In New York City, for example, a woman told the police that she had just been raped at gunpoint. She then saw her attacker run into a supermarket. The police ran into the supermarket and arrested Benjamin Quarles. Quarles matched the woman's description, but he had no gun—he was wearing an empty holster. One officer asked, "Where is the gun?" Quarles pointed and said, "The gun is over there." The officers found the revolver, read Quarles his Miranda warnings, and took him away.

After he was convicted, Quarles protested that he had been questioned before hearing the Miranda warnings. Therefore, his statement about the gun should not have been used as evidence. The Supreme Court disagreed. It held that the officer had to ask about the gun immediately to protect the public safety. The officer's question was not the kind of question that the Miranda warnings were designed to protect against; that is, it was not intended to trick Quarles into making a confession. Therefore, the Court ruled that Quarles's answer could be used as evidence.

Prohibition against Excessive Bail

At the beginning of this chapter, you read that defendants are often released from custody after they deposit a sum of money called bail. When they show up for the trial, the bail money is returned to them. The bail system is intended to make sure that defendants will not run away or disappear before they are tried. At the same time, it ensures that people accused of crimes—people who, under the law, are still innocent—do not have to spend time in jail.

Illustration 3-5   Many people who must post bail get the money from a bail bondsperson, who, for a fee, pays the bail to the court.

Setting the amount of bail is a delicate matter. For the system to be effective, the amount of bail must be relatively high. Otherwise, many defendants would be willing to give up the money as the price of avoiding a trial. By contrast, if the amount of bail is set *too* high, a defendant might not be able to pay it.

The Eighth Amendment, which deals with the subject of bail, says very little about it. It says, "Excessive bail shall not be required," but it doesn't define *excessive*. Some courts have said that those arrested for similar crimes should pay similar amounts of bail. Others have said that a judge should set bail according to a defendant's ability to pay. In this case, if a defendant can't afford to pay bail at all, some alternative must be made available.

The Supreme Court has held that a judge may deny bail entirely to certain people. Defendants who can't be trusted to return or who are so dangerous that releasing them would endanger lives can be locked up without bail. Similarly, harmless or trustworthy defendants may be released without having to pay bail.

REVIEW QUESTIONS

1. Define *self-incrimination*.
2. What rights do you have if you are arrested for a crime and you can't afford a lawyer?
3. What are the Miranda warnings? When must a police officer recite them?
4. Under what circumstances can a judge deny bail to a defendant?

DURING AND AFTER THE TRIAL

The Fifth, Sixth, and Eighth amendments include more rights than we've talked about so far. These additional rights can protect you during and after a trial.

Trial Rights

The Sixth Amendment gives you the right to a "speedy and public trial, by an impartial jury." The meaning of *speedy*, however, has never been made clear. As you've already read, time will always pass between the day you are arrested and the day of your trial. In most cases, you wouldn't have to spend that time in jail; instead, you'd be released on bail.

Even so, the longer your trial is delayed, the more difficult it may be to defend yourself. Crucial pieces of evidence may be lost or damaged; some witnesses' memories may fade; other witnesses may die, disappear, or move far away. If a long delay in your trial makes your defense more difficult, the Sixth Amendment gives you the right to ask that the case against you be dropped.

The right to a "public trial" means that the public—including reporters—must be allowed to see everything that goes on in court. This right is based on the idea that you are more likely to be treated fairly at a public trial than at a secret trial. According to the Supreme Court, however, trials may be closed to the public in certain circumstances. In rape cases or child abuse cases, for example, the need to protect the victim from public embarrassment may outweigh the right of the public to watch the trial.

The right to a trial by jury is one of the few rights mentioned in the original Constitution as well as in the Bill of Rights. (The use of juries to decide criminal cases dates back nearly a thousand years.) The Constitution says little about how a jury is to be used, so most of those details vary from state to state. Some states require that a jury consist of 12 people; others require only 6. Some states require that a jury's verdict be unanimous; others require only a majority vote. The Supreme Court has held that juries may not be required at trials for very minor offenses.

The Sixth Amendment says that "the accused shall enjoy the right . . . to be confronted with the witnesses against him." In practice, this means that you are entitled to be present at your own criminal trial. It also means that people who testify against you must do so in person so that you (or your lawyer) can question them. There are, of course, exceptions to these rules. If a defendant becomes disruptive, he or she may be removed from the courtroom. If a witness needs special protection (for example, if the witness is a child), he or she may be allowed to testify in private or on videotape.

Posttrial Protections

If you are convicted of a crime, a judge will decide how you are to be punished. According to the Eighth Amendment, your punishment cannot be "cruel and unusual." The Constitution offers no guidance, however, about what punishments fall into this category. The Supreme Court has ruled that torture, flogging, long periods of solitary confinement, and forced sterilization are cruel and unusual punishments. It has also held that punishments that don't "fit the crime"—such as a 20-year sentence for possessing a small amount of marijuana—are cruel and unusual.

Some human rights activists have argued that **capital punishment**, the death penalty, is cruel and unusual and should be prohibited. The Supreme Court has never interpreted the Constitution that way. It has, however, restricted the use of capital punishment. The Court requires that certain strict legal procedures be followed before a person can be sentenced to death. (Table 3-1 shows state-by-state information on the death penalty.)

Suppose you are tried for a crime and **acquitted**—that is, declared not guilty. In that case, the Fifth Amendment protects you from being tried again for the same crime. (The Fifth Amendment says that no defendant "shall . . . be twice put in jeopardy of life or limb." As a result, being tried twice for a single crime has become known as **double jeopardy**.) Of course, if you are a bank robber who has robbed the same bank twice, you can be tried separately for each robbery. If you are tried for one robbery and acquitted, however, you can't be tried again for the same robbery—even if new evidence turns up that clearly proves you committed the crime.

There are exceptions to the double jeopardy rule. For example, if a jury can't agree on a verdict, your trial may be declared a **mistrial**—an unsuccessful trial. In that case, you may be tried again for the same crime, with a new jury.

REVIEW QUESTIONS

1. Under what circumstances might a trial be closed to the public?
2. What does it mean to confront witnesses?
3. What is capital punishment? Is it ever legal?
4. What is double jeopardy?

Table 3–1 Capital Punishment in the United States, 1976 to April 1991

State	Capital Punishment Permitted?	Number on Death Row	Executions Since 1976[1]	State	Capital Punishment Permitted?	Number on Death Row	Executions Since 1976[1]
Alabama	Yes	109	8	Montana	Yes	6	
Alaska	No			Nebraska	Yes	12	
Arizona	Yes	96		Nevada	Yes	60	5
Arkansas	Yes	35	2	New Hampshire	Yes		
California	Yes	299		New Jersey	Yes	13	
Colorado	Yes	2		New Mexico	Yes	2	
Connecticut	Yes	2		New York	No		
Delaware	Yes	7		North Carolina	Yes	99	3
District of Columbia	No			North Dakota	No		
Florida	Yes	295	26	Ohio	Yes	99	
Georgia	Yes	113	14	Oklahoma	Yes	122	1
Hawaii	No			Oregon	Yes	20	
Idaho	Yes	21		Pennsylvania	Yes	132	
Illinois	Yes	136	1	Rhode Island	No		
Indiana	Yes	53	2	South Carolina	Yes	43	3
Iowa	No			South Dakota	Yes		
Kansas	No			Tennessee	Yes	85	
Kentucky	Yes	27		Texas	Yes	335	38
Louisiana	Yes	34	19	Utah	Yes	11	3
Maine	No			Vermont	No		
Maryland	Yes	16		Virginia	Yes	45	11
Massachusetts	No			Washington	Yes	9	
Michigan	No			West Virginia	No		
Minnesota	No			Wisconsin	No		
Mississippi	Yes	52	4	Wyoming	Yes	2	
Missouri	Yes	73	5	U.S. Military	Yes	5	
				Totals		2,470[2]	145

1. After a ten-year suspension of executions, the Supreme Court, in the 1976 case *Gregg v. Georgia*, provided the constitutional basis for resuming the death penalty.
2. The actual number of people on death row is 2,457. The difference in totals is due to the fact that some inmates are under sentence of death in more than one state.

Source: NAACP Legal Defense and Educational Fund, Inc.

Viewpoints on Capital Punishment

As of 1991, more than 2,400 convicted criminals were waiting on death row. One of them was Wilbert Lee Evans. Evans had been convicted of the 1981 shooting murder of Deputy Sheriff William Truesdale. After being sentenced to death, Evans remained on death row for nearly ten years while his lawyers filed appeals. Finally, in October 1990, Wilbert Lee Evans was executed in Virginia's electric chair.

Virginia is one of 36 states that currently have death penalty laws. In almost all these states, the death penalty is reserved for the crime of murder. All 36 states must comply with a 1976 Supreme Court ruling that requires special procedures in death penalty cases. The subject of capital punishment continues to be hotly debated around the country. Is the death penalty just what a murderer deserves? Or is execution an example of cruel and unusual punishment?

The Argument for Capital Punishment

Supporters of capital punishment believe that it is needed to protect members of our society. They argue that it is the right and duty of a civilized society to punish terrible crimes with a sentence of death. Death penalty supporters believe that capital punishment deters criminals in two important ways. First, some criminals may be stopped from committing murder because they know their actions may be punished by death. Second, the only sure way to stop cold-blooded murderers is to put an end to their lives. Otherwise, they might escape or they could be released in time, only to kill again.

People who support capital punishment believe that enough safeguards are built into the system to prevent innocent persons from being executed. They believe that there are plenty of chances for an unjust verdict to be overturned before an execution occurs.

Supporters of the death penalty also point out that opinion polls show that up to 75 percent of Americans favor capital punishment for certain crimes. Capital punishment, therefore, expresses the wishes of the nation's people.

The Argument against Capital Punishment

Many people oppose the death penalty on moral grounds. They point out that a society that respects life should not take an individual's life even if that person has committed a violent crime. They argue that the death penalty is no more than state-sponsored murder and that it violates the U.S. Constitution, which forbids cruel and unusual punishment.

Opponents do not believe that the death penalty protects society any more effectively than life imprisonment does. They point out that no study has proved that the death penalty deters crime. In fact, the murder rates in states that have death penalty laws are just as high as those in states without such laws.

People who oppose the death penalty also express concern that innocent persons might be executed. They believe that *not* executing the guilty is necessary to avoid the risk of executing an innocent person.

Critics of the death penalty note that when poll questions offer life in prison without parole as an alternative to the death penalty, American support for the death penalty drops below 50 percent—proof, say the critics, that support for capital punishment is not overwhelming.

Capital Punishment and the Law

In 1987 the Supreme Court heard the most recent challenge to the constitutionality of capital punishment. The case involved a furniture store robbery in which a white police officer was shot and killed. One of the four robbers, who was black, was convicted of murder and sentenced to death. A study of this and other murder cases concluded that killers of whites are four times more likely to receive death sentences than killers of blacks are. The case brought before the Supreme Court challenged the constitutionality of the death penalty on the grounds that statistics showed that it was not applied fairly. The Court's decision found that the unfair application of the law was not sufficient cause to strike it down. Even so, the issue continues to spark strong feelings in many Americans.

Chapter Review

Chapter Summary

- The Fourth, Fifth, Sixth, Eighth, and Fourteenth amendments to the U.S. Constitution protect us from unfair treatment within the criminal justice system.

- The Constitution has very broad rules about the treatment of criminal suspects. The Supreme Court interprets those rules—sometimes loosely, sometimes strictly.

- The Constitution sets minimum standards for protection. State laws and other federal laws may give us more rights than the Constitution does.

- According to the Supreme Court, our privacy rights under the Fourth Amendment depend on how much privacy we can *reasonably expect* in a given situation.

- The Fourth Amendment allows law enforcement officers to search or seize only (1) when they do so without invading anyone's privacy, (2) when they have a warrant, or (3) when certain special circumstances demand it.

- A judge can issue a warrant to an officer only if that officer can show probable cause.

- Anything seized illegally is subject to the exclusionary rule. It cannot be used as evidence in court.

- If you are arrested, the police must notify you of your rights by reciting the Miranda warnings. Until they have done so, they may not ask you any questions.

- The Fifth Amendment protection against self-incrimination allows you to remain silent while in police custody. If you choose to speak, anything you say may be used as evidence against you.

■ The Sixth Amendment gives you the right to be defended by a lawyer. If you can't afford to hire a lawyer, the government must hire one for you.

■ The Eighth Amendment gives you the right to reasonable bail. Judges are permitted to deny bail to dangerous or untrustworthy defendants.

■ The Sixth Amendment entitles you to a speedy, public trial by an impartial jury. It also gives you the right to confront witnesses against you.

■ The Eighth Amendment forbids "cruel and unusual punishments" such as torture and excessively long sentences. It does not forbid capital punishment.

■ The Fifth Amendment protects your right to due process. It also protects you against double jeopardy (being tried twice for the same crime).

Understanding Legal Terms

On a separate sheet of paper, match the terms below with the definitions that follow.

acquit	mistrial
arrest	probable cause
bail	self-incrimination
defendant	waive
double jeopardy	warrant

1. A person who has been charged in court with a crime
2. Saying something that links you with a crime
3. To take into custody
4. The reasonable belief that a crime has been committed or that a particular person has committed a crime
5. To give up, as an individual right
6. Being tried twice for a single crime
7. A sum of money deposited with the court that is returned when the accused person shows up for trial
8. A court order, signed by a judge, that authorizes a search or an arrest
9. To declare not guilty
10. A trial that is unsuccessful, for example, because the jury can't agree on a verdict

Applying the Law

1. Loretta checks into a hotel room. The hotel manager, thinking Loretta's behavior is suspicious, calls the police. A police officer arrives without a

search warrant. While Loretta is out to dinner, the manager lets the officer into Loretta's room. The officer searches the room and finds a small amount of cocaine. Loretta is arrested and tried for illegal possession of a controlled substance. Can the cocaine be used as evidence at Loretta's trial? Explain your answer.

2. A deputy sheriff, driving on a residential street, sees a man having a yard sale on his front lawn. Among the items for sale are several old rifles. In this state, only licensed retailers may legally sell firearms. The deputy gets out of the car, seizes the rifles, and arrests the man who is selling them. Is this a legal search and seizure? Explain your answer.

3. Officer Brandon has been watching a certain apartment building for several weeks. He sees heavily made up women going in and out at all hours of the day and night, each time with a different man. He knows that there is a prostitution ring in the area, and he thinks it may be run from this apartment building. Officer Brandon wants to search the building to get more information. What steps must he take before he can enter the building?

4. Officer Martin sees Wayne walk into a convenience store and point a gun at the cashier. The officer enters the store and says, "Stop right there. You're under arrest." She says nothing else to Wayne. She takes him to the police station, where she and other officers begin to ask him questions. How has Officer Martin violated Wayne's constitutional rights?

5. Five years ago, Roland was arrested on charges of burglary and was released on bail. Now, five years later, his case is finally coming to trial. Roland's defense is that he could not have committed the burglary because he was caring for his mother that night. Roland had planned to call his mother as a witness at the trial, but she died during the five-year delay. What can Roland do to protect himself?

6. The FBI suspects Patrice of having committed murder. They arrest her, question her, gather fingerprints, question witnesses, and collect other evidence. Patrice is tried for the murder and found not guilty. After the trial is over, a witness comes forward with new evidence that Patrice is guilty. Can Patrice be tried again? Explain your answer.

Case Studies

1. Three men stood on a street corner in Cleveland, Ohio, near a large store. One at a time, each man strolled down the street, peered into the store's window, walked a short distance, turned back, peered into the window again, and then went back and talked with the others. Officer McFadden, noticing the men's strange behavior, watched them from a distance. In less than 15 minutes the men made roughly a dozen trips past the store window. From the officer's experience, it was clear that the men were "casing" the store, that is, planning a robbery. He finally approached the three men, questioned them, and frisked them for weapons. Did the officer need a warrant to do what he did? Explain your answer.

2. Jesse James Gilbert was arrested for robbing a bank. The police read him his Miranda warnings and took him to the police station for questioning. During the questioning, they asked Gilbert to provide a handwriting sample. Later, in court, the prosecutor showed a hand-drawn map of the bank that had been found at the scene of the crime. He then showed that Gilbert's handwriting sample matched the handwriting on the map. Gilbert protested that the handwriting sample should be excluded from the evidence because it was self-incriminating. Was he right? Explain your answer.

3. John Garvey was caught picking flowers in a public park in New Orleans. The judge sentenced him to six years in prison. The usual punishment for violating a park rule was 30 days. Which constitutional amendment gives Garvey the right to protest his sentence?

Unit 2

Criminal Law

Chapter 4

Types of Crimes

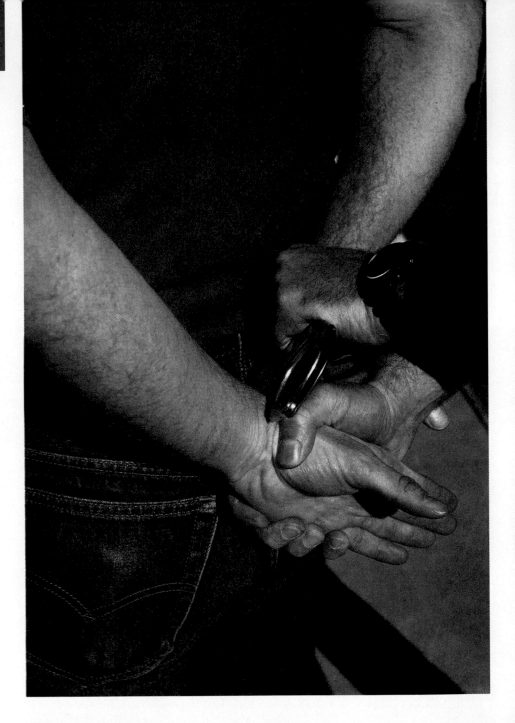

Chapter Objectives   When you have read this chapter, you should be able to:

■ Explain the differences between a felony and a misdemeanor.

■ Define the two basic elements of a crime.

■ List the parties to a crime.

■ Explain the differences between murder and manslaughter.

■ Describe four types of crimes against property.

■ Describe five defenses against criminal charges.

Case Study

Cody v. State, 605 S.W.2d 271 (Texas 1980).

On October 6, 1977, a student named Robert Lee Cody went to a dance at Sunset High School in Dallas, Texas. While at the dance, he got into an argument with the adults at the front door about whether he had paid the admission fee. The argument made Cody angry. He went to a gas station near the school and filled a jug with gasoline. He then took the jug back to the high school and went upstairs.

Police officer Bernardo Silva was assigned to handle security at the dance. From outside the school building, Silva saw Cody pouring something on the second-floor balcony. He went upstairs and found that the entire floor was covered with gasoline. He stopped Cody, searched him, and discovered that Cody had matches in his pocket.

Silva arrested Cody on the charge of attempted arson. Cody was tried, found guilty, and sentenced to two years in prison.

Cody appealed his conviction. He said that he couldn't be guilty of attempting to burn the school, because he'd never even taken the matches out of his pocket. The appeals court disagreed. It is true, the court said, that planning or preparing to commit a crime is not in itself a crime. Nevertheless, taking a substantial step toward committing a crime—such as, in this case, pouring gasoline on the floor—constitutes a crime called *attempt*. Cody's conviction was allowed to stand, and Cody was ordered to serve a prison term.

GENERAL RULES OF CRIMINAL LAW

A crime is an act that the government forbids and that the government can punish. Every state and local government, along with the federal government, has a set of laws defining which acts are crimes. In this chapter, you will read about some of the most common crimes. In Chapter 5, you will find out what happens after a crime is committed and how a person who commits a crime is tried and punished.

Classification of Crimes

Except for very minor crimes (such as parking violations), all crimes.are classified as either misdemeanors or felonies. These classifications indicate the maximum penalty that can be imposed for the crime. A **misdemeanor** is any crime for which the maximum penalty is less than a year in jail. A **felony** is any crime for which the punishment may be imprisonment for a year or longer or death.

Felonies are more serious than misdemeanors in a number of ways. A person convicted of a felony may be barred from certain types of work, such as the practice of law or police work. Some states will not permit anyone convicted of a felony to hold public office. As you will see in Chapter 5, the arrest and trial processes are also somewhat different for felonies than they are for misdemeanors.

Illustration 4-1   Some states have regulations about the records of people who hold public office.

Elements of a Crime

With a few exceptions, a person can be convicted of a crime only if he or she (1) does something that violates a criminal law and (2) does it intentionally. These two requirements are called *criminal act* and *criminal intent*.

Criminal Act   It is not a crime in the United States to think bad thoughts. In the opening case, Robert Cody tried to burn down a school. If all he had done was *think* about burning it down—even if he had planned every detail down to which pocket he would carry the matches in—he would not have been guilty of a crime. It is only because Cody took some action beyond thinking about it that he was convicted and imprisoned.

Normally, you can be found guilty of a crime only because of something you do—not because of something you *don't* do. For example, you have no legal duty to try to stop a crime or to help an injured person.

In some cases, however, people do have a legal duty to act. Parents, for example, have a duty to get medical care for their children when the children are ill. If a parent fails to carry out this duty, he or she may be guilty of a crime.

Criminal Intent　　Even if you've done something that violates a criminal law, you may not have committed a crime. Your action is a crime only if you *meant* to do what you did. Criminal law isn't designed to punish people who do things accidentally. It is meant to punish people who do things intentionally (on purpose) or, in some cases, recklessly (by taking an unreasonable risk).

Suppose you're at a party given by your friend Dionne. You've brought some new CDs along, and as you play them during the party, they get mixed in with Dionne's CDs. When you collect your CDs, you accidentally pick up one of Dionne's disks. You leave without noticing that you've taken her disk with you. In this case, even though you've walked away with someone else's property, your action is not a crime. You took the CD by mistake. You had no intent to take something that belonged to someone else.

There are some crimes for which you can be found guilty without criminal intent. These are called **strict liability** crimes. Most of these are crimes that threaten the safety or welfare of other people. Driving faster than the speed limit, for example, is always a crime—even if you didn't know the speed limit and didn't intend to exceed it.

Act plus Intent　　A crime can take place only if a criminal act and criminal intent occur at the same time. For example, suppose your friend Dionne has a CD that you really want. Many times in the past, you've thought about stealing it. Then, one night, you go to her party and accidentally take it home. Because you didn't intend to steal the CD at the time you actually took it, you haven't committed a crime. (Of course, if you ever do find that you've taken someone's property accidentally, you must return it as soon as possible. Failure to do so *is* a crime.)

Parties to a Crime

In 1972 Arthur Morrow and three friends entered an apartment building in Cambridge, Massachusetts. They beat and robbed a number of people. While they were in the building, one of the men raped a woman.

The four men were arrested, charged, and found guilty of a number of crimes, included armed robbery and rape. Morrow appealed his conviction on the charge of rape. He said that he was not a rapist—it was one of his friends who had attacked the woman.

The appeals court did not accept Morrow's argument. According to the court, the evidence showed that Morrow had been present during the rape and that he might even have helped or encouraged his friend. His presence and encouragement made Morrow guilty of the crime of rape.

The person who actually commits a crime is called the **principal**. Anyone who helps the principal complete the crime is called an **accomplice**. That person is also guilty of the crime. Accomplices can help the principal in any number of ways. Some help at the scene of the crime—for example, by acting as a lookout or driving the getaway car. Others help away from the scene of the crime—for example, by helping to plan the crime or by supplying equipment that is used in the crime.

Anyone who knowingly helps a criminal *after* a crime has been committed—for example, by hiding the criminal, destroying evidence, or lying to a police officer—is called an **accessory after the fact**. Unlike accomplices, accessories after the fact are responsible only for their own actions, not for the original crime.

REVIEW QUESTIONS

1. What is the basic difference between a felony and a misdemeanor?
2. What does *criminal intent* mean? Give an example.
3. What is an accessory after the fact?

CRIMES AGAINST PEOPLE

Earlier in this chapter you read that all crimes are classified either as felonies or as misdemeanors. Crimes—both felonies and misdemeanors—are also categorized as being against people or against property. First we'll discuss crimes against people.

Homicide

Homicide is the act of killing another person. Until about two hundred years ago, anyone who killed another person would be punished by death. Today, homicide is divided into categories based on the circumstances of the killing and the intent of the killer. The punishment for an act of homicide depends on the category it falls into.

The most serious type of homicide—in which the criminal intent is greatest and for which the punishment is most severe—is called murder. Less serious killing is called manslaughter.

Murder   **Murder** is generally defined as killing with the intent to kill or to cause serious bodily harm. Let's say, for example, that Crystal walks into a bar with a gun, walks up to James, and shoots him. If James dies, Crystal has committed murder.

Most states recognize different levels, or degrees, of murder. The most serious level—**first-degree murder**—is defined as killing that is not merely intended but also premeditated.

An act that is **premeditated** is one that has been thought about beforehand. A premeditated murder is committed by someone who has had some time to reflect on what he or she is doing. It is sometimes called "killing with a cool mind."

For example, James Blaikie Jr., a resident of Brookline, Massachusetts, was deeply in debt. In December 1974 he borrowed $6,000 from his friend Caesar DeWilde. When the time drew near to pay DeWilde back, Blaikie was even deeper in debt. He phoned DeWilde at work, told him he had the money he owed him, and asked him to come over. When DeWilde arrived, Blaikie shot him in the back of the head, wrapped him in plastic, and buried him in the basement of his house. Because Blaikie owed money to DeWilde and appeared to have planned the murder, a court found Blaikie guilty of first-degree murder.

Murder that is not premeditated is usually called **second-degree murder.** In most states, second-degree murder includes killing by outrageously reckless conduct even if there was no intent to kill or cause harm. For example, let's say Crystal walks into the bar and begins shooting randomly. She doesn't aim at anyone and doesn't mean to hurt anyone, but one of her bullets hits and kills James. Because of her reckless conduct (sometimes defined as "conduct that shows extreme indifference for human life"), she is guilty of murder. Similar examples of reckless conduct might include throwing stones from the top of a tall building or driving a car on a sidewalk.

A person who kills while committing a felony may be guilty of **felony murder**. Let's say Crystal decides to break into James's house and steal his valuables. James finds Crystal in his home, and they fight. During the fight, Crystal throws a heavy lamp at James. If James dies from the blow, Crystal is guilty of felony murder. In many states, felony murder is considered as serious a crime as first-degree murder.

Manslaughter   The law recognizes that when people are angry or upset, they sometimes lose their sense of reason or their self-control. They do things that they normally would not do. Courts refer to this temporary mental state as the "heat of passion." A killing committed in the heat of passion is usually considered **voluntary manslaughter** rather than murder.

Let's say Anthony comes home and finds his wife, Shannon, in bed with Damon. In a fury, Anthony grabs a baseball bat and attacks Damon. Damon dies. Because the killing took place in the heat of passion, Anthony would most likely be found guilty of voluntary manslaughter.

The courts have defined *heat of passion* as a temporary state of mind that wears off in time. Therefore, in order for a killing to be considered voluntary manslaughter, the killer must not have had time to cool off. Suppose Anthony finds Damon in bed with Shannon, waits a week, and then goes to Damon's house and kills him. Because Anthony had plenty of time to get his feelings under control, a court would probably find him guilty of premeditated murder—not voluntary manslaughter.

Another type of manslaughter is called involuntary manslaughter. (*Involuntary* means "not intentional.") **Involuntary manslaughter** is a killing that happens accidentally, as a result of someone's gross negligence or reckless behavior. This category is very much like second-degree murder. The only difference, in fact, is the degree of recklessness involved.

On December 17, 1977, Edward Leon Puryear was driving past a field in western Arizona. He saw what he thought was a goose. He stopped his car, took out a rifle, and shot into the field. The "goose" he shot at was actually a goose decoy that several hunters had set up. His gunshot hit and killed one of the hunters.

If Puryear had shot wildly and randomly into the field, he might have been charged with second-degree murder. In this case, however, he had reasonably aimed at what seemed to be a goose. His real crime was that he failed to take proper precautions; that is, he failed to make sure that what he was shooting at really *was* a goose. Therefore, he was eventually found guilty of the lesser crime of involuntary manslaughter.

Noncriminal Homicide   There are times when killing another person is not a crime. Homicides conducted in the line of duty by soldiers and law enforcement officers generally fall into this category. Suppose, for example, that a kidnapper is holding a gun to the head of a hostage. If a police officer shoots and kills the kidnapper, the officer is not considered to have broken the law. Other instances of noncriminal homicide include executing a person condemned to death and killing an enemy soldier in wartime.

Assault and Battery

Battery is physical contact with someone against his or her will. (Like homicide, battery is normally considered a crime only if it is intentional or reckless.) An **assault** is an act that makes someone fear that he or she will be a victim of battery. Although it is possible to commit an assault without battery—or vice versa—many states combine the two into a single crime called *assault and battery*.

Assault and battery is usually classified as a misdemeanor. There is, however, a more serious form of assault and battery—called aggravated assault and battery or first-degree assault and battery—which is considered a felony. In some cases, aggravated assault and battery means attacking someone with the intent to kill or cause serious bodily harm. In other cases, it means attacking someone with a deadly weapon.

Certain acts of assault and battery are not considered crimes. For example, it is not a crime for parents to spank their children. It is not a crime for police officers to use force on an individual who resists arrest. It is also not a crime for players in a contact sport to shove or tackle each other.

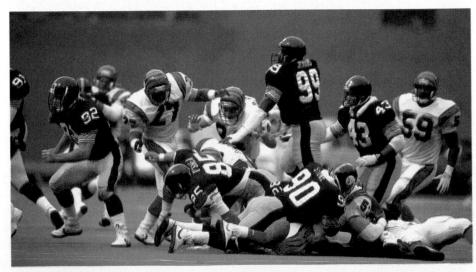

Illustration 4-2   It is not a crime for players in contact sports to shove or tackle each other.

Rape

When a man forces a woman to have sexual intercourse or has intercourse with her without her consent, he has committed the crime of **rape**. Rape is a very serious form of aggravated battery for which the penalties are usually severe.

In most cases, it's clear whether a woman has consented to a sexual act. A woman who struggles to get away from a stranger in a dark alley has clearly not consented. Sometimes, however, a woman is raped by a friend, a date, or a neighbor. This sort of sexual attack is often called *date rape* or *acquaintance rape*. In cases like these, it is often difficult for a woman to prove in court that she didn't consent to the act. (This is especially true if the woman is romantically involved with the man who raped her or if she has consented to sexual relations with him in the past.) Many women fail to report acquaintance rapes, either out of fear or embarrassment or because they don't realize that acquaintance rape is a crime.

Girls under a certain age (usually 16, but the limit varies from state to state) are considered to be too young to consent to sexual intercourse. Having sex with anyone under that age is called **statutory rape**. Statutory rape is a crime regardless of whether force was used. It is usually a strict liability offense. In other words, it's a crime even if the girl's sexual partner truly believes the girl is old enough to consent.

Rape laws are always changing. In the past, for example, the only way a woman could prove that she didn't consent to intercourse was to prove that she struggled and resisted as hard as she could. Now, lawmakers recognize that such resistance—especially when the man has a deadly weapon—may make the situation worse. Many states now require only evidence of reasonable resistance.

Another modern change involves the "marital exemption" rule. This rule states that a man's sexual intercourse with his own wife—with or without force—can never constitute rape. Recently, states have begun to limit the marital exemption. Some states will not apply it to couples who are legally separated or living apart. Others will not apply it when the husband uses physical force. Of course, regardless of the state law, any husband who uses force on his wife, for any reason, can be guilty of assault and battery.

The biggest change in this area is an expansion of the definition of rape. Michigan, for example, has redefined rape to include any criminal sexual conduct committed by any person (of either sex) against another person (of either sex).

REVIEW QUESTIONS

1. What does it mean that a murder is premeditated? Give an example of a premeditated murder.
2. What is felony murder?
3. Define *assault* and *battery*, and explain why these two crimes are often combined.
4. Define *statutory rape*, and explain why it is usually a strict liability crime.

CRIMES AGAINST PROPERTY

Crimes against property include burglary, vandalism, and theft crimes such as larceny, forgery, and embezzlement. One particular crime—robbery—is an offense against both people and property. As you'll see, for that reason it is treated differently than other property crimes.

Theft Crimes

Deliberately taking or keeping property that doesn't belong to you is a crime called **theft**. Like homicide, theft is divided into categories (such as larceny, embezzlement, and robbery) based on the circumstances of the crime.

Within each category, thefts are classified as felonies or misdemeanors depending on the value of the stolen property. In most cases, it is a felony to steal something that is valued at over $100. Stealing something of lesser value is generally a misdemeanor.

Larceny   On March 29, 1952, Thomas Hufstetler drove into a service station in northeastern Alabama. He asked the attendant to fill his tank with gas and to add engine oil. The attendant filled his tank and went to get oil. While the attendant was away from the car, Hufstetler drove off without paying for the gas. He was arrested, tried, and found guilty of the crime of larceny.

Larceny is taking someone else's property with the intent to keep it. The most common form of larceny is shoplifting. **Shoplifting** is taking an item from a store without paying for it, or concealing something while in a store with the intent to steal it. Other forms of larceny include picking someone's pocket and leaving a restaurant without paying the bill.

Illustration 4-3   The most common form of larceny is shoplifting.

Because the definition of larceny includes "intent to keep," borrowing property without permission is generally not considered larceny. Many states, however, have made **joyriding** (borrowing a car without permission) a criminal act. Although joyriding is a less serious act than larceny, it still is a crime punishable by law.

Embezzlement is a crime closely related to larceny. **Embezzlement** is keeping property that you're legally allowed to use but that doesn't belong to you. Suppose, for example, that Jason works in an office with several other employees. All the employees have free access to the supply cabinet and are allowed to take whatever supplies they need to do their work. Every time Jason goes to the cabinet, he pockets a few extra pens and pencils and takes them home. Even though these pens and pencils may not be worth very much, Jason is guilty of embezzlement.

Theft by Deception   On February 3, 1986, Patricia Miles obtained a money order that was made out to Ericka Nickerson. (A money order is similar to a check.) Miles took the money order to a store in Columbus, Georgia, signed the name Ericka Nickerson on the back, and asked a clerk to cash it. The clerk did so, and Miles walked out with $290 belonging to Nickerson. Miles was later arrested and found guilty of the crime of forgery.

Forgery is making, altering, or signing a legal document with the intent to defraud. Changing a date on a bus pass and signing someone else's name to a letter are examples of forgery.

Passing a bad check is a crime similar to forgery. In every state, it's a crime to write a check if you know the check will bounce—that is, if your account lacks enough funds to cover the check.

The crime of using trickery or lies to acquire someone else's property is called **false pretenses**. For example, a butcher who rests a thumb on the scale while weighing meat is guilty of false pretenses.

Extortion   **Extortion**, also known as blackmail, is the use of threats to take away someone's property. A schoolyard bully who says, "Give me your lunch money or I'll beat you up after school," is committing the crime of extortion.

Receiving Stolen Property   If someone offers to sell or give you stolen property, you should turn down the offer. It is a crime to receive property that you know is stolen. It is also a crime to receive property that you *have reason to believe* is stolen. Suppose, for example, that a person on the street offers to sell you an expensive name-brand watch at an extremely low price. You don't know for sure that the watch is stolen, but your common sense should tell you that the offer is too good to be true. If you buy a watch anyway—and it turns out to be stolen—a court could find you guilty of receiving stolen property.

Robbery

When a mugger stops you and says, "Your money or your life," he or she is committing the crime of robbery. **Robbery** is taking something from another person through the use of force or threats. Because it combines the act of assault with the act of larceny, robbery is considered a particularly serious crime in most states.

An even more serious form of robbery is aggravated robbery. Aggravated robbery (known in some states as first-degree robbery) is robbery in which the robber intends to, or actually does, inflict serious bodily injury. The most common form of aggravated robbery is robbery with a deadly weapon (also called armed robbery).

Burglary

In everyday speech, we tend to confuse burglary with robbery. In criminal law, however, the two words have different meanings. It is possible for someone to commit a burglary without stealing anything or without even intending to steal anything.

In general, **burglary** is defined as entering someone's property with the intent to commit a crime. The details of the definition vary from state to state. In some states, for example, simply entering someone's property is enough. In other states, the burglar must enter by force, for instance, by picking a lock or breaking a window. In some states, the property must be a dwelling; in others, a car or an office would qualify as well. In some states, "intent to commit a crime" is replaced by "intent to commit a felony."

Some states' laws define a more serious form of burglary called aggravated burglary or first-degree burglary. A burglary may be aggravated if it occurs at night or if the burglar is armed with a deadly weapon.

Damaging Property

Destroying or damaging someone's property—either intentionally or through reckless behavior—is called **vandalism** or **malicious mischief**. Examples of vandalism include throwing stones through the windows of houses or cars, breaking off car antennas, and marking up walls with graffiti.

Destroying or damaging someone's property by means of fire or explosives is called **arson**. Occasionally, people have been known to burn their own buildings to collect money on a fire insurance policy. For this reason, burning one's own property may be considered arson.

Entering someone's property without permission is called **trespassing**. Trespassing is a crime even if you don't cause any damage to the property.

Illustration 4-4   Vandalism is the crime of destroying or damaging someone's property.

Computer Crimes

Oliver, a college student, has a personal computer and a modem. (A *modem* is a device for transmitting computer data over the telephone.) One night, Oliver discovers the access code to get into the college administrator's computer system. He explores the system and reads the records that are kept on the students. He then logs off, leaving everything just the way he found it. Even though he has changed nothing, Oliver has committed a crime by accessing a computer system without permission.

In today's world, nearly all the information needed to run schools, businesses, and governments is stored in computers. Many of these computers are tied together by means of satellites, data networks, and ordinary phone lines. Under these circumstances, one person's misuse of a personal computer can cause a tremendous amount of damage.

Most people would agree that breaking into a computer system is wrong, even if no damage is done, as in Oliver's case. Until recently, however, there were few or no laws dealing specifically with computer crime.

In many cases, people who have misused computers have been found guilty of breaking traditional laws. For example, Oliver, who accessed a computer system without permission, would be guilty of trespassing. If he had changed or deleted any information—or had planted a "virus" that damaged the system—he might be guilty of forgery or malicious mischief. If he had stolen information from the system, he might be guilty of larceny.

Many legal experts, however, aren't sure that these older laws really apply to computer crimes. For example, how could Oliver be accused of trespassing if he'd used his own computer in his own room? If Oliver had stolen information by copying computer files, would he really have committed larceny? (After all, the original files would still be there for the college administrator to use.) Because of questions and doubts like these, many people who have clearly misused their personal computers have been able to avoid punishment.

In recent years, nearly every state has solved this problem by passing criminal laws dealing specifically with computers. Under these laws, any unauthorized use of computer hardware or software is a crime. Any unauthorized entry into a computer system is also a crime, even if no information is changed, copied, or deleted. People who break these "computer crime laws" can be punished severely—even if, like Oliver, they meant no harm.

Illustration 4-5   In recent years, most states have passed laws dealing specifically with the unauthorized use of computer hardware and software.

REVIEW QUESTIONS

1. Why is robbery considered a more serious crime than other theft crimes?
2. Define *burglary*, and explain how this definition varies from state to state.
3. Describe two ways a person can commit crimes using a computer.

OTHER CRIMES

Not all actions are crimes just because they involve injuries to people or property. Some activities are classified as crimes simply because they are dangerous or because they lead to more serious crimes. These activities are crimes even if no one gets hurt and no damage is done.

Substance Abuse

The use of alcohol and other mind-altering drugs leads to tens of thousands of deaths and injuries every year. In an effort to protect people from the effects of these dangerous substances, every state has passed strict laws limiting their use and sale.

Illustration 4-6   In an effort to protect people from the effects of dangerous substances, every state has passed strict laws limiting their sale and use.

Every state has set a minimum drinking age, generally 21. No one under this age is allowed to buy or possess alcoholic beverages. If an underage person buys alcohol by borrowing someone else's identification, the buyer, the seller, and the owner of the identification can all be found guilty in court.

Possession of certain other drugs—such as marijuana, cocaine, and heroin—is illegal for anyone of any age. The penalties for possessing these drugs vary from state to state. If you possess an illegal drug, the penalty will generally depend on the type of drug, the amount you possess, and what you intended to do with the drug. In some states, for example, possession of a drug for personal use is a misdemeanor. If you intended to sell or distribute the drug, however, your crime becomes a felony.

Motor Vehicle Crimes

Motor vehicle crimes are generally divided into two categories: moving violations (crimes committed while the vehicle is in motion) and nonmoving violations. Moving violations are considered especially serious. They include drunk driving, driving through a red light, driving at excessive speeds, and leaving the scene of an accident in which you were involved.

If you cause a death by driving recklessly, you may be charged with involuntary manslaughter in addition to your moving violation. (As you read earlier in this chapter, involuntary manslaughter means causing a death through reckless or grossly negligent behavior.) Some states have a separate law under which causing death by auto is prosecuted. **Vehicular homicide** is causing a death through negligent use of a motor vehicle. You may be charged with vehicular homicide even if your driving wasn't reckless or grossly negligent. If you drive carelessly (for example, by trying to read a map while you drive) and you hit and kill someone, you may be guilty of vehicular homicide.

Drunk Driving   On the afternoon of June 30, 1972, Joe Taylor Jr. was so drunk that his speech was slurred and he couldn't stand without help. Despite his condition, he decided to drive home. He drove through the streets of Philadelphia at speeds up to 80 miles an hour. Speeding past a neighborhood park, Taylor rammed into two boys who were leaving the park on their bicycles. Ronald Beatty, age 13, and Herbert Palmer, 14, were thrown about 100 feet, and Palmer was killed. Taylor was convicted of murder in the second degree and of driving under the influence of alcohol. Taylor received 10 years' probation on the murder charge and was sentenced to 23 months in prison on the charge of driving under the influence.

Drunk driving, sometimes called driving under the influence (DUI) or driving while intoxicated (DWI), is a crime even when no one is injured or killed. Every state has its own definition of drunk driving, based on the concentration of alcohol in a driver's blood. The blood alcohol concentration (BAC) can be determined through tests of the driver's breath, urine, or blood. In most states a BAC of 0.10 is the legal limit, although the trend is to lower it to 0.08.

If you are driving a car, and your blood has a higher concentration of alcohol than the law permits, you are guilty of drunk driving—regardless of how sober you feel. If you drive with any amount of an illegal drug in your system, you are committing an equally serious crime.

The penalties for driving under the influence or driving while intoxicated depend on the state you live in and on how many times you have committed the crime. Your license may be revoked or suspended, you may be fined, or you may go to jail.

Attempt, Conspiracy, and Solicitation

As you read earlier in this chapter, it is perfectly legal to plan a crime in your own mind. If your planning goes beyond the thinking stage, however—for example, if you discuss your plan with other people or if you actually begin to carry out your plan—you are breaking the law.

Suppose Carlos and Dean both want to kill Bryce. They discuss the matter, and they decide that Alicia is the best person to do the killing. Carlos convinces Alicia to buy a gun and shoot Bryce. Alicia does so, but when she fires her gun at Bryce, she misses.

Even though no one was injured, Alicia, Carlos, and Dean are all guilty of crimes. Alicia's crime is attempted murder. Carlos and Dean are guilty of conspiracy to commit murder. Carlos may also be guilty of solicitation.

Attempt   If you try and fail to commit a crime, you are guilty of **attempt**. The reason for your failure doesn't matter. Alicia, for example, failed to shoot Bryce because her aim wasn't good enough. Robert Cody, in the case study that opened this chapter, failed to burn the school because a police officer stopped him. Both Alicia and Cody are guilty of attempt.

If you succeed in committing a crime, you can't be found guilty of attempt. Suppose Alicia had been successful in killing Bryce. In that case, a court could find her guilty of murder, but it could not find her guilty of murder *and* attempted murder.

Conspiracy   When two or more people work together to plan a crime, they are guilty of **conspiracy**. They don't have to take any steps toward actually committing the crime. When Carlos and Dean began to talk about killing Bryce, they immediately became guilty of conspiracy. They would have remained guilty even if they had given up the idea after one conversation.

Conspiracy, unlike attempt, remains a crime regardless of whether the plan succeeds. If Carlos and Dean had personally carried out their plan to kill Bryce, they would have been guilty of murder *and* conspiracy to commit murder.

Solicitation   **Solicitation** is the act of persuading others to commit a crime. When Carlos talked Alicia into buying a gun and shooting Bryce, he became guilty of solicitation. He would have remained guilty even if Alicia had decided not to shoot Bryce.

REVIEW QUESTIONS

1. Under what circumstances might possession of an illegal drug be a felony?
2. How does a law enforcement officer determine whether you're too drunk to drive?
3. Define *solicitation* and *conspiracy*.

DEFENSES

As you read in Chapter 3, people who are accused of a crime have the right to a fair trial. At the trial they are given the opportunity to explain and defend their actions. If they have a defense—an acceptable excuse for what they did—they will not be found guilty and will not be punished.

Defending Yourself, Others, or Property

It is legal to injure someone—or even to kill someone—if you are acting in self-defense. As a general rule, you may use whatever force is reasonable to defend yourself against harm. If you are threatened with **deadly force** (force that might cause death or serious bodily injury), you have the right to use deadly force in return.

Generally, the same rule applies if you are defending other people or protecting property: you may use as much force as necessary, but no more than is necessary. Because property is considered less important than human life, the use of deadly force to protect property is illegal in most cases.

Lacking Criminal Responsibility

As you read at the beginning of this chapter, a person generally cannot be convicted of a crime unless he or she had criminal intent. The law recognizes, however, that some people aren't capable of criminal intent. For example, people with certain mental illnesses and people under a certain age may not understand that what they are doing is wrong. When these people are put on trial for criminal acts, the court may decide that they are not responsible for the things they did.

Insanity   People who were insane when they committed a crime are not held responsible for their actions. If a court rules that a defendant is "not guilty by reason of insanity," the defendant is usually confined to a mental institution until he or she is judged to be sane.

In modern psychiatric practice, of course, there is no such thing as insanity. The ideas of "craziness" and "madness" have, for the most part, been replaced with a more humane, scientific concept of mental illness. Criminal law, however, still treats insanity as a real, identifiable condition. Different states have different legal definitions of insanity. These definitions generally include the inability to tell right from wrong or the inability to control one's impulses.

Some people think the insanity defense is unfair because it lets criminals off too lightly. For example, a murderer who is declared to be insane might spend 10 years in a mental institution rather than 30 years in prison. Some states have responded to this criticism by permitting a verdict of "guilty but mentally ill." A defendant who is guilty but mentally ill is sentenced like any other criminal but serves the sentence in an appropriate psychiatric treatment facility. If the defendant is restored to mental health, he or she serves the remainder of the sentence in prison.

Youth   Some states consider people under a certain age too young to form criminal intent. Also, in every state, young people who commit crimes are dealt with not by criminal courts but by the state's juvenile justice system. This system—which prescribes treatment instead of punishment—is discussed in Chapter 6.

Intoxication   If you commit a crime while under the influence of drugs or alcohol, you may be able to use your intoxication as a defense. If you were so intoxicated that you didn't realize what was going on—that is, if you weren't aware that you were committing a criminal act—a court might decide that you lacked criminal intent.

This defense is an extremely limited one. To use it, you must be able to show that you wouldn't have committed the crime if you hadn't been intoxicated. If you first decided to commit a crime and then drank alcohol to get up your nerve, your intoxication wouldn't be considered an acceptable excuse.

The intoxication defense also doesn't apply to crimes in which recklessness, rather than criminal intent, is the issue. If you kill someone while driving drunk, for example, you can't use your intoxication as a defense. Drunk driving is reckless behavior, and you are responsible for the consequences of that behavior—even if you didn't intend those consequences.

Mistake

As you read earlier in this chapter, criminal laws are not meant to punish people who do things by mistake. If you commit a criminal act accidentally, you are not guilty of a crime. (The exceptions to this rule, as you have learned, are reckless actions and strict liability crimes.)

Committing an act by mistake, however, is not the same as being mistaken about the law. Suppose you decide to hitchhike to the beach. As you stand on the edge of the highway and signal passing cars, a police officer pulls over and arrests you for hitchhiking. You say, "I'm not guilty, Officer; I just made a mistake. I didn't know that hitchhiking was against the law." This defense would not hold up in court. After all, you knew you were hitchhiking. Your only mistake was failing to understand the law.

Duress and Necessity

If you are forced to commit a crime—either by another person or by unavoidable circumstances—a court will generally not hold you responsible for your actions.

To claim the defense of **duress**, you must show that someone was threatening you with immediate harm if you refused to follow instructions. Suppose a robber points a gun at a bank teller and says, "Give me all the money in the safe." As soon as she hands money to the robber, the teller becomes an accomplice to the crime. No court would convict her, however, because her actions were performed under duress.

If you are forced to commit a crime because of natural events, you can claim the defense called **necessity**. Fire fighters, for example, must sometimes burn a piece of property that is in the path of a fire. Doing so is the only way to stop the fire from spreading. Although the fire fighters are committing arson, their arson is necessary—and therefore the fire fighters would not be found guilty in court.

REVIEW QUESTIONS

1. Why do some people object to the insanity defense?
2. Under what circumstances can a person use the intoxication defense?
3. What is the difference between the defense of necessity and the defense of duress?

Latest in the Law: Sobriety Checkpoints

In recent years, many local police departments have begun setting up sobriety checkpoints to search for drunk drivers. At these checkpoints, the police stop cars randomly as they pass by—perhaps every car or every fifth car or every tenth car. Stopped drivers are asked to produce their driver's licenses and perform simple tests of coordination, such as touching the nose with the index finger or maintaining balance while counting backward. Drivers who fail the roadside sobriety tests are arrested. They are taken to the police station, and they may be asked to take a Breathalyzer test. This test checks the amount of alcohol in a person's blood.

Are Checkpoints Constitutional?

Some legal experts have argued that such checkpoints are unconstitutional because they violate the protection of the Fourth Amendment against unreasonable search and seizure. That amendment says, "The right of the people to be secure in their persons, houses, papers, and effects, against unreasonable searches and seizures, shall not be violated, and no Warrants shall issue, but upon probable cause. . . ."

These experts argue that the police cannot stop a driver to check for drunk driving unless the officers have some concrete reason—such as erratic driving or speeding—to believe that the driver is drunk. When the police stop drivers at random, these experts contend, police power is being misused to harass and frighten innocent people.

Supporters of sobriety checkpoints argue that the checkpoints are constitutional as long as the police treat everyone equally. The police would be out of line, for example, if they stopped only people driving Fords or if they stopped only young male drivers. In addition, supporters believe that checkpoints are no more of an inconvenience than the security gates used at airports are.

The Supreme Court Says Yes

In 1990 the U.S. Supreme Court ruled in *Michigan Department of State Police v. Sitz* that the use of sobriety checkpoints to search for drunk drivers is constitutional and does not violate the Fourth Amendment protection against unreasonable search and seizure. In the 6 to 3 majority opinion, Chief Justice William H. Rehnquist said that the Court believed that the interest of the state in deterring drunk drivers outweighed the inconvenience to innocent drivers. "No one can seriously dispute the magnitude of the drunken driving problem or the states' interest in eradicating it [wiping it out]," he wrote. Later in the opinion, Rehnquist said, "Conversely, the weight bearing on the other scale—the measure of the intrusion on motorists stopped briefly at sobriety checkpoints—is slight."

The three justices who dissented in the case agreed that drunk driving is a serious problem. Drunk drivers kill more than twenty thousand people each year. The justices questioned, however, whether the Court was justified in making sobriety checkpoints constitutional when they are not very effective in stopping drunk drivers.

Some police experts have testified that only about 1 percent of those stopped at sobriety checkpoints are arrested for drunk driving and that other methods of pursuing drunk drivers are more effective.

Now that sobriety checkpoints have been ruled constitutional, many police departments are using them or planning to use them, especially during holidays when many people drink and drive. Police officials claim that even if the checkpoints result in only a handful of arrests, they will still have a powerful deterrent effect. Law enforcement officials believe that people will drink less if they think that they may have to pass a police checkpoint to get home. As a result of the Court's decision, sobriety checkpoints may become very common sights along our nation's highways.

Chapter Review

Chapter Summary

- A crime is an act that the government forbids and can punish.

- Crimes are classified as felonies or misdemeanors in accordance with the penalty that the government can impose. Crimes may also be classified by degree, depending on the circumstances surrounding the crime.

- In general, a crime can take place only if a criminal act and criminal intent occur at the same time. An exception to this rule is strict liability crimes, which are crimes regardless of intent.

- Accomplices can be found guilty of any crime they help principals carry out.

- Homicide is the killing of another person. It is generally subdivided into murder and manslaughter.

- Murder is homicide with the intent to kill or to cause severe bodily harm. Murder that is premeditated is called first-degree murder. Killing someone through outrageous recklessness or while committing a felony is also murder.

- Voluntary manslaughter is homicide committed in the heat of passion. Homicide that occurs through extreme negligence is called involuntary manslaughter.

- Battery is intentional or reckless physical contact with another person. Assault is an act that places someone in fear of such contact.

- When a man forces a woman to have sex with him, he commits the crime of rape. Sex with a girl under a certain age is also rape, even if it is not forced.

- Larceny is deliberately taking someone else's property. Embezzlement is keeping property that you have the right to use but not to keep.

- Forgery is making, altering, or signing a legal document with the intent to defraud.

- False pretenses is the crime of using trickery or lies to acquire someone else's property.

- Extortion is the use of threats to take someone's property.

- It is a crime to receive property that you know, or have reason to believe, is stolen.
- Robbery is taking property from someone through the use of force or threats.
- Burglary is generally defined as entering someone's property with the intent to commit a crime.
- Damaging property through vandalism or arson is a crime whether the damage is intentional or is caused by reckless behavior. Trespassing on someone's property is a crime even if no damage occurs.
- Many states have passed laws making unauthorized use of computers or computer systems a crime.
- Every state has laws that strictly limit the use of alcohol and other drugs.
- Drunk driving and other motor vehicle crimes may carry severe penalties.
- A person who tries to commit a crime but docs not complete it may be guilty of the crime of attempt.
- A person who plans a crime with another person may be charged with conspiracy. A person who persuades another person to commit a crime may be charged with solicitation.
- Defenses to crimes include self-defense, defense of others, defense of property, insanity, youth, intoxication, mistake, duress, and necessity.

Understanding Legal Terms

On a separate sheet of paper, match the terms below with the definitions that follow.

accomplice	forgery
burglary	larceny
conspiracy	principal
embezzlement	robbery
felony	solicitation

1. Person who actually commits a crime
2. Person who helps complete a crime
3. The act of taking someone else's property with the intent to keep it
4. The act of taking something from another person through the use of force or threats
5. The act of entering someone's property with the intent to commit a crime
6. The act of persuading others to commit a crime
7. The action of two or more people to plan a crime
8. The act of keeping property one is legally allowed to use but not to keep
9. The act of making, altering, or signing a legal document with the intent to defraud
10. Any crime for which the punishment may be imprisonment for a year or longer or death

Applying the Law

1. Felice goes into a restaurant and leaves her coat on a rack by the front door. When she leaves, she takes a coat that she thinks is hers but is

actually Heather's. Later in the day, she discovers that she took the wrong coat. What crime, if any, has Felice committed?

2. Todd, armed with a gun, robs a bank. He then jumps into a car and drives away. As he speeds down the street, he accidentally hits and kills a pedestrian. Todd is guilty of armed robbery, which is a felony. What other crime has he committed?

3. Amber owns a small gift shop. One of her customers, Jaime, pays for his purchase with a credit card. Before Jaime signs the credit card slip, Amber writes on it the amount of Jaime's purchase—$13.45. After Jaime leaves, Amber changes the credit card slip by making the 1 into a 7. She then submits the altered slip to the credit card company and collects $73.45. What crime has Amber committed?

4. Keisha spends an evening drinking with some friends. As she drives home, a police officer notices that her car is weaving unsteadily from lane to lane. The officer pulls Keisha over and tells her she is under arrest for drunk driving. He takes her to the police station, where a blood test reveals that the concentration of alcohol in her blood is 0.16—twice the state's legal limit. Keisha insists that she hasn't hurt anyone, so she hasn't committed a crime. Is she right? Explain your answer.

5. Martha and Brent decide to rob a bank. They meet a couple of times at Martha's house and work out several possible ways to do the job. They invite two friends to help plan the robbery. At this point, are Martha and Brent guilty of any crime? Explain your answer.

6. Luis, Jason, and Gabriel are in a bar. Jason becomes angry at Gabriel and begins to hit him. Luis tries to break up the fight. He pulls Jason away from Gabriel and hits him with a bottle. Is Jason guilty of any crime? Is Luis guilty of any crime? Explain.

Case Studies

1. One night, Dorsey Palmore came home and heard his wife, Carlister, talking with a man inside the house. Moments later, he saw a man running out the back door. Dorsey and Carlister argued heatedly over who the man was and why he was visiting when Dorsey wasn't home. Four days later, while they were out for a walk, Dorsey stabbed Carlister in the back of the neck and killed her. What type of homicide did Dorsey commit?

2. On August 5, 1955, Reyes Moriel Silva went into a liquor store in Los Angeles. He pointed a gun at John Mrotek, who was working behind the counter, and demanded money. Mrotek gave Silva $38. Silva left the store and got into a car driven by Rueben Ramirez Hernandez. Hernandez drove the car away. What crime, if any, did Silva commit? What crime, if any, did Hernandez commit?

3. Equinees Anthony Boyles stood on the stairway above Curley's Tavern in Milwaukee. He was waiting for Harvey Rotter, the owner of the bar, to return from a nearby bank. When Rotter approached, Boyles came down the stairs and demanded the sack of money Rotter was carrying. Boyles tried to pull out his gun, but it got stuck in his pocket. While he struggled, Rotter ran away and disappeared into the bar. Boyles got no money. Was he guilty of any crime? Explain your answer.

Chapter 5

Criminal
Procedure

Chapter Objectives   When you have read this chapter, you should be able to:

- Describe the steps of the criminal procedure from the arrest to the trial.

- Describe the roles of the prosecutor and the judge in a criminal case.

- Give four reasons for punishing criminals.

- Explain the difference between a determinate sentence and an indeterminate sentence.

- Define *probation*, and describe three conditions that may be put on a sentence of probation.

- Describe the services and programs available to crime victims.

Case Study

Whitfield v. State, 781 P.2d 913 (Wyoming 1989).

Between 1:30 and 7:00 on the afternoon of April 2, 1988, Mark George Whitfield went drinking. After stopping at two bars in his hometown of Torrington, Wyoming, he drove to a bar in a nearby town. Driving home to Torrington, Whitfield lost control of his car. He hit another car and killed its driver.

The police arrested Whitfield. They tested his blood alcohol concentration and found that it was 0.29. This was nearly three times the level Wyoming defines as legally drunk. Whitfield went before Judge John Langdon and pleaded guilty to aggravated vehicular homicide, the crime of killing someone through drunk driving.

Under Wyoming law, the maximum sentence for the crime was 20 years in prison. This meant that Judge Langdon had the authority to sentence Whitfield to a prison term of any length up to 20 years. The judge also had the authority to sentence him to probation or to let him go without any sentence at all.

Whitfield's lawyer requested that Whitfield be sentenced to a term of probation, with no time in prison. The lawyer said that probation was an appropriate sentence for a man like Whitfield, who was not a violent criminal but "essentially a nice person who just got in serious trouble for the first time."

Before deciding on the sentence, Judge Langdon asked for some information on Whitfield's background and criminal record. He learned that Whitfield had a record of eight speeding tickets, one previous charge of driving while intoxicated, and several other instances of substance abuse.

Judge Langdon decided that even if Whitfield was "essentially a nice person," he had a history of drinking and driving. This time his drunk driving had killed someone. Anyone who kills through drunk driving deserves to be punished, the judge said. He also said that by sentencing Whitfield to prison, he would set an example that would make Whitfield and others think twice before deciding to drink and drive. Therefore, he sentenced Whitfield to a prison term of three to five years.

THE ROLE OF THE POLICE

As you read in Chapter 4, the government has the right to punish anyone who commits a crime. In day-to-day life, however, it's not always easy to know who has committed a crime. Not all criminals are caught by the police, and not everyone caught by the police is a criminal. In the United States, we sort out the criminals from the noncriminals by holding a trial. No one can be punished for a crime until he or she has received a fair trial and been declared guilty.

The process by which suspected criminals are identified, arrested, accused, and tried in court is called the **criminal procedure**. This process is designed to punish the guilty without taking away the constitutional rights of either the guilty or the innocent. The process includes many steps, beginning with a police investigation and ending with the sentencing of the guilty party. (Figure 5-1 shows a diagram of the steps in the system.) At each step, there are strict rules to ensure that everyone involved is treated fairly.

You've already read about some of the most common criminal laws. In this chapter, you'll find out what happens to people who are accused of breaking those laws.

The Police Investigation

Enforcing criminal law is the responsibility of law enforcement officers employed by the government. There are law enforcement officers at every level of government—for example, federal agents, state troopers, and county sheriffs—but the job of fighting crime in most communities belongs to the local police. The police are responsible for preventing criminal activity, investigating crimes, and arresting anyone who is suspected of having committed a crime.

The role of the police in the criminal procedure begins with the investigation of a crime. Police investigations serve several goals. First, they help determine whether a crime has been committed and who may have committed it. Second, they allow officers to identify evidence that can be used in a criminal trial. Third, they may establish probable cause to arrest suspects and seize evidence. (The probable cause requirement, as you read in Chapter 3, helps protect the rights of individuals by placing certain limitations on police officers' activities.)

Arrest and Custody

When a police officer has probable cause to believe that someone has committed a crime, the officer may arrest that person. You read in Chapter 3 that the Constitution gives certain rights to an arrested person, such as the right to have the advice of a lawyer before answering any questions. At the time of the arrest, the officer must explain those rights by reciting the Miranda warnings.

After the arrest, the officer generally takes the suspect to the police station for booking. **Booking** is a clerical procedure in which the police make a formal record of the arrest. A booking officer records the name of the suspect; the name of the arresting officer; the date, time, and place of the arrest; and the reason for the arrest.

As part of the booking process, police officers photograph and fingerprint the suspect. Depending on the crime, they may also take a sample of the suspect's blood, urine, hair, or clothing. These samples may be used as evidence at a criminal trial.

At the time of booking, police officers usually spend some time questioning the suspect. If there was a witness to a crime, the police may also place

Figure 5-1 The Criminal Justice System

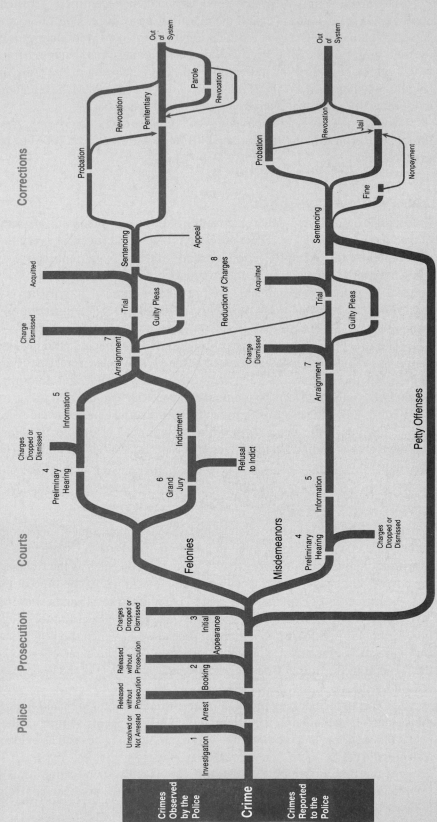

Police   Prosecution   Courts   Corrections

Crimes Observed by the Police

Crime

Crimes Reported to the Police

Investigation 1
Arrest
Released without Prosecution 2
Booking
Released without Prosecution
Charges Dropped or Dismissed 3
Initial Appearance
Unsolved or Not Arrested

Felonies

Preliminary Hearing 4
Charges Dropped or Dismissed
Information 5
Grand Jury 6
Indictment
Refusal to Indict
Arraignment 7
Charge Dismissed
Guilty Pleas
Trial
Acquitted
Reduction of Charges 8
Sentencing
Appeal
Probation
Revocation
Penitentiary
Parole
Revocation
Out of System

Misdemeanors

Preliminary Hearing 4
Charges Dropped or Dismissed
Information 5
Arraignment 7
Charge Dismissed
Guilty Pleas
Trial
Acquitted
Sentencing
Probation
Revocation
Fine
Jail
Nonpayment
Revocation
Out of System

Petty Offenses

1. May continue until trial.
2. Administrative record of arrest. First step at which temporary release on bail may be available.
3. Before magistrate, commissioner, or justice of the peace. Formal notice of charge, advice of rights. Bail set. Summary trails for petty offenses usually conducted here without further processing.
4. Preliminary testing of evidence against defendant. Charge may be reduced. No separate preliminary hearing for misdemeanors in some systems.
5. Charge filed by prosecutor on basis of information submitted by police or citizens. Alternative to grand jury indictment. Often used in felonies; almost always used in misdemeanors.
6. Reviews whether government evidence is sufficient to justify a trial. Some states have no grand jury system; others seldom use it. In some states, both a preliminary hearing and a grand jury are used.
7. Appearance for plea; defendant elects trial by judge or jury (if available): counsel for indigent usually appointed here in felonies. Often not at all in other cases.
8. Charge may be reduced at any time before the trial in return for plea of guilty or for other reasons.

Note: Procedures in individual jurisdictions may vary from the pattern shown here.
Source: Adapted from President's Commission on Law Enforcement and Administration of Justice, *The Challenge of Crime in a Free Society*, Washington, D.C.: U.S. Government Printing Office, 1967.

the suspect in a lineup. This means placing the suspect with several similar-looking individuals and asking the witness to pick out the suspect.

Illustration 5-1   A suspect has the right to have an attorney present during questioning.

The Right of the Accused to a Lawyer

As you read in Chapter 3, the Sixth Amendment gives you the right to a lawyer from the moment you are accused of a crime. You have this right not only during police interrogations but at every important step of the criminal procedure—from the time you are formally charged to the time you are sentenced.

Your lawyer's primary role at these times is to make sure the police, the attorney for the government, and the judge treat you fairly. Therefore, when there is no opportunity for unfair treatment, there is no need for a lawyer. For example, you don't have the right to a lawyer while police are taking blood, hair, or clothing samples.

REVIEW QUESTIONS

1. Define *criminal procedure*.
2. List three goals of police investigations.
3. What happens during the booking process?

BEFORE THE TRIAL

There are many legal steps between arrest and trial. During these procedures, the judge and the attorneys for both sides examine all the facts of the case against the suspect and evaluate the evidence. (After a suspect has been charged with a crime, he or she is referred to as the **defendant**.) In some cases, the charges are dropped. In other situations, an agreement is made between the defendant and the court, and the case doesn't reach the trial stage.

Initial Court Appearance

As soon as possible after the arrest, the defendant is brought before a judge for the initial court appearance. This appearance usually takes place within 12 to 72 hours after the arrest.

The initial court appearance is usually brief. The judge explains to the defendant exactly what the charges are—that is, what crimes the defendant is accused of committing. (These charges are submitted by the police.) The judge informs the defendant of his or her constitutional rights, such as the right to counsel and the right to remain silent. At this point, if the defendant can't afford a lawyer, the judge may appoint a public defender. (In some states, a public defender is not appointed until later in the process.)

If the defendant is charged with a misdemeanor, the judge asks the defendant to plead guilty or not guilty. If the defendant pleads guilty, the judge hands down a sentence and the process is complete.

If a defendant pleads not guilty, the judge asks whether the defendant wants to waive, or give up, the right to a jury. If the defendant agrees to waive that right (and if the defendant's lawyer is present), the judge may hold the trial immediately. If the defendant requests a jury trial, however—or if the defendant needs more time to prepare a defense—the judge will schedule a trial for a future date.

The process is somewhat different for defendants who are charged with felonies. In this case, the judge doesn't ask the defendant to plead guilty or not guilty. Instead, after explaining the charges, the judge sets a date for the defendant's next court appearance.

Particularly dangerous defendants may be held in jail until the next court appearance. Usually, however, the judge sets bail and gives the defendant an opportunity to pay it. As you read in Chapter 3, a defendant who pays bail is allowed to go free while waiting for his or her trial.

The Prosecutor

After the arrest and before the trial, the government assigns a prosecutor to the case. The **prosecutor**—sometimes called the district attorney or the state's attorney—is a lawyer who represents the government. The prosecutor's job is to prove that the defendant is guilty of the crimes he or she is charged with. Once the prosecutor takes over, the police are no longer involved in the case (except, perhaps, as witnesses at the defendant's trial).

The prosecutor begins by reviewing the police records of the case. He or she must make sure that the police had probable cause for arresting the suspect and that all evidence in the case was obtained legally. Because police officers often move quickly when conducting searches or making arrests, they sometimes make mistakes. They may, for example, seize evidence without probable cause or without a warrant. The exclusionary rule prevents such illegally seized evidence from being used in court.

After setting aside any evidence that must be excluded, the prosecutor decides whether there is enough evidence remaining to prove the case against the defendant. Suppose, for example, a prosecutor named Peter Espinoza is reviewing the police report of a homicide case. According to the report, Officer Karen Maynard investigated the scene of the crime and found a bloody knife with fingerprints on it. She also found a sleeve that had been torn from a shirt. Later, she got a description of the killer from a witness.

Based on the witness's description and on the fingerprints, Officer Maynard had probable cause to believe that a man named Marcus was the killer. She got a warrant and arrested Marcus. Afterward, she searched Marcus's girlfriend's house and found the rest of the torn shirt.

In reviewing this police report, Espinoza realizes that Officer Maynard didn't have a warrant to search Marcus's girlfriend's house. Therefore, the torn shirt was seized illegally and would have to be excluded from the trial. However, the shirtsleeve, the knife, and the witness's description of the killer can still be used as evidence.

If Espinoza thinks this evidence is enough to prove Marcus guilty, he will continue to work on the case. If not, he will probably drop the charges and let Marcus go—even if he still believes Marcus is guilty. Without sufficient evidence, it wouldn't make sense to take this case to trial. Marcus would most likely be found not guilty, and many people's time would be wasted—including that of Espinoza and the judge. For similar reasons, a great number of criminal cases are dropped at this stage.

If a prosecutor decides that a case is worth pursuing, he or she must decide exactly what charges to bring against the defendant. Marcus, for example, may originally have been charged with first-degree murder by the police. When Espinoza looks at the facts of the case, he may decide to change the charge to felony murder or voluntary manslaughter. He may also decide to add other charges, such as aggravated assault and battery. After making these decisions, the prosecutor sends a revised list of charges to the judge who will preside over the trial.

Determining Probable Cause

The need for probable cause doesn't apply only to police procedures. Once a prosecutor takes over the case, he or she must have probable cause to bring the defendant to trial. In other words, the prosecutor must show—based on available, legally obtained evidence—that there is reason to believe the defendant is guilty. If the prosecutor can't show probable cause, there can be no trial.

Within a few weeks after the arrest, the trial judge holds a hearing to decide whether there is probable cause for a trial. This hearing, called a **probable cause hearing**, can take one of two forms. At a **preliminary hearing**, the judge hears both sides of the case and decides whether there is probable cause.

At a **grand jury hearing**, a jury makes that decision. The type of hearing a defendant receives depends on state law.

Preliminary Hearing   A preliminary hearing is conducted much like a trial. First, the prosecutor presents evidence that shows that the defendant is guilty. This evidence may include testimony by a victim, testimony by witnesses, and items gathered in a police investigation. Next, the defense attorney presents evidence to show that the defendant is not guilty. After listening to both sides, the judge decides whether there is probable cause to hold a trial. If the judge concludes that there is no probable cause, the charges are dropped and the defendant is released.

Although a preliminary hearing resembles a trial, its purpose is very different. The purpose of a trial is to determine whether the defendant is guilty of a crime. The purpose of a preliminary hearing is to decide whether it is *reasonable to believe* that the defendant committed a crime.

This is often a difficult distinction to make. For example, the police department in Benton Harbor, Michigan, received evidence that Vertis McManus had failed to file a state income tax return. In January 1980, a police officer and two tax investigators got a warrant to search McManus's personal records. While looking through McManus's desk drawer, they found a vial of cocaine. They seized the vial and later arrested McManus for possession of an illegal drug.

After his arrest, McManus was brought before Judge Julien Hughes for a preliminary hearing. At the hearing, the prosecutor explained how the police had found the cocaine. Judge Hughes decided that there was not sufficient evidence to bring McManus to trial because it wasn't clear that the drug belonged to McManus. The cocaine could have belonged to his wife or his son. The prosecutor disagreed with Judge Hughes's decision and appealed the case.

The appeals court held that Judge Hughes was wrong, because a preliminary hearing is different from a criminal trial. At a trial, the prosecutor must prove beyond a reasonable doubt that the defendant is guilty. At a preliminary hearing, however, the prosecutor must prove only that there is probable cause to believe the defendant committed a crime. In this case, the court said, the prosecutor had clearly shown that there was probable cause.

Grand Jury Hearing   A grand jury hearing differs from a preliminary hearing in two important ways. First, at a grand jury hearing, only the prosecutor gets to present evidence. (The defendant and the defense attorney are not even allowed to attend.) Second, the outcome of the hearing is decided not by a judge but by a grand jury. A **grand jury** is a randomly selected group of 16 to 23 citizens. After hearing the prosecutor's case, the grand jury decides whether there is probable cause to bring the defendant to trial.

Documentation of Charges

If the judge or grand jury decides that there is no probable cause to hold a trial, the charges against the defendant are dropped. If the judge or jury decides that there *is* probable cause, the prosecutor moves on to the next step: making a formal list of the charges against the defendant.

The prosecutor must list each crime the defendant is charged with. (Each item on the list is called a **count**.) For each count, the prosecutor must specify when, where, and how the crime was committed.

If the probable cause hearing was held in front of a grand jury, the prosecutor's list of charges is called an **indictment**. If the probable cause hearing was held by a judge (or if there was no probable cause hearing), the list of charges is called an **information**. The prosecutor gives the indictment or information to the trial judge. The judge will read the list of charges to the defendant at the next step in the process—the arraignment.

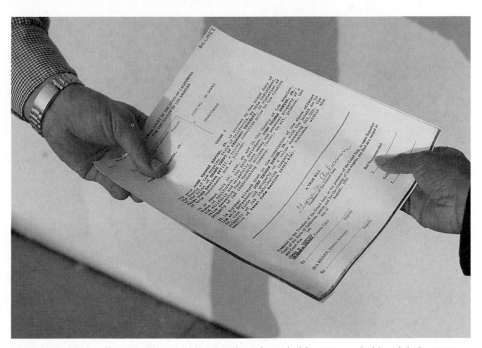

Illustration 5-2   If a grand jury decides that there is probable cause to hold a trial, the prosecutor prepares a formal list of charges called an indictment.

Arraignment

Kenneth Rayford was arrested in Kansas City, Missouri, and charged with killing William Medina. After a preliminary hearing, the prosecutor prepared an information against him. Then, on January 17, 1970, Rayford appeared before Judge James Moore.

Judge Moore read the list of charges to Rayford. He asked Rayford, "Did you kill Medina?" Rayford said, "Yes." The judge, the prosecutor, and Rayford's lawyer then asked a series of questions. In response to these questions, Rayford said he understood the charges against him. He said he understood that by pleading guilty, he could be punished with ten years to life in prison. He said that he understood that he was entitled to a speedy trial by jury and that by pleading guilty he was waiving that right. After listening to Rayford's answers, Judge Moore was satisfied that Rayford was pleading guilty "voluntarily and intelligently." The judge accepted the plea and prepared to pass sentence.

An **arraignment** is a pretrial court appearance during which a judge reads the charges against a defendant. Judge Moore's questioning of Rayford is a typical example of what happens during an arraignment. The judge reminds the defendant of his or her constitutional rights. The judge then asks the defendant to plead guilty or not guilty to each charge listed in the indictment or information.

Like Kenneth Rayford, most defendants plead guilty at the arraignment. When that happens, the judge must take certain precautions before accepting the plea. The judge needs to be sure that the defendant knows his or her constitutional rights. The judge must carefully explain the consequences of a plea of guilty and must make sure the defendant understands everything he or she has been told. If the judge fails to do these things, the defendant's plea of guilty may not be valid.

In 1978, for example, Clarence Wells and Reginald Rolsal were arrested and charged with robbery. At their arraignment, they pleaded guilty. Although the judge did question the two men about their pleas, he didn't tell them the maximum sentence they could get for their crime. For this reason, an appeals court later found that the defendants' guilty pleas weren't valid. Wells and Rolsal had to be arraigned a second time.

Plea Bargaining

In September 1988 Wayne Alan Hanks was arrested in Carson City, Nevada. He was charged with a felony—possessing a controlled substance. Before Hanks's trial, the prosecutor offered him a deal. If Hanks agreed to plead guilty to the charge of conspiracy to possess a controlled substance (a misdemeanor), the prosecutor would drop the felony charge.

If he accepted this deal, Hanks would give up his right to a trial. By pleading guilty to a misdemeanor, however, Hanks would be sure to get a very light sentence. Hanks accepted the deal. He pleaded guilty to the misdemeanor charge and was sentenced to probation.

A deal like this one, in which a prosecutor gives a defendant a "break" in exchange for pleading guilty, is called **plea bargaining**. Plea bargaining takes different forms. Sometimes a defendant agrees to plead guilty to the crime he or she is charged with. In exchange, the prosecutor promises to ask the judge for a light sentence. Other defendants, like Hanks, agree to plead guilty to a lesser crime for which the sentence is automatically lighter. If a defendant is charged with several crimes, he or she may agree to plead guilty to one charge if the prosecutor drops the others.

Although plea bargaining is sometimes controversial, it is the most practical way to prevent the courts from being crowded with a huge number of cases. It would seem that everybody benefits from a plea bargain: the prosecutor wins the case, the defendant gets a lighter sentence, and the government is spared the time and expense of a long trial.

REVIEW QUESTIONS

1. What happens at the initial court appearance? At a preliminary hearing? At an arraignment?
2. What is the role of the prosecutor in the criminal process?
3. What is a grand jury, and what does it do?
4. What is a plea bargain?

TRIAL AND SENTENCING

As you read in Chapter 3, the Constitution guarantees all criminal defendants the right to a trial. In reality, most defendants choose to waive this right and to plead guilty as part of a plea bargain. Many, however, choose to plead not guilty, and their cases eventually come to trial.

Burden of Proof

Under our system of criminal law, anyone accused of a crime is innocent until proved guilty. Therefore, a defendant at a criminal trial is never required to prove that he or she is innocent. Instead, it is the prosecutor's responsibility to prove that the defendant is guilty. This responsibility is called the **burden of proof**.

For a defendant to be found guilty, the prosecutor must prove *beyond a reasonable doubt* that the defendant committed a crime. If the prosecutor shows only that the defendant possibly—or even probably—committed a crime, the court is not allowed to find the defendant guilty.

The Trial

American courts use an adversary process to decide whether a defendant is guilty of a crime. The two adversaries, or opponents, are the prosecutor and the defendant (or, in most cases, the defendant's attorney). The prosecutor's role is to use the evidence gathered by the police to prove that the defendant is guilty. The defendant's role is either to show that the facts are not as the prosecutor says or to offer a valid defense against the charges. (You read about defenses against criminal charges at the end of Chapter 4.)

All trials are conducted according to strict rules. You will read about those rules and find out more about the trial itself in Chapter 19.

The Purposes of Punishment

Phillip Toohill was 20 years old when a court in Minidoka County, Idaho, found him guilty of second-degree burglary. Before Judge Sherman Bellwood sentenced Toohill, he reviewed his criminal record. The judge found that Toohill had a history of juvenile and adult offenses. The judge also found that after having been arrested for this burglary and released on bail, Toohill had committed two misdemeanors. Taking these facts into account,

Illustration 5-3   The prosecutor, or district attorney, represents the government in a criminal case; the defense attorney represents the person who has been accused.

Judge Bellwood sentenced Toohill to the maximum sentence for second-degree burglary—a prison term of up to five years.

Toohill appealed this sentence, saying it was unreasonably long for the crime of second-degree burglary. In reviewing the judge's decision, the appeals court examined the reasons for criminal punishment. Prison sentences, the court said, serve a number of purposes. They protect the public; they deter, or discourage, the individual offender—and others—from committing the same crime; they help rehabilitate the offender; and they punish the offender for his or her offense. Putting Toohill in prison would serve all those purposes. Considering the defendant's background, the court said, the sentence was not unreasonable.

The primary role of the criminal justice system is to punish people who commit crimes. If a defendant is found guilty, it is the responsibility of the trial judge to decide on an appropriate punishment. This is one of the most difficult decisions a judge must make.

Punishment can serve a number of purposes.

■ Its most immediate goal is **incapacitation**—preventing a criminal from committing more crimes. By placing criminals under lock and key, the criminal justice system helps keep the rest of us safe. Of course, unless an offender is sentenced to death (or to life in prison without parole), the incapacitation is only temporary.

- A second goal of punishment is **deterrence**—teaching the criminal a lesson so that he or she will be discouraged from breaking the law again. Punishing one offender has the added advantage of setting an example for others, so would-be criminals are likely to think twice before committing a crime.

- A third goal of punishment is **rehabilitation**—helping an offender become a law-abiding member of society. Today's prisons, known as *corrections facilities*, generally offer psychological counseling and special programs designed to help prisoners lead a normal life. In some cases, judges may sentence offenders to a specific treatment—such as traffic school or drug counseling—rather than prison.

- A final goal of punishment is **retribution**—"getting back" at a criminal for what he or she has done. Although retribution accomplishes nothing, it is part of human nature. If somebody makes us suffer, we want that person to suffer in return. Retribution is probably the oldest reason for punishment, and it remains important to many people.

In deciding on a sentence, a judge usually tries to serve more than one of these purposes. In the case that opened this chapter, for example, Judge Langdon's stated goals in sentencing Mark Whitfield to prison were deterrence and retribution.

The Presentence Report

In order to choose fair, appropriate sentences, judges need to have as much information as possible. Often a judge will ask for facts about an offender's background before deciding on a sentence. In the opening case, for example, Judge Langdon handed down a harsh sentence because of Whitfield's history of driving violations and substance abuse.

If a judge needs background information about a defendant, he or she asks a probation officer to gather the information. A **probation officer** is a social services professional who supervises criminal defendants and helps with their rehabilitation. At the judge's request, the probation officer finds out as much as possible about a particular defendant. The officer puts this information into a document called a **presentence report**.

A presentence report usually begins with basic facts about the defendant's background, such as his or her age, employment history, level of education, and criminal record. If the defendant has been asked to take psychological tests, the results of those tests are included in the report. The report may include comments about the defendant's attitude and willingness to cooperate during the time leading up to the trial. It may also include information about the defendant's family—for example, whether there are children who may be left without support if the defendant is imprisoned.

In determining a sentence, the judge is free to use any of the information in the presentence report. In addition, the judge may use information that wasn't included in the report.

In 1982, for example, Gregory Reid forced his way into an apartment in western Maryland. He found a 17-year-old girl alone inside the apartment. Reid tied her up, raped her, and sexually molested her. He then ransacked the apartment. A jury found him guilty of first-degree rape, first-degree sexual offense, and robbery with a deadly weapon.

Before passing sentence, Judge Calvin Sanders reviewed a presentence report on Reid. He also reviewed a statement from the girl who had been attacked. In her statement, the girl described how the attack had changed her life. The attack, she said, made her afraid of being home alone at night or driving by herself. In fact, she continued, the attack permanently changed her daily life and the lives of her family members. Based on this statement and other information, Judge Sanders sentenced Reid to life in prison.

Sentencing Restrictions

Judges have a great deal of freedom in sentencing, but their sentences must stay within certain limits. One limit is imposed by the Eighth Amendment to the Constitution. This amendment, which you read about in Chapter 3, prohibits "cruel and unusual punishments."

Other limits may be imposed by specific laws. When a legislature passes a criminal law, it almost always specifies a maximum sentence. (Some laws, as you will see, include minimum sentences as well.) In the case that opened this chapter, for example, Wyoming law set the maximum sentence for aggravated vehicular manslaughter at 20 years in prison.

Incarceration

In most cases, **incarceration**—confinement to a jail or prison—is the most severe sentence a judge can impose. There are basically two kinds of prison terms—indeterminate and determinate.

Illustration 5-4   In most cases, incarceration is the most severe sentence a judge can impose.

An **indeterminate term** is the more common type of sentence. It is stated as a range of time, such as *5 to 10 years* or *20 years to life*. The underlying idea is that prisons are places for rehabilitation and that prisoners who "turn over a new leaf" should be released sooner than those who don't. A prisoner who is sentenced to an indeterminate term is watched closely by prison officials, especially after he or she has served the minimum number of years. At that point, the prisoner may be released whenever the authorities think he or she is ready to live in the community.

In recent years, some people have become dissatisfied with indeterminate terms. These people say that indeterminate terms are unfair because two individuals who commit the same crime may spend vastly different amounts of time in prison. They also say that indeterminate sentences allow criminals to get out of prison too early. In response to these criticisms, some states now require judges to hand down **determinate**, or fixed-length, **sentences**—for example, *15 years* rather than *10 to 20 years*.

No matter which type of sentence they receive, most offenders are released from prison after serving only part of the term. They are released under a system called **parole**, which rewards good behavior in prison. Prisoners who are released on parole must agree to follow certain rules. They must, for example, meet regularly with parole officers. They may be prohibited from using alcohol or drugs or from having contact with other ex-convicts. An offender who violates any condition of parole is sent back to prison.

Alternatives to Incarceration

Most people agree that incarceration isn't the best treatment for all criminals. For first-time offenders and for those who commit nonviolent crimes, judges often pass sentences that do not involve prison time. In many cases, for example, a person who commits a minor crime is required only to pay a fine.

For serious crimes, the most common alternative to a prison term is **probation**. A person sentenced to probation is permitted to stay out of jail so long as he or she follows certain rules. The rules are usually similar to the rules of parole. Offenders may be required to meet regularly with a probation officer and to avoid the use of alcohol or drugs.

For example, on June 13, 1976, police officers found drugs and drug paraphernalia in Michael Joseph Donovan's house. They also found evidence that he was selling drugs. They arrested Donovan, and he was eventually found guilty of possession of narcotics and possession of marijuana for sale. Judge Jack Arnold sentenced Donovan to five years of probation.

The judge placed six conditions on Donovan's probation. Donovan had to meet regularly with a probation officer. He had to move out of his own house and live with his parents. For the first eight months of probation, he had to be home by ten o'clock every night. He had to continue school and get an after-school job. Finally, he could no longer see his ex-girlfriend, who had also been charged with drug violations. If he violated any of those conditions, Donovan would have to serve time in prison.

Within the limits set by the Eighth Amendment, judges are free to place almost any conditions on a term of probation. For example, a judge may require

Illustration 5-5   The most common alternative to prison is probation, which may include regular meetings with a probation officer.

that an offender receive psychological counseling or enroll in a drug treatment program. As in the case of Michael Donovan, a judge may require that the offender follow a certain schedule and avoid seeing certain people. In many cases, offenders are required to pay back the victims of their crimes. (Repaying a victim for items stolen or for damage done is called **restitution**.)

Judges are sometimes quite creative in setting conditions for probation. In 1979, for example, Rae Morgan was convicted of prostitution in New Orleans. As a condition of her probation, Judge Frank Marullo required her to stay away from the French Quarter, a part of the city known to be a center for prostitutes. Such unusual rules are perfectly legal because offenders are always given a choice: if they don't want to accept the conditions of probation, they can choose to go to prison instead.

An increasingly common condition of probation is community service—volunteer work that helps the community. Judges often require offenders to perform a particular kind of community service that relates to the crime they committed. People guilty of vandalism may be required to spend a certain number of days cleaning graffiti from walls. People convicted of drunk driving may have to spend time at a physical rehabilitation clinic, helping to treat victims of car accidents.

For certain offenders—especially those without a criminal record—a judge may order a suspended sentence rather than probation. A **suspended sentence** allows an offender to stay out of prison with no special conditions or requirements. Like probation, a suspended sentence lasts for a fixed amount of time. If the offender commits another crime during that time, the sentence may be "unsuspended." In such a case, the offender will have to serve two prison terms—one for the original crime and one for the second crime.

As jails and prisons become increasingly crowded, the number of sentencing alternatives continues to grow. Some prisoners are allowed to leave each day to work at a job outside the prison. Other offenders are allowed to live at home during the week and serve the prison sentence on weekends. Some states are experimenting with house arrest programs that require offenders to wear electronic bracelets. With the help of special transmitters and monitoring equipment, parole officers can make sure an offender remains at home during certain hours.

Probation, community service, house arrest, and other alternatives to prison are not always popular. Many people criticize these kinds of sentences for not being tough enough on criminals. In recent years, some state legislatures have responded by passing mandatory sentencing laws. These laws require people who commit certain crimes to spend time in jail, with no possibility of alternative sentences. The Massachusetts gun control law, for example, requires anyone who carries a gun illegally to spend 1 to 2 ½ years in prison. Many states have passed similar laws for possession of illegal drugs or for driving while intoxicated.

Capital Punishment

Some states allow criminals to be sentenced to death for especially serious crimes. The death penalty—also called **capital punishment**—is used very rarely. It is most often reserved for cases of first-degree murder in which the criminal's behavior was particularly brutal. The usual sentence for first-degree murder is life in prison, sometimes without the chance for parole.

REVIEW QUESTIONS

1. What does it mean to say that the prosecutor has the burden of proof?
2. What is the difference between parole and probation?
3. What is community service? Give two examples.
4. Define *determinate sentence*, *indeterminate sentence*, and *suspended sentence*.

WITNESSES AND VICTIMS

To operate effectively, the criminal justice system requires the work of trained professionals such as police officers, prosecutors, and judges. However, it also needs the cooperation of two groups of ordinary citizens—victims of crimes and witnesses to crimes. Without the help of victims and witnesses, very few criminals would be convicted and punished.

Police investigators depend on witnesses and victims to watch for suspicious activity, report crimes, and help with investigations. Prosecutors depend on witnesses and victims to testify against defendants. When the charges against a defendant are dropped before a trial, it is usually because a victim or an important witness has decided not to testify. (Of course, the best way to help yourself and the police is not to become a victim. See Table 5-1 for tips on preventing crime.)

Witnessing a Crime

Some people who witness crimes don't want to get involved. They refuse to cooperate with the police or to testify about what they saw. In many cases, they are worried about their own safety. They may have been warned by the defendant to keep quiet, or they may believe that the defendant will try to harm them if they help the police.

To deal with this fear, many states and the federal government have enacted witness protection laws. (The 1982 Federal Victim and Witness Protection Act is the best-known example.) These laws make it a serious crime to retaliate against a victim or witness who testifies at a criminal trial.

Help for Victims

The criminal justice process is intended to punish criminals. It is not designed to aid the victims of crimes. Ordinarily, when people lose property or suffer physical injury because of a criminal act, the only way they can receive compensation is to sue the criminal in a civil court. (You'll read about civil suits in Chapters 7 and 8.)

In recent years, states have begun to find other ways to help crime victims. You read about one way—restitution—earlier in this chapter. As a condition of probation, many judges require criminals to pay back the victims of their crimes. Often, however, restitution by the criminal isn't possible. To handle cases like these, most states have developed victim compensation programs. Under these programs, states compensate victims for medical bills and lost income resulting from crimes. They may also compensate the families of people who are killed by criminals. Because these programs are very expensive, each state has strict rules about who is eligible and how much compensation a victim may receive.

Crime victims in many cities and towns can get nonfinancial aid from local victim assistance programs. These programs generally offer a combination of practical help and psychological counseling. They may, for example, help victims deal with insurance companies, lawyers, or the state program for victim compensation. They may also encourage victims to testify by explaining the process, calming their nerves, and even helping them get to court on time. In addition to these programs, rape crisis centers and other private support services can help individuals deal with the emotional, physical, and legal problems that crime victims face.

REVIEW QUESTIONS

1. What role do witnesses and victims play in the criminal procedure?
2. What is a victim compensation program?
3. List three ways a victim assistance program can help a crime victim.

Table 5-1   Ways to Protect Yourself and Your Property against Crime

Common sense is often the best defense against crime. Below are some ideas on how to lessen your chances of becoming a victim.

Keep your house or apartment secure:
- Secure your home or apartment with proper locks, chains, and peepholes.
- Lock all doors and windows when you are leaving the house, even just briefly.
- Secure other entries into your home, such as skylights and pet doors.
- Don't hide keys outside.
- Don't leave notes on the door, letting strangers know you're not home.
- Use outdoor lighting at night.
- Make your home seem occupied when you're out: leave the TV or a radio on; hook up lights to timers.
- Don't give out personal information over the phone. Don't tell strangers that you are home alone.
- Don't invite strangers into your home. Verify the identity of service people.
- Use a phone answering machine to take messages when you're not home.

If you plan to be away for an extended period of time:
- Don't tell other people about your travel plans.
- Have a neighbor keep an eye on your home while you're gone.
- Have your yard cared for, and don't let newspapers and mail accumulate.
- Remove valuables from the house.
- Keep a car parked in the driveway.

On the streets and in public places:
- Walk in a confident manner, and be alert to your surroundings. You may be considered an easy target if you are distracted.
- Keep away from large bushes, alley entries, dark doorways, and other places where an attacker might hide.
- Carry a whistle.
- Don't display your valuables.
- Take the elevator instead of the stairs if you can. To escape an attacker on a stairwell, use the fire exit.

- In an elevator, stand near the control panel. Push buttons to get off if you sense danger. Don't get into an elevator with someone who acts suspiciously.
- While waiting for a bus or train, stand with other people. On the vehicle, try to sit near the driver or conductor. Don't fall asleep.
- Never hitchhike.
- In public rest rooms, don't hang your handbag or other valuables where they can be grabbed from the outside.

In your car:
- Keep your car well maintained to reduce the chance of a breakdown.
- Keep the gas tank filled.
- Keep packages and other valuables out of sight.
- Don't stop to help stranded drivers.
- When you reach your destination, park as close as possible to the entrance.
- Be sure no one is hiding in the backseat before you get in your car.
- After you get in the car, lock the car doors.

Other tips:
- Your chances of being confronted by a violent criminal are slight. Most criminals won't harm you if you cooperate. Do everything you can to avoid violence. Nothing is worth the risk of physical injury.
- The less you carry with you, the less you have to lose. Avoid carrying too much cash, personal checks, credit cards, and ATM cards.
- You might want to carry "mugger money" with you. This is cash ($20 perhaps) that can be handed over quickly. Your chances of being hurt may be greatly reduced. Having no money may put you in jeopardy if the attacker is violent.
- Form a neighborhood watch program.
- Investigate self-defense training. Organizations such as the YMCA, the YWCA, and Women against Rape offer classes that teach practical techniques and "street smarts" to people. With this instruction, you will feel that you are not helpless.

Viewpoints on Gun Control

Firearms have played a role in American life from the Revolutionary War through the taming of the continent to the gun battles between warring drug gangs on our city streets today. Experts estimate that Americans own about 200 million guns, nearly one for every man, woman, and child in the country.

Many people believe that they have a right to own guns—a right based on the Second Amendment to the Constitution. This amendment states, "A well regulated Militia, being necessary to the security of a free State, the right of the people to keep and bear Arms, shall not be infringed." By contrast, people who support gun control argue that this amendment was intended to protect a state's right to use guns to maintain peace, not the right of an individual to own firearms.

Many Americans are passionately for or against gun control. Those at one pole of the debate argue that there should be no laws regulating gun ownership. Those at the other pole would like to see a ban on all guns. The majority of Americans believe there should be some regulation but disagree on exactly which laws to impose.

The Case for Gun Control

Advocates of gun control believe that something must be done to make guns less available to criminals and the violent mentally ill. Each year more than 9,000 people are murdered with guns in the United States. In Great Britain and Switzerland, by contrast, where guns are banned, fewer than 20 people are murdered with guns each year.

Gun control supporters believe that one way to make guns less available to those who would use them to break the law is to impose a nationwide waiting period for the purchase of all guns. This would give local police the chance to check the backgrounds of the purchasers and provide a cooling-off period for angry or desperate buyers. A national waiting period, they claim, would prevent criminals from avoiding local and state laws by going to other cities or states to buy guns.

The Case against Gun Control

Opponents of gun control laws contend that such laws would merely inconvenience and punish law-abiding gun owners, since they are the only ones who would obey them. Criminals, on the other hand, would continue to get guns illegally. Opponents of gun control contend that state and local governments should punish only those who use guns to commit crimes. They could do this by imposing stiff mandatory prison sentences.

Gun control opponents also argue that law-abiding people want and need guns to protect themselves and their families from criminals. They point out that violent crime continues to rise in places where gun control laws have been passed. The laws, they say, do not deter criminals and may hamper the ability of victims to defend themselves.

The Courts and Legislatures

The gun control battle is fought by two powerful lobbies in the state and federal legislatures. The National Rifle Association (NRA) opposes gun control, while Handgun Control, Inc., favors gun control laws. The latter group is aided by James and Sarah Brady. James Brady, formerly President Ronald Reagan's press secretary, was shot and seriously injured during the assassination attempt on the President in 1981.

At present, gun control laws differ from state to state. In recent years, the trend has been toward stricter gun control laws. Nearly half the states have enacted laws that require a waiting period before the purchase of a gun. Some states have a total ban on certain kinds of guns, such as semiautomatic assault weapons. Gun control supporters continue to try to pass a national law requiring a waiting period before a handgun purchase. Their opponents work to defeat this measure.

Chapter Review

Chapter Summary

- The criminal procedure begins with the police investigation and arrest. When suspects are arrested, they are taken to the police station for booking.

- Soon after being arrested, suspects are brought before a judge for an initial court appearance. The suspects are informed of their constitutional rights and told what they have been charged with. Suspects who have been charged with misdemeanors are asked to plead.

- Suspects charged with felonies are entitled to a probable cause hearing. Probable cause is determined by a judge at a preliminary hearing or by a grand jury.

- At the arraignment, felony suspects are told of the charges against them and are asked to plead. Most defendants plead guilty, often as part of a plea bargain arranged with the prosecutor.

- If a defendant pleads not guilty, his or her guilt must be determined through a criminal trial. At the trial, the prosecutor must prove beyond a reasonable doubt that the defendant is guilty.

- When a defendant is found guilty, the judge reviews the defendant's background before determining the sentence.

- Incarceration is the usual punishment for serious crimes. The term of imprisonment may be determinate or indeterminate. After serving some portion of the term, most offenders are released early, on parole.

- Offenders found guilty of less serious offenses may not be incarcerated. Instead, they may pay a fine, receive a suspended sentence, or serve a term of probation. Most offenders who are put on probation must agree to specific conditions.

- Witness protection laws make it safer for witnesses and victims to testify in criminal cases. State and local programs can provide compensation and assistance for victims.

Understanding Legal Terms

On a separate sheet of paper, match the terms below with the definitions that follow.

arraignment	incarceration
booking	plea bargaining
deterrence	probation
grand jury	restitution
incapacitation	retribution

1. Group of citizens who decide whether there is enough evidence to bring a defendant to trial
2. A goal of punishment that prevents a criminal from committing more crimes by locking the criminal in prison
3. Process in which the police make a formal record of a person's arrest at the police station
4. Pretrial court appearance during which a judge reads the charges against a defendant and asks the defendant to state his or her plea
5. A deal in which a defendant's sentence is reduced in exchange for pleading guilty and avoiding a trial
6. A goal of punishment that seeks to discourage a criminal from committing crimes again
7. A goal of punishment that seeks to "get back" at the criminal
8. Confinement to jail or prison
9. Repayment by a criminal to victims for property taken or damage done
10. A sentence that involves no jail time but consists of rules that must be followed by the person who is sentenced

Applying the Law

1. Nancy Diaz, a prosecutor, is preparing for a probable cause hearing in the case against Clifford Block. Block was arrested for possession of cocaine. The only evidence Diaz has is a small quantity of cocaine that the police found in Block's house. In reviewing the police records, Diaz finds out that the police seized the cocaine during an illegal search. Therefore, she can't use the cocaine as evidence against Block. What should she do?
2. Alexis Boone is arrested and charged with attempted murder. At her arraignment, Judge Raj Masir reads the charges against Boone and asks her how she pleads. She responds, "Guilty." Judge Masir asks, "Are you sure?" She says, "Yes." The judge accepts her plea and sets a date for sentencing. Did Judge Masir do anything wrong? Explain your answer.
3. Larson Puller is found guilty of the crime of arson, a serious crime that can be punished by 5 years to life in prison. Before sentencing Puller, Judge Lisa Prince reviews his criminal record. She finds that Puller has been convicted twice for burglary and three times for assault and battery. After considering these facts, Judge Prince sentences Puller to 30 years in prison. Puller protests that he was on trial for only one crime—arson. He says that the judge has no right to take his past crimes into account when determining his sentence. Is Puller right? Why or why not?
4. Raul Martinez hot-wires a neighbor's car and drives off in it. When the police pull him over, he says he only "borrowed" the car and was planning to return it later that day. He is arrested and found guilty of joyriding. Judge Harold Quan reviews Martinez's report and finds that Martinez is a good citizen who, until now, had no criminal record. Judge Quan therefore sentences Martinez to a six-month suspended sentence. Three weeks later, Martinez is arrested again for taking a car without permission. If he is found guilty, what may happen to his suspended sentence?

5. Mary Ming is found guilty of driving while intoxicated. Before sentencing her, Judge Ed Lynch reviews her presentence report. He finds that she was convicted of drunk driving once before but has no other criminal record. He also notes that when she was arrested, her blood alcohol concentration was measured at 0.09, which is very slightly over the state limit. State law requires that anyone convicted of drunk driving a second time serve 90 days in jail. Can Judge Lynch, based on Ming's record, order a sentence of probation for Ming? Explain your answer.

6. Patrick McGee attacks Ellen Moffit one night. He knocks her to the ground, breaking her collarbone. Moffit has very little money and can't afford to pay for medical treatment. Is there anything she can do? Explain.

Case Studies

1. James Nelson approached two young boys who were riding their bicycles. He looked threatening. As one boy rode away to get help, Nelson drew a gun and shot him in the leg. The boy returned later and found his friend dead. Nelson was arrested. At Nelson's preliminary hearing, he said that there was no evidence to prove he had killed the second boy. Therefore, he said, there was no probable cause to charge him with murder. Was he correct? Explain your answer.

2. Charles Norval was arrested and charged with assault with a deadly weapon. For this serious crime, the penalty was a minimum of five years in prison. He made a deal with the prosecutor. He agreed that he would plead guilty to second-degree assault, a much less serious crime. In return the prosecutor agreed to drop the original charges and ask the judge to give Norval a light sentence. Was this agreement legal? Explain your answer.

3. Phillip Reynolds was convicted of receiving stolen property. Before sentencing Reynolds, the judge reviewed his criminal record. The judge found that alcohol had "played a substantial role" in his criminal behavior. The judge therefore sentenced Reynolds to one year in jail plus five years of probation. As a condition of probation, Reynolds would not be allowed to drink alcohol. Reynolds was 25 years old and therefore of legal drinking age. Did the judge have the right to prevent him from drinking alcohol? Why or why not?

Chapter 6

Juvenile Justice

Chapter Objectives

When you have read this chapter, you should be able to:

- Give a brief history of juvenile courts, and explain how they differ from criminal courts.

- Describe the limits of a juvenile court's jurisdiction.

- Explain the reasons for transferring a case from juvenile court to adult criminal court.

- Describe each step of the juvenile justice process.

- Describe four kinds of dispositions that a juvenile judge may order.

Case Study

In the Interest of M.D., 441 N.E.2d 122 (Illinois 1982).

M.D., a 15-year-old boy, lived in Chicago. (Courts often do not release the names of juveniles involved in court cases.) M.D. had gotten into trouble with the police several times, once for burglary. He had also been involved in several fights with a local gang called the Vice Lords. On January 26, 1981, M.D. and his friend Izear Sewell confronted two gang members in a Laundromat and shot and killed them.

Sewell, who was 22 at the time of the shooting, was tried in an adult criminal court. However, according to Illinois state law, M.D. was too young to go through the criminal justice system. In every state, if a person is below a certain age when he or she is accused of a crime, that person is considered legally a juvenile—a child. As in the case of M.D., that person's case must be taken to the state's juvenile court.

Unlike an adult in criminal court, a child in juvenile court is not put on trial and cannot be punished. Instead, a judge orders whatever treatment will help rehabilitate the child. However, if the judge believes that the child will not respond to rehabilitation, the judge can transfer the case to an adult court. There the child can stand trial and, if found guilty, be punished—just as an adult would be.

When M.D.'s case came before the juvenile court, the prosecutor asked the judge to transfer the case to criminal court. He reminded the judge of the seriousness of M.D.'s offense. He also pointed out M.D.'s history of offenses. He said that with such a background, M.D. should be tried as an adult in criminal court.

Before deciding whether to transfer the boy, the judge heard testimony from a probation officer, two mental health professionals who had examined M.D., and M.D.'s mother. They all testified that M.D. was childish and immature but not a hardened criminal requiring punishment. They felt that he could be rehabilitated if he lived in a structured environment and had positive role models and firm moral instruction. The judge therefore decided that long-term placement in a state school would be in the best interest of both the boy and the community. The judge denied the prosecutor's request to transfer the case to criminal court.

JUVENILE COURTS

Throughout early American history, children who committed crimes were tried and punished as if they were adults. In the nineteenth century, social reformers became concerned about this practice. They felt that it was unfair to treat children so harshly, because children were too young to be responsible for their actions. Children's criminal activities were a result of bad upbringing, the reformers said. It was clearly unfair to punish a child for having received improper supervision or training.

Illustration 6-1   At one time, juveniles who committed crimes were treated as adults; today that is not always true.

The reformers also pointed out the cruelty of subjecting young criminals to adult punishment. Young children locked away with adult criminals often were abused physically and sometimes were abused sexually. Also, by spending time with hardened criminals, many children who had been arrested for petty crimes learned to commit more serious crimes.

The reformers believed that if a child was given proper training, attention, and education, he or she could be made into a good citizen. By contrast, if the child was labeled a criminal at an early age, that label might stick for life. These beliefs became the basis of a specialized court system for children and adolescents. This system, which now exists in every American state, is called the **juvenile justice system**.

History of Juvenile Courts

In 1899 Illinois established this country's first juvenile court. This court had jurisdiction, or authority, over children who committed crimes in the state. It was also responsible for handling children who were homeless. When any such child was brought to the juvenile court, a judge would review the child's history. With the help of social workers, the judge would determine the treatment that would be most likely to rehabilitate the child.

Early juvenile court hearings looked more like meetings than like criminal trials. Unlike criminal trials, juvenile hearings did not use an adversary process, in which opposing sides present their cases to determine guilt or innocence. In fact, juvenile proceedings were not even held in a courtroom. Instead, a judge conducted an informal hearing, often in his or her office. The idea was to place the child in a caring atmosphere and show the child that no one was determining guilt or fixing blame. Children who had broken the law were not labeled guilty of a crime or sentenced to a punishment. Instead, they were declared to be juvenile delinquents—children who had broken the law and were in need of rehabilitation. These juveniles were ordered to undergo treatment.

Because a juvenile hearing was not considered a criminal matter, the criminal rights guaranteed by the U.S. Constitution did not apply. The child had no right to a lawyer or a jury. Often there was no prosecutor. Generally, the only participants were a judge, the child, the child's parents, probation officers, and social workers.

Juvenile Institutions

Juvenile court judges did not send delinquent children to jail. Some children were given a stern warning and sent home with their parents. Others were ordered to serve a term of probation. With probation, a child was allowed to stay out of a government institution as long as he or she followed certain rules. Children who were most in need of rehabilitation were sent to live in state-run juvenile institutions. Those institutions were designed to house, raise, control, and educate problem children.

In the early years, juvenile institutions focused mostly on giving children moral and religious training. In later years, they began to place greater emphasis on education and vocational training. Today, every state's juvenile facilities employ psychologists to diagnose and treat children's problems. By tracing the roots of a child's behavior, the psychologists try to help that child change his or her behavior.

Constitutional Rights of Juveniles

On June 8, 1964, a woman living near Phoenix, Arizona, told the police that she had received an obscene phone call. She said that her neighbor, a 15-year-old boy named Gerald Gault, had placed the call. The police took Gerald into custody without giving him (or his parents) any information about the crime he was accused of.

If Gerald had not been a juvenile, he would have been tried in a criminal court. There he would have had the protections of a formal trial. For example, he would have had the right to hire a lawyer. He would have been allowed to question his neighbor about her accusation. He would have had a chance to speak in his own defense or to take advantage of his Fifth Amendment right to remain silent.

Because of Gerald's age, however, his case was heard in juvenile court. There Gerald had no right to a lawyer and no right to question the witness.

Instead, he and his mother met with the judge and two probation officers and discussed the matter informally. Based on what the officers reported, the judge decided that Gerald was delinquent. Therefore, the judge ordered that Gerald be sent to the State Industrial School until he turned 21. Gerald would have to stay at the institution for six years unless he showed signs of early rehabilitation.

Gerald and his parents appealed the judge's decision, and the case eventually came before the U.S. Supreme Court. Until that time, the Supreme Court had held that the due process rights of adults do not apply in juvenile court. According to the Supreme Court, the juvenile justice system was not an adversary system in which the prosecutor and defense attorney argue for and against the guilt of the defendant. It was designed to help children, not to punish them. Therefore, it had no need to give children the same kinds of protection that the Constitution provides for adults.

Although this principle seemed reasonable, it clearly didn't work well in practice. Children such as Gerald Gault received none of the protections that criminal defendants would have received. However, after brief questioning, a judge could send them away for years for even a minor offense.

After the Supreme Court heard Gault's case, it ordered some changes. For the first time, the Court gave children certain constitutional rights that had applied only to adults. Children in juvenile court now have the right to receive notice of the charges against them. They have the right to a lawyer or, if they can't afford a lawyer, a public defender. They have the right to remain silent during police interrogations and at hearings. They also have the right to confront witnesses.

Since its 1967 ruling on the Gault case, the Supreme Court has extended the rights of juveniles even further. For example, in 1970, the Court ruled that a child cannot be considered delinquent unless the prosecutor proves beyond a reasonable doubt that the child broke the law. Before that ruling, the prosecutor only had to present evidence that the child *probably* broke the law.

Not *all* rights guaranteed to adult criminal defendants have been extended to children, however. The Supreme Court has held that children do not have the right to bail, a grand jury indictment, a public trial, or a trial by jury. (Individual states, however, may choose to grant these rights to children.)

REVIEW QUESTIONS

1. Why did reformers feel it was necessary to develop a separate legal system for children?
2. Describe three ways in which early juvenile court hearings differed from adult criminal trials.
3. Name two constitutional rights that adult defendants and juveniles have in common.
4. Name two constitutional rights of adult defendants that are not granted to juveniles.

JUVENILE COURT JURISDICTION

Each state's juvenile courts have jurisdiction over children who are under a specified age. That age varies from state to state, but it is typically 16 or 17. Anyone older who is accused of a crime is treated as an adult and must stand trial in criminal court.

Juvenile courts hear cases involving three different types of children: delinquents, status offenders, and neglected or abused children.

Delinquents

A child who commits any act that would be considered a crime if done by an adult can be declared a **delinquent**. He or she then comes under the jurisdiction of the juvenile courts. Delinquency offenses include serious crimes such as robbery, selling drugs, and homicide. Less serious crimes, such as shoplifting and trespassing, are also considered delinquency offenses if committed by a child.

Status Offenders

Every state has laws that apply only to children. For instance, every state requires that children attend school until they reach a certain age. Every state sets a minimum age for drinking alcohol or driving a car. Other laws require that children obey their parents, not run away from home, obey curfews, and stay away from certain places (such as tattoo parlors).

Children who break these laws are said to commit **status offenses**. In most states, status offenses are considered less serious than criminal offenses, and juvenile courts treat status offenders less harshly than they do delinquents. Status offenders are referred to in the juvenile justice system as PINS, CHINS, or MINS: persons (or children or minors) in need of supervision.

Status offenses include not only specific acts but also patterns of improper behavior. For example, some states have laws defining status offenders as any children who are out of control, unmanageable, or "in danger of leading an idle or immoral life."

Illustration 6-2   Children who are abused, neglected, or abandoned come under the jursidiction of the juvenile courts.

Neglected and Abused Children

Since their role is to protect children, juvenile courts also have jurisdiction over cases involving children who are abused, neglected, or abandoned by their parents. Children who are not receiving proper food, shelter, medical care, or education may be brought before a juvenile court judge. The judge will then find a way to help those children. You'll read more about how the juvenile court system handles neglected and abused children in Chapter 11.

Transfer of Jurisdiction

Not every child who breaks the law can be helped by the juvenile justice system. Some children who commit more serious crimes or who have a history of repeated offenses are considered **incorrigible**—unlikely to respond to rehabil-itative treatment. Most states allow these children to be transferred to criminal court, where they can be tried and punished as an adult would be.

In some states, any child over a certain age (usually 14 or 16) who is ac-cused of committing a serious offense is automatically transferred to criminal court. In some states, the serious offense must be a felony; in others, it must be a crime punishable by death or life imprisonment; in others, it may be any crime other than a status offense.

Some states treat children and adults alike in regard to certain specific ac-tivities. For example, certain states require all licensed drivers, regardless of age, to face criminal charges for breaking traffic laws. In these states, a 16-year-old who drives recklessly will be treated the same as a 26-year-old who drives recklessly.

Generally, however, the decision about whether to transfer a case is made by the juvenile court judge. In the opening case, for example, the juvenile court judge held a hearing to decide whether M.D. should be tried in criminal court. At that hearing, the judge considered M.D.'s age and the nature of the offense he committed. The judge also reviewed M.D.'s history and heard rec-ommendations from various witnesses. On the basis of all this information, the judge decided to keep M.D.'s case in juvenile court.

Although transfer to criminal court may sound like harsh treatment, chil-dren often benefit from it. Once a child is transferred to adult criminal court, he or she is entitled to the same constitutional rights as an adult. Also, criminal ju-ries are often sympathetic to young offenders and may be more lenient than a juvenile court judge would be.

REVIEW QUESTIONS

1. What is the difference between a delinquent and a status offender?
2. What does it mean to transfer jurisdiction?
3. List three things a judge may consider in deciding whether to transfer jurisdiction.

THE JUVENILE JUSTICE PROCESS

The juvenile justice process is similar to the adult criminal justice process in many ways. Nearly every step that you read about in Chapter 5—the probable cause hearing, the indictment, the trial, and so on—has an equivalent step in the juvenile court system. (See Figure 6-1 for a description of the basic juve-nile justice process.)

The Police

The police are responsible for investigating any violation of the law, whether the law is broken by an adult or a child. In most cases, however, police officers treat young offenders more leniently than they would treat adults. They may let

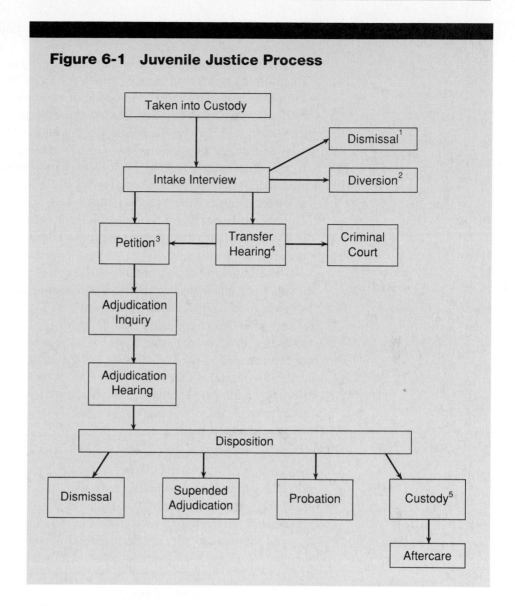

Figure 6-1   Juvenile Justice Process

1. May involve informal probation.
2. Case is referred to drug rehabilitation, social service, or other treatment program.
3. Charges are listed and filed with the court.
4. Hearing to decide whether to transfer the case to criminal court. Each jurisdiction decides who is subject to transfer hearings.
5. May be a secure or a nonsecure facility.

a child off with a warning, or they may take the child home to his or her family for treatment and discipline. If a child has committed a particularly serious offense, a police officer will generally take that child to the police station.

To distinguish itself from the criminal justice system, the juvenile justice system often uses different words to describe similar procedures. For example, when a police officer takes an adult to the police station, that action is called an arrest. When a police officer takes a child to the police station, however, the procedure is called *taking into custody*.

Once a child has been taken into custody, he or she has most of the same constitutional rights that an adult would have. In some cases, children receive even more protection than adults do. For example, the police in Shreveport, Louisiana, suspected that 13-year-old Andrew Dino had killed a 9-year-old girl. On August 2, 1977, the police asked Andrew's mother to bring him to the police station. At the station, Mrs. Dino was asked to wait outside while two officers questioned Andrew. Less than ten minutes later, the officers had a confession from Andrew. Ordinarily, this confession wouldn't be acceptable as evidence, because Andrew didn't have a lawyer with him when he confessed. The police officers, however, had anticipated this problem. Before listening to his confession, they had gotten Andrew to sign a document waiving his Miranda rights.

The Dinos protested that the officers had taken advantage of Andrew's inexperience and hadn't explained the consequences of signing the document. Nevertheless, the juvenile court allowed Andrew's confession to be used as evidence. The Dinos appealed that decision, and the case was eventually reviewed by the Louisiana Supreme Court. The court agreed that Andrew had not been treated fairly. It ruled that, unlike adults, children cannot waive their constitutional rights unless they have had "a meaningful consultation" with an attorney, an informed parent, or another adult interested in the child's welfare.

Intake Interview

Soon after a child is taken into custody by the police, he or she has an intake interview. An **intake interview** is similar to an adult's preliminary hearing. Its purpose is to determine whether formal charges should be brought against the child. The interview is usually conducted not by a judge but by a referee. A **referee** is a person with a background in social services and in law.

At the intake interview, the referee meets with the child and the child's parents. (A probation officer or a prosecutor may also be allowed to present evidence.) The referee reviews the accusations against the child and examines the child's background, school performance, and peer relationships. The referee also considers whether the child is hostile or cooperative and whether the child admits responsibility or shows remorse. After weighing all this information, the referee may take one of three actions: he or she may dismiss the case, divert the case, or file a petition.

Dismissal   If there is no probable cause to hold the child, the referee will dismiss the case. Probable cause is the reasonable belief, based on legally obtained evidence, that the child has committed a crime. Even if there is probable cause, the referee may dismiss the case if the offense is minor or if it is a first offense. The referee may also dismiss a case if the child's parents seem willing and able to discipline the child themselves.

Sometimes the referee will dismiss a case only if the child agrees to an informal probation. A child on **informal probation** is released without a trial.

In return, the child agrees to report to a probation officer and abide by the rules set up by the probation department.

Diversion   In about half the cases they hear, referees recommend diversion. **Diversion** is transferring a child out of the juvenile justice system and into the care of another agency. Depending on the child's needs, a referee may send the juvenile to a mental health, educational, job development, drug rehabilitation, or social service agency for treatment. A child who is diverted to one of these agencies does not have to appear in court. In most cases, the child can live at home while receiving treatment instead of being sent to a state institution. Diversion is especially common for children accused of a status offense.

Illustration 6-3   Following the intake interview, a referee may decide to divert a juvenile's case to a drug rehabilitation center.

Filing a Petition   Referees generally do all they can to avoid sending a child to court. In some cases, however—particularly when a child is accused of an especially serious offense or has a history of offenses—dismissal or diversion may not be appropriate. In cases like these, the referee may decide to file a petition. A **petition** is similar to an indictment or information in the criminal justice system. It is a document that lists the charges against a child and states the facts that support the charges. After the petition has been filed with the court, the child must attend a formal hearing in juvenile court.

Most children are released to their parents to await the hearing. (No bail payment is required.) If there are no responsible adults to care for a child, the child may have to stay in a juvenile detention center until the hearing. A child may also be sent to a detention center if he or she seems likely to run away or commit other crimes before the hearing.

Adjudication Hearing

Shortly after his or her petition is filed, a child must appear in court for an adjudication inquiry. An **adjudication inquiry** is similar to a criminal arraignment. The judge tells the child exactly what he or she is accused of and explains the child's constitutional rights.

The adjudication inquiry is followed by an **adjudication hearing**—the juvenile court equivalent of a criminal trial. At this hearing, just as at a trial, a judge listens to the testimony of various witnesses. Those witnesses may include the child, the child's parents, probation officers, social workers, and other people familiar with the child's behavior and background. On the basis of this testimony, the judge must decide whether or not the child is delinquent, in need of supervision, or abused or neglected.

REVIEW QUESTIONS

1. Under what circumstances might a referee dismiss a case at the intake interview?
2. What does it mean for a referee to divert a case?
3. Under what circumstances would a child await a court hearing in a juvenile detention center rather than at home?
4. What is the purpose of an adjudication inquiry? An adjudication hearing?

DISPOSITION

If a judge rules that a child is delinquent, in need of supervision, or abused or neglected, the judge must develop a treatment plan for the child. This treatment plan is called a **disposition**. Although a disposition is not intended to be a punishment, it is similar in some ways to the sentence that a judge hands down at the end of a criminal trial. (See Figure 6-2 for the disposition of some typical juvenile offenses.)

In order to come up with an appropriate disposition, the judge must know as much as possible about the child. He or she can get background information by consulting a social report. A **social report** is similar to a presentence report in criminal court. It contains summaries of the child's prior court history, family situation, school record, and psychological profile.

Based on the information in the social report as well as the seriousness of the offense and the child's behavior in court, the judge determines a disposition. In general, the judge has four options: he or she can order a dismissal, a suspended adjudication, a term of probation, or custody.

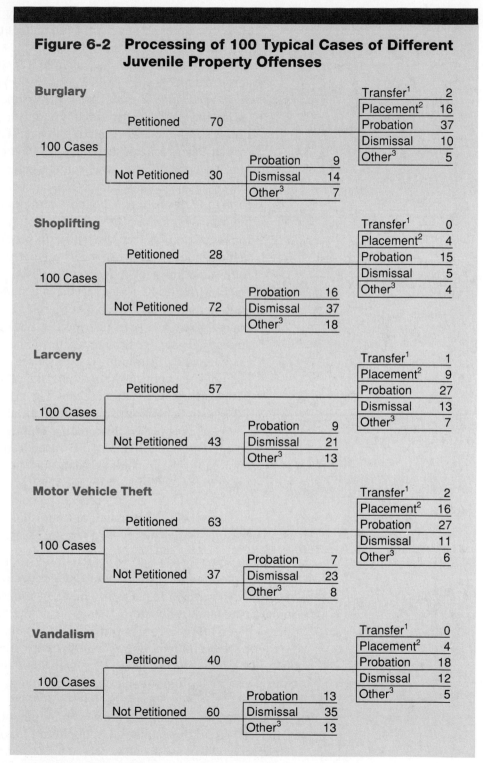

Figure 6-2   Processing of 100 Typical Cases of Different Juvenile Property Offenses

Burglary

100 Cases
- Petitioned 70
  - Transfer[1] 2
  - Placement[2] 16
  - Probation 37
  - Dismissal 10
  - Other[3] 5
- Not Petitioned 30
  - Probation 9
  - Dismissal 14
  - Other[3] 7

Shoplifting

100 Cases
- Petitioned 28
  - Transfer[1] 0
  - Placement[2] 4
  - Probation 15
  - Dismissal 5
  - Other[3] 4
- Not Petitioned 72
  - Probation 16
  - Dismissal 37
  - Other[3] 18

Larceny

100 Cases
- Petitioned 57
  - Transfer[1] 1
  - Placement[2] 9
  - Probation 27
  - Dismissal 13
  - Other[3] 7
- Not Petitioned 43
  - Probation 9
  - Dismissal 21
  - Other[3] 13

Motor Vehicle Theft

100 Cases
- Petitioned 63
  - Transfer[1] 2
  - Placement[2] 16
  - Probation 27
  - Dismissal 11
  - Other[3] 6
- Not Petitioned 37
  - Probation 7
  - Dismissal 23
  - Other[3] 8

Vandalism

100 Cases
- Petitioned 40
  - Transfer[1] 0
  - Placement[2] 4
  - Probation 18
  - Dismissal 12
  - Other[3] 5
- Not Petitioned 60
  - Probation 13
  - Dismissal 35
  - Other[3] 13

1. Transfer to criminal court.
2. Custody.
3. Referrals to other agencies, fines, restitution, etc.
Note: Detail may not add to totals because of rounding.

Source: U.S. Department of Justice, Office of Juvenile Justice and Delinquency Prevention.

■ *Dismissal.* Even when a child is clearly delinquent, the judge may choose to order no treatment at all and let the child go without restrictions. A judge may do this if he or she feels that the juvenile process itself is enough to teach the juvenile a lesson or if the child's parents agree to supervise the child more closely in the future.

■ *Suspended adjudication.* If a child seems relatively trustworthy, the judge may order a suspended adjudication. A **suspended adjudication** is similar to a suspended sentence: It allows a child to go without restrictions as long as the child stays out of trouble. If the child commits a second offense, however, the judge will consider both the original offense and the second offense in deciding the disposition.

■ *Probation.* Probation is the most common disposition for a delinquent child. It is often coupled with a term of community service or an order for restitution or a fine. A child on probation is permitted to live at home as long as he or she meets regularly with a probation officer and follows the rules the judge imposes.

■ *Custody.* James K. was a 15-year-old student at Milwaukee Technical High School in Wisconsin. On March 1, 1974, he admitted in juvenile court that he had been distributing LSD, a dangerous drug, to other students. The judge declared James to be delinquent.

Because distributing drugs is a serious crime and because James had not been cooperative in court, the judge felt that probation would not be enough to rehabilitate him. He ordered that James be sent to the Wisconsin School for Boys until he turned 18.

James appealed this order, claiming that it was unfair. An adult charged with distributing LSD faced a maximum penalty of $250 or one year in jail. In contrast, James had been committed to almost three years in the state school for the same crime. The Wisconsin Supreme Court upheld the judge's order. The court explained that time spent in a state school is treatment, not punishment. Therefore, James had no reason to compare it with a term of incarceration.

Judges are reluctant to remove a child from his or her home unless it is absolutely necessary. However, when judges decide that a child must be placed in custody, they prefer to place the child in a nonsecure facility such as a group home, foster home, or boarding school. A nonsecure facility is a residential facility with no locked doors or restraints; it lets children come and go freely.

For some children, however (especially those who are seriously delinquent, like James K.), a judge may feel that a secure, or locked, facility is more appropriate. In most states, secure juvenile facilities are called training schools.

A juvenile is usually sent to a training school for an indeterminate period of time. The child is held at the school until he or she is rehabilitated or becomes an adult. In most states, people age 18 or older are considered adults. Some children are released early from training school, just as some adults are released from prison on parole. This sort of early release, under the supervision of a juvenile probation officer, is called **aftercare.**

Illustration 6-4 For juveniles who are seriously delinquent, a judge may decide that a locked state training school is the most appropriate disposition.

The Child's Best Interest

No matter which of these alternatives a judge chooses, the disposition must satisfy several requirements. It must be suited to the problems of the specific child rather than to delinquent children in general. It must be in the best interest of the child, the child's family, and the community. It must restrict the child's freedom as little as possible.

For example, 15-year-old Randy Groves lived in Gaston County, North Carolina. At his adjudication hearing on December 31, 1987, he admitted that he had stolen five cartons of cigarettes while on probation for earlier crimes. He also admitted that he was a drug addict. The juvenile court judge declared Randy to be delinquent.

The judge talked with a psychologist, Randy's lawyer, and Randy himself. He also read Randy's social report. On the basis of all this information, the judge determined that Randy's drug addiction had caused his delinquency. He ordered Randy to spend two years at a state training school that offered drug treatment. Randy appealed the judge's order.

When the North Carolina Supreme Court reviewed Randy's case, it found that the judge had overlooked many less restrictive alternatives. There were several good community-based programs available. For example, Randy could be sent to a group home or a substance abuse facility, or he could be hospital-ized for drug treatment. The court ordered the juvenile court judge to reexam-ine Randy's case and look for treatment options that were less restrictive than training school.

Juvenile Records

Many people think of juvenile delinquents as criminals and treat them that way. Some employers, for example, are reluctant to hire anyone who has a record of delinquency. Some colleges refuse to admit people who have a juve-nile record.

Most juvenile justice authorities believe, as the nineteenth-century re-formers did, that a child's misbehavior is not the child's fault. Therefore, it is wrong to hold a person's record of juvenile delinquency against that individual as he or she goes through life. For this reason, every state has taken steps to protect the identities of juvenile offenders.

As you have seen in this chapter, court records often refer to children by their initials rather than their full names. Most states refuse to release the names of juvenile offenders to anyone, except when absolutely necessary. For further protection, most states prohibit prosecutors from introducing evidence that an adult criminal defendant has a history of delinquency charges.

In most states, it is illegal to use a person's juvenile record to deny that person any rights, such as the right to vote, obtain a driver's license, get credit, or get housing. In addition, many states permit juvenile records to be sealed permanently or destroyed after a certain amount of time has passed. (In some states, this is done automatically. In other states, the individual must ask to have it done.) Once a person's juvenile record is sealed or destroyed, that per-son can act as if the record never existed.

REVIEW QUESTIONS

1. What is a social report?
2. What is the difference between a secure facility and a nonsecure fa-cility?
3. For how long may a child be committed to a training school?
4. Why don't juvenile courts publicize the names of the juveniles who come before them?

Latest in the Law: Working as a Probation Officer

In the juvenile justice system, a probation officer is a type of social worker who oversees children who have gotten into trouble with the law. The probation officer's main task is to make sure that the child and his or her family are following the rulings of the juvenile court. Probation officers form close relationships with the juveniles in their care. They provide aid and counseling to both the juveniles and their families.

The Nature of the Work

A probation officer's job usually starts when a juvenile is taken into custody or when the child appears for an intake interview. At that point, the probation officer may be assigned to investigate the child. This information will help the juvenile court judge or referee determine the disposition of the case. The probation officer's investigation may include interviews with the parents, the child, school officials, friends, and witnesses to the incident that brought the child to the court.

By being assigned to a case from the start, the probation officer is able to become completely familiar with the case and begin building a relationship with the child and the child's parents. If the judge or referee orders the juvenile to serve a term of probation, the probation officer makes certain the terms of probation are being carried out. The juvenile is usually required to report to the probation office regularly. During those visits, the probation officer tries to help the juvenile find ways to stay out of trouble. The probation officer also makes sure that the child completes any community service that the court has assigned. During the probation period, probation officers also visit the child's home and work with officials at the child's school.

Probation officers typically have 20 or more cases under their supervision at any one time. Some cases may require more supervision than others, depending on the nature of the misbehavior and the child's home situation. Part of a probation officer's job is to help the juvenile adjust to his or her environment. Probation officers may help some youngsters return to school. They may help others find jobs or learn to avoid troublesome friends. Officers also help parents deal with family conflicts that may be contributing to the juvenile's problems. Sometimes the probation officer acts as the juvenile's advocate in an adjudication hearing. In some smaller towns, probation officers also serve as intake interview referees.

Education and Training

To qualify for a job as a probation officer, applicants usually need a minimum of a bachelor's degree in liberal arts or the social sciences, such as psychology or sociology. More and more applicants have a master's degree in social work as well. Most juvenile probation departments also provide on-the-job training and some in-service training, such as seminars and workshops.

Personal Attributes

Effective probation officers genuinely like people and work easily with all kinds of individuals. Like other social workers, probation officers often deal with people who have experienced tragedies or who have very difficult problems. They must remain sympathetic toward their clients. At the same time, they have to avoid becoming so involved emotionally that they lose their objectivity.

Probation officers should be prepared to work in less than ideal conditions. In some municipalities, probation officers carry heavy caseloads and must make visits to unsafe neighborhoods. Probation officers must be emotionally mature enough not to become discouraged by the difficult circumstances they see every day or by the fact that some problems remain unsolved. Despite these demands, many juvenile probation officers report that they receive a great deal of satisfaction from the job. This is especially true when a probation officer helps a youngster overcome his or her difficulties and start on the road to a more fulfilling life.

Chapter Review

Chapter Summary

■ Originally, children who committed crimes were treated the same way as adults who committed crimes. Around the turn of the twentieth century, states established juvenile justice systems to separate children from adults and to provide treatment, rather than punishment, for juvenile offenders.

■ At first, the juvenile justice system was informal. None of the rules of criminal procedure were observed.

■ By the middle of the twentieth century, the Supreme Court had held that children accused of crimes must be given some of the same rights as adults accused of crimes. Children have the right to an attorney, the right to be informed of the charges against them, and the right to confront witnesses. They do not, however, have the right to bail, a grand jury indictment, a public trial, or a jury trial.

■ The age at which juvenile courts no longer have jurisdiction over a person varies from state to state, but it is generally 16 or 17.

■ Juvenile courts have jurisdiction over children who may be delinquent, status offenders, or abused or neglected. Delinquents are children who commit crimes. Status offenders are children who break laws that apply only to children.

■ Some juvenile cases may be transferred to criminal court. For example, children who repeatedly commit offenses or who commit particularly serious offenses may have to stand trial in criminal court.

■ The juvenile justice process begins when a police officer takes a juvenile into custody. Later, the juvenile comes before a referee at an intake interview.

■ When there is no probable cause to hold the child or when the child's offense is minor or a first offense, a referee will dismiss the case. Sometimes the referee will divert the case to a community agency through which the child can receive treatment.

- If the referee decides not to dismiss or divert the case, he or she must file a petition for the child to have a court hearing.

- At the adjudication hearing, the judge considers the facts of the case and determines whether the juvenile is a delinquent, in need of supervision, or abused or neglected. If this is the case, the judge must order a disposition.

- The most common dispositions are dismissal, suspended adjudication, a term of probation, and custody in a secure or nonsecure facility.

- Unlike a criminal record, a juvenile record may not be used against a person later in life. Many states offer special protection for juveniles who appear in court, such as not releasing their names.

Understanding Legal Terms

On a separate sheet of paper, match the terms below with the definitions that follow.

adjudication hearing	incorrigible
aftercare	intake interview
delinquent	petition
disposition	referee
diversion	status offense

1. A treatment plan for a juvenile judged to be delinquent, in need of supervision, or neglected or abused
2. Early release from a juvenile detention facility, similar to parole for adults
3. An act that can be considered wrong only when done by a juvenile
4. Action of transferring a child out of the juvenile justice system and into another agency's care
5. A juvenile who commits an action that would be considered a crime if done by an adult
6. Juvenile court equivalent of a criminal trial
7. Person who conducts an intake interview when a juvenile has been taken into custody
8. Unlikely to respond to rehabilitative treatment
9. Procedure conducted to decide whether formal charges should be brought against a juvenile
10. A document, filed with the court, that lists the charges against a juvenile and facts that support the charges

Applying the Law

1. Doris, a 15-year-old girl, is accused of stealing a car. At her adjudication hearing, the judge listens to the evidence showing that she did steal the car. He also listens to Doris's defense. He decides that Doris did steal the car and declares her to be a delinquent. Doris appeals the judge's decision, saying that she was denied her constitutional right to a trial by jury. Is she right? Explain your answer.

2. Sarita is 17 years old and has a valid driver's license. One evening, Officer Harold Gold pulls Sarita over for driving while intoxicated. In her state, any licensed driver accused of violating motor vehicle laws must be tried in criminal court. Sarita, however, is legally considered a juvenile until she turns 18. Will Sarita's case be heard in juvenile court or criminal court? Why?

3. Officer Joyce Barkley sees Craig, a 14-year-old boy, in a video arcade on a Tuesday morning. Local law prohibits any school-age child from being in an arcade before three o'clock on weekdays. Discuss the three ways Officer Barkley might handle the situation.

4. Officer Boyce catches Art, age 15, shoplifting and takes him into custody. At the intake interview, the referee reviews Art's background. She finds that Art has been detained for shoplifting four times before and that he is currently on probation for one of those offenses. She also finds that Art seems not to realize the seriousness of shoplifting. What action will the referee probably take?

5. Judge Tyler declares Trent to be delinquent, based on evidence that Trent murdered a young girl. Trent is 15 years old. Judge Tyler orders that Trent be committed to the state training school for boys. How long will Trent spend at the school? Explain your answer.

6. Roy is 24 years old. When he was younger, he committed a series of juvenile offenses. Since that time, he has broken no laws. A landlord finds out about Roy's juvenile record and refuses to rent him an apartment. If Roy's state is like most other states, is the landlord's action legal? Explain your answer.

Case Studies

1. Nina Blondheim had run away from home six times by the time she was 17. On November 30, 1973, she was taken to juvenile court. The judge ruled that Nina was beyond the control of her parents and ordered her to serve a two-year term of probation. Nina appealed this disposition, saying that running away is not a crime and that she was being punished illegally. Was she right? Why or why not?

2. In 1974 Robert Earl Anthony was accused of stabbing Jeffrey Bawak to death in Black Hawk County, Iowa. Robert was 17½ years old. Under Iowa law, juvenile courts had jurisdiction over all individuals under 18 years old. Nevertheless, Robert was tried in adult criminal court. Why?

3. When M.C. was 17, he admitted to possessing a small amount of marijuana. The Colorado juvenile court declared him delinquent and ordered two years of probation. M.C. appealed this disposition. He said that if he had been 18, he would have been tried as an adult, and the maximum punishment he could have received would have been a $100 fine. Therefore, he said, his two-year term of probation was unfair. Did the court of appeals agree with him? Why or why not?

Unit 3

Tort Law
And Contracts Law

Chapter 7

Civil Law

Chapter Objectives When you have read this chapter, you should be able to:

■ Describe the purpose of civil law.

■ Explain how civil trials differ from criminal trials.

■ Describe six kinds of remedies that a plaintiff might ask for in civil court.

■ Define *damages*, and explain what kinds of costs may be included in damages.

■ Describe the disadvantages of litigation, and discuss three alternatives.

Case Study

Cecil v. State, 350 S.W.2d 614 (Arkansas 1961); *Cecil v. Headley*, 373 S.W.2d 136 (Arkansas 1963).

Belton Cecil started a fire on his property to burn off some dead grass. The fire quickly got out of control. It spread beyond Cecil's property and burned 475 acres of his neighbors' land. It also destroyed a neighbor's house and most of the belongings inside.

Under Arkansas law, it is a misdemeanor to allow a fire to get out of control. Cecil was charged with violating this law and was found guilty at a criminal trial. His punishment was a fine of $99.

Cecil's neighbors, Kenneth Headley and others, then sued Cecil for the damage he had caused to their property. At a civil trial, they proved that Cecil was responsible for burning land, destroying a building, and destroying personal property. The judge ordered Cecil to pay his neighbors a total of $5,466 to cover the damage.

DIFFERENCES BETWEEN CIVIL LAW AND CRIMINAL LAW

If you watch television newscasts, you may get the impression that the chief task of the American legal system is to fight crime. (The past few chapters, which talked about crimes and criminal law, may have reinforced that impression.)

In reality, most laws have nothing to do with crime. Instead, they deal with disagreements between people. Courts play an important role in settling disputes about property ownership, contracts, and physical injuries. They also help settle family matters such as divorce, adoption, and child custody.

To resolve these kinds of disputes, the courts rely on a type of law called civil law. **Civil law** deals with the rights of private citizens in disputes with other citizens, with businesses, or with governments. Some civil laws—such as the laws that protect freedom of religion and freedom of expression—come directly from the Constitution. However, most civil laws—such as labor laws, zoning laws, and contract laws—are passed by the federal, state, and local governments.

People accused of breaking civil laws are tried in civil court, just as people accused of crimes are tried in criminal court. In civil court, a judge listens to both sides of the dispute and decides whether a law has been broken. If it's not clear how the law applies to a particular dispute, the judge *interprets* the law by considering two questions: First, what are the precedents? (In other words, how has this law been applied in the past?) Second, what is fair in this case? (In other words, is there a commonsense solution to the dispute?) If someone is found to have broken a civil law, he or she may be required to offer a **remedy**—a way to make up for the damage that has been done.

Let's look at a typical civil law case. Gerald and Ann Fields opened an animal shelter in a residential neighborhood in an Atlanta suburb. Residents of the neighborhood complained. They said that the shelter had an offensive odor and that the noise from the animals kept them awake at night. They also worried that the animals might spread disease through the neighborhood.

Finally, the neighbors took their case to court. Their county had a zoning law banning businesses in residential neighborhoods. The neighbors claimed that the Fieldses' shelter violated that law. The Fieldses disagreed. They said that they were not running a business; they were simply providing a place for homeless animals to live.

After listening to both sides, the judge interpreted the zoning law to mean that residential neighborhoods are for private homes only. Even if the Fieldses' animal shelter wasn't strictly a business, it was more than just a private home. Based on this interpretation of the law, the judge ordered a remedy: the Fieldses had to close their shelter.

Civil law and criminal law are meant to accomplish very different things. The main purpose of criminal law is to punish people who do harm to others. An important goal of civil law, however, is to compensate, or repay, the people who have been harmed. **Compensation** is payment for the loss or injury they have suffered.

The Fieldses' animal shelter did not do lasting harm to the neighborhood, so the Fieldses were not required to compensate their neighbors. Many civil cases, however, involve serious accidents or injuries. If you are hit by a car, for example, you can take the driver of the car to court. If the judge finds the driver **liable**—legally responsible—for the accident, the driver may be required to compensate you for your injuries.

In many cases, the person who causes an accident is tried in both criminal court and civil court. At a criminal trial, the defendant may be declared either guilty or not guilty. If found guilty, he or she is punished—usually by a fine or a prison term. At a civil trial, the defendant may be declared either liable or not liable. If found liable, he or she must provide the necessary remedy.

In the case study that opened this chapter, for example, Belton Cecil let a fire get out of control. At his criminal trial, he was found guilty of violating a criminal law. As punishment, he was ordered to pay a relatively small fine. At Cecil's civil trial, he was found liable for the damage to his neighbors' property. As a result, he was ordered to pay a much larger amount of money. This second sum of money was not intended to punish Cecil; instead, it was meant to compensate his neighbors for their losses.

Illustration 7-1   In many cases, the person who causes an accident is tried in both criminal court and civil court.

REVIEW QUESTIONS

1. Name three kinds of cases that may be tried in a civil court.
2. What are the main purposes of civil law, and how are they different from the purpose of criminal law?
3. Describe an incident that may lead to both a criminal trial and a civil trial.

A CIVIL TRIAL

Peter is about to leave for a vacation. He offers to let his friend Diane stay in his apartment while he is away. When Peter returns a few weeks later, he finds that his kitchen table is cracked, his microwave oven is broken, and some jewelry is missing. He pays a carpenter $150 to fix the table. The microwave oven can't be fixed; it costs Peter $300 to buy a new one. The value of the missing jewelry is $5,000. Peter asks Diane to pay him $5,450 to compensate him for his losses. Diane refuses. She says that she left his apartment exactly the way she found it. Peter decides that his only option is to **sue** Diane—that is, to take her to court.

The process of resolving a dispute in civil court is called **litigation** or a **lawsuit**. The person who begins the litigation—in this case, Peter—is called the **plaintiff**. The person who is being sued—Diane—is the **defendant**.

The process begins when Peter (or his lawyer) files a **complaint**—a written notice to the court that explains his side of the story. Peter's complaint, for example, describes what was damaged and what was missing in Peter's apartment. It explains why he thinks Diane is responsible. It also states the remedy he wants from Diane—specifically, that he wants her to pay him $5,450.

After the court receives Peter's complaint, it notifies Diane that she is being sued. At this point, Diane may hire a lawyer to defend her. If she does hire a lawyer, she must do so at her own expense. The Sixth Amendment right to a court-appointed lawyer does not apply in civil cases. (The same is true for most of the constitutional safeguards that you read about in Chapter 3: they apply only to criminal cases.)

The court allows Diane (or her lawyer) to file an **answer**—a written response to Peter's complaint. In her answer, Diane may deny Peter's charges. (For example, she may say that she never saw the jewelry that Peter claims is missing.) She may also offer a defense to Peter's charges. (For example, she may admit that she broke the kitchen table but insist that it was such an old, wobbly table that it would have broken anyway.) Finally, she may dispute the amount or type of compensation that Peter is asking for. (For example, she may claim that he could have replaced the microwave oven for less than $300.)

After the complaint and answer are filed, both parties begin to prepare for the trial. In a process called **discovery**, the plaintiff and defendant gather as many facts as possible about the case. Peter's lawyer may want to question Diane's friends about her recent activities. Diane's lawyer will want to see the carpenter's repair bill and some proof that Peter owned jewelry. Both lawyers will probably want to question neighbors about what they saw or heard while Diane was staying at the apartment.

The trial itself is very similar to a criminal trial. (The steps in a typical trial will be discussed in more detail in Chapter 19.) Both parties present evidence and call witnesses to support their sides of the story. For example, Peter tries to prove that Diane is responsible for the damaged and missing property. He also tries to prove that $5,450 is reasonable compensation. Diane tries to prove that she is not liable for the loss and damage. She may also try to prove that Peter is asking for too much compensation—that the table, oven, and jewelry were worth less than $5,450. If the evidence presented by one side conflicts with the evidence presented by the other, the judge (or, in some cases, the jury) must decide which side is telling the truth.

That decision is made differently in a civil trial than in a criminal trial. As you read in Chapter 5, a defendant can be convicted of a crime only if the prosecutor proves guilt "beyond a reasonable doubt." In a civil case, however, a defendant can be held liable on the basis of a **preponderance of the evidence**. In other words, the evidence doesn't have to *prove* the plaintiff's case; it only has to support the plaintiff's case better than it supports the defendant's case. Even if Peter can't prove beyond a reasonable doubt that Diane caused the damage in his apartment, Diane may still be held liable.

HOFFMAN, MARKS, & COLETTI
1900 PRINCETON PIKE
TRENTON, NEW JERSEY 08648
(609) 555-1000
ATTORNEYS FOR PLAINTIFF(S)

Plaintiff
RUTH M. HANNON

vs.

Defendant
VALLEY REAL ESTATE, JAMES GROVER and
MELINDA GROVER, his wife.

SUPERIOR COURT OF NEW JERSEY
MERCER COUNTY, LAW DIVISION

Docket No. L89-47280

CIVIL ACTION

COMPLAINT

The plaintiff, residing at 29 Allwood Avenue in the Township of Lawrence, County of Mercer and State of New Jersey, by way of Complaint, alleges and says:

1. On or about June 26, 1989, the plaintiff was a business invitee lawfully upon certain premises owned by the defendants, James Grover and Melinda Grover, his wife, commonly known as 20 Anthony Lane, Hightstown, New Jersey, upon their express and/or implied warranty that said premises were safe and fit to come upon and use.

2. At the time and place aforesaid, the defendants, Valley Real Estate, were realtors engaged in the business of conducting an "Open House" and other services upon said premises, upon their express and/or implied warranty that said premises were safe and fit to come upon and use.

3. At the time and place aforesaid, the defendants were careless and negligent, breached their warranties and/or created and maintained a nuisance, and negligently failed to warn plaintiff of hazards.

4. As a proximate result of the aforesaid negligence, carelessness, breach of warranties, maintenance of a nuisance, and failure to warn of hazards by the defendants, the plaintiff sustained serious personal injuries, both internal and external, and suffered great pain, shock and mental anguish and will continue to suffer for a long time to come and has been permanently injured. The plaintiff has, in the past, and will, in the future, be required to obtain medical, hospital and nursing care and has been prevented from performing her usual duties and will be so prevented for a long time to come.

WHEREFORE, plaintiff demands judgment against the defendants for damages, together with interest and costs of suit.

CERTIFICATION

Pursuant to the provisions of Rule 4:5-1, the undersigned attorney certifies that to the best of his knowledge, the above matter is not the subject of any other action pending in any court or of a pending arbitration proceeding, nor is any other action or arbitration proceeding contemplated.

DESIGNATION OF TRIAL COUNSEL

Pursuant to the provisions of Rule 4:35-4, the Court is advised that Alfred P. Coletti is hereby designated as trial counsel.

Hoffman, Marks, & Coletti
Attorneys for Plaintiff

BY: *Alfred P. Coletti*
ALFRED P. COLETTI

Illustration 7-2   In a civil suit, the plaintiff files a complaint.

REVIEW QUESTIONS

1. What is the first step in a civil trial? Who takes that step?
2. What is the purpose of discovery?
3. What does *preponderance of the evidence* mean?

CIVIL REMEDIES

As you read earlier in this chapter, when a defendant is held liable in a civil case, he or she may have to offer a remedy. One common remedy is compensation, in which the plaintiff recovers for a wrong or a loss by getting money or by having his or her goods returned. Other remedies seek to prevent or correct a wrong or a loss.

Types of Compensation

In most civil cases, compensation takes the form of money. Money paid as compensation is called **damages**. For example, in the opening case Belton Cecil was required to pay his neighbors $5,466 for burning their property. Diane may be required to pay Peter $5,450 for his lost and damaged belongings.

The amount of damages a defendant must pay depends on many factors. Let's begin with a simple example. Steve Downey and Victoria Sklebar were neighbors in St. Louis. During a quarrel, Downey shot Sklebar and wounded her. Sklebar went to a hospital and was treated for her injury. After she recovered, Sklebar sued Downey. Downey was required to pay $1,500 in damages to cover Sklebar's medical expenses.

Although $1,500 may seem like a good deal of money, Downey could have been required to pay much more. For example, if his gunshot had also damaged Sklebar's home or property, he might have had to cover the cost of repairs. If the shooting had caused Sklebar to miss several days of work, Downey might have had to compensate her for lost wages. If Sklebar had needed someone to cook and clean while she was recovering, Downey might have had to pay for a housekeeper as well.

In addition to covering Sklebar's expenses, he might have had to compensate her for other losses. Suppose, for example, that Downey's bullet had hit Sklebar in the eye and blinded her. No amount of money could buy her a new eye or restore her sight. Nevertheless, Downey would have been required to pay damages—probably amounting to many thousands of dollars—to compensate her for the loss of her eye. In addition, he might have been required to compensate Sklebar for mental distress or for pain and suffering resulting from the injury.

In many states, a defendant who is found liable in a civil case must pay all the costs of the lawsuit, including the fees for the plaintiff's attorney. In especially serious cases, the defendant may also have to pay punitive damages.

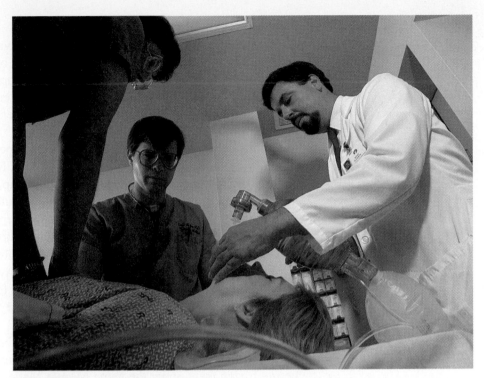

Illustration 7-3   If someone is hurt by another person, the injured person can sue for damages in order to recover the medical costs.

Punitive damages is money that the defendant must pay as punishment for breaking the law. Unlike a fine, this money is paid to the plaintiff rather than to the court.

Occasionally a person may break a civil law without causing any real damage or injury. In those cases, the defendant may be required to pay nominal damages. **Nominal damages**, or "damages in name only," is a small amount of money the defendant must pay just for having been wrong. Often these damages amount to no more than a dollar.

Courts may order other kinds of compensation besides damages. Suppose George's engraved pocket watch—a family heirloom—stops running. He takes it to a repair shop. The shop holds on to his watch for months without repairing it. George finally asks the shop to give back his broken watch. The shop manager refuses. He says that he's already ordered the necessary part and that he won't return the watch until it's fixed.

George can sue the repair shop to get his watch back. The remedy he would ask for is not damages but **restitution**—the return of a piece of property. Plaintiffs often ask for restitution when someone else has an item that belongs to them, especially if the item is unique. George's pocket watch, for example, has sentimental value—no amount of money could replace it. If a court finds that the repair shop is holding the watch illegally, it can force the shop to return it. (Of course, if the shop has lost or destroyed the watch, restitution isn't possible. In that case, the only remedy available to George is damages.)

Other Remedies

Compensation is not the only kind of remedy available in civil cases. Some remedies are meant to prevent or correct a wrong or a loss. For example, an **injunction** is a court order requiring a person to stop doing something. You may recall the Fields case from earlier in this chapter, in which a court ordered Gerald and Ann Fields to close their animal shelter. That court order was an injunction.

Injunctions are used in many different types of cases. In Little Rock, Arkansas, for example, two co-workers named E. M. Webber and George Gray had a short romance. Gray ended the relationship, but Webber refused to accept that it was over. She did everything she could to get back together with Gray. Gray married another woman 11 years later, but Webber still didn't give up. She followed the couple around town and phoned their house constantly. She sat outside their door for hours at a time, waiting to speak with Gray.

After years of pleading with Webber to leave him alone, Gray went to court to get an injunction against her. The court forbade Webber to have any further contact with Gray. She was not allowed to approach him, call him, write to him, or even park her car on his street.

Businesses sometimes get injunctions to stop illegal picketing or unfair trade practices. In one case, a meat-packing company in Florida began marketing frozen meat under the name Minute Made. The Minute Maid Corporation, best known for its frozen orange juice, sued the meat company for using a name so similar to its own. Minute Maid claimed that consumers would be confused and that the meat company would profit unfairly from the millions of dollars spent on advertising by Minute Maid. The court ordered the meat company to stop using the Minute Made name.

The past few examples have shown how injunctions can stop an action that is already happening. Just as often, however, an injunction is used to stop an action before it begins. In 1973, for example, a psychotherapist in New York City wrote a book about a former patient and her family. She used the patient's record of therapy as source material for the book. The patient sued to stop the book from being published. She said that the book invaded her privacy and that publishing the book would damage her relationship with her friends and family. The court agreed. It issued an injunction that prevented the therapist from publishing the book.

Another type of court order is called specific performance. **Specific performance** is an order requiring a person to do something (unlike an injunction, which is an order *not* to do something). Specific performance is the usual remedy when a defendant has signed a contract and then refuses to carry it out.

For example, Brenda and Barry Minkin signed a contract at the time of their marriage. The contract stated that if they ever decided to end their marriage, they would go through the steps of a traditional Jewish divorce. They did split up years later, but Barry refused to follow the Jewish divorce procedure. Because of Brenda's beliefs, she would never be able to marry again unless her divorce followed the traditional rules.

Brenda took Barry to court and asked the judge to enforce the contract they had signed. Because no other remedy would work, the court ordered Barry to follow the rules of a Jewish divorce.

In some contracts disputes, a better remedy is **rescission**. With this remedy, the contract is canceled, or rescinded. When a contract is rescinded, the parties who signed the contract are no longer required to carry out the agreement. For example, suppose the owner of a computer store signs a contract with a supplier. In the contract, the supplier agrees to deliver five IBM computers a month at $1,000 a computer. The store owner sends the supplier $5,000 for the first month's shipment. When the shipment arrives, however, the store owner discovers that she has not received genuine IBM computers. Instead, she has received low-quality imitations designed to look like IBM computers.

The store owner can sue the supplier for having broken the contract. She would ask the court to rescind the contract—to put both parties where they were before the contract was signed. The store owner would return the computers, the supplier would return the $5,000, and there would be no further shipments.

Sometimes a plaintiff in a contracts case will ask for **reformation**—a court-ordered change in the contract. Suppose the same store owner signs a contract with another supplier. Once again, the supplier agrees to deliver five IBM computers a month at $1,000 each. Because of a typographical error, however, the contract lists the price of each computer as $100 instead of $1,000. Both parties sign the contract without noticing the mistake.

Later, the store owner discovers the error and realizes that it will save her an enormous amount of money. She sends the supplier $500 instead of $5,000 for the first shipment of computers. The supplier says that the price in the contract was a mistake and that he can't sell computers at that price. He delivers five computers and sends the store owner a bill for $4,500. When the store owner refuses to pay the bill, the supplier takes her to court.

The supplier can ask the court to rescind the contract. In this case, however, a better remedy is to reform the contract—to change the price back to $1,000 a computer. When the court orders this change in the contract, both parties are required to accept it.

Exceptions to Remedies

In some cases, a plaintiff may sue a defendant without seeking a remedy. The plaintiff may simply want the court to make a decision about his or her legal rights. For example, in 1921 Charles Baumann left his wife, Berenice, after 12 years of marriage. Charles went to Mexico to get a divorce. He then came back to the United States and married another woman. Berenice, who had not wanted the divorce, sued Charles. She claimed that the Mexican divorce was not valid and that she was still married to Charles. The court agreed. It declared that Berenice was Charles's legal wife and that his second marriage was void.

Illustration 7-4   If there is a dispute about a signed contract, remedies may include rescinding or reforming the contract.

Enforcing Remedies

When a court makes a decision in a civil case, it has the power to enforce that decision. If a defendant refuses to pay damages, the court may send law enforcement officers to seize the defendant's property. The court may then hold on to the property until the defendant pays the plaintiff. If the defendant still refuses to pay, the court may sell the defendant's property and give the plaintiff the money from the sale.

In some cases, the court can order the defendant's employer to collect the damages. The employer does this by taking a certain amount of money out of each paycheck the defendant receives. The employer gives this money directly to the plaintiff. This process may continue for weeks, months, or years until the plaintiff is compensated fully.

A defendant who violates a court-ordered injunction may be fined or jailed until he or she complies. A defendant who refuses to obey an order of specific performance may suffer the same penalty.

REVIEW QUESTIONS

1. Describe three types of costs that may be included in damages.
2. Give an example of a case in which a plaintiff would want restitution.
3. What is the difference between an injunction and specific performance?
4. What is the difference between rescinding a contract and reforming a contract?

ALTERNATIVES TO LITIGATION

Litigation is not the only way to settle disputes, and it is certainly not the best way. Most legal experts would agree that a lawsuit should be a last resort, to be used only if all attempts to settle a dispute have failed. In fact, most people are able to settle their differences informally, without having to go to court.

Litigation has several serious disadvantages.

Illustration 7-5   Litigation can be expensive because of lawyers' fees and possible court fees.

1. *Litigation is time-consuming.* Courts all over the United States are flooded with more cases than they can handle. Every new lawsuit must be added to a long waiting list. Years may pass before the case comes before a judge. (The Sixth Amendment guarantee of a "speedy trial" doesn't apply to civil cases.) As the lawsuit drags on, the dispute that started it may become worse instead of better. If the dispute is between friends, neighbors, or family members, the relationships among those people may be damaged beyond repair.
2. *Litigation is expensive.* Except for the very simplest cases, most lawsuits cannot be settled unless each side hires a lawyer. Lawyers' fees for an ordinary civil case can amount to thousands of dollars. Court fees and the costs of gathering evidence can add to the expense of a lawsuit.
3. *Litigation does not always lead to the best solution to a dispute.* Suppose a boy hits a ball through a neighbor's window. There are many possible ways to settle this problem. For example, the boy could work off the cost of a new window by mowing the neighbor's lawn for a month. A court, however, is not equipped to offer this kind of creative solution. If the neighbor takes the boy to court, the only remedy she can ask for is damages—money to cover the cost of replacing the window.

Fortunately, most disputes can be settled without the time and expense of a civil trial. There are several different ways to settle disputes, some more formal than others.

The most common and informal way to settle a dispute is **negotiation**—working out an agreement through discussion. Though you may not realize it, you spend much of your life negotiating with others. For example, you may disagree with other members of your family about which TV programs to watch. If your sister wants to watch her favorite comedy series while you want to watch *Monday Night Football*, you don't threaten to take her to court. Instead, you work out a compromise. You may agree to watch comedy and football on alternate weeks, or you may offer to do your sister's chores in exchange for her letting you watch the game.

Negotiation is often used to settle business and employment disputes. For example, new employees negotiate with employers about pay and benefits. In many stores, customer service representatives negotiate with customers about problems with a store's products or services. Insurance companies negotiate with hospitals and auto repair shops about how much they will pay to settle claims. Negotiation works in all these cases because the parties want to stay on good terms with each other and are therefore willing to compromise.

Although negotiation is a common technique for resolving disputes, it is not always successful. There are times when people's points of view are so far apart that they can't find a compromise acceptable to both parties. In such a case, the conflicting parties may decide to bring in a third party called a **mediator**. A mediator is a good listener who is skilled at solving problems. He or she is neutral, having no reason to favor one side over the other. The mediator plays an active role in the negotiation between the two parties. He or she listens to the arguments on both sides and suggests solutions that the parties themselves may not have thought of. The use of a mediator to help people negotiate is called **mediation**.

Illustration 7-6   When negotiation is not successful, a mediator can be called in to help both parties reach an acceptable compromise.

Suppose Joe and Hilda are neighbors in an apartment building. Hilda drives to work every morning at 5:30. Joe's bedroom is directly above the building's garage, so he is awakened at 5:30 every morning by the sound of Hilda's car. They've talked about the problem, but they can't find a practical solution. Joe refuses to look for another apartment, and Hilda refuses to look for another job.

Finally, they invite their neighbor Nolan to mediate. Because Nolan isn't emotionally involved in the dispute, he is better able to point out possible solutions. He may suggest that Joe wear earplugs or that Hilda have her car tuned so it runs more quietly. He may suggest that Hilda and Joe share the cost of a parking spot in a commercial lot outside the building. If either Hilda or Joe had come up with these ideas, the other person might have been too angry to listen. However, since the suggestions are being made by a neutral party, Hilda and Joe may be willing to take them seriously.

Professional mediators are often hired to help labor unions negotiate with employers or to help divorcing couples make decisions about property and child custody. In many communities, business organizations (such as the Better Business Bureau) or local media (such as newspapers and radio stations) hire mediators to help consumers settle disputes with local businesses. Because mediation has proved so successful, many high schools now teach mediation techniques. The students use these techniques to help settle disputes between other students.

In some cases, the parties involved in a dispute will bring in an **arbitrator** rather than a mediator. Like a mediator, an arbitrator is a neutral third party. Unlike a mediator, an arbitrator acts as a judge: he or she listens to both sides and then makes a final decision. Usually the decision of the arbitrator is binding—that is, the disputing parties have agreed beforehand that they will accept what the arbitrator decides. Settling a dispute in this way is called **arbitration**.

Arbitration has many advantages over a civil trial. It can usually be accomplished quickly, before a dispute has a chance to get out of control. It is much less expensive because cases settled by arbitration usually don't require lawyers. An arbitrator can also order more flexible remedies than a civil judge can.

Because of these advantages, many business contracts now include an arbitration clause. If there are disagreements about the contract, this clause requires that they be settled by arbitration rather than by a lawsuit. (For the same reasons, people often put arbitration clauses into their wills.) In recent years, some states have tried to take pressure off the courts by requiring arbitration in certain cases. For example, any dispute that involves an amount under $10,000 may have to be settled by an arbitrator rather than a judge.

For the many minor disputes—such as those between tenants and landlords or between consumers and businesses—a good alternative to a regular civil trial is small claims court. **Small claims court** is a court designed to handle disputes about small amounts of money, usually no more than $2,000. The legal procedure in small claims court is less complicated than that followed in ordinary courts. It involves less paperwork and does not require lawyers. As a result, a trial in small claims court is quicker and much less expensive than an ordinary trial is.

Small claims court has an important limitation, however. The only remedy a plaintiff can ask for is damages. A small claims court cannot order an injunction, demand specific performance, or reform a contract.

Despite all these alternatives, many people still decide to sue when they are involved in a dispute. Even after starting a lawsuit, however, a plaintiff may continue to negotiate with the defendant. If the plaintiff and defendant reach an agreement, they can end the lawsuit immediately. An agreement that is reached in this way is called an **out-of-court settlement**. Judges encourage disputing parties to settle their case out of court even if the trial has already begun. By ending the trial early, both parties save time and money. They also allow the court to move on more quickly to the next case on the waiting list.

REVIEW QUESTIONS

1. What are some disadvantages of litigation?
2. Name and describe three alternatives to litigation.
3. What does it mean for arbitration to be binding?
4. What is the purpose of small claims court?

NAME AND ADDRESS OF COUNSEL FOR PLAINTIFF

Robert Zeigler
89 Parkway Avenue, Suite 100
Trenton, NJ 08650

NAME AND ADDRESS OF COURT
SUPERIOR COURT OF NEW JERSEY
SPECIAL CIVIL PART
209 SOUTH BROAD STREET ROOM 110
TRENTON, NEW JERSEY 08650

From Plaintiff:

Alvin White
Name

20 Anthony Lane
Address
Lawrenceville, NJ 08648

555-1861
Phone No.

STATE OF NEW JERSEY

SUPERIOR COURT, LAW DIVISION
SPECIAL CIVIL PART

____Mercer____ County

SMALL CLAIMS SECTION

SC- __1556__ Docket No.

v.

CIVIL ACTION

COMPLAINT

To Defendant:

Lauren Johnson
Name

7 W. Welling Ave.
Address
Pennington, NJ 08534

555-0328
Phone No.

(✓) Contract

( ) Security Deposit

COMPLAINT

$ __200__ plus costs
Demand

Defendant signed contract agreeing, for a fee of $500, to provide catering services for a graduation party on June 22, 1991. Defendant called three hours before the party and said she would not be able to provide the service. Plaintiff paid $750 to another caterer to handle the party on short notice.

IMPORTANT: All plaintiffs and defendants must bring all witnesses, photos, documents, other evidence to the hearing.

Alvin White
PLAINTIFF'S SIGNATURE

Illustration 7-7   Small claims court is designed to handle disputes about small amounts of money, usually less than $2,000.

Latest in the Law: High Punitive Damage Awards in Civil Suits

In 1981 an agent of Pacific Mutual Life Insurance Company sold an insurance package to the town of Roosevelt, Alabama. Premiums paid by the town's employees were sent to the agent, who was supposed to forward them to the insurer. The agent soon stopped forwarding the payments. As a result, the policy was canceled. The problem was discovered when an employee tried to collect $3,800 in medical payments and was told she was uninsured. The woman sued both the agent and Pacific Mutual to recover the payment. The jury awarded her damages of $1.04 million, $840,000 of which was punitive damages.

In recent years, juries in civil suits have been returning record-high punitive damage awards, especially in fraud, personal injury, and products liability cases. Lawyers for the companies involved complain that the amounts of money awarded are unfair and ultimately crippling to the business community.

The Punitive Damage System

When a jury decides in favor of a plaintiff in a civil case, it may award actual damages—the amount of money necessary to replace the damaged property or make the injured person well again. Juries may also award punitive damages. These are damages over and above the actual costs involved. Their purpose is to punish the defendant for past wrongdoing and to deter the defendant—and others—from similar actions in the future.

Lawyers for large corporations are troubled by the fact that the law does not limit the amount of damages juries can award. Companies complain that they are being exploited and that an upper limit should be set on punitive damage awards. At least, many claim, the damage award should be related in some reasonable way to the harm done to the plaintiff.

The Supreme Court's View

Some hard-hit defendants have appealed their cases to the U.S. Supreme Court. They claim that very large awards violate the Eighth or Fourteenth amendments to the U.S. Constitution. The Eighth Amendment prohibits excessive fines, and the Fourteenth Amendment states that due process of law must be followed.

In the Pacific Mutual case, the insurance company appealed the $840,000 punitive damages judgment. The company claimed that the award was so extreme that it violated ideas of fundamental fairness that are implied under due process of law. The Supreme Court, however, disagreed. In March 1991 the Court refused to abolish or even set definite limits on punitive damage awards.

The State Legislatures

With no clear ruling from the Supreme Court, there is much variety among state legislatures in regard to punitive damage awards. Since 1986, at least 25 states have attempted to enact limits on punitive damage awards. Some states have merely limited the amount of money that may be awarded. Others have tied the amount of punitive damages to the amount of actual damages. Virginia, for example, places the limit for punitive damages at $350,000. Florida, by contrast, sets the limit at three times the amount of the actual damages.

Several states also require that a percentage of the punitive damages be given to the state or to a state agency. These laws are designed to discourage people from seeking punitive damages in the hope of getting rich. In Georgia, 75 percent of punitive damage awards in products liability cases go to the state treasury (after legal fees are deducted).

Overall, state legislatures are not prepared to ban punitive damage awards altogether. Many states, though, seem ready to limit the amounts or to demand that there be a reasonable relationship between the actual injuries and losses that have occurred and the punitive damages awarded.

Chapter Review

Chapter Summary

- Civil law deals with the rights of private citizens in disputes with other citizens, with businesses, or with governments.

- Whereas criminal law is intended to punish wrongdoers, civil law is intended to compensate people for injuries or losses caused by others.

- Civil actions are called lawsuits. The plaintiff begins a lawsuit by filing a complaint. The defendant named in the complaint is given an opportunity to answer.

- Before the trial, both parties engage in discovery—that is, they collect evidence that will support their side of the dispute.

- At the trial, the defendant is declared liable if a preponderance of the evidence supports the plaintiff's case.

- A common remedy in civil cases is compensation. Usually the compensation takes the form of damages. Damages may include medical expenses, costs to replace or repair property, compensation for pain and suffering, the costs of the lawsuit, and punitive damages.

- Sometimes a plaintiff sues to recover property that is being held by the defendant. In seeking this form of compensation, the plaintiff is suing for restitution.

- A plaintiff may ask for an injunction (a court order requiring that the defendant *not* do something) or for specific performance (a court order requiring the defendant to do something).

- Contract disputes may be settled by rescinding (canceling) or reforming (changing) the contract.

- A defendant who refuses to obey a court order can be fined or jailed. If the defendant refuses to pay damages, the court may seize the defendant's property.

■ Because litigation is expensive and time-consuming, most disputes are settled through less formal means, such as negotiation, mediation, and arbitration.

■ Negotiation is discussion between the disputing parties, with the hope of reaching a compromise.

■ Mediation is negotiation with the help of an outside party.

■ Arbitration is similar to mediation, except that the outside party acts as a judge and decides how the dispute will be resolved. The disputing parties agree beforehand to accept the arbitrator's decision.

■ Small claims court is a good alternative to formal litigation for disputes that involve small amounts of money.

■ At any point during litigation, the disputing parties may decide to discontinue the suit and settle the case out of court.

Understanding Legal Terms

On a separate sheet of paper, match the terms below with the definitions that follow.

arbitration   negotiation
discovery   punitive damages
injunction   reformation
liable   remedy
litigation   specific performance

1. A way to make up for damage that has been done
2. Legally responsible
3. The process of resolving a dispute in civil court
4. The process during which a plaintiff and defendant gather facts about the case
5. Money paid to a plaintiff by a defendant as punishment for breaking the law
6. A court order requiring a person to stop doing something
7. A court order requiring a person to do something
8. A court-ordered change in a contract
9. The process of working out an agreement through discussion between people who have a disagreement
10. The process of resolving a dispute by having a neutral party act as a judge and make the decision

Applying the Law

1. Brian knocks down Gretta, an elderly woman, and snatches her purse. The fall causes Gretta to break her leg. As a result, she must pay for expensive hospital treatment. Brian is arrested, tried, and found guilty of

robbery. He is sentenced to six months in jail. What other legal action can be taken against Brian?

2. Frank slips on a skateboard that was left in front of his door. He sues Michelle, his next-door neighbor, claiming that she left the skateboard there. Michelle denies the charge and says that the skateboard isn't hers. At the trial, both sides present evidence to prove their claims. How will the jury decide who is right?

3. Dwight drives through a red light and hits Paula's car. The car is destroyed, and Paula is seriously injured. She is hospitalized for a week and misses two weeks of work. What damages can Paula collect from Dwight?

4. Drew buys a VCR from Ace Electronics. The first time he uses it, it "eats" his videotape. Drew takes the VCR back to the store. He asks the store manager to take back the VCR, return his money, and pay for the damaged tape. The manager isn't sure whether the VCR was faulty or Drew broke it. What will the store manager be more likely to do: compensate Drew or take the case to court? Explain your answer.

5. Every day, when Marcy lets her puppy outside, the dog runs over to Roberta's rose garden and digs up roses. Name two ways in which these neighbors could settle the matter without going to court.

6. Doris works part-time for Madden Company one summer. When she leaves that job, the company still owes her $500. The company refuses to pay her. She tries several times to negotiate a settlement, but nobody at the company will talk to her. Doris is a student and cannot afford the expense of a lawsuit. Is there any action Doris can take to get the $500 she's owed? If so, describe it.

Case Studies

1. Richard Maretti decided to build an addition to the upper story of his house. Maretti's neighbor, Glenn Prah, objected. Prah used solar energy to heat his house. The energy came from sunlight collected by solar panels on Prah's roof. Prah complained that Maretti's addition would block the sunlight that his heating system depended on. Before Maretti could begin construction, Prah took him to court. What kind of remedy did he request?

2. Don Cumbest and Bedford Harris signed a contract. In the contract, Cumbest agreed to give Harris a sum of money by June 7. The contract said that if Harris received the money by that day, Harris would give Cumbest a stereo system he had acquired. On June 7, Cumbest made every effort to give the money to Harris. Harris, however, deliberately stayed away from Cumbest so that he wouldn't have to give up the stereo. Cumbest sued Harris. He demanded that the court force Harris to accept the money and give him the stereo, as they had agreed. The stereo was

unique—built from rare parts over a 15-year period—so Cumbest was not willing to settle for damages. What kind of remedy was he asking for?

3. The Dover family hired John Leavitt to construct a well on their property. Everyone thought this would be a relatively simple task. However, when Leavitt began to dig the well, he hit quicksand. The quicksand made the construction much more difficult and expensive. Leavitt finished the well, but he felt he deserved more money because of the extra work involved. What remedy did he ask for in court?

Chapter 8

Torts: Duties to Others

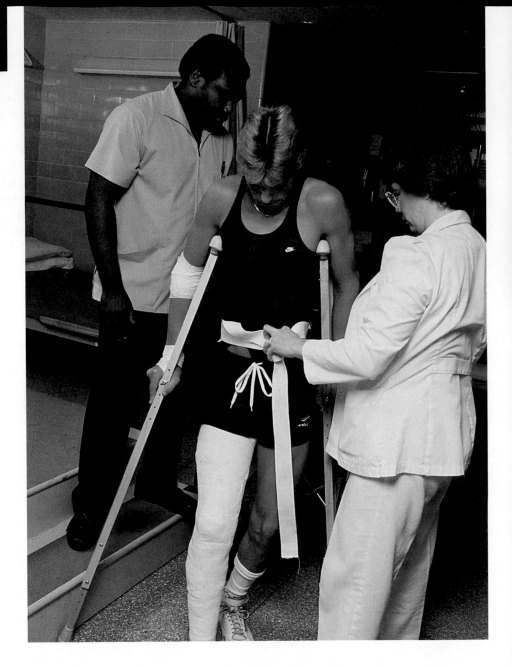

Chapter Objectives   When you have read this chapter, you should be able to:

■ Explain the purpose of tort law.

■ Define *intentional tort*, and name at least two kinds of intentional torts.

■ Describe how a court decides whether a person has acted negligently.

■ Describe the special types of liability that apply to manufacturers of products.

■ Define *defamation*, and describe two defenses to a charge of defamation.

■ Describe three types of damages for which a plaintiff may sue.

■ Explain the purpose of liability insurance.

Case Study

Garratt v. Dailey, 279 P.2d 1091 (Washington 1955).

Brian Dailey was 5½ years old. He spent one summer afternoon visiting his elderly aunt, Ruth Garratt.

Ruth invited Brian to meet her friend Naomi, who was sitting on the porch. Just as Ruth was about to sit in the chair next to Naomi, Brian picked up the chair, moved it a few feet, and sat down on it. Ruth, caught off balance, fell and broke her hip.

Ruth sued Brian for $11,000 to pay for treatment of the injuries from her fall. In court, Ruth told the judge and jury that Brian caused her injuries when he moved the chair.

Brian explained in court that he hadn't intended to make his Aunt Ruth fall. In fact, when he realized that she wanted the chair, he tried to put it back. Unfortunately, he wasn't quick enough to get it under her before she fell.

Ruth's lawyer asked Brian a few questions: "Brian, did you intend to move the chair?" Brian said, "Yes, I did." The lawyer then asked, "Brian, do you know that if you move a chair that someone is about to sit in, that person might fall?" Brian answered, "Yes, I know that."

On the basis of Brian's answers, the judge concluded that Brian was legally responsible for Ruth's injuries. The fact that he hadn't intended to hurt his aunt didn't matter. What mattered was that he had moved the chair. By moving the chair, he had hurt Ruth. Therefore, he was required to pay $11,000 to cover Ruth's medical expenses.

WHAT IS A TORT?

Every day—at school, on the street, at the store, or on the job—we do things that might injure another person or damage someone's property. A student late for school, for example, may start running and then carelessly collide with a passerby. A boy who wants to be left alone may lock his little sister in her bedroom, forcing her to break a window to get free. An overtired baby-sitter may fall asleep, allowing the toddler he's watching to go tumbling down a flight of stairs.

Legally, all these actions are called torts. A **tort** is any unreasonable action that hurts someone or does damage to a person's property. (As you'll see later, causing injury or damage by *failing* to act in a certain way may also be considered a tort.)

Under tort law, we have a duty to act *reasonably* at all times in order to ensure the safety of other people and their property. Violations of this duty are called **wrongful acts**. People's duties to others involve not intentionally causing injury to a person or damage to a person's property. They also include not acting in a careless or negligent way that causes injury or damage. In addition, some people have special duties. A doctor, for example, has the duty to perform certain tests when a patient comes in for a checkup. The manufacturer of a product has a duty to ensure that the product is safe. A store owner has a duty to keep the floor clean so shoppers won't slip and fall. People who don't exercise reasonable care may be liable, or legally responsible.

Illustration 8-1   Under tort law, store owners have a duty to keep their premises clean and safe so that shoppers won't injure themselves.

In addition to imposing these duties, tort law gives us certain rights. We have the right to go about our daily lives without fear of being injured by someone else. If we are injured because of someone's unreasonable, wrongful actions, tort law gives us the right to be compensated. *Compensation* is payment for an injury or a loss.

The earliest tort laws came from medieval English common law. By offering a legal procedure for settling disputes, these laws kept citizens from "taking the law into their own hands." Over the centuries, legislatures in the United States have added to, and changed some, common law torts. The U.S. Constitution and the courts have also helped shape modern tort law. The lawmakers, through statutes, and the judges, in their court decisions, attempt to ensure that people do not violate their duty to act reasonably.

Tort law is a type of civil law. As you remember from Chapter 7, the legal action taken in civil cases is called a lawsuit. The person who brings the lawsuit is called the plaintiff, and the person who is sued is called the defendant.

REVIEW QUESTIONS

1. What is a tort?
2. Under tort law, what general duty do we have toward other people?
3. What two general rights do we have under tort law?

INTENTIONAL TORTS

At the beginning of this chapter, you read about how Brian Dailey injured his aunt by pulling a chair out from under her. Brian's action is known as an **intentional tort**—a wrong done to another person on purpose. For an intentional tort to take place, the following elements must be present:

1. The defendant commits a certain act.
2. The defendant means to commit that act.
3. The defendant's act causes injury to the plaintiff.

Brian's action clearly fit this definition: He moved the chair; his action was intentional (that is, he did it on purpose); and his action injured his aunt.

In the law of torts, to do something intentionally means to do it voluntarily. The *reason*, or *motive*, for the action doesn't matter. What matters is that something was done and that it wasn't an accident. Brian Dailey, for example, said that he took the chair because he needed it and that he wouldn't have taken it if he'd known his aunt was about to sit in it. The judge held him liable anyway. Regardless of the reason, Brian had *intended* to move the chair. Age is also not a factor in intentional torts. Brian, who was only 5½ years old at the time of the incident, was held liable because he knew his action could have caused harm.

For another example, imagine that a student throws a smoke bomb into a classroom in order to annoy a teacher. The teacher isn't there, but another student chokes on the smoke. The first student did not intend to hurt the other student, but he did intend to throw the bomb. Therefore, he has committed an intentional tort. He is liable for the injuries he caused.

Some Intentional Torts

In Chapter 7, you found out that some criminal acts also violate civil laws. Many intentional torts fall into that category—that is, they are crimes as well as torts.

Assault and battery are good examples. Under tort law, **battery** is defined as physical contact with someone against his or her will. (You don't have to touch someone to commit battery; Brian's injuring his aunt by pulling her chair away is legally an act of battery.) In contrast, an **assault** is an act that puts someone in fear that he or she will be a victim of battery.

For example, Robert spots his girlfriend, Sheila, across the schoolyard with a boy named John. Robert races toward them, throws his books on the ground, pulls off his jacket, and waves a fist under John's face. Robert is committing an assault: he's putting John in fear of being hit.

Illustration 8-2   Many intentional torts, such as assault and battery, are crimes as well as torts.

The single phrase *assault and battery* is often used because these acts frequently occur together. (In a typical case of assault and battery, a person follows through on a threat and hits another person.) There can, however, be cases of battery without assault—for example, if Robert sneaks up behind John and hits him. There can also be cases of assault without battery—for example, if Robert waves his fist at John but doesn't touch him.

Although assault and battery are the most common intentional torts, there are many others. **False imprisonment**, for example, means keeping someone in a confined space against his or her will. (Despite its name, it doesn't necessarily involve locking someone behind iron bars.) Earlier in this chapter, we mentioned a boy who locked his sister in her bedroom so she would leave him alone. This is a case of false imprisonment.

Intentional infliction of emotional distress is another common intentional tort. In 1897 Mr. Downton went to Mrs. Wilkinson's house to play a practical joke. He told Mrs. Wilkinson that he had seen her husband lying on the ground with both legs broken. He then advised her to rush over and pick up the pieces. On hearing this news, Mrs. Wilkinson suffered a serious nervous shock and physical illness. Because his joke was responsible for her illness, a court held Mr. Downton liable for Mrs. Wilkinson's medical care.

To make sure that the courts aren't cluttered with cases of hurt feelings, the law strictly limits the definition of emotional distress. The action must be outrageous, and the damage must be extreme distress. Just because someone is rude to you or insults you does not mean you can take that person to court.

Not all intentional torts involve illness or injury to a person. An intentional tort may harm property or cause economic damage. These torts include trespassing on someone's property and taking, keeping, or destroying property that belongs to someone else.

Invasion of privacy is another tort that may cause emotional injury or economic damage. A person can be liable for intruding on someone's private life. These intrusions may include spying, eavesdropping, electronic monitoring, reading someone's mail or diary, and going through someone's wallet without permission.

Defenses to Intentional Torts

Not every action that causes injury or property damage is a tort. In many cases, people have valid **defenses**—excuses or explanations—for their actions.

Consent   The most common defense is **consent**, or permission. For example, you might tell a friend, "Go ahead, punch me as hard as you can." If your friend does punch you, you can't take him or her to court for any injury you sustain.

Consent is a valid defense only if it is given freely. Suppose a thug tells a mother to stay inside her car if she ever wants to see her child again. The mother nods and does not leave the car. The thug has nevertheless committed the tort of false imprisonment because the mother was forced into giving her consent.

In addition to consenting freely, a person must understand what he or she is consenting to. He or she must give **informed consent**—that is, consent based on complete information. Before doctors perform surgery, for example, they must explain to the patient all the potential problems the surgery might cause. The patient cannot legally sign a consent form allowing the surgery until he or she understands all the risks.

Consent doesn't always have to be spoken or written. It can be **implied**, or assumed because of the situation. One type of implied consent is expressed through actions. If you put on boxing gloves and enter a boxing ring, for example, you are clearly consenting to be punched by the other boxer. If you climb into a roller coaster, you are consenting to be placed in fear or emotional distress. If you send someone a party invitation, you are allowing that person to enter your property. In all these cases, your consent is assumed to have been given through your behavior.

Just by living in a community, we offer implied consent to many things. When we get on a bus, for example, we can expect a little jostling from the other passengers. We can also expect that another passenger may tap us on the shoulder to ask directions. By deciding to ride the bus, we are clearly consenting to these kinds of touching. Therefore, these touches—no matter how unwelcome they are—are not considered acts of battery.

A second type of implied consent is assumed when a person cannot speak or act. Let's say William is hit by a car and hurt badly. He is unconscious.

Illustration 8-3   If you climb into a roller coaster, you are consenting to be placed in fear or emotional distress.

Paramedics take him to a hospital, where doctors perform emergency surgery and save his life. William clearly never consented to being touched by the paramedics. He also never consented to surgery. However, these actions were necessary to save his life. William most likely would have consented if he had been able to do so, but he was unconscious. For this reason, he was considered to have given implied consent. That is, his consent was assumed to have been given even though it was not stated directly.

The defense of implied consent has limitations. A boxer in the ring has clearly consented to be punched by the other boxer, but he has not consented to be punched by someone outside the ring. Similarly, William's implied consent extends to emergency surgery only. While William is unconscious, doctors cannot draw his blood and give it to another seriously ill patient. The doctors cannot assume that William would have consented to this procedure, and the procedure is not necessary to save his life. Therefore, taking William's blood without his permission—even if it might save someone else's life—would be a tort.

Other Defenses to Intentional Torts   Another set of defenses to intentional torts includes *self-defense, defense of others,* and *defense of property.* The law of torts recognizes that if someone attacks you or another person, you have the right to defend yourself or the other person in a reasonable manner. You can also protect your property in a reasonable way. As in criminal law, you have the right to use as much force as is necessary but no more than is necessary.

Because property is considered less valuable than human life, the right to protect it is quite limited.

Necessity may also be a defense. In 1849 a fire was blazing on a street in San Francisco. To keep the fire from spreading, the mayor ordered the fire department to blow up Mr. Surocco's home with dynamite. With the house gone, the fire was prevented from moving farther along the street, and fire fighters were able to put it out. Mr. Surocco sued the mayor for destroying his home. The mayor's defense was one of public necessity—his action was necessary to save the city.

Performing an action in the line of duty is another defense. A police officer may detain someone, arrest someone, monitor someone's activities, or even enter a person's home on the reasonable belief that it is necessary for public safety. When law enforcement officers follow proper criminal procedures, their actions are not considered torts.

Another defense is discipline. Parents have the right to use reasonable physical force to discipline their children. As long as parents don't resort to unreasonable measures (such as beating or starvation), their disciplinary actions are not torts.

One excuse that will not hold up in court is "I made a mistake." Error, no matter how innocent, is never a defense. For example, Barbara sues Monica for cutting down one of Barbara's trees. Monica admits that she cut the tree but says she thought the tree was on her own property. Like Brian Dailey, Monica didn't intend to do any harm. Nevertheless, she is liable for the cost of replacing the tree she cut down.

REVIEW QUESTIONS

1. Can a person commit an intentional tort without meaning to do harm? If so, give an example.
2. What is the difference between *assault* and *battery*?
3. What does it mean to have a defense to a tort?
4. Name, and give examples of, two defenses to intentional torts.

NEGLIGENCE

Allen is driving his car down Main Street. He sees his friend Paula on the sidewalk and waves to get her attention. Because he has taken his eyes off the road, Allen doesn't see that there's a red light ahead of him. His car goes through the red light and rams into Betty's car, injuring Betty and damaging her car.

Allen's case is different from the torts we've looked at so far, because his action wasn't intentional. If he had deliberately run the red light, his action would have been an intentional tort (even if he didn't mean to hit Betty's car). However, Allen didn't go through the red light on purpose; he just forgot to watch where he was going.

Although his action wasn't intentional, Allen may be liable for a tort called negligence. **Negligence** is the failure to act with reasonable standards of care for the safety of others. Anyone who endangers others by being careless—or by committing other unintentional acts—may be sued for negligence.

In reviewing a case such as Allen's, a court would have to ask four questions:

1. Did Allen, the defendant, have a duty in this case?
2. Did Allen **breach**, or fail to do, his duty?
3. Did Allen cause the harm?
4. Did Betty, the plaintiff, suffer damages?

Clearly, Allen did have a duty in this case. As you read at the beginning of this chapter, everyone has a general duty to act in a way that doesn't injure others. When we get behind the wheel of the car, we have a number of specific duties. For example, we are expected to drive the car carefully, to remain alert, and to obey all traffic laws.

Did Allen breach his duty? In order to decide whether someone failed to do a duty, a court asks what a reasonable person would have done under the circumstances. Under tort law, a "reasonable person" is one who takes care not to injure others and acts sensibly. A reasonable person isn't the same as an ordinary person or an average person. Even if most people in Allen's circumstances would have turned to wave to Paula, a reasonable person probably would not.

We know people should act reasonably, but exactly what is reasonable behavior, and how does the court decide whether a person has acted sensibly and used good judgment? To reach a decision, a judge and jury must look at each negligence case individually, with all its special circumstances. In this case, Allen was clearly negligent; a reasonable person would have kept his or her eyes on the road. Imagine, however, that the facts were different: What if Allen had gone through the red light because his brakes failed and he lost control of the car? The question before the court now becomes: Would a reasonable person go through a red light if his brakes failed? The answer to this question is clearly yes. In this case, most juries would not consider Allen's action to be negligent.

Most cases are not so clear-cut. What if Allen had gone through the red light because he was rushing his daughter to the hospital emergency room? In that case, the jury might see his actions as reasonable. What if he had rushed through the light because he was late for a baseball game? Chances are that this would not be seen as the action of a reasonable person.

Once the court has determined that Allen was negligent, it has to decide whether the defendant caused the harm and whether the plaintiff suffered damages. In Allen's case, it is clear that he caused the injury by his action. It is also clear that there was damage to Betty and to her car.

Let's consider another case of negligence. Billy is 10 years old. He's playing in the front driveway of his house, which slants down to the street.

He climbs into his father's car, which is parked in the driveway. While he's playing in the car, he releases the emergency brake. The car rolls down the driveway and hits Juanita's car, damaging the car and injuring Juanita.

A reasonable person would not have released the emergency brake in a car parked on a slant. The courts, however, have found that it is unfair to expect small children to behave like reasonable adults. They therefore use a slightly different standard when children are involved. Courts look at what a reasonable person of similar age, experience, and maturity would have done. Under this principle, a jury would probably not find Billy negligent. (It might, however, find Billy's parents negligent in letting him play unsupervised and in leaving the car unlocked.)

There is an important exception to this "reasonable child" rule. If the child is engaged in an adult activity, such as driving a car or steering a motorboat, the child is held to adult standards. For example, a 16-year-old licensed driver is still legally a child. If that teenage driver causes an automobile accident, his or her liability will be no different from that of an adult.

Some people are expected to know more than the reasonable person. For example, Faith takes George for a flight in her helicopter. She goes off course, and the helicopter crashes, injuring George.

When Faith is tried for negligence, the court does not ask what a reasonable person would have done. (After all, even the most reasonable people don't necessarily know how to fly a helicopter.) Instead, the court asks what a "reasonable pilot" would have done. All professionals, such as doctors, nurses, lawyers, and pilots, are held to higher levels of what is reasonable.

Failure to Act

Tort law requires that when we act, we must act reasonably. We can, however, choose to do nothing at all in most situations. Because there is no general "duty to act," failure to do something is usually not a tort. For example, a driver who sees a disabled car on the side of the road does not have to stop and offer help. A passerby who sees a woman drowning in a lake has no legal duty to jump in and save her.

There are several exceptions to this general rule. One is that someone who begins to rescue another person may not give up and abandon the rescue. Imagine, for example, that you see a man collapse on a city street. You shout, "I'll call an ambulance!" and you run off in search of a phone. A crowd gathers around the man, waiting for the ambulance to arrive. Meanwhile, you decide not to make the phone call after all. Even if someone else eventually makes the call, the ambulance will arrive much later than it would have otherwise. The delay in the man's treatment is your responsibility, and you may be held liable for his medical problems.

Another exception to the rule is that owners of public places—such as schools, museums, hospitals, and theaters—must keep those places safe for visitors. Store owners, for example, have a special duty to inspect their stores and be sure that they pose no danger to customers. They must look for and clean up slippery floors and broken glass; they must keep public areas well lit. When they can't fix a problem right away, they must warn visitors of the danger. (This is why we often see DANGER: SLIPPERY FLOOR or LOW CEILING signs in stores and buildings.)

People whose job it is to protect safety and provide aid to people in trouble also have a special duty to act. Lifeguards, paramedics, and fire fighters, for example, must attempt to save a person as part of their job.

Illustration 8-4   People whose job it is to provide safety, such as lifeguards, have a special duty to act and must try to save people as part of their job.

Laws passed by federal, state, and local governments often impose specific duties to act. For example, most states require car owners to take their cars for periodic safety inspections.

To discourage drunk driving, many states have passed **dram shop laws**. (*Dram shop* is an old English term for bar or saloon.) Under these laws, bartenders and bar owners have a duty to keep their customers from driving while intoxicated. If a bartender knowingly lets a drunk customer drive and the customer causes an accident, the bartender may be held liable.

Some laws don't impose a duty to act but do encourage people to help others. For example, many states have passed **Good Samaritan laws**. These laws protect doctors or nurses who volunteer to help others in an emergency.

(In some states, this protection is extended to other health care workers.) Suppose a doctor sees an auto accident and stops to help the injured victims. One of the victims later dies, in part because the hurried doctor didn't treat the injuries properly. Ordinarily the doctor could be held liable for the victim's death. Good Samaritan laws protect the doctor from liability in cases like this.

Other duties are imposed by customary practice. For example, it's customary for a doctor to take x-rays before putting a broken arm in a cast. If a doctor sets a broken arm without taking x-rays, he or she may be found negligent.

Defenses to Negligence Torts

You'll recall that a person accused of committing an intentional tort can offer a number of defenses in court. The same is true of a person accused of negligence. If the defendant can show that his or her actions were reasonable or necessary, that defendant may not be held liable.

The reasonable person standard, which we discussed earlier in this chapter, frequently serves as a defense. Defendants often try to show that any reasonable person would have done what the defendant did. If the jury is convinced, it will decide that the defendant was not negligent.

Another common defense is to show that both the plaintiff and the defendant were at fault. Suppose two drivers are involved in a collision. One driver sues the other for negligence. In court, the jury determines that both drivers had been speeding. Who is liable? The answer depends on state law, but some courts will say that the plaintiff's negligence relieves the defendant of all liability. In other words, one negligent person can't be compensated for the negligence of another. Courts in other states might split the cost, assigning half the liability to the plaintiff and half to the defendant. Other courts might split the liability proportionally, depending on who was more negligent.

REVIEW QUESTIONS

1. What is the difference between an intentional tort and a tort based on negligence?
2. What does the term *reasonable person* mean? When is it used?
3. What special duties might an architect have? A pharmacist? A lifeguard?
4. What are dram shop laws?

OTHER TYPES OF LIABILITY

People who commit intentional wrongs or acts of negligence are liable for damages. There are other situations in which individuals and businesses may be held liable. For instance, a person may be held accountable for damage caused by acts that are by their very nature dangerous. Companies are responsible for making or selling products that cause harm. Finally, individuals and the media may be held responsible for injuring the name and reputation of another person through lies.

Strict Liability

Some activities—such as using dynamite and storing flammable liquids—are considered to be extremely dangerous. For people who engage in activities like these, the reasonable person standard does not apply. Instead, these people are automatically held liable for any injuries or damage caused by their actions. They are liable even if they took all possible care to prevent the damage.

This form of liability is known as **strict liability**—liability for dangerous actions that involve no negligence or bad intent. It is sometimes called liability without fault.

Keeping dangerous animals is one common activity for which people may be held strictly liable. Under tort law, there are two categories of dangerous animals. The first is wild animals; the second is domestic animals that are known to be dangerous.

If you keep a wild animal, such as a lion or tiger, you are strictly liable. Even if you've trained the animal and take special care to keep it from injuring people, you must pay for any injuries the animal causes.

Domestic animals, such as dogs and cats, are usually not considered dangerous. However, if you know that your pet is dangerous—for example, if the animal has already bitten or injured someone—you are strictly liable for any further injury the animal causes. This rule is sometimes expressed as "every dog is allowed one bite." After your pet has bitten one person, you are liable for all future bites.

Other forms of strict liability have been imposed by state laws. For example, most states have child labor laws that try to discourage employers from hiring minors (people under a certain age, usually 18). Some of these laws make an employer strictly liable for injuries to a minor on the job—even if the employer did not cause the injury or didn't know the employee was a minor.

Dram shop laws, which we discussed earlier in this chapter, also impose strict liability. A bartender is strictly liable for auto accidents caused by drunk customers even though he or she may be nowhere near the accident.

Products Liability

Products liability is another area of tort law. It protects consumers from being injured by defects in the products they buy. Products liability uses a principle similar to strict liability: when manufacturers make a defective product—even if they don't know the product is defective—they are liable for any injuries caused by using the product.

Imagine that Jim borrows his mother's sewing scissors to cut pictures out of a magazine. While he is cutting, the scissors break in half and Jim is badly cut. Who is liable for Jim's injury?

The answer depends on why the scissors broke. They may have been designed wrong: perhaps the screw that holds the two pieces together was too short. There may have been an error in the manufacturing of the scissors: perhaps the metal in the blades was defective. In either event, the manufacturer of the scissors may be liable.

However, it is possible that the product wasn't defective at all. Suppose Jim's little brother, Joey, had been playing with the scissors and had loosened the screw that holds the blades together. In this case, Joey may be responsible for Jim's injury. Manufacturers cannot be held liable for a product that has been altered or misused by the consumer.

Of course, it's not always clear when a product has been misused. For example, sewing scissors are designed to cut cloth, but Jim used them to cut paper. Is Jim therefore responsible for his own injury?

Under products liability law, Jim is not responsible. The law requires that products be able to withstand any "reasonably expected" use—even if it's not the use that the product was made for. A chair, for example, should not fall apart if somebody stands on it rather than sits on it. A screwdriver should not break if it is used to pry open a can of paint.

In Jim's case, the manufacturer of the sewing scissors should expect that the scissors might be used to cut paper. The manufacturer must therefore design the scissors so they can do that job without falling apart. Other reasonably expected uses for scissors might be punching holes in cardboard or sharpening a crayon.

It is not reasonable, however, to expect someone to use sewing scissors for cutting sheet metal or opening cans. If Jim were injured by trying to use the scissors in one of these ways, the manufacturer would probably not be held liable.

In one unusual case, a woman tried to kill herself by locking herself in the trunk of her car. After some time, she changed her mind and tried to free herself from the trunk. The trunk, however, had no latch on the inside. As a result, she remained locked inside the trunk until someone discovered her and let her out. The woman later sued the car manufacturer, saying that the lack of an escape latch in the trunk was a dangerous defect. The court decided that the manufacturer was not liable, because locking oneself in the trunk is not a reasonably expected use for a car.

Even when a product is designed and made properly, a manufacturer may be required to warn consumers about the risks of using the product. For example, liquid drain opener (which is made from corrosive chemicals) must be labeled with a warning such as "Caution: Harmful if swallowed. May burn eyes or skin on contact." If a bottle of drain opener lacks this warning, it is considered to have a dangerous defect for which the manufacturer may be liable.

Similarly, a product that can injure a person if it is used incorrectly must be labeled with clear instructions for use. For example, electric clothes dryers often have labels that warn against placing rubber or dry-cleaned items in the dryer. If a dryer lacks this warning and if someone starts a fire by drying a pair of rubber-soled sneakers, the manufacturer may be liable.

It isn't necessary to warn consumers of very obvious dangers. A scissors manufacturer, for example, is not required to label its scissors with "Caution: if

Illustration 8-5 Manufacturers put warning labels on products to reduce their liability for a consumer's injury.

used incorrectly, this product may cut skin." Similarly, there is no need to print "Danger: Flammable" on a book of matches. A carton of milk doesn't need to say "Do not drink if allergic to dairy products." When in doubt, however, manufacturers tend to protect themselves by labeling.

Whenever they label or advertise products, manufacturers must be careful to avoid misrepresentation. **Misrepresentation** is saying something that is untrue or exaggerated. For example, a diet product may be labeled "This product will reduce your waist by 2 inches within six weeks." If you buy the product and it doesn't reduce your waist by 2 inches, the manufacturer has committed a tort. For this reason, you rarely see such promises. Instead, you typically see something like "When used as directed, this product may reduce your waistline by up to 2 inches."

Some products are extremely dangerous even when carefully manufactured and properly labeled. Guns are a good example; they are *intended* to be dangerous. In recent years, several injured individuals have tried to show that the manufacture of guns in itself is a tort. They believe that gun manufacturers should be held liable for every injury and death caused by guns. Similarly, a growing number of people believe that cigarette manufacturers should be held liable for every death caused by smoking. So far, the courts have disagreed.

Generally, whenever manufacturers are held liable for dangerous or mislabeled products, the sellers of those products are liable as well. For example, if you buy a new car that has a dangerous defect, you are entitled to sue both the manufacturer and the car dealer. Like manufacturers, sellers may be held liable even for defects they don't know about.

This rule, however, applies only to "regular sellers"—that is, people whose business is selling products. "Occasional sellers"—for example, a person who sells her own used car or sells something at a yard sale—are usually not held liable for a defect unless they knew of that defect when they made the sale.

Today consumers are given additional protection by consumer product safety acts; motor vehicle acts; food, drug, and cosmetics acts; and other federal and state legislation. In many cases, these laws give consumers rights that aren't covered by traditional tort law.

Defamation

John is the editor of his high school paper. Angry at Simon, a classmate, John prints a story that says that Simon cheated on the chemistry final. He publishes this story even though he knows it isn't true.

This is an example of defamation—a very different kind of tort. In Chapter 2, we discussed defamation as a form of speech that is not protected by the First Amendment to the Constitution. As you may recall, defamation means telling lies that hurt someone's interests or reputation. The lies may be spoken (slander) or written (libel).

For a statement to be considered defamation, someone else must hear or read the statement. If John writes in his diary that Simon cheated on the chemistry test, that is not defamation. It's also not defamation for John to accuse Simon personally of having cheated on the test (as long as no one else hears the conversation).

In addition, a statement is considered defamation only if it is clear who is being named in the statement. Suppose John had said in his newspaper that "a certain football player whose father teaches English in the school" had cheated on the chemistry final. If Simon is the only person who fits that description, John's statement would be libel.

In contrast, suppose John had written that "some seniors" had cheated on the final. This description would not be enough to identify Simon, and it probably would not be considered libel.

Defamation can come in the form of words, actions, or even pictures. A cartoon of Simon reading answers from his shirtsleeve during the exam, for example, could also be considered defamatory.

The best defense against a claim of defamation is truth. If what you say or write about someone is true, it cannot be called defamation.

Another defense is called **privilege**, or protection from legal liability. There are times (for example, when you are testifying in court) when it's important to be able to speak freely. At these times, what you say is privileged. That is, you're given absolute freedom to talk, and you can't be sued for defamation.

Statements made in the interest of others are also privileged as long as they are made without malice. (**Malice** is the willful intent to hurt someone.) For example, suppose you believe that a student has been selling drugs in school and you tell the school principal. Later, it turns out that your belief was untrue. Your statement to the principal is not slander, because you were speaking honestly in the interest of protecting the school. However, suppose you had talked to the principal because you wanted to get a particular student in trouble. In that case, your statement might be slander, because it was made with malice.

Another type of privilege is granted by the First Amendment. As you'll recall, the First Amendment protects freedom of speech and freedom of the press. The Supreme Court has interpreted these freedoms to include the right of fair comment.

Fair comment permits the media to make a broad range of statements about public officials, public figures (such as celebrities), and people involved in public activities. As long as these statements are made without malice, they cannot be considered defamation—even if they turn out to be untrue.

Fair comment protects statements of opinion as well as statements of fact. As a result, critics are free to be honest in their reviews of movies, shows, and books; and political commentators are free to state their opinions about public affairs.

REVIEW QUESTIONS

1. Define *strict liability*.
2. Who might be liable if a new ladder broke the first time it was used?
3. Describe a use for a skateboard (other than the use it was made for) that a manufacturer should reasonably expect.
4. Name two circumstances under which a defamatory statement might be privileged.

Illustration 8-6   Fair comment, a privilege granted by the First Amendment, protects statements of fact and of opinion that the media make about public figures as long as malice is not intended.

OTHER ISSUES IN TORTS

As you read at the beginning of this chapter, tort law was developed as a way to keep people from taking the law into their own hands. It brought people into the courts to settle matters fairly, with the help of a judge. Today we use courts less and less to settle disputes. Torts cases, in particular, tend to be settled long before they reach the courtroom.

The primary reason is cost. Lawsuits are expensive for both the plaintiff and the defendant. It's usually cheaper and faster to settle the matter privately. If both parties can agree on who is at fault, they can usually agree on how much money the injured party should receive. If both parties have liability insurance, the matter may be settled entirely by the insurance companies.

Whether a torts case is settled privately or in court, both parties should be familiar with tort law. They should know what kind of remedies they can expect, and they should understand the role of insurance in torts.

Remedies

As you'll recall from Chapter 7, one difference between crimes and torts is the remedy for the wrongful act. A person who is guilty of a crime has committed a wrong against the community. It is the government—not the victim of the crime—that brings an action against the wrongdoer. The remedy for a crime is usually some form of punishment, such as a fine or a prison sentence.

In contrast, a tort is a wrong against an individual or a group of individuals. The court action is brought by the injured person or group. A person found liable for a tort will not be imprisoned, but he or she is required to compensate the injured party. This compensation most often takes the form of money, or damages.

Sometimes money will not make up for a tort that someone committed. In those cases, plaintiffs may ask for other remedies, such as restitution (the return of personal property) or an injunction (a court order requiring a person to stop doing something). You read about these remedies in Chapter 7.

Insurance

Being held liable for a tort can be very expensive. For example, suppose a soda-bottling company puts too much gas into a bottle of soda. Lucy buys the bottle. When she opens it, the bottle explodes, spraying glass all over Lucy and her kitchen. The bottling company will be liable to Lucy for all her physical injuries, plus all damages to her home. If she is seriously hurt, the company may be liable for the days of work she misses. If she is permanently injured (for instance, if the flying glass blinds her), the company's liability will be much greater. In addition, the court may require the bottling company to pay for Lucy's pain and suffering and to reimburse her for the costs of the lawsuit.

Having to pay these large amounts of money would put many companies out of business. For this reason, most manufacturers purchase liability insurance. **Liability insurance** is a contract with an insurance company. Under this contract, the insurance company agrees to pay the damages for which the insured party is held liable. If the soda-bottling company has liability insurance, the insurance company—not the bottling company—will pay damages to Lucy.

People who buy insurance pay for a specific amount of coverage. The insurance company will pay an injured person up to the limits of the policy. If the damages exceed the policy limits, the policyholder must pay the additional amount.

In some states, businesses that have a good chance of being sued (such as soda-bottling companies and construction companies) are required to have liability insurance. In this way, innocent victims like Lucy are sure to be compensated for all their injuries.

State laws sometimes require that individuals buy insurance as well. For example, in most states, licensed drivers must be covered by liability insurance. Doctors also carry liability insurance. Liability insurance can be expensive, but it is much less expensive than having to pay damages to the victim of a tort.

REVIEW QUESTIONS

1. What is the main type of compensation given to a victim of a tort?
2. Give an example of a tort for which a plaintiff would sue for damages.
3. If a defendant has liability insurance, who pays the damages?
4. Name three types of liability insurance.

Latest in the Law: Parental Liability Laws

In May 1976, three boys broke into Piscataway High School in New Jersey, damaging the building and the equipment inside it. The Piscataway Township board of education sued the parents of the boys for damages. The board cited a New Jersey law that imposed liability on the parents of pupils who damage school property. The parents went to court to have the law declared unconstitutional. They claimed that the law violated due process because there was no logical relationship between holding parents liable and deterring delinquent behavior. The New Jersey Supreme Court disagreed. It held the parents liable for the torts of their sons.

Different States, Different Laws

Forty-nine states have parental liability laws that allow parents to be sued under certain circumstances when their children cause bodily injury or damage to property. No single rule defines parental liability for torts in all states. New Hampshire has no law defining the responsibility of parents for their children's torts. By contrast, both Hawaii and Louisiana impose strict parental liability. (Strict liability means that the parents are responsible even though they didn't know about or approve of their children's actions.) Each of the other states defines parental liability in a slightly different way. In most cases, however, parents cannot be held liable for their children's torts simply because of the family relationship. Certain factors must be present. For example, parents may be liable if they direct a child to take the action, cause the child to act as their agent, or provide an instrument (such as

a gun) to a child knowing that it is likely to be used in a dangerous way.

Parents may also be held liable if—as in the New Jersey case—the child is found to have caused destruction maliciously or willfully. Such liability laws serve two purposes. They discourage destructive behavior, and they allow the victims of malicious acts to be compensated for their injuries or for other damages.

In most states that have parental liability laws, the amount of damages that parents have to pay is limited. The limits range from $250 per child in Vermont to $15,000 plus court costs and attorneys' fees in Texas. Only Hawaii and Louisiana set no limits on the amount of damages a plaintiff can collect.

Liability Laws and Public Policy

Why should parents be held liable for their children's torts at all? When a child does damage under direction from a parent, the reasons are clear. However, many people believe that parental liability is closely connected to parental responsibility. Since children can't be expected to show the same degree of judgment and maturity as adults, most states expect parents to guide and control their children and to be responsible for the children's actions. In the New Jersey case, the judge cited two concerns—deterring destructive behavior and encouraging parents to guide and control their children—as reasonable bases for the New Jersey statute. Parental liability laws and the court decisions that support them, then, provide incentives for parents to exercise responsibility for the actions of their children.

Chapter Review

Chapter Summary

- Torts are unreasonable acts that cause injury to people or their property. People who fail to act with reasonable care may be liable for damages.

- Under tort law, a type of civil law, we have a general duty to exercise reasonable care for the safety of other people and their property. We also have the right to live our lives without being injured by others, and we have the right to be compensated if we are injured.

- A person has committed an intentional tort if he or she commits an act, means to commit that act, injures another person through that act, and has no valid defense for having committed the act.

- Intentional torts against individuals include battery, assault, false imprisonment, intentional infliction of emotional distress, and invasion of privacy. Intentional torts against property include trespassing and taking, keeping, or destroying something that belongs to someone else.

- Consent is a defense to an intentional tort. Consent is a valid defense only if it is given freely and if the person understands what he or she is agreeing to.

- Consent often is implied by a person's actions. Implied consent is also assumed to be given in certain situations (such as medical emergencies) in which a person is unable to consent by speaking or acting.

- Other defenses to intentional torts include self-defense, defense of property, defense of others, necessity, line of duty, and parental discipline. Error is not a defense.

- The law of negligence requires everyone to act with reasonable standards of care for the safety of others. To be negligent, a person must have a duty, breach the duty, and cause the harm that results in damage being suffered by another person.

- Children are expected to behave like reasonable children of similar age, maturity, and experience. People with special knowledge, such as doctors and pilots, are expected to behave like reasonable people with that special knowledge.

- The law does not generally impose a duty to act. There are many exceptions to that general rule. Bartenders and shop owners, for example, have special duties that require them to act. If they breach those duties, they may be liable for injuries that result from their failure to act.

- When both the plaintiff and the defendant are negligent, the defendant may be relieved of some or all liability.

■ Strict liability is imposed for extremely dangerous activities, such as keeping wild or dangerous animals at home.

■ Manufacturers and sellers of products are required to make sure that their products are safe. They may be liable for any injury caused by defects in design, manufacturing, or labeling. They may be liable for any misrepresentation on which a consumer relied. They are also liable for injuries resulting from "reasonably expected" misuse of their products.

■ Lying about someone is a tort if the lie hurts that person's reputation or interests.

■ Truth is a defense to the tort of defamation. Other defenses are privilege—statements made in the public interest or in the interest of others—and fair comment, which allows the media to make unmalicious statements about public figures.

■ An injured plaintiff can sue a defendant for damages, for restitution, or for an injunction.

■ Many individuals and companies purchase liability insurance. The insurance company then pays, up to the limits of the policy, damages for which the insured party is liable.

Understanding Legal Terms

On a separate sheet of paper, match the terms below with the definitions that follow.

breach	malice
Good Samaritan law	negligence
implied consent	privilege
informed consent	strict liability
intentional tort	wrongful act

1. Violation of the duty to act reasonably in order to ensure the safety of people and property
2. A wrong done to another person on purpose
3. Consent based on information
4. Consent that is assumed because of the situation
5. Failure to act with reasonable standards of care
6. To fail to perform a duty
7. Law that protects doctors and nurses who volunteer to help others in an emergency
8. Legal responsibility for dangerous actions that involve no negligence or bad intent
9. Protection from legal liability
10. The willful intent to hurt someone

Applying the Law

1. Charlie Luka is run over by a train. His foot is crushed. By the time he reaches the hospital, he is unconscious and bleeding to death. The doctor

in charge, Dr. Lowrie, determines that the only way to save Charlie's life is to amputate his leg. Later, Charlie sues Dr. Lowrie for battery, claiming that the doctor amputated his leg without his consent. Does Dr. Lowrie have a defense? If so, what is it?

2. Anita is camping. She builds a campfire and cooks dinner. After dinner, she goes to sleep, leaving the campfire lit. During the night, the fire ignites some trees and spreads to a nearby house. The owner of the property and the owner of the house sue Anita for negligence. What technique will the jury use to decide whether Anita breached her duty?

3. The city of Springfield operates a public swimming pool during the summer. One day Martin swims into the deep end of the pool and can't swim back. He calls out for help. There are only two other people present. One is Brad, a championship swimmer, who is preparing for an upcoming meet. The other is Laura, the pool's lifeguard. Neither Brad nor Laura helps Martin. Can either Brad or Laura be held liable? If so, for what?

4. In order to reach the cookie jar, 6-year-old Mary climbs up on the kitchen table. The table collapses beneath her. Mary falls, breaking her leg. How will a jury decide whether the manufacturer of the table is liable for Mary's injury?

5. Carol is planning to marry Peter. Jason, who has known Peter a long time, tells Carol that Peter is a compulsive gambler who is in constant trouble with the police. He warns Carol that she will ruin her life if she marries Peter. What tort may Jason have committed? What defenses might Jason have?

6. While shopping at Eddie's grocery store, Gary slips on a wet floor and breaks his arm. Eddie has liability insurance in the amount of $5 million. If Gary sues Eddie for $500,000 and the court finds that Eddie is liable for Gary's broken arm, what amount will Eddie pay in damages?

Case Studies

1. At an annual family picnic, a number of guests start a softball game. Leland gets a hit, crosses first base, and tries to slide into second. Al is standing on second base. Leland slides directly into Al, knocking him over and breaking his arm. For what tort could Al sue Leland? Would Leland have any defense? If so, what would it be?

2. Cicero Fredericks owns a resort in Pennsylvania. He has a dog named Sport. Sport isn't a friendly dog. When guests try to pet him, he usually snarls at them and then backs away. He's never bitten anyone. Vincent Zarek comes to stay at the resort. He see Sport and pets him. Instead of backing away, Sport bites Vincent. Is Cicero liable for the bite? Explain your answer.

3. Sam Baxter buys a new Ford car. One of the advertised features of the car is that the windshield is made of shatterproof glass. The owner's manual says that the glass in the windshield will not break, fly, or shatter if hit. Despite this, the first time the windshield is hit by a loose pebble, it cracks and a small sliver of glass flies into Sam's eye. Sam loses vision in that eye. Will the Ford Motor Company be held liable for Sam's injury? Why or why not?

Chapter 9

Contracts

Chapter Objectives

When you have read this chapter, you should be able to:

- Explain what a contract is and how it differs from a promise.

- Explain the importance of an offer and an acceptance in making a contract.

- Explain the role of consideration in making a contract.

- Name three types of contracts that a court may reform or rescind.

- Describe the rights of minors who make contracts.

- Define *breach*, and explain what remedies a court may order if one party breaches a contract.

Frostifresh Corporation v. Reynoso, 274 N.Y.S.2d 757 (New York 1966).

Luis and Teresita Reynoso needed to buy a refrigerator. The couple, who lived in New York, spoke and read only Spanish. They went to an appliance store and discussed refrigerators with a Spanish-speaking salesman. They told him that since Luis was about to lose his job, they couldn't afford any of the refrigerators in the store.

The salesman told the Reynosos that he would give them a refrigerator for nothing. All they had to do in exchange was persuade their friends and neighbors to shop at his appliance store. Every time one of their friends made a purchase, the Reynosos would earn $25 toward the cost of their own refrigerator. The Reynosos accepted the salesman's offer.

The salesman then asked the Reynosos to sign a written contract. Because the document was entirely in English, the Reynosos couldn't read it. The salesman assured them that it was simply a summary of the agreement they had just made. In reality, it was a sales contract. The contract required the Reynosos to pay $900—plus a $245.88 credit charge—for the refrigerator that was supposed to cost them nothing.

Soon afterward, the Reynosos began receiving bills for the refrigerator. Because they had been told that the refrigerator was free, the Reynosos ignored the bills. Eventually the appliance store took them to court.

At the trial, a lawyer for the store argued that the contract the Reynosos had signed was valid and binding. The court agreed that the document seemed legal but that simply looking at the piece of paper was not enough. To rule on this case, the court had to consider how and why the agreement had been made.

After hearing the evidence, the court decided that the Reynosos had been treated unfairly. The salesman had tricked them into signing a contract they didn't understand. The contract was therefore unfair, and the court refused to enforce it. Instead, the court allowed the Reynosos to keep the refrigerator and to pay what the store had paid for it—only $348.

MAKING A CONTRACT

A **contract** is an agreement that can be enforced by a court. The agreement may be between two or more parties. (For the sake of simplicity, this chapter will deal only with two-party contracts.) When you make a contract with someone, you take on a legal responsibility. If you fail to carry out that responsibility—that is, if you don't do what you've agreed to do—you can be held liable.

The Wheatman Corporation

August 28, 1991

Mr. Russell Kennedy
K & R Cleaning Services
P.O. Box 3201
Princeton Jct., NJ 08550

Dear Mr. Kennedy:

This will serve as renewal of our contract for the cleaning of our offices at Bldg. 4, Franklin Park.

You will provide cleaning services three times per week as follows:

1. Empty ashtrays and trash cans, vacuum all floors, and clean both bathrooms.
2. Dust desks, tables, cabinets, and shelves.
3. As needed, wipe spills on walls and furniture.

You will provide all cleaning materials and equipment needed for the performance of these duties. You will also provide us with evidence that you have secured the necessary insurance.

Your fee for these services will be $735.00 per month. The terms of this agreement are effective from September 1, 1991 through December 31, 1992 or until notified in writing by The Wheatman Corporation.

Please return one signed copy of this letter to me to indicate your acceptance of this agreement.

Sincerely,

Patricia R. Blackwell

Patricia R. Blackwell
Controller

Accepted By:

Russell Kennedy   *8/28/91*

Russell Kennedy   Date

14 WASHINGTON ROAD • BOX 2321 • PRINCETON, NEW JERSEY 08543 • 609-799-9200

Illustration 9-1   A contract is an agreement that can be enforced in court. Many contracts are written down as a record of the agreement.

You will make contracts throughout your life. When you take a job, you'll make a contract with your employer to do certain work in exchange for a certain amount of money. When you buy or rent a place to live, you'll make a contract with the seller or landlord. If you buy insurance or take out a loan, you'll make a contract with the insurance company or bank. If you get married, you may make a marriage contract with your spouse.

This chapter will concentrate on the general rules that apply to all contracts. Keep in mind, however, that the federal and state governments have passed many laws that apply only to certain types of contracts. (For example, all the contracts mentioned in the preceding paragraph—employment contracts, rental and sales contracts, loan and insurance contracts, and marriage contracts—must follow special rules.) We'll discuss some of these special types of contracts and the rules that apply to them in Units 4 and 5 of this book.

Agreement

To be enforceable by a court, a contract must be *mutual*—that is, it must be agreed to by both parties. Both parties must take some action to show that they agree to the contract. That action may be as simple as signing a document or saying okay.

A contract must also be *voluntary*—that is, both parties must agree to it of their own free will, with full knowledge of what they are doing. A court will not allow anyone to be forced or tricked into making a contract.

For example, the J.C. Durick Insurance Company sent Peter Andrus a contract for fire insurance. The contract said that if Andrus *didn't* want the insurance policy, he would have to notify the company. Otherwise, the company would assume that Andrus had agreed to buy the insurance. When Andrus received the contract, he ignored it. The company interpreted Andrus's silence as acceptance and began sending him bills.

After a few bills went unpaid, the company took Andrus to court. The company said that Andrus had broken the contract by not paying for his fire insurance. The court held that Andrus owed nothing because there was no contract to break. Andrus had not voluntarily agreed to buy insurance.

In deciding whether a contract is mutual and voluntary, a court looks at more than just the words of the contract. It looks at how the contract was made. With the help of witness testimony and written evidence, the court tries to reconstruct the steps that led to the contract.

According to contracts law, the process of making a contract must include two steps: an *offer* and an *acceptance*. When one party makes an offer and the other party accepts that offer, the result is a legal contract. (There may, of course, be many steps between the offer and the acceptance. We'll discuss those additional steps later in this chapter.)

An offer without an acceptance is not a contract. In the case of Peter Andrus, for example, Andrus didn't accept the company's offer to sell him insurance. Therefore, he was not required to pay the bills the company sent him.

Offers   An **offer** is a legally binding proposal. If you were interested in buying a friend's car, you might say, "I'll pay you $500 for your car." An employer who wants to hire you might say, "I'll pay you $5 an hour to work in my store."

There are no magic words that turn an ordinary statement into an offer. The difference between a casual comment and a serious offer depends largely on the intention of the person who is speaking. If a person intends a statement to be legally binding and if that intention is clear to the listener, a court will usually consider the statement to be an offer.

A statement that is clearly a joke or a wish cannot be considered an offer. For example, suppose your friend Eduardo wins two tickets to the Super Bowl in a raffle. When you congratulate Eduardo on his win, you say, "You're so lucky! I'd pay a million dollars for tickets to the Super Bowl." Eduardo says, "Okay, it's a deal," and hands you the tickets.

Because Eduardo accepted your "offer," are you now legally bound to pay him a million dollars? No, because your statement was clearly just a wish—and Eduardo knew it. Eduardo can't create a contract by accepting an offer you didn't intend to make.

Similarly, an off-the-cuff "ballpark estimate" is not an offer. Suppose you take your car to a mechanic because it isn't running properly. The mechanic listens to your description of the problem and says, "I won't know for sure until I look at the engine, but I think the repair will cost about $500." The mechanic makes this statement as a courtesy, to let you know what to expect. It is not an offer to fix your car for $500.

To be considered an offer, a statement must be clear and definite. It must include all the information that the other party needs in deciding whether to accept. For example, "I'll buy your bicycle" is not an offer. It includes no mention of the price or even of which bicycle the buyer wants. In contrast, "I'll give you $100 for that red ten-speed" would be a legally binding offer.

Acceptances   When one party makes an offer, the other party can create a legal contract by accepting the offer. The contract exists from the moment of **acceptance**. It doesn't have to be written down, signed, or witnessed by anyone other than the two parties.

As with offers, there is no magic formula to indicate acceptance. In most cases, people accept offers orally by saying "I accept," "Okay," or even "What time is good for you?" In other cases, people accept offers in writing, often by signing a printed contract.

It's often possible to accept an offer by actions rather than words. For example, Barry puts an ad in the newspaper that says "$25 reward for finding my lost dog." Sharon finds the dog and brings it to Barry's house. By doing so, Sharon has accepted Barry's offer. He now owes her $25.

In some cases, it's possible to accept an offer by silence. For example, Jane offers Neil $10 to drive her to the train station that night. Neil says, "Let me look at my schedule. If you don't hear from me within the hour, assume I'll do it." If Neil doesn't call Jane within the hour, his silence becomes an acceptance of her offer.

(Note, however, that only Neil can decide to accept by silence. As you saw in the case of Peter Andrus and the insurance company, the principle doesn't work in reverse. Jane can't tell Neil, "I'll give you $10 to drive me to the train station tonight. If I don't hear from you in an hour, I'll assume you've accepted.")

Although the person who makes an offer can't decide that silence will be an acceptance, he or she *can* decide what other forms an acceptance may take. A college can require, for example, that any student who is offered a scholarship accept it in writing.

The person who makes an offer can also limit the offer to a specific person. Suppose, for example, you offer to sell your radio to Gina for $50. Esther, who is listening nearby, accepts your offer. Esther's acceptance doesn't create a contract, since your offer was made only to Gina.

Anyone who makes an offer is free to **revoke** it—that is, to take the offer back—at any time. You can't make a legal contract by accepting an offer that's been revoked. Even if you accept an offer before it's revoked, your acceptance may come too late. To create a contract, you must accept the offer within a reasonable amount of time. (How much time is reasonable depends on the circumstances.)

For example, an official at the Dexter Savings Bank in Maine was murdered. The bank offered a reward for information leading to the capture of the murderer. Twelve years after the offer was made, John Mitchell came to the bank with information and tried to collect the reward. The bank refused to pay him.

Mitchell sued the bank. He claimed that the bank had not revoked its offer and that it therefore owed him the reward money. The court disagreed, saying that it wasn't reasonable to expect the bank's offer to last 12 years.

Counteroffers

As we noted earlier, many contracts don't result from a simple offer and acceptance. There are often other steps in between. Suppose, for example, your neighbor offers you $5 to shovel his driveway after a snowstorm. You don't want to accept his offer because you don't think $5 is enough money. Instead, you say you'll do the job for $20. This is called a **counteroffer**—a proposal that is different from the original offer.

Your neighbor may accept your counteroffer, or he may make a counteroffer of his own. He may, for example, offer you $10. These negotiations can continue as long as necessary, until one of you accepts the counteroffer made by the other.

Once you've made a counteroffer, you can't change your mind and decide to accept the original offer. Suppose your neighbor gets tired of negotiating with you. He says, "I don't like greedy people. I'll give you $2 to shovel the driveway. Take it or leave it." You can't say, "Let's make believe these negotiations never happened. I'll accept your original offer of $5." Legally, that original offer no longer exists. Your only options are to accept the latest offer of $2 or decide not to take the job.

In a real-life example, William and Katherine Horan wanted to sell their house in Newport, Rhode Island. They offered the house to Ernst Ardente for

$250,000. Ardente said that he would accept as long as the price included the furniture in the dining room and on the porch. The Horans refused to include the furniture and then refused to sell the house to Ardente at all.

Ardente took the Horans to court. He asked for specific performance of their original offer—the house alone for $250,000. The court held that Ardente had made a counteroffer. In doing so, he had eliminated the original offer. The Horans could repeat their offer if they wished, but they were not legally required to do so.

Written Contracts

When nonlawyers use the word *contract*, they usually mean a written document that is signed by both parties. (For the sake of simplicity, we sometimes use *contract* in that way in this book.) To a lawyer, however, a contract is never a piece of paper. It is an agreement between two parties, created as soon as one party accepts an offer made by the other. Contracts are often written down so that both parties (and a court, if necessary) will have a record of what was agreed to. The real contract, however, continues to exist even if the piece of paper is lost or torn up.

A contract does not have to be written down to be enforceable by a court. If the court has no written document to look at, it will rely on other evidence (such as letters, receipts, the testimony of the people who made the contract, and the testimony of witnesses) to find out what has been agreed to. It is easier for everyone, however, if the contract has been written down and signed by both parties. This is especially true for complicated contracts and for contracts involving large amounts of money.

Most states have passed laws requiring certain types of contracts to be in writing. The kinds of contracts covered by these laws include real estate purchases, long-term rentals, and contracts that will take over a year to complete. If these contracts are not written down and signed, no court will be able to enforce them.

REVIEW QUESTIONS

1. What is a contract?
2. Make two statements that a court would interpret as offers.
3. Describe two situations in which an acceptance of an offer would not create a contract.
4. What is a counteroffer?

CONTRACTS AND PROMISES

An offer and an acceptance do not in themselves make a contract. You must also agree to exchange something of value.

In some cases, however, contracts are made even when there is no clear-cut offer and acceptance. Sometimes a promise will be considered a contract. At other times, a contract will be implied by the circumstances.

Consideration

Charley Dougherty and his aunt, Helena Dougherty, were very close. As a reward for his loyalty over the years, Aunt Helena gave Charley a note promising him $3,000 after her death. When Aunt Helena died, Charley took the note to Emma Salt. Salt was Helena's **executor**—the person responsible for settling her finances after her death. Charley asked Salt for the money his aunt had promised him. Salt refused to give him the money. She said that promises, unlike contracts, are not enforceable. Charley took Salt to court. The court agreed with Salt, holding that Charley was not entitled to any money.

At around the same time, another young man, Willie Story, had a talk with his uncle, Bill Story. Willie was 15 years old. His uncle made a deal with him: If Willie would not drink, use tobacco, swear, or gamble until he was 21, Uncle Bill would give him $5,000. After Willie turned 21 but before he had a chance to collect the money, Uncle Bill died. Willie asked his uncle's executors to pay him the money. The executors refused.

Like Charley Dougherty, Willie Story went to court. The court, however, treated this case very differently from Charley's case. Charley had not been awarded any money because his aunt had merely made him a promise. In Willie's case, however, there was more than a promise—there was an agreement. Willie had agreed to give up legal rights in exchange for a sum of money. The court held that Willie's agreement with his uncle was a legal contract. As a result, the executors had to pay Willie the money he was owed.

As you can see, there is an important difference between a promise and a contract. A promise is a statement by one party that he or she will do something. A contract is a agreement between two or more parties in which each party agrees to exchange something of value for something else of value. The legal term for "something of value" is **consideration**.

In most contracts, consideration takes the form of money, property, or a service. When you hire a painter to paint your house, for example, you and the painter offer consideration to each other. You offer money, and in exchange the painter offers a service.

While consideration must be something of value, it doesn't have to be of much value. In fact, consideration can be something that is of value to only one party. Sally, for instance, attended a rock concert. She wants to put a ticket stub from the concert into her scrapbook, but she lost her stub. She offers Ron $3 for his ticket stub. The stub is worthless to Ron, but it has value to Sally. Therefore, Ron's acceptance of Sally's offer would make a legal contract.

If a service is offered as consideration, that service must be legal. For example, no court will enforce a contract that requires either party to kill someone, print counterfeit money, or sell illegal drugs.

Consideration doesn't always take the form of money, property, or services. In Willie Story's contract with his uncle, for example, Willie's consideration was the giving up of his legal rights to smoke, drink, swear, and gamble. Any time you agree *not* to do something that you have a right to do, you are offering consideration. Similarly, any time you agree to do something you don't already have to do, you are offering consideration. For example, if a friend paid you money in exchange for your keeping a secret, that contract could be

Illustration 9-2   A homeowner and a roofer can have a legal contract when the roofer agrees to repair the roof in exchange for payment by the homeowner.

enforced in court. However, if a passenger in your car paid you to obey the speed limits, that contract would not be enforceable. (You already have a legal duty to obey speed limits.)

A similar rule applies to services. If you offer a service as consideration, it must be a service that you were not already required to perform. For example, Theresa Martino's jewelry was stolen in Atlantic City, New Jersey. Martino offered a reward to anyone who could find the jewelry and return it to her. A police officer assigned to her case found the jewelry and tried to collect the reward. Martino refused to pay, because looking for the jewels was the policeman's job. He would have found them even if she hadn't offered the reward. A court ruled in Martino's favor.

Detrimental Reliance

When John Devecmon was a young man, his uncle, John Combs, suggested that he take some time off to see Europe. Combs offered to cover the cost of the trip. He told his nephew to keep track of his expenses in Europe and promised to reimburse him (to pay back what he had spent) when the trip was over.

Devecmon went to Europe. When he returned, he told his uncle how much the trip had cost and asked to be reimbursed. Combs died before paying his nephew, and Combs's executors refused to pay for the trip. They said that Combs's agreement with Devecmon had been a promise, not a contract, because Devecmon had offered no consideration in return. Combs therefore was not legally required to pay anything.

Devecmon brought the case to court. The court agreed that Combs had made only a promise and not a legally binding contract. Devecmon, however, had relied on his uncle's promise and had spent a substantial amount of money because of it. (Devecmon clearly would not have gone to Europe and would not have spent his own money if his uncle had not agreed to repay him.) For this reason, the court ruled that Combs's promise was enforceable. The court ordered Combs's executors to pay Devecmon the money he was owed.

This example demonstrates an exception to the rule that promises can't be enforced. If someone makes a promise to you and you spend or lose money because you are relying on that promise, the promise may become enforceable. (Your behavior in this situation is called **detrimental reliance**, because your *reliance* on the promise has caused you to suffer a *detriment*—a loss.) In a case such as this, the person who made the promise may be required to compensate you for your loss.

Implied Contracts

Sometimes a court will decide that a contract exists between two parties even if those parties haven't agreed to make a contract. This kind of contract—which is "understood" but not stated explicitly—is called an **implied contract**.

One day Sosa Crisan collapsed while shopping in a grocery store in Detroit. She was rushed by ambulance to the city hospital. After remaining in a coma for nearly a year, Crisan died. The city hospital sent a bill to Crisan's executor for the cost of the ambulance and medical care. Crisan's executor refused to pay. He said that there was no contract because Crisan had been unconscious the entire time and couldn't have agreed to anything.

The hospital took Crisan's executor to court. The court said that in cases of medical emergency, there is an implied contract between the patient and the health care provider. Under this implied contract, Crisan's executor was required to pay the hospital bill.

Even when two parties have agreed on a contract, there may be additional contracts—implied contracts—between the parties. Suppose, for example, you agree to vacuum a neighbor's four-room apartment for $10. After you have cleaned two rooms, your vacuum cleaner breaks down. You tell your neighbor that she owes you $5 because you were able to finish only half the job. Your neighbor replies that the contract required you to vacuum four rooms. Since you haven't done the job you agreed to do, she refuses to pay you anything. Who is right?

In this case, a court would probably decide that you are right. When you offer your services to an employer, there is an implied contract that entitles you to be paid. Even though you failed to carry out the agreed-upon contract, your neighbor must still pay you for the work you did under the implied contract.

REVIEW QUESTIONS

1. What is the difference between a contract and a promise?
2. Name three types of consideration.
3. Define *detrimental reliance*, and explain how it affects a promise.
4. Describe two situations in which an implied contract exists.

REFORMING AND RESCINDING CONTRACTS

Not every contract is a good contract. For example, some contracts have mistakes in them. Others may be unfair to one party.

Courts are not generally willing to enforce contracts that contain serious problems. In some cases, a court may have to reform (change) a contract before the contract can be enforced. In other cases, the court may decide to rescind (cancel) the contract.

Keep in mind that a contract does not have to go to court to be modified. The parties who have made a contract are free to change it in any way they want as long as they both agree on the changes. If they find a mistake, they can correct it. If the contract seems to be unfair, they can change a few words or cancel the entire contract. If they have an idea for a better agreement, they can throw out the existing contract and make a new one.

Often, however, only one of the two parties wants to make a change. One party may feel that the contract is unfair, while the other feels that it is perfectly fine. In that case, going to court may be the only way to resolve the problem.

Illustration 9-3   The parties who have made a contract are free to change it in any way as long as they both agree on the changes.

Unfair Contracts

If a contract is unfair to one or both parties, a court will not enforce it. This is true even when both parties have willingly agreed to the contract.

Why would anyone agree to an unfair contract? The case study that opened this chapter gave you one answer: people don't always understand what they're agreeing to. Unfortunately, people are often tricked, forced, or blackmailed into making contracts. One party may lie or withhold important facts in order to get the other party to agree to a contract. In some cases, one party may not even know that he or she is making a contract.

For example, Otto Schupp had a large tree in his front yard. A worker from the Davey Tree Expert Company, who was driving by Schupp's house, noticed that the tree was diseased. He stopped and talked to Schupp. He offered to do some minor tree surgery, which he said would cost very little. Without discussing the worker's fee, Schupp agreed to let him work on the tree.

Hours later, Schupp found that the work was taking much longer than he had been led to believe it would. He ordered the worker to stop at once. The worker said that his company had very strict rules about finishing jobs once they had been started. He would not be able to stop in the middle of the job unless Schupp signed a form ordering him to leave. Schupp signed the form.

Schupp found out later that the form he had signed was actually a contract. It required him to pay for 220 hours of tree surgery at a cost amounting to hundreds of dollars. Schupp refused to pay, saying that he had been tricked into signing the contract. The Davey Tree Expert Company took him to court, claiming that Schupp had signed voluntarily and that the contract was therefore legal.

The court told Schupp that he should not have signed the document without reading it first. The court also said, however, that Schupp's carelessness wasn't an issue here. The contract, as it stood, was unfair because it charged Schupp for much more time than the job had actually taken. The court ordered that the contract be changed to reflect the actual amount of time the worker had spent on the tree. As a result, Schupp was required to pay only $100.

Occasionally a court will decide that a contract is **unconscionable**—so unfair that it offends public standards. For example, a contract that required an employee to work 100 hours a week would be unconscionable. The same would be true of a contract that required a borrower to pay 200 percent interest on a loan. A court will not enforce an unconscionable contract even if both parties understand the contract and have agreed to it voluntarily.

In 1955 Claus Henningsen bought a new Chrysler car from Bloomfield Motors in New Jersey. At the time he paid for the car, he read and signed a standard Chrysler sales contract. Ten days later, when Henningsen's wife was driving the car, she heard something in the steering column crack. The car swerved out of control and crashed into a brick wall. Mrs. Henningsen was injured and hospitalized.

The Henningsens went to court and demanded compensation from Chrysler Corporation. They said that the car was defective and that Chrysler was liable for Mrs. Henningsen's injuries and the damage to the car. Chrysler's lawyer admitted that a flaw in the steering column had caused the accident. He pointed out, however, that the sales contract Mr. Henningsen had signed clearly limited Chrysler's liability. According to the contract, Chrysler was required to replace any parts of the car that proved to be defective. Chrysler was not, however, required to pay for injuries or damage resulting from the defective parts.

Illustration 9-4   Courts will not enforce unconscionable contracts—for example, a contract that would require an employee to work 100 hours a week.

The court ruled that the Chrysler contract was unconscionable. In our society, the court said, manufacturers are expected to take responsibility for injuries and damage caused by their products. Therefore, even though Mr. Henningsen had freely signed the contract, the court would not enforce it. The court ordered that the paragraphs limiting Chrysler's liability be removed from the contract. It also ordered Chrysler to pay for all medical expenses and damage caused by the defective steering column.

The contract Claus Henningsen had signed is called a contract of adhesion. A **contract of adhesion** is a contract in which one party makes all the rules and the other party is given the choice to accept or not to accept. (Many sales contracts are of this type. In the case study that opened this chapter, for example, the Reynosos were asked to sign a contract of adhesion when they bought a refrigerator.) Because contracts of adhesion don't allow a buyer and seller to negotiate equally, they tend to be unfair to the buyer. You'll find out more about contracts of adhesion and your rights as a consumer in Chapter 15.

Illustration 9-5   Many sales contracts are contracts of adhesion, in which one party makes all the rules and the other party chooses to take it or not to take it.

Mistakes in Contracts

People often make mistakes even when they are doing something as important as making a contract. If a court finds that there has been a serious mistake—either in the contract itself or in the events leading up to the contract—it usually will not enforce the contract. Instead, the court will try to reform, or change, the contract to eliminate the mistake. In some cases, it may rescind, or cancel, the contract.

George Smith had a large collection of antique violins. Efrem Zimbalist, a world-famous violinist, visited Smith to look at his collection. Zimbalist recognized two of Smith's violins as especially valuable instruments, made in Italy in the early eighteenth century. He offered Smith $8,000 for the two violins. Although Smith said that $8,000 was a low price for two such precious violins, he accepted Zimbalist's offer. Zimbalist gave him $2,000 and promised to pay the remaining $6,000 over the next six months.

Zimbalist took the violins home. After playing them and inspecting them more closely, he discovered that they were not genuine eighteenth-century violins. Instead, they were modern imitations worth not more than $300.

Having discovered his mistake, Zimbalist refused to pay Smith any more money. Smith said that he, too, had been fooled; he had truly believed that the violins were antiques. Nevertheless, he reminded Zimbalist that they had made a contract, and he insisted that Zimbalist stick to it. He sued Zimbalist for the remaining $6,000.

The court decided that because both men had made a serious mistake, their contract could not be enforced. Smith had not simply offered violins as consideration; he had offered *antique* violins. Because the violins in question were not true antiques, Smith's consideration didn't exist. Without consideration, there could be no contract. Therefore, the court ordered Zimbalist to return the violins and ordered Smith to return the $2,000 Zimbalist had paid.

Often—especially in cases involving written contracts—one party will make a mistake that the other party is unaware of. The party who writes the contract may accidentally change a date or a dollar amount, and the other party may sign the contract without noticing the error. In these cases, a court may decide that the party who made the error must suffer the consequences of that error.

For example, Clarence Hetchler bought a $12,000 life insurance policy from the American Life Insurance Company. He paid for insurance through March 13, but the company mistakenly sent him a contract that said he was insured through May 13. When Hetchler died in April, his widow asked the company for the money it owed her. The company looked at its records and found that Hetchler's insurance policy had expired in March. It told Mrs. Hetchler that she could not collect on an expired policy. Mrs. Hetchler showed the company her husband's copy of the contract, which had an expiration date of May 13. The company said that the date in the contract was a mistake.

When the company still refused to pay, Mrs. Hetchler went to court. The court decided that the insurance company was at fault for putting the wrong date in the contract. If Mr. Hetchler had known his policy was about to expire, he would have renewed it. Therefore, the court ordered the company to extend the policy to May 13 and to pay Mrs. Hetchler the $12,000.

Not every mistake is as important as those in the preceding two examples. People who want to get out of a written contract sometimes look for minor mistakes in the contract, such as a spelling error or a misplaced comma. They think that by bringing such a mistake to the attention of a court, they can get the court to rescind the contract. This scheme rarely works, however. Unless the mistake is important or significant, a court will usually enforce the contract as it is.

Vague Contracts

In some cases, a court may refuse to enforce a contract because the contract isn't specific enough. For example, William Factor hired a company called Peabody Tailoring System, Inc., to make him a custom-made suit. He and the company signed a written contract in which he agreed to pay for the suit in weekly installments. The contract said nothing, however, about what material the suit would be made from. When Factor saw the suit in progress, he thought the fabric Peabody was using was unacceptable. He refused to continue paying for the suit.

The company took Factor to court, demanding payment. The court decided that the contract was too vague to be enforceable. It rescinded the contract and ordered Peabody to return the payments Factor had made.

Whenever possible, a court will try to "fill in the blanks" of a vague contract rather than rescind the contract entirely. For example, the actor Roy Scheider made a contract with Metro-Goldwyn-Mayer (MGM) in which he agreed to star in a television series. In the contract, Scheider agreed to make one episode of the series (the pilot) and to appear in further episodes if the series was bought by a network. The contract didn't mention the starting date for filming the series.

The pilot was successful, but Scheider refused to perform in the series. He admitted that he had made a contract, but he said that the contract wasn't enforceable because it was vague about the starting date for filming. MGM sued Scheider for breaching the contract.

The court agreed with MGM that the contract was enforceable. It pointed out that the television industry nearly always follows the same schedule for filming TV series. (When a television series premieres in the fall, for example, filming for the series always starts during the preceding summer.) Both parties to this contract were in the television business and could reasonably be expected to know this schedule. Therefore, the court ruled that Scheider had breached his contract, and it ordered him to compensate MGM for the losses he had caused.

Contracts with Minors

A teenager named Arnede McNaughton got her first job in the early 1930s. As soon as she made some money, she went to Granite City Auto Sales to buy a car. She picked out a car that cost $150 and made a deal with the car salesman to pay for it in installments of $3 a week. Several months after making that contract, McNaughton lost her job. She had paid $41, but she would not be able to pay any more. She asked Granite City Auto Sales to cancel the contract and to give her money back. The company refused, and she sued.

Normally, both parties are bound to a contract the minute they agree to it. Neither party has the right to come back later and say, "I changed my mind" or "I was only kidding." This rule, however, does not apply to minors. (A **minor** is someone who has not yet reached the age of legal adulthood. That age, which is determined by state law, is usually 18.) If you are a minor, you have the right to **disaffirm** (cancel) any contract you have entered into.

Because Arnede McNaughton was a minor, Granite City Auto Sales could not hold her to the contract it had made with her. The court rescinded the contract and ordered both parties to act as if it never had existed. McNaughton didn't get the car, and Granite City Auto Sales was required to return all the money she'd paid for it.

The rule that a minor can disaffirm a contract was developed by the courts to protect young people. Unfortunately, it sometimes has the opposite effect—it makes life more difficult for minors. Knowing that a minor can disaffirm a contract, many businesses refuse to deal with young people. If a minor wants to make a contract involving a large amount of money—such as a loan, a large purchase, or a lease—he or she must usually have an adult cosign the contract. (The adult cosigner is legally bound to the contract even if the minor disaffirms it.)

Note that only a minor has the right to disaffirm a contract. If a contract is made between a minor and an adult, the minor can disaffirm it but the adult

Illustration 9-6   Most banks require minors who apply for a loan to have an adult cosigner who will be legally responsible for that contract.

cannot. Even if the minor has tricked the adult into making the contract—for instance, by lying about his or her age—the adult remains bound by the contract. (The adult can, however, sue the minor for fraud. **Fraud** is the use of lies or dishonest statements for personal benefit.)

Over the years, the federal and state governments have passed a number of laws that limit a minor's right to disaffirm contracts. For example, minors can no longer disaffirm contracts for insurance, bank loans, or educational loans. If a minor joins the military, he or she can't disaffirm the enlistment. If a young athlete, actor, or model makes a professional contract, he or she is bound to it just as an adult would be.

REVIEW QUESTIONS

1. How does a court handle an unfair contract?
2. How does a court handle a contract in which only one party has made a mistake?
3. What can a court do with a vague contract other than reform or rescind it?
4. Name two types of contracts a minor cannot disaffirm.

BREACHING A CONTRACT

When two people make a contract, each takes on a responsibility. Each person agrees to do something—for example, to perform a service or to give up something of value. Sometimes, however, one person may **breach** the contract—that is, fail to do what he or she has agreed to do. When that happens, the other party may go to court and demand compensation.

Although breaching a contract is a serious matter, people who breach contracts are not necessarily bad people. As you might expect, some people breach contracts on purpose, just as some criminals break laws on purpose. More often, however, people breach contracts because of bad planning, bad health, or bad luck.

For example, suppose Michael hires Joey to help move furniture. They agree that Joey will arrive at Michael's house at eight o'clock on Saturday morning and move furniture for three hours. In return, Michael will pay him $60.

Joey may breach this contract for several reasons. His alarm may not go off, causing him to oversleep and show up half an hour late. He may misunderstand the agreement and show up at noon instead of eight o'clock. He may be too ill to work at all. Even though none of these problems is Joey's fault, Joey is legally responsible for his actions. If he causes Michael any harm by breaching the contract, he must compensate Michael for that harm.

If both parties are unable to carry out a contract, the contract is automatically canceled. Imagine, for example, that a nightclub hires a rock band to play for four nights. Before the first night, the club burns down. The band can't perform, and the club can't pay the band. In this case, neither party has breached the contract, because there is no longer a contract to breach.

Remedies

When one party breaches a contract, the other party is entitled to compensation. That compensation most often takes the form of damages (money). The amount of the damages depends on how much money the nonbreaching party has lost as a result of the breach.

To return to our earlier example, suppose Joey breaches his furniture-moving contract by arriving half an hour late. Michael may be annoyed, but he hasn't lost anything except time. Joey doesn't have to compensate Michael at all.

Suppose, however, that Michael has rented a moving van by the hour. If Joey arrives half an hour late, Michael may have to pay an extra hour's rent on the van. In this case, Joey will have to compensate Michael for the extra rent.

In either of these situations, Joey's lateness would be considered a minor breach—a breach that doesn't cause any significant problems. Despite Joey's late arrival, both parties would remain bound to the contract. Joey would still have to move furniture for three hours, and Michael would still have to pay him $60.

Suppose, however, that Joey shows up four hours late instead of half an hour late. In doing so, he may be committing a major breach. (Unfortunately, there are no hard and fast rules to distinguish a minor breach from a major breach. If the parties cannot reach this decision by themselves, a judge or a jury may have to do it for them.)

When one party commits a major breach, the other party has a legal right to rescind the contract. Michael, in other words, has a choice: he can allow Joey to work for three hours and pay him $60, or he can cancel the contract and tell Joey to go home. Either way, Joey is still required to compensate Michael for his losses (such as four hours' extra rent on the moving van).

If a contract is canceled because one party has committed a major breach, the other party has the right to make a new contract with someone else. In some cases, the new contract costs more than the original contract. If that happens, the party who breached the original contract must pay the extra cost of the new contract.

For example, Stanley hires Cindy, a carpenter, to repair a leak in his roof. After agreeing to fix the leak for $1,000, Cindy breaks her leg and can't do the work. Stanley looks for a replacement, but the least expensive carpenter he can find charges $1,500 for the same job.

In other words, Stanley's contract with the new carpenter costs him $500 more than his contract with Cindy. Because she breached the original contract, Cindy is responsible for this extra cost. Therefore, she must pay Stanley $500 in damages.

Cindy may have to pay other damages as well. Suppose she was to fix Stanley's roof in the early spring. After she breaches the contract, it takes two months for Stanley to find another carpenter willing to do the work. During that time, spring rains penetrate the leaky roof and cause Stanley's living room ceiling to collapse. Because the ceiling would not have fallen if Cindy had fixed the roof, she may have to pay for repairs to Stanley's living room.

No matter which party breaches a contract, both parties must try to **mitigate** (reduce) the amount of damage that results from the breach. Stanley, for example, must try to protect his living room furniture (perhaps by moving it away from the leak or covering it with plastic). He can't simply let his sofa be dripped on and then demand that Cindy pay to replace it. For her part, Cindy must do all she can to help Stanley find another carpenter.

If a party doesn't try to mitigate damages, a court is likely to rule in favor of the other party. For example, a farmer named James Wavra ordered seeds from Lyon Karr. When Wavra received the seeds, he could tell that they were of poor quality. He planted the seeds anyway, but the few crops that grew from them were not good enough to sell.

Wavra sued Karr for the loss of a year's worth of crops. The court refused to award any damages to Wavra, saying that Wavra had not tried to mitigate the damage. According to the court, Wavra shouldn't have planted the seeds if he knew they were faulty. Instead, he should have refused to buy Karr's seeds and bought better seeds elsewhere.

When two parties make a contract, they may decide in advance what the damages will be if either party breaches. The amount of money they agree on is called **liquidated damages**. Courts generally allow parties to agree on liquidated damages as long as the amount is fair to both parties.

Damages are not the only possible remedy for a breach of contract. As you read earlier in this chapter, a court may decide to reform or rescind a

Illustration 9-7   When a contract is breached, both parties must try to reduce the amount of damage from the breach, regardless of who committed the breach.

contract instead of awarding damages. Another option, which you read about in Chapter 7, is specific performance—a court order to do what was agreed to in the contract.

REVIEW QUESTIONS

1. What does it mean to breach a contract?
2. If one party breaches a contract, what kinds of compensation might the other party be entitled to?
3. What does it mean to mitigate damages? Give an example.
4. Define *liquidated damages*.

Latest in the Law: Working as a Court Reporter

A court reporter is a stenographer who takes down word-for-word statements, in shorthand, at legal proceedings such as criminal trials, civil trials, and court hearings. Later the court reporter transcribes the shorthand notes into an accurate written record of the trial.

Court reporters are expected to record testimony very swiftly, perhaps at the rate of 140 to 200 words a minute. For this reason, virtually all court reporters use stenotype machines. These machines are like small typewriters that print shorthand symbols at the stroke of a key. The court reporter uses the symbols to produce a written transcript. In some court systems, computers do the work of translating the stenotype symbols into a printed transcript. Other court systems do not require court reporters to take dictation at trials. These courts use electronic tape recorders to record court proceedings. Reporters are still needed, however, to transcribe the audiotapes of a trial into a printed record.

Working Conditions

During trials, court reporters sit in the front of the courtroom, where they can hear clearly. They are usually required to sit and take dictation for several hours at a time. When they are not in the courtroom, court reporters work in pleasant, comfortable offices. Some court reporters also work on a freelance basis. They are required to take their equipment to different work sites. They may be sent to a lawyer's office for an out-of-court proceeding, to a business office to record an annual meeting, or to a hotel conference room to record a seminar or a professional gathering.

Education and Training

People who plan a career in court reporting should begin training in high school. They should take a basic secretarial course that includes typing, shorthand, and business English. After they graduate from high school, they should take additional training at a business school, college, or vocational school. They should learn how to operate a stenotype machine as well as a range of word processing equipment. Court reporters may be employed by a local, state, or federal court system or by a private firm specializing in legal transcription. Most employers administer tests during the interview process because applicants must meet strict standards of accuracy and speed in shorthand and typing.

Personal Attributes

Court reporters need excellent shorthand and typing skills, along with hand and finger dexterity. They must have a good grasp of spelling and grammar and should be familiar with legal terminology. They also need to be accurate and able to pay close attention to details. Judges and attorneys will not tolerate mistakes or sloppiness, since a transcript must be an exact record of what took place during the trial. Employers also look for court reporters who demonstrate responsibility, honesty, and good judgment.

The need for court reporters is not expected to grow dramatically in the near future. Reporters will continue to be needed, however, to replace people leaving the profession and to help the courts deal with an increasing caseload of civil and criminal trials.

Chapter Review

Chapter Summary

- A contract is an agreement that is enforceable by a court.

- A contract is enforceable only if both parties have agreed to it voluntarily and have taken some action to show that they agree.

- A contract is created when one party makes an offer and another party accepts that offer.

- An offer is a proposal that clearly states the terms of the contract.

- An acceptance may be made orally, in writing, by action, or (in some cases) by silence.

- An acceptance may be made only by the party to whom an offer was made.

- An acceptance must be made before the offer has been revoked. Even if the offer is not revoked, the acceptance must be made within a reasonable period of time.

- A counteroffer cancels the original offer.

- Most contracts are valid whether they are oral or written. Certain types of contracts—for example, real estate purchases and contracts that will take over a year to complete—must be in writing to be enforceable.

- For an agreement to be a contract, both parties must offer consideration. If only one party offers consideration, the agreement is a promise rather than a contract.

- Consideration can be money, services, or anything of value, including the giving up of legal rights.

■ A promise is not enforceable unless someone has relied on the promise. Reliance on a promise is called detrimental reliance.

■ An implied contract is a contract that is understood through the circumstances. A contract may be implied when one party clearly has benefited from the services of another and should expect to pay for those services.

■ A court will not enforce unfair or unconscionable contracts. Such contracts will be reformed or rescinded.

■ Contracts that include serious mistakes may be reformed or rescinded. If a mistake was made by one party, the contract may be enforced in favor of the other party.

■ A vague contract may be reformed or rescinded. In some cases, a court will try to "fill in the blanks" of a vague contract to make it enforceable.

■ Minors can disaffirm most contracts for any reason. They cannot disaffirm certain contracts having to do with loans, employment, and military enlistment.

■ When one party breaches a contract, the other party is entitled to compensation.

■ If it becomes impossible for both parties to carry out a contract, the contract is canceled.

■ If one party commits a minor breach, the other party remains bound to the contract. If one party commits a major breach, the other party has the option to cancel the contract.

■ No matter which party has breached a contract, both parties have a duty to mitigate the damage caused by the breach.

Understanding Legal Terms

On a separate sheet of paper, match the terms below with the definitions that follow.

acceptance	fraud
consideration	mitigate
contract	offer
counteroffer	revoke
disaffirm	unconscionable

1. An agreement between two or more people that can be enforced by a court
2. A legally binding proposal
3. The act of agreeing to an offer
4. To take back an offer

5. Something of value that is exchanged by parties to a contract
6. Grossly unfair, to the point of offending public standards
7. To reduce, as the amount of damage caused by a breach of contract
8. The use of lies or dishonest statements for personal benefit
9. To cancel a contract, as by a minor
10. A proposal that differs from the original proposal

Applying the Law

1. Peter sells apples to grocery stores. A good friend of his, Ted, is a grocery store manager. One evening, when Peter and Ted are at dinner, they begin joking about work. Peter says, "Ted, I'll be glad to sell you apples for 25 cents a pound." Ted says, "Great. It's a deal." Both Peter and Ted know that Peter is joking. Both men know that Peter buys apples for 35 cents a pound, so he'd lose money selling them for 25 cents. Can Ted enforce this agreement? Explain your answer.

2. Alex rents an apartment from Fran. Fran decides to sell the apartment and offers it to Alex at a reasonable price. Alex says that he needs to think it over. Six months later, he still has not given Fran an answer. Finally, Fran tells Alex that she is revoking her offer and plans to sell the apartment to someone else. Alex tells her that that won't be necessary because he has decided to buy the apartment after all. The next day, Fran sells the apartment to a man named Larry. Alex sues Fran, claiming that she had no right to sell the apartment to Larry. Will he win in court? Explain your answer.

3. Owen offers Marie a job as a cashier for $5 an hour. Marie makes a counteroffer. She says, "I'll take the job if you pay me $6 an hour." Owen says, "Forget it. I'll find someone else to be my cashier." Marie says, "All right, I'll take the job for $5 an hour." Have Owen and Marie made a contract? Give reasons for your answer.

4. Karl's grandmother says to Karl, "Because you've been such a good boy, I'm going to give you a television on your next birthday." Karl's next birthday comes and passes, and his grandmother gives him nothing. If Karl sues his grandmother, will the court order her to give him a television? Why or why not?

5. Audrey has a diamond ring that she believes to be genuine. Her friend Trudy has always wanted a diamond ring. She offers Audrey $1,000 for the ring, and Audrey accepts. After Trudy buys the ring, she takes it to a jeweler to be appraised. The jeweler tells her that the stone is glass and that the ring is worth only $50. Can Trudy get her money back from Audrey? Explain your answer.

6. Stacy hires Joseph to paint her house for $500. After they make the agreement, but before Joseph begins to paint, the house is destroyed by a hurricane. Is Stacy required to pay Joseph the $500? Explain your answer.

Case Studies

1. Albert Goodman decided to open an electronics store. He applied for permission from Emerson Radio Corporation to sell Emerson radios. An Emerson representative said that Goodman's application looked fine and that a shipment of radios was on its way. Thinking that the radios would arrive soon, Goodman spent money to hire a sales staff and to advertise the radios. Soon afterward, the Emerson representative told Goodman that he had changed his mind—he would not grant the application, and he would not send any radios. What rights did Goodman have?

2. Jack Freeman manufactured clothing. He hired Murray Stone as a broker. (The job of a broker is to find companies that are willing to sell the manufacturer's products. Each company's representative is called a buyer.) Freeman and Stone agreed that, if necessary, Stone would bribe buyers— that is, pay them money illegally—if their companies agreed to sell Freeman's goods. Freeman would then reimburse Stone for the amount of the bribe. When Stone did bribe a buyer, however, Freeman refused to reimburse him for the entire amount. Stone took Freeman to court. Did the court award any damages to Stone? Why or why not?

3. Stanley Barr was a minor. He bought a motor scooter from Allen Hurwitz. Barr discovered that the scooter was defective. He took it back to Hurwitz and demanded a refund. Hurwitz refused to give him any money, so Barr sued him. Could the court order Hurwitz to give Barr a refund? Explain your answer.

Unit 4

Family Law

Chapter 10

Marriage Issues

Chapter Objectives

When you have read this chapter, you should be able to:

■   Explain how state and federal laws protect and restrict the right to marry.

■   Identify who can get married.

■   Explain what a prenuptial agreement is.

■   Describe the difference between a ceremonial marriage and a common law marriage.

■   Explain how the rights of married women have changed over the last 150 years.

■   Identify the financial responsibilities you assume when you get married.

■   Define the concept of domestic partners, and explain the differences between the rights of domestic partners and those of a married couple.

Case Study

Zablocki v. Redhail, 434 U.S. 374 (1978).

When Roger Redhail was in high school, he and his girlfriend had a child. He was ordered by the court to pay money to support the child. He was unable to do so because he didn't have a job and was extremely poor. About two years later, Redhail met a woman he wanted to marry. Redhail and the woman he wanted to marry were expecting a child. They applied for a marriage license, but their application was turned down because of a law then on the books in Redhail's home state of Wisconsin.

At that time in Wisconsin, a male resident who had a child not in his custody, and whom he was required to support, could not marry without first getting permission from the court. To get permission, a Wisconsin resident in this situation had to prove two things. First, he had to show that he had paid all the money he was supposed to pay to support the child. Second, he had to show that the child was not receiving welfare and was unlikely ever to be on welfare. Redhail could not prove either. Because he was unemployed, he had not been supporting his child, and the child was receiving public assistance. Therefore, the court would not give him permission to marry.

Redhail challenged the Wisconsin law and sued the state (in the name of Thomas E. Zablocki, the county clerk who refused to issue the marriage license). Redhail thought the Wisconsin statute infringed on his right to marry.

When Redhail won in federal district court, the state of Wisconsin appealed to the U.S. Supreme Court. The Supreme Court agreed with the lower court's ruling. The Court stated that no one can be denied the right to marry without a compelling reason on the part of the state. In the Court's view, Wisconsin's law was an illegal and unconstitutional restriction. The Court reasoned that the state law unfairly and unnecessarily deprived a particular group of people—the very poor—of a basic liberty—the right to marry.

The state of Wisconsin felt that its law was needed to make sure children received support payments. The Supreme Court, by contrast, felt that such a law did not necessarily ensure payment of support. Rather, it prohibited poor people from marrying solely because of their inability to pay. Also, the Court felt that the state had other ways to collect child support that were probably more effective than forbidding someone to marry. For example, the state could take something out of a person's paycheck or could seek criminal penalties.

In addition, the Court determined that the law would not prevent this person from having more children whom he would have to support. It would just mean that those children would be born out of wedlock. For these reasons, the Supreme Court held that the Wisconsin law was not justified by the interest it was supposed to further. It said the law was unconstitutional.

LEGAL RIGHTS AND RESPONSIBILITIES OF MARRIAGE

Illustration 10-1 Most people who fall in love don't think about the legal aspects of marriage.

The law places a high value on marriage. Marriage is considered the foundation of the family and of society. Because marriage is so important to the preservation of society, every state has laws for people about to marry, for those who are married, and for those whose marriage is about to break up. The states' regulations are based in large part on a desire to protect the family unit created through marriage and to protect any children born of that marriage.

Marriage is also a very personal right that the courts have held must be protected. The freedom of two people to marry and start a family is basic to the well-being of those individuals and to the well-being of society as a whole. Therefore, as you read in the opening case, marriage laws must be fair and reasonable.

Most people who fall in love and plan to marry don't even think about the legal aspects of that decision. However, the law views marriage as a type of contract. Like other agreements, the marriage contract carries with it mutual rights and responsibilities. Unlike most contracts, however, the marriage contract cannot be created solely by the voluntary agreement of two individuals. For a marriage to be valid, the state must give its consent. If children are born, the state has laws about a parent's responsibility to raise and support them (Chapter 11). The state also has laws about dissolving the contract (Chapter 12).

Who Can Marry?

Each state has its own laws specifying who can get married. Some requirements are the same in every state. Others vary from state to state.

In all states, a marriage must be between a man and a woman. A person may not legally marry another person of the same sex.

A person cannot legally marry if he or she is already married. Having two spouses at the same time is **bigamy**. **Polygamy** is having more than two spouses at once. Both are criminal offenses in every state.

All states forbid a couple to marry if they are closely related by blood. This is called **consanguinity**. The following relatives cannot marry in any state:

■ Parent and child
■ Brother and sister
■ Grandparent and grandchild
■ Aunt and nephew
■ Uncle and niece

In some states, first cousins cannot marry.

The laws of consanguinity are enforced whether the relatives are related by whole blood or half blood. Being related by half blood means you share a blood relative on one side of the family only. For example, if you and your sibling (brother or sister) have the same mother but different fathers, you are related by half blood.

People may also be related by **affinity**, or marriage. In some states, certain people who are related in this way may not marry each other. For example, John is planning to marry Amelia. John has a son, Peter, from a previous marriage. Amelia has a daughter, Sara. When John and Amelia marry, Peter and Sara become stepbrother and stepsister. Theirs is a relationship of affinity. In some states, Peter and Sara would not be able to marry. Other relatives by affinity who cannot marry in these states are:

- Stepparent and stepchild
- Step-grandparent and step-grandchild
- Mother-in-law and son-in-law
- Father-in-law and daughter-in-law
- Grandmother-in-law and grandson-in-law
- Grandfather-in-law and granddaughter-in-law

In states that have marriage restrictions based on affinity, it would be illegal for Sara and Peter to marry even if John and Amelia's marriage ended in death or divorce.

All states have age requirements for those who want to get married. In almost all states, both people must be 18 to marry without the consent of their parents. People under the age set by their state may marry if they have parental consent. However, the need for parental consent may be set aside in certain circumstances, such as when the underage couple are expecting a child or have a child.

In all states, only people who have the mental capacity to understand what they are doing may marry. For example, in many states, state law forbids the county clerk to issue a marriage license if either applicant is under the influence of drugs or alcohol. People in this condition cannot understand what they are doing and so are, at least temporarily, not competent to make the decision to marry.

Couples in all states must also meet the intent requirement. That is, both people must voluntarily agree to get married. Remember, marriage is a contract. There is no agreement if one or both parties do not have the mental ability to understand the nature and obligations of marriage and if either or both people do not intend to meet those obligations. If there is no agreement, there can be no contract.

Deciding Not to Marry

When two people exchange the promise to marry, they become engaged. For many reasons, a person who has agreed to get married may change his or her mind. If one party breaks the engagement, can the other person sue for breach of contract? It depends on the law of their state.

Most states used to allow a suit for the breach of a promise to marry. These suits were called "heart balm" actions. If you were engaged and your fiancé (e) broke the engagement, you could sue for damages. You could be compensated for the damage to your reputation caused by the broken engagement. You could also get back money you lost as a result of the broken engagement.

For example, you could be paid the money you spent on a wedding dress or the money you lost because you quit your job to get married.

Some states still allow heart balm actions, but the trend is to abolish them. Many states have decided that the breach of a promise to marry is too personal in nature for the state to get involved. They have decided that it is better for the two people to work it out themselves. Other states limit recovery to out-of-pocket losses. In those states, you can get back only the money you lost directly as a result of the broken engagement, such as money spent on wedding preparations.

Couples often exchange gifts when they become engaged and during the engagement. For many couples, the most expensive of these gifts may be the engagement ring. What happens to the ring if the engagement is broken? In most states, state courts, rather than state statutes, decide these cases. Most states will let the donor, or giver, have the ring back. These states consider the gift to be conditional. That is, the gift was given on the understanding that a marriage was going to take place. If there is no marriage, then the condition for the gift has not been met. The gift must be returned. In some states, the donor is entitled to get the ring back regardless of why the engagement was broken or who broke it. In other states, however, the recipient is allowed to keep the engagement gift if the engagement is broken by the donor.

For example, Tom and Susan agree to get married. They are going to live in Tom's apartment. This will mean that Susan can no longer walk to work. Two weeks before the wedding Tom gives Susan a car. He tells her it is her "diamond." Then, the day before the wedding, Tom tells Susan he has met someone else and no longer wants to marry her. Does Susan have to return the car? It depends on the law of the state where they live. If they live in a state like Ohio, where the reason for the broken engagement is immaterial, Susan must return the car. The car was the equivalent of an engagement ring, and thus the gift was conditional on the marriage taking place. However, if they live in a state like Colorado, where the donor cannot get the gift back if he or she broke the engagement, Susan can keep the car.

Prenuptial Agreements

Sometimes, before the wedding, the bride and groom decide to put some of the rights and responsibilities of their marriage agreement in writing. This document, called a **prenuptial agreement** or **antenuptial agreement**, usually focuses on financial issues. However, any topic—even who will do the dishes—may be included as long as it isn't illegal or harmful to the public good.

In general, when people get married, each person acquires certain rights over the other person's property. Often, people want this to happen. They get married because they want to share their lives, including their material possessions.

Sometimes, however, this is not what they want. For example, if a person has been married before and already has children, that person may want his or her property to go to these children, not to the new spouse. If a person who is extremely wealthy marries someone who is not very well off financially, the wealthy person may want to keep some of the possessions that he or she had before the marriage. A prenuptial agreement spells out whether some or all of a couple's individually owned property will be kept separate after they marry. Prenuptial agreements may also explain what will happen to property the man and woman acquire during the marriage.

Courts will enforce prenuptial agreements, but only if certain conditions are met. First, these agreements must be in writing. Second, both parties have to be fully informed about the other party's wealth. For example, suppose a millionaire pretends to be poor so that his or her intended spouse will sign a prenuptial agreement giving up all rights to the millionaire's property. The court won't enforce such a contract. Both sides have to fully understand what they are doing. To understand what you are doing, you must know what you may be giving up.

Also, both sides have to sign the agreement voluntarily and of their own free will. If you force or trick your intended spouse into signing, the agreement is not binding. Finally, the agreement cannot be **unconscionable**. This means that it cannot be grossly unfair to either side. To avoid the possibility of having a court view a prenuptial agreement as being unfair to one side or as having been signed under pressure, each person should have his or own lawyer.

Sometimes the prenuptial agreement says what will happen to the couple's property when one of them dies. Other times it says what will happen to their property if they get divorced. Some states will not enforce a prenuptial agreement that says what will happen if the couple get divorced. These states think that agreements that talk about what happens during a divorce will encourage divorce. Specific rules on when and whether a prenuptial agreement will be enforced depend on state law.

Getting Married

As we have seen, both the bride and the groom must meet all the requirements of the state where they want to marry, such as age, mental capacity, and intent.

Then, assuming a couple are eligible to marry in their chosen state, they must observe the formalities required by that state in order to be legally married. First, all states require the couple to apply for and obtain a marriage license. They usually get the license from the county clerk in the county where the wedding will take place. The requirement of a marriage license enables the state to monitor who gets married. It allows the state to make sure that the people who marry there meet the state's requirements.

Some states require the parties to have blood tests before they can get a marriage license. The blood test is often done to find out if either party has a venereal disease. Some states do not allow a person to marry if that person has a venereal disease that is or may become communicable.

A few states test for diseases that can cause risks to any children the couple may have after they are married. Tests may be done for such diseases as German measles (which can cause birth defects) and sickle-cell anemia (a genetic disease). If the results of the tests are positive, some states offer counseling to tell the couple about the risks to the future children. Other states require

New York State Department of Health

Certificate of Marriage Registration

District Name   City of Kingston

District No.   5501

Local Register No.   929

This is to certify that the persons identified below were married on the date and at the place specified as shown by the duly registered license and certificate of marriage on file in this office.

Groom Name   Michael   A.   Sodano, Jr.

First   Middle   Premarriage Surname

New Surname (if applicable)   [X] Check box if same as premarriage surname

Residing at   Oneonta, New York   Trenton, New Jersey

City, Town or Village/State or County

Date of Birth   9/12/1960   Place of Birth

Month Day Year

Bride Name   Mary Lyn   Lovak

First   Middle   Premarriage Surname

New Surname (if applicable)   Sodano   [ ] Check box if same as premarriage surname

Residing at   Oneonta, New York   Troy, New York

City, Town or Village/State or County

Date of Birth   3/21/1959   Place of Birth

Month Day Year

Date of Marriage   9/29/1992   Cohoes,   NEW YORK

Month Day Year   Place of Marriage   City, Town or Village

(SEAL)   City Clerk   *Kathleen A. Rose*   Oct. 9, 1992

Month Day Year

Any Alteration Invalidates This Certificate Issued Pursuant to Section 14-a, Domestic Relations Law

DOH-130 (9/86) (Formerly VS-12)

Illustration 10-2   All states require couples to obtain a marriage license before they wed.

the clerk who issues the marriage license to give applicants a brochure providing information about testing and treatment for genetic diseases and AIDS. At least one state does not allow a person with AIDS to marry.

Many states have a waiting period of not more than a few days. Usually the waiting period takes place between the time the license is issued and the time of the wedding ceremony. This gives the couple a chance to reflect on the seriousness of marriage so they won't rush into it without thinking.

Once the license has been obtained and the waiting period has passed, the marriage can be **solemnized**. The marriage is solemnized by having a wedding ceremony. All states require a ceremony for a valid ceremonial marriage. The marriage can be solemnized by a civil authority (for example, a judge or a mayor) or by a religious authority (for example, a minister, a priest, or a rabbi). When the marriage has been solemnized, the couple are officially married. Finally, the marriage is registered at the county clerk's office.

If you are legally married in one state and then move to another state, the marriage is valid in the new state even if the two states have different requirements. As you read in Chapter 1, under the Full Faith and Credit Clause of the Constitution, states honor each other's laws.

What happens if a man and woman who live in one state travel to another state to get married? The answer depends on their reasons for going to another state and on whether they meet the requirements for a valid marriage in that state. For example, Anita and Max, who live in Illinois, want to get married in Vermont because they met and fell in love there. They are free to do so as long as they meet Vermont's requirements for a valid marriage.

What happens, though, if a couple go outside their state just to avoid a law at home that prohibits their marriage? It depends on state law. Suppose Gene and Carol, who are first cousins, live in a state that will not let them marry. They go to a neighboring state that does permit such marriages. According to the laws in most states, their marriage would be considered valid in their home state. However, in some states, the marriage would not be recognized when they returned home—if the couple went to another state for the sole purpose of avoiding the law at home *and* if the different requirement is more than just a formality.

Common Law Marriages

Like a ceremonial marriage, which you just learned about, a **common law marriage** is an agreement between a man and a woman to get married. The difference is that a common law marriage is not solemnized. There is no license and no wedding ceremony. All states recognize ceremonial marriages. Only about a quarter of the states recognize common law marriages.

If you enter into a valid common law marriage in a state that recognizes such marriages, the marriage is as legally binding as a ceremonial marriage would be. The financial rights and obligations are the same as those for a ceremonial marriage.

If you have a valid common law marriage in one state and then move to another state, the marriage will be valid in the new state. This is true even if the

Illustration 10-3 Couples who live together without a marriage license may have a common law marriage in some states.

new state does not allow its residents to enter into common law marriages. Again, one state honors another state's laws under the Full Faith and Credit Clause of the Constitution.

In states that recognize common law marriages, a man and woman have a common law marriage if they meet the following requirements:

- They hold themselves out to the public as husband and wife. This means that they tell other people they are married. It means they do things a married couple would do, such as opening a joint checking account.
- They live together as husband and wife.
- They intended to enter into a marriage relationship at a certain moment in time.

The last requirement is interpreted differently in different states. Some states require the parties to state that they intend to be married. Other states infer the intent to be married from the situation.

For example, Darlene and Paul live together. They open a joint bank account and rent an apartment together. However, Darlene tells everyone that she never wants to get married and that she does not believe in the institution of marriage. Paul says that he has been married once and that once is enough. Darlene and Paul do not have a common law marriage (even if they live in a state that recognizes common law marriages) because they do not intend to be married.

As with a ceremonial marriage, a valid common law marriage can be ended only by the death of one of the parties or by a legal divorce granted by a court of law.

Spouses Who Disappear

Sometimes a person will disappear and never be heard from again. In some cases, a person may disappear only to return years later, after everyone believes that person is dead. What happens to that person's spouse? Is the spouse still legally married as long as the person is missing?

Once again, it depends on the law of the state where the couple lived. Years ago, if the spouse who was left behind remarried, he or she took the risk of being a bigamist if the absent spouse ever returned.

Today most states have laws that protect an innocent spouse whose partner disappears. Some state laws say that a person who marries a second spouse after the first one has been missing for a period of time cannot be prosecuted for bigamy even if the first spouse reappears. However, in these states, the second marriage is still invalid.

In other states, a deserted spouse can ask the court to dissolve the marriage after a certain period of time has passed. If the court agrees that the absent spouse is probably dead, the court will dissolve the first marriage. Then the surviving spouse can legally marry again. Still other states will declare the absent spouse legally dead if certain conditions are met.

REVIEW QUESTIONS

1. What is the main reason that states regulate marriage?
2. Name three marriage regulations that all states have.
3. What are three marriage formalities that couples must observe?
4. How is a common law marriage different from a ceremonial marriage?

THE CHANGING FACE OF MARRIAGE

The roles of men and women in marriage in the United States have changed dramatically since the nineteenth century. Until the middle of that century, a woman gave up many rights when she married. For one thing, her personal property became the property of her husband. If she owned any land, her husband took control of it. He was also entitled to keep any profits from her land. A married woman lost the right to make contracts. She could not sue on her own—she had to join her husband as a party to the lawsuit. She could not make a will. Even her children were generally considered as "belonging" to the husband/father.

In return for giving up these rights, a woman was supposed to be taken care of by her husband. She also acquired what were called **dower rights** in her husband's land. This meant that upon his death a wife was entitled to use one third of her husband's lands during her lifetime. Finally, her husband was responsible for her antenuptial debts and her torts, or civil wrongs.

These rules were based on the common law system that had been brought over from England by the colonists. By the late 1800s, many states began to think that these rules were unfair and started passing laws to remedy the situation. Today, in the United States, women (married or single) can own and manage their own property, sell their property, make contracts, bring lawsuits in their own names, and make wills. Now married women are entitled to essentially the same rights as married men.

With these rights come responsibilities. Married women are responsible for their own torts and their own antenuptial debts. As we will see, they have obligations of support, just as their husbands do.

A Married Woman's Name

Traditionally, when a woman married, she took her husband's name. Some states required her to do this. In other states, it was a social custom. Today, when a woman marries, she has a choice. She may keep her maiden name, use her husband's name, or use a hyphenated last name made up from her name and her husband's name. Also, a husband may decide to take his wife's name.

In fact, in most states, anyone can take any name he or she chooses as long as it's not done for the purpose of defrauding another person.

The Obligation to Provide Financial Support

Illustration 10-4 In many families today, both the husband and wife work outside the home.

Traditionally, the duties of a married couple were divided according to gender. The wife was supposed to run the household and raise the children. In return for those services, the husband was supposed to earn the money necessary to support the family.

Today the situation is quite different. In some families, it is still the wife who stays home and cares for the children. In other families, the husband takes on the role of homemaker. In many cases, both husband and wife work outside the home.

In the past, the husband's duty to provide was enforced by the common law **doctrine of necessaries**. According to this doctrine, the husband was required to pay for necessary items that the wife bought. For example, if the husband refused to buy food for the family, the wife could go to the grocery store and charge the food. The husband would then be responsible for the bill.

What happens today if a husband or wife doesn't support his or her spouse? What can the needy spouse do? Once again, the remedies depend on the state where the couple live. Some states still recognize the traditional view of the doctrine of necessaries. According to the laws in these states, the husband is solely responsible for the wife's debts. When this doctrine was challenged in Virginia's state courts, the rule was abolished in that state as being unconstitutional. It violated the Equal Protection Clause of the U.S. Constitution because it required only the husband to support the wife and not vice versa. If this law were challenged in other states where it is in force, it would probably be declared unconstitutional there too.

Some states have modified the doctrine of necessaries and now make both husband and wife responsible for each other's essential needs. In some states, the husband is primarily liable, but the wife is now secondarily liable. In other words, the merchant must try to collect from the husband first. If unsuccessful, the creditor can try to collect from the wife. The theory behind this version of the doctrine of necessaries is that because men typically earn more than women do, they should be primarily responsible.

Other states make the spouse for whom the expenses were necessary primarily responsible. The other spouse is secondarily liable. For example, in these states, if the wife had hospital bills, the hospital would have to try to collect from her first. If unsuccessful, the hospital could then try to collect from the husband.

A few states hold husband and wife jointly liable. This means that the business, hospital, or other creditor can collect from either husband or wife or both as long as the amount collected does not exceed the amount owed.

There are other methods of getting a spouse to provide support. In some states, the wife (or husband) can bring a civil suit for support without filing for divorce and without separating. In other states, if the couple decide to live apart, one spouse can ask the court to require the other spouse to provide support as part of a court-ordered separation. You will read more about this arrangement in Chapter 12.

Finally, a person may face criminal penalties for failing to support his or her family. In most states, failure to support a spouse is a misdemeanor. In some states, it is a felony. To be criminal, nonsupport must be willful. That is, the person must be able to support the spouse but choose not to do it. However, if the person doesn't have the means to provide support, he or she can't be punished for failing to do so. As you will read in Chapter 11, it is a crime in all states not to support one's children.

Nontraditional Living Arrangements

You may think of a family as including only people related by blood or marriage. According to this definition, your family consists of your blood relatives (mother, father, siblings, grandparents, aunts and uncles, and so forth) and your spouse and his or her relatives. This definition is often the one used by the law. For example, state inheritance laws provide that if you die without a will, your property will pass to certain people to whom you are related by blood or by marriage (see Chapter 13). Also, insurance policies provide coverage to "family members" in accordance with this definition.

Today many people not related by blood or marriage live together and share a life together. For example, some unmarried couples live together as a family unit. They may even have children. These couples choose not to marry for many reasons. In the case of a homosexual couple, they *cannot* enter into a legal marriage because all states deny people of the same sex the right to marry. These couples may consider themselves as life partners, or domestic partners, but the state does not recognize the relationship as a marriage.

What are the rights of nontraditional couples who live together as a fam-

Illustration 10-5 Even though they live together as a family unit, unmarried couples do not have the same rights as married couples.

ily unit but are not legally married? In most cases, they do not have any of the rights of a married couple. They do not inherit from each other. They will typically not be given insurance coverage that would be available to a legal spouse. If one partner dies, the remaining partner will probably not be entitled to survivor's benefits from the deceased partner's employer or from social security. If an unmarried couple split up, their property will probably not be divided as it would be in the case of a married couple. Also, the non–wage earner will probably not be entitled to alimony.

There may be nonfinancial consequences too. For example, a hospital may refuse to allow someone to visit the person he or she has been living with for years because they are not "family" according to the traditional definition. Also, a court may deny a domestic partner visitation rights with a child of the other partner, as happened in New York in 1988. Alison D. and Virginia M., who began living together in 1978, wanted to raise a child. They decided that Virginia would have the child by means of artificial insemination. (With this procedure, a woman becomes pregnant without sexual intercourse.) In 1983, when the child was two years old, the couple separated. At first, Alison had visitation rights with the child. Then, in 1987, Virginia would not let Alison have any contact with the child. When Alison sued, the court held that only Virginia, the biological mother, was a parent. It stated that Alison had no parental rights, including the right to see the child. In 1991, after Alison D. appealed to New York State's highest court, the lower court's decision was upheld.

Today, under certain specific circumstances, a domestic partner may be officially recognized and afforded a few of the benefits of a spouse. For example, in California, couples who are living together are using an old law to register with the state as an unincorporated, nonprofit association. They use the word *family* in the association title. This registration may allow a couple to be treated as a family in some situations, such as for hospital visits. A few cities allow an unmarried couple to register what is called a **domestic partnership** with the city clerk. To do this, a couple go to city hall. There they sign an affidavit affirming that they share a close personal relationship, meet the age requirement, are not married, and are competent. The partners can be of the same sex or different sexes. If one or both partners want to terminate the relationship, they do this by signing a form at the city clerk's office.

Registration as a domestic partner does not mean that the couple are legally married, but it may help them obtain some benefits. The benefits vary from place to place. In Seattle, Washington, a city employee who registers a domestic partnership can obtain health insurance benefits for his or her domestic partner. The employee can take leave to care for a partner who is ill or to attend the funeral of a partner. In Madison, Wisconsin, community pools and other public accommodations that offer family memberships must recognize domestic partners.

In 1989 New York's highest court interpreted a New York City rent control law to include unmarried lifetime partners in the definition of family. According to New York City's rent control law, when a person who lives in a rent-controlled apartment dies, the landlord cannot evict that person's spouse or any other family member who has been living with the tenant. Two men, Leslie and Miguel, began living together in a rent-controlled apartment in 1975. Leslie was the tenant of record of the apartment. For over ten years, the two men considered each other as spouses and shared all obligations, including financial ones. When Leslie died in 1986, the owner of the apartment building tried to evict Miguel because Miguel wasn't the deceased tenant's spouse or relative. The court held that the landlord could not evict Miguel just because the men were not "family" in the traditional sense of being related by blood or marriage. In this case, the court used a functional definition of family, saying that the men lived as a family for all practical purposes.

Today situations in which an unmarried couple are given rights typically reserved for a married couple are the exception and not the rule.

REVIEW QUESTIONS

1. In the nineteenth century, what rights did a woman give up when she married?
2. What is the doctrine of necessaries?
3. What is the purpose of a domestic partnership?

THE PROBLEM OF DOMESTIC VIOLENCE

Illustration 10-6 In 95 percent of the cases of domestic violence, the victim is a woman.

Beating or assaulting another person is wrong, and it is a crime. Until recently, however, people—even those in law enforcement—were inclined to place domestic violence in a separate category that was outside government involvement. (Domestic violence involves the abuse of spouses, ex-wives and ex-husbands, and people who are living together.) Many people believed that what went on in a family was a private matter. It was also felt that a man had certain rights over his spouse. As you read earlier in this chapter, at one time a wife and children were considered a husband's property. The law even allowed the male head of the household to use violence against his wife and children. (Although men have been victims of domestic violence, women are the victims of 95 percent of all assaults of this type.)

These attitudes toward domestic violence are changing slowly. At the same time, the letter of the law has changed. Today all states have laws to protect battered spouses. Some laws provide a civil remedy. For example, under one law, the court can issue an injunction, or court order, forbidding someone to beat a spouse or housemate. If the person violates the injunction, he or she can be sent to jail, fined, or both. In many states, an abused person can also bring a civil suit for money damages against the abusive spouse.

Criminal remedies are also available. For example, a spouse abuser can be arrested and charged with assault and battery. In some places, a police officer may arrest someone without a warrant if the officer has reasonable cause to believe that an assault has been committed and if the person who has committed the assault is the spouse or former spouse of the victim. Some laws offer even more protection. For example, a city ordinance in Ann Arbor, Michigan, requires a police officer to arrest a spouse abuser if the victim has visible signs of abuse or if the abuser has a gun. In most communities, however, the police are not required to make an arrest. The officers may try mediation or may remove the abuser from the home for a time. If the police refuse to make an arrest, the abused victim may press criminal charges against the abusive spouse.

Even with state and local laws on the books, the legal system's response is sometimes hampered by the view that families should solve their own problems. For example, some prosecutors may be reluctant to bring the case to court. Some judges may give a more lenient sentence to a spouse abuser than they would to a person who has assaulted a stranger. However, the attitudes of police officers, district attorneys, and judges are changing. Many communities have special prosecution units to help the abused person through the criminal process.

Often the victim doesn't report abuse from a spouse or housemate. The victim may not realize it's a crime or may not think the legal system will offer protection. Many victims accept serious physical violence as a normal part of family life—perhaps because as children they saw one of their parents being abusive or being abused. Some victims feel that they deserve the abuse because they have made their spouses angry.

Every person who is being abused must remember that help is available. Most programs are set up to help women in trouble because the overwhelming majority of battered spouses are women. Many communities have a crisis hotline number that women can call if they are being abused by their husbands or boyfriends. There is also the National Domestic Violence Hotline number: 1–800–333–SAFE. Often communities also have shelters where battered women can go with their children to escape violence. The locations of these shelters, sometimes called safe houses, are kept secret so that the women do not have to worry about more beatings while they try to find a permanent solution to the problem. Sometimes counseling is available to both parties to help them learn more constructive ways of dealing with their feelings.

REVIEW QUESTIONS

1. Why has domestic violence been treated differently than the assault of a stranger?
2. What civil remedies are available to abused spouses?
3. Name three methods of help for an abused spouse.

Latest in the Law: Marital Rape

Rape is a very serious crime in which a man forces a woman to have sexual intercourse or has intercourse with her without her consent. However, until very recently, all 50 states had an exception to this law called the marital exemption rule. This rule holds that a man's sexual relations with his own wife can never be considered rape even if he uses force. This rule, arising from English common law, states that by marrying, a woman consents to having sexual relations with her husband. It further states that a wife cannot withdraw that consent as long as she remains married.

The Need for Change

With the growth of the civil rights and women's liberation movements of the 1960s and 1970s, courts and state legislatures began to rethink the marital exemption rule. It became apparent that no woman, whether married or not, should be subjected to sexual assault. The judges and legislators began to realize that rape can indeed occur within marriage—for example, when a husband forces his wife to have sexual intercourse during a beating or other type of violent act.

The courts and legislatures also began to recognize that there are several circumstances within a marriage in which a woman may no longer consent to have sex with her husband. Traditionally, women who had legally separated from their husbands, who had filed for divorce, or who had changed their residences were still legally married and therefore subject to the marital exemption rule in all states. Some states began to consider that these women were not bound by marital consent because they no longer enjoyed a loving relationship with their husbands.

Opponents of abolishing the marital exemption argued that by eliminating the rule, the courts and legislatures were violating the privacy of marriage. They also feared that wives would fraudulently claim rape in bitter divorces. Those who favored abolishing the marital exemption countered that wives have as much right to be protected from rape by their spouses as unmarried women have to be protected from rape by boyfriends, dates, or acquaintances. They also argued that wives are no more likely to bring false charges than anyone else is.

New Laws

Beginning in the late 1970s, several states, including New Jersey, Montana, and Oregon, either repealed the marital exemption law outright or deleted the rule from their statutes. Many other state legislatures enacted new laws limiting the marital exemption to specific circumstances. For example, Virginia allows the state to prosecute a husband for rape if the couple live apart or if he batters his wife during the rape. Pennsylvania enacted a law which says that if a husband is living with his wife, he cannot be prosecuted for rape. He can, however, be prosecuted for a new crime called spousal sexual assault. This offense carries a lesser penalty than rape does.

In a few states, the marital exemption rule has been overturned in court. In New York, the court struck down this rule because it said the rule violated the Equal Protection Clause of the Fourteenth Amendment. The court held that the rule unfairly protected unmarried women, but not married women, against rape.

By 1990, 24 states had abolished the marital exemption rule altogether. Twenty states had modified or limited the exemption so that it no longer applies to couples who are living apart or who have filed for divorce, annulment, or separation. Only three states retain the marital exemption rule regardless of circumstances. In addition, three other states have extended it to apply to unmarried partners who are living together.

Chapter Review

Chapter Summary

- Marriage is considered by the law as the basic building block of the family. Marriage is regulated by state law to protect the family unit.

- State laws on marriage must be reasonable and fair to protect what is considered a basic personal right.

- Marriage is a type of contract. This agreement between two people must be validated by the consent of the state.

- In all states, marriage is permitted only between a man and a woman. No state allows a person to be married to more than one person at a time. All states have age requirements for marriage.

- Laws of consanguinity forbid people who are closely related by blood to marry. All states have these laws.

- To marry, people must be competent and must do so voluntarily.

- The right to sue for breach of contract because of a broken engagement has been abolished in many states.

- States vary in their laws about the return of engagement gifts when an engagement is broken. Most states will let the giver have the engagement ring back.

- Some couples choose to prepare prenuptial agreements that set down in writing the rights and responsibilities of each person in the marriage. Courts will enforce prenuptial agreements only if certain conditions are met.

- People who are eligible to marry must observe formalities, including getting a license and taking blood tests. After the marriage is solemnized in a ceremony, it is registered.

- Marriages that are valid in one state are valid in other states. In some states, however, if a couple go to another state to marry just because the law prohibits their marriage at home, the marriage may not be valid in the home state.

- Common law marriage is an agreement between a man and a woman to marry without solemnization. Only about a quarter of the states recognize common law marriages.

- In the past, wives took care of the house and children, and husbands supported the family. The doctrine of necessaries required the husband to pay for items needed by his wife.

■ Today some states still make the husband solely responsible for the wife's debts. Other states make wives responsible if their husbands can't pay. In some states, husband and wife are equally responsible.

■ Unmarried couples who live together do not, in most cases, have any of the rights of married couples. In some communities, these couples are allowed to register as domestic partners.

■ Domestic violence is the assault or other abuse of a spouse. Laws allow spouses to file civil actions or criminal charges against the abuser.

Understanding Legal Terms

On a separate sheet of paper, match the terms below with the definitions that follow.

affinity	domestic partnership
bigamy	dower rights
common law marriage	polygamy
consanguinity	prenuptial agreement
doctrine of necessaries	solemnize

1. Having more than two spouses at one time
2. Blood relationship
3. Relationship through marriage
4. Having two spouses at the same time
5. Written agreement made before marriage that explains the rights and responsibilities of the bride and groom
6. To have a wedding ceremony before a civil or religious authority
7. Agreement between a man and a woman to be married without a license or a ceremony
8. Right of a wife to use one third of her deceased husband's lands during her lifetime
9. Rule that enforces the duty of a husband or wife to be responsible for his or her spouse's debts
10. Agreement, registered at city hall, in which two people of the same sex or different sexes affirm a close personal relationship

Applying the Law

1. Melanie, age 25, and Rick, age 27, are planning to marry. Neither has been married before. To celebrate, they throw a big party for their friends. At the party, which lasts all night, they drink too much and become intoxicated. On the spur of the moment, they decide to go to the county clerk's office after the party to apply for a marriage license. The clerk refuses to issue it to them. Why is the clerk able to refuse Melanie and Rick a license? What requirements for marriage have they not met?

2. Mildred, a black woman, and Richard, a white man, wanted to get married. They met all their state's requirements except one. Their state had a law forbidding interracial marriages. Was such a law constitutional? Explain your answer.

3. Bill and Sandra lived together in a state that recognizes common law marriages. When they had a child, Bill filed an acknowledgment of paternity. In it, he said that he was the child's father. Later the couple separated. Sandra took Bill to court, claiming they had a common law marriage. Sandra said that Bill told her they were "married in the eyes of God." Bill denied that he said this. Most witnesses testified that Bill and Sandra did not hold themselves out as husband and wife. Did they have a valid common law marriage? Explain your answer.

4. Beth and William agree to marry. William gives Beth an engagement ring. Then Beth breaks the engagement but refuses to give back the ring. Can William get the ring back? Why or why not?

5. Dennis is Sharon's half brother. They have the same mother but different fathers. They are separated when Sharon is adopted at the age of only 10 days. Sharon and Dennis meet again when they are adults. They fall in love and decide to marry. Can they marry? Why or why not?

6. John has had a terrible day at work. He hates his job anyway, but today was especially bad. He did not get an important assignment done, and his boss told him that if he missed another deadline he would be fired. He has to keep the job because he has a wife and four children to support. After work, he goes out with some friends and has too much to drink. When he gets home, his children are cranky, the house is messy, and his wife starts yelling at him for getting home late. This makes John even madder, and he hits his wife. Was this assault justified? Explain your answer.

Case Studies

1. When Reginald and Donna agreed to marry, Reginald bought wedding and engagement rings. Donna began wearing the engagement ring. Sometime later, Reginald broke the engagement. They continued to see each other and tried to work things out, but eventually they broke off the relationship completely. When Reginald asked for the ring back, Donna refused. In fact, Donna became engaged to another man, and they used the ring as a trade-in on a new set of rings for their wedding. Reginald sued to get his ring back. Who would win? Give reasons for your answer.

2. Betty and Dominic were married for 38 years before they started living apart. They were separated for four years, although they never signed a legal separation agreement and never got divorced. Dominic died. Betty had nothing to do with the funeral arrangements and, in fact, did not even attend the funeral. Dominic did not leave enough money in his estate to pay for his funeral and burial expenses. Is Betty obligated to pay these expenses? Explain your answer.

3. James and Judith were engaged. James is a businessman and politician. Judith is a secretary. James wanted a prenuptial agreement to protect the interests of his sons from a previous marriage. He did not tell Judith that he intended to make certain that everything he obtained after their marriage, as well as everything he had at the time of the marriage, would go to his sons. He suggested that a lawyer who was his friend and business attorney draw up the agreement. Judith agreed because this attorney had handled her divorce and she trusted him. James rushed Judith into signing the agreement on the eve of the wedding. It stated that James could keep everything he had or acquired and that Judith could keep everything she had or acquired. After 13 years of marriage to Judith, James sued for a divorce. By that time, James was worth about $830,000 and Judith had only her personal effects. James asked the court to enforce the prenuptial agreement. Judith objected. Is the agreement enforceable? Why or why not?

Chapter 11

Responsibilities of Parents to Their Children

Chapter Objectives

When you have read this chapter, you should be able to:

■ List the rights and duties that parents have in raising their children.

■ Describe the circumstances under which the government may interfere in a parent's child-raising decisions.

■ Define *adoption*, and describe the precautions a state takes before permitting a person to adopt a child.

■ Explain why it is sometimes hard to identify a child's legal parents.

■ Give examples of child abuse and child neglect.

■ Describe how the government responds to suspected cases of child abuse and child neglect.

Case Study

People v. Tomlianovich, 514 N.E.2d (Illinois 1987).

Eleven-year-old Jeremy Tomlianovich lived with his mother and stepfather in western Illinois. In May 1986 Jeremy's mother hit him with a wooden paddle. She beat him so hard that he needed emergency treatment at a hospital. At the hospital, Dr. Carlos Almeida examined and treated him. Soon afterward Jeremy's mother was arrested for cruelty to her child.

At her trial, Jeremy's mother explained that she had hit Jeremy to punish him for playing with matches and smoking. Dr. Almeida testified that the bruises he had found on Jeremy were the most severe he had ever seen. The prosecutor displayed photographs of the bruises, which were solid red and purple. On the basis of this evidence, the jury found Jeremy's mother guilty of the felony of cruelty to children.

Jeremy's mother appealed her conviction, saying that she had the right to discipline her own child without outside interference. The appellate court agreed that parents have the right to discipline their children and that discipline can include spanking and other forms of punishment. However, a parent's right to discipline a child is not without limits. Vicious paddling that causes severe injury is abuse, not punishment.

Jeremy's mother was sentenced to two years' probation. She was required to pay $250 in fines and court costs. As a condition of her probation, she had to continue to get mental health counseling, and she had to cooperate fully with the state Department of Children and Family Services.

CHILDREN

In colonial days, parents were free to treat their children in whatever way they chose. The government never interfered. Children were considered the property of their parents, no different from horses or mules. Parents could require their children to work for the family in return for room and board, as if the children were indentured servants. Parents were free to punish or discipline their children in any way they wished.

In the nineteenth century, states began passing laws to protect children. As you read in Chapter 6, some of these laws established juvenile justice systems to rehabilitate delinquent children. Other laws, called **child welfare laws**, limited the amount of power parents had over their children. The first child welfare laws concerned education and child labor. Every state passed mandatory education laws requiring that children be kept in school up to a certain age. Every state also passed child labor laws that limited the number of hours a parent or employer could require a child to work.

Over the years, states have passed more and more child welfare laws. Some laws, for example, require children to be vaccinated against certain childhood diseases. Other laws, as you saw in the opening case, limit a parent's right to discipline a child. As each new law is passed, parents lose a little more of the right to raise their children in any way they want. Some parents have argued that these laws are an illegal intrusion on the privacy of the family.

As you've read in previous chapters, the U.S. Supreme Court considers the right to family privacy to be a fundamental right. The government may not intrude on this right any more than it may intrude on the constitutional rights to free speech and freedom of religion. In other words, the government must have a compelling reason to justify restricting the right to family privacy.

The issue of raising children involves two important interests: a parent's right to keep family matters private and the state's duty to protect the welfare of children. As you will see in this chapter, these two interests often come into conflict.

Emancipation

Parents are responsible for their children (and have authority over them) only until the children become adults. Becoming an adult is called **emancipation**. The most common way to become emancipated is to reach a certain age, called the age of majority. At the **age of majority**, which is determined by state law, a person gets all the rights and responsibilities of an adult. In most states, the age of majority is 18.

There are ways in which a child may become emancipated before reaching the age of majority. When a child marries, for example, he or she is considered emancipated. Enlisting in the armed forces is another way to become emancipated. Children may also become emancipated by becoming self-supporting. A child who is self-supporting pays his or her own living expenses with no financial support from parents.

Some states permit partial emancipation. A child who is partially emancipated is treated as an adult for certain specific purposes only. California, for example, permits children over age 15 to be partially emancipated for the purpose of making medical decisions. These children may decide for themselves (without the need for parental consent) whether to undergo surgery. This partial emancipation does not permit them to disobey their parents in any other matter, however. It also does not relieve the parents of any obligations toward their children.

REVIEW QUESTIONS

1. Give two examples of child welfare laws.
2. Define *emancipation*, and list three ways in which a child can become emancipated.
3. What is partial emancipation?

Illustration 11-1   Enlisting in the armed forces is one way for children to become emancipated.

PARENTS

A child's parents share equally the duties and the privileges of raising the child. When a child is born into a traditional family, with a clearly identifiable mother and father, there is usually no question about who will support and care for the child. In recent times, however, many family arrangements have become much less traditional. An increasing number of families are headed by unmarried parents. In addition, the rising numbers of divorces, remarriages, and adoptions have complicated the rules of child support and custody.

Changes in medical science have added further complications. More accurate blood tests have made it easier to determine whether a particular man is the father of a particular child. At the same time, advances in fertility science have made it more difficult for courts to decide who should be called the mother of a child.

Parents Living Apart

On August 1, 1978, in Bethlehem, Pennsylvania, Orlanda Hughes gave birth to twins. She and Carl Hutt, the babies' father, were not married. Hutt refused to give the twins financial support. He said that he had told Hughes that he didn't want children. Hughes had promised to use birth control, but she had stopped using it without telling him. After she had become pregnant, Hutt had asked her to have an abortion and she had refused. Hutt said that for these reasons he shouldn't be required to support the children. Hughes took Hutt to court. The court ruled in Hughes's favor, saying that both parents are responsible for all the children they produce.

Parents may live apart for several reasons. In some cases, as in the case of Hutt and Hughes, the parents may not be married. In other cases, they may be married but separated, or they may be divorced. Generally, when the parents of a child live apart, one parent has custody of the child. That parent takes the primary responsibility for raising, educating, and caring for the child. Both parents, however, remain responsible for supporting the child financially. (You'll read more about child custody and child support in Chapter 12.)

Sometimes, as in the case you just read, a parent who doesn't have custody refuses to help support his or her child. When that occurs, the other parent can sue for child support. Parents can also sue to protect other rights. For example, if the parent with custody denies the noncustodial parent the right to visit their child, the parent without custody can sue to protect that right. Parents can also sue for the right to make decisions about their child's upbringing.

Sometimes a man refuses to support a child because he denies that he's the child's father. In that case, the mother may sue him to prove that he really is the father. To settle the suit, a court must decide whether that man should legally be considered the father of the child. A lawsuit of this type is called a **paternity suit**.

A man who is the defendant in a paternity suit is usually required to offer a blood sample. A laboratory compares this sample with a blood sample taken from the child. Each blood cell contains a chemical called DNA, which holds the genetic code that is passed down from parents to children. By comparing the man's DNA and the child's DNA, a laboratory can determine whether the man is the father of the child. If the blood test reveals that the man is the father, the court will order him to support the child financially until the child is emancipated.

This test is called **DNA fingerprinting** because each person's DNA is unique, like a person's fingerprints. DNA fingerprinting is a relatively new technique that is being accepted by an increasing number of courts.

Parents by Adoption

Adoption is the process by which a person who is not a child's biological parent becomes that child's legal parent. A person who adopts a child is called an **adoptive parent**. When a child is adopted, the adoptive parent takes on all the rights and obligations of a biological parent. Adoption also eliminates all legal ties between the child and the child's biological parents.

Children are adopted for a number of reasons. Orphaned children may be adopted into a new family. Children who have only one living parent may be adopted by that parent's new spouse. Parents who cannot care for their children may permit them to be adopted by someone who can.

The Need for Consent   Before a child can be adopted, the biological parents must give up their rights to that child. In certain cases, which you will read about later in this chapter, parents are ordered by a court to give up their children. More often, however, biological parents willingly consent to give up

Illustration 11-2   After adopting a child, the adoptive parents take on all the rights and responsibilities of biological parents.

their children. This often occurs when one member of a divorced couple remarries. It is also common for an unmarried woman to give up an infant for adoption if she feels she won't be able to care for the child.

Some states require the consent of the child as well as the consent of the biological parents. When children are over a certain age (generally 10 to 14), a judge may ask them how they feel about being adopted and how they feel about the person who wants to adopt them.

Investigating Adoptive Parents   State laws place very few restrictions on who may adopt a child. States do, however, try to make sure that a child is adopted by a family that best meets that child's needs. Therefore, no state will permit a person to adopt a child until that person's background has been investigated thoroughly. The investigation is usually conducted by a social worker, who may be employed by the state or by a state-approved adoption agency.

In determining whether a person is suited to adopt a child, social workers take many factors into account. One important factor is whether the person is married. (Although states do not prohibit a single person from adopting a child, they prefer to place a child with two parents.) Other factors include the adoptive parent's age and health and whether he or she has enough money to care for the child. Social workers also try to match children with families of the same race and religion.

Finding Biological Parents or Children   Sometimes a child who has been adopted develops an interest in finding his or her biological parents. In some cases, a biological parent wants to locate a child he or she gave up earlier in life. In either case, the desired information may be difficult to get.

In most states, adoption records are sealed, and no one is permitted to see them. This policy is meant to protect the privacy of the people involved. Some courts feel that permitting access to adoption records might weaken the bond between the adoptive parent and the child.

Although adoption records are sealed, they are not destroyed. They can be opened if there is a good reason. For example, if a child needs to know whether he or she carries a hereditary disease, state law may permit a court to examine the adoption record. Even then, the court will reveal all the necessary information about the parents' health but will not reveal the parents' names.

In recent years, courts have been more willing to open adoption records. Some states actively assist adopted children in locating their biological parents once the children have become adults. In a few states, the court may act as an intermediary between biological parents and their grown children. A representative of the court may locate a child's biological parents and ask if they will agree to have their identities revealed. Similarly, a court representative may locate a grown adopted child at the request of the child's biological parents.

Some states have established voluntary adoption registries. Biological parents who want to find their children can register. Adopted children who want to find their biological parents can do the same. If a child and the child's parent both register, the registry will arrange for them to meet.

New Forms of Conception

Over the past few decades, innovations in science and law have made it easier for couples to have children. In some cases, though, these innovations have made it difficult to determine who should be considered a child's legal parents. The most important of these innovations are artificial insemination, in vitro fertilization, surrogate mothering contracts, and sperm donors.

Artificial insemination is the reproductive process by which a woman's egg is fertilized by a man's sperm without sexual intercourse. Most often the sperm is placed inside the woman's body by medical personnel. It is sometimes possible, however, to fertilize an egg outside the woman's body—that is, in a laboratory. This process is technically called **in vitro fertilization**, though it is popularly known as test-tube fertilization. An egg fertilized in this manner is placed into the womb of a woman. She then carries the child through a normal pregnancy.

In most cases, these procedures are done with the egg and sperm of the couple who plan to raise the child. When this can't be done because of a medical problem, another person may be involved. Couples may use sperm banks, which provide the sperm of usually anonymous donors. In other cases, the couple have a woman carry and give birth to a child for them.

Surrogate mothering is a contractual arrangement in which a woman agrees to carry and give birth to a child for another woman. Suppose Joy has a medical condition that makes it impossible for her to have a child. She and her husband, Tom, make an arrangement for Sally to be a surrogate mother. They agree to pay Sally $20,000 plus all her medical expenses. In exchange, Sally agrees to carry a child for them and to give up the child as soon as it is born.

Sally may then be impregnated with Tom's sperm through artificial insemination. Alternatively, she may have Joy's egg (which has been fertilized in the laboratory) implanted in her womb.

Legal Consequences   The medical procedures of artificial insemination and in vitro fertilization make it possible for a child to have more than one "father" or "mother" or to be born to a woman who is not biologically related to the child. Such situations have brought about some complex court cases. For example, some sperm donors have sued for the right to raise their biological children. At the same time, some husbands of women who have been artificially inseminated with donors' sperm have refused to support those children.

Most courts and legislatures have settled the matter as simply as possible. They have ruled that when a woman is artificially inseminated and her husband consents to the procedure, she and her husband are the legal parents. The sperm donor, by contrast, has no parental rights or responsibilities.

The use of surrogate-mother contracts has also resulted in lawsuits over parental rights. Occasionally a surrogate mother decides to ignore the contract she made and keep the child she carried and gave birth to. In a case like this, the other party to the contract may sue to get custody of the child.

In 1985 Mary Beth Whitehead agreed to be a surrogate mother for a New Jersey couple named William and Elizabeth Stern. She was artificially inseminated with William Stern's sperm. After she gave birth to a baby girl, she decided to keep the baby. William Stern sued her for breach of contract.

The New Jersey trial court ruled that the contract had to be enforced. It gave custody of the baby to the Sterns. Whitehead appealed the trial court's decision, and the case eventually reached the state's highest court. The court pointed out that Whitehead was the baby's biological mother and that her contract with the Sterns required her to sell her parental rights. However, it has never been legal for a mother to sell her child for money. Therefore, the court called the surrogate mother contract invalid and refused to uphold it.

There remained the question of who should have custody of the baby—the father (Stern) or the biological mother (Whitehead). The court treated the case as if it were a divorce case. It reviewed the family situation of both parents to determine who could best care for the baby. The court finally gave custody to Stern and visitation rights to Whitehead.

Another case a few years later had a different result. In 1990 Anna Johnson agreed to be a surrogate mother for a California couple named Mark and Crispina Calvert. Through the process of in vitro fertilization, Crispina's egg was fertilized with Mark's sperm and implanted in Johnson's body. Therefore, unlike Mary Beth Whitehead, Johnson was not biologically related to the baby she carried.

When Johnson gave birth and refused to give up the child, the Calverts sued. The court said that because the surrogate mother was not the baby's biological mother, she had no parental rights. Therefore, the court gave custody of the child to the Calverts.

Legislatures and courts continue to struggle with the problems arising from artificial insemination, in vitro fertilization, surrogate mother contracts,

Illustration 11-3   When surrogate mother Mary Beth Whitehead, above, decided to keep the child she gave birth to, the baby's biological father sued her for breach of contract.

and sperm donors. Some states have outlawed surrogate mother contracts entirely, but many people feel that this is not the best long-term solution. It remains to be seen whether state governments can come up with clear, widely acceptable rules for dealing with these complex issues.

REVIEW QUESTIONS

1. What is DNA fingerprinting? What is it used for?
2. Who must consent before a court will allow a child to be adopted?
3. What does it mean to "seal" adoption records?
4. Describe a situation in which it might be unclear who should be considered the mother of a child.

RIGHTS AND DUTIES OF PARENTS

Robin Strasser's grandmother was worried about Robin's upbringing. She felt that the child's mother was not caring for her properly. In 1951, when Robin was 6 years old, her grandmother took action. She notified the New York State authorities.

The grandmother told the authorities that Robin's mother did not stay at home with her little girl during the day. She held a full-time job (which was uncommon for women at that time). Each day, when Mrs. Strasser went to work, she dropped Robin off at a nursery school. The grandmother also reported that although Mrs. Strasser was Jewish, she did not give her daughter any religious training. The grandmother noted that when Robin was 4 years old, Mrs. Strasser married a man of a different race and different religious beliefs.

When the authorities received this complaint, they sent social workers to investigate Robin's home. The social workers found that the home was kept clean. Nothing there seemed harmful to Robin. A medical examination of Robin showed that she was well fed, healthy, and well adjusted.

Despite the social workers' findings, the court ruled that Robin's mother was not fit to raise the girl. The court said that the grandmother would be a better parent because she would be home during the day to care for Robin. She could also give Robin the proper religious upbringing. The court decided to remove Robin from her mother's house and give custody of the girl to her grandmother. Robin's mother appealed the decision.

The court of appeals reversed the lower court's decision and returned Robin to her mother's home. The court said that a child should be removed from his or her parent only for the gravest reasons. As long as the child is cared for, the way in which the parent chooses to bring up the child is not for anyone else to judge.

The case of Robin Strasser, and other cases like it, upheld the right of parents to raise their children as they choose. It is not the place of the court—or anyone else—to tell parents how they should run their families. It is entirely up to the parents to decide how much, if any, religious training to give their children.

Parents have the right to decide how to discipline their children. Parents also have the right to decide where their children live, what they wear, what they eat, and where they go to school.

The government may interfere with these rights only when a parent's actions put a child's welfare at risk. It is the duty of the state to make sure that every parent provides his or her child with sufficient food, clothing, shelter, medical care, education, and discipline.

Education and Religious Training

Parents have the duty to make sure their children get a proper basic education. Most parents fulfill this duty by sending their children to public school. Parents who can afford to do so may send their children to a private school as long as the education given by that school meets all state requirements. Some states permit parents to educate their children at home. These parents must prove, however, that they are giving their children as good an education as a public school would provide. They must also show that their children are being taught all the same subjects they would be taught in public school.

Illustration 11-4   Parents have the duty to make sure that their children get a proper basic education.

Parents have the right to choose what religious training to give their children. This right includes the freedom to raise children without any religion or with a nontraditional religion.

Medical Care

Parents have a duty to see that their children get proper medical care. Parents also have the right to make medical decisions for their children. Except in an emergency, a doctor may not treat a child without first getting permission from the child's parent.

Sometimes a parent will refuse to consent to a certain type of medical treatment. This happens most often when the medical treatment interferes with the parent's religious beliefs. The faith of Jehovah's Witnesses, for example, prohibits the use of blood transfusions. Because blood transfusions may be necessary in surgery, Jehovah's Witnesses will not consent to surgery for their children.

Sometimes doctors can find an alternative to surgery. At other times, unless a child receives surgery, the child may suffer or die. Doctors often bring these cases to court. A court has the power to permit surgery on a child without the parent's consent. In making this decision, however, the court must weigh two important interests: (1) the state's interest in the child's health and (2) the right of parents to raise their children according to their own religious beliefs.

Courts have consistently ruled that if a child's life is at stake, the state has the right to order surgery despite the parent's objections. However, if the surgery isn't necessary but merely recommended or desirable, courts are more willing to uphold the parent's point of view. For example, Naomi Green was a Jehovah's Witness living in Philadelphia. Her son, Ricky, had polio when he was a child. The polio caused his spine to curve, and Ricky could no longer walk. When Ricky was 16, his doctor asked Naomi for permission to operate on the boy's spine. The doctor said that without the surgery, Ricky might be confined to bed for the rest of his life.

Naomi wanted the best for her son, but she refused to permit the surgery because of her religious beliefs. The doctor notified the state authorities, and the matter went to court. The court said that Ricky's life would be more difficult without the surgery but that there was no reason to believe he would die. Therefore, the court refused to allow the operation. The court also pointed out that the doctor and Ricky could discuss the matter again in a few years, when Ricky was an adult.

In making this decision, the court considered Ricky's feelings as well as those of his mother. Ricky was 16 years old and did not want the operation. Courts often take an older child's feelings and religious beliefs into account. In recent years, legislatures and courts have allowed even younger children to have a say in their own medical treatment. This is considered particularly important in cases involving abortion, treatment for venereal disease, treatment for alcohol or drug abuse, and mental health services.

Discipline and Control

When children misbehave, parents have the right—and the duty—to discipline them. Parents may use any form of discipline they wish as long as they do not abuse their children. Parents may spank their children, "ground" them, or require them to stay in their rooms. Parents may punish children by depriving them of an occasional meal, although they cannot starve a child as a form of punishment.

When necessary, parents can get help from the courts in disciplining their children. As you read in Chapter 6, state laws require children to obey their parents. A parent who has difficulty controlling his or her child can file a petition with the juvenile court. If the juvenile court judge finds that the child is "out of control," he or she can order the child to undergo whatever treatment is necessary. Although the usual treatment is counseling or probation, some unruly children must spend time in a state institution for juveniles.

If parents fail to control their children, the legal consequences can be serious. If a child commits an intentional tort—that is, injures someone by an intentional action—the child may be held liable for damages. In many states, the child's parents are responsible for paying those damages, up to a certain limit. In addition, the parents may be held liable for negligence because they failed to prevent their child from causing the injury.

Services and Money

Parents have a right to expect their children to do chores around the house. When parents permit their children to get jobs outside the home, they have the right to take all the money made by their children. (Of course, most parents permit their children to keep the money they earn.)

Parents do not have the right to take other money that belongs to their children. For example, if a child inherits money, only the child may spend that money.

REVIEW QUESTIONS

1. List four duties that parents have toward their children.
2. Under what circumstances may a parent teach a child at home?
3. When can a doctor treat a child without getting the parent's permission?
4. What restriction is there on a parent's right to discipline a child?

CHILD ABUSE AND CHILD NEGLECT

A parent who does not give his or her child proper care may be guilty of **child neglect**. When a parent or other person mistreats a child, that person may be guilty of **child abuse**. Every state has laws prohibiting child neglect and child abuse. These laws provide protection for the child and treatment or punishment for the neglectful or abusing adult.

Child Abuse

In the opening case, you read about a parent who abused her young son by beating him so hard that he needed medical treatment. Not all child abuse is

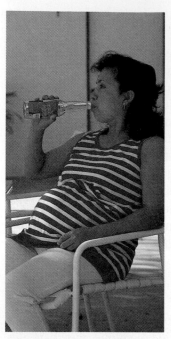

Illustration 11-5   The child of a woman who drinks or takes drugs during pregnancy may be born with serious medical problems.

physical, however. A parent can also abuse children emotionally by deliberately making them feel unloved or unwanted. A continuing pattern of screaming at, belittling, or ignoring a child can lead to serious emotional injury.

Another form of child abuse is sexual abuse. Any form of sexual contact between an adult and a child is considered sexual abuse. Sexual abuse not only may cause physical harm to a child, it also may cause severe emotional problems that persist throughout the child's life.

Abuse of an Unborn Child   A pregnant woman who uses drugs or alcohol can seriously harm her unborn child. The children of drug users often are born addicted to drugs. They may suffer brain damage, birth defects, or other serious medical problems. The child of a woman who drinks during pregnancy may be born with a serious medical condition called **fetal alcohol syndrome**. A child with fetal alcohol syndrome is usually smaller than most babies and may suffer from nervous system disorders, retardation, or other birth defects. In an effort to prevent these problems, some states have defined the use of drugs or alcohol by pregnant women as a form of child abuse.

Child Neglect

More children die from being neglected than from being abused. A parent's failure to provide adequate food, clothing, medical care, nurturing, education, or shelter is considered neglect.

Parents may neglect their children for a variety of reasons. Some parents are not aware that they are being neglectful. They may be mentally retarded or may be addicted to drugs or alcohol. Some parents are unable to provide for a child's needs because of a physical handicap. Some parents just don't care about the welfare of their children.

It's not always easy to tell whether a parent is being neglectful. In making this judgment, a court must often look at the parent's financial situation. Suppose a young girl has no boots to wear in the snow. If the girl's parents are wealthy, a court may consider them neglectful for failing to give her boots. If the girl's parents can't afford boots, however, a court will probably not consider them neglectful.

Reporting Abuse or Neglect

State authorities can't stop abuse and neglect unless they know which children are being mistreated. For this reason, states depend on the eyes and ears of teachers, doctors, nurses, social workers, and day care workers. It is the duty of these people—and others who spend time with children—to watch for signs of possible mistreatment. Anyone who suspects that a child has been abused or neglected must notify the police or a local child welfare agency. Failure to do so is a violation of state law. (See Table 11-1 for signs of child abuse and neglect.)

On April 26, 1971, when Gita Landeros was 11 months old, her mother brought her to San Jose Hospital in California. The emergency room doctor, Dr. Flood, examined Gita. Her leg bones appeared to have been twisted; they

Table 11-1 Signs of Possible Child Abuse and Child Neglect

Children who are abused or neglected may exhibit a number of physical and behavioral signs, such as those listed below. Children who are not abused or neglected may also show these signs. However, a combination of these symptoms is a strong indication that a child is suffering from abuse or neglect.

Physical Abuse

Physical Indicators
- Has unexplained bruises (in various stages of healing), black eyes, welts, human bite marks, bald spots
- Has untreated sores or infections
- Has burns on the arms or back, especially cigarette burns or burns resulting from contact with a hot liquid
- Has unexplained fractures, deep cuts, or abrasions

Behavioral Indicators
- Is self-destructive
- Is sometimes withdrawn and at other times aggressive
- Is uncomfortable with normal physical contact
- In adolescents, runs away chronically
- Complains of soreness and moves uncomfortably
- Wears clothing inappropriate to the weather
- Destroys school property
- Steals the personal belongings of others
- Seems fearful of authority
- Misses school to care for brothers and sisters
- Misses school or is frequently late for school without reason
- Has a short attention span
- Is not enrolled in school even though this is required for child's age

Physical Neglect

Physical Indicators
- Is consistently not being supervised by a parent or other adult
- Has medical needs that are not being taken care of
- Is consistently hungry or eats only junk food
- Dresses inappropriately
- Has poor hygiene
- Has parasites such as head lice
- Doesn't have a proper immunization record
- Has a swollen stomach
- Looks very thin
- Is dehydrated and undernourished
- Is not the appropriate height and weight for child's age

Behavioral Indicators
- Doesn't have basic skills other children of the same age have
- Has no energy, is listless
- Steals food, begs
- Reports that no caretaker is home
- Is self-destructive
- In adolescents, drops out of school
- Consistently hangs around school after everyone has left, possibly as a result of being thrown out of home
- Constantly looks to adults such as teachers or neighbors for attention and affection
- Generally seems unhappy or ill

Source: U.S. Department of Health and Human Services.

were splintered in several places. Gita also had bruises all over her back. She appeared to be afraid of people. These were signs that Gita probably had been beaten. Dr. Flood treated Gita's injuries and let her go home with her mother.

California law requires any doctor who suspects child abuse to report it to the police or the juvenile authorities. Dr. Flood violated this law by failing to report Gita's condition. Two months later, Gita's mother rushed Gita to a different hospital. This time the doctor in charge realized that Gita had been beaten and notified the local police. After an investigation, Gita's mother was found guilty of child abuse. Dr. Flood was charged with violating California's reporting laws.

Investigation of Child Abuse or Child Neglect

As soon as they receive a report of possible child mistreatment, the police or juvenile authorities send a social worker to investigate. The social worker's first concern is the child's safety. If the child appears to be in immediate danger, the social worker may remove the child from the home and investigate later.

When a social worker finds that a child is being mistreated, he or she tries to resolve the problem informally with the parents. The social worker may recommend child care training or counseling for the parent. Some parents, however, refuse to work with a social worker or accept help from other professionals. In these cases, the state's only option is to take the parents to court.

Juvenile Court Action

As you read in Chapter 6, juvenile courts have jurisdiction over cases of child abuse and child neglect. The court's first step in such a case is to appoint a **guardian ad litem** (guardian for the legal matter) to serve as the child's advocate. This person's role is to speak for the child in court and protect the child's interests. He or she may also counsel the child and help the child understand what is going on.

Juvenile Court Dispositions

If the juvenile court finds that parents have been abusive or neglectful, the judge must decide how to handle the matter. Before ordering a disposition, or treatment plan, the judge usually listens to the advice of several different parties. The social workers involved in the case tell the judge what sort of treatment they recommend to improve the parents' behavior. The guardian ad litem gives the judge his or her opinion about what would be best for the child. On the basis of this information, the judge orders a disposition that will help rehabilitate the parent without hurting the child further.

Parental Counseling or Probation   Whenever possible, the judge looks for a solution that does not disrupt the family or require the child to be removed from the home. In most cases, the parents are ordered to get counseling or child care training. Some judges require the parents to serve a form of probation. During this time, social workers may visit the home to check on the family's progress.

Foster Care   If the judge feels that leaving the child in the parents' care is dangerous, he or she may order that the child leave the home temporarily. The child may then be placed in foster care. **Foster care** is any placement away from the family. The three most common types of foster care are foster families, group homes, and residential facilities. A child in a foster family lives with a couple who may have children of their own. In a group home, a child lives with a couple who care for several other foster children. A children's residential facility is more like a residential school. It cares for larger numbers of children.

Parents whose children are placed in foster care are permitted to visit the children and must continue to support the children financially. When the court believes that the situation at home is no longer dangerous, these children may be returned to their parents.

Termination of Parental Rights   Courts are very reluctant to take children away from their parents permanently. This action may be necessary, however, if parents remain abusive after repeated attempts to rehabilitate them. It may also be necessary if the parents have seriously harmed or abandoned a child. In these cases, the government's interest in protecting children outweighs the parents' right to custody of a child.

Many courts will not remove a child from the home permanently unless there is another family willing to adopt that child. When only one parent has been abusive, the court may require that parent to leave either temporarily or permanently. This solution, which permits the child to stay in his or her home with one parent, usually eases the disruption in the child's life.

A court will never take a child away from a parent simply because the parent is poor or uneducated or because someone else could provide a better life for the child. The only reason for removing a child from a parent, either permanently or temporarily, is that the parent is endangering the child's welfare. If the court believes that a parent is honestly trying to improve, it will not permanently take away that parent's child.

Criminal Court Actions

Juvenile courts cannot punish parents for mistreating children; they can only offer rehabilitation and treatment. Sometimes, however, a parent's behavior is so morally offensive that treatment alone doesn't seem to be a strong enough response. If a parent tortures or abandons a child or repeatedly abuses a child, most people feel that the parent ought to be punished.

Every state has criminal laws against child abuse. If a parent is found guilty of violating those laws, he or she may be sent to prison. Like juvenile courts, however, most criminal courts try to disrupt the child's life as little as possible. Therefore, many abusive parents are sentenced to a fine or probation rather than a prison term.

In recent years, some states have incorporated treatment goals into the criminal process. In these states, a parent may agree to participate in a treatment program in return for a suspended sentence or probation.

REVIEW QUESTIONS
1. Give two examples of child abuse.
2. How can a woman abuse her child before the child is born?
3. What is a guardian ad litem?

Viewpoints on Adoption Record Laws

Elizabeth B. had just gotten her children off to school when the doorbell rang. She opened it to find a young woman looking at her expectantly. "Mrs. B.?" the young woman asked with a nervous smile. "My name is Rebecca. I'm the daughter you gave up for adoption 22 years ago. May I come in?"

Elizabeth was too shocked to answer. Memories and painful feelings came flooding back—her panic at a high school pregnancy, the confusion surrounding the birth, the baby she never saw. Was this young woman really that child? How had she found Elizabeth after all those years?

Stories like this one are becoming more common every day. More than sixty thousand adoptees and parents in the United States are searching for their past. An increasing number of states are helping adopted children and their biological parents locate each other. This search is a highly emotional one—and one that is controversial as well.

The Case for Opening Adoption Records

Many people feel strongly that adoption records should be opened to allow adult adoptees and their biological parents to locate each other. Some adoptees feel robbed of a right that other people take for granted—the right to know and understand their past. Biological parents may long for the child they gave up, remembering the child's birthday and wondering if every child they see who is the same age might be their own.

Mothers who as teenagers were shamed or forced into giving up a baby may have a strong desire to see the child again. Many adoptees yearn to find out about the circumstances of their birth and learn why their parents felt they had to give them up.

In addition, many adopted children want to know about their biological parents when they begin their own families. They want to know about any hereditary medical problems. Sometimes biological parents want to pass on such information to their children.

The Case for Sealing Adoption Records

Just as some people yearn to recover their past, others want to keep the past locked firmly away. Some biological parents want to forget the difficult circumstances of the pregnancy—especially if incest or rape was a factor. Other biological parents have made new lives for themselves. They may not have told their spouses or other children about the first birth. They would prefer not to have the past come looking for them.

Some adoptees feel the same way. They feel secure in their adoptive families and believe that contact with their biological parents could threaten that security. They don't want to hurt the parents who raised them. Indeed, having a child search for his or her biological parents—or vice versa—can be painful and threatening for adoptive families.

Not all searches end happily. Some parents have looked long and hard only to find that their children have been abused or that they resent their parents bitterly for having given them up. Adoptees who, like Rebecca, locate their parents may end the search by having doors slammed in their faces.

The Search Continues

Adoption record laws still aim at maintaining confidentiality for both parents and children. Nevertheless, a number of adoptees and biological parents continue to search for connections through state registries, special support groups, and even private "search consultants."

The experiences and reactions of those involved will continue to be highly personal—as varied as the individuals who want to remember or to forget.

Chapter Review

Chapter Summary

- Until the nineteenth century, parents could raise their children in any way they wanted, without interference from the government.

- In the nineteenth and twentieth centuries, state governments passed many child protection laws. These laws often permit the government's interest in protecting a child to override the parents' interest in family privacy.

- Emancipation is the process by which a child becomes an adult. A child is emancipated by reaching the age of majority, marrying, joining the armed forces, or becoming self-supporting.

- A child's father and mother share the responsibility for supporting and raising that child.

- If one parent refuses to support a child, the other parent can sue for child support. If a man denies that he is the father of a child, the mother may bring a paternity suit to determine whether he is the father.

- Adoption is a legal process that creates a parent-child relationship. Before a child can be adopted, his or her biological parents must give their consent. The child's consent may also be required. States look into the fitness of adoptive parents before permitting them to adopt.

- Some states assist adopted children and their biological parents in locating each other later in life.

- When a child is conceived through artificial insemination or in vitro fertilization, there may be some question about who should be considered the child's father or mother. Courts and legislatures are trying to develop solutions for the problems that these medical procedures have created.

- As long as a child's welfare is not at risk, parents have the right to raise the child in any way they see fit. Parents have the duty to provide food, clothing, shelter, medical care, education, and discipline.

- Except in an emergency, no one can give a child medical care without permission from the child's parent. When a parent refuses to consent to a child's medical treatment, a court may permit the treatment if it is necessary to save the child's life.

- By law, anyone who has contact with children must report any signs of child abuse or child neglect to the authorities.

- A parent who abuses or neglects a child may be given training, counseling, or a form of probation. If these solutions don't work, a court may take a child away from the parent either temporarily or permanently. In some cases, the parent may face criminal charges.

Understanding Legal Terms

On a separate sheet of paper, match the terms below with the definitions that follow.

adoption   foster care
artificial insemination   guardian ad litem
DNA fingerprinting   in vitro fertilization
emancipation   paternity suit
fetal alcohol syndrome   surrogate mothering

1. The act of becoming an adult
2. Type of artificial insemination in which a woman's egg is removed from her body and fertilized by a man's sperm in a laboratory
3. Person who serves as a child's advocate in court in a child abuse or child neglect case
4. Medical condition that may affect a newborn whose mother drinks liquor during pregnancy
5. Temporary placement of a child away from his or her parents
6. Reproductive procedure in which a woman's egg is fertilized by a man's sperm without sexual intercourse
7. Process by which a person who is not a child's biological parent becomes the child's legal parent
8. A blood test that can be used to determine who the father of a child is
9. Contractual agreement in which one woman carries and gives birth to a child for another woman
10. Lawsuit brought by the mother of a child to prove that a certain man is the child's father

Applying the Law

1. Lauren, a 16-year-old girl, marries Luis. They get an apartment together but have trouble finding jobs. Lauren asks her parents to give her money for rent and food. They refuse. She says they can't refuse because parents have a duty to support their children. Is she right? Explain your answer.
2. Pavel is 15. His parents are divorced. He lives with his mother. When his mother decides to remarry, her new husband, Don, wants to adopt Pavel. Who must consent to the adoption before it will be permitted?
3. Darlene is 7 years old and has appendicitis. The doctor tells her parents that if she does not get medical attention soon, she may die. Darlene's parents refuse to consent to medical treatment. Their religion teaches that all illnesses should be treated only through prayer. The doctor takes the case to court, hoping to get permission to treat Darlene. How will the court make its decision? What will the court probably order?
4. Audrey is 9 years old. Four times in one month, Audrey's parents catch her smoking cigarettes. As punishment, they spank her and prohibit her from going out after school or on weekends. Audrey complains that her

parents are abusing her. Should she take her complaint to a social service agency or to the police? Explain your answer.

5. Noelle gives birth to a boy. Her son is relatively small for a newborn. He cries continuously and, within hours after he is born, begins to show signs of drug withdrawal. The doctor asks Noelle whether she abused drugs during her pregnancy, and she admits that she did. What may happen to Noelle?

6. Twice a year the school nurse does a brief health check on every student. While examining Eric, she notices that he looks underfed. He is wearing clothes that are dirty and inappropriate for the weather. Looking more closely, she finds a number of cuts and bruises all over his body. She thinks that Eric may be a neglected or abused child. What should she do?

Case Studies

1. Joann Nancy Chattman was a married woman who was thinking of having children. Because Chattman had been adopted when she was a child, she didn't know if she carried any hereditary diseases that she might pass on to her children. She went to court and asked for permission to see her adoption records. The court denied her request, saying that the records were sealed. Chattman appealed this decision, and the appeals court decided that there was good cause to open the records. Could Chattman find out the names of her biological parents? Why or why not?

2. Mr. and Mrs. S. agreed to have a baby through artificial insemination. Mrs. S. was inseminated by sperm from an anonymous donor. On December 28, 1980, the baby was born. Later, when Mr. and Mrs. S. were divorced, Mr. S. refused to continue to support the child. He said that because he was not the child's biological father, he owed the child no financial support. According to the decisions of most state courts, was he right? Why or why not?

3. John, Thomas, and Robert H. were all between the ages of 10 and 13. In 1974 their parents took them out of school and began teaching them at home. The parents taught them English, math, science, singing, and acting. They did not teach them history or geography, although books on those subjects were available in the house. The principal of the neighborhood public school asked the family court to investigate the quality of the boys' education. Did the court permit the parents to continue teaching their sons at home? Give reasons for your answer.

Chapter 12

Separation and Divorce

Chapter Objectives   When you have read this chapter, you should be able to:

- Explain the difference between annulment and divorce.

- Discuss the types of legal agreements married couples may make when they separate.

- Explain the concept of no-fault divorce.

- Discuss the financial consequences of divorce.

- Explain the rights of unmarried couples who split up after living together.

- Explain the laws regulating child support.

- Discuss the different types of child custody arrangements.

Case Study

Neudecker v. Neudecker, _____ N.E.2d _____, 17 Fam. L. Rep. (BNA) 1195 (Ind. Ct. App. 1991).

Rolland Neudecker was a divorced parent who lived in Indiana. He was paying child support as required by Indiana law. When his daughter was ready for college, Rolland's ex-wife asked for an increase in child support to pay for their daughter's college expenses. She based her request on a state law that says child support can include sums for a college education where appropriate.

Rolland challenged the law that allowed the court to order him to pay for his daughter's college expenses. He argued that it was unconstitutional to force him to pay for a child's college expenses when the court could not order a parent who was not divorced to pay for those expenses.

The court disagreed. It said that in an intact family, children can usually count on their parents to help them with college expenses, even at a sacrifice. This was not necessarily true with divorced parents. Therefore, the law served to protect the children of divorced parents against some of the hardships of divorce. Rolland's daughter had the aptitude and ability to go to college, and her father had the ability to pay for it. The court therefore ordered Rolland to pay these expenses.

ENDING A MARRIAGE

The breakup of a marriage is a very upsetting time for the man and woman whose marriage is ending as well as for any children they might have. While facing the emotional upheaval, couples must decide how to best care for the children and how to split up the property and money they have accumulated. The rights and responsibilities of people in this situation are determined by the laws of the state in which they live.

Marriages fail for different reasons. Sometimes one party refuses to honor the couple's wedding vows or walks out when the going gets tough. Sometimes people marry when they are very young and discover that they aren't ready for the responsibilities of marriage. Sometimes people marry the first person who comes along without getting to know the person. In some cases, couples simply "grow apart."

When a married couple aren't getting along and don't want to live together, they can agree to separate. With this arrangement, they stay married but live apart either temporarily or permanently. Other couples decide to end a marriage through a divorce, which is a court order that legally ends a valid marriage. In some situations, couples may have a third option—annulment.

Annulling a Marriage

An **annulment** is a declaration by the court that a marriage never existed. An annulment is different from a divorce because a divorce ends a valid marriage. With an annulment, the court declares the marriage void—it never happened in the eyes of the law.

In many cases, a person who seeks an annulment does so for moral or religious reasons. For example, Jill and Bob want to get married, but Bob was married before and has been divorced. The church Jill belongs to will not allow them to marry because it does not believe a person can end a marriage by divorce. Bob is still married in the eyes of this church, so he cannot marry someone else. However, if Bob's first marriage had been annulled, the church would allow him to marry Jill because the annulment would say that he had never been married in the first place.

When a Marriage Can Be Annulled   State law determines when a marriage can be annulled. The **grounds**, or the legal basis, for annulment vary from state to state. The grounds for annulment must have been present at the time of the marriage ceremony.

As you learned in Chapter 10, states require that a couple meet certain requirements for their marriage to be valid. These requirements include that the couple are a man and a woman who are both single, are not closely related, are old enough, and are mentally capable of understanding the responsibilities of marriage and intend to meet those responsibilities. An annulment may be granted if it can be shown that one or both parties did not meet one of these conditions.

Courts also issue annulments if one of the parties lies to the other before the wedding about something that would have caused the person being lied to to cancel the wedding. This is called fraud in inducing the marriage. However, the lie must be about something that is essential to the marriage relationship. Essential lies include telling a future spouse that you want to have children when you know that you don't intend to have them. Because having children is a basic part of married life, this action would be considered grounds for annulment.

Courts will examine the facts of each case to determine whether the lie was essential. For example, Linda and George Woy were married in 1980 and lived in Missouri. After several years, George filed for divorce. During testimony in the divorce case, Linda mentioned that she had engaged in lesbian activities before she married George. When George found out what Linda had said, he changed his request for a divorce and asked for an annulment. He claimed that he wouldn't have married Linda if he had known about this activity. George also stated that her premarital affairs affected an essential element of their marriage relationship—their sexual relationship. He admitted, though, that their sexual relationship had been satisfactory during the marriage. The court refused to annul the marriage. It said that chastity before the marriage was not vital to the marriage relationship. The court also stated that the fraud was not serious enough to warrant an annulment, especially since it had not affected the parties' sexual relations.

Consequences of Annulment   As you have seen, an annulment declares that the parties were never married. What happens to the children of parents whose marriage is annulled? As you read in Chapter 11, a parent has a duty to support his or her child whether the parents are married or single.

What happens to the couple? In some states, alimony cannot be given to people whose marriage is annulled. **Alimony** is money paid by one spouse to support the other spouse when the marriage ends. If there was no marriage, there is nothing on which to base an award of alimony. For the same reason, most states do not distribute property obtained during a marriage when the marriage is annulled. Therefore, courts look very carefully at requests for annulment. They want to be sure that a person such as George Woy, who was earning $500,000 a year, isn't seeking an annulment just to avoid paying alimony.

Illustration 12-1   Because an annulment is a declaration by the court that a marriage never existed, the laws of most states do not allow distribution of the couple's property when an annulment is granted.

Sometimes the rules about alimony and property settlement can cause serious financial hardship for one of the parties in an annulment. This is especially true when one of the people has been dependent on the other. For example, Betty, who is married to Joe, takes care of the house and their children. She doesn't have a job outside the home. If the court grants Joe an annulment in a state that doesn't allow alimony in such cases, Betty will be left with nothing. She will get no share of the house or of Joe's salary, pension, or insurance benefits. In part because of these consequences, annulments are usually granted only in rare cases.

Separation

When a couple are having problems in their marriage, they may decide to separate to give each person some breathing space. The couple stop living together but are still legally married. When a couple separate, they often have a written **separation agreement** drawn up. This agreement is a contract that spells out alimony payments to a spouse and child support and custody arrangements. It may also divide any property the couple acquired during the time they lived together. To be sure that each side's interests are protected, couples often have lawyers write or review these agreements. In some states, an agreement of this type may become part of a divorce decree if the couple aren't able to work out their problems.

Some couples seek a **judicial separation**, which is a court-ordered or court-approved decree. This type of judicial decree is also called a decree of separate maintenance, a divorce from bed and board, or a legal separation. A judicial decree lists the rights and responsibilities of the couple just as a separation agreement does. This agreement may also be converted to a divorce decree. Unlike a private separation agreement, however, a judicial decree may be obtained only when a couple have grounds. In some states, a spouse may have to show grounds, such as physical cruelty, that indicate wrongdoing by one spouse. In other states, the couple may only have to show that they have been living apart for a certain period of time.

Of course, a married couple can simply start living apart and not bother with a separation agreement or a judicial decree. However, if one spouse depends on the other for support, it is probably a good idea to have an agreement in writing. Otherwise, the dependent party may find herself or himself without any money, or the wage-earning spouse may find that he or she is responsible for the other party's debts even though they have been living apart.

Marriage Counseling   Couples who are separated or are having trouble may try marriage counseling in the hope that an unbiased, specially trained person can help them work out their problems. Sometimes the judge may suggest or even require a couple to undergo counseling before a divorce is granted. This is done because the law views marriage as a serious commitment that should not be dissolved without careful thought. Sometimes couples benefit from counseling and get back together. Other couples remain separated permanently because they no longer want to live together but don't believe in divorce. Many couples, however, divorce.

Even when counseling cannot save a marriage, it is often a good idea. The counselor may be able to help the couple feel less angry. Then they can have a "better" divorce. This is especially important if there are children. If parents are very angry when they get divorced, the divorce is much more difficult for their children.

Getting a Divorce

A **divorce** is a court order that legally ends a valid marriage. If a couple want to divorce, one of them must file a lawsuit with the court. If both husband and

Illustration 12-2   Sometimes a judge will suggest or even require a couple to go to a marriage counselor before granting a divorce.

wife agree on everything, including how they will divide their property and debts and how their children will be provided for, the court will grant them a judgment of divorce. The court will usually allow the terms to which the couple have agreed. If the couple do not agree on any of the financial or child care issues, they will have to go to trial. The judge will decide any issues that the couple cannot resolve.

If you want to get divorced, all states but one require that you be a resident of that state before the court will hear your divorce case. You become a resident by living in a state for a period of time. For purposes of divorce law, this is most commonly six months. Alaska does not require you to be a resident when you file for divorce, but you must intend to become a resident.

You must also establish that there are grounds for the court to grant you a divorce. Each state has laws that specify exactly what the grounds for divorce are in that state. Until recently no state would allow the courts to grant a divorce unless one spouse was at fault. That meant that one spouse had to prove that the other one had done something wrong. Examples of grounds for a divorce under a fault-based system are adultery, desertion, mental or physical cruelty, habitual drunkenness, and drug addiction. (Adultery is sexual intercourse between a married person and someone other than that person's spouse.)

Today all states have adopted the concept of **no-fault divorce**. This means that you do not have to prove fault in order to get a divorce. Many states allow you to get a divorce if one party says that the marriage is over and there is no hope of a reconciliation. Other states require that the parties live apart for a period of time, often a year, before they will allow them to divorce.

Some states still allow fault-based divorce as well as no-fault divorce. Even in states that have only no-fault divorce, courts may consider fault in deciding how to divide property or how much alimony to award.

Some years ago, when proof of fault was required for a divorce and when most states had much longer residency requirements, people who could afford it sometimes went to other states or even foreign countries to get a divorce. Today the "quickie" out-of-state divorce is less common because you can get a divorce in your own state relatively easily.

REVIEW QUESTIONS

1. What is the difference between an annulment and a divorce?
2. What are three situations in which a court may grant an annulment?
3. What is the difference between a private separation agreement and a judicial separation decree?
4. What is a no-fault divorce?

LIVINGSTON, NEWMAN & DE VITO
A PROFESSIONAL CORPORATION
300 BROAD STREET
P.O. BOX 1800
BLOOMFIELD, N.J. 07003
(201) 555-1200
ATTORNEYS FOR   Plaintiff

Plaintiff DAVID WALTER *vs.* *Defendant* CAROL WALTER	SUPERIOR COURT OF NEW JERSEY CHANCERY DIVISION MORRIS COUNTY *Docket No.* FM– *C92 – 8443* *CIVIL ACTION* COMPLAINT FOR DIVORCE

The plaintiff, David Walter, residing at 25 Marigold Court, Florham Park, County of Morris and State of New Jersey, by way of Complaint against the defendant says:

1. He was lawfully married to Carol Sutton Walter, the defendant on August 17, 1968, in Jersey City, New Jersey in a religious ceremony.

2. He was a bona fide resident of the State of New Jersey when this cause of action arose, and has ever since and for more than one year next preceding the commencement of this action, continued to be such bona fide resident. ...

Illustration 12-3   If a couple want to divorce, one of them must file a lawsuit with the court.

FINANCIAL EFFECTS OF DIVORCE

When a couple split up, there are many financial considerations. They must divide their property, including houses, cars, furniture, and savings accounts. If there are debts, they must decide what to do about them. In addition, there are often support issues to be resolved. The money that supported one household now has to support two. The same amount of money that paid for one house and one car cannot pay for two houses and two cars. For most people, divorce has very real and often very difficult financial consequences.

State law provides guidance on issues such as how the property should be divided and whether one spouse should get support payments. It is difficult, though, to set hard and fast rules because every case is different. What is fair in one case may not be fair in the next. Courts look at the contributions of both spouses to the marriage. Whether both worked outside the home or whether one spouse stayed home to care for the children and house, both spouses made contributions. Often it is the judge who must decide what is fair.

Property Division

State law determines how the property should be divided in a divorce. Some states require the court to divide all the property a couple have regardless of who acquired it or when it was acquired. Most states, however, make a distinction between marital property and separate property in deciding the property settlement of a divorce. Marital property is property that is acquired during the marriage. Separate property is property each party owned before the marriage (unless one spouse makes a gift of the property to the other spouse). Other items that are usually considered separate property include gifts and inheritances received by only one spouse during the marriage.

Sometimes it isn't easy to determine what constitutes property, let alone decide how to divide it fairly. In some cases, courts may be asked to consider things that wouldn't normally be thought of as property. These items include future pensions, professional licenses, academic degrees, and career advancement potential. Courts don't always agree on these issues. For instance, when Terry and Gary Lewis divorced in 1987 after 21 years of marriage, Gary had acquired three academic degrees, including a master's degree in business administration (MBA). A Michigan court awarded Terry one half the value of the MBA as part of the divorce settlement. Terry had helped her husband obtain the degree by taking care of the house and children so he could study. She did this because she believed the family would be more secure financially if her husband had an MBA. The court said that since she had helped acquire this common goal, she should share in the rewards. In this case, the value of the degree was calculated by determining the difference between what Gary would make with the degree and what he would make without it.

A New Jersey court reached a different conclusion in the divorce of the Mahoneys. During the nine years Melvin and June Lee Mahoney were married, Melvin also earned an MBA. While he was in school, June Lee supported them. In 1982 the New Jersey court said that the advanced degree was not property. Instead, the court viewed it as nothing more than the possibility of earning more money. Therefore, it declined to award June Lee a share of any value the degree might have. However, the court said that Melvin had to pay June Lee back for the financial contributions she had made toward his education. In similar situations, other courts have decided that the help a partner gives toward advancing the career of the other spouse has no value at all as part of a property settlement.

Systems of Property Division   Once either the couple or the courts have determined what property is to be divided, they must decide what part of the property belongs to each person. There are two main methods of determining property division, depending on the state. Most states follow an **equitable distribution system**. Some states with this system require the court to divide the marital property equally (50-50) unless there are reasons why this would be unfair. However, equitable doesn't always mean equal. The judge can take into account many factors in deciding how to divide the property fairly. These factors usually include the length of the marriage; the contribution of each party toward the acquisition of the property; the age, health, and needs of each party; and the reason why the marriage is breaking up. Sometimes the judge may even award one party's separate property to the other party if this is required for a just result.

In states that have a **community property system**, the goal—fair distribution of property—is the same as in states with equitable distribution. The basic difference is in the concept of ownership of property. Eight states have a community property system: Arizona, California, Idaho, Louisiana, Nevada, New Mexico, Texas, and Washington. Under the community property system, property acquired by either spouse as a result of that spouse's efforts during the marriage belongs to both spouses equally. For example, if Melinda works outside the home and Dennis stays home to take care of the children and the house, everything they buy with the money Melinda earns belongs to both of them equally. This is true from the moment they get married. If they divorce, this joint, or community, property is split, usually more or less equally.

In a noncommunity property state that has equitable distribution, Melinda may buy a car with the money she earns and put the title in her name. This means Melinda is the legal owner of the car, and during the marriage she will have the right to control the use of the car. However, if they get divorced, Dennis will probably be entitled to a share of the value of the car because it will be considered marital property regardless of who the technical owner is.

When a couple who live in a community property state divorce, each spouse already owns half the community, or marital, property. In theory, the judge just has to decide who gets what. As in the other states, each spouse gets to keep his or her separate property. However, the judge has the freedom to deviate from a 50-50 split of joint property if this is necessary to reach a fair result. Thus the result in a community property state may not be all that different from the result in a noncommunity property state with equitable distribution.

Judges have to look at many factors in reaching a just property division. For example, the Carrikers, who divorced in the 1980s, lived in Arizona, a community property state. Both the husband, Frederick, and the wife, Kathleen,

Illustration 12-4   In a divorce, courts interpret state law in order to divide the couple's property fairly.

were doctors. Frederick was 17 years older than Kathleen and had some health problems, but the court still divided their property 50-50 as required by state law.

William and Diane Hentges also lived in a community property state, Idaho. State law required substantially equal division of marital property unless there were compelling reasons not to divide it equally. When the Hentgeses divorced in 1984 after 19 years of marriage, the court awarded 70 percent of the community property to William. He was paralyzed from the neck down because of a work-related accident that occurred several years before the divorce. He required constant assistance, had no reasonable hope of employment, and might have even greater needs in the future. Diane was in good health and could work to support herself.

William and Joan Brooks, who lived in South Carolina, an equitable distribution state, divorced in 1984 after 24 years of marriage. Joan was in good health and earned more than William, who was in poor health and was scheduled to retire soon. Joan got 35 percent of the property and was allowed to keep as her separate property the money she had inherited from her father.

Diane and Alan Weiss also lived in an equitable distribution state, New Jersey. They separated in 1985 after 18 years of marriage and later divorced. Their biggest asset was their house. They had made a joint decision to buy the house for their marital residence, but Alan had purchased the house with his money four months before they got married. The deed was in his name. Both Alan and Diane made improvements to the house before and after they were married, and they lived in it during the entire marriage. The court said that the house was a marital asset under the circumstances and ordered that the value of the house be split 50-50.

As you can see from these cases, each situation is different and requires the court's interpretation of state law to reach a fair settlement. As a general rule, once a judgment of divorce is final, the property settlement cannot be modified or changed.

Alimony

Alimony is money paid by one former spouse to support the other. As you read earlier in this chapter, it may also be paid by a spouse when a couple separate. Alimony is also called spousal support or maintenance because it is money paid by the spouse who has money to the spouse who is not working or does not earn enough to support himself or herself. It is usually paid periodically and is used for housing, food, clothing, and other living expenses.

In the past, only the husband had to pay alimony. That is no longer true. In 1979 the U.S. Supreme Court held that a state cannot require only husbands to pay alimony.

Unlike a property settlement, alimony may be changed or stopped under certain conditions.

Illustration 12-5 In 1979 the U.S. Supreme Court held that a state cannot require only husbands to pay alimony.

■　*Death.* If the spouse receiving alimony dies, alimony stops. However, if either spouse dies before the property has been divided as ordered in the divorce judgment, the property still gets divided, although the deceased spouse's share goes to his or her estate.

- *Remarriage.* Often alimony stops if the spouse receiving the payments remarries. However, if either spouse remarries before all the property has been divided, the property still gets divided as ordered.
- *Bankruptcy.* If the person paying alimony declares bankruptcy, that person still has to make the support payments. However, he or she may get out of the property settlement debt in some cases.
- *Change of circumstances.* If circumstances change in a significant way after a divorce, the amount of alimony can be modified or changed. For example, if the court has awarded the former wife $500 a month of alimony and she loses her job after the divorce, the amount may be increased. The court will look at why she lost her job, her chances of getting a new job, and the former husband's ability to pay more. If the ex-husband loses his job, the amount of alimony may be decreased, depending on why he lost his job, the needs of the former wife, and how likely he is to find another job.

The court has a great deal of freedom in deciding whether to grant alimony, and if so, how much. Most courts consider a number of factors, including the ability of the wage-earning spouse to pay, the ability of the non-wage-earning spouse to earn money, the length of the marriage, the age and health of the parties, each party's needs, the reason for the divorce, the conduct of the parties (in some states), and any other factors the court thinks should be taken into account.

Courts sometimes look at alimony and property settlement as a package deal. The spouse needing support may get more than a "fair share" of property instead of alimony, for example. Some courts think it's better to make a final financial break rather than keep one spouse dependent on the other after the divorce.

It used to be that a wife who had been married a long time and had stayed home might get alimony for the rest of her life. This was true particularly if the husband was the one who wanted the divorce. Today the trend is toward **rehabilitative alimony**. This is alimony that is paid for a short period to give a spouse a chance to enter (or perhaps reenter) the work force and become self-supporting. For example, Tim and Elizabeth Addis lived in Arkansas. Married in 1966, the couple divorced some 20 years later. Tim was a veterinarian. Elizabeth, who had no job skills, was unemployed. The court awarded Elizabeth about 25 percent of her husband's salary for five years to allow her to receive training and enter the job market.

Palimony   Traditionally, when an unmarried couple who lived together, even for a long time, split up, they each took their own things and started over. This situation still occurs and can sometimes have harsh consequences. Suppose Susan gives up her career to stay home and take care of the house she shares with John. Should he get to keep everything they have acquired through their joint efforts when they split up after many years just because everything is held in his name? In many states, the answer is yes. The courts are reluctant to step in and protect the non–wage earner in these situations because of the strong preference of society that couples who are living together be married.

However, in one famous case in California, the court said that a person who lives with someone in a nonmarital relationship may acquire financial rights in some circumstances. These financial rights include a share in property acquired during the relationship and, possibly, support payments. Payments made by one member of an unmarried couple to the other are called **palimony**.

A singer named Michelle Triola and an actor named Lee Marvin lived together for seven years during the 1960s. Michelle claimed that they had agreed verbally to share whatever they accumulated as a result of their joint efforts. She said that she gave up her career as a singer and became a companion and homemaker for Lee and that he agreed to support her for the rest of her life. During the time they lived together, they acquired over a million dollars' worth of property, all of which was held in Lee's name.

When Lee broke off the relationship, Michelle sued to enforce the oral contract she claimed they had made. She asked the court to give her half the property they had acquired during the time they lived together and to order support payments. In 1976 the court said that divorce laws governing division of property and awards of support did not apply because Lee and Michelle had never been married. However, it held that a contract between an unmarried couple regarding their financial affairs is enforceable. This type of contract is called a **cohabitation agreement**. Even if there was no contract, the court could divide their property if fairness required it to do so.

However, courts have been reluctant to apply this principle unless there is clear evidence of a contract or unless it is very clear from the facts that it would be grossly unfair not to divide the assets. For example, in the Marvin palimony case, which established the principle, the court refused to give Michelle a share of the property. She was granted $104,000 to help her learn a job skill but lost that amount when Lee Marvin appealed. The court found that the parties did not have a contract as Michelle had claimed and that Lee had not agreed to support her for the rest of her life. In addition, the court said that Michelle had benefited both economically and socially from their relationship and that there were no equitable, or fair, reasons to order Lee to support her or give her some of the property.

Since the Marvin case, a number of courts have considered the rights of unmarried people who live together. In some of these cases, the courts have divided property. For example, in a Florida case, Douglas Evans and Kathie Wall lived together for five years. During that time, Kathie contributed her salary to household expenses and contributed household services (cooking, washing, and cleaning). She also worked in Douglas's mango grove and helped him build a new house. When he ordered her out in 1987 because he had met someone else, she sued him for the value of what she had contributed to his land. The court awarded her some money to repay her for her contributions.

Illustration 12-6 In general, a noncustodial parent must pay child support until each child reaches the age of majority.

Child Support

Parents have a legal duty to support their children. As you read in Chapter 11, this duty exists even if the parents never marry. By the same token, a parent's obligation to support his or her children does not stop if the parents divorce. In almost every case, the judge who grants a divorce will order a parent who does not live with the children (the noncustodial parent) to contribute financially to the support of his or her minor children. **Child support** is money paid by the noncustodial parent to the parent with whom the children live (the custodial parent) for the benefit of the minor children.

How long a parent must pay child support depends on state law. In general, a noncustodial parent must pay child support for all of his or her children until each child reaches the age of majority (18 in most states). However, many 18-year-olds are not financially independent. Many states recognize this, although in different ways.

In New York, for example, a noncustodial parent is obligated to pay child support until the child is 21 years old, even though the age of majority in New York is 18. Other states require support until the child graduates from high school or attains age 19 (or 19½), whichever comes later. In some states, child support can continue indefinitely if the child is either physically or mentally disabled. As you read in the opening case, a few states allow the court to order a divorced parent to pay college expenses for a child beyond the age of majority.

The amount of support a noncustodial parent had to pay used to be set by the court. Amounts of support varied enormously depending on the state or city and even on the judge deciding the case. In some cases, the amounts were extremely low. The federal government has stepped in to try to make payments more even and to ensure that the children of divorced parents are provided for adequately.

The Child Support Enforcement Act (amended by the Family Support Act of 1988) requires each state to establish child support guidelines for the courts of that state to follow. If the courts don't follow these guidelines, they have to state in writing why an amount listed in the guidelines would be unfair in a certain situation. Therefore, a judge still has some freedom in setting support in a particular case, but much less than before the use of guidelines.

In establishing child support guidelines, most states take into account the parents' income and the family size. Some states base support on a percentage of the income of the noncustodial parent. This percentage varies according to the number of children. Other states have a chart that bases the amount of support on how much money each parent makes and on the number of children. Other states require each parent to contribute a percentage of their combined incomes. Each state is supposed to review its guidelines every four years to make sure that the amounts called for are still appropriate. As with alimony, child support can be modified if there is a significant change in circumstances, such as a change in the custodial parent's income.

Traditionally, noncustodial parents were supposed to pay child support on a regular basis (usually once a month). If a parent didn't pay voluntarily, it could be very difficult to collect the money. In 1988 less than half of all custodial parents received part or all of their child support. For many children, this has meant a drastically reduced standard of living after their parents' divorce. As a practical matter, it also means that many custodial parents bear an unfair share of the financial responsibility of raising their children.

The Child Support Enforcement Act also makes the following provisions for collecting unpaid child support and for tracking down missing parents who owe child support money.

- Beginning in 1994, all states must have set up systems that provide for employers to withhold child support money from the paychecks of people who owe support. The employers will send the money directly to the state agency responsible for collecting and distributing child support. This rule will, for the most part, apply to new orders for child support. For certain kinds of cases, income withholding began in 1991.
- Overdue child support can be withheld from a parent's state and federal tax refunds.
- States are required to set up procedures for imposing liens, or legal claims, against the property of a parent for the amount of past-due support.
- The Parent Locator Service has been set up to help find absent parents who refuse to support their children. Certain agencies are permitted to track down an absent parent by using that parent's social security number.

In addition, it is much easier for states to collect support from an out-of-state parent because of the Revised Uniform Reciprocal Enforcement of Support Act. Most states have adopted this act. It allows states to enforce each other's support orders. When a person paying child support moves to another state, the court in the home state can register the support order in the new state. The new state can then collect child support and forward it to the home state for payment to the former spouse. States also have laws that allow for civil and criminal actions to help enforce child support.

REVIEW QUESTIONS

1. What factors do divorce courts look at when deciding how to divide property fairly?
2. What are three differences between a property settlement and alimony?
3. What is palimony?
4. Name two ways in which the Child Support Enforcement Act provides for the collection of unpaid child support.

CHILD CUSTODY

When parents split up, a major consideration is which parent the children will live with. The traditional arrangement is for the children to live with one parent, who has sole custody, and for the noncustodial parent to have visitation rights.

However, the trend now is to award joint custody. The parents can have joint legal custody, joint physical custody, or both. **Joint legal custody** means that both parents have equal rights and responsibilities regarding their children. It means they share decision making about the children, such as where they will go to school, what extracurricular activities they will participate in, and what health care they will receive.

If the parents also have **joint physical custody**, the children live with each parent about half the time. Another possibility is for the parents to have joint legal custody but for the children to have their principal home with just one parent. For example, if Meredith's parents live in different towns, an arrangement for joint physical custody would probably not work. If she attended school in her father's town, transportation would be a problem when she was living with her mother. It would be hard for Meredith to see her friends from school when she was living with her mother. In this case, joint physical custody would not work very well, but it might be possible for the parents to share legal custody.

Yet another possibility when there are at least two children is split custody. This means that each parent has custody of at least one child.

More than half the states have statutes allowing the courts to order joint custody. Some of these statutes favor joint custody; others offer it as an option without stating a preference. Joint custody is supposed to encourage both parents to stay involved with their children after a divorce. Sometimes it works. However, some courts are reluctant to order joint custody. They feel that parents who could not cooperate enough to stay married probably won't be able to cooperate once they are divorced.

How Courts Decide Custody

If the parents agree on who should have custody, the court will usually go along with their decision. If the parents don't agree, the court must make the decision for them. Generally, courts use a standard called "the best interests of the child" in making custody decisions. This means that the court is supposed to base the decision on what is best for the child, not on the parents' desires.

Most states tell the courts what factors they should consider in determining the child's best interests. These factors typically include the ability of each parent to be a good parent, the strength of the existing ties between each parent and the child, and the willingness of each parent to help the child have a continuing relationship with the other parent. The child's own preference can be weighed heavily by the court, especially when the child is older.

As with child support and alimony, custody orders can be modified if there has been a significant change in circumstances and if the change is in the best interests of the child.

The noncustodial parent is granted visitation rights. Sometimes the court will simply give the noncustodial parent "reasonable rights of visitation," and the parents can work out the details. If the parents cannot cooperate, the court may grant specific visitation rights. For example, the noncustodial parent may see the child every other weekend from Friday after school until Sunday at 6 p.m., every other holiday, and for an extended period in the summer.

Some states have laws that allow people other than parents to have visitation rights in certain circumstances. Most common is a law that gives grandparents the right to see their grandchildren if the parents divorce. The failure of a parent to comply with a court order for visitation may result in court action to enforce the visitation rights.

Problems with Enforcing Custody Orders

Illustration 12-7 In recent years, many laws have been passed to try to stop parents from kidnapping their children.

Sometimes when parents lose a child custody battle, they decide to take the law into their own hands. A parent who was not awarded custody may kidnap the child and move to another state, hoping to get a favorable custody order in the new state. To prevent this from happening, all states have enacted the Uniform Child Custody Jurisdiction Act. This law indicates when a new state can hear a custody dispute and when the new state must recognize the order of the home state. It also specifies when a court can modify the custody order of another state.

The Parental Kidnapping Prevention Act, which was passed by Congress in 1980, is another attempt to stop parental kidnapping. The law requires states to give full faith and credit to the custody orders of other states, provided that certain conditions are met. This is important because custody orders are not final orders—that is, they can be modified—and the full faith and credit laws apply only to final orders.

In addition, Congress has permitted authorized state agencies to use the Parent Locator Service to find an absent parent or child when a custody order has been violated or when a child has been kidnapped by the noncustodial parent. Finally, Congress has said that people who kidnap their children may be subject to the same fines and jail terms given to people found guilty of fleeing prosecution.

State statutes also address this problem. For example, it is a crime in many states for a noncustodial parent to keep a child if doing so violates a custody order.

The International Child Abduction Remedies Act offers help to citizens whose children are kidnapped to a foreign country. This law also helps secure visitation rights for parents whose minor children are abroad. To date, 14 nations have accepted this law. However, parental kidnapping can be a difficult problem, especially if the children are taken out of the country.

REVIEW QUESTIONS

1. How might joint legal custody differ from joint physical custody?
2. Name three factors courts consider when awarding custody of children in a divorce.
3. Name two steps Congress has taken to help states prevent parental kidnapping.

Viewpoints on Joint Physical Custody

Ethan's parents are getting a divorce. They have told him that they are considering asking the court for joint physical custody. If they make this arrangement, Ethan will live part of each week with each parent. Ethan wonders how this will change his life. He likes the idea of living with each of his parents. He has concerns, though. Which house will be his real home? Will he have to pack and unpack his belongings as he moves from place to place? Where will he keep his stereo and his computer? If his parents can't agree on Ethan's care, will he be caught in the middle of their battles?

The Case for Joint Physical Custody

Supporters of joint physical custody point out that this arrangement lets the children of divorced parents have sustained, frequent contact with both parents. Some supporters believe that this arrangement forces the parents to cooperate. Thus, they avoid postdivorce court disputes, which can be especially disturbing for children. In a recent California study of custody cases, only 16 percent of parents with joint physical custody came back to court because of a dispute. In contrast, 32 percent of sole custody parents returned for further court battles.

Children aren't the only ones who benefit from joint physical custody, say its supporters. When one parent has sole custody, all the day-to-day care of the children falls to that parent. At the same time, the other parent is almost totally left out of his or her child's daily life and growth. With joint physical custody, both parents can stay involved in their children's lives.

However, because they are sharing custody, both parents have built-in free time when the other parent has the children. As a result, both may be able to devote more time to their careers and may find it easier to start dating again. They can do these things without feeling guilty that their children are alone or with baby-sitters too often.

The Case against Joint Physical Custody

Many people feel that joint physical custody is bad for everyone involved. They argue that divorce is enough of a disruption for children without adding to it the confusion about where they will be this week or month and which parent's rules they must obey. Some people worry that these children will feel there is no place they can call home. Others are concerned that if the parents can't get along as they try to make joint child care decisions, they will end up making their children pawns in their continuing fights. After all, critics say, the parents got divorced because they couldn't get along well.

Parents also lose out in joint physical custody awards, some claim. With joint physical custody, both parents must maintain larger homes, and this can be costly. When one parent's salary is much higher than the other's, the parent with the lower income spends a larger proportion of money for the child's expenses. Parents who are sharing custody often experience the constant stress of dealing almost daily with an ex-spouse. In addition, joint physical custody restricts a parent's ability to move, which may affect both the individual's social life and his or her career.

The Courts and Legislatures

More than half the states have passed joint custody statutes. These laws try to address the needs of divorcing parents who both have careers and who both want to be involved on a daily basis with their children's upbringing. In some states, these statutes offer joint custody as an option to the courts but state no preference for or against it. Other states' statutes have a preference only when both parents want joint custody. Still other states have a preference for joint custody generally. In states without joint custody statutes, the courts may use general custody statutes or their own discretion to choose joint custody. Most legislatures and judges agree on one point: Joint custody works best when the parents are able to negotiate differences and agree on solutions that benefit everyone involved.

Chapter Review

Chapter Summary

- Marriages can end through annulment or divorce. When an annulment is granted, the court declares that the marriage never existed.

- Couples who aren't getting along may separate either temporarily or permanently. They live apart but remain married. Some couples have a written separation agreement. Some get a judicial separation ordered or approved by a court.

- Divorce legally ends a valid marriage. People who seek a divorce must meet the grounds for divorce that are set by their state.

- No-fault divorces are available in all states. People who are divorcing no longer have to prove wrongdoing by one spouse.

- The financial aspects of divorce involve the division of marital property and the payment of support to one spouse by the other spouse.

- Most states distinguish between property acquired during the marriage and property each spouse owned before the marriage.

- In community property states, marital property is automatically owned by both spouses equally. In equitable distribution states, spouses can own property they acquired during the marriage individually. This may affect property distribution at a divorce, although all states try to be fair.

- Alimony is money paid to a spouse who is not working or who can't earn enough to support himself or herself.

■ Unmarried couples who live together may acquire financial rights to joint property in some circumstances.

■ After a divorce, parents must still support their children. The parent who does not live with the children is almost always ordered to pay child support.

■ Both state and federal laws have been enacted to ensure that parents pay child support.

■ The children of a divorced couple may be in the sole custody of one parent, or the parents may have joint custody. Another option is split custody, with each parent having custody of at least one child.

■ The parent who doesn't have custody has visitation rights.

■ Federal and state laws protect against the kidnapping of children by a divorced parent.

Understanding Legal Terms

On a separate sheet of paper, match the terms below with the definitions that follow.

alimony	joint physical custody
annulment	judicial separation
child support	no-fault divorce
grounds	palimony
joint legal custody	separation agreement

1. Money paid by one spouse to support the other spouse when the marriage ends
2. A court-ordered or court-approved decree listing the rights and responsibilities of a married couple who have separated
3. Money paid by one member of an unmarried couple to the other when they split up
4. A declaration by the court that a marriage never existed
5. A divorce in which neither party has to prove wrongdoing
6. A written agreement, drawn up by a married couple or their lawyers when the couple decide to stop living together, that spells out alimony and child support payments
7. Situation that occurs after a divorce in which both parents have equal rights and responsibilities toward their children
8. The legal basis for an annulment or a divorce
9. Money for the care of the minor children, paid by the noncustodial parent to the custodial parent
10. Situation that occurs after divorce in which the children live with each parent about half the time

Applying the Law

1. When Judith and James got married, Judith told James that her first husband was dead. James later found out that Judith's first husband was not dead at all. Instead, Judith was divorced from him. She told James that her first husband died because James was a practicing Roman Catholic and would not have married her if he had known she was divorced. Can James get an annulment of this marriage? Give reasons for your answer.

2. When Justin and Lara get married, Justin is working as an electrician. Lara is a secretary, but she wants to go to law school. Justin says he will support her and pay her law school expenses, which he does. After they have been married 10 years, Justin is still an electrician earning $30,000 a year. Lara is a lawyer and earns $60,000 a year. They get divorced. Will Justin receive any compensation for putting Lara through law school? Explain your answer.

3. Barbara and Dale Sullivan divorced after 29 years of marriage and four children. The court included in the marital property some farmland that Barbara's father had given Barbara and her brother. Dale never had anything to do with the operation of this farmland during the marriage. Barbara thought that this land should not have been considered marital property. She appealed the court's decision. Did Barbara win her appeal? Explain your answer.

4. Loretta and Dwight Heim were married for 35 years. Loretta stayed home and raised the couple's six children. She had no professional skills and had never earned more than $600 a month. During the marriage, Dwight earned a Ph.D. and pursued his career. At the time of their divorce, he was earning $5,600 a month and had living expenses of $2,000 a month. The trial court awarded Loretta $500 of alimony a month. Was this result fair? Give reasons for your answer.

5. Mr. Smith pays child support for his son, Greg. They live in a state where the age of majority is 18, but Greg will not graduate from high school until he is almost 19. Must Mr. Smith pay child support for Greg after Greg turns 18 but is still in high school? Explain your answer.

Case Studies

1. Anthony and Josephine Stegienko were married on October 29, 1938. Two days later, Anthony filed for annulment, claiming fraud. Anthony told the court that before the marriage Josephine had said that she wanted to have children. Anthony was delighted because he wanted a family very much. After the marriage, however, Josephine refused to have sexual intercourse without the use of contraceptives. She said she did not want to have children. Anthony couldn't agree to this because of his desire to have children. He filed for annulment. Josephine filed for divorce on the grounds of extreme cruelty. When the case came to court, who won? Explain your answer.

2. David and Carolyn Morrison were married for 35 years. They lived in Texas, a community property state. The marriage broke up because of

David's adultery and alcoholism. During the time they were married, David spent substantial amounts of marital funds on other women. He took the women on expensive trips, gave them money, and bought them expensive gifts. The divorce court awarded Carolyn 83.5 percent of the community property. Was this a fair division of property? Give reasons for your answer.

3. Maureen Sullivan and James Rooney had a relationship that lasted about 14 years, including the 7 years they lived together. Maureen gave up her job as a flight attendant to keep house for James. When they bought a house, they considered it a joint purchase. Maureen put all her earnings and savings into the house, paid for food and household supplies, and did all the housework. James paid the mortgage, taxes, utilities, and insurance on the house. However, the deed to the house was in James's name alone. He said that this was done because he could get better financing. He promised to put the property in both their names several times but never did. After they separated, Maureen sued James to obtain joint title to the house. Would Maureen win her suit? Why or why not?

Chapter 13

Preparing for Death

Chapter Objectives

When you have read this chapter, you should be able to:

- Explain what happens to your property when you die.

- Describe the requirements for making and changing a will.

- Explain what it means to have the right to die.

- Define *euthanasia*, and explain how it is different from refusing medical treatment.

- Explain the differences between a living will and a durable power of attorney.

263

Case Study

In re Estate of Ervin, 399 N.W.2d 200 (Minnesota 1987).

Valley Ervin died in Minnesota in 1984. He had no wife. He had a son named Virgil Israelson, but Ervin had abandoned him when the boy was 5 years old and never saw or spoke to him again.

When Ervin died, he had property worth $60,000. In his will, he stated that his two nieces, Donna Mae Och and Mary Miller, should share that property. He did not mention Israelson in the will.

Israelson took the matter to court. Minnesota law (and the law of nearly every state) protects children from being accidentally omitted from a parent's will. Any child left out of a parent's will has the right to take a share of the parent's property unless the will clearly states that the child was left out intentionally. The child is entitled to the same share that he or she would have received if the parent had left no will at all.

The court found no clear evidence that Ervin had intended to omit his son from the will. It therefore set aside the will and gave Israelson what he would have been entitled to if there had been no will. In this case, Israelson was entitled to all the property. Och and Miller received nothing.

DYING WITHOUT A WILL

Over the course of your life you will accumulate many things. You may have money in the bank. You may have personal property with material or sentimental value. You may have a home or a car. Together, all the money and property you own is called your **estate**. When you die, the people who take or share your estate are called **heirs**. The money or property they receive is their **inheritance**.

If you've written a will, that document will tell others what to do with your estate after your death. Although everyone should have a will, many people die without having written one. Dying without a will is called dying **intestate**. When people die intestate, the state government is responsible for distributing their property.

Each state's laws of **intestate succession** provide very specific instructions about how property should be divided. Like marriage laws, laws of intestate succession (and laws of wills) vary considerably from state to state.

Laws of Intestate Succession

The laws of intestate succession give your property to your closest relatives without taking into consideration how much you like or dislike those individuals.

In most states, if you are married and have no children, all of your estate goes to your spouse when you die. In other states, your estate may be divided between your spouse and other close relatives, such as your parents.

Illustration 13-1   Under the laws of intestate succession, if you are married and have no children when you die, most states will give all of your estate to your spouse.

If you have biological or adopted children, your spouse generally gets one third (in some states, one half) of your estate and the children get equal shares of what remains. If your children have died but have left children of their own, their children share what your children would have inherited.

If you have no spouse or **direct descendants** (children or grandchildren), your parents inherit your estate. In some states, they must share the estate with your brothers or sisters if you have any.

Some people die without leaving behind any close relatives. In that case, some states permit more distant relatives to inherit. Under the laws of those states, a person you never met could be heir to your entire estate. Other states don't permit anyone more distantly related than a grandparent, aunt, uncle, or first cousin to take a share of an estate.

If no relatives can be found who are qualified to inherit under state law, the estate goes to the state government.

Administering an Estate

In every state, certain courts have jurisdiction over matters involving the property of those who die. These courts are called **probate courts**. When someone dies intestate, the probate court's first task is to appoint an estate administrator.

The job of the **administrator** (sometimes called the administratrix if she is female) is to settle all matters having to do with the estate of the deceased person. The administrator has several duties:

1. To make an inventory of the estate and determine its value
2. To collect any money or property that others owed the deceased person
3. To withdraw money from the estate to pay any bills or taxes the deceased person owed

Although any adult can serve as an administrator, probate courts most often appoint a spouse or other close relative.

REVIEW QUESTIONS

1. What does it mean to die intestate?
2. In most states, who is most likely to inherit the estate of an adult who dies without a will?
3. What are direct descendants? What happens to your property if you have no direct descendants?
4. What is the role of a probate court?

WILLS

As you have seen, without a will, you have no control over what happens to your estate. State law determines who gets what and in what amounts. That is why it is so important to make a will, no matter how little property you have. By making a will, you can decide who will inherit your money and property when you die. When you leave a will, your heirs—the people (or organizations) to whom you leave your money and property—are called your **beneficiaries**.

The Purpose of a Will

A person who writes a will is called a **testator**. (A female testator is sometimes called a testatrix.) If you write a will, you, as the testator, can do three very important things. First, as you have seen, you can dictate how your property will be distributed when you die.

Second, if you have a child, you can appoint someone to become the child's legal guardian. That person will be responsible for raising the child if you and the child's other parent both die. If both parents die without naming a guardian in their wills, the probate court must decide who will raise the child.

Third, you can appoint someone to take charge of your estate after your death. The person you appoint is called the **executor**. (A female executor is sometimes called a executrix.) The executor's duties are similar to those of an administrator—that is, keeping records, paying bills and taxes, and collecting whatever is owed. In addition, the executor is required to distribute your property according to the instructions in your will. The executor carries out these duties under the supervision of a probate court judge.

Choosing Beneficiaries

You can make your will as detailed or as simple as you want. You can leave all your property to one person, or you can dictate how several people should divide the property. You can leave specific items to specific people. You can make gifts to charities or corporations. You can also place conditions on the gifts as long as the conditions are not illegal or against public policy. For example, you can say, "I leave my car to my son provided that he give his car to my daughter." You cannot say, "I leave $1,000 to my brother provided that he kill his wife."

I, THOMAS MULHOLLAND, do hereby make, publish and declare this to be my Last Will and Testament and do revoke any and all other Wills and Codicils heretofore made by me.

ARTICLE 1

1.1   I direct payment of my debts, funeral expenses and expenses for administration of my estate.

ARTICLE 2

2.1   I give the rest of my estate to my wife, CYNTHIA SHELMIRE MULHOLLAND. If she predeceases me, I give the rest to my children, equally, share and share alike.

2.2   If any beneficiary shall fail to survive me by 45 days, it shall be deemed that such person shall have predeceased me.

2.3   If neither my wife nor issue survive me, I direct that the rest be divided into 4 equal parts. I give one part to my wife's parents, or the survivor; one part to my father; one part to my wife's brother, STEPHEN; and one part to my sister, MARION.

ARTICLE 3

3.1   I appoint my wife Executrix of this Will. If she predeceases me, I appoint my friends (a) MERCEDES COLLINS and her husband, LOUIS, to said office, and (b) as guardian of the person of each of my children. I direct that no appointee hereunder shall be required to give bond for the faithful performance of the duties of said office.

3.2   As often as the executor shall deem such action to be advantageous to any beneficiary, the executor may, by written notice resign and appoint as substitute executor, with respect to all or part of the corpus any person or bank, within or outside the State of New Jersey. The substitute executor shall have all of the title, powers and discretion of the original executor, who shall act as adviser to the substitute executor. The adviser may resume the office or may continue to act as adviser and appoint another substitute executor. ...

Illustration 13-2   Wills can be as short and simple as one page, or they can be very detailed and complicated.

Most states have established certain other limitations on how people's estates may be distributed. For example, if you are murdered, the murderer cannot inherit any portion of your estate. (This is true even if the murderer is named in your will or if you die without a will.) There are special rules designed to protect spouses and children as well.

Spouses   Most states will not allow you to exclude your spouse from getting a fair share of your estate. If you die and leave little or nothing to your spouse in your will, your spouse may demand his or her **elective share**.

Taking an elective share, or **taking against the will**, means asking the probate court to ignore the will and give the surviving spouse his or her rightful share of the estate. (Depending on the state, a spouse's rightful share is usually one third or one half.) Once the spouse has received his or her elective share, the court distributes the remainder of the estate in accordance with the will's instructions.

For example, suppose Teresa's will says that her property should be divided equally among her three sisters, but it does not mention her husband, Safwan. When Teresa dies, she leaves $12,000 worth of property. Safwan demands his elective share—which, in his state, is half the estate. The probate court therefore gives Safwan $6,000 and divides the remaining $6,000 among the three sisters. Each sister gets $2,000. If Safwan hadn't demanded his elective share, each sister would have received $4,000.

Sometimes married couples agree to waive their rights to an elective share. (This arrangement may be written into a prenuptial agreement or a contract made during the marriage.) Such agreements are especially common when each member of the couple wants to leave his or her estate to children from a previous marriage.

Only legally married spouses have the right to an elective share. Unmarried couples who live together do not have this right.

Children   Unlike spouses, children are not guaranteed a share of their parents' estates. A parent can choose to omit a child from the will, or **disinherit** the child. Some parents make their desire to disinherit a child very clear. They may state in the will that they choose to leave nothing to a particular child, or they may leave the child a very small amount (such as a dollar).

In some cases, however, parents leave children out of a will by mistake. Some parents write a will before their children are born and then forget to change the will afterward. Other parents may be unaware—or may have forgotten—that a particular child exists. (An example is the case of Valley Ervin, which you read about at the beginning of this chapter.)

Nearly every state has laws that protect children from being accidentally left out of their parents' wills. These laws are called **pretermitted heir** statutes. If a child isn't mentioned in a parent's will, these laws allow a probate court to decide whether the omission was intentional or accidental. If the court decides that the omission was accidental, the child is given a share of the parent's estate—the same share that he or she would have received if there had been no will.

To avoid accidentally leaving a child out of a will, many people use the phrase "all my children." By leaving property to "all my children" (rather than "my two children" or "my children, Alex and Jamie"), a parent can make sure that children born after a will is written will not be excluded.

Making a Will

Many people ask a lawyer to prepare a will for them. It is possible to write a simple will yourself, however, provided that you follow certain rules. These rules vary from state to state.

Illustration 13-3   Many people ask a lawyer to prepare their wills even though an individual may write his or her own simple will.

Most states permit only adults to make wills. In addition, to make a valid will, you must have sufficient mental capacity. That is, at the time you sign the will, you must have a "sound mind" and the ability to understand what you're doing. If you sign a will when you are under the influence of drugs or alcohol, the will may not be valid. The same is true for a will signed by a person who is considered insane.

A will may be invalid if it is made under undue influence or if fraud is involved. For example, Dorothy Mae Baker died on February 15, 1978, leaving an estate valued at $73,131. She had no husband or children. Her closest relatives were her brother, Clarence Coleman, and her cousin, David Lee. In her will, however, Baker left less than $10,000 to Coleman and his family and $1,000 to Lee. She left her home and nearly everything else to Alta Potter, a friend.

While such a will normally would be perfectly valid, Coleman and Lee felt that Potter had tricked Baker into giving her so much. They took the matter to court. In court, they showed that Potter had claimed to be able to speak to the dead. Potter had convinced Baker that Baker's mother had sent messages from beyond the grave explaining how Baker should write her will. Potter had claimed that Baker's mother "was earthbound and could not go on to a higher plane" unless Baker followed her instructions.

The jury decided that Baker had written the will under the undue influence of another person, who stood to benefit from the will. Because of that undue influence, the court set aside the portions of the will that left property to Potter. (The rest of the will remained valid.) The property left to Potter was distributed to Baker's heirs as it would have been if Baker had died intestate.

Formalities of a Will

In nearly every state, a will is valid only if it is signed by the testator. In addition, each state requires several witnesses (usually two or three) to sign the will. The witnesses do not need to see the contents of the will; their signatures are needed only to certify their belief that the testator is of sound mind. To avoid any appearance of undue influence or fraud, it is best that the witnesses not be beneficiaries of the will.

A will that a testator has written entirely by hand (rather than with a typewriter or word processor) is called a **holographic will**. In some states, holographic wills are considered valid even if they have not been signed by witnesses.

Changing a Will

No matter what your wishes are at the time of your death, a probate court will enforce only the words you have put down on paper. For this reason, it's important to keep your will up to date. Suppose Giovanni writes a will in which he leaves all his possessions to his girlfriend, Lisa Marie. Several months later, they break up and Giovanni becomes involved with Angela. If Giovanni dies without changing his will, all his possessions will go to his former girlfriend, Lisa Marie, not to Angela.

The most common way to change a will is to write a codicil. A **codicil** is an amendment to a will. To be valid, a codicil must be made with the same formalities as a will—that is, it must be signed and witnessed.

Making additions or changes to the original will—for example, by adding or crossing out words—is not permitted. When a probate court sees such changes, it will enforce the will as it was originally written. For example, Richard Collins died in New York on February 5, 1982. He left a typewritten will dated August 14, 1970. The will contained numerous handwritten changes. Collins had crossed out sections dealing with specific gifts of money and with guardianship of his minor children. The probate court refused to honor Collins's cross-outs and changes. Only the portions that had been typewritten in 1970 were considered valid.

You can **revoke**, or cancel, a will at any time. Revoking a will is most easily done by tearing it up or destroying it. Another way to revoke a will is to make a new will that states, "This document supersedes and revokes any wills that are dated earlier."

Probating a Will

A will has no legal effect until it is probated, that is, approved by a probate court. When a will is presented for **probate**, the court reviews the will and all its codicils, decides whether they are valid, and interprets any parts that are unclear. The court may also listen to testimony from people who object to the will.

Anyone who has reason to believe that a will is invalid may **contest**, or fight, the will. This occurs most often when a spouse or child finds that he or she has been omitted from the will. Other interested parties may argue that when the testator wrote the will, he or she acted under undue influence, was defrauded, or was not of sound mind. If these claims can be proved (as in the case of Dorothy Mae Baker, which you read about earlier in this section), the court will set aside all or part of the will. It will then distribute the estate according to the parts of the will that remain valid and according to the rules of intestate succession.

REVIEW QUESTIONS

1. What does it mean to "take against the will"? Who has the right to do so?
2. What is the clearest way to disinherit a child?
3. List three requirements for making a valid will.
4. What is a codicil?

THE RIGHT TO DIE

Peter Cinque suffered from a combination of serious medical conditions. Thirty-five years of living with diabetes had caused him to go blind, lose both legs, lose the use of his kidneys, and suffer from heart problems. He was in constant pain. In addition, because his kidneys had failed, he required an uncomfortable medical treatment called hemodialysis. He was hooked up to a hemodialysis machine for four hours a day, three days a week.

In October 1982 Cinque decided that he no longer wanted to live in such pain. He chose to stop the hemodialysis treatment, knowing that he would die in a week without it. When he refused hemodialysis, the hospital asked for a court order to force him to continue the treatment. The court would not issue such an order. All American adults, the court said, are entitled to **personal autonomy**—the right to make decisions about themselves, their bodies, and their property. The right to personal autonomy includes the right to refuse medical treatment even if that refusal results in death.

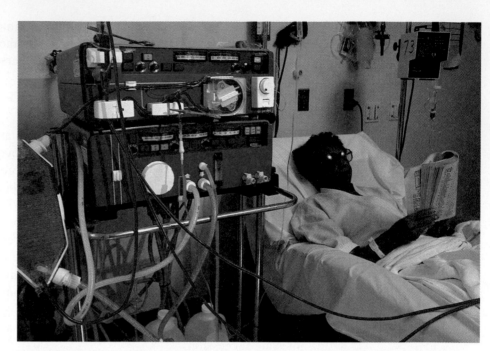

Illustration 13-4   All American adults are entitled to personal autonomy in the right to make decisions about themselves and their bodies, including the right to accept or refuse medical treatment.

Although personal autonomy is not mentioned in the Constitution, it has long been considered a fundamental right of all people. Your right to write a will—to decide who gets your possessions after your death—is part of your right to personal autonomy. Personal autonomy includes many other rights, including the right to make decisions about how and when you will die.

Making Medical Decisions

Advances in medical technology have made it possible to extend people's lives through the use of surgery, drugs, and other treatments. People can now survive illnesses and injuries that would have been fatal 10 or 20 years ago. In many cases, medical treatment can make people well. In other cases, such as that of Peter Cinque, medical treatment can keep people alive, but only in severe pain or with extreme disabilities.

A doctor may not treat you until that doctor has gotten your informed consent. **Informed consent** requires two steps. First, a doctor must tell you what treatment he or she is planning, what the risks are, and how likely it is that the treatment will work as planned. Second, you, the patient, must confirm that you understand the risks and consent to the treatment.

If you are an adult and are considered competent (mentally fit), you have the right to refuse to consent to medical treatment—for any reason or for no reason at all. You may refuse surgery or blood transfusions. You may refuse to take prescribed medicine. As in the case of Peter Cinque, you may refuse to be treated at all even if that refusal will cause your death.

Incompetent Individuals

On April 15, 1975, when Karen Quinlan was 21, she suddenly stopped breathing. By the time she arrived at the hospital, the lack of oxygen to her brain had caused severe, permanent brain damage. She was in what doctors call a persistent vegetative state. This meant that her brain was still working but she was not able to respond to anything around her. She was fed through a tube and could not breathe without the help of a respirator.

Medical experts agreed that she would never regain consciousness and that nothing could be done to improve her condition. Karen's father, Joseph Quinlan, knew that Karen would not want to be kept alive in this artificial way. Because she could not make her wishes known, he spoke for her. He asked her doctor to remove the respirator and let Karen die naturally. The doctor refused, saying that turning off a respirator is not proper medical procedure. The doctor was also concerned that he or the hospital could be held criminally liable for causing Karen's death.

Joseph Quinlan went to court, hoping to get a court order that would require Karen's doctor to turn off the respirator. The New Jersey Supreme Court agreed with Quinlan that incompetent individuals—people who are incapable of making or expressing their own decisions—should not lose their right to personal autonomy. Since Karen could not speak for herself, the court said, another person should be appointed to speak for her. The court authorized Joseph Quinlan to make decisions for his daughter, including the vital decision of whether she should be allowed to die.

Deciding for Others　　There is no generally accepted rule about who should make medical decisions for incompetent patients. Some people feel that a family member (such as Karen Quinlan's father) is most likely to know what the patient wants and should be allowed to speak on the patient's behalf. Others feel that the doctor knows what is best and should have the right to make decisions for the patient.

Some courts have suggested that all decisions about incompetent patients be made by a court in order to protect the parties involved from criminal or civil liability. Other courts have recommended that every hospital establish an ethics committee to review the cases of incompetent patients. An ethics committee is a group of lawyers, doctors, and religious experts who consider the doctor's diagnosis, the family's wishes, and their own beliefs about what is right and wrong. On the basis of all this information, the ethics committee recommends a course of action.

How Courts Decide　　When a court must make a decision for an incompetent patient, it tries to find out what decision the patient would have made. If the patient has left written instructions about his or her wishes, the court will usually rely on those instructions. Otherwise, the court must rely on other evidence of the patient's desires and beliefs. Courts differ greatly on what kinds of evidence they accept. Some courts are satisfied with a family member's testimony about what the patient would have wanted. Others require much more convincing evidence.

Illustration 13-5   In some hospitals, ethics committees review the cases of incompetent patients.

For example, on January 11, 1983, Nancy Cruzan was in a car accident in southwestern Missouri. The accident caused severe, permanent brain damage. Like Karen Quinlan, Nancy remained in a persistent vegetative state and was fed through a tube. After she had remained in this condition for over four years, her parents, Lester and Joyce Cruzan, asked her doctors to remove the feeding tube and let her die. The doctors refused.

The Cruzans took the case to court. In court, Nancy's former roommate testified that Nancy had once talked about what to do if she were seriously injured. According to the roommate, Nancy had said that she would not want to continue her life unless it could be at least "halfway normal." The trial court held that this was sufficient evidence of Nancy's wishes. The court ordered the feeding tube removed.

Nancy's doctors refused to remove the tube. Instead, the hospital appealed the decision to the Missouri Supreme Court. That court said that the testimony of Nancy's roommate was not sufficiently clear and convincing. The court indicated that much more reliable evidence was necessary. Nancy's parents argued that in the absence of clear evidence, they should be allowed to speak for Nancy, as Joseph Quinlan had spoken for his daughter. The court disagreed and reversed the lower court's decision.

The Cruzans appealed the case to the U.S. Supreme Court. The nation's highest court upheld the Missouri Supreme Court's decision. It said that every state has the right to set its own standards in cases involving incompetent patients. Some states may accept casual conversations as evidence of a patient's wishes or may permit family members to speak for incompetent individuals. Other states have the right to set stricter requirements. Therefore, the Court said, the state of Missouri was perfectly justified in rejecting the testimony of Nancy's roommate and in rejecting the Cruzans' request to speak for Nancy.

Deciding for Those Who Were Never Competent   It is often impossible for a court to find out what an incompetent patient would have wanted. Some people have never expressed their feelings about being kept alive artificially. Others—such as newborn babies and severely retarded adults—have never been competent to develop opinions on the subject.

When a court must make decisions for an individual who has never been competent, it does not try to figure out what the patient would have wanted. Instead, it makes a decision that seems to be in the best interests of the patient. In making this decision, the court considers how the patient feels—for example, whether he or she is in pain—and how much the treatment or continued care will prolong or improve the patient's life. The court weighs the benefits of continued treatment against the burdens of that treatment.

For example, Joseph Saikewicz, age 67, was so severely retarded that he was considered to have the mental abilities of a 2-year-old. In April 1976 Saikewicz was found to have leukemia. Without chemotherapy treatments, he would die within a few months. Chemotherapy could extend his life another year or so. Cancer chemotherapy, however, causes discomfort and is often painful. It has many side effects and is difficult to endure even for someone who understands its purpose. Because of Saikewicz's mental state, the treatment would be even more difficult and frightening. For these reasons, Saikewicz's doctors went to court to ask if they could permit Saikewicz to die without treatment.

The court decided in this case that the burdens of treatment exceeded the benefits and that Saikewicz's leukemia should be allowed to progress naturally. Even though Saikewicz would die a year sooner, the court decided that it was in his best interest to spare him the pain and terror of chemotherapy.

Euthanasia

Euthanasia is the act of ending a person's life to relieve incurable or insufferable pain—for example, by giving the person a lethal drug dose. When euthanasia is used to relieve the suffering of an incompetent person, it is often called *mercy killing*. When it is used at the request of a competent person, it is usually called *assisted suicide*.

Euthanasia is not the same as removing artificial life support devices, such as a respirator or a feeding tube. Removing artificial life support simply allows the natural process of death to occur. Euthanasia, no matter how well intentioned, is a form of killing. For this reason, even people who approve of withholding medical treatment from incompetent patients often do not approve of euthanasia.

You read earlier in this chapter that everyone has the right to personal autonomy. Nevertheless, suicide and attempted suicide were long considered criminal acts. Although taking one's own life is no longer illegal, people who attempt suicide are often hospitalized and receive psychiatric care for their own protection. In addition, it is still a crime in some states to help someone commit suicide.

In 1990 Janet Adkins was suffering from Alzheimer's disease, an incurable illness that affects the mind. It makes people forgetful at first and, within a few years, leaves them totally dependent on others for care. Adkins did not want to go through that experience. She met with Dr. Jack Kevorkian, a physician who had developed what became known as a "suicide machine." On June 4, 1990, Kevorkian hooked Adkins up to the machine. Then Adkins flipped a switch, permitting a painless drug to enter her bloodstream and kill her. After Adkins's death, Kevorkian was arrested for helping her commit suicide. Although criminal charges were eventually dropped, a Michigan court prohibited Kevorkian from using that or any device to assist a person in committing suicide.

There has been no uniform agreement about how to handle euthanasia cases. However, such cases very rarely come to the attention of a criminal court. In reality, many physicians and nurses are willing to honor the requests of patients who want to die. They do so quietly, without drawing attention to their actions. Therefore, they are very rarely prosecuted.

REVIEW QUESTIONS

1. What is informed consent?
2. Why might a doctor treating a person in a persistent vegetative state not want to turn off a respirator?
3. How does a court make medical decisions for a formerly competent person who becomes incompetent?
4. How does a court make medical decisions for someone who was never competent?

MAKING YOUR WISHES KNOWN

What will happen if you become so seriously ill that you can no longer express your wishes? As you have seen, it is likely that a court will have to make medical decisions for you. The court will try to figure out what you would have wanted. If that's not possible, it will try to act in your best interests.

You can avoid these possibilities by expressing your wishes now, in writing, while you are still able to do so. By writing a legal document called an **advance directive**, you can let others know how you want to be treated if you become incompetent. The two most common types of advance directive are the living will and the durable power of attorney. Advance directives may also be written to donate your body or body parts after you die.

Living Wills

A **living will** is a set of instructions describing what kind of medical care you want if you become incompetent. In 1975 Francis Landy wrote a living will saying that he did not want to be kept alive by artificial means. He signed the document in front of witnesses. Six years later, Landy became seriously ill and was admitted to a Florida hospital. Within two days, he had stopped breathing. The only thing keeping him alive was a respirator. His wife showed his living will to Landy's doctor and asked to have the respirator turned off.

Concern for Dying
TO MY FAMILY, MY PHYSICIAN, MY LAWYER, AND ALL OTHERS WHOM IT MAY CONCERN

Death is as much a reality as birth, growth, maturity, and old age—it is the one certainty of life. If the time comes when I can no longer take part in my decisions for my own future, let this statement stand as an expression of my wishes and directions, while I am still of sound mind.

If at such a time the situation should arise in which there is no reasonable expectation of my recovery from extreme physical or mental disability, I direct that I be allowed to die and not be kept alive by medications, artificial means, or "heroic measures." I do, however, ask that medication be mercifully administered to me to alleviate suffering even though this may shorten my remaining life.

This statement is made after careful consideration and is in accordance with my strong convictions and beliefs. I want the wishes and directions here expressed carried out to the extent permitted by law. Insofar as they are not legally enforceable, I hope that those to whom this Will is addressed will regard themselves as morally bound by these provisions.

Signed _George Evans_

_9/16/91_
Date

Melanie Khoo
Witness

Bruce Goldberg
Witness

Copies of this request have been given to

Alma Evans
Melanie Khoo
Bruce Goldberg
Winifred Evans

Excerpted from *Personal Forms on File*, by Facts on File, Inc.

Illustration 13-6   A living will is a legal document that describes what kind of medical care you want to have if you become incompetent.

Because there was no state law concerning the validity of living wills, the hospital administrator did not want to honor the document. He feared that if Landy died when the respirator was turned off, the doctor or the hospital might be held liable. He asked a court whether he could legally rely on Landy's living will. The court ruled that a hospital may honor a living will without prior approval of a court and without fear of liability.

Since that time, many states have passed laws permitting medical personnel to honor living wills. These laws differ from state to state, however. Some states accept living wills in all cases. Others allow living wills to be honored only when a patient is terminally ill. This restriction would exclude people like Francis Landy and Karen Quinlan, who are not considered terminally ill because they could live for years with the aid of artificial life support.

Even if you live in a state that does not accept living wills, it's still a good idea to write one. If you become incompetent and a court or family member must make decisions for you, the document will provide valuable evidence about what you would have wanted. For example, the U.S. Supreme Court noted that if Nancy Cruzan had written a living will, that document could have provided sufficient evidence of her wish to be allowed to die.

Durable Power of Attorney

As you have read, some states will not honor living wills under some circumstances. Another type of advance directive, however—the durable power of attorney—is accepted at all times in every state. A **durable power of attorney** is a legal document in which you appoint another person to speak on your behalf. This person is called your **proxy**.

If you become incompetent, a hospital must treat your proxy's requests in the same way it would treat your own. In 1983, for example, Hilda Peter signed a durable power of attorney. She named her close friend Eberhard Johanning as her proxy. A year later she collapsed and was kept alive by a respirator in a nursing home. Johanning, based on his conversations with Peter, knew that she would not want to be kept alive in that way. He asked to have the respirator turned off. When the nursing home refused to do so, Johanning went to court. The court ordered the nursing home to follow Johanning's instructions and turn off the respirator.

Once you sign a durable power of attorney, it's important that you explain to your proxy exactly what your wishes are. (Hilda Peter, for example, had told Eberhard Johanning that she did not want to be kept alive artificially.) If you appoint a proxy but do not give him or her any instructions, you put the proxy in a difficult position. He or she may have to make life-or-death decisions for you without knowing what you would have wanted.

Making Patients Aware

Despite the importance of the right to refuse treatment, very few people are aware that they have such a right. Even fewer have written advance directives to protect them if they become incompetent. As you have read, not having an advance directive can create many problems for family members, medical providers, and courts.

Because of this, Congress recently passed a law that requires hospitals and other medical facilities to tell new patients about their rights. These rights include the right to refuse treatment, the right to have a durable power of attorney, and, in most states, the right to write a legally binding living will.

Anatomical Donations

In addition to writing a living will or durable power of attorney, many people choose to make another kind of advance directive—an offer to donate their bodies or body parts after death. If doctors act quickly enough after a patient has died, they can remove the heart, kidneys, and other organs and transplant them into living patients who need them. In this way a dead person can save the life of someone who is dying.

Even if your internal organs are not healthy enough at death to be used for transplant, other parts of your body—for example, your corneas or skin— may be. Medical schools also can use bodies or body parts for research or education.

Of course, doctors may not use parts of your body unless they have your permission—or, if you are unable to consent, the permission of your family. Many states have passed laws requiring hospital personnel to ask the relatives of deceased patients for permission to use a patient's body parts. To save your family from dealing with such issues at the time of your death, you may want to make your wishes known ahead of time.

Every state has enacted an **anatomical gift act**—a law that makes it easy for individuals to donate body parts. If you are an adult, you can make a gift of any or all usable body parts upon your death. You can make this donation in your will, or you can sign an organ donor card. In many states, people who wish to donate organs may say so on their driver's licenses.

<table>
<tr><td colspan="2">AFFIX CORRECTION STICKER</td></tr>
<tr><td colspan="2">D1435920</td></tr>
<tr><td>Upon my death I am willing to donate the following:</td><td>☒ Eyes ☒ Kidney
☒ Liver ☐ Any organ
☒ Heart ☐ None</td></tr>
</table>

WEIGHT CODES

0 - under 121 lbs.
1 - 121 to 140 lbs.
2 - 141 to 160 lbs.
3 - 161 to 180 lbs.
4 - 181 to 200 lbs.
5 - 201 to 220 lbs.
6 - over 221 lbs

CONDITION AND/OR RESTRICTION CODES

0 - No restriction
1 - Must wear corrective lenses
2 - Prosthetic device
3 - Mechanical device

4 - Hearing impaired
8 - Attached endorsement (special restrictions and/or combination of restrictions)

X _____ *Robert Edwards* _____

Please use BALL POINT pen to sign.

Illustration 13-7   In many states, people who wish to donate organs may say so right on their driver's licenses.

Some people choose to make general donations, allowing any or all of their body parts to be used for any purpose. You may, however, limit your donation to certain organs or to certain purposes, such as transplant, research, or education.

REVIEW QUESTIONS

1. What is a living will?
2. What is a durable power of attorney?
3. List two ways in which a person's body or body parts can be used after the person's death.

Viewpoints on Doctors and the Right to Die

Timothy Quill, a doctor from Rochester, New York, described in a March 1991 *New England Journal of Medicine* article how he helped a cancer patient commit suicide. The 45-year-old woman had refused a difficult treatment program for a severe type of blood cancer. As her pain became unbearable, the woman asked Dr. Quill to help her commit suicide. Dr. Quill discussed the patient's decision with her and her family, trying to make sure that her mind was clear and that she understood what she was doing. When he was satisfied, Dr. Quill wrote the patient a prescription for sleeping pills, making sure she knew what quantity would be needed to bring about her death. She died peacefully at home after saying good-bye to her husband and her son.

The issue of a person's right to die creates agonizing dilemmas for doctors such as Dr. Quill. Some patients ask their physicians to withhold treatment, such as chemotherapy. Those patients may feel that such treatment will be too painful and that they will die anyway. Some patients may ask not to be revived if the heart or lungs fail. The families of some comatose patients ask doctors to help by turning off life-sustaining machines. Some patients, like Dr. Quill's, ask their doctors to prescribe a sufficient amount of barbiturates so that they can take a lethal overdose.

The Case against Allowing or Helping Patients to Die

Those who are opposed to having doctors allow or actively help people to die say that it goes against everything a doctor should stand for—healing and a respect for the sanctity of life. They think such actions are morally, ethically, and legally wrong.

Some people worry that a policy that begins with helping an alert, willing patient commit suicide may be abused. They fear how doctors, other medical personnel, or family members would decide that a patient who could not express his or her wishes would be "better off" dead.

Doctors also fear that they will be held legally responsible. They may be sued for malpractice, or they may lose their licenses. They may also be brought up on criminal charges. Twenty-six states have laws prohibiting doctors from assisting patients in committing suicide.

The Case for Allowing or Helping Patients to Die

Some physicians believe that terminally ill patients have a right to die in as little pain as possible and with dignity. They believe that it is right to honor a patient's desire not to lose control of his or her body. These doctors believe that when a person who is suffering greatly with an incurable disease wishes to die, doctors should be able to relieve that suffering. This relief may involve helping such patients end their own lives.

Most doctors who hold this view believe that certain conditions should be met, however. They must know the patient well and for a long period of time. They must have discussed the treatment options and the chances for survival thoroughly with the patient. These doctors have to be convinced that the patient is completely rational and alert when making the decision.

Some doctors are concerned that because hospitals and doctors fear legal action or just because the technology is available, they will take extraordinary measures to save a life even if that life would be as a permanently comatose individual.

A Continuing Debate

Dr. Quill's article generated much controversy in the medical community. Physicians who have wrestled with the same decisions applauded Dr. Quill for bringing the issue into the open, where it could be widely discussed. Perhaps from this debate an ethical standard may emerge. This standard would help physicians know what to do when patients or their families ask doctors to allow life to end without treatment or even to hasten its end.

Chapter Review

Chapter Summary

- If you die without a will, the laws of intestate succession determine what happens to your estate. Usually your property goes to your spouse and your children, if you have any.

- If you have no spouse or direct descendants, your property may go to your parents or more distant relatives or to the state.

- Probate courts are responsible for handling matters dealing with the estates of those who die.

- By writing a will, you can determine what happens to your property after your death.

- Even if you leave nothing to your spouse, your spouse has a right to a portion of your estate.

■ State laws protect children from being accidentally disinherited. Unless a parent's will specifically excludes a child, that child is entitled to a share of the parent's estate.

■ Any adult who is competent may make a will. A will may be invalid if it is made under undue influence or if fraud is involved.

■ Wills can be changed only through codicils or revocation. A probate court will not honor changes that have been made improperly.

■ Every adult has the right to make decisions about what happens to his or her body. This includes the right to refuse medical treatment even if that refusal results in death.

■ A family member or doctor may be permitted to make medical decisions for a person who is incompetent. In some cases, these decisions must be made by a court or a hospital ethics committee.

■ Unlike withholding medical treatment, which allows the natural process of death to occur, euthanasia is an act that kills a seriously ill person.

■ Every state honors some form of advance directive that permits individuals to let their wishes be known if they become incompetent. The most common advance directives are the living will and the durable power of attorney.

■ Every state permits individuals to donate their bodies or body parts after death.

Understanding Legal Terms

On a separate sheet of paper, match the terms below with the definitions that follow.

codicil	holographic will
contest	intestate
durable power of attorney	living will
estate	probate
executor	testator

1. Dying without a will
2. All the money and property a person owns
3. Procedure in which a court establishes a will's validity and distributes the estate
4. To oppose the validity of a will
5. A will that is written entirely by hand
6. Addition to a will
7. Person who writes a will
8. Person who is appointed in a will to take charge of the deceased's estate

9.   A set of instructions that describe the kind of medical care a person wants if he or she becomes incompetent

10.   A legal document in which a person appoints another person to speak on his or her behalf

Applying the Law

1.   Reiko is divorced and has two children. She dies without having made a will. At the time of her death, she had a close relationship with her son, but she and her daughter did not get along. How will her estate be divided between her daughter, her son, and her ex-husband?

2.   In his will Ahmed leaves one third of his estate to his wife, one third to Najib (his only child), and one third to charity. Najib murders Ahmed. How will the probate court distribute Ahmed's estate? Why?

3.   In her will Beverly leaves $10,000 to her sister Sandra on the condition that Sandra use the money to go back to school. Sandra is not interested in going back to school. Can she use the money to start a business instead? Why or why not?

4.   Bruce dies, leaving an estate worth $50,000. In his will he leaves $3,000 to his wife, Laura. He leaves the rest to charity. Laura feels that her husband should have left her more. What, if anything, can she do?

5.   Marla wrote a will in 1988. In the will she left all her property to her son, Jeremy, who was her only child. In 1990 she adopted a second child, Seth. Marla died in 1991 without changing her will. Will the probate court give Seth a portion of Marla's estate? Why or why not?

6.   Juan has a terminal illness. He knows that he will die within a year. While he is still competent, he follows all state requirements for writing a durable power of attorney. He names his wife, Elena, as his proxy. Four months later Juan falls into a persistent vegetative state and is placed on a respirator. Elena shows Juan's doctor the durable power of attorney and asks the doctor to turn off the respirator. Must the doctor do so? Why or why not?

Case Studies

1.   Before they were married, Jack and Bernice Lopata signed a prenuptial agreement that met all the requirements of state law. In the agreement, each waived the right to take against the other's will. Jack died several years after they were married. In his will, he left only a small portion of his estate to Bernice. Bernice contested the will. She claimed that as Jack's spouse, she had a right to a larger share of his estate. Did the probate court grant her a larger share? Why or why not?

2.   Nancy Yett wrote a will on June 11, 1976. On October 1 of that year she died. In her will she left a large portion of her estate to her son Stephen and a small portion to her son David. David knew that his mother had

suffered from some memory lapses and disorientation in the last year of her life. For this reason he believed that she was not of sound mind when she wrote the will. What could David do?

3. Abe Perlmutter had Lou Gehrig's disease. By 1977 the disease had left him permanently paralyzed. He could speak and he remained competent, but he could not breathe without the help of a respirator. Without the respirator, he would die within an hour. He asked his doctors to turn off the respirator and let him die, but the doctors refused. What, if anything, could Perlmutter do?

Unit 5

The Law
In Everyday Life

Chapter 14

Your Rights and Responsibilities as an Employee

When you have read this chapter, you should be able to:

- Name four federal laws that protect employees against unfair discrimination.

- List the techniques that employers might use to screen job applicants, and identify those techniques that are illegal.

- Describe the legal relationship between an employer and an employee, and explain how labor unions affect that relationship.

- Explain how federal and state laws protect employees' rights to safety and privacy.

- Describe the legal rights of employees who are fired or laid off.

Case Study

Phipps v. Clark Oil & Refining Corp., 408 N.W.2d 569 (Minnesota 1987).

Mark Phipps worked at a gas station in Brooklyn Park, Minnesota. On November 17, 1984, a motorist drove into the station and asked for gas. Phipps's manager, Leroy Chmielewski, told Phipps to pump leaded gas into the automobile. The car was designed to run on unleaded gas only, and putting leaded gas into the car would have been a federal offense. Rather than break the law, Phipps refused to do what Chmielewski had ordered.

Chmielewski fired Phipps for refusing to follow his instructions. Believing that he had been fired unfairly, Phipps sued the oil company that owned the station.

Phipps had not signed an employment contract with the oil company. Under Minnesota law (and the law of most states), if there is no written employment contract, an employer can fire an employee at any time—for any reason or for no reason at all. Based on that law, the trial court found that the oil company had a legal right to fire Phipps. Phipps appealed the case.

The appeals court reversed the trial court's decision. The appeals court agreed that when there is no employment contract, employers have the right to fire employees for any reason. However, it pointed out that there are exceptions to that rule. For example, an employer may not fire an employee simply because of the employee's race, religion, national origin, or sex. There are several other exceptions, including one that was relevant to this case: An employer may not fire an employee for refusing to commit an illegal act.

Because of this exception, the court ruled that Phipps had been fired illegally.

DISCRIMINATION IN HIRING, PROMOTION, AND FIRING

Two centuries ago, people who were looking for work had very few rights. If an individual was offered a job, he or she had to "take it or leave it"—either accept the job on the employer's conditions or find someplace else to work. Since that time, the federal government and state and local governments have passed a great number of laws that regulate the relationship between employers and employees. These laws affect nearly all employers, with a few exceptions (for example, those who run very small businesses).

Many employment laws are intended to prevent certain types of discrimination. They apply not only to people who have been hired but also to people who apply for jobs. Before you read about the laws concerning getting a job, keeping a job, and leaving a job, it's important to know how the antidiscrimination laws protect your rights.

Title VII

The most important antidiscrimination law is **Title VII of the Civil Rights Act**. Passed by Congress in 1964, it has been amended several times to expand the scope of its protection. Title VII forbids employers to consider a person's race, religion, national origin, or sex when making employment decisions. The law applies to decisions involving hiring, promotion, working conditions, and firing.

Illustration 14-1   Title VII of the Civil Rights Act protects employees from discrimination based on race, religion, national origin, or sex.

Let's say Brian is the manager of a store. He has two employees—Gloria and Herb. He wants to promote one of them to assistant manager. An assistant manager must stay at the store late at night, and Brian thinks it's dangerous for a woman to stay that late. Therefore, he promotes Herb instead of Gloria. Brain has violated Title VII, and Gloria has the right to take legal action against him.

Title VII protects employees and job applicants from discrimination based on race, religion, national origin, and sex but not from other types of discrimination. An employer still has the right to fire an employee who does poor work or is dishonest. An employer also has the right not to hire someone who appears to be unqualified for the job. For example, if Brian chooses Herb over Gloria because Herb has more experience or is better with customers, Brian has done nothing illegal.

Unintentional discrimination that hurts a particular group of people is also a violation of Title VII. Suppose Sid owns a factory. All his employees are white. When a job opens up, Sid doesn't advertise for new employees. Instead, he tells his current employees about the opening and asks them to recommend people for the job. Because of this practice, very few nonwhite individuals hear about job openings at Sid's factory. Sid is committing a Title VII violation.

Title VII prohibits all kinds of on-the-job harassment, including sexual, racial, and religious harassment. An employer can be held liable not only for personally harassing employees but also for allowing other employees to do so. Title VII also forbids employers to make hiring, promotion, or firing decisions on the basis of an employee's granting of sexual favors.

Equal Pay for Women

Traditionally, men earned money for the family, and women stayed home to raise children. When women did work outside the home, their earnings were often considered supplemental income—not a significant means of support for the family. Many employers therefore paid women less than they paid men. In 1963 Congress put an end to that practice by passing the Equal Pay Act. This law states that a man and a woman who work in the same place and do substantially the same work—work that requires equal skills, effort, and responsibility—must receive equal pay.

In the 1970s, the John J. Kane Hospital in Allegheny County, Pennsylvania, employed six people to style and cut patients' hair. Three male barbers tended to male patients, and three female beauticians cared for the female patients. The men were paid $165 a month more than the women, even though they did substantially the same work. The women took the matter to court. They showed that their educational requirements were the same, their work requirements were the same, and their hours were the same. The court forced the hospital to pay the beauticians the same salary that it paid the barbers.

Women and men are entitled to the same pay only if they do the same work. For work that is different in a substantial way (such as a night shift), different pay is permitted. However, both sexes must have the opportunity to do the better-paying work.

The Equal Pay Act does allow pay differences that are not based on an employee's sex. Many employers, for example, pay experienced employees more than new employees, even though their responsibilities are the same. This sort of discrimination is permitted under the law.

Age Discrimination

Stereotypes about age often lead employers to hire younger people rather than older people. Employers sometimes think that older employees may be out sick more often or may be slow to learn the job routine. Some employers prefer to hire younger workers on the assumption that they'll stay with the company longer. In 1967 Congress passed the Age Discrimination in Employment Act to end discrimination based on these assumptions. Specifically, the act prohibits discrimination in hiring against people over the age of 40. It does not offer similar protection for younger workers (although some state laws do).

Illustration 14-2 The Equal Pay Act states that men and women who work in the same place and do the same work must receive equal pay.

At the same time, state and federal **child labor laws** *require* age discrimination in hiring young people. Federal law generally prohibits children under age 14 from working. Children under 16 may work, but only for a limited number of hours and never overnight. Federal law prohibits anyone under 18 to work at jobs designated as hazardous, such as jobs that require the use of heavy equipment. Exceptions to these age restrictions permit young children to deliver newspapers, work on farms, work for their parents, and perform as models and actors. Some state child labor laws are more restrictive.

Discrimination against the Handicapped

The Rehabilitation Act, passed by Congress in 1973, prohibits discrimination against mentally or physically handicapped individuals. This law applies only to federal offices and federal contractors. Most states have similar laws that apply to *all* employers, both public and private.

In 1990 Congress extended the rights of the handicapped with the Americans with Disabilities Act. This law requires all employers to make reasonable accommodations for employees with disabilities. These adjustments may include making the workplace wheelchair-accessible, modifying work schedules, and hiring readers or interpreters for blind or deaf employees. Under the law, employers must have made these changes by 1995 at the latest.

Bona Fide Occupational Qualifications

Discrimination is not illegal when it serves a legitimate purpose. In certain careers—for example, modeling, acting, and police undercover work—a person must often be of a particular sex, age, or race in order to do a job. In these cases, the employee's sex, age, or race is known as a **bona fide occupational qualification** (BFOQ). An employer may take BFOQs into account when making hiring or promotion decisions. The federal government severely limits the kinds of situations in which a person's physical characteristics are considered BFOQs.

In addition to the federal laws discussed so far, many antidiscrimination laws have been passed by states and cities. Some of these laws prohibit discrimination based on sexual preference or marital status, for example.

Enforcement and the EEOC

The Equal Employment Opportunity Commission (EEOC) oversees Title VII and many other federal employment laws. (Some employment laws, such as the Rehabilitation Act and child labor laws, are enforced by the U.S. Department of Labor.) To find out when employment laws have been broken, the EEOC relies mostly on complaints from individuals. If you feel you are being discriminated against in getting a job or if you have questions about your treatment on the job, you should call the local EEOC office.

If you complain to the EEOC about an employer, the EEOC will ask you to fill out a document explaining what the employer has done. The EEOC will then send an investigator to talk to the employer about why he or she took that particular action. If the employer's action appears discriminatory, the investigator will negotiate on your behalf. If negotiations don't succeed, the EEOC may sue the employer.

Through negotiation or litigation, the EEOC can require the employer to compensate you for having been the victim of illegal discrimination. You may be entitled to back pay (money you would have earned if the discrimination had not occurred). If you were unfairly fired or refused a promotion, the employer may have to reinstate (rehire) you or give you the promotion. If the employer's discriminatory action is part of an overall employment policy, the employer will be required to change that policy.

REVIEW QUESTIONS

1. What types of discrimination are prohibited by Title VII?
2. What is unintentional discrimination?
3. What is the Equal Pay Act?
4. What are the main restrictions made by federal child labor laws?

GETTING A JOB

In the United States, there is no promise of a job for every citizen. Once you have a job, there is no promise that it will be yours for life. The laws you've read about so far guarantee only that you will be given an equal opportunity in the workplace. Getting and keeping a job are up to you.

Illustration 14-3   Most employers require people who are looking for a job to fill out a job application before the initial interview.

Interviewing

Most employers will want to interview you before they decide to hire you. An employer may want to know about your education, training, experience, availability to work, and career plans. These kinds of questions are permitted, but certain other kinds are not. The laws against discrimination forbid employers to ask about your race, religion, national origin, or marital status. (They may not even ask such questions indirectly—for example, by asking, "What does your husband do for a living?")

Some kinds of questions are permitted even though they seem discriminatory. Because of child labor laws, employers must ask about your age if they suspect you are under 18. While they cannot ask about your national origin, it is proper for employers to ask if you are an American citizen. In 1986 the federal government passed the Immigration Reform and Control Act, a law making it illegal for an employer to hire anyone who is not a citizen or does not have proper work authorization. Before you will be permitted to work, you will be required to prove your citizenship. If you are not a citizen, you must show that you have the proper work permits.

Applicant Testing

Some employers may want to test your aptitude for a job before offering you the position. For example, if you are applying for a job as an editor, an employer may give you a sample manuscript to edit. Some employers may require you to take psychological tests that are designed to measure your honesty, morality, or aptitude for the job. Such tests are very common and are perfectly legal.

Until recently, some employers might also have asked you to take a **polygraph** (lie detector) **test**. During a polygraph test, a trained examiner asks a number of questions. Some of the questions are straightforward, such as "What is your name?" or "What is today's date?" Other questions are much more challenging, such as "Have you ever thought about taking something that wasn't yours?" During the questioning, a machine measures any changes in the job applicant's breathing rate, pulse, and blood pressure. If those measurements change significantly, the examiner may conclude that the applicant is not answering certain questions truthfully.

Many job applicants felt that polygraph tests were an unfair invasion of their privacy. In response to these concerns, Congress passed a law in 1988 that made it illegal for employers to give polygraph tests to job applicants. (The law makes an exception for certain types of jobs, such as security guards and government employees.) Many states also have passed laws restricting the use of polygraph tests.

Increasing concern about drug abuse has led some employers to give drug tests to job applicants. Like polygraph tests, drug tests have been prohibited or restricted by a number of states. Generally, though, drug tests can be given to applicants for government jobs and high-security jobs. As you will read later, however, the laws concerning polygraphs and drug tests are different for employees than they are for job applicants.

REVIEW QUESTIONS

1. What topics may an employer *not* ask a job applicant about?
2. What does the Immigration Reform and Control Act require employers to do?
3. Name four types of tests an employer may want a job applicant to take.

THE EMPLOYMENT AGREEMENT

The relationship between an employer and an employee is a contract: The employee agrees to do a particular job. In return, the employer agrees to pay compensation in the form of money. Sometimes the contract is spelled out very carefully in a written document. More commonly, the employer and employee agree on a few main points but say nothing about many details.

Individual Written Employment Contract

A written employment contract is a document that lists the specific agreements between the employer and the employee. It usually describes the employee's job responsibilities and states the amount and type of compensation the employee will receive. It may also include other agreements, such as how much vacation the employee can take and how often the employer will review the employee's work. Some employment contracts (such as those for summer jobs) specify how long the term of employment will be. Even for a long-term job, the employment contract may expire after a certain amount of time (for example, a year). At that time, the employer and the employee may renew the contract or renegotiate their agreement.

Implied Contract

If you do not have an individual written employment contract, you are an **employee-at-will**. This is the most common form of employment arrangement. Generally, the employer or the employee-at-will can end the employment relationship at any time—for any reason or for no reason at all. You will read about exceptions to this rule later in this chapter.

Even without a written contract, an employee-at-will may have certain rights under an implied contract. An **implied contract** is an agreement between parties that is understood but not stated explicitly. Oral promises made by employers or supervisors, statements made in employee manuals, and long-standing company policies may be considered parts of an implied contract. Every state allows implied employment contracts to be enforced in court.

For example, early in 1978, Richard Mettille took a job with the Pine River State Bank in St. Paul, Minnesota. He had no individual written employment contract and was therefore an employee-at-will. Later in the year, the bank distributed an employee handbook to all its employees. The handbook contained information about the bank's employment policies, including rules concerning vacations, sick leave, telephone manners, and personal appearance. It also contained a section on disciplinary policy. It described a three-step procedure that the bank promised to follow before an employee could be fired.

On September 28, 1978, the president of the bank fired Mettille without following the procedure outlined in the employee handbook. Mettille later claimed in court that he had been fired illegally. The bank argued that the handbook was for information only and was not meant to be part of an employment contract. The court, however, ruled that the handbook contained promises to employees and that those promises were binding on the bank. The court said that once Mettille had been notified about the disciplinary procedure, the bank could not discharge him without following the procedure.

Illustration 14-4   When union members are unhappy with an employer, they sometimes picket or refuse to work until the working conditions are changed.

Union Contracts

For many years, an employee who was unhappy with his or her working conditions had no choice but to quit and find another job. There was nothing to prevent employers from taking unfair advantage of their employees.

Some employees have dealt with this problem by joining together to negotiate with their employers. This process, called **collective bargaining**, succeeds because an employer is more likely to listen to a group of employees than to a single employee.

A group of workers that engages in collective bargaining is called a **labor union**. The union's goal is to make sure that its members get fair wages and good working conditions. About one fifth of American workers belong to labor unions.

Each labor union elects representatives to negotiate with the employer on behalf of its members. When the employer and the union representatives reach an agreement, they write a document called a union contract. A **union contract** is similar to an ordinary employment contract except that it applies to all members of the labor union, not just to one employee.

If an employer cannot reach an agreement with the union—or refuses to bargain with the union at all—the union can take action against the employer. Union members can **strike**, or refuse to work until conditions are changed. They can also **picket**, or march in protest, to make others aware of the employer's labor practices.

Compensation

Before you take a job, you should find out what kind of **wages**, or payment, the employer is offering. You may be paid by the hour, or you may be paid a **salary** (a fixed amount of money per month or per year). In either case, the federal Fair Labor Standards Act (FLSA) will protect you from being paid too little. This law establishes minimum wages and rules concerning overtime payments.

Minimum Wages and Overtime   The federal minimum wage in 1991 was $4.25 an hour. Except for those discussed below, all employees, whether they receive a salary or are paid by the hour, must be paid at least the minimum wage.

Also, any nonsalaried employee who works more than 40 hours in a week is entitled to extra compensation called **overtime payments**. The FLSA requires overtime payments to be one and a half times the employee's normal hourly rate. Some union contracts require a higher overtime rate; some employers voluntarily pay a higher rate.

Who Is Not Covered   The FLSA does not apply to **independent contractors**, that is, people who are self-employed. For example, if you hire yourself out as a baby-sitter, you are not covered by FLSA rules. Also, farm workers, trainees, and (in some cases) full-time students may be paid less than the minimum wage.

Employees who receive tips are another important exception to the minimum wage law. Waiters, for example, may be paid less than the minimum wage as long as their total hourly income (wages plus tips) equals or exceeds the minimum wage.

Payroll Deductions and Employee Benefits

The wages you take home each payday will always be less than the amount you were promised. Employers are required by law to withhold from your paycheck income tax payments and social security payments. In some states, a disability insurance tax is also withheld. You'll read more about these required payroll deductions in Chapter 17.

With your permission, your employer may take additional money out of your paycheck. You may designate money to be given to charity, put into a savings account, or contributed to a **pension plan** (a plan that puts money away for your retirement).

In many cases, pension plans and other extras are provided completely or partially by the employer. These forms of additional compensation are called **benefits**. Many employers, for example, provide health insurance for their full-time employees. Some employers pay the educational expenses of employees who decide to go back to school. Most employees get a certain amount of paid vacation each year, and those who work in retail stores often are entitled to discounts on purchases made in the store. Some employers promise to give their employees a sum of money called **severance pay** if those workers are fired or laid off.

No law requires employers to give benefits to their employees. Most employers have found, however, that offering benefits allows them to attract better employees. Many union contracts also require employers to offer certain benefits to union members.

REVIEW QUESTIONS

1. List three items an individual written employment contract may include.
2. What is an employee-at-will?
3. What is the purpose of a labor union?
4. What are the two ways in which the Fair Labor Standards Act protects workers?

SAFETY AND PRIVACY ON THE JOB

Many workers, especially those who work with machinery or hazardous chemicals, are concerned about the danger of being killed or injured on the job. Many other workers are concerned about employers' invasion of their privacy by means of electronic surveillance systems and intrusive searches. In response to these concerns, the federal and state governments have passed a number of laws that protect employees' rights to safety and privacy.

A Safe Workplace

You have the right to work in a safe place. The 1970 Occupational Safety and Health Act, enforced by the Occupational Safety and Health Administration (OSHA), sets minimum requirements for workplace safety. It requires that employers follow certain rules, such as providing protective clothing for workers or installing shut-off valves on machinery. A number of labor unions have expanded these rules, adding extra protection for union members.

Although factories present the greatest dangers to employees, offices can present health hazards as well. A number of office workers have reported physical problems resulting from extended exposure to video display terminals. (Video display terminals, or VDTs, are the screens attached to most office computers.) VDT-related problems include eyestrain, backaches, headaches, and increased stress. In response to these problems, some legislatures have passed laws to protect employees who work with VDTs. These laws require employers to provide adjustable desks and chairs, install glare-reduction devices, and provide periodic breaks for employees who work with VDTs.

Federal law requires employers to keep records of all injuries and illnesses that employees report. OSHA inspectors may examine those records if they have reason to believe that a certain workplace is hazardous. They may also examine the workplace.

Although OSHA sometimes conducts random inspections of workplaces, it most often finds out about potentially hazardous conditions through employee complaints. To encourage employees to report workplace hazards, federal law makes it illegal for an employer to fire, demote, mistreat, or discriminate against an employee for filing a complaint.

Workers' Compensation   Even in the safest workplaces, employees may occasionally be hurt. If you are injured at your workplace—even during a break—you may be entitled to workers' compensation. **Workers' compensation** is money that covers wages and medical expenses for an employee who is injured on the job. (The cause of the injury doesn't matter.) Workers who contract job-related illnesses, such as coal miners who develop black lung disease, are also entitled to workers' compensation.

Workers' compensation is an **exclusive remedy** for on-the-job injuries. That means that if you file for workers' compensation, you cannot also sue your employer for the injury. In nearly every state, employers are required to provide workers' compensation for their employees by purchasing workers' compensation insurance or by contributing to a state workers' compensation fund.

Illustration 14-5   Some local and state governments require employers to separate smokers from nonsmokers or to ban smoking completely in the workplace.

A Smoke-Free Workplace   In 1984 Lorraine Lapham was a program monitor for the Berks County Employment and Training Office in Reading, Pennsylvania. She was surrounded by co-workers who smoked cigarettes. The smoke in the office was making her sick. She asked her supervisor to give her office space away from the smokers, but no such space was available. Lapham left her job.

When she applied for unemployment compensation (payments to people who lose a job through no fault of their own), the unemployment board refused her application. No one who quits a job may collect unemployment, the board members said, without having a compelling reason for leaving the job. According to the board, Lapham's reason was not compelling.

Lapham took the matter to court. The court reversed the unemployment board's ruling. It pointed out that tobacco smoke is poisonous not only to smokers but also to nonsmokers who are exposed to it. The court ruled that being forced to sit near a smoker was a compelling reason for Lapham to leave her job and that she was therefore entitled to unemployment compensation.

In recent years, more people have become concerned about the potential dangers of **secondhand smoke** (smoke from other people's cigarettes). Lawsuits like Lapham's have become common. Some workers have succeeded in getting workers' compensation benefits for illnesses caused by secondhand smoke. Others have worked with their unions to require employers to regulate or restrict smoking in the workplace.

In response to this concern, state and local governments around the country have begun establishing rules about smoking in the workplace. In some cities and towns, employers are required to separate smokers from nonsmokers or to ban smoking altogether.

Privacy Rights

Irresponsible or dishonest behavior by employees can cause great financial losses for employers. Some of these losses are due to outright theft by employees; others result from employees slacking off on company time.

Some employers have tried to cut down on stealing by searching their employees' clothing, desks, and lockers. Others have tried to increase productivity by monitoring their employees electronically. It has long been possible for employers to watch workers through video cameras and to listen in on their phone conversations. In recent years, however, electronic surveillance has gotten more sophisticated. In computer-based workplaces, employers can secretly read their employees' electronic mail, examine their files, and even keep track of how many words they have typed per hour.

In general, all these forms of surveillance are legal as long as the employer makes the employees aware of them. According to many court decisions, if employees are informed that they may be searched or monitored, they cannot claim that these actions are invasions of privacy.

Searches   Congress has passed no laws that prohibit employers from searching employees. Government agencies, however, are restricted by the Fourth

Amendment rules on searches and seizures. Government agencies may search employees, their desks, and their property, but only when they have probable cause to conduct a search.

Private (nongovernment) employers are not bound by the Fourth Amendment. They are generally permitted to conduct searches as long as the employees are informed that they may be searched.

Surveillance   There are no laws that prevent employers from watching their employees work. Employers may legally use cameras, one-way windows, guards, and computers to monitor their employees' activities. Employers are even permitted to listen in on employees' phone calls.

As with searches, the regulations for government agencies are stricter than those for private companies. In general, however, most surveillance techniques are permissible.

Polygraph Tests   As you read earlier, polygraph testing of job applicants is almost always illegal. Once an applicant has been hired, however, most states allow employers to give the employee polygraph tests.

Different states regulate polygraph testing in different ways. Some states limit the number of questions that can be asked; others restrict the types of questions. Some states permit polygraph tests only if the employee consents. (In those states, an employer cannot fire or punish an employee for refusing to consent.)

Some states bar the use of polygraphs by employers altogether. Others bar polygraph testing for all employees except those who work in law enforcement and government jobs.

Drug and Alcohol Testing

Another controversial issue is whether employers should be permitted to test their employees for drug or alcohol use. Federal law generally allows private employers to test employees unless a union contract forbids it. The Fourth Amendment restriction on searches and seizures puts some limits on federal and state government agencies and government contractors.

State regulation of drug testing varies considerably. Some states permit random drug testing of all employees. Others permit employers to test individual employees only if there is evidence that those employees have been using drugs or alcohol on the job. Most states allow routine drug testing of workers whose jobs affect the safety of others—for example, truck drivers, airline pilots, and workers in nuclear power plants.

Even when employers are allowed to test employees for drug use, many states protect employees who test positive from being disciplined unfairly. For example, an employer may not be allowed to fire an employee for drug abuse until the employee has tested positive for drugs twice or even three times. In many states, an employee who tests positive for drug use must be given a chance to get professional help. Only after treatment or counseling has proved unsuccessful can the employee be disciplined or fired.

Illustration 14-6   Most states allow routine drug testing of workers whose jobs affect the safety of others.

REVIEW QUESTIONS

1. What is OSHA, and what does it do?
2. What is workers' compensation?
3. List three ways in which states restrict polygraph testing of employees.
4. Who is more likely to have to take a drug test—a train engineer or a librarian? Why?

LEAVING THE JOB

In the United States, it is rare for a person to take a job for life. Most people—especially younger people—leave jobs frequently. They may do so in order to get a better job, change careers, return to school, or stay home to raise children.

Sometimes the employer decides that an employee should leave. An employer may fire an employee whose job performance has been unsatisfactory. An employer may also dismiss an employee for economic reasons.

Regardless of who makes the decision, federal and state laws protect the rights of both employers and employees when an employee leaves the job.

Resigning

If you have an individual written employment contract, that contract may prohibit you from leaving your job before a certain date. If you quit before that date, you may have to compensate your employer for the losses caused by your early departure. For example, you may have to pay for the cost of finding someone to replace you. You may also have to pay for the time lost between your departure and the replacement's arrival.

If you are an employee-at-will, you can leave your job at any time and for any reason. You can do so without liability. Most employees give their employers **notice**, or advance warning that they will be leaving the job. Some employment contracts require employees to give two weeks' notice or even more.

Wrongful Discharge

If you have a written employment contract that expires on a certain date, your employer must allow you to work until that date. He or she can fire you earlier only if he or she has **good cause**—that is, a legitimate reason. Chronic absenteeism, violation of safety rules, unsatisfactory job performance, dishonesty, and fighting are examples of good cause for firing. Even if an employment contract has no expiration date, it may state that the employee cannot be fired without good cause.

If you don't have an individual employment contract, your employer can fire you at any time, even without good cause. As you read earlier, an employer can usually fire an employee-at-will for any reason or for no reason at all. There are, however, a number of exceptions to this rule. For example, government employees may be fired only for good cause. The same is true for many union members.

There are other exceptions as well. As you read at the beginning of this chapter, employees may not be fired because of race, religion, national origin, sex, or age (if they are over 40). Employees may not be fired for joining a union, making a complaint to OSHA, filing for workers' compensation, protesting an invasion of their privacy, or suing an employer for unfair treatment. As was illustrated by the case that opened this chapter, employees may not be fired for refusing to do something illegal. Firing an employee for any of these reasons is called **wrongful discharge** and is against federal law.

Layoffs

Occasionally, an employer must let a number of employees go in order to reduce costs. This reduction in staff is called a **layoff**. Laying off employees is different from firing them. It has nothing to do with an individual's job performance. Also, unlike firings, layoffs are often meant to be temporary. In many cases, the employer agrees to reinstate the laid-off employees as soon as possible.

Layoffs can be especially devastating to a community when a large factory closes or reduces its work force. Many people lose their jobs all at once. To help reduce the impact of sudden layoffs, Congress passed the Worker.Adjustment and Retraining Notification Act in 1988. This law requires factories employing more than 100 people to give at least two months' notice of a shutdown or cutback in staff.

Unemployment Compensation

Employees who are laid off are usually entitled to receive unemployment compensation. **Unemployment compensation** is a series of payments that the government gives to workers who lose their jobs through no fault of their own. You'll read about the funding for this program in Chapter 17.

Illustration 14-7   Employees who are laid off from their jobs are usually entitled to receive unemployment compensation for a certain period of time.

Employees who were fired for misconduct are not eligible for unemployment compensation. Employees who quit their jobs are also not eligible unless they had good cause for quitting. For example, you read earlier in this chapter about Ms. Lapham, who resigned because the cigarette smoke in her office made her ill. The court ruled that she was entitled to unemployment compensation because she had good cause for leaving her job.

Unemployed workers receive unemployment payments only for a limited period of time and only if they can prove that they are ready and willing to work. If they do not actively look for work or if they turn down jobs for which they are suited, their unemployment payments may be cut off.

REVIEW QUESTIONS

1. List four things an employee might do that would give an employer good cause to fire that employee.
2. Describe two exceptions to the rule that an employee-at-will can be fired for any reason.
3. What is unemployment compensation? Who is entitled to receive it?

Latest in the Law: Parental Leave

More than half of all women in the United States work. Millions of these women are single parents who must work full-time to support their families. For many working women, life requires a constant juggling of the demands of their jobs, their families, and their homes.

One of the most important job benefits for working women is the right to take time off from work after they have given birth or when they must care for sick children, parents, or spouses. This time off—called parental leave, maternity leave, or family leave—may range from a one-day absence because the baby-sitter didn't show up to a year's leave after the birth or adoption of a child. Increasingly, male workers are also feeling the need to take time off from work to care for children or deal with family crises.

Most workers cannot take this time off unless they know their job will be waiting for them when they are ready to return to work. Some cannot do it in any case unless the time off is paid for by the company.

Business Is Slow to Respond

Many believe that American business has not been meeting the need for parental leave very well. In a 1988 survey, only 36 percent of full-time workers in medium-size and large companies were found to be covered by parental leave policies. Most of these policies provided between 6 and 26 weeks of leave for women who needed to take time off after childbirth—and this leave was unpaid.

American parental leave policies contrast sharply with those of other industrialized nations. In most of these other countries, new parents receive generous paid parental leave. Sweden, for example, provides 90 percent of a worker's salary for nine months plus a flat rate of pay for three additional months.

In the mid-1980s, organizations began to lobby Congress and state legislatures for laws that would compel private corporations to grant unpaid parental leave to their employees. Most business groups strongly opposed mandatory parental leave laws. They argued that such laws would cause great hardship to, and even bankrupt, small companies that had to hire temporary employees while holding jobs open for workers on long-term leave.

Those who favored the proposed laws argued that workers faced great hardships when they had to lose their jobs and income in order to take care of their children and handle family crises. Those in favor of parental leave also argued that paternal leave would be cheaper for most companies in the long run because it would reduce costly employee turnover.

Action in Congress and State Legislatures

There is no federal family leave law on the books. In 1990 one was passed by Congress, requiring companies to provide men and women with up to 12 weeks of unpaid parental leave. President George Bush vetoed that law.

Meanwhile, about one third of the states have enacted some version of a parental leave law. Many other states are considering enacting such laws.

All state parental leave laws cover government employees. North Dakota, for example, provides up to four months of unpaid parental leave to state employees. Some of these state laws also require private employers to provide parental leave. In Maine, private employers with 25 or more workers must provide up to eight weeks of unpaid leave. All the state laws require employers to reinstate employees to the same or equivalent jobs when they return to work.

The number of single-parent families and two-earner families is expected to continue to grow. This indicates that the need for parental leave will continue to increase.

Chapter Review

Chapter Summary

■ Federal and state laws protect employees and job applicants against unfair discrimination. Title VII of the Civil Rights Act of 1964 prohibits employers from taking a person's race, religion, national origin, or sex into account when making decisions regarding hiring, promotion, working conditions, or firing.

■ The Equal Pay Act requires that men and women who do the same work, or substantially the same work, receive the same compensation.

■ The Age Discrimination in Employment Act protects workers over 40 years old from being discriminated against because of their age.

■ Child labor laws prohibit employers from hiring people under age 18 for certain dangerous jobs or jobs that require long hours.

■ The Rehabilitation Act and the Americans with Disabilities Act guarantee fair treatment of employees and job applicants who are handicapped.

■ Employers may interview job applicants and give them aptitude tests or psychological tests. Employers' rights to require polygraph testing or drug testing of applicants are limited by law.

■ An individual written employment contract describes the employer's and the employee's rights and duties. An employee without a contract is an employee-at-will. An employee-at-will may have certain rights under an implied contract.

■ Many employees are members of labor unions. Union members may achieve higher wages and better working conditions through the process of collective bargaining.

■ The Fair Labor Standards Act requires that employers pay the workers in most jobs no less than the federal minimum wage. It also provides that nonsalaried workers who work more than 40 hours a week receive extra compensation in the form of overtime payments.

■ Many employers provide benefits for their employees, such as tuition reimbursement, insurance coverage, and vacation pay.

■ The Occupational Safety and Health Administration (OSHA) ensures that all employees work in a safe environment. It monitors employee injuries and requires employers to provide certain safety features at the workplace. Employees who are injured are entitled to workers' compensation.

■ Employers have the right to monitor their employees' work and, in most cases, to search their employees. Some states restrict employers' rights to give polygraph tests or drug tests to employees.

■ An employer may fire an employee at any time if there is good cause. An employer may fire an employee-at-will even without good cause unless doing so is prohibited by a union contract or an implied contract. No employer may fire an employee if that firing violates Title VII or any·other antidiscrimination act.

■ An employer may not fire an employee for filing a complaint or joining a union. An employer may not fire an employee who refuses to perform an illegal act.

■ An employee who is laid off and is willing and able to work may be entitled to unemployment compensation.

Understanding Legal Terms

On a separate sheet of paper, match the terms below with the definitions that follow.

collective bargaining	polygraph test
employee-at-will	severance pay
good cause	union contract
independent contractor	workers' compensation
notice	wrongful discharge

1. Series of questions asked of a person who is hooked up to a machine, done to determine whether the person is lying
2. A legitimate reason to fire an employee
3. Process in which employees join together to negotiate with their employer
4. An agreement between an employer and employees who are organized in a group
5. Person who is self-employed
6. Sum of money given by an employer to an employee who is fired or laid off
7. Money paid to an employee who is injured on the job
8. Advance warning given to an employer by an employee who is leaving a job
9. Unlawful firing of an employee
10. Worker who does not have an individual written employment contract with an employer

Applying the Law

1. Les decides to promote one of his two assistant managers to manager. One assistant, Annette, is 26 years old. The other, Clifton, is 35 years old. Because Les thinks a younger person is more likely to stay with the firm longer, he offers the promotion to Annette. Clifton feels that he has been the victim of age discrimination. What, if anything, can he do?

2. All the employees in Max's department store belong to a labor union. When Max decides to eliminate health insurance as an employee benefit, the employees complain that they are being treated unfairly. Max refuses to discuss the matter. What can the employees do?

3. Mandy runs a restaurant. She pays her waiters $2.50 an hour. They also earn about $5.00 an hour in tips. One day Mandy decides that the practice of tipping waiters makes her customers uncomfortable. She announces to the customers and staff that tipping is no longer permitted in the restaurant. After setting this new policy, what other change must Mandy make?

4. Kim applies for a job as a correctional officer at the county jail. Timothy, the warden, calls her in for an interview. He asks Kim about her education and training for the job. He gives her a written exam to test her understanding of jail policies. He asks her if she is an American citizen. He requires her to take a psychological test, a polygraph test, and a drug test. Has Timothy done anything that violates federal law? Explain your answer.

5. Michael is an employee-at-will at a company that rents boats on the bay. At the end of each day, he must inspect and wash each boat. To save time, Ryan, the manager, tells Michael to dump the dirty wash water into the bay. Michael knows that dumping anything into the bay is illegal. When he refuses to follow Ryan's instructions, Ryan fires him. Is Ryan's action legal? Explain your answer.

6. Ted works in a soda-bottling factory. The bottle-capping machine is malfunctioning. Every once in a while, it spits a bottle cap out toward the workers. The workers have complained, but the factory owner says she can't afford to fix it. One day the machine spits out a cap and hits Ted, injuring his eye. What should Ted do?

Case Studies

1. Brenda Phillips worked as a janitor in Ray Smalley's company. Every week, Smalley called Phillips into his private office and asked her questions about her sex life. He made sexual advances. When Phillips refused to have sex with Smalley, he fired her. Did Smalley violate any laws? If so, what could Phillips do?

2. Loveman's Department Store in Montgomery, Alabama, hired women to sell women's clothing and men to sell men's clothing. The saleswomen were paid less than the salesmen were paid. The department store defended this action, saying that selling clothes to women is not the same thing as selling clothes to men. Was the department store's policy permissible? Why or why not?

3. Ulysses Grant worked nights at a juvenile detention center in Washington, D.C. After twice catching Grant sleeping on the job, his supervisor fired him. Grant went to the District of Columbia Department of Employment Services to collect unemployment compensation. Did the department accept Grant's application? Why or why not?

Chapter 15

Consumer Law

Chapter Objectives When you have read this chapter, you should be able to:

■ Describe how federal and state laws and agencies protect the rights of consumers.

■ Explain what a warranty is, and name the kinds of warranties that come with the goods people purchase.

■ Describe the restrictions that the federal government places on the advertising, pricing, and labeling of products.

■ Give three examples of what the Federal Trade Commission can do when it discovers an unfair business practice.

■ Explain what it means to make a purchase on credit, and describe what can happen if a buyer doesn't make credit payments on time.

Case Study

Warner-Lambert Company v. Federal Trade Commission, 562 F.2d 749 (District of Columbia Cir. 1977).

The Warner-Lambert Company produces Listerine Antiseptic mouthwash. For over 50 years, its advertisements for the mouthwash said that Listerine "kills germs on contact." The ads claimed that gargling with Listerine would help cure and prevent colds and sore throats. In 1972 the Federal Trade Commission (FTC), a federal agency that regulates businesses, investigated Warner-Lambert's claim that Listerine cured colds.

After reviewing Warner-Lambert's scientific studies and consulting with experts, the FTC concluded that although Listerine may indeed kill germs and soothe throat irritation, it does not cure or prevent colds or sore throats. Warner-Lambert's ads, therefore, were false and were misleading the public. The FTC ordered the company to stop running those ads immediately.

Further, the FTC ordered Warner-Lambert to run corrective advertising for the next several years. During that time, the company had to include the following statement in its Listerine ads: "Listerine will not help prevent colds or sore throats or lessen their severity." The FTC said that in print ads (ads in newspapers and magazines and on billboards), the statement had to appear in a type size at least as large as the rest of the text in the ad. In television ads, the statement had to be shown and spoken simultaneously. In this way, Warner-Lambert could correct the public's mistaken beliefs about Listerine that resulted from years of false advertising.

SALES AGREEMENTS

Traditionally, when a person bought a product, it came with no guarantees. It might work; it might not. **Caveat emptor**, a Latin phrase meaning "let the buyer beware," ruled transactions between buyers and sellers. Today, however, caveat emptor is no longer the rule. Over the years, many federal, state, and local laws have been developed to protect consumers. (A **consumer** is someone who buys a product or service for personal use.)

An important step forward in consumer protection occurred in 1952, when a group of lawyers, judges, and businesspeople developed the Uniform Commercial Code. The **Uniform Commercial Code (UCC)** is a set of laws that establish the rights and duties of people who buy or sell products. (The UCC does not apply to sales of real estate, services, or money.) Every state except Louisiana has made the UCC into state law. Therefore, nearly all American consumers receive the same protection no matter where they live.

Hundreds of other consumer laws, both state and federal, protect consumers' rights. In addition, the federal and state governments have established agencies to help consumers who have trouble with goods or services. As you read in the opening case, the Federal Trade Commission (FTC) regulates businesses throughout the country. At the state level, state attorneys general and offices of consumer affairs can be extremely effective. These agencies make sure that companies deal fairly and honestly with the public.

The Sales Contract

You read in Chapter 9 about contracts and how they are made. A sale is a particular kind of contract. Therefore, all the rules you read about contracts apply to sales. There must be an offer (most often in the form of a price tag), an acceptance, and consideration. As with any other contract, you have the right to cancel a sales contract that you are pressured into or deceived about. If you are a minor, you may have the right to change your mind and cancel a sale for any reason.

Most sales contracts do not have to be written. However, the UCC requires written contracts for sales of goods worth more than $500. Without a written contract, you may not be able to enforce your contractual rights in court.

Nearly every written sales contract is a **contract of adhesion**—a contract in which one party makes the rules and the other must "take it or leave it." Sellers usually use standard, preprinted contract forms that are designed to protect the seller. Therefore, the UCC includes special protection for buyers who sign those contracts. If a contract of adhesion turns out to be **unconscionable**, or grossly unfair, the buyer can go to court. The court may undo, or rescind, the unfair part of the contract or cancel the contract entirely.

Special Kinds of Sales

Before buying a major item, such as a car or a stereo system, most people go from store to store to compare models and prices. They then buy from the seller who gives them the best deal. Not all sales are made in stores, however. In fact, many consumers purchase certain kinds of goods without leaving their homes.

Door-to-Door Sales   **Door-to-door salespeople** are sales representatives who go from house to house, demonstrating and selling products to neighborhood residents. Buying something from a door-to-door salesperson is convenient, but it also can be risky. You don't have the opportunity to comparison shop, and you may not be aware of competitors' prices for the same item. In addition, you may feel pressured to buy something simply to get the salesperson out of your home.

For all these reasons, in 1974 the FTC developed a set of rules to regulate door-to-door sales. Under these rules, any door-to-door salesperson who sells you goods worth more than $25 must allow you a three-day **cooling-off period**. During this period, you have the right to change your mind and cancel

Illustration 15-1   Many people purchase goods through the mail.

the sale for any reason. The salesperson must notify you in writing of your right to a cooling-off period and explain the procedure for canceling orders.

Mail-Order Sales   Another common way to purchase items is through the mail. Many consumers read catalogs or watch "home shopping" programs on television and then order goods by calling or writing to a company. The company then delivers the goods directly to the consumer's home.

Some companies used to try to trick consumers into paying for goods they didn't order. A company would send an item to a consumer, along with a bill. Many consumers wouldn't ask questions—they would simply keep the merchandise and pay the bill.

Congress put an end to this practice in 1970, when it passed the Postal Reorganization Act. Under this law, if you receive an unordered item through the mail, you are under no obligation to pay for it or return it. Instead, you can treat the item as a gift. You are free to keep it or throw it away.

Some mail-order companies—particularly those that sell books or CDs—get around this restriction by using a **negative option plan**. Under this plan, a company sends out products on a regular schedule, and customers must let the company know when they *don't* want to receive a product. For example, Donny signs up with the Bailey Book Club. The club agrees to notify Donny each month about a new book it intends to send him. Donny then has a short time to let the company know that he does not want the book. If he does nothing, the book will come automatically and Donny will be required to pay for it.

REVIEW QUESTIONS

1. What does *caveat emptor* mean?
2. What is the Uniform Commercial Code?
3. What special rule applies to door-to-door sales that does not apply to other types of sales?
4. What is a negative option plan?

CONSUMER PROTECTION

The main purpose of the UCC is to require that sellers treat buyers honestly and fairly. The UCC enforces this requirement by providing certain remedies for buyers who are deceived or cheated by sellers.

The UCC rules apply to all sales, involving anything from a diamond necklace in a jewelry store to an old iron at a garage sale. In many instances, however, the UCC requirements are stricter for **merchants** (people who are in the regular business of selling) than they are for occasional sellers (people who are selling something but don't do so for a living). For example, if you decide to buy a used car, you may be better protected if you buy it from a used car dealer than if you buy it from a neighbor.

Express Warranties

On August 10, 1975, James Ewers went to the Verona Rock Shop in Madison, Wisconsin. He wanted to buy some decorations to put in his saltwater aquarium with his tropical fish. The sales clerk told him that the shells, coral, and driftwood he picked out "had come from salt water and were suitable for salt-water aquariums."

Ewers took the items home and put them in his aquarium. A week later, all his fish were dead. He found out that the water was polluted. Tiny creatures inhabiting the shells and coral had decayed, releasing toxic matter into the water. That toxic matter had killed the fish.

Ewers sued the store. The court held the store responsible for the death of Ewers's fish. The court said that a buyer should be able to rely on any statement a seller makes about the condition or quality of the goods being sold. The sales clerk at the Verona Rock Shop had made a clear statement that the shells and coral were suitable for Ewers's fish tank. That statement was an express warranty.

An **express warranty** is a seller's promise that a product will function in a particular way. For example, most new cars come with a warranty that the car will run properly for 12 months or 12,000 miles. If the car fails to function properly, the seller promises to fix the defects at no charge. If the seller promises to repair or replace any defective part, he or she is offering a **full warranty**. If the seller promises to repair or replace only certain parts, he or she is offering a **limited warranty**.

GLOBAL ELECTRONIC CORPORATION OF AMERICA
Also known as GECA
GLOBAL ELECTRONIC OF CANADA LIMITED
Also known as GECL

WARRANTY

GLOBAL ELECTRONIC CORPORATION OF AMERICA (GECA) guarantees that each Global product for home use will be free of defects in materials or workmanship. GECA agrees to remedy any such defect or to provide a new or equal part in exchange. All repairs covered by this warranty must be performed at one of our authorized service agencies.

This warranty covers labor costs for 90 days and parts for 1 year from the date of original purchase, provided that the product is purchased and used within the United States of America or Canada.

This warranty does not apply to any product damaged following the time of sale either in transit or because of accident, misuse, fire, flood, or acts of God.

GLOBAL ELECTRONIC CORPORATION OF AMERICA (GECA)
GLOBAL ELECTRONIC OF CANADA LIMITED (GECL)

Illustration 15-2   An express warranty, which may be oral or written, is a seller's promise that a product will function in a certain way.

Though sellers generally offer express warranties only for new products, some sellers offer them for used products as well. For example, many car dealers offer limited warranties for used cars.

Express warranties may be oral, like the one made to James Ewers, or they may be written. Written contracts are subject to the rules of the Magnuson-Moss Warranty Act. This act, passed in by Congress in 1975, applies to any written warranty for a product that costs $15 or more. The law requires that a warranty explain clearly what the warranty covers, what it does not cover, when it expires, and how to make claims on the warranty. Of course, a seller is not required to make an express warranty at all.

Implied Warranties

According to the UCC, you have the right to expect certain things about the products you buy. If you buy a can opener, for example, you have the right to expect that it will open cans—even if the seller doesn't specifically promise that it will. This sort of assumption, which is "understood" by the buyer without being explicitly stated, is called an **implied warranty**. Whether or not the seller offers an express warranty, every product you buy comes with a number of implied warranties. The three most important are warranty of title, warranty of merchantability, and warranty of fitness for a particular purpose.

Warranty of Title   A person can't sell something that he or she doesn't own. The **warranty of title** is a promise that the seller legally owns the property he or she is selling. (**Title** is legal ownership.) Suppose your neighbor borrows a friend's drill and then sells it to you at a yard sale. When the friend finds out what happened, she calls you and demands that you give back her drill. At that point, you have the right to get back the money you paid to your neighbor.

Warranty of Merchantability   Paul Vlases lived in western Pennsylvania. In 1961 he decided to raise chickens. After building a large chicken coop, he ordered and received 2,200 baby chicks from Montgomery Ward & Company. Within a few weeks, the chicks began to look unhealthy. Medical examinations revealed that the chicks were afflicted with avian leukosis, a fatal disease. All the chicks died. Vlases sued Montgomery Ward.

In court, a veterinary expert testified that Montgomery Ward could not have known about, caused, prevented, or cured the avian leukosis. Therefore, the company claimed that it could not be held liable for the death of the baby chicks. The court disagreed. It said that every time a merchant sells a product, there is an implied warranty that the product can be used for its "ordinary purpose"—that is, the purpose it is generally used for. This is called the implied **warranty of merchantability**.

Under the warranty of merchantability, the scissors you buy should cut paper, tape should stick, and baby chicks should grow into chickens. If something you buy from a merchant doesn't work as it's supposed to, the merchant may have breached this warranty. Even if the merchant was unaware of the defect, he or she is still required to fix it, give you a replacement, or return your money.

Only merchants—professional sellers—are held to the implied warranty of merchantability. Occasional sellers are not.

Warranty of Fitness for a Particular Purpose   Charlie wants to go hiking in Alaska. He goes to a sporting goods store, explains what he plans to do, and asks for help in picking out boots for the excursion. Denise, the store owner, sells Charlie a pair of boots. Though they are well made, these particular boots are meant for warm, dry hikes, not for Alaskan weather. Charlie wears them to Alaska, and they soak through and fall apart halfway through his hike. Denise may be liable for a breach of **warranty of fitness for a particular purpose**. That is, Denise incorrectly promised Charlie that the product he bought would work not only for their ordinary purpose (hiking) but for his particular purpose (hiking in a cold, wet climate).

The warranty of fitness for a particular purpose applies whenever a buyer tells a seller about a specific need and then relies on the seller's skills and judgment in making the purchase. Both merchants and occasional sellers may be held to this warranty.

Disclaimers

A buyer can rely on a seller's express and implied warranties unless the seller explicitly limits them. For example, you may see an item in a store marked "as is." This is a **disclaimer**, or a notice that some warranties do not apply. To be valid, a disclaimer must be clearly visible and stated in simple English. Disclaimers are often included in sales contracts or on tags. They are usually printed in large type or in a different color to draw the buyer's attention.

The UCC does not permit disclaimers to be hidden in fine print or expressed in difficult language. Courts nearly always consider such disclaimers unconscionable and therefore invalid.

Products Liability

You read in Chapter 8 about **products liability**. As you may recall, if a product causes injuries or damage, the product's manufacturer or seller may be held liable. This is true regardless of express or implied warranties.

Product Standards

In 1972 Congress passed the Consumer Product Safety Act. This law set up the Consumer Product Safety Commission (CPSC), whose responsibility is to create and enforce standards for consumer products. Manufacturers are required to design and build their products in accordance with these standards.

Occasionally, as a result of consumer complaints, a manufacturer may discover that one of its products does not meet CPSC standards. When that occurs, the manufacturer must report the problem to the CPSC. The CPSC may then require the manufacturer to **recall** the product—that is, ask consumers to bring the product back to the seller. The seller must then repair or replace the product without charge or refund the purchase price.

Other federal agencies provide consumer protection as well. For example, the Food and Drug Administration (FDA) has developed standards for food, drugs, and cosmetics. It regulates the ingredients that go into these products and the production methods that are used to manufacture them.

Lemon Laws

Cars are complicated machines that often suffer from design or manufacturing flaws. Some new cars are particularly prone to problems. Even after repeated repairs, they still don't work properly. These cars are commonly referred to as "lemons." Most states have passed **lemon laws** to protect people who buy chronically defective cars. Under these laws, the manufacturer must refund the buyer's money or replace the car in the following situations: (1) if a substantial defect in a new car cannot be repaired after a given number of tries or (2) if the defect causes the car to be in the repair shop for more than 30 days in its first year.

Regulating Services

You read earlier in this chapter that the UCC applies only to the sale of products. To provide further protection to consumers, many states regulate the sale of services as well.

The most common way to regulate services is through licensing. In every state, for example, people who want to practice medicine, dentistry, law, engineering, or similar professions must be licensed. To qualify for a license, they must take exams or demonstrate in other ways that they meet professional standards. If they perform poorly or act in an unprofessional manner, their license can be taken away.

Many types of businesses are licensed as well. For example, hospitals, schools, banks, and auto mechanics must meet state standards before they can offer their services to consumers.

REVIEW QUESTIONS

1. Give an example of an express warranty.
2. What is the difference between a warranty of merchantability and a warranty of fitness for a particular purpose?
3. What is a disclaimer? What type of disclaimer might a court rule to be unconscionable?
4. How do states regulate sellers of services?

Illustration 15-3 Sellers are required by law not to deceive customers in advertising or in labeling their products.

RESTRICTED BUSINESS PRACTICES

Sellers are required to do more than offer good-quality products. The FTC and other agencies require that businesses treat consumers fairly and avoid misleading them through advertising. They must not use sales tricks to attract customers. They must also label their products accurately so that consumers know what they are getting for their money.

Deceptive Advertising

The purpose of advertising is to increase the sales of a product. Some advertisements do this by offering information to show how the product is superior to competing products. Others do it by using attention-getting devices to make the product seem fun, sexy, or desirable. In some cases, advertisers simply repeat the product's name over and over again. All these techniques are permissible under federal law as long as advertisers don't make false claims about their products. If an advertiser says things that are clearly untrue (as Warner-Lambert did in its ads for Listerine), its advertising is considered deceptive. Deceptive advertising is prohibited by FTC regulations.

There is a difference between deceptive advertising and puffery. **Puffery** is exaggerated sales talk—for example, referring to an item as "the world's best" or "the most comfortable you'll ever own." Statements such as these are considered to be opinions rather than facts, and giving an opinion is not illegal.

Bait and Switch

Some dishonest sellers engage in a practice called **bait and switch**. They advertise a very low price on a certain product in order to lure customers into the store. Once a customer arrives, the seller finds an excuse not to sell that product. (In some cases, the low-priced product doesn't even exist.) The seller then persuades the customer to buy a higher-priced product instead.

For example, suppose you see a newspaper ad for Stan's Butcher Shop. It says that Stan is selling a choice cut of meat for only $3.50 a pound, when the usual price is $7.50. When you go to the store and ask to see the advertised meat, Stan tells you it's sold out, or he shows you a steak that is so fatty that it appears inedible. Then he shows you another cut of meat that was not advertised and is not on sale. It's clear that Stan had no intention of selling the meat that he advertised. He was using it as bait to get you into his shop.

The practice of bait and switch is against FTC regulations. If a seller advertises a low-priced product, he or she must describe it honestly and be prepared to sell it to customers who want it.

Pricing Practices

Niresk Industries was a mail-order company that sold kitchen appliances. During 1957 it advertised the Merit cooker-fryer for sale at prices of $6.95 to $8.95. The advertisements said that the regular value of the appliance was $39.95. In fact, Niresk had never sold the cooker-fryer for $39.95, nor had any other merchant. Similar appliances on the market were sold at that price, but the Merit cooker-fryer had never been sold for more than $20.00. The FTC decided that Niresk's ads were deceptive and ordered that they be stopped.

It is perfectly legal for a store to reduce its prices and advertise both the original price and the sale price. However, a store may not invent fictitious "regular" prices or make misleading price comparisons with other products. Doing so is against FTC regulations.

Labeling

The FTC requires products to be labeled clearly and honestly. For example, in 1960 Bantam Books published two kinds of paperback books. Some were full-length reprints of previously published hardback books; others were abridged (shortened) versions of the hardback books. One of the abridged books did not indicate anywhere on the cover that it was abridged; others were labeled "abridged," but only in small, hard-to-read print. The FTC decided that this practice was deceptive. It ordered Bantam to indicate clearly on the cover of every abridged book that the book was abridged.

The FDA also has rules about labeling. All food, drug, and cosmetic products must be labeled to warn consumers about any known harm that may result from using those products. Labels on diet foods, for example, must indicate which artificial sweeteners the foods contain, because some people are allergic to certain sweeteners. Labels on cleaning products must give directions for using the products safely and explain the dangers of using them improperly.

REVIEW QUESTIONS

1. Give an example of puffery.
2. Define *bait and switch*.
3. Why does the federal government require certain information on labels for consumer products?

CONSUMER REMEDIES

As you read in Chapter 7, if you have a dispute with someone, such as with a seller of a product or service, you can sue that person in civil court. If the amount is small enough, usually $2,000 or less, you can go to small claims court. Going to court should be done only as a last resort, however. Very often, the problem can be solved by other means, such as negotiation or mediation.

If you are not satisfied with a product or service, the first thing you should do is negotiate with the seller. In most cases, he or she will be willing to repair or replace the product, or redo the service, at no charge to you. You may also contact the manufacturer of the product. Many manufacturers have toll-free telephone numbers—often listed on the product package—for questions or complaints. In some cases—for example, if you are having a problem with a chain store outlet—you can contact the company headquarters to issue your complaint. Many of these companies also have toll-free numbers.

If you are not satisfied with the seller's or the company's response, you can seek the help of a private organization that handles consumer complaints, or you can contact a government agency. These organizations and agencies will also be able to help you if you are the victim of deceptive advertising, bait and switch practices, mislabeling, or other unfair business practices.

Private Business and Consumer Groups

If informal negotiation isn't successful in resolving a problem with a merchant or manufacturer, you may want to seek help from a private business group or consumer organization. Companies that manufacture similar products, such as clothing or cars, and those that offer similar services, such as travel agents or insurance companies, often belong to industry associations. These groups help resolve problems between their members and consumers. They may offer mediation and arbitration. Professional associations, such as those representing doctors, lawyers, and accountants, may also have consumer-help services. For service providers who must be licensed, such as electricians and beauticians, licensing boards have a procedure for handling consumer complaints.

The Council of Better Business Bureaus, a nonprofit national organization with local and regional offices, also offers mediation and arbitration services. Local Better Business Bureaus also can help you avoid trouble if you contact them before buying a product or service. The BBB provides background information on local businesses. It keeps records of complaints issued against companies and of how those companies resolved the problems. Figure 15-1 lists the 20 types of businesses about which the Better Business Bureaus received the most complaints in 1990.

Many local newspapers and radio and television stations have action lines or hotlines for consumers. However, they usually handle only the most severe or the most common problems.

Government Agencies

Government agencies can be especially helpful to consumers with problems. Unlike private organizations, these agencies have the power of the government behind them. The CPSC, FDA, and FTC, along with similar agencies on the state level, have broad powers to protect consumers. When necessary, they can force sellers to act fairly. For example, the FTC can order a merchant to return your money for a defective product. As you'll read in Chapter 18, government agencies are often willing to help with a consumer's problem through negotiation or by suing a company or seller on behalf of the consumer.

If the FTC finds that a merchant has been guilty of deceptive advertising, false labeling, or other illegal practices, it will request that the merchant sign a **consent order**—a voluntary agreement to stop the practice.

For example, in 1970 Standard Oil ran a series of television commercials to show how its new gasoline additive, F-310, made engines run more cleanly. In one commercial, demonstrators attached a transparent balloon to the exhaust pipe of a car that had its engine running. The balloon filled up with black smoke. Then the gas tank was refilled with Standard Oil's gasoline containing F-310. This time, when the balloon was attached, it filled with a colorless vapor.

FIGURE 15–1   Major Areas of Consumer Complaints in the United States

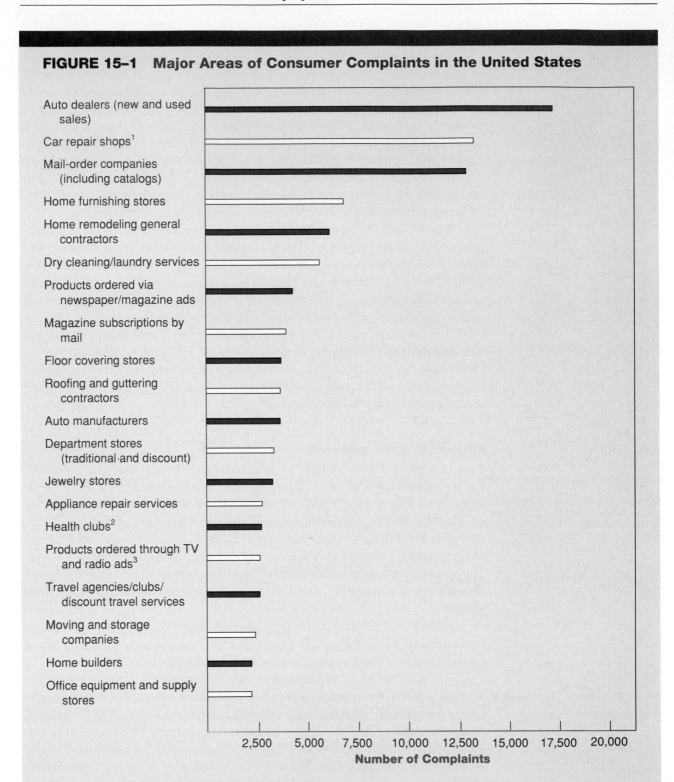

1. Includes transmission and body and paint shops.
2. Includes tennis and racquetball clubs and fitness and exercise class companies.
3. Includes "30-minute commercials."

Source: Selected data extracted from the Council of Better Business Bureaus, Inc. , *Annual Inquiry and Complaint Summary—1990.*

What the commercial didn't mention was that the car in the commercial was at first filled with an unusual gasoline—a formula designed to expel dark smoke from the car. If the car had been filled with ordinary gasoline, its exhaust wouldn't have been nearly as dirty. When the FTC commented on this, Standard Oil consented to superimpose on the screen "very dirty engine purposely used to provide severe test."

Unlike Standard Oil, some sellers may refuse to agree to a consent order. Others may break a consent order to which they have agreed. In such cases, the FTC can make a **cease and desist order** that requires the sellers to stop their illegal practices.

If the FTC has reason to doubt the claims in an advertisement, it may ask the seller for **advertising substantiation**—proof that the claims are true. If the seller can't prove the claims, the FTC can require that an **affirmative disclosure**—a statement of the product's limitations—be included in the advertisement. For example, many magazine ads for television sets include the phrase "TV picture simulated." This is an affirmative disclosure designed to warn the consumer that the real television picture may not be as sharp as the one shown in the ad.

As you saw in the case of Listerine Antiseptic, the FTC may require **corrective advertising** in certain cases. That is, the FTC may require a seller to run ads that correct misstatements made in earlier ads.

REVIEW QUESTIONS

1. What is the first thing you should do if you find that a product you bought doesn't work properly?
2. What is the first thing the FTC will do when it finds that a company is engaging in an unfair trade practice?
3. What is advertising substantiation? Affirmative disclosure?

USING CREDIT

Some products and services are too expensive for the average consumer to pay for all at once. The biggest purchases most people make are homes and cars. Even a college education may cost tens of thousands of dollars. Many people pay for these kinds of items on **credit**. That is, they receive an item in exchange for a promise to pay for it over a period of time. (Credit is also the money that is lent.)

Suppose you decide to buy a new car. The car you want costs $15,000, but you have only $1,000 in the bank. If you have a good job and sufficient income, the car dealer may agree to let you buy the car on credit. However, in almost every case, you'll have to pay a portion of the purchase price right away. You can then pay the rest of the price in monthly installments over a period of years. In the meantime, the car is yours to use.

You and the car dealer must agree on how much you will pay per month. Each monthly payment covers part of the price of the car, plus interest. (**Interest** is the money you pay for the right to buy on credit.)

When you make a purchase on credit, you become a **debtor**. The person or business that provides credit (in this case, the car dealer) is called a **creditor**. Besides getting credit at the place of purchase, you can also borrow money from banks, credit unions where you work, and finance companies.

Secured Credit

Creditors may require collateral before agreeing to give you credit. **Collateral** is a valuable item that you agree to give the creditor if you fail to pay the money you owe. In the example of your buying a car on credit from a car dealer, the dealer will probably require the car as collateral. With such an arrangement, you must sign an agreement stating that you are giving the dealer a security interest in the car. The security interest gives the dealer the right to **repossess** the car—that is, take it away from you—if you stop making payments.

Illustration 15-4   If you stop making installment payments on your car, the creditor may repossess it.

After repossessing the car, the dealer must sell it to someone else. From the money he or she receives, the dealer can keep the amount you owe on the car, plus the costs of repossessing and selling the car. The dealer must then return any remaining money to you. In this example, the item being purchased is the collateral. In other cases, you may have to put up an item you already own, such as stock, jewelry, or a piece of land, as collateral when you borrow money.

Credit that requires collateral is called **secured credit**.

Unsecured Credit

Many people carry **credit cards** that allow them to buy goods and services on credit. Some credit cards, such as those issued by department stores, may be used only in one particular store. Other credit cards, issued by banks, can be used at thousands of places around the world.

The most common bank credit cards are MasterCard and VISA. When you pay for an item with a bank credit card, the merchant collects the purchase price from your bank. The bank then sends you a bill for the amount you owe. This type of credit is called **unsecured credit**, because neither the merchant nor the bank requires collateral.

The bank or company that issues your credit card will generally impose a **credit limit**—a limit on how much you can buy with the card. (The amount of the credit limit depends primarily on your income.) Before letting you buy something with a credit card, most stores will check that the amount of the purchase does not exceed your credit limit. If it does, you will not be able to use the card to make that purchase.

When you receive a bill for a purchase you made with a credit card, you can do either of two things. You can pay the bill right away, or you can pay it off little by little, in monthly installments. You can spread the payments over as many months or years as you wish, as long as you make a certain minimum payment each month.

Most issuers of credit cards don't charge interest if you pay your bills right away. If you choose to pay in installments, however, you will have to pay interest on the money you owe. The longer you take to pay for the item, the more interest you will have to pay. Interest rates for credit cards are higher than those for almost any other form of credit.

Debit Cards

More and more Americans are paying for purchases with **debit cards**. Although debit cards look much like credit cards, they operate very differently. When you use a debit card, the amount of the purchase is deducted by computer from your bank account. You never have to pay interest on debit card purchases.

Until recently, debit cards were used almost exclusively to withdraw cash from a "bank machine." They are still known to most people as automated teller machine (ATM) cards or electronic funds transfer (EFT) cards. Today, however, the uses of these cards are expanding. Many gas stations, supermarkets, and convenience stores now permit consumers to use debit cards to make purchases.

Applying for Credit

Before a creditor will give you credit, he or she will want to be sure that you can make all the monthly payments. In order to find out about as much as possible about your finances, the creditor will ask you to fill out a credit application.

On the application, you will have to state the name of your employer, the length of time you've worked for that employer, and your current salary. You will have to list any other creditors to whom you owe money and state how much you owe each one. The application may also ask about your **credit his-**

tory—that is, whether you've bought things on credit before and whether you made the payments on time.

If the creditor has any reason to think that you are a bad risk, he or she will deny your application. Under federal law, the creditor can consider only your financial situation and credit history in deciding whether to give you credit. The Equal Credit Opportunity Act, passed by Congress in 1974, prohibits creditors from taking your race, sex, national origin, religion, or marital status into account when making credit decisions.

Credit Bureaus

A creditor cannot always be certain that you are telling the truth on your application form. In most cases, he or she will want to verify the facts by checking other sources. For example, the creditor will probably call your employer to find out what your salary is. He or she may also consult a credit bureau to find out about your credit history.

A **credit bureau** (sometimes called a consumer reporting agency) is a company that collects information on consumers. If you've ever borrowed money or used a credit card, a credit bureau probably has information about you in its files. Credit bureaus keep watch over your bank accounts, marital status, occupation, and income. They keep records of any lawsuits you have been involved in. They also keep records of your educational background, health status, arrests, convictions, and any other factors that may help indicate whether you are a good credit risk.

When a creditor asks a credit bureau for information about you, the bureau prepares a **credit report** based on the information in your file. The creditor pays the bureau for this report.

The reports issued by credit bureaus are sometimes inaccurate. These errors cause consumers embarrassment and financial problems. In 1970 Congress passed the Fair Credit Reporting Act to remedy this situation. This law requires credit bureaus to check their information carefully and to delete information that is no longer relevant. It also requires creditors to tell you that they intend to contact a credit bureau about you.

If a creditor rejects your application because of information in a credit report, the law requires that the creditor tell you the reason for the rejection. In addition, the creditor must give you the name and address of the agency that made the report.

If your credit application is rejected, the Fair Credit Reporting Act gives you the right to see most of the information in your file, free of charge. (Even if your application has not been rejected, the credit bureau must allow you to see your file at any time. It may, however, charge you a small fee.) You have the right to know where the credit bureau got its information about you. You also have the right to know who has requested and received your credit report recently.

If you find a mistake in your file, you should notify the credit bureau immediately. The bureau must then investigate the mistake and make any necessary corrections. If the credit bureau disagrees with you and insists that its information is accurate, you have the right to add a brief statement to your file. You can use this statement to give your side of the story.

For example, let's say Nora applies for a credit card and is rejected. The credit card company tells her that she was rejected because of information about her employment history. It tells her that it got the information from the Investigative Credit Bureau.

Nora calls Investigative Credit and demands to see her file. The file includes a note that she had been fired from a job because she was caught stealing supplies. Nora tells the bureau that the information is inaccurate. She says that she quit that job because of personal differences with her boss.

An investigator from the credit bureau speaks to Nora's former boss. Based on this conversation, the investigator says that the bureau's information is correct—Nora had indeed been fired. The bureau therefore refuses to change Nora's file.

Nora now has the right to place a written statement in her file saying that she quit the job, that she was not fired, and that she never stole supplies. From now on, whenever anyone requests Nora's credit report, the bureau must include Nora's statement as part of the report.

Credit Protection

Federal and state laws protect consumers from paying excessive amounts of interest. Creditors face stiff penalties for violating these laws.

The federal Truth in Lending Act requires a creditor to tell you how much interest you will have to pay. The creditor must also let you know whether there will be any charges in addition to interest.

The Fair Credit Billing Act requires a creditor to send you monthly statements—written notices stating how much you've paid and how much you still owe. It's important that you examine these statements carefully and watch for errors. If you disagree with the creditor about how much you owe, you should notify the creditor immediately. Under the Fair Credit Billing Act, the creditor must respond to your notice within 90 days. You have the right not to pay the disputed amount until you and the creditor reach an agreement.

Federal law also protects you if your credit card is lost or stolen. As soon as you realize that your card is missing, you should notify the bank or company that issued the card. (MasterCard and VISA offer telephone hotlines that you can call at any time of the day or night.) The company will immediately cancel your credit card number and issue you a new one.

If someone uses your credit card before you report it missing, you are responsible for paying for only $50 worth of the unauthorized purchases made with that card. You do not have to pay for any purchases made after you report that the card is missing. Table 15-1 gives suggestions on how to protect yourself from credit card fraud.

Table 15-1 Consumer Tips about Credit Cards

1. In a safe place, keep a list of your credit card numbers, expiration dates, and the phone number given by each card issuer to be used if your card is lost or stolen.

2. Credit card issuers offer a wide variety of terms (annual percentage rate, methods of calculating the balance subject to the finance charge, minimum monthly payments, and actual membership fees). When selecting a card, compare the terms offered by several card issuers to find the card that best suits your needs.

3. When you use your credit card in a store, watch the card after giving it to a sales clerk. Take the card back promptly after the clerk is finished with it and make sure it's yours.

4. Tear up the carbons when you take your credit card receipt.

5. Never sign a blank receipt. Draw a line through any blank spaces above the total when you sign receipts.

6. Open credit card bills promptly and compare them with your receipts to check for unauthorized charges and billing errors.

7. Write the card issuer promptly to report any questionable charges. Written inquiries should not be included with your payment. Instead, check the billing statement for the correct address for billing questions. The inquiry must be in writing and must be sent within 60 days to guarantee your rights under the Fair Credit Billing Act.

8. Never give your credit card number over the telephone unless you made the call. Never put your card number on a postcard or on the outside of an envelope.

9. Sign new cards as soon as they arrive. Cut up and throw away expired cards. Cut up and return unwanted cards to the issuer.

10. If any of your credit cards are missing or stolen, report the loss as soon as possible to the card issuer. Check your credit card statement for a telephone number for reporting stolen credit cards. Follow up your phone calls with a letter to each card issuer. The letter should contain your card number, the date the card was missing, and the date you called in the loss.

11. If you report the loss before a credit card is used, the issuer cannot hold you responsible for any unauthorized charges made after the time of the report. If a thief uses your card before you report it missing, the most you will owe for unauthorized charges on each card is $50.

Source: U.S. Office of Consumer Affairs.

Debt Collection

People who buy on credit sometimes spend more than they can afford. You may someday buy an expensive item on credit and then find that you can't make the monthly payments. If that occurs, the creditor will have to take steps to collect the money that you owe.

Generally, the creditor will send you several written notices that your payments are overdue. If you still don't pay, the creditor must take more forceful action. If you offered collateral in exchange for credit, the creditor may choose to repossess it. If there is no collateral, the creditor may hire a **collection agency**—a business that specializes in collecting debts. The collection agency may write or phone you to discuss the matter.

The Fair Debt Collection Practices Act, passed by Congress in 1978, forbids collection agencies to use harassment, abusive language, or threats of violence to force you to pay. It also forbids them to contact your friends, family, or employers. They cannot call you at work or disturb you at unreasonable hours of the night.

If all else fails, the creditor can go to court to collect the debt. The court may allow the creditor to **garnish** your wages—that is, to collect a portion of each paycheck you earn until the debt is paid off. By law, a creditor can garnish up to 25 percent of your wages.

Bankruptcy

If you owe more money than you can afford to pay, you may have to declare bankruptcy. **Bankruptcy** is a legal procedure that relieves you of debt. When you declare bankruptcy, a court takes charge of your finances. The court may **liquidate** your assets (turn them into cash) by selling your valuables. It will then pay whatever debts it can with the money earned from those sales. Some of your creditors may never be paid back. Some debts, however, are not wiped out. Taxes, alimony, child support, and judgments in drunk driving cases must be repaid, as must most student loans. This procedure is called a Chapter 7 bankruptcy. (Federal bankruptcy law is divided into chapters.)

Declaring a Chapter 7 bankruptcy may seem like a way of "beating the system," because it allows you to accumulate large debts and then avoid paying them. Bankruptcy has serious consequences, however. A declaration of bankruptcy will stay in your credit report for ten years. During that time, you will probably find it impossible to get credit or borrow money. Even after the ten years are over, it may be difficult to reestablish yourself as a good credit risk.

If you have too many debts and cannot pay all your bills but you are working regularly, you may be able to declare a less drastic type of bankruptcy. This is called a Chapter 13 bankruptcy. With this modified bankruptcy, you agree to pay off some of what you owe to each creditor or to pay all your debts over an extended period of time. With this court-supervised plan, you do not lose all your possessions, and your credit rating is not as seriously damaged as it is with total bankruptcy.

REVIEW QUESTIONS

1. What is the difference between secured credit and unsecured credit? Give an example of each.
2. What is a debit card?
3. Name three types of information a credit bureau might keep in your file.
4. What is liquidation?

Working as a Paralegal

A paralegal is a person who assists lawyers by performing much of the background and routine legal work in a law office. Because of the work paralegals do, lawyers are free to concentrate on highly skilled legal work, including giving legal advice to clients and appearing in court and at hearings. Paralegals research cases, draft contracts and wills, prepare financial reports, and perform a wide variety of other tasks. Paralegals are sometimes called legal assistants.

Many law offices hire paralegals to assist their lawyers because paralegals can do much of the same work lawyers do but can be paid lower salaries. This enables a law office to keep expenses down and thus provide clients with legal services at a reasonable cost.

The Nature of the Work

Paralegals work under the supervision of lawyers. They cannot accept cases, represent clients in court, or give legal advice. However, they can do nearly everything else that a lawyer does. Some paralegals work in large law offices where they specialize in one or two areas of the law, such as contracts or corporate taxes. Others are employed in small offices where they perform a wide variety of tasks. Most paralegals spend a large amount of time in law libraries researching laws and cases and gathering facts for their employers. They may also assist lawyers in preparing legal briefs and other court documents.

Education and Training

The paralegal is a relatively new career category. In the past, legal secretaries performed many paralegal duties along with their clerical work. Some law firms trained their legal secretaries to become paralegals and promoted them to legal assistant positions. Gradually, this position came to be recognized as a separate job category, calling for a person who did less clerical work and more of the day-to-day legal work of a law office. Schools and colleges began to develop specific training courses for paralegals. Today more than 450 colleges, law schools, and private schools offer paralegal programs. The programs range in length from one to three years; most are completed in two years. Many schools require that their paralegal students be college graduates, while others accept students with a high school diploma.

Job Opportunities

The paralegal profession has been growing very rapidly in the last ten years. The need for paralegals is expected to continue to increase substantially in the future. In addition to private law firms, many government agencies, insurance companies, and accounting firms employ paralegals.

The possibilities for advancement vary. A few paralegals return to school and become lawyers. Others move from small law firms to larger ones. Some large law offices promote paralegals to the supervisory position of law office manager. Still other paralegals specialize in one area of law and then go into business for themselves. They sell their paralegal services to lawyers and law offices.

Personal Attributes

People who are interested in becoming paralegals will benefit from having a broad range of knowledge. Since they write reports and draft legal documents, they should be able to communicate effectively. Typing and word-processing skills are also important. Because paralegals spend much of their time doing detailed research, they need to have a lot of perseverance and patience. They must also be self-starters, able to work independently without close supervision.

For a person with these attributes, paralegal work can be very satisfying and fulfilling. Paralegals are a very important part of the American legal system and will continue to contribute greatly to it in the future.

Chapter Review

Chapter Summary

- A sale is a type of contract. Therefore, all the rules of contracts apply to sales.

- Sales contracts need not be in writing unless they involve goods worth more than $500.

- The Federal Trade Commission (FTC) requires door-to-door salespeople to inform customers of their right to a cooling-off period, during which they may cancel the purchases they made.

- If you receive merchandise in the mail that you didn't order, you have the right to keep it without paying for it. The only exceptions are items sent under a negative option plan.

- Express warranties may be oral or written. If the warranty is in writing, it must clearly explain the consumer's rights under the warranty. A seller does not have to offer an express warranty.

- All sellers are held to the implied warranty of title—that is, the promise that the seller owns what is being sold. Merchants are held to an implied warranty of merchantability—that is, the warranty that the product will do what it is intended to do.

- Sellers who sell a buyer an item after being told the buyer's specific need are held to the implied warranty of fitness for a particular purpose.

- Sellers can disclaim any express or implied warranties, as long as the disclaimer is clear.

- The Uniform Commercial Code (UCC) is the set of laws that list the rights and duties of buyers and sellers, including rules about contracts and warranties. Consumer product laws and lemon laws provide additional guarantees of products' effectiveness and safety. State licensing laws regulate providers of services.

- The FTC prohibits unfair or deceptive advertising, including bait-and-switch advertising. It also regulates sellers' pricing and labeling practices.

- When you have a problem with a product, you should first speak to the seller. If the seller refuses to repair or replace it or return your money, you should contact the manufacturer or company headquarters. If these methods don't work, you should seek the assistance of a private consumer or business group or a government agency.

- When the FTC finds that a business is engaging in an unfair or deceptive practice, the agency will request a consent order. If the company refuses or breaks that order, the FTC can make a cease and desist order.

- Many consumers pay for major purchases on credit. Credit is an agreement by which you receive an item in exchange for a promise to pay for it over a period of time, often with interest.

■ Secured credit is credit for which there is collateral. Unsecured credit, such as that obtained with a credit card, requires no collateral.

■ Before offering you credit, a creditor will investigate your ability to pay. He or she may consult a credit report that provides information about your finances, personal life, and credit history. If you appear to be a bad credit risk, the creditor will not offer you credit.

■ If you fail to make payments on secured credit, the creditor may repossess the collateral. If you fail to make payments on unsecured credit, the creditor may hire a collection agency to collect what you owe.

■ Bankruptcy is a legal procedure that relieves you of debt. When you declare bankruptcy, a court takes over your finances and may sell your assets to pay some of your creditors. You may also choose a less drastic plan, in which you keep your possessions and agree to a court-supervised repayment plan.

Understanding Legal Terms

On a separate sheet of paper, match the terms below with the definitions that follow.

bait and switch   negative option plan
caveat emptor   puffery
disclaimer   Uniform Commercial Code (UCC)
express warranty   warranty of merchantability
lemon law   warranty of title

1. The rule that buyers have no protection when they purchase a product from a seller
2. Set of laws that establish the rights and duties of people who buy and sell products
3. Agreement by which customers will receive products unless they notify the seller that they don't want the items
4. Oral or written promise made by a seller that a product will work in a certain way
5. Implied promise of the seller that he or she legally owns the item that is being sold
6. Implied promise of a seller that the item being sold can be used for its normal purpose
7. A notice that some warranties do not apply
8. Law that protects buyers who buy chronically defective cars
9. Exaggerated claims made by a seller
10. Sales practice of getting a buyer to take a higher-priced product instead of the low-priced advertised item

Applying the Law

1. Fran buys $50 worth of cosmetics from a door-to-door salesperson. Later that day, Fran examines her purchases. She finds that she really doesn't like the cosmetics she bought. What, if anything, can she do?

2. Jason buys a new car. After three weeks, the transmission breaks down. He takes the car to the dealer for repairs. He gets it back in a week, but the transmission soon breaks again. This happens several times during the next few months, and the car spends a total of six weeks in the shop. Jason becomes fed up with the car. He demands his money back. The dealer refuses to give him a refund but offers to continue to repair the transmission at no charge. What state law might the dealer be violating? Under this law, what should the dealer do?

3. Mae's Shoes advertises its product as "the world's most comfortable shoe." Hailey buys a pair and finds that they are comfortable but not the most comfortable shoes she owns. What, if anything, can Hailey do?

4. In order to make its prices look especially inviting, Sherman's Department Store writes on the price tag for its dresses, "Was $120. Now $49." The dresses never sold for $120. Is Sherman's violating an FTC rule? If so, what is the rule?

5. Grace buys a car on credit. The car dealer requires the car as collateral. For the first nine months, Grace makes all her monthly payments on the car. After that, she stops making payments. What, if anything, can the car dealer do?

6. Randy applies for a bank credit card. A bank representative investigates his history and finds that Randy has never kept a job for more than six months. The representative fears that Randy may soon be unemployed again and may be unable to pay for what he buys on credit. The bank therefore refuses Randy's application. Is the bank's action legal? Why or why not?

Case Studies

1. Ruby Dempsey bought a pedigreed puppy from the American Kennels pet store. She planned to breed the puppy and show him at dog shows. Later, she learned that the puppy had a hereditary defect that he would pass on to his offspring. The defect also made the puppy ineligible to be shown at dog shows. Dempsey demanded a refund from American Kennels, but the store refused to take back the puppy. Dempsey sued the store owner. What did the court decide?

2. J. B. Williams Company, the manufacturer of Geritol tablets, advertised that Geritol could energize people who felt worn out and tired. In truth, however, Geritol could help only people who had particular vitamin or iron deficiencies. Only a small number of people who feel worn out and tired suffer from those deficiencies. Therefore, Geritol could do nothing for the vast majority of people. What was the FTC able to do about those ads?

3. Josephine Rutyna received medical treatment from the Cabrini Hospital Medical Group. The medical group billed her for the service, but Rutyna did not pay the bill. The medical group hired a collection agency called Collection Accounts Terminal to collect the debt. In August 1978 the collection agency wrote a threatening, intimidating letter to Rutyna. The letter said that collections investigators would talk to her neighbors and employer about her debts unless she paid what she owed immediately. Was Collection Accounts Terminal's action legal? Why or why not?

Chapter 16

Housing Law

Chapter Objectives

When you have read this chapter, you should be able to:

- List the factors to consider before renting a place to live.
- Describe the rights and duties of landlords and tenants.
- List three advantages of buying a home over renting a home.
- Describe what a real estate agent does.
- Explain what a mortgage agreement is.
- Name three government programs that help low-income individuals pay for a place to live.

Case Study

Pugh v. Holmes, 384 A.2d 1234 (Pennsylvania 1978).

In November 1971 Eloise Holmes agreed to rent an apartment from J. C. Pugh in Chambersburg, Pennsylvania. By September 1975 the apartment had developed a number of serious problems, including a leaking roof, a lack of hot water, infestation by cockroaches, and hazardous steps and floors. Holmes complained about each of these problems, but Pugh did nothing to correct them. In response, Holmes stopped paying rent.

Pugh went to court to force Holmes to pay her rent. Holmes claimed that she owed Pugh nothing because her apartment was not fit to live in. The court agreed with Holmes. It said that when a landlord accepts rent from a tenant, the landlord makes an implied promise to keep the property in livable condition. Pugh had broken that promise by not properly maintaining the apartment. Therefore, Holmes was entitled to withhold the rent until Pugh made the necessary repairs.

RENTING A HOME

A **rental agreement** is a contract. It gives a **tenant** the right to live temporarily on property owned by a **landlord**. In exchange, the tenant must pay **rent**—a sum of money—to the landlord. People most often rent apartments in multiunit buildings, although some people rent houses, parts of houses, single rooms, or other kinds of property.

Many people, especially young people, rent their homes instead of buying them. One reason is that rental agreements are usually short-term. When you rent property, you're usually free to move out after a year or even less, depending on the agreement.

Another reason many people rent is cost. Buying property is always expensive, and the additional costs of owning a home—such as taxes and maintenance—may vary widely from year to year. If you rent, however, your expenses are fixed, predictable, and usually well below the cost of buying.

In addition to paying rent, you may also have to pay for **utilities** such as heat, electricity, and water. These, however, are your only housing expenses. The landlord pays all taxes on the property and is responsible for most repairs as well.

The Lease

Although oral rental agreements are usually valid, the tenant and the landlord are both better protected if they put the agreement in writing. A written rental agreement is called a **lease**. At a minimum, your lease should state the address of the property you are renting, how much the rent is, and how often the rent payments must be made. Most leases include other rules and restrictions as well.

APARTMENT LEASE

This Lease is made on   February 1   , 19 90

      BETWEEN the Tenant(s)

         RISA SINGER, SUSAN PHILLIPS, AND HILLARY GOSS

whose address will be   300 Stonefield Lane, East Brunswick, NJ

                                      referred to as the "Tenant",

      AND the Landlord

         WILLIAM KOVAK AND ESTHER KOVAK

whose address is   250 Dominica Drive, Manalapan, NJ

                                    referred to as the "Landlord".

The word "Tenant" means each Tenant named above.

1. Property.   The Tenant agrees to rent from the Landlord and the Landlord agrees to lease to the Tenant the apartment located at   300 Stonefield Lane, East Brunswick, NJ

                                  referred to as the "Apartment".
The Tenant shall take possession and use the Apartment only as a private residence.

2. Term.   The term of this Lease is for   one (1) year   starting on   February 1   , 19 90 and ending   January 31   , 19 91 .

3. Rent.   Rent for the Term is $ 10,800.00   . It is payable as follows: $ 900.00   per month, due on the   first   day of each month. The first payment of rent and any security deposit is due upon the signing of this Lease by the Tenant. The Tenant must pay a late charge of $ 25.00   for each payment that is more than   5   days late. This late charge is due with the monthly rent payment.

4. Security Deposit.   The Tenant will give to the Landlord $ 1,350.00   as security that the Tenant will comply with all the terms of this Lease. If the Tenant complies with the terms of this Lease, the Landlord will return this deposit within 30 days after the end of the Lease, including any extension. The Landlord may use as much of the deposit as necessary to pay for damages resulting from the Tenant's occupancy. If this occurs prior to the Lease termination, the Landlord may demand that the Tenant replace the amount of the security deposit used by the Landlord. If the Landlord sells the property, the Landlord shall turn over the security deposit amount plus Tenant's interest to the new Landlord. The Landlord will notify the Tenant of any sale and transfer of the deposit. The Landlord will then be released of all liability to return the security deposit. The Landlord will fully comply with the Rent Security Law *(N.J.S. 46:8-19 et seq.)*. This includes depositing the security deposit in an interest bearing account, and notifying the Tenant, in writing, of the name and address of the banking institution and the account number. Interest due the Tenant will be credited as rent on each renewal date of this Lease.

5. Utilities.   The Landlord will pay for the following utilities: The Tenant will pay for the following utilities:
         ( ) water   ( ) water
         ( ) electricity   ( ) electricity
         ( ) gas   ( ) gas

6. Eviction..   If the Tenant does not pay the rent withing   30   days after it is due, the Tenant may be evicted. The Landlord may also evict the Tenant if the Tenant violates any agreement in this Leases and for all other causes allowed by law. If evicted, the Tenant must continue to pay the rent for the rest of the term. The Tenant must also pay costs, including reasonable attorney fees, related to the eviction and the collection of any moneys owed the Landlord, along with the cost of re-entering, re-renting, cleaning and repairing the apartment. Rent received from any new tenant will reduce the amount owed the Landlord.

Illustration 16-1   It is wise to put a rental agreement in writing in the form of a lease.

Term of the Rental   You and the landlord must agree on the term—the length of time—of your rental agreement. **Fixed-term leases**—those which specify a definite preset term—are the most common type. Most fixed-term leases specify one year. However, leases can specify terms of six months, two years, five years, or any length of time to which the landlord and tenant agree. At the end of the term, the tenant and the landlord are free to end the agreement or extend it for another fixed term. Neither the tenant nor the landlord has to give **notice**, or warning that he or she intends to end the contract.

If you aren't sure how long you plan to stay, you may want to ask the landlord for a month-to-month lease. A **month-to-month lease** is an open-ended rental agreement. Most month-to-month leases require the tenant or landlord to give 30 days' notice.

Financial Arrangements   Your lease should specify when each rent payment is due. Even if you are renting the property for a fixed term, you will probably pay the rent month by month. Landlords usually require that rent be paid by the first day of each month.

Many landlords require tenants to make additional payments when the lease is signed. For example, your landlord may ask you to pay the first month's rent and the last month's rent before you move in. Your landlord also may ask for a **security deposit**. If you do any damage to the property, the landlord can use the security deposit to pay for repairs. If you owe rent when you move out, the landlord can use the security deposit to cover that rent.

If no repairs are needed and no rent is due, the landlord must refund the security deposit to you shortly after you move out. Some state and local laws require the landlord to pay interest on the security deposit. Some laws also limit the amount of a security deposit to the equivalent of one or two months' rent.

Some landlords include the cost of utilities in the rental price. Others may bill you separately for utilities or require you to pay the utility companies on your own. Because the costs of gas, electricity, and other utilities can greatly increase a tenant's monthly expenses, it's important to know how utilities will be handled before you sign a lease.

Before Signing a Lease

Most landlords will want to look into your background before accepting you as a tenant. They will want to make sure that you're a responsible and trustworthy person who is able to pay the rent. A landlord may ask you to fill out an application form with information about your finances, your job, and any previous rentals you have had. He or she also may ask for personal and bank references. All these actions are permitted by law.

Just as a landlord must be cautious in deciding whether to accept you as a tenant, you should be cautious when dealing with a landlord. Before you sign a lease, always inspect the rental property carefully. Make sure to note

Illustration 16-2 Prospective renters should examine the property they want to rent and note any problems.

anything that's broken or in bad repair. If you don't bring these problems to the landlord's attention before moving in, the landlord may later hold you responsible for them.

Read the lease carefully before you sign it. Most landlords use standard, printed lease forms. These forms are almost always written to protect the landlord's rights. To protect your own rights, if there is anything in the lease that you don't understand or don't agree with, discuss it with the landlord.

If you have any special needs, ask the landlord to let you write them into the lease. If the landlord has agreed to allow you to keep a pet, for example, it's a good idea to get that permission in writing.

Ending the Rental Agreement

If you've signed a fixed-term lease, you're free to move out at the end of the term. If you leave before the term is over, you remain responsible for paying the rent through the end of the term (unless you and the landlord agree to cancel the lease early).

If you have a month-to-month lease, you must usually pay rent for an entire month even if you move out before the end of that month. If you fail to give the landlord notice before you move out, you may have to pay rent for the time you would have been living in the apartment. (For example, if you were supposed to give a month's notice, you may have to pay an additional month's rent.)

Either party can end a rental agreement if the other party **breaches** (breaks) the agreement in a substantial way. Later in this chapter, you'll read about what happens when a rental agreement is breached.

Assigning and Subletting

Once you've signed a lease, you have a legal right to live in a particular house or apartment. If you wish, you may transfer that right to somebody else. For example, Dorothy is a college student. She has a one-year lease for an apartment a few blocks from school. The lease runs from September 1 to August 31, but Dorothy will graduate in May and wants to take a job in another city. She offers to give the apartment to her friend Lorraine.

Dorothy is offering to **assign** her lease—that is, to give someone else her legal rights and duties under the rental agreement. If she assigns her lease to Lorraine, Lorraine will have the right to live in the apartment and the duty to pay the rent.

In addition to the right to assign your lease, you have the right to sublet the property you're renting. When you **sublet**, you keep your legal right to occupy the property but you allow someone else to live there. For example, Dylan has a one-year lease for an apartment. He plans to go on vacation during July and August, but he intends to return to the apartment in September. He sublets the apartment to Maury for July and August. During those two months, Maury is responsible for paying the rent. When September comes, Maury is required to move out and let Dylan move back in.

You may assign your lease or sublet your apartment at any time unless your lease forbids you to do so. Many landlords refuse to allow assignments and subletting because they don't want their property to be occupied by people they don't know and trust. Other landlords permit assignments or subletting but reserve the right to meet and approve the new tenants.

REVIEW QUESTIONS

1. List three basic items that should be included in a lease.
2. What is the purpose of a security deposit?
3. Explain how a month-to-month lease differs from a fixed-term lease.
4. What does it mean to assign a lease?

RIGHTS AND DUTIES OF LANDLORDS AND TENANTS

Most leases spell out the basic duties of the landlord and the tenant. Often, however, disputes arise over matters that weren't discussed and weren't included in the rental agreement.

Federal, state, and local laws give tenants and landlords certain rights even when those rights aren't specifically mentioned in a lease. (For example, as you read earlier in this chapter, tenants have the right to assign their leases.) Landlords and tenants also have a number of remedies at their disposal when the other party breaches a rental agreement. For example, as you saw in the opening case, tenants may be permitted to withhold rent payments. Landlords, in turn, may be able to **repossess** the property—that is, require a tenant to move out. If a tenant refuses to leave, the landlord can seek a court order that will force the tenant off the property. Such a court order is called an **eviction**.

Tenants' Rights

As a tenant, you have the right to live in the rented property without being disturbed by the landlord or anyone else. This is called the **right to quiet enjoyment**.

The right to quiet enjoyment prevents the landlord from repossessing the property before the term of the lease is over. It also prevents the landlord from doing anything that makes it difficult or impossible for you to use the property. Any such action by the landlord (or by others, with the landlord's permission) is called **constructive eviction**.

For example, on August 18, 1978, Jerry and Diane Trinkle rented an apartment in St. Joseph, Illinois, from Merwin Glasoe. By the time winter came, the apartment had developed a number of problems. The heating system often didn't work. Even when it did work, the heat seeped out of the apartment through holes in the windows and doors. Because of defective plumbing, the toilet overflowed. Sewage leaked through the ceiling in one of the bedrooms. There were holes in the floor, and the apartment was infested with cockroaches and rats. At one point, the bathroom ceiling collapsed. The Trinkles reported these problems to Glasoe, but he did nothing about them.

The Trinkles stopped paying rent in July 1981. In October, Glasoe sued them for the unpaid rent. The Trinkles said they had no obligation to pay because it was practically impossible for them to live in the apartment. The court agreed, saying that Glasoe had constructively evicted the Trinkles and that he therefore had no right to demand rent from them.

Tenants have many of the same rights that consumers have. You read in Chapter 15 that most items you buy come with an implied warranty of merchantability. Similarly, rental property comes with an **implied warranty of habitability**. In other words, you have the right to expect that the home you are renting is livable. Exactly what constitutes "livable" varies from case to case. Generally, courts have held that buildings without heat or running water, buildings infested with rats or cockroaches, and buildings with dangerous structural conditions violate this warranty.

Many jurisdictions have established **housing codes** that set minimum standards for residential property. Among other things, these codes usually require that a home have safe electrical wiring, a working heating system, a sanitary plumbing system, and rooms that are of a reasonable size. In these jurisdictions, any property that falls below the standards of the housing code is not considered livable.

The implied warranty of habitability continues throughout the term of the lease. If anything breaks or deteriorates in a way that makes the property less livable, the landlord must fix it. If you notice a problem or a defect, you should tell the landlord about it immediately. Courts have held that the landlord must be allowed a reasonable time to make repairs. However, the amount of time that is "reasonable" depends on how dangerous the problem is.

In addition to fixing problems within individual apartments, landlords are responsible for maintaining common areas. In a multistory apartment building, for example, the landlord must maintain the stairways, the laundry rooms, the elevators, and the roof. If anyone is injured because of unsafe conditions in a common area, the landlord is liable for those injuries.

Illustration 16-3   In many cases, renters may pay to have a problem fixed and charge the landlord for the repair.

Tenants' Remedies

If your landlord refuses to make repairs to the property you're renting, there are several things you can do. First, you can report the problem to the local housing authority. An inspector will examine the property to see whether it satisfies the housing code. If it doesn't, the housing authority will order the landlord to make repairs. In many jurisdictions, the housing authority can impose civil or criminal penalties for housing that is not "up to code."

If you live in an area without a housing code—or if the housing code doesn't apply in your case—there are other alternatives. If the property is in extremely bad condition, the landlord's failure to repair it may be considered a constructive eviction. In that case, you can ignore the rental agreement, move out, and pay no more rent. If the problems are less severe, you can withhold part or all of the rent until the defects are fixed. You can sue the landlord for specific performance—that is, you can ask a court to order the landlord to make the repairs. You can also sue for damages to cover any costs you've incurred or any inconvenience you've suffered because of the defects. In some cases, you can sue for punitive damages as well.

Another option is to pay for the repairs yourself and deduct the cost from the rent. For example, on June 25, 1969, Alice Ireland noticed a crack in the toilet in her apartment in Camden, New Jersey. Water was leaking onto the bathroom floor. After several unsuccessful attempts to notify her landlord, Joseph Marini, she decided to take action herself. She hired a plumber to repair the toilet and paid the bill, which came to $85.72.

Ireland's rent was $95.00 a month. When the next rent payment was due, she mailed Marini a check for $9.28 and a copy of the plumber's bill. Marini took her to court for failure to pay the rent. The court ruled that Ireland had done the proper thing. Without a working toilet, the property was not livable. Since she was unable to notify the landlord, she had the right to make the repair herself and deduct the cost from her rent.

Retaliation

When a tenant sues a landlord or reports the landlord's actions to the local authorities, the landlord is likely to be upset. He or she may respond by threatening the tenant, raising the tenant's rent, or refusing to renew the tenant's lease. The landlord may also try to evict the tenant. (Doing so is called **retaliatory eviction**.) Taking revenge on a tenant in these or other ways is against the law.

Landlords' Rights

You have already read that landlords have the right to collect rent in exchange for the use of their property. Landlords have a number of other rights as well.

Use Restrictions Landlords have the right to put reasonable restrictions on the use of their property. For example, your landlord can prohibit you from keeping pets on the property, installing large appliances (such as a washing machine), and making holes in the walls. As you'll read later in this chapter, however, a landlord may not make restrictions that discriminate against certain groups of people, such as members of a particular race.

Repairs   As you read earlier in this chapter, landlords are responsible for keeping the rental property in livable condition. This responsibility includes making repairs resulting from wear and tear—that is, ordinary deterioration or aging of the property.

The tenant, however, also has certain responsibilities in terms of maintaining the building. You must repair any damage you cause—either to the rental property or to any common areas. You must also give the landlord notice of any defects that he or she wouldn't otherwise know about. Let's say Demos rents an apartment in a building owned by Julie. The shower in his apartment develops a leak. Because Demos is busy, he fails to tell Julie about the leak. Instead, he just mops up the water each morning. In time, the leak worsens, weakens the floor, stains the ceiling underneath, and begins dripping into the apartment below. Although Julie is responsible for fixing the leak, Demos may be liable for repairs to the floor, the ceiling, and any damaged property in the apartment below.

Alterations and Improvements   A landlord has the right to get his or her property back in the same condition it was in when the tenant moved in. In general, a tenant cannot make any substantial changes without the landlord's permission even if those changes might raise the value of the property. For example, if you install kitchen cabinets, the landlord can require you to take them out before you leave and to repair any damage they caused to the kitchen walls.

Of course, the landlord may like the cabinets and may allow you to leave them in the kitchen when you move out. In that case, however, the landlord has no duty to pay for the cabinets or for the time and money you spent installing them.

Landlords' Remedies

If you cause damage, fail to pay rent, or breach the rental agreement, your landlord can remedy the situation in a number of different ways. He or she can take you to court to recover damages. He or she can also get an injunction to stop you from breaking the agreement.

In some cases, the landlord may choose to repossess the property and demand that you leave. Some states permit landlords to use peaceful means or reasonable force to remove a tenant. (These states differ, however, on what is "peaceful" or "reasonable.")

State governments generally want to discourage landlords from breaking down doors, climbing through windows, or throwing a tenant's personal property onto the street. They prefer that tenants be evicted by court order. For this reason, every state offers a streamlined court procedure through which landlords can evict tenants quickly, without the time and expense of a full trial.

If your landlord wants the court to evict you, he or she must first give you notice of the eviction and explain what you have done to make it necessary. You then have a short time (often just three to five days) to remedy the situation. For example, if you have put up wallpaper without the landlord's permission, you can remedy the situation by removing the wallpaper and repainting the walls.

If you don't remedy the situation within the specified time period, the matter will come before the court. Unless you have a good reason for having breached the rental agreement, the court will order an eviction. The court may also order you to pay damages such as overdue rent or the cost of repairs. In some cases, you may also be ordered to pay punitive damages.

Raising the Rent

If you've signed a fixed-term lease, the landlord is not permitted to raise your rent until the lease expires. At that time, you and the landlord can renegotiate the lease. Often the landlord will ask for a slight increase in rent. If you have a month-to-month lease, the landlord may raise the rent at any time, as long as he or she gives you proper notice.

In recent years, many state and local legislatures have enacted **rent control laws**. These laws protect tenants by limiting landlords' ability to raise rents. Rent control laws often restrict rent increases to a certain percentage of the total rent or tie them to increases in the cost of living.

REVIEW QUESTIONS

1. What two basic rights of tenants are implied in every rental agreement?
2. Give an example of constructive eviction.
3. What is retaliatory eviction?
4. Give an example of a use restriction that a landlord might impose.

BUYING A HOME

Buying a home requires a much greater commitment than renting. Not only is buying more expensive, it also restricts your freedom to leave. Unlike renters, buyers can't just give notice and move out. There are, however, many advantages to buying a home. For one thing, buying a home is an investment. In most cases, you will be able to sell your home for much more than you originally paid for it.

There are also a number of tax advantages to owning a home. If you borrow money to purchase a home (as nearly everyone does), the interest you must pay on the borrowed money is deductible on your annual income tax. Property taxes that you must pay are tax-deductible as well.

Homeowners have fewer restrictions than renters do. Owners are free to repaint, remodel, keep pets, and plant gardens without asking permission from a landlord. There are, however, many local laws that restrict what homeowners can do with their property. Some of these are health and safety laws, which prevent homeowners from doing things that might endanger themselves or others. If a homeowner installs new windows, for example, local laws may require that they be made of shatter-resistant glass.

Cities and towns usually also have **zoning laws** that restrict what property can be used for. For example, zoning laws may prohibit you from running a business in your home or turning your house into an apartment building. Zoning laws may also restrict your right to build a pool, a fence, or a new garage on your property.

Illustration 16-4   Local zoning laws restrict a property owner's use of a piece of land and the buildings on it.

Choosing a Home

Buying a home is not like buying a stereo or computer. You can't simply go to the store, decide what features you need, and choose a model that has those features at a reasonable price. Every home is different. Even two homes with identical layouts may have different locations or different views or may be in different condition. The only way to choose is to visit many places, compare the features, and do careful inspections. Also, homes don't come with fixed price tags. Buying a home often requires a great deal of negotiation between the buyer and the seller.

Many people shop for homes with the help of **real estate agents**—experts in finding, buying, and selling homes. Real estate agents have up-to-date listings of available homes, and they are familiar with the advantages and disadvantages of different neighborhoods. Once you explain to an agent what you are looking for, he or she can help you find homes that you might like. The agent can also help you make financing arrangements and deal with the often complex legal procedures for buying a home.

Illustration 16-5   Real estate agents help people buy and sell homes, often assisting with the complex legal aspects of these procedures.

Title

Once you have found a home you like, you and the seller must agree on a price. You must also agree on what the price includes. For example, you may be willing to pay more for the property if the seller agrees to leave some appliances that he or she installed. The seller may accept less for the home if you agree to repair the broken plumbing instead of asking the seller to do it. Finally, you and the seller must agree on a closing date—the date when the seller will transfer legal ownership of the property to you.

Legal ownership of a home is called **title**. There are several different types of title, each of which gives the homeowner different rights. For example, if you and someone else (such as a friend or a spouse) buy a home together, you may arrange for a **joint tenancy**—ownership shared by two people. Under this arrangement, if one of you dies, the entire property automatically becomes the property of the other.

Another type of ownership agreement is **tenancy in common**. Under this arrangement, each owner has separate title to the home. If one owner dies, his or her title passes, not to the other owner, but to the deceased owner's heirs.

Joint tenancy and tenancy in common are only two of many types of ownership arrangements. The kind of title you choose will affect your taxes, the rights of your heirs, and your rights to make changes in or sell the property. Before you buy a home, it's important to talk with a real estate agent, an accountant, or a lawyer and decide which form of ownership is best for you.

Mortgage Agreements

Very few people can afford to pay for a home with money they have saved. Instead, they need to borrow money from a bank or other lender. In most cases, a lender will not lend the entire purchase price of a home. You, the buyer, must pay a certain percentage of the purchase price out of your own pocket. The portion of the purchase price that you pay yourself is called a **down payment**.

In order to borrow the rest of the money, you must make a **mortgage agreement** with the lender. Under this agreement, the lender agrees to lend you a certain amount of money. You agree to repay the loan, plus interest, in monthly installments. If you **default** on the loan—that is, if you stop making monthly payments for any reason—the lender may take possession of your home. Taking a home away from someone who has defaulted on a loan is called **foreclosure**.

Banks and other lenders want to avoid foreclosure whenever possible. Therefore, before a lender will lend you money, he or she will want to make sure that you are able to pay back the money you borrow and all the interest. The lender will ask you a variety of questions and then do a background check to make sure your answers are accurate. Among other things, the lender will ask about your annual income, how much money you have saved, and how long you've held your job. The lender will want to know whether you're currently paying back any other loans (for example, for a car or for college). The lender will also check to see whether you've defaulted on any loans in the past.

Lenders are free to ask virtually anything as long as their questions do not violate federal, state, or local antidiscrimination laws. You'll read about those laws later in this chapter.

Closing Costs

In addition to making monthly mortgage payments, you'll have to pay certain one-time costs when you buy a home. These are called **closing costs** or settlement costs. They may include mortgage application fees, title search fees, insurance premiums, real estate agent's fees, and inspection fees.

Types of Property

Because the prices of single-family houses have risen so high, more and more people are buying other types of homes. The most common alternatives to traditional houses are mobile homes, condominiums, and cooperative apartments.

Mobile homes, or manufactured housing, are houses that are built in a factory and towed to a location selected by the owner. They are much less expensive than houses that are built on a piece of land from the ground up. However, the price of a mobile home does not include land. A mobile home owner must buy or rent a plot of land, usually in an area that has been zoned for this type of housing.

A **condominium** is an apartment that is owned, rather than rented, by the people who live in it. Though a condominium is part of a multiunit building, the owner has title only to the individual apartment. When you buy a condominium, you assume responsibility for all upkeep and repairs within the apartment. You can sell your condominium at any time, without consulting anyone else.

A **cooperative apartment** (usually called a co-op) is similar to a condominium, except that the apartment isn't owned by an individual resident. Instead, a corporation owns the building, and all the building's residents share ownership of the corporation. Each resident is a stockholder or **shareholder**. If you want to sell your share in the building to someone else, the sale may have to be approved by the other members of the cooperative.

Owners of co-ops and condominiums share responsibility for common areas of the building, such as the hallways, stairways, and grounds. Generally, owners deal with this responsibility by organizing an owners' association. The association collects a monthly fee from its members and uses the money to pay for the care and upkeep of the common areas. The association may also place restrictions on what changes the owners may make to the property.

Illustration 16-6   Owners of condominiums and cooperatives share responsibility for common areas, often through an owners' association.

REVIEW QUESTIONS

1. What does a real estate agent do?
2. What is title?
3. What can a lender do if a homeowner defaults on a mortgage agreement?
4. What is the difference between a condominium and a cooperative apartment?

GOVERNMENT-ASSISTED HOUSING

Housing is usually a person's biggest expense. Many people spend nearly half their income on rent or mortgage payments. As the cost of housing increases, more and more people are finding that they can't afford a place to live. The rising cost of housing is one of the major causes of homelessness in the United States. To combat homelessness, the federal and state governments have developed a number of low-cost housing programs.

Government-Sponsored Rental Housing

Public housing is a general term for government-owned houses or apartments that are available for rental by low-income families. (The definition of "low-income" depends on the size of the family.) A local public housing authority acts as the landlord. It resolves tenants' problems, maintains the buildings, and collects rent.

The biggest provider of public housing is the U.S. Department of Housing and Urban Development (HUD), which has built housing projects since 1937. Many other housing projects have been built by state and local governments.

Unfortunately, there is not enough low-income housing for everyone who needs it. For this reason, HUD also provides **rent supplements**. Under this program, low-income tenants live in apartments owned by private landlords. The tenant pays a portion of the rent, and HUD pays the rest.

Mortgage Guarantee Programs

As you read earlier, not everyone can borrow money to buy a home. Lenders offer loans only to qualified people—people who, in the lender's opinion, are fairly certain to pay the loans back. Lenders are almost never willing to risk lending money to people with a low income.

The Federal Housing Administration (FHA), a part of HUD, has dealt with this problem by providing loan insurance. The FHA guarantees the lender that if the borrower does not pay back the loan, the federal government will. **FHA-insured loans** are available only to low-income people who are trying to buy a first home. A lower than usual down payment of 5 percent is required.

The U.S. Department of Veterans Affairs offers similar loans, called **VA loans**, to military veterans. The Department of Veterans Affairs guarantees the loan; in addition, the borrower is not required to make a down payment.

REVIEW QUESTIONS

1. What is public housing?
2. How does HUD's rent supplement program operate?
3. How does the FHA make it easier for low-income families to borrow money?

HOUSING DISCRIMINATION

Federal, state, and local laws protect buyers and renters from certain types of discrimination. The most important of these laws is the Fair Housing Act, which was passed by Congress as part of the Civil Rights Act of 1968. The Fair Housing Act outlaws discriminatory practices by landlords, real estate agents, and lenders. These people must not consider an individual's race, religion, sex, or national origin in any matter involving the rental or sale of housing. They also must not discriminate against people with handicaps or families with children.

Many states have expanded these protections. Some state and local laws prohibit discrimination based on political affiliation, sexual orientation, personal appearance, or source of income.

Permissible Discrimination

Some forms of discrimination are permitted under the Fair Housing Act. A lender has the right to deny a loan to someone who appears to be unable to pay it back. A landlord can refuse to rent an apartment to a family that is clearly too large to live in that apartment. Retirement communities—housing developments designed for people over a certain age, such as 55—have the right to exclude people under that age. (All other "adults only" policies that discriminate against people with children are illegal.)

Illustration 16-7   In retirement communities, discrimination against people below a certain age is permitted.

There are a few other minor exceptions to the Fair Housing Act. For example, landlords of buildings with fewer than four rental units do not have to follow the antidiscrimination rules.

Illegal Discriminatory Practices

A number of common discriminatory practices were made illegal by the Fair Housing Act. Some landlords charge different rents to members of different races—for example, they may charge a black tenant more than a white tenant for the same apartment. This practice is against federal law.

Some discriminatory practices are more subtle. For example, some real estate agents guide people of different races to different neighborhoods. When black people want to buy a house, the agent will take them to one part of town; when Hispanic people want to buy a house, the agent will take them to another part of town. This practice, called **steering**, is illegal.

Some landlords lie about apartments in their buildings. If a member of one group asks to rent an apartment, the apartment is unavailable, but if a member of another group asks about the same apartment, it suddenly becomes available again. A landlord may lie because of his or her own prejudices or because the other residents of the building ask the landlord to do so. Either way, this practice is illegal.

Bankers and other lenders are sometimes guilty of an illegal practice called redlining. **Redlining** is refusing to make loans to people who buy homes in certain neighborhoods. For example, in 1974 John Harrison decided to buy a house in Toledo, Ohio. He went to the Otto G. Heinzeroth Mortgage Company and applied for a loan. John Haugh, a representative of the company, asked Harrison where the house was located. When Harrison named the location, Haugh commented that it was "a bad area" with a history of racial problems. For this reason, Haugh said that the company would not give Harrison a loan unless he made a very large down payment. If Harrison chose a house in a different neighborhood, he could get a better deal.

Harrison sued the company for violation of the Fair Housing Act. He won both actual and punitive damages.

When Discrimination Occurs

If you feel that a landlord, a real estate agent, or anyone else has discriminated against you in a housing matter, you can file a complaint with HUD. HUD will investigate the problem and attempt to resolve it informally. If that attempt is unsuccessful, HUD may sue on your behalf. In most cases, you can seek help from your state or local housing authority as well.

REVIEW QUESTIONS

1. Give two examples of permissible discrimination in housing.
2. What is a retirement community?
3. Define *redlining*.

Latest in the Law: The Right to Shelter

Do the homeless in the United States have a legal right to shelter? If they cannot provide housing for themselves, does the government have an obligation to provide it? These questions have been debated in recent years in courtrooms, in the halls of Congress, and in state legislatures all over the nation.

The homeless population in the United States—numbering in the hundreds of thousands, perhaps the millions—skyrocketed during the 1980s as developers tore down thousands of low-cost SRO (single-room-occupancy) hotels to build new high-rise office buildings. During the same period, state-run mental hospitals inadvertently contributed to the problem by releasing many mentally ill patients without providing them with a place to live. As real estate values rose faster than many people's incomes, whole families found themselves homeless when they could no longer afford to pay their monthly rent or mortgage payments.

In addition, the amount of money available for federally subsidized housing was reduced—funds were cut 75 percent between 1981 and 1988. Religious organizations and various private groups have tried to meet people's needs, but they seem to be unable to handle the problem.

A Right to Shelter?

As the homeless population increased, lawyers representing homeless clients began to look for ways to force federal, state, and city governments to help. One way to do this was to try to prove that homeless Americans have a fundamental right to shelter. However, there is no clause in the U.S. Constitution that can be interpreted as a right to shelter. Few state constitutions contain such a clause either.

Some advocates for the homeless argue that the government is obligated now to provide shelter for the homeless since it had undertaken a similar role in the past. For decades, the federal government has, in fact, been providing low-cost public housing for the nation's poor. In addition, all states have laws that provide welfare payments, food stamps, and other aid to certain categories of the poor—children, the elderly, the disabled, and the unemployable. The homeless, however, often seem to fall through the cracks in this system.

The Government Responds

In 1987 Congress, yielding to public pressure, passed the McKinney Homeless Assistance Act. It provides hundreds of millions of dollars annually for emergency shelters, food, health care, and job training for the homeless. The McKinney Act requires that states establish programs for the homeless and share the costs equally with the federal government.

Most large cities have assumed an obligation to provide some housing for homeless people. Some have opened emergency shelters where the homeless can stay for a few days. Others also provide transitional housing where families can stay for up to six months. The city of Los Angeles, California, put a five-year ban on the destruction of old SRO hotels in 1989. Nonprofit and tax-supported organizations in that city are working to renovate these and other buildings to provide housing for the homeless. Programs in Minneapolis, Minnesota, funded by private foundations, have set up emergency shelters and drop-in centers that provide meals. One Minneapolis program targets specific groups for aid—for example, homeless mothers who have small children. However, many of the nation's large cities are now experiencing financial crises. Advocates for the homeless worry that housing programs will be the first to go when cities tighten their belts.

For many people, the issue of whether Americans have a right to shelter comes down to this: Will we let the poorest among us forage for food among garbage cans? Will we let them freeze to death in our cities' streets? Or is there something we can do?

Chapter Review

Chapter Summary

- A rental agreement gives a tenant the right to live on property owned by a landlord. In exchange, the tenant must pay rent.

- Many landlords require tenants to pay the first month's rent and the last month's rent plus a security deposit before moving in.

- Two common kinds of rental agreements are fixed-term and month-to-month.

- Landlords usually check into the background of prospective tenants before offering them a lease. Many landlords do not permit tenants to assign the lease or sublet the property.

- Tenants have the right to quiet enjoyment of the property. They also have the right to a warranty of habitability. Any serious breach of these rights may be considered constructive eviction.

- If a landlord breaches the rental agreement, the tenant's remedies include filing a complaint with the housing authorities, withholding rent, moving out, and suing the landlord.

- A landlord may not retaliate against a tenant for reporting housing code violations or suing the landlord.

- Landlords have the right to collect rent in a timely manner, to set restrictions on the use of their property, and to have their property returned in the same condition it was in when the tenant moved in.

- A landlord's remedies for a tenant's breaches include suing for damages, suing for an injunction, and obtaining an eviction.

- Every state has a streamlined court procedure that permits landlords to evict tenants who breach a rental agreement.

- In some areas, rent control laws restrict landlords' right to raise rents.

- Legal ownership of a home is called title.

- Because most people cannot afford to pay for a home by themselves, they must make a mortgage agreement with a lender. If they default on the loan, the lender can foreclose.

■ Public housing is government-owned housing that is rented to low-income families. Some low-income people receive HUD rent supplements.

■ Two mortgage guarantee programs offered by the federal government are FHA-insured loans and VA loans.

■ The Fair Housing Act prohibits landlords, real estate agents, lenders, and others from discriminating in housing on the basis of race, religion, sex, national origin, handicap, or number of children.

■ Illegal discriminatory practices include steering (showing a person housing only in certain neighborhoods) and redlining (refusing to make loans to individuals who buy homes in certain neighborhoods).

Understanding Legal Terms

On a separate sheet of paper, match the terms below with the definitions that follow.

assign   security deposit
constructive eviction   sublet
joint tenancy   tenancy in common
lease   title
retaliatory eviction   zoning law

1. Written rental agreement
2. Money a renter pays to a property owner before moving in, to cover any damage that the renter may do to the property
3. To give someone else the tenant's rights and duties under a rental agreement
4. Action by the owner of a rental unit that prevents the renter from having undisturbed use of the unit
5. To retain certain tenant's rights under a rental agreement while allowing someone else to occupy the rental unit
6. Action by the owner of a rental unit to remove a renter as revenge for the renter's complaints
7. Local law that restricts property use
8. Legal ownership of a home
9. Ownership shared by two people whereby when one dies, the other becomes the sole owner
10. Agreement by which two people hold separate title to the same property

Applying the Law

1. Kathy signs a lease in which she agrees to rent Stephen's house from December 1 to May 31. She pays Stephen a security deposit before moving in. She pays all her rent on time and does no damage to the house. On May 31 she moves out. Stephen refuses to return her security deposit because she failed to give notice before moving out. Is Kathy entitled to the return of her security deposit? Explain your answer.

2. Martin wants to rent an apartment from Josie. Josie tells him to fill out a rental application. The application asks for Martin's current address, his employer's name, his salary, the addresses of his previous rentals, the names of personal references, and the amount he has in his savings account. Is it legal for Josie to require this information from Martin? Explain your answer.

3. Daniel, a landlord, provides a garbage dumpster for his tenants to use. The dumpster is old, rotting, and infested with mice. The tenants complain to Daniel, but he does nothing about it. Is Daniel responsible for fixing the dumpster? If so, what can the tenants do if Daniel doesn't correct the problem?

4. Chris owns his home. He decides to build a pool in the backyard. Can the local government place any restrictions on his right to build the pool even though the pool is on his own property? Explain your answer.

5. Brook and Edward buy a house together. They decide to share title as joint tenants. A few years later, Edward dies. In his will, he leaves all his property to his son, Oliver. Oliver claims that he now shares ownership of the house with Brook. Brook says that when Edward died, she became the sole owner of the house. Who is correct, and why?

6. Jo is an Asian-American woman. She asks Keith, a real estate agent, to help her buy a house. Keith shows her several houses in a neighborhood where most of the residents are Asian-American. Jo asks to see houses in other neighborhoods, but Keith tells her he knows of no other suitable houses in her price range. Later that day, Keith shows houses—in other neighborhoods and in the same price range—to a white woman named Leslie. Has Keith done anything illegal? If so, what?

Case Studies

1. In August 1981 Sonia Engstrom signed a one-year lease for a house owned by Donald Graber. After she moved in, the condition of the house deteriorated. The floor rotted, rats moved in, and the house soon became unlivable. She complained to Graber, but he didn't make the necessary repairs. Engstrom moved out in December and paid no more rent. Graber sued Engstrom, saying that the lease required her to pay rent for one year. Was he right? Why or why not?

2. When Wilma King moved into a New York City apartment in 1969, she signed a lease that prohibited her from keeping pets in the apartment. Nevertheless, she moved her dog in with her. Whenever the landlord reminded her of the "no pets" rule, she put the dog in a kennel for a few days and then returned it to her apartment. Was the restriction against dogs legal? If so, what action could the landlord take against King?

3. In 1980 Andrew and Theresa Oliver asked to rent a unit in an apartment complex managed by Walter Shelly. Shelly refused to rent the apartment to the Olivers because they were an interracial couple. He said that he had had interracial couples in the building before and that other tenants had complained. To avoid problems, he had decided not to rent to any more interracial couples. Was Shelly's practice legal? Why or why not?

Chapter 17

Paying Taxes

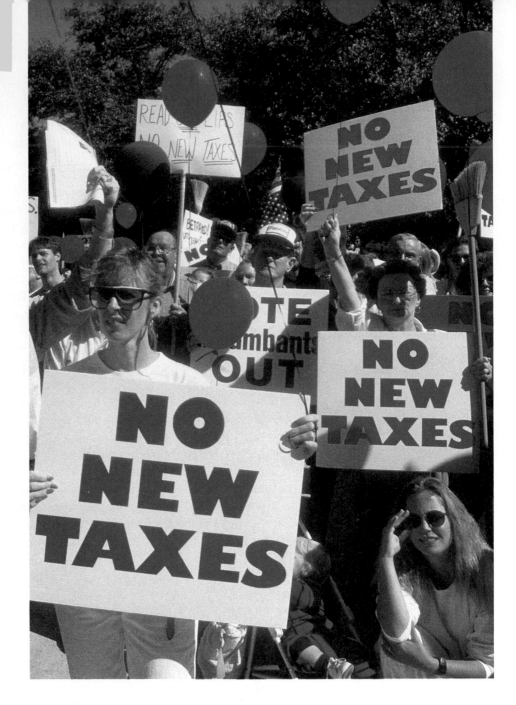

Chapter Objectives

When you have read this chapter, you should be able to:

- Name five kinds of taxes.

- Explain how taxes are collected and from whom they are collected.

- Explain how the federal and state governments use taxes.

- Describe how to file an income tax return, and explain how returns are processed.

- List some of the penalties the federal government can impose on people who do not pay their taxes.

Case Study

Autenrieth et al. v. Cullen, 418 F.2d 586 (9th Cir. 1969).

Neila Autenrieth was a conscientious objector to the war in Vietnam. She believed the war was morally wrong. Because of this belief, she claimed she was exempt, or excused, from participating in military activity in any way, including paying money to support the war.

At that time, there was a law requiring men in a certain age range to serve in the armed forces, with some exceptions. One of those exceptions said that a conscientious objector could be exempted from combat duty in the military. Ms. Autenrieth felt that under the Equal Protection Clause of the Fourteenth Amendment, she should not have to support the war financially. She also felt that requiring her to pay taxes to support the war was a violation of her First Amendment freedoms, especially the free exercise of religion.

Using these arguments, Ms. Autenrieth and a group of 123 other citizens asked for a tax refund of the portion of their tax money that was being used in the war effort. When their claim for a partial refund was denied, they took the case to court. The court held that they had to pay their taxes, even if they did not agree with the way Congress was spending the money. It said that the Constitution does not prohibit Congress from taxing all persons to raise money to support the general activities of government, regardless of the taxpayers' religious beliefs. The court pointed out that some person or group might object to almost every government activity. If people could refuse to pay taxes because they disapproved of the way the government used the money, the ability of the government to function would be seriously impaired, or maybe even destroyed.

TYPES OF TAXES

No one wants to pay taxes, but in the United States taxes are required. The government relies largely on money raised through taxes to produce revenue. **Tax revenue** is money that governments collect to provide services and to pay for public expenses. You will learn more about the ways in which all levels of government use taxes later in this chapter.

The authority of the federal government to tax the people comes from the Constitution. Article I, Section 8, says: "The Congress shall have Power To lay and collect Taxes, Duties, Imposts and Excises, to pay the Debts and provide for the common Defence and general Welfare of the United States. . . ."

The federal government is not the only one that has the power to tax. Both state and local governments may also impose and collect taxes. As you read in Chapter 1, the states get their power to tax from the U.S. Constitution. Local governments get their power to tax from the states. State and local taxes are limited by provisions in state constitutions and state statutes.

The federal, state, and local governments impose many different kinds of taxes. For example, you may have to pay:

- Income taxes
- Payroll taxes
- Sales taxes
- Excise taxes
- Wealth taxes

Income Taxes

The federal government gets its power to collect **income tax** from individuals and corporations through the Sixteenth Amendment, which became law in 1913. The most common forms of income that are taxed are:

- Wages and business income
- Interest and dividends on investments
- Gains from the sale of stocks and other items

The federal government collects income taxes from the residents of all 50 states. In addition, almost all states collect income taxes from their own residents. The few states with no personal income tax receive the revenue they need from other types of taxes. Florida, for example, collects sales, rental, and admissions taxes from its tourism activity. Alaska collects an oil and gas properties production tax.

Local governments also have the authority to collect income taxes. Relatively few cities use this power. However, some larger cities, such as New York City and Detroit, as well as some smaller cities do have income taxes.

Because of these differences in state and local policies, where you live greatly affects how much income tax you must pay. For example, in 1990 a resident of New York City making $50,000 per year paid about 19 percent of his or her income in federal tax, 6 percent in state tax, and 3 percent in city tax, for a total of approximately $14,000. A resident of a state and city without an income tax who was making the same amount of income paid only federal tax of less than $10,000.

Sources of Income   The Sixteenth Amendment provides that taxes will be collected on income "from whatever source derived." That means that most of the money you earn is considered income for tax purposes. As you just read, the most common forms of income that are taxed are wages you earn at your job or money you earn in your business and interest and dividends and gains from the sale of items such as stocks. Tips, such as those received by restaurant and hotel employees, are also taxed as income. Lottery, bingo, and horse-racing winnings are taxed. Prizes and awards are also taxed whether won at random or for a special achievement. Other, less common types of income may be taxed also, including money a person receives from the sale of his or her blood.

In addition, money earned from illegal activities—such as drug sales, robbery, and embezzlement—is just as taxable as money received from legal activities. During 1978 and 1979, Glen D. Wood made $600,000 selling marijuana. After a federal investigation, he was sentenced to four years in prison and was fined $30,000. Also, under a law allowing the government to seize money and possessions acquired illegally, the money Wood earned from selling marijuana was taken. In 1985 the IRS audited, or reviewed, Wood's personal tax returns. The agency discovered that Wood had not paid taxes on the money he had made selling marijuana. Wood stated that this income should not be taxed because the government had already seized it. Wood took the case to court. The court said that since Wood had had the benefit of the money during 1978 and 1979, he had to pay tax on it. With interest and penalties, Wood had to pay more than $735,000.

However, not all income is taxable. Certain items are excluded under the law. For example, inheritances and gifts a person receives are exempt, or free, from income tax. Also, amounts a person gets because he or she has been physically injured in an accident are not taxable.

How Income Taxes Are Collected   How the taxes on income are collected varies according to the type of income and the way in which the income is earned. Employers are required to withhold federal and state income taxes from their employees' paychecks. Employers send this money, referred to as **tax withholding**, to the federal and state governments. By paying this money out of each paycheck, employees are paying their taxes as they earn the income rather than paying all at once at the end of the year.

To find out how much to withhold from each paycheck, employers give their employees a Form W-4 at beginning of each year. Using a worksheet on the form, employees figure the number of **withholding allowances** they can claim and still have enough money withheld to pay the correct amount of tax. (The more allowances you take, the less money will be deducted from your paycheck.) Employers then use government-provided tables—which take into account an employee's number of withholding allowances, wages, and marital status—to determine the correct amount to withhold each pay period. Table 17-1 shows a portion of a typical table used by employers for this purpose. Brenda, who is a single woman, earned $225 a week and had one withholding allowance in 1991. She had $24 in federal income tax withheld from her paycheck each week in 1991.

Some people do not have to have money deducted because they do not pay income tax. If you can prove that you will not owe taxes and if you did not owe any tax the previous year, you can ask your employer not to withhold money.

Self-employed individuals who do not work for a company must make income tax payments four times a year directly to the government. These are called quarterly estimates and, as with the amounts withheld by employers, are intended to pay in advance the total year's tax liability.

How Much Will You Owe?   Your exact **tax liability**, which is the amount you must pay, is determined at the end of the year when you prepare an income

Table 17-1　Portion of an Income Tax Withholding Table

Single Persons—Weekly Payroll Period
(For Wages Paid after December 1990)

And the wages are—		And the number of withholding allowances claimed is—										
At least	But less than	0	1	2	3	4	5	6	7	8	9	10
		The amount of income tax to be withheld shall be—										
$0	$25	$0	$0	$0	$0	$0	$0	$0	$0	$0	$0	$0
25	30	1	0	0	0	0	0	0	0	0	0	0
30	35	1	0	0	0	0	0	0	0	0	0	0
35	40	2	0	0	0	0	0	0	0	0	0	0
40	45	3	0	0	0	0	0	0	0	0	0	0
170	175	22	16	10	4	0	0	0	0	0	0	0
175	180	23	17	11	4	0	0	0	0	0	0	0
180	185	24	18	11	5	0	0	0	0	0	0	0
185	190	25	18	12	6	0	0	0	0	0	0	0
190	195	25	19	13	7	0	0	0	0	0	0	0
195	200	26	20	14	7	1	0	0	0	0	0	0
200	210	27	21	15	9	2	0	0	0	0	0	0
210	220	29	22	16	10	4	0	0	0	0	0	0
220	**230**	30	**24**	18	12	5	0	0	0	0	0	0
230	240	32	25	19	13	7	1	0	0	0	0	0

Source: Internal Revenue Service.

tax return. The amount of tax is based on your taxable income. **Taxable income** is less than total income because certain deductions and exemptions are allowed. These deductions and exemptions reduce the amount of income that is taxed. You get a deduction for various types of payments, such as interest expense paid on a home mortgage and contributions to charities. Many expenses paid by employees while doing their jobs may be deductible if their employers do not reimburse them. These expenses include the cost of work uniforms, gloves, and shoes. Medical expenses are also deductible. If the amount of these deductions doesn't reach a specified level, you get a **standard deduction** instead. (For example, the standard deduction for a single person for 1991 was $3,400.)

Besides these deductions, each taxpayer receives a **personal exemption**, or allowance, for himself or herself and for each dependent. (The personal exemption for 1991 was $2,150.) A **dependent** is someone you support. It can be a child or any other legal relation such as a parent, sister, or grandchild. There are also limits on the amount of income a person claimed as a dependent can earn. (In 1991 the amount was $2,150. Students, however, can earn more.)

Once you have calculated your taxable income, you can figure the amount of tax owed by using a tax schedule provided by the government. In Table 17-2, the tax table shows that for 1990, a single person who had taxable income of $10,000 paid $1,504 in tax. You'll learn more about paying income taxes later in this chapter.

In theory, the income tax is a **progressive tax**. This means that the more you make, the greater the percentage of tax you pay. This type of tax is considered the most fair because it requires the people who can best afford it and who have the greatest resources to pay the most.

The liability for tax is also affected by whether an individual is married or single. A single individual pays more on a given amount of income than a married couple does.

Certain states collect income tax based on a "flat" percentage of income. That is, the percentage is the same for everyone regardless of the amount of income. This is called a **proportional tax**.

Table 17-2 Portion of 1990 Federal Tax Table

If line 37 (taxable income) is—		And you are—			
At least	But less than	Single	Married filing jointly *	Married filing separately	Head of a house-hold
			Your tax is—		
8,000					
8,000	8,050	1,204	1,204	1,204	1,204
8,050	8,100	1,211	1,211	1,211	1,211
8,100	8,150	1,219	1,219	1,219	1,219
8,150	8,200	1,226	1,226	1,226	1,226
8,200	8,250	1,234	1,234	1,234	1,234
8,250	8,300	1,241	1,241	1,241	1,241
8,300	8,350	1,249	1,249	1,249	1,249
8,350	8,400	1,256	1,256	1,256	1,256
8,400	8,450	1,264	1,264	1,264	1,264
8,450	8,500	1,271	1,271	1,271	1,271
8,500	8,550	1,279	1,279	1,279	1,279
8,550	8,600	1,286	1,286	1,286	1,286
8,600	8,650	1,294	1,294	1,294	1,294
8,650	8,700	1,301	1,301	1,301	1,301
8,700	8,750	1,309	1,309	1,309	1,309
8,750	8,800	1,316	1,316	1,316	1,316
8,800	8,850	1,324	1,324	1,324	1,324
8,850	8,900	1,331	1,331	1,331	1,331
8,900	8,950	1,339	1,339	1,339	1,339
8,950	9,000	1,346	1,346	1,346	1,346

Table 17-2 Continued

At least	But less than	Single	Married filing jointly * Your tax is—	Married filing separately	Head of a household
9,000					
9,000	9,050	1,354	1,354	1,354	1,354
9,050	9,100	1,361	1,361	1,361	1,361
9,100	9,150	1,369	1,369	1,369	1,369
9,150	9,200	1,376	1,376	1,376	1,376
9,200	9,250	1,384	1,384	1,384	1,384
9,250	9,300	1,391	1,391	1,391	1,391
9,300	9,350	1,399	1,399	1,399	1,399
9,350	9,400	1,406	1,406	1,406	1,406
9,400	9,450	1,414	1,414	1,414	1,414
9,450	9,500	1,421	1,421	1,421	1,421
9,500	9,550	1,429	1,429	1,429	1,429
9,550	9,600	1,436	1,436	1,436	1,436
9,600	9,650	1,444	1,444	1,444	1,444
9,650	9,700	1,451	1,451	1,451	1,451
9,700	9,750	1,459	1,459	1,459	1,459
9,750	9,800	1,466	1,466	1,466	1,466
9,800	9,850	1,474	1,474	1,474	1,474
9,850	9,900	1,481	1,481	1,481	1,481
9,900	9,950	1,489	1,489	1,489	1,489
9,950	10,000	1,496	1,496	1,496	1,496
10,000					
10,000	**10,050**	**1,504**	1,504	1,504	1,504
10,050	10,100	1,511	1,511	1,511	1,511
10,100	10,150	1,519	1,519	1,519	1,519
10,150	10,200	1,526	1,526	1,526	1,526
10,200	10,250	1,534	1,534	1,534	1,534
10,250	10,300	1,541	1,541	1,541	1,541
10,300	10,350	1,549	1,549	1,549	1,549
10,350	10,400	1,556	1,556	1,556	1,556
10,400	10,450	1,564	1,564	1,564	1,564
10,450	10,500	1,571	1,571	1,571	1,571
10,500	10,550	1,579	1,579	1,579	1,579
10,550	10,600	1,586	1,586	1,586	1,586
10,600	10,650	1,594	1,594	1,594	1,594
10,650	10,700	1,601	1,601	1,601	1,601
10,700	10,750	1,609	1,609	1,609	1,609
10,750	10,800	1,616	1,616	1,616	1,616
10,800	10,850	1,624	1,624	1,624	1,624
10,850	10,900	1,631	1,631	1,631	1,631
10,900	10,950	1,639	1,639	1,639	1,639
10,950	11,000	1,646	1,646	1,646	1,646

*This column must also be used by a qualifying widow(er).
Source: Internal Revenue Service.

Payroll Taxes

Employees and the companies they work for are required to pay **payroll taxes**. These are payments made to the government to finance programs that benefit workers.

The federal government collects two types of payroll taxes: social security tax (also known as FICA tax, from the Federal Insurance Contributions Act passed by Congress to establish the tax) and federal unemployment insurance tax.

Social security taxes fund two programs that benefit workers. One program pays retirement benefits to workers who have reached the age of 65 (or who have chosen to receive reduced benefits at age 62 or who are disabled). Benefits are also paid to the families of workers who have died.

The second program funded with social security taxes is health insurance (Medicare) for retired individuals. This program pays a certain percentage of a retired worker's medical bills.

The social security tax is paid by both the employee and the employer. A fixed percentage of a worker's wage is withheld from the paycheck and sent to the government. An identical amount is paid by the company employing the worker.

Self-employed individuals must also pay social security. However, because they do not work for a company, they must pay the same amount that would have been withheld plus the company's portion.

Federal unemployment insurance tax is paid by the employer only. The funds are used by the federal government to provide temporary support for workers who have lost their jobs.

The states also have payroll taxes. States differ slightly in which of these taxes they collect and in how they collect them. Basically, though, there are two types of state payroll taxes: state unemployment and state disability.

When an individual loses his or her job, both the federal government and the state in which the individual worked share in the cost of providing temporary financial support and, if necessary, retraining. Therefore, the states collect a tax directly from employers to fund these costs.

A few states also collect a disability insurance tax to aid workers who become disabled and are unable to work. This tax is withheld from employees' paychecks in certain states. In other states, the tax is paid by employers only.

Sales Taxes

Sales tax is money paid by a buyer purchasing goods. The retailer selling the goods is required to collect the tax and send the funds to the state government periodically. Almost every state and numerous cities collect sales tax.

The amount of sales tax collected depends on the state and local government imposing the tax. For example, sales tax in Connecticut is 8 percent; in Louisiana, it's 4 percent. Sales tax is a flat-rate, or proportional, tax. That means that all income groups pay the same percentage of tax on a product. In practice, though, sales tax is a **regressive tax**. Because the tax is assessed against goods that everyone uses regardless of income level, poorer individuals often pay a larger share of their income in sales tax than wealthier individuals do.

Illustration 17-1   In cities and states with a sales tax, buyers pay the tax on goods when they purchase the items.

Each state and local government decides which goods will be subject to sales tax. Certain states do not impose a sales tax on necessities such as food and medicine. Also, sales tax is not charged on goods sold directly to a resident of another state. For example, Midori and Akeo live in Michigan. Through mail-order catalogs, they buy a camera from a store in New York City and a computer from a company in Chicago. These purchases are free from sales tax.

A variation of the sales tax is called the **use tax**. This tax is payable in two circumstances. It is imposed by the state on goods that are rented or leased to the public. It is also imposed on purchases from another state. As you just read, a resident of one state doesn't pay sales tax on an item bought in another state. Many states require the purchaser to pay a use tax instead. In the previous example, when the Michigan couple Midori and Akeo bought by mail, they didn't have to pay sales tax to New York or Illinois. Their home state of Michigan, however, requires that they pay use tax. Some states rely on the individual to tell the state about these purchases. Other states send people a general letter informing them about the law and asking them to comply. Cars and boats purchased in another state are easier to track because the owners have to register those items with their home state.

Excise Taxes

Excise taxes are imposed on the production, sale, or consumption of selected goods and services. Examples of items subject to excise tax are cigarettes, alcohol, gasoline, tires, and telephone service. It is difficult to explain why some items are subject to this tax while others are not. It will become a little clearer later in this chapter, when we discuss the uses and functions of taxes. Although these taxes are collected from the manufacturer or distributor of the goods or service, it is generally assumed that the cost is passed on to the consumer as an increase in the sales price. Excise taxes are collected by both the federal and state governments.

Wealth Taxes

Besides taxing the money you make every year and many of the goods and services you purchase, the government also collects taxes on certain possessions that you own. These are called wealth taxes. The wealth tax that is the greatest source of revenue for local governments is the real estate tax, or **property tax**. This tax is based on the value of a piece of land and the buildings on it. For this reason, property tax is sometimes called an ad valorem tax, meaning "according to value."

Illustration 17-2   Property tax is based on the value of a piece of land and the buildings on it.

Typically, the property's value is determined by a local **tax assessor**. Rarely is the assessed value (the value used for tax purposes) as high as the price for which the property could be sold on the open market. Each local government decides what percentage of the market value is subject to tax. The local government also determines the rate at which property will be taxed. For example, in a community in which assessed value is one third of the market value, a home that would sell for $90,000 would have a taxable value of $30,000. If the tax rate for properties in the community is $50 per $1,000 of taxable value, the property tax on that home would be $1,500.

Transfer tax is a wealth tax imposed when property changes hands in the form of an inheritance or a gift. The three most common transfer taxes are the federal estate tax, state inheritance taxes, and the federal gift tax. These taxes are based on the value of the property and are usually reserved for large.gifts and inheritances.

REVIEW QUESTIONS

1. What are three kinds of income that can be taxed?
2. Why is taxable income lower than total income?
3. What are two programs funded by social security taxes?
4. Why is property tax sometimes called an ad valorem tax?

BENEFITS AND USES OF TAXES

The most obvious use of your tax dollars is to pay for the operation of federal, state, and local governments. The main use for the money these governments collect in taxes is to provide goods and services to the public. Taxes pay for education; highways and public transportation; public welfare programs such as social security, unemployment benefits, and public housing; and health, police, and fire protection. Tax money also pays for the daily operating expenses of government, such as the salaries of government employees and interest owed on government debt. In 1991, for example, the federal government's budget called for 32 percent to be spent on social security payments and on unemployment and retirement benefits. About 20 percent was allotted for defense spending, and 14 percent was paid in interest on the national debt. The rest was spent on health, commerce, education, veterans' benefits, the environment, international affairs, and other programs.

At the state and local levels, the greatest percentage of tax dollars is spent on education. Other major uses for taxes at these levels include public welfare, health protection, and highway construction and repair.

Another major objective of the tax system is to give incentives to activities that Congress believes are good for the nation and to discourage activities that are not. For example, an extra tax deduction for the purchase of equipment by businesses was passed to help stimulate growth of the economy. Similarly, credits, which lower taxes, are given to employers who hire certain handicapped or economically disadvantaged people. Activities that Congress wishes to discourage, such as the overconsumption of gasoline, are limited by the imposition of an additional or increased tax. In an attempt to discourage industrial use of chlorofluorocarbons, which endanger the earth's ozone layer, Congress has placed a tax on these chemicals.

You read earlier in this chapter that with progressive taxes, such as the income tax, the more one makes, the greater the percentage of tax one pays. When wealthier taxpayers are taxed at a greater rate than the poor, there is actually a redistribution of wealth. Many people feel that a redistribution is required to maintain a desired level of economic health, as well as being a socially beneficial thing to do.

REVIEW QUESTIONS

1. What is government's main use of taxes?
2. What did the federal government spend the largest percentage of its tax money on in 1991?
3. What do state and local governments spend the greatest percentage of tax dollars on?

RESPONSIBILITIES AND RIGHTS OF INCOME TAX PAYERS

The federal income tax system is based on voluntary cooperation and compliance. This doesn't mean that you can pay your taxes only if you want to. What it does mean is that the tax system works because each year most people compute their taxes, file their tax returns, and pay any amounts due.

As you saw in the opening case, everyone must pay taxes, even when a person is morally opposed to how the government uses those taxes. There have been many other cases fought over the constitutionality of required taxation. The courts have been unanimous in ruling that moral, philosophical, or financial objections are no excuse for failing to file income tax returns.

In order for people to comply with their legal responsibilities, the tax law must be both fair and firm. The laws must be fair so that people won't resent paying the government what they owe. The laws must be firm so that those who refuse to cooperate will be punished. The only fair system is one that makes sure everyone complies.

The federal government agency that collects taxes and administers tax law is the **Internal Revenue Service (IRS)**. The IRS is a major agency in the Department of the Treasury and is organized into seven regions across the country. Those regions, in turn, are further divided into districts and local offices.

Your responsibilities and requirements regarding the tax law are spelled out in the Internal Revenue Code, which is written by Congress. The IRS interprets the legal wording of the tax code and writes rules and regulations that also become part of the law.

Filing a Tax Return

The cooperative tax process starts when you file your **income tax return** every year. This return is a formal statement telling the government how much you earned and the deductions for which you qualify. Depending on your situation, you will file the return on Form 1040, Form 1040A, or Form 1040EZ. It must be filed by April 15 for the previous calendar year. If you are unable to complete the return on time, extensions of time of four to six months may be granted by the IRS.

Department of the Treasury - Internal Revenue Service

Form
1040EZ

Income Tax Return for
Single Filers With No Dependents (L)   **1990**

Name &
address

Use IRS label (see page 9). If you don't have one, please print.

Print your name (first, initial, last)

Home address (number and street). (If you have a P.O. box, see page 9.)   Apt. no.

City, town or post office, state, and ZIP code. (If you have a foreign address, see page 9.)

Please print your numbers like this:

$9\ 8\ 7\ 6\ 5\ 4\ 3\ 2\ 1\ 0$

Your social security number

Please see instructions on the back. Also, see the
Form 1040EZ booklet.

Presidential Election Campaign (see page 9)
Do you want $1 to go to this fund?

Note: *Checking "Yes" will*
not change your tax or
reduce your refund. ▶

Report
your
income

Attach
Copy B of
Form(s)
W-2 here.
Attach tax
payment on
top of
Form(s) W-2.

Note: You
must check
Yes or No.

1   Total wages, salaries, and tips. This should be shown in Box 10
of your W-2 form(s). (Attach your W-2 form(s).)   **1**

2   Taxable interest income of $400 or less. If the total is more
than $400, you cannot use Form 1040EZ.   **2**

3   Add line 1 and line 2. This is your **adjusted gross income.**   **3**

4   Can your parents (or someone else) claim you on their return?

☐ **Yes.** Do worksheet on back; enter amount from line E here.

☐ **No.** Enter 5,300.00. This is the total of your standard
deduction and personal exemption.   **4**

5   Subtract line 4 from line 3. If line 4 is larger than line 3,
enter 0. This is your **taxable income.**   **5**

Figure
your
tax

6   Enter your Federal income tax withheld from Box 9 of your
W-2 form(s).   **6**

7   **Tax.** Use the amount on **line 5** to find your tax in the tax table
on pages 14–16 of the booklet. Enter the tax from the table on
this line.   **7**

Refund
or
amount
you owe

8   If line 6 is larger than line 7, subtract line 7 from line 6.
This is your **refund.**   **8**

9   If line 7 is larger than line 6, subtract line 6 from line 7. This is the
amount you owe. Attach your payment for full amount payable to
"Internal Revenue Service." Write your name, address, social security
number, daytime phone number, and "1990 Form 1040EZ" on it.   **9**

Sign
your
return

Keep a copy
of this form
for your
records.

I have read this return. Under penalties of perjury, I declare
that to the best of my knowledge and belief, the return is true,
correct, and complete.

Your signature   Date

X

For Privacy Act and Paperwork Reduction Act Notice, see page 4 in the booklet.   Form 1040EZ (1990)

Illustration 17-3   Form 1040EZ is the simplest tax return form and is used by many single people who meet certain income and other requirements.

The IRS mails the tax forms to people who have previously filed returns. However, you are responsible for getting the needed forms if you don't receive them by mail. Forms are available at post offices, libraries, banks, and local IRS offices.

Almost everyone who earns income must file a tax return. In 1990 you did not have to file an income tax return if your wage and investment income for the year was $500 or less. If your income was more than $500, whether you had to file depended on the type of income you had (wages or investment income), how much income you received, and whether your parents claimed you as a dependent on their return.

If you worked during the year, your employer must send you Form W-2 by January 31 of the next year. This form shows the amount of wages you were paid during the last year and how much income tax (federal and state) was withheld from your paycheck. If you had any bank interest or investment dividends, you also receive Form 1099-INT or Form 1099-DIV, showing the amount of interest or dividends you earned for the year.

1 Control number		OMB No. 1545-0008	
2 Employer's name, address, and ZIP code		6 Statutory employee ☐ Deceased ☐ Pension plan ☐ Legal rep. ☐ 942 emp. ☐ Subtotal ☐ Deferred compensation ☐ Void ☐	
		7 Allocated tips	8 Advance EIC payment
		9 Federal income tax withheld	10 Wages, tips, other compensation
3 Employer's identification number	4 Employer's state I.D. number	11 Social security tax withheld	12 Social security wages
5 Employee's social security number		13 Social security tips	14 Nonqualified plans
19 Employee's name, address and ZIP code		15 Dependent care benefits	16 Fringe benefits incl. in Box 10
		17	18 Other
20	21	22	23

24 State income tax	25 State wages, tips, etc.	26 Name of state	27 Local income tax	28 Local wages, tips, etc.	29 Name of locality

Copy 1 For State, City, or Local Tax Department

Dept. of the Treasury—Internal Revenue Service

Form **W-2 Wage and Tax Statement 1990**

Employee's and employer's copy compared ☐

Illustration 17-4 Form W-2, sent by employers to employees by January 31 of each year, shows the amount of wages the employee was paid during the previous year.

After you have this information and the correct tax forms, you're ready to complete the return. Basically, you fill in your name, address, social security number, and the amounts of your different types of income. You subtract your exemptions and any deductions you are allowed from your total income.

Then you figure your tax from tables included with the income tax form. You compare the amount of tax shown with the tax your employer withheld (plus any estimated payments you may have made). If you had too much withheld, you are due a **refund**. If not enough was withheld, you must pay the government the difference.

You must attach certain forms, such as the W-2, sign the return, and mail it. As long as the return is postmarked and mailed by April 15, the return is considered to have been filed on time, even if it is not received by the IRS until later.

Help for Taxpayers   It is often a difficult task to complete an income tax return accurately. The tax law has become so complex and it changes so often that many people pay professional return preparers to complete their returns.

To assist taxpayers, the IRS issues—at no cost—publications, news releases, pamphlets, and handbooks designed to clarify the many complex issues. Also, the IRS maintains a taxpayer assistance program that will answer many questions either by telephone or in person.

However, you are responsible for keeping thorough records and for seeing that your return is accurate and complete. When you sign your return, you declare that the return and all attachments are "to the best of my knowledge and belief, . . . true, correct, and complete."

If you do *not* sign the return, the IRS may take the position that you did not file a valid return. You may be subject to penalties for not filing. In one case, the IRS was investigating Peter Vaira's tax returns for 1959 and 1962. During the examination, the IRS noted that Vaira had not signed his return for 1962. When his case came to court, the court said that since the return was not signed, the IRS could treat it as an unfiled return and impose a penalty of 25 percent of the tax due.

Personal Responsibility for Your Return   You are personally responsible for your tax return. This is true whether you prepare your own return or have someone else prepare it for you. In one case, Robert Boyle, who was the executor of his mother's estate, hired Ronald Keyser, a lawyer, to file a tax return for the estate in 1979. Boyle provided the attorney with all the necessary information. He contacted Keyser several times to ask about the progress of the return. Each time, Keyser assured Boyle that he would file the return in plenty of time. However, because of a clerical oversight, Keyser did not file the return until three months after it was due. The IRS charged Boyle with a penalty for late filing that in this case amounted to over $17,000. Boyle felt that he had a reasonable excuse for not having filed on time. He took his case to court to get the amount of the penalty back. He claimed that the penalty was not justified because he had reasonably relied on his attorney to file the return on time. The case went all the way to the U.S. Supreme Court, which held in 1985 that Boyle had to pay the penalty. The Court said that it might be reasonable to rely on an attorney for legal advice about a tax law issue. If that happened, the taxpayer might avoid a penalty for late filing. However, you do not have to be a tax expert to know that tax returns have fixed filing dates and that any tax due must be paid on time. Therefore, the taxpayer, Boyle, was responsible for filing the return on time. Because the return was late, he was liable for the penalty for late filing.

According to government regulations, you are usually responsible for your return even if you are given incorrect information by an accountant, a lawyer, or even the IRS. This includes information provided through IRS publications or its taxpayer assistance program. You can rely on the IRS's information only when you have received in writing an answer to a specific question—and then only if you have provided the IRS with correct and complete facts.

Suppose Alicia calls the IRS taxpayer assistance service and asks whether she must declare as income alimony she received from her ex-husband. The IRS representative answers incorrectly that she doesn't have to include the alimony on her return. If her return is later questioned or audited, Alicia will owe additional tax, interest, and perhaps penalties on the omitted income, even though she acted in good faith in relying on the IRS information.

Time Limit on Applying for a Refund   If you discover a mistake in your favor or want to amend, or change, your return, there is a time limit on applying for a refund from the IRS. The statute of limitations is the later of these two dates: three years after you file your return or two years after the tax is paid. Judith Roach was unsure whether the money she received as child support was taxable income to her. Because, as the court documents stated, she wanted to pay her taxes "carefully and scrupulously," Roach included this amount as income on her tax returns for 1979 through 1983. In 1983 the IRS told Roach that child support was not taxable to her and gave her a refund for that year. In 1984 Roach learned that she could file amended returns for 1979 through 1982 and get a refund for those years. After she filed, the IRS sent her a refund for 1981 and 1982, but not for 1979 and 1980. Roach sued for a refund for the remaining two years, but she lost. The court said that her claims for 1979 and 1980 were barred by the statute of limitations. She had filed the amended returns for 1979 and 1980 more than three years after she had filed those tax returns.

How Your Return Is Processed

Once your return has been received by the IRS at one of its regional service centers, computers perform several calculations and reviews. First, the arithmetic and calculations on the return are verified. Also, the information contained in the return is matched with information the IRS has. For example, employers are required to send a copy of Form W-2 to the IRS. Banks and other financial institutions also must provide the IRS with information.

Any mathematical errors or discrepancies with IRS information will result in a notice of correction being sent to you. This can result in either a refund or an additional amount due.

Illustration 17-5   Computers are used by the IRS to help process the vast numbers of tax returns it receives—200 million in one recent year.

How Returns Are Selected for Audit   After this preliminary review, your return is sent to the classification division. There returns are reviewed to determine whether they should be audited. Returns that are not selected for audit are provisionally accepted and filed.

Only about 1 percent of all personal income tax returns are audited. This is due to the financial and workload limitations of the IRS relative to the large number of returns filed. An **audit** is the review of a tax return and the records supporting the information on that return. Certain returns with obviously unallowable items are audited by mail. Usually, additional information regarding one or two items on the return is requested.

Returns that have a high chance of being selected for audit include those with unusually high deductions relative to the income reported and those with an unusually high deduction relative to the same deduction on other people's returns. If Harvey, who earns $30,000 a year, claims $10,000 in deductions for charitable contributions, his return may be selected for review. Also, in general, the higher the income on the return, the greater the chance of audit.

Some returns are selected for audit even though they do not appear to be incorrect or unusual in some way. Some are picked purely at random. Others are audited to provide the IRS with additional information so that it can make more accurate selections of returns to be audited in the future.

Tax Audits

Returns that are selected for audit are forwarded to a local IRS office near the taxpayer's home. In many cases, the examination is held at this office. When the taxpayer has extensive records or when a large business is being audited, the audit may be held at the taxpayer's place of business or in the office of the accountant or lawyer who prepared the return.

Whether an examination occurs inside or outside the IRS office, the process is the same. The agent begins by asking a series of questions to gather general information. For example, you may be asked if you had any bartering income. (Bartering is trading one item or service for another.) Since bartering income is taxable and since many people barter to avoid paying taxes, this is an important issue to the IRS. For example, if Jack paints a house in exchange for receiving groceries from Bill, Jack has taxable income on the value of the groceries he received, as if he had received cash and then had gone out and bought the food. Bill also owes tax on the value of the paint job.

After that, the scope of the audit depends on the particular items on the return. It is the examining agent's goal to determine that all income has been reported and that all the deductions taken are allowable and are supported by documentation.

During the audit, you may be represented by an attorney, a certified public accountant (CPA), or another authorized person. In most cases, your representative can attend the meeting alone—you are not required to be there.

The audit can have four different results:

1. The agent may recommend that no changes be made to your return.
2. The agent may find that you have overpaid your taxes and will recommend a refund.
3. The agent may propose adjustments that increase your tax, and you agree.
4. The agent may propose adjustments that increase your tax, and you don't agree.

In the first three cases, you will be asked to sign a form stating that you agree with the result. In the fourth case, when you don't agree with the agent's findings, you have several ways to proceed. One method is to meet with a member of the IRS's appeals office. Appeals agents, who have the power to settle cases, may override an examining agent's findings.

When an agreement is not reached at the appellate office level, your dispute can go to court. Most people choose to go to the U.S. Tax Court. People can save money in this court because the tax doesn't have to be paid before going to court. Disputes can also be taken to either a U.S. district court or the U.S. Claims Court. In these courts, however, the tax must be paid in advance.

Generally, according to the statute of limitations on audits, the IRS cannot audit a return more than three years after that return is filed. However, if no return has been filed or if a person attempts to evade taxes, the IRS can charge tax or start a court proceeding at any time. (Keep in mind that, as you read earlier in this chapter, an unsigned return can be treated as an unfiled return.)

IRS Penalties for Not Paying Taxes

The IRS has many strict penalties and remedies if you fail to file a return or if you don't pay all the taxes you owe. If you file a return on time but don't send your entire payment, you will be charged interest that is higher than the interest banks charge. In addition to interest charges, late payments are also subject to penalty charges. However, if you file late, the penalties are even higher. Therefore, it is important to file your income tax return on time even if you can't pay the amount due. Although the IRS has great power to seize property (including your home and your car), bank accounts, and wages to collect overdue taxes, the agency may agree to let you pay what you owe on an installment plan. The IRS prefers, however, that you borrow the money or sell something you own to pay immediately.

Illustration 17-6   The IRS can impose severe penalties for failing to pay income taxes.

Penalties for Tax Fraud   If you don't pay what you owe because of carelessness or negligence, you will have to pay interest and possibly penalties. However, the consequences of fraud are the greatest. **Tax fraud** occurs when people intentionally and knowingly conceal income or otherwise falsify their return in order to avoid paying taxes. This would include tax protesters or resisters who do not disclose income to the government or who lie about their income. The case that opened this chapter is *not* an example of fraud, in that those protesters paid their tax and then filed for a refund on moral grounds. In the case of Kathleen Hadden, the court *did* find that the taxpayer had fraudulently failed to pay her taxes. Hadden was a successful Florida real estate salesperson for 20 years. During that time, she filed and paid taxes. Then she decided to earn some fast money in drug trafficking. She made about $120,000 from drug deals in 1981. Hadden did not report this money as income on her 1981 tax return. When the IRS investigated, Hadden denied that she had committed fraud. The U.S. Tax Court held otherwise. Hadden was experienced in business matters. She had to know that her taxes would be underpaid when she omitted the $120,000 from her return. She did not tell the accountant who prepared her return that year that she made money from illegal drug dealings. The court found that she had intentionally underpaid her taxes and that the underpayment was due to fraud.

The financial penalties for fraud are extremely severe. If the IRS proves that any part of any underpayment of a tax is due to fraud, it adds an additional penalty in the amount of 75 percent of the portion of the underpayment that is due to fraud. This penalty can apply only to tax returns that are actually filed. However, fraudulent failure to file a return is also subject to a 75 percent penalty.

In addition to the civil penalties, it is a crime to commit fraud against the IRS. A willful evasion of or failure to pay taxes is a felony with a penalty of up to five years' imprisonment or a fine of $100,000 or both.

Taxpayers' Rights

Despite the great powers possessed by the IRS, you as a citizen and a taxpayer also have certain rights. Two basic ones are the right to privacy and the right to appeal IRS findings you disagree with. Under the right to privacy, information given to the IRS on a tax return must remain confidential, although the agency can share the information with state tax agencies. You also have the right to plan your finances so that you pay the lowest amount of tax that is due under the law. That is, you have to pay what you owe, but not one penny more than you owe. You also have the right to influence tax policies by contacting elected representatives or by joining tax groups that influence legislation.

In addition, taxpayer safeguards were updated and expanded in the Omnibus Taxpayer Bill of Rights Act passed by Congress in 1988. You already read about some of these additional safeguards earlier in this chapter. For example, you learned that you have the right to choose to stay away from your audit and send an accountant or lawyer in your place. Also, penalties are not charged if you acted on incorrect information that the IRS gave you in writing.

Another very important protection offered under this bill of rights is that all notices for tax collection sent by the IRS must be written in clear, nontechnical language. These notices must tell you how to appeal and how to file a complaint. They also must contain a complete description of the IRS's collection procedures. Also, if you give advance notice, you may make an audiotape of your audit. You also have the right to the fair collection of tax, which includes the right to collect damages from the government if the IRS intentionally fails to follow certain collection laws.

REVIEW QUESTIONS

1. What is the extent of your responsibility for your tax return?
2. What three types of tax returns have a high chance of being audited?
3. What are the four possible results of an audit?
4. Name three rights taxpayers are given through the Taxpayer Bill of Rights.

Latest in the Law: A Friendlier IRS?

To the average American taxpayer, dealing with the Internal Revenue Service can be a terrifying experience. Taxpayers view the IRS as a sprawling, faceless bureaucracy with enormous power. The IRS also has a reputation for being ruthless in its pursuit of delinquent taxpayers. People know that if a taxpayer owes the government money, the IRS can take away nearly everything that person owns. A greater fear is that of people who worry about being caught in an IRS mistake. They have heard that trying to get an agency error corrected can be a nightmare.

A few years ago, taxpayers by the thousands told congressional investigators hair-raising stories of IRS errors and abuses. In one case, Alex Council, a man involved in a dispute caused by an IRS clerical error, committed suicide after receiving a tax bill for $289,282. In another case, the IRS told an elderly Maine couple that they owed more than $9,000 in overdue taxes and more than $20,000 in interest and penalties. It took the couple 15 months to convince the IRS that they had in fact paid their taxes on time and didn't owe the IRS anything.

Stories like these led Congress to pass the Omnibus Taxpayer Bill of Rights Act in 1988 so that taxpayers would know what their rights are when dealing with the IRS. The bill of rights specified some definite rules about how the IRS must treat delinquent taxpayers. For example,

the IRS must wait 30 days—rather than 10—after giving a taxpayer notice that it intends to seize the taxpayer's property or wages. (An exception to this rule occurs if the IRS feels its chances of getting paid are in jeopardy—then it can make a seizure immediately.)

Better Public Relations

The IRS was stung by people's criticisms and by the fact that the American people felt they needed to be protected from the agency. As a result, the IRS is not simply complying with the bill of rights. It is doing much more than trying to change its tarnished image. Its "one-stop service" program, for example, enables taxpayers to deal with just one IRS agent instead of being shunted from office to office or from phone extension to phone extension.

The IRS has also started the Problem Resolution Program (PRP). Three hundred IRS employees serve as advocates for taxpayers. These problem-resolution officers are assigned to help distraught taxpayers deal with the IRS when they have a serious problem, such as not receiving a refund that is overdue.

The IRS has also conducted a series of town meeting and telephone surveys to ask taxpayers how it can serve them better. One result is that the IRS will now speed the payment of refunds to people with hardships. A person who needs money, perhaps to fly to a funeral or to pay for a medical emergency, can obtain his or her refund in less than two days instead of the usual ten weeks. Some IRS offices offer classes that teach people how to fill out their tax returns. The Baltimore, Maryland, district office even places agents on commuter trains during the tax season (February to April) to help commuters with their tax returns.

Continuing Problems with the System

Despite the bill of rights and public relations changes, the IRS still has two major problems:

(1) the government's overly complicated tax code and (2) the agency's outdated computer equipment. Congress has made the Internal Revenue Code so complicated that most people have great difficulty preparing their tax returns correctly. Each year, Congress changes or add dozens of provisions to the tax code. These changes require taxpayers, tax accountants, and IRS agents to relearn the regulations continually. The IRS can't do much to simplify the tax code, but it is planning to spend up to $8 billion in the next ten years to upgrade its technology and services. IRS officials hope that these changes will result in more accurate tax payments and less friction between the agency and taxpayers.

Chapter Review

Chapter Summary

- The federal government receives the power to tax the people from the U.S. Constitution. States and local governments also impose and collect taxes.

- The main types of income that are taxed are wages, business income, interest and dividends on investments, and gains from the sale of stocks.

- Employers are required to withhold income taxes from employees' paychecks throughout the year.

- Each taxpayer determines his or her exact income tax liability once a year when preparing a tax return.

- A taxpayer's tax liability is reduced by deductions and exemptions. Because of deductions and exemptions, taxable income is less than total income.

- Payroll taxes are paid by employers and employees to finance federal and state programs such as social security, unemployment insurance, and disability insurance.

- Many states and some cities collect sales tax on certain goods that consumers purchase. Use tax is paid on rental items and on goods purchased outside one's state.

- Excise tax is imposed on the production, sale, or consumption of selected goods such as cigarettes and gasoline.

■ Property tax is based on the value of a piece of land and the buildings on it.

■ Taxes allow all levels of government to provide goods and services to the public.

■ Tax laws must be fair so people won't resent paying what they owe; tax laws must be firm by penalizing those who don't pay their share.

■ Congress writes the tax code, which spells out tax law. The Internal Revenue Service (IRS) collects taxes and administers tax law.

■ You are personally responsible for your tax return. There are penalties for not filing (and for filing late) and for not paying what you owe.

■ A tax audit is a review by the IRS of a tax return to verify the information on the return and to examine the supporting documentation.

■ If you don't agree with the outcome of an audit, you can go to the IRS appeals office or to court.

■ There are both civil and criminal penalties for tax fraud.

■ Taxpayers have the right to have their return kept confidential and to appeal IRS findings. Additional rights granted under the 1988 Taxpayer Bill of Rights Act include that notices from the IRS must be clear and in nontechnical language.

Understanding Legal Terms

On a separate sheet of paper, match the terms below with the definitions that follow.

progressive tax	taxable income
property tax	tax fraud
proportional tax	tax liability
regressive tax	transfer tax
sales tax	withholding allowance

1. A tax that takes a larger percentage of income from high-income people than from low-income people
2. The amount of tax you must pay
3. After deductions and exemptions, the amount on which you must pay taxes
4. A tax that takes a larger percentage of income from low-income people than from high-income people
5. A tax that takes the same percentage of income from everyone regardless of income
6. A tax that is based on the value of a piece of land and the buildings on it
7. The intentional misrepresentation of income in order to avoid paying taxes

8. Claim made by an employee that reduces the amount of income tax money that is taken out of each paycheck
9. A tax imposed when property changes hands in the form of an inheritance or a gift
10. Tax paid by a buyer purchasing goods

Applying the Law

1. Cynthia believed the 1991 war with Iraq was wrong. She thought the United States had no right to interfere with the affairs of other countries. Also, her religion forbade fighting and killing under any circumstances. When she filed her tax return for 1991, she signed it. However, she also stated that she could not pay her tax because of a religious and moral conviction that it is wrong to spend money on a war effort. She donated the amount of the taxes for that year to her church. Will she be excused from paying taxes? Explain your answer.

2. In appreciation for Hiram's 25 years of achievement at the Walker Widget Company, the company president gave Hiram and his family a trip to Florida. The value of the trip was $4,500. Does Hiram have to pay tax on the value of the award? Explain your answer.

3. Jorge recently accepted a job that paid $500 every two weeks. He was looking forward to the first payday. However, when he looked at the check, he was very disappointed. He was taking home much less than he thought he would. What had been taken out of his paycheck that gave Jorge less than the $500 he was expecting?

4. Willie was offered a job as a counter worker at a fast-food restaurant. The pay wasn't too bad, but when the boss explained to Willie that he would have to pay for his own uniforms, Willie wondered whether to take the job. He needed the money, though, so he took it. What may Willie be able to do to get back the money he has to put out for his work uniforms?

5. Marcia and Evan have asked Evan's mother, whose health is failing, to come live with them. Even though Evan's mother has an income of $15,000 a year from her investments, Marcia and Evan are planning to provide for all of the mother's needs, including food and medical care. Can Evan and Marcia claim Evan's mother as a dependent on their income tax return? Explain your answer.

6. Sally and Tom have been going together for several years. Usually, they take care of their own tax returns. One year Sally asks Tom, who is an accountant, to prepare and file her return because she is preoccupied with a book she is writing. Tom is happy to help out. He prepares the return and gives it to Sally to sign, telling her he will mail it the next day, April 1. The envelope containing the return falls under the front seat of Tom's car, and it doesn't get mailed until Sally discovers it six months later. Is she liable for a penalty for late filing? Explain your answer.

Case Studies

1. Judy Webb was a cocktail waitress in a gambling casino. Besides her wages, she received tips. Many customers gave her tips in the form of gambling chips. When the amount of tips Judy claimed on her income tax return wasn't what the IRS thought it should have been, the agency investigated. Judy stated that she didn't report all her tips as income because she often got drunk right after work and gave the gambling chips away. Does she owe income tax on the value of the gambling chips she gave away? Explain your answer.

2. Sandra Jenkins filed her income tax return for 1980 on time, but she did not sign the return. She calculated the tax incorrectly on the return and didn't pay enough. In 1986 the IRS sent Jenkins a notice that she owed additional taxes. Jenkins claimed that the IRS could not come after her for those taxes because the three-year statute of limitations had run. Would Jenkins win in court? Explain your answer.

3. For years, Phillip Lloyd paid taxes on his earnings. In fact, he always had his tax returns prepared by an accountant, who advised him on tax matters. Then he met a man who was a member of a tax protest movement and who claimed to know ways to avoid paying taxes. Lloyd went to several meetings of this group and was given ideas about how to avoid having money withheld. He heard arguments about how wages are not income and income tax is unconstitutional. Lloyd decided to try some of the methods of this group one year. He claimed an extremely high, and false, number of withholding allowances so no money would be withheld from his wages. Then he didn't file a return. The IRS accused Lloyd of fraud. Who would win in court? Explain your answer.

Unit 6

Using The Law

Chapter 18

Working with a Lawyer

Chapter Objectives
When you have read this chapter, you should be able to:

- Explain what a lawyer does, and describe several circumstances under which a person might need a lawyer's services.

- Describe the steps by which a person can find and hire a suitable lawyer.

- Explain the differences between hourly fees, flat fees, and contingency fees.

- Describe the rights and responsibilities of clients in an attorney-client relationship.

- Describe the rights and responsibilities of attorneys in an attorney-client relationship.

- List five less expensive alternatives to hiring a lawyer.

Case Study

National Organization for Women, Essex County Chapter v. Little League Baseball, Inc., 318 A.2d 33 (New Jersey 1974).

For many years, Little League baseball teams were limited to boys only. In the early 1970s, several young girls in New Jersey asked to try out for Little League teams. The league refused to let them.

The girls felt that they were being treated unfairly, but they didn't know what to do about it. They turned to the county chapter of the National Organization for Women (NOW) for advice. NOW had a long history of working for women's rights and fighting to end sex discrimination. NOW told the girls that the Little League's boys-only rule violated New Jersey's civil rights laws. The organization suggested that the girls take the Little League to court, where the rule could be declared illegal.

The girls' families told NOW that they couldn't afford to hire lawyers to sue the Little League. Because this was an important case that could affect girls throughout the state, NOW didn't want to let the matter drop. After some discussion, the organization volunteered to have its own lawyers handle the case at no cost to the girls.

In 1974 NOW's lawyers argued the girls' case before the Superior Court of New Jersey. The court ruled that the Little League's discrimination against girls was illegal. From then on, girls all over New Jersey were allowed to try out for Little League teams.

WHAT A LAWYER CAN DO FOR YOU

A lawyer is a person trained in law. Lawyers advise people on how to proceed in legal matters such as buying a house, adopting a child, and settling a dispute. They write legal documents such as wills and contracts. They also speak for their clients in court.

To work as a lawyer, a person must be licensed by the state **bar** (or bar association). The bar is an official agency that oversees lawyers and the practice of law in a particular state. Each state bar has different rules about who can and who cannot be licensed as a lawyer. In most states, a person who wants to be a lawyer must attend a law school and get a law degree. He or she must then pass a two- or three-day examination on legal knowledge. Finally, he or she must pass a background and character check.

Illustration 18-1   In most states, a person who wants to be a lawyer must attend law school and get a law degree.

Preventive Law

Many people never pay attention to legal matters until they have a legal problem. If you have been arrested, if you are being sued, or if you have been injured through someone else's negligence, you will certainly need a lawyer. In many cases, however, careful preparation before a crisis occurs—including, perhaps, a visit with a lawyer for some general advice—will make you less likely to need expensive legal services later. This kind of advance preparation is sometimes called **preventive law**.

Preventive law is especially important if you go into business. Imagine, for example, that you've finished school and have decided to start your own catering business. You know a lot about cooking but not much about starting a business. You know you'll need to sign a contract with your customers, but you don't know what sort of contract you should ask your customers to sign. You don't know if there are tax rules, health codes, or local regulations that affect new businesses in your area.

To avoid getting into legal trouble, you'll want to find out the answers to these questions long before you accept the first catering job. There are several ways to get the information you need. You can hire a lawyer; you can research the issues yourself; you can talk to other professionals, such as an accountant or financial adviser; or you can talk to the government agencies that make the rules and regulations. Each option has advantages and disadvantages.

A lawyer can tell you about all the federal, state, and local regulations that affect a catering business. He or she can help you draft a standard contract to use with your customers.

A lawyer's advice on these matters is certainly helpful, but it is usually expensive. If you don't have much money, you may be better off doing your own legal research. In many cases, you can find out everything you need to know without the help of a lawyer.

Your public library and local bookstores have a wealth of information on law-related topics. You can find books on how to start a business, write a will, or even handle a divorce without a lawyer. Many libraries have legal forms, reference manuals, and other resources for people who want to handle their own legal affairs.

If you want free advice about matters such as taxes, insurance, licenses, and business regulations, you can call a government agency. Many federal, state, and local government agencies are likely to have branch offices in or near the town where you live. The names of state and local agencies vary from place to place, but many telephone directories now have special government sections, which may be called the Blue Pages, where you can find the agency you're looking for. Agencies that may give you legal advice include the state insurance bureau, the state department of commerce, the state office of economic development, and the local license and permit bureau. If you're not sure who can help you with a particular matter, ask a librarian or call your local government center (such as the city or town hall) for a recommendation.

Keep in mind, however, that books and government agencies can give only general advice. They can't anticipate your special needs the way a lawyer can. Before you decide to handle a legal matter on your own, consider how complicated your situation is. Figure out how much time it will take to do the work yourself and how serious the consequences will be if you make a mistake. One option is to do as much legal work as you can on your own and then pay a lawyer to check and complete the work. For example, hiring a lawyer to review the contract you've prepared for your catering business would be much less expensive than having the lawyer write the contract from scratch.

For some matters, you may get better advice by talking to someone other than a lawyer. Suppose you're confused about the tax laws that may apply to your catering business. Most lawyers know something about tax law, but an accountant may know even more. In addition to answering your tax questions, a good accountant can give you money-saving ideas, help you apply for business loans, and offer many other kinds of financial assistance that a lawyer usually doesn't handle. In most cases, you'll pay less for an accountant's services than for a lawyer's services.

When Should You Hire a Lawyer?

As you read in Chapter 7, most disputes can be settled privately, without the use of lawyers. You may be able to settle through negotiation, mediation, or arbitration or by going to small claims court. However, if you have been unsuccessful with these alternatives or if your case involves a greater amount of money than the limit allowed in small claims court, you may have to go to regular court.

In general, whenever you have to go to court, you should hire a lawyer to represent you. (The only exceptions to this rule are small claims court and, in most cases, traffic court.) Although you have the right to represent yourself in civil and criminal trials, it is never a good idea to do so. Courtroom rules are complicated and are usually too difficult for a nonlawyer to handle. Also, when you are personally involved in a case, you may not be able to think and act objectively. Even a plaintiff or defendant who is a trained lawyer will usually choose to be represented by another lawyer.

If you're involved in a civil dispute that may lead to a court case, you should hire a lawyer as soon as possible. Federal and state laws called **statutes of limitations** set time limits for many kinds of legal action. These laws state that if you want to sue someone, you must do so within a certain number of years. (Depending on the state and the matter involved, the limit may range from 2 years to more than 20 years.) If you fail to take action before the time runs out, you lose the right to sue.

If you are the defendant in a civil case, you may be faced with a much shorter time limit. When the plaintiff files a complaint against you, you must answer that complaint within a certain amount of time—sometimes as little as 30 days. If you fail to answer a complaint in time, you will lose the right to defend yourself in court. The judge will automatically rule in favor of the plaintiff. Answering a complaint is not something you should do on your own— you'll need a lawyer to do it for you.

If you are the defendant in a criminal case, you have the constitutional right to be represented by a lawyer. You should get a lawyer immediately after you are arrested or charged with a crime. If you can't afford a lawyer, the court will appoint one for you without charge. Later in this chapter you'll learn about some of the options if you are involved in a civil dispute and can't afford to pay for the services of a lawyer.

REVIEW QUESTIONS

1. What qualifications must a person have to practice law?
2. Describe one advantage and one disadvantage of handling a legal matter yourself, without the help of a lawyer.
3. What is a statute of limitations?

FINDING A LAWYER

Let's return to the earlier example in which you've decided to start a catering business. Suppose you've made a contract with Alicia Jenkins to cater her party for $3,000. For the party, you prepare dinner for a hundred people and hire three people to help you cook and serve. After the party is over, Jenkins refuses to pay you. You try to resolve the matter with her informally, but she refuses even to discuss it. Because there is a large amount of money involved, you decide to hire a lawyer.

You will have to choose your lawyer carefully. If this case goes to court, you and your lawyer may be working together closely for some time. You'll want a lawyer who is affordable, trustworthy, easy to work with, and experienced with this type of case.

The best way to choose a lawyer is to talk to a few different lawyers and compare them. You can get the names of lawyers from newspaper advertisements or from listings in the Yellow Pages. Better yet, ask for recommendations from friends, members of your family, local businesspeople, and neighbors.

Illustration 18-2   A good way to find a lawyer is to ask for recommendations from friends and family members.

Don't just collect names; ask questions. Suppose your uncle Joseph recommends his lawyer, Allen Kopec. Ask your uncle what type of case he hired Kopec for. (Since your case involves a contract dispute, you wouldn't want a tax lawyer.) Ask also why your uncle recommends Kopec and whether there were any problems when they worked together.

If you have friends or relatives who practice law, you may consider hiring one of them to handle your case. That is not a good idea. Lawyers and their clients often disagree, and such disagreements may permanently harm a friendship. In addition, you may have trouble being completely truthful with a friend. It's essential that you be able to tell your lawyer all the facts about the case, even facts that may be too embarrassing to tell a friend. For these reasons, don't ask someone close to you to be your lawyer. Ask him or her to recommend a good lawyer instead.

You can also contact state or local bar associations, most of which offer **lawyer referral services**. These services help match lawyers with potential clients. If you call one of these services and briefly describe the facts of your case, you can get the names of several suitable lawyers in your area. Other sources for recommendations include a local law librarian, court clerk, or law school professor. These people work with local lawyers frequently, and they will probably know which ones are best suited to take your case.

Once you have a list of four or five possible lawyers, you can narrow down the list by conducting brief telephone interviews. The purpose of these interviews is to learn more about each lawyer and to decide which ones are worth the time and expense of a personal meeting.

It's a good idea to list your lawyers in order of preference, from those you're least likely to hire to those you're most likely to hire. Call the least desirable lawyers first so that you'll have extra practice when you call the others.

Before you make the first call, prepare for the interview. Know the specific facts of your case—the dates, the names of the parties involved, the amount of money involved, and the exact sequence of events that led to the dispute. Write those facts down so you'll be prepared for any question the lawyer may ask. The more questions you can answer in the phone interview, the more effectively a lawyer can measure the complexity of your case.

Let's say you decide to speak first to Allen Kopec, the lawyer your uncle recommended. When you call, introduce yourself and explain that you are looking to hire a lawyer. Briefly describe your problem and ask Kopec whether he would have the time to handle your case. If he is too busy (or simply not interested), he may be able to recommend someone else for you to call.

If Kopec tells you he is available, ask him what kinds of cases he generally handles. Lawyers usually identify themselves as either general practitioners or specialists. A **general practitioner** is like a family doctor: he or she handles most routine legal matters. A **specialist**, by contrast, has developed expertise in one limited area, such as criminal law, immigration, personal injury, real estate, or divorce.

For this case, you'll want a lawyer with experience in contract disputes. You may want to hire a contracts specialist, or you may prefer a general practitioner who has handled a number of contracts cases. (Your decision will probably depend at least partly on the lawyer's fees. A specialist will probably charge more per hour, but his or her experience may make the work go faster. As a result, you may end up paying less for a specialist than for a general practitioner.)

Suppose Allen Kopec is a general practitioner. Having heard that your case involves a breach of contract, he may tell you that he has experience in contracts law. If this happens, don't settle for vague information about his experience. Ask Kopec how many years he has practiced law. Ask him how many contracts cases he has handled and how recently he has dealt with a case like yours.

Ask Kopec for a rough idea of how much time and work your case would require and how much he charges for his time. Based on his experience with similar cases, Kopec should be able to give you an estimate of what his services will cost you. Of course, no lawyer can tell you exactly what it will cost to handle a complex case, especially during a brief phone interview. Kopec should, however, be able to give you at least a ballpark figure: for example, a few hundred dollars, $1,000, or more than $5,000. This estimate will give you some idea of whether you can afford his services. If Kopec says his minimum fee is $5,000 and your catering contract was for only $3,000, there's no reason to discuss the matter further.

If you are satisfied that Kopec can handle your case and if you can afford his rates, you'll want to set up a personal meeting. Some lawyers charge a small fee for this kind of meeting; others will meet with you once at no charge.

REVIEW QUESTIONS

1. Name three good ways to get the names of recommended lawyers.
2. What is the difference between a general practitioner and a specialist?
3. Why is it important to interview lawyers over the phone before meeting them in person?

INTERVIEWING A LAWYER

After talking with four or five lawyers on the phone, you'll probably find at least two who seem worth the time and cost of a personal meeting. These meetings will be very much like job interviews, where you will play the role of the employer. Before you agree to hire a lawyer, you will want to find out as much as possible about what he or she can do for you.

Experience and Qualifications

Suppose you set up an interview with a lawyer named Sheila Franks. On the phone Franks told you that she is a general practitioner with a good deal of experience in contract disputes. When you meet with her in person, you'll want to find out more about her experience. Ask her to describe any cases she has handled that were similar to yours.

Keep in mind that laws differ from state to state. Most lawyers are qualified to practice in only one state; others belong to the bars of two or more states. If the party you catered was in another state, Franks may not be able to handle your case. Ask Franks which state's laws apply to your case and whether she is qualified to practice law in that state.

Find out whether Franks works alone, in a small partnership, or as a member of a large firm. There are advantages and disadvantages to each type of arrangement. Lawyers in large firms can get help and support from hundreds of other lawyers and legal researchers. If Franks works for a large firm, however, she may not handle your case herself—instead, she may hand it over to an assistant or to a less experienced lawyer.

Illustration 18-3 Whether people choose a lawyer who works alone or one who has many partners, there are both advantages and disadvantages.

If Franks works with only a few partners or if she works alone, you are likely to get much more personal attention. She may not be able to handle your case as quickly as a large firm can, but her hourly rate is likely to be lower. You will have to decide which kind of arrangement best suits your needs.

Tasks and Time Involved

At the meeting you and Franks will have to discuss your case in some detail. Remember that before you conducted your phone interviews, you made a list of the facts of your case. Bring that list with you to the meeting, along with any documents that are relevant to the case.

Tell Franks the names of the people involved in your dispute. You should end the meeting with Franks immediately if she knows or has worked with any person involved in the case. Her connection with one of those people could bias her against you.

After you describe your case to Franks, the first thing you should ask is whether you really need a lawyer. Franks may recommend that you try to settle the matter on your own through negotiation, mediation, or arbitration. She may also recommend alternatives you haven't thought of. For example, she may suggest that you sue Jenkins for $2,000 rather than the full $3,000 Jenkins owes you. If you do this, you'll lose $1,000—but you'll be able to sue Jenkins in small claims court without having to pay a lawyer's fees.

If Franks thinks it makes sense for you to hire a lawyer, ask her how she would handle the case. Don't expect her to give you free legal advice during the meeting. She should, however, be able to describe the steps she would take to resolve your problem.

Be suspicious if the first thing Franks suggests is a lawsuit. A good lawyer will usually suggest simpler alternatives first, such as a phone call or a letter. (If Jenkins gets an intimidating letter from a lawyer, she may decide to pay you right away, without your having to sue her.) Ask Franks how long each step of the case would take and how much it would cost.

It's essential that you speak openly at this first meeting. Tell Franks the good and the bad. Suppose the truth is that Jenkins didn't pay the bill because you showed up six hours late. You may be tempted not to mention your lateness—either because you think it's not important or because you want to make yourself look good. Remember, however, that all the facts will come out eventually and that your lawyer will have to be prepared for them. If you hold back the truth now, your case may become much more complicated and expensive later on.

Personal Relationship

One of the most important parts of a face-to-face meeting is getting a feel for the person you may be working with. When you talk to Franks, make sure she is someone you like and can work with easily.

■ Does she answer your questions in a way you can understand?
■ Does she treat you patiently and respectfully?

■ Does she seem trustworthy?

■ Does she give you her full attention, or does she interrupt your meeting by taking phone calls?

If you are uncomfortable with Franks during your first meeting, you're not likely to be happy with her over the long term.

Fees

Like many people, you may be uncomfortable talking about money. At some point during your meeting, however, you should discuss fees more thoroughly than you did during the phone interview. Even for simple cases, a lawyer's time can be expensive. The more difficult your case is, the more you can expect to pay for Franks's services.

Lawyers charge for their work in three different ways: flat fees, hourly fees, and contingency fees. A **flat fee** is a fixed price for a service. You pay the same flat fee regardless of how long the lawyer takes to complete the task. Some lawyers charge flat fees for simple tasks such as writing a standard will, filing for a name change, and handling an uncontested divorce.

For most other services, lawyers generally charge an **hourly fee**—a fee per hour of work. The amount they charge per hour depends on many factors, including the complexity of the case, the lawyer's level of expertise, and—in some cases—your ability to pay. If Franks charges by the hour, ask her to estimate the number of hours she expects to spend on your case. Ask if there's anything you can do to help her handle the case more quickly.

Some lawyers who charge hourly fees will guarantee a fixed maximum charge. In other words, they will bill by the hour up to a limit that you have agreed upon in advance. If handling your case takes longer than the agreed number of hours, the lawyer will do the additional work free.

Under a third type of billing arrangement, lawyers receive a **contingency fee**. This fee is a percentage of the money they collect for you. If you lose the case and collect nothing, the lawyer also gets nothing.

Illustration 18-4 Lawyers charge for their work in three different ways: flat fees, hourly fees, and contingency fees.

Contingency fees are allowed only in cases that involve money, such as personal injury and debt collection. Because your catering dispute involves a sum of money, it is possible that Franks will agree to take your case on contingency. If Franks succeeds in collecting your $3,000 from Jenkins, she will receive a percentage of that sum—most likely a third, or $1,000.

The amount of a contingency fee varies from case to case and from lawyer to lawyer. While 33 percent is a common rate, different lawyers may ask for as little as 20 percent or as much as 50 percent of whatever they collect.

Some lawyers change their contingency fees in accordance with how much work they've done on a case. For example, if a case is settled in the client's favor before trial, the lawyer's fee may be 25 percent. If a case goes to trial and the court rules in the client's favor, the lawyer may collect 33 percent. If a case goes through one or more appeals before a court rules in the client's favor, the lawyer may take as much as 40 or 50 percent.

No matter what kind of payment a lawyer asks for—a flat fee, an hourly fee, or a contingency fee—you may have to pay additional charges to cover the lawyer's expenses. Depending on the type of case, those expenses may include the costs of filing court papers, traveling, conducting investigations, taking photographs, making photocopies, hiring expert witnesses, and processing documents. Find out how many of these expenses will be billed separately. Remember that even if your lawyer fails to collect a contingency fee because of losing the case, you may still have to pay the lawyer's expenses.

Some lawyers may ask you to pay them part of their fee in advance, before they do any work on the case. This partial payment is called a **retainer**.

If you think you'll have trouble paying a lawyer's fees and expenses, explain those financial problems during the first meeting. Many lawyers—especially those who work alone—are willing to negotiate fees. Other lawyers offer long-term payment plans that allow you to pay in monthly installments.

When talking about fees, ask your lawyer whether you might qualify for a special rate. Some lawyers offer special rates for students, members of particular unions, or members of other organizations. Other lawyers offer sliding fee scales—that is, the fee depends on how much you can afford to pay.

Putting It in Writing

Let's say that after meeting with several different lawyers, you decide to hire Sheila Franks to handle your case. To prevent any misunderstandings later, the first thing you should do is write down, clearly and specifically, everything you and Franks have agreed on.

The written agreement should list the responsibilities of each party. (You, as the client, do have certain responsibilities—for example, to speak truthfully to your lawyer and to supply all relevant documents.) The agreement should include an estimated timetable for the handling of your case and a description of your payment arrangements. It should list the expenses that are included in Franks's fees and those you are expected to pay. Finally, it should explain how any disputes between you and Franks will be resolved. (Many lawyers and clients prefer that such conflicts be handled through mediation or arbitration.)

If Franks offers to write the agreement, make sure she uses plain English rather than legal jargon, or legalese. Read over the agreement to make sure you understand exactly what it says. (If you don't trust Franks to write the agreement in a way that's fair to both of you, perhaps you shouldn't hire her.) If you decide to write the agreement yourself, you may want to look at a sample lawyer-client contract. You can find such samples in legal self-help books, or you can get them from certain consumer organizations and bar associations.

REVIEW QUESTIONS

1. Name four kinds of information that you should discuss with a lawyer during the first meeting.
2. Explain the differences between a flat fee, an hourly fee, and a contingency fee.
3. What is a retainer?

WORKING WITH YOUR ATTORNEY

As soon as you hire Franks to handle your case, she becomes your attorney. (An **attorney** is a lawyer who represents a client in a legal matter.) Although you are paying Franks for her legal expertise, you can't just sit back and wait for her to settle the case. In order to do her job effectively, she will need your help. The attorney-client relationship is a partnership.

Keep Franks informed about your case. Give her any contracts and other documents that you think will be helpful. If new information comes in, don't hold it back. For example, if Jenkins decides she wants to talk with you about the case, tell Franks about it.

Learn all you can about the legal issues involved, and don't be afraid to ask questions. Remember, your attorney works for *you*. While it's important that you take her advice seriously, the final decisions—such as whether to appeal or whether to settle—are yours to make. To make these decisions intelligently, you'll need to pay attention to all the details of the case.

If you held back any facts during the initial interview, tell your attorney immediately—especially if you know you've done something wrong. You may be tempted to withhold facts from Franks or even to lie to her. You may think that if you convince her that you're blameless, she'll have a better chance of winning the case. In reality, exactly the opposite is true. If you lie to your attorney, she'll have a much harder time presenting your case in court.

Let's say a young man named Jason is arrested for stealing beer from a liquor store. He tells his attorney, Hector Rivera, the truth: he didn't steal the beer. To protect himself further, however, he tells a lie: he says that he wasn't even *in* the liquor store the night the beer was stolen. At Jason's trial, Rivera allows Jason to testify that he wasn't in the store. Unfortunately, three witnesses—including a police officer—testify that they did see Jason in the store that night. On hearing this testimony, the jury concludes that Jason lied about everything that happened. As a result, Jason is found guilty.

If Jason had told his attorney the truth, Rivera could have defended him much more effectively. He could have presented evidence that Jason was in the store but didn't steal the beer. The testimony of the three witnesses would have supported that story, and the jury might have been much more likely to find Jason innocent.

Attorney-Client Privilege

Suppose you made a terrible mistake when you catered Alicia Jenkins's party. Instead of refrigerating the hors d'oeuvres until serving time, you let them sit at room temperature for most of the day. Some of the hors d'oeuvres spoiled, and several guests became mildly ill from eating them. This is why Jenkins refused to pay you for the catering job.

These are facts that Franks, your attorney, must know in order to handle the case. You, however, don't want to tell her what really happened. You are afraid that she'll tell other people about the spoiled food and that you'll never get a catering job again. Even worse, you're afraid that Franks—or someone she talks to—will report you to the board of health and that you'll suffer serious consequences.

Fortunately for you, Franks is not allowed to repeat anything you say about your case. Discussions of legal matters between lawyers and their clients must remain strictly private. This rule of confidentiality is called **attorney-client privilege**.

In 1953, for example, Harry Kor was arrested and charged with possession of heroin. He phoned a lawyer, Joseph Rosen, and told him what had happened. At Kor's trial the prosecutor called Rosen to the witness stand and asked him to repeat what Kor had said after the arrest. He wanted to know whether Kor had admitted to possessing heroin.

Rosen refused to answer. He claimed that their discussion had been private and that to repeat what Kor had said would violate the attorney-client privilege. The judge disagreed and ordered Rosen to answer the questions. Rosen then admitted that Kor had told him that the heroin was his.

As a result of Rosen's testimony, Kor was found guilty. Kor appealed. The appeals court overturned the conviction. It stated that Rosen's testimony had indeed violated attorney-client privilege and that the trial judge had been wrong in forcing him to testify.

The attorney-client privilege applies whenever a lawyer gives legal advice to a client or handles a case for a client. All conversations and documents relating to a case—including the lawyer's notes—are confidential. For practical reasons, the attorney-client privilege also covers people who work with attorneys, such as secretaries and law clerks. These people are allowed to know what went on in private discussions between an attorney and a client, but they are not allowed to repeat it to anyone.

There are, of course, exceptions to attorney-client privilege. Not every conversation you have with your attorney is confidential. To be protected by attorney-client privilege, a conversation must deal specifically with legal matters. Similarly, attorney-client privilege does not protect your conversations with anyone who happens to be a lawyer. The lawyer must be acting as your attorney.

The case of Tom Watkins, a Florida farmer, illustrates this second exception. Watkins's life insurance policy guaranteed that his wife would receive a sum of money when he died unless Watkins died by suicide. On December 15, 1940, Watkins was found dead. Medical examiners discovered traces of poison in his body, but they couldn't tell whether he had poisoned himself accidentally or had intended to kill himself. The insurance company declared Watkins's death a suicide and refused to pay his widow. She sued the company.

Errol Willes, a local lawyer, was Watkins's friend. The day before his death Watkins had gone to visit Willes. Watkins had asked to borrow some money, and the two men had talked for a while. In court, the life insurance company asked Willes to testify about his chat with Watkins. Willes was asked whether Watkins had mentioned suicide during their conversation. Willes refused to answer. He said that because he was a lawyer, his conversation with

Watkins was protected by attorney-client privilege. The court decided, however, that Watkins had been talking to Willes as a friend, not as an attorney.
After being ordered to answer the question, Willes admitted that Watkins had
indeed talked about suicide.

Conflict of Interest

Lawyers have a duty to help their clients in every way possible. Sometimes,
however, other interests may interfere with that duty. For example, suppose
Sheila Franks is a friend of Alicia Jenkins. As your attorney, Franks is required to take your side against Jenkins. As Jenkins's friend, however, Franks
is expected to take Jenkins's side against you. Franks is caught in a difficult situation—she can't be a good attorney and a good friend at the same time. This
sort of situation, in which two duties or desires conflict with each other, is
called a **conflict of interest**.

Most responsible lawyers will refuse to represent you if they think that taking your case will create a conflict of interest. To protect yourself, however, you
should keep an eye out for conflicts of interest that the lawyer may not be aware
of. Earlier in this chapter you were advised not to hire a lawyer who knows or
has worked with any of the parties involved in your case. This advice applies
even after you have hired a lawyer. If you discover that your attorney (or anyone
in your attorney's firm) has a connection with your adversary or with your adversary's attorney, you should find a new lawyer as soon as possible.

Occasionally, lawyers are caught in a conflict between their clients' interests and their own self-interest. James Horan, for example, was a lawyer and
a good friend of Wellington Barnes. During the late 1950s, Barnes asked
Horan to write a will for him. When Barnes died in 1959, his relatives expected to inherit a good deal of money. Instead, when the will was read, they
discovered that Barnes had left much of his money to Horan. The relatives
complained that they were the victims of a conflict of interest. Horan's duty as
Barnes's attorney was to write a will that distributed the wealth fairly. Horan's
self-interest, however, compelled him to take much of that wealth for himself.

Problems with Your Attorney

In 1958 Mrs. Garfield Green hired a California lawyer named Wallace Rock to
handle a real estate matter for her. Soon afterward, she discovered that he was
nearly impossible to reach by telephone. The few times she did manage to talk
to him, he assured her that he was working diligently on her case. The truth
was that he was doing nothing. He continued to avoid Green's calls for nearly
two years. Finally, Green reported Rock's behavior to the California state bar.
The bar reviewed her case and found out that other clients had made similar
complaints about Rock. The bar held a disciplinary hearing and decided that
Rock had been extremely negligent. Rock's license to practice law was suspended for two years.

Very few lawyers are as negligent as Rock, but problems with lawyers
sometimes occur. Lawyers and their clients may disagree about fees, delays, or

simple matters of opinion. Sometimes a lawyer and client just don't work well together.

What can you do if, after hiring Franks as your attorney, you decide you don't like the way she's handling the case? One option is to fire her. As the employer, you have the right to fire your attorney at any time. Firing a lawyer in the middle of a case, however, may cause more problems than it solves. You'll have to face delays in the handling of the case. You'll have to pay for the work Franks has already done—and then pay for the same work again when another lawyer takes the case. (Even lawyers hired on contingency fees must be paid a reasonable sum when they are fired.) You'll also be faced with the task of finding another lawyer. You may find that some lawyers are reluctant to take a case from which another lawyer was fired. For these reasons, firing your attorney should never be your first choice.

Instead, if you and Franks have a dispute about her handling of the case or about fees, try to resolve it yourselves. Many attorney-client disputes result from poor communication that leads to misunderstandings. By discussing your differences openly and honestly, you may be able to settle the dispute and continue your relationship.

Some problems, of course, are too serious to be settled by negotiation. In some cases—such as the case of Wallace Rock at the beginning of this section—it may be clear that your attorney is acting improperly. Under these circumstances, you should fire your attorney immediately and file a complaint with the state bar. The bar will investigate your charges and may hold a formal disciplinary hearing. If the bar finds that your attorney is guilty of neglect, breach of confidence, misconduct, conflict of interest, unethical behavior, illegal actions, or incompetence, it will declare that you had "good cause" to fire your attorney. A lawyer who is fired for good cause is not entitled to be paid.

The bar may also decide to discipline your attorney. For a minor offense, the punishment may consist of a simple letter of warning. For a moderate offense, the lawyer may receive a public reprimand. For a very serious offense, the lawyer may be temporarily or permanently suspended from practicing law. Permanent suspension is called **disbarment**.

Suppose your attorney, Franks, takes a very long time to prepare your case against Alicia Jenkins. By the time Franks is ready to file the proper papers with the court, your deadline under the statute of limitations has passed. As a result, you lose the right to sue for the $3,000 Jenkins owes you.

You can file a complaint with the state bar, and Franks may be disciplined for her behavior. The bar may also decide that you don't have to pay Franks for her work on your case. Still, you have lost $3,000 because of Franks's negligence. The only chance you have to recover that money is to sue her for legal malpractice.

To prove malpractice in court, you must show that your attorney's actions were negligent, incompetent, or dishonest. You must also show that you suffered a loss because of those actions. Simply showing that your attorney lost a case or made errors in judgment is not enough.

Malpractice suits, like other kinds of lawsuits, tend to be time-consuming and expensive. It's never a good idea to sue a lawyer for malpractice unless you have exhausted all other ways of resolving the problem.

Withdrawal by Your Attorney

Although you are free to fire your attorney at any time, your attorney does not have equal freedom to end the relationship. According to rules agreed on by all state bars, a lawyer may not withdraw from a case unless there is a very good reason to do so.

Conflict of interest is a good reason for a lawyer to withdraw from a case. Client misconduct is another. A lawyer may refuse to work for a client who is uncooperative or unwilling to pay the lawyer's bills. A lawyer may also withdraw from any case that seems unethical—for example, a case the client has invented for the sole purpose of harassing another person.

If Franks withdraws from your case, she must do everything possible to minimize the problems caused by her withdrawal. She must, for example, tell you in advance about her plans to withdraw. She must also cooperate fully with any lawyer you hire to replace her.

REVIEW QUESTIONS

1. What is the attorney-client privilege, and what is its purpose?
2. Give an example of conflict of interest.
3. Describe three things you can do if you think your lawyer has behaved improperly.
4. What might a state bar do if it decides that a lawyer has been negligent?

ALTERNATIVES TO PAYING FOR A LAWYER

As you've learned in this chapter, legal services are expensive. Although access to a lawyer has become increasingly important in today's society, many Americans simply can't afford the fees that lawyers charge.

The Constitution does not guarantee a lawyer to people involved in civil suits, as it does to those accused of a crime. If you find it necessary to sue someone—or, worse, if someone decides to sue *you*—you must provide your own lawyer. Fortunately, there are several alternatives for people who can't afford to pay for legal services.

Legal Aid

Legal aid societies are not-for-profit organizations that provide free legal services for low-income people. They are usually funded by federal, state, or local governments or by private contributions. Your local bar association can help you find out about legal aid services in your area.

Legal Clinics

Legal clinics offer low-cost legal services to anyone, regardless of income. They prepare wills, handle uncontested divorces, and take care of other routine matters at a fraction of standard prices. Some legal clinics may also represent plaintiffs or defendants in simple lawsuits. Most, however, will not handle unusual cases or prepare complex documents.

Illustration 18-5   Legal clinics offer low-cost legal services to anyone, regardless of income.

"Storefront" legal clinics can often be found in malls and shopping centers. They may offer evening hours, quick service, and other conveniences. Some law schools set up legal clinics to give their students experience in practicing law. The students work under the supervision of lawyers.

Legal Plans and Legal Insurance

Some law firms offer prepaid legal plans to individuals and groups. In exchange for an annual fee, paid in advance, the law firm will provide routine legal services similar to those offered by legal clinics. The law firm may also provide more complicated services (such as writing complex documents or handling large lawsuits) at a discounted hourly rate. Some employers pay for these legal plans as a benefit for their employees, and some colleges and universities provide them for their students.

Instead of belonging to a legal plan, some people prefer to buy legal insurance. Legal insurance is similar to medical insurance. In exchange for paying regular premiums, you get legal coverage up to a certain limit. Unlike a prepaid legal plan, legal insurance allows you to choose your lawyer. If the lawyer's charges are reasonable, the insurance company will pay your legal bills.

Of course, many people take out liability insurance policies. If they are sued, lawyers hired by the insurance company will represent the insured and handle the case under the terms of the policy.

Payment by the Other Party

As you read in Chapter 7, a defendant who is found liable in a civil case may have to pay the plaintiff's attorney's fees. If the case involves family matters, welfare benefits, or discrimination based on sex, race, or age, a federal rule *requires* that attorney's fees be included in the damages.

In other words, suppose you've brought a lawsuit against your employer for sex discrimination. If the court rules in your favor, the employer will have to reimburse you for all the money you paid your attorney. (Of course, your employer will probably have to pay other damages as well.) This rule helps encourage lawsuits by people who could not otherwise afford to bring them.

Help from Government Agencies

Federal, state, and local government agencies are often willing to help citizens resolve legal problems. Suppose you are injured by a product you bought from a national manufacturer. You may want to contact your state or local department of consumer affairs, the state attorney general's office, the Federal Trade Commission (FTC), or the Consumer Product Safety Commission (CPSC). Any of these agencies will be able to give you legal advice, and one of them may be willing to sue the manufacturer on your behalf.

For help with disputes involving food or drug products, you can contact the Food and Drug Administration (FDA). If you have a dispute with your employer, call the National Labor Relations Board (NLRB) or the Equal Employment Opportunity Commission (EEOC) for assistance and advice. You can find the addresses of these and other agencies in the government section of the telephone book.

Occasionally, several government agencies will cooperate to end injustice against individuals. In 1974, for example, workers at several steel plants in Alabama were concerned about their treatment. They felt that the plant managers discriminated against female, black, and Hispanic employees in hiring and promotion. They saw that ethnic minorities and women were restricted to the worst jobs at the plants and that only white males had any chance for advancement. They complained to the EEOC, the U.S. Department of Justice, and the U.S. Department of Labor. When these federal agencies investigated the complaints, they found that what the employees had said was true: the plants' practices directly violated federal civil rights laws.

The agencies negotiated with the steel plants to change their practices. When negotiation didn't work, they brought a lawsuit. Eventually, the agencies succeeded in having the discriminatory practices stopped permanently. They also won $30 million in back pay for those employees who had been unfairly passed over in hiring and promotions.

Help from Private Organizations

If you are involved in a dispute involving race or sex discrimination, environmental issues, or constitutional rights, a number of private organizations may be willing to give you legal assistance. These organizations are sometimes called special-interest groups because each is dedicated to a narrowly defined issue or goal.

In the case that opened this chapter, for example, you read about the National Organization for Women. NOW's primary goal is to end discrimination against women. One way to achieve this goal is to bring legal action against people and organizations that discriminate on the basis of sex. For this reason, NOW was willing to handle the case of the girls who were not allowed to try out for Little League teams.

Other organizations are also willing to take legal action on behalf of individuals. For example, the Native American Rights Fund and the National Association for the Advancement of Colored People (NAACP) work to end discrimination against Native Americans and African Americans. The American Civil Liberties Union (ACLU) assists people of all backgrounds who feel that their constitutional rights have been violated. These organizations have offices throughout the United States. If you can't find them in the phone book, your state or local bar association can probably help you find the nearest local office.

Illustration 18-6　　The American Civil Liberties Union assists people of all backgrounds who feel that their constitutional rights have been violated.

REVIEW QUESTIONS

1. What are the differences between a legal aid society and a legal clinic?
2. What are the differences between a prepaid legal plan and legal insurance?
3. Why would private organizations be interested in helping an individual with a legal problem?

Working as a Lawyer

When many people think about what lawyers do for a living, they envision dramatic courtroom battles like those shown on television and in films. Of the more than half million lawyers who practice law in the United States, relatively few are involved in scenes like those. The basic tasks of lawyers are to give legal advice, help clients understand their legal rights and responsibilities, and represent clients in a legal setting such as a court or a special hearing.

The majority of lawyers practicing law today work for corporations. Corporate lawyers handle legal matters for businesses—issues involving taxation, property purchases, employee contract negotiations, corporate policy, and government regulation. Lawyers may, however, specialize in a variety of fields. Some of these specialties include the following:

■ *Civil lawyer.* Civil lawyers may specialize in areas such as divorce cases, real estate transactions, or tax matters. These lawyers may also represent clients in civil suits, in which they seek remedies such as damages or recovery of property. Civil lawyers also draft documents such as wills, mortgages, and contracts.
■ *Criminal lawyer.* These are lawyers who represent defendants accused of crimes.

They prepare a defense for their clients and present arguments in court before a judge or jury. Some criminal lawyers work as public defenders, representing people who cannot afford to hire their own attorneys.
■ *District attorneys.* These lawyers, also called prosecuting attorneys or prosecutors, are hired by the city, county, state, or federal government to represent the government's side in criminal cases. They collect and present evidence in court to prove a defendant's guilt.

Education and Training

To become a lawyer, a person must graduate from high school and college. Those planning to become lawyers can major in almost any subject in college. Many prospective lawyers choose to major in English, history, political science, or another liberal arts subject. These subjects teach them to sharpen their communication skills, think logically, and gain an understanding of how society functions.

After college, law students must attend law school. If they attend full-time, it takes three years. Some law students go part-time, usually taking four years to complete the coursework. To practice law, graduates of law school must take a state bar examination. When individuals pass the test, they are said to have been "admitted to the bar." Then they are allowed to practice law in that state. They do not, however, have the right to practice in any other state.

Beginning lawyers may start out as law clerks to state or federal judges. A law clerk does much of the routine legal work required by the judge while continuing to gain a background in law. Some lawyers begin as assistants in a private law firm. There they do research and handle routine cases. They may advance within the firm or begin their own law practice.

Personal Attributes

Lawyers must be able to write and speak clearly and with precision. Trial lawyers in particular must be persuasive speakers. Lawyers must be able to think logically and analyze complicated legal documents. Because of the complexity of the law, lawyers must be thorough in their research of the law. Because of the role lawyers play in law enforcement, they are expected to live up to a high standard of ethical conduct.

Lawyers should be willing to work hard and put in long days. They must continue to study and learn since the law changes all the time.

Lawyers should be able to understand all types of people. They may have to defend people they dislike or positions they disagree with. Lawyers should also be objective, putting aside their personal feelings so that they can serve their clients well.

Chapter Review

Chapter Summary

- A lawyer is someone who is trained in law. To practice law, a lawyer must be licensed by the state bar.

- The best way to deal with legal problems is to prevent them before they happen. You can do this by paying a lawyer for legal advice, talking to professionals other than lawyers, doing your own legal research, or getting help from government agencies.

- Whenever you are involved in a court case (except for small claims court and minor traffic court cases), it's best to hire a lawyer.

- Statutes of limitations specify how long a plaintiff can wait before taking legal action. Court rules specify how long a defendant can wait before answering a civil complaint.

- The first step in hiring a lawyer is getting recommendations. Friends, family members, acquaintances, lawyer referral services, and people in the legal community are good sources for recommendations.

- A general practitioner handles most routine legal matters; a specialist handles cases involving a particular area of the law.

■ Before you hire a lawyer, find out about the lawyer's experience and qualifications, get an idea of the time and tasks that will be necessary for your case, get an estimate of what you will have to pay for the lawyer's time and expenses, and get a feel for the lawyer's personality.

■ A lawyer may charge a flat fee, an hourly fee, or a contingency fee. In a contingency fee arrangement, the lawyer gets a percentage of any money that is won in the suit. Contingency fees are limited to cases that involve money.

■ In addition to paying a lawyer's fees, you may have to pay for the lawyer's expenses. Some lawyers will ask you to pay a retainer before they begin work on your case.

■ Always put an agreement with a lawyer in writing.

■ As the client, you have the right to make all final decisions in your case. You have the duty to be truthful and to tell your attorney everything that may affect the case.

■ The attorney-client privilege requires lawyers to keep secret any conversations with their clients that concern legal matters.

■ If you discover that the lawyer handling your case has a conflict of interest, you should find another lawyer immediately.

■ If your attorney acts improperly, you should file a complaint with the state bar. If your attorney is found guilty of neglect or misconduct, the bar will allow you to fire him or her without pay. The bar may also take its own disciplinary action.

■ If your attorney's negligence, incompetence, or dishonesty caused you to suffer a loss, you can sue him or her for legal malpractice.

■ Alternatives to hiring a private lawyer include legal aid, legal clinics, prepaid legal plans, and legal insurance. Special-interest groups and government agencies may be willing to handle your legal matters for you.

Understanding Legal Terms

On a separate sheet of paper, match the terms below with the definitions that follow.

attorney
attorney-client privilege
bar
conflict of interest
contingency fee

disbarment
flat fee
legal aid society
retainer
statute of limitations

1. Official agency that oversees lawyers and the practice of law in a state
2. Law that sets time restrictions for a legal action
3. Amount of money paid to a lawyer that is a percentage of the money the lawyer collects for a client in a lawsuit

4. Partial payment made by a client to a lawyer before any work is done on the client's case
5. Situation in which a lawyer has opposing duties or desires in a case
6. Rule of confidentiality between a lawyer and the person he or she represents
7. Permanent suspension from practicing law
8. A fixed price for a service
9. A lawyer who is representing a client in a legal matter
10. Nonprofit organization that offers free legal services to low-income people

Applying the Law

1. Stan has bought a small piece of land and is interested in building a house on it. He knows that there are many local laws that will affect his plans to build a house: zoning laws, building codes, environmental regulations, tax laws, and so on. How can he find out about these laws and regulations and figure out which ones apply to him?
2. Georgette breaks Franklin's valuable vase. When Franklin asks Georgette to pay for the broken vase, she refuses. Franklin is too busy with other things to take legal action against Georgette. Ten years later he decides to sue Georgette for the cost of the vase. What problem might Franklin have in bringing the lawsuit?
3. Joan hires a lawyer named Bernard to handle a tax matter for her. The next day she finds out that a man named Henry intends to sue her for breach of contract. She also finds out that Bernard is Henry's attorney. What should Joan do?
4. Sandra slips on a loose tile while shopping in a department store. She breaks both her legs, and her medical treatment costs $10,000. She decides to sue the department store. A lawyer named Morton offers to represent her if she will give him one third of whatever damages the court awards her. Morton tells her that if she collects no damages, she will not have to pay him anything. Is this arrangement legal? Explain your answer.
5. Gary is looking for a lawyer to handle his divorce. He finds two lawyers with whom he is equally satisfied. The only difference between the two is the fees they charge: one lawyer will take Gary's case for a flat fee of $2,000; the other charges $100 an hour. How can Gary choose between the two lawyers?
6. Myrna hires a lawyer named Stella to write a legal document. Stella agrees to write the document for a flat fee of $500. While Stella is working on the document, Myrna finds another lawyer, Daniel, whom she likes better. She fires Stella and asks Daniel to write the document. Stella demands to be paid for her work. Myrna says that because Stella didn't finish the document, she's not entitled to be paid. Who is right, Stella or Myrna? Give reasons for your choice.

Case Studies

1. Joanne Kinoy was wanted for questioning by the FBI. (She was not charged with a crime.) To avoid talking to the FBI, she went into hiding. Her father, Arthur Kinoy, was a lawyer who had sometimes represented Joanne in legal matters. FBI agents asked Arthur where they could find Joanne. He refused to answer, claiming that the attorney-client privilege prevented him from revealing anything Joanne had told him. Was Arthur right? Explain your answer.

2. Two different clients had hired William O'Malley to handle legal matters for them. Each had paid him a retainer. Whenever the clients checked in with him, O'Malley told them he was working on their cases. The truth was that he hadn't done anything on either case. He even made up stories about the progress of the cases. This situation went on for several months before the clients learned the truth. What could these two clients do?

3. Robert Wells and Stuart Goldstein were a homosexual couple who lived in a New York City apartment. The apartment's lease was in Goldstein's name. When Goldstein died, the landlord told Wells that he would have to leave. New York City law allowed family members to stay in an apartment after the death of the person named on the lease. A recent court case had extended the term *family* to include some gay relationships. Wells couldn't afford a lawyer, but he wanted to take action to keep the apartment. What could he do?

Chapter 19

The Trial

Chapter Objectives   When you have read this chapter, you should be able to:

- Explain the purpose of discovery.
- Identify everyone in the courtroom during a trial.
- Describe how a jury is selected.
- List the steps in a trial from opening statements to final judgment.
- Describe three rules of evidence.

Case Study

Hauter v. Zogarts, 534 P.2d 377 (California 1975).

When her teenage son Fred showed interest in golf, Louise Hauter bought him a "Golfing Gizmo" for Christmas in 1966. The Gizmo was a simple device— a golf ball attached to a long string. The string was tied to an elastic cord anchored between two pegs. According to the instruction book, a golfer could hit the ball "with full power," and the ball would fly into the air and then spring back to its original position. A note on the cover of the instruction book said, "COMPLETELY SAFE BALL WILL NOT HIT PLAYER."

On July 14, 1967, Fred Hauter was practicing with the Gizmo outside his Los Angeles home, as he had done about a dozen times before. He followed all the rules in the instruction book. He swung his club, and the ball flew up, hitting him in the head. Hauter became unconscious and suffered brain damage as a result of the injury. He sued the Gizmo's manufacturer, Rudy C. Zogarts.

At the trial, Hauter accused Zogarts of negligence for stating in the instruction book that the Gizmo was "completely safe." Zogarts argued that Hauter had misunderstood the note in the instruction book. According to Zogarts, the note meant that the Gizmo was safe *only when the golfer hit the ball correctly*. Golf is a dangerous sport, he said, and Hauter should not have assumed that golfing with the Gizmo would be any less dangerous. On the basis of this testimony, the jury decided that Zogarts was not liable for Hauter's injuries.

After a jury announces a verdict, the judge must review the verdict and make a final judgment. In this case, the judge decided that the jury's verdict was wrong. According to the law of products liability, the manufacturer was clearly responsible for the player's injuries. The judge realized that the jury had either misunderstood the law or failed to follow it. Therefore, he disregarded the jury's decision and held the manufacturer liable. Zogarts was ordered to pay damages to Hauter.

BEFORE THE TRIAL

Every courtroom trial must accomplish two things. First, it settles questions of fact—that is, it determines what happened in a particular case. Usually the two sides in a criminal case or civil case have conflicting versions of the events. At the trial, each side presents his or her version of the story. The judge or jury must then decide which side to believe.

Second, a trial settles questions of law. Once the facts have been determined, the judge must decide which laws apply to those facts. He or she looks at statutes (federal, state, or local laws) and precedents (previous court decisions) that seem to fit the case. The judge then instructs the jury about the applicable laws.

To make sure every trial is fair, the federal and state governments have set up strict rules about how a trial must be conducted. The rules are similar for both civil and criminal trials. In this chapter, you will read about the steps of a trial, from pretrial preparations through the final judgment.

These steps are meant to protect the interests of all the parties in a trial. In a civil case, the **parties** are the people who have a dispute—that is, the defendant and the plaintiff. These parties are usually represented by lawyers. In a criminal case, the defendant and the prosecutor are the parties. The prosecutor, who is the lawyer for the government, is considered a party because crimes are wrongs against the people. The victims of crimes are considered witnesses, not parties.

Discovery

As you read in Chapter 7, the process that leads to a civil trial begins when the plaintiff's lawyer files a complaint with the court. In criminal cases, as you read in Chapter 5, the process begins when the accused is arrested and appears at pretrial hearings.

After the complaint or arrest and before the trial, both sides conduct discovery. **Discovery** is the process by which the lawyer for each party questions the other party and any witnesses who may testify on behalf of the other party. This process permits both lawyers to find out as much as possible about the other side's case. As part of discovery, one side may require the other to produce certain documents, undergo medical examinations, or permit an inspector to examine a particular location.

Illustration 19-1   Before a trial, lawyers for both sides may take testimony from the parties and from witnesses to find out about the other side's case.

Suppose Suzy trips over a loose floor tile in her accountant's office. She suffers a wrist injury that she later claims is serious and permanent. She sues Steve, the owner of the building. During discovery, Suzy's lawyer will probably want to see the building maintenance records and have building experts examine the office. Steve's lawyer will probably hire a doctor to examine Suzy to find out if her medical injury is as serious as she says it is.

Discovery helps eliminate the element of surprise. It often simplifies and shortens the courtroom process. It also serves to bring out the weaknesses of each side. As a result, it often leads one or both parties to choose to settle, rather than continue, the case.

The two most common forms of discovery are depositions and interrogatories. A **deposition** is testimony given out of court. Before trial, it is common for the lawyers for each side to take depositions from the other party or the other party's witnesses. Although there is no judge present, the process of taking a deposition resembles a trial in many ways. Before the questioning begins, the person testifying must take an oath to tell the truth. Both lawyers have the opportunity to question that person, and a court reporter records every question and answer.

Interrogatories are written questions that the other party must answer completely and honestly. Lawyers often use interrogatories because they are easier to set up and less expensive than depositions. Interrogatories, however, may be used to question only the plaintiff or the defendant—not witnesses.

Information gathered through depositions and interrogatories serves two purposes. First, it helps each side gather evidence for the trial. Second, in some cases it may be used as evidence during the trial. For example, if a witness is too ill to attend a trial, the judge may permit the witness's deposition to be used in place of trial testimony.

Occasionally, a person's testimony at trial may contradict what he or she said during discovery. If this occurs, a lawyer may introduce that person's deposition or interrogatory as evidence. The lawyer may then point out the differences between the person's present statements and those made earlier. Those differences may convince the judge or jury that the person is lying or has a faulty memory.

Judgment without Trial

Sometimes one of the parties in a civil case feels that there is nothing in dispute and that the matter doesn't need to go to trial. In that case, the party may ask the judge to make a summary judgment. Making a **summary judgment** means concluding the case before the trial begins. A judge can grant a summary judgment only if he or she believes that both parties agree about the facts of the case. The judge must then settle the questions of law. That is, he or she must look at applicable laws and decide which party is legally entitled to win the case. For example, Georgette Nabhani sued the members of the school board of District 89 in Illinois. She claimed that on October 26, 1981, they had held a school board meeting and had not permitted her to attend. This, she said, was in violation of Illinois law, which requires all school board meetings to be open to the public.

The meeting in question had been a political gathering at which the school board members discussed upcoming local elections. All the members of the school board had attended, but so had many other people. The board members were not there in their official capacity, and no school business was discussed that evening.

The trial judge found that there was no dispute about what had happened that evening. The dispute was simply over a question of law: Was the gathering an official school board meeting? Illinois law defines a "school board meeting" as a meeting at which the board discusses school business. Since no school business was discussed, the gathering was, by definition, not a school board meeting. Therefore, it did not have to be open to the public. The judge made a summary judgment in favor of the school board, and the matter was concluded without the need for a trial.

REVIEW QUESTIONS

1. What are the two goals of a trial?
2. What is the purpose of discovery?
3. What are the two most common forms of discovery?
4. When may a judge make a summary judgment?

THE COURTROOM

Illustration 19-2   The judge has the final word on everything that happens in the courtroom.

Historically, courtroom procedures were very formal. Judges and lawyers wore black robes and powdered wigs and addressed each other in formal terms. Today much, but not all, of that formality is gone. In most courts, the judge still wears a black robe. Each trial begins with the clerk or bailiff formally calling the court to order. The judge is traditionally the last person to enter the courtroom, and everyone is expected to rise when the judge enters. The language used in the courtroom remains formal. For example, "Your Honor" is the proper way to show respect when addressing a judge.

People in the Courtroom

If you ever attend (or participate in) a trial, you'll see that the process involves a great number of people. Knowing who these people are and what their roles are will help you understand the trial.

The judge presides over the entire trial. It is the judge's responsibility to make sure the trial is fair. The judge decides all questions of law and, if there is no jury, questions of fact. He or she settles all disputes during the trial. Unless a case is appealed later, the judge has the final word on everything that happens in the courtroom.

The **court clerk** is the judge's assistant. He or she handles all court papers and watches over any physical evidence that is presented during the trial. The court clerk is usually responsible for calling and swearing in all witnesses and jurors.

Illustration 19-3 The court reporter's transcript is a record of everything that is said during a trial.

The **bailiff** is the officer of the courtroom. The bailiff's job is to keep order. If anyone—including parties, lawyers, jurors, witnesses, and observers—misbehaves or causes trouble, it is up to the bailiff to handle the problem.

The **court reporter** keeps a record of the trial. He or she must write down every word that is said during the trial. The court reporter's record of the trial proceedings is called a **transcript**. The transcript becomes very important if there is a question about what was said during the trial or if there is an appeal.

Because most trials are public, there are often observers in the courtroom. These observers may include representatives of the news media, students, friends of the participants, and members of the general public. In most courtrooms, observers must sit in the back of the room so they do not interfere with the trial.

Parties and Their Lawyers

During a civil trial, the parties usually sit with their lawyers to clarify facts and answer any questions the lawyers may have. In a criminal trial, the prosecutor usually sits alone or with his or her assistants. Even though the plaintiffs and defendants have the biggest stake in the outcome of a trial—and are almost always present in the courtroom—they generally have the smallest role. In court, each lawyer speaks for his or her side. The defendants, plaintiffs, and victims speak only if they are called to testify on the witness stand.

Witnesses

Witnesses are extremely important to the trial process because they provide most of the facts of a case. Most witnesses are ordinary people who happened to see something relating to the case. In a trial for the armed robbery of a store, for example, the cashier who was robbed and a customer who was in the store at the time of the incident might be witnesses. Parties, of course, may also be called as witnesses.

Expert witnesses are people with special knowledge, training, or skills—for example, a surgeon or an engineer. They are used at some trials to answer questions about technical matters.

Sometimes people who have witnessed important events or who have important documents may not want to participate in a trial. The court can force these people to cooperate by issuing a document called a subpoena. A **subpoena** is a court order requiring a person to come to court or to deliver a document to the court on a specific date. A person who does not obey a subpoena can be arrested.

The Jury

The **jury** is a group of citizens randomly selected from the community. It usually consists of 12 people, though some jurisdictions require only 6. The jury is responsible for listening to the testimony from both sides of a case and then deciding all questions of fact.

Not every trial has a jury. You read in Chapter 3 that the Sixth Amendment guarantees criminal defendants the right to a trial by jury. Often, however, defendants waive that right. Parties in many civil cases are also entitled to a jury. Because jury trials often cause extreme delays, however, many people choose to have their civil cases decided by a judge.

Selecting the Jury   Any adult U.S. citizen can be called to serve on a jury. Most courts select potential jurors from county voting lists or lists of licensed drivers.

Before a trial starts, a large number of potential jurors (usually 40 to 100) are called into the courtroom. From this group, the lawyers and the judge select a jury through a process of questioning called **voir dire**. The process varies from jurisdiction to jurisdiction, but it generally includes the following steps.

The court clerk calls 12 people at random from the group. Those people sit in the jury box. The judge begins the voir dire by explaining a little about the case without revealing any details. Then the judge asks each potential juror to state his or her name and occupation. The judge asks other questions about the potential jurors' lives—for example, whether they have had personal experience with cases similar to this one.

Ordinarily, the judge will dismiss anyone who has reason to be biased against either party. For example, a woman who has been the victim of a rape will probably be dismissed from a rape trial. If the judge believes that the trial will last more than a few days, he or she may also dismiss people whose lives would be seriously disrupted by long jury service.

The parties' lawyers then have an opportunity to question the prospective jurors. Each lawyer may issue **challenges**. That is, the lawyer may ask the judge to dismiss some individuals from the jury. There are two kinds of challenges—a challenge for cause and a peremptory challenge. Lawyers use both types to eliminate potential jurors who are likely to be biased.

A **challenge for cause** is a challenge for which the lawyer states a reason. If the judge agrees with the reason, he or she will dismiss the potential juror. For example, if a potential juror knows one of the parties in a civil case, the other party's lawyer will probably challenge that person for cause. Both lawyers can make an unlimited number of challenges for cause.

A **peremptory challenge** is a challenge for which the lawyer does not give a reason. Each lawyer is permitted a limited number of peremptory challenges (usually 3 to 6 in a civil trial and up to 20 in some murder cases). If a lawyer has a gut feeling that a potential juror is biased, he or she will often use a peremptory challenge to keep that person off the jury.

As each challenged individual is dismissed, he or she is replaced by another individual from the larger group. Once the proper number of individuals has been approved by both lawyers, those persons become the jury.

If the trial is expected to be a long one, the lawyers will select one or two additional people to be alternate jurors. The alternates sit with the rest of the jury throughout the trial. If a regular juror becomes unable to serve (because of illness or other reasons), an alternate can take over with no loss of trial time.

Behavior of Jurors   Jurors are expected to respect the rules of the court. In the courtroom, they must remain silent and pay close attention to the proceedings. They must never talk with the judge, lawyers, parties, or witnesses. Outside the courtroom, jurors must never discuss the case with anyone—even with other jurors. They must not investigate the case on their own.

REVIEW QUESTIONS

1. Describe the roles of the court clerk, the bailiff, and the court reporter.
2. What is an expert witness?
3. Describe the process of voir dire.

THE TRIAL

The procedure for a trial is basically the same in every state. The lawyers for both sides make opening statements. Each lawyer then has an opportunity to call witnesses, question them, and question the witnesses called by the other side. Finally, both lawyers have an opportunity to make a closing statement.

Opening Statements

The lawyers for both sides begin the trial by making opening statements. An **opening statement** is an outline of the case that the lawyer intends to present during the trial. The plaintiff's lawyer (or, in a criminal trial, the prosecutor) speaks first. Because the opening statement by the plaintiff's lawyer or the prosecutor is the first thing the jurors hear, it can have a powerful influence on them.

The defendant's lawyer speaks next, telling the defendant's side of the story. In some trials, the defendant's lawyer does not present an opening statement until the plaintiff's lawyer or the prosecutor has called all of his or her witnesses.

Direct Examination

After the opening statements, each side presents its case. Depending on the case, the presentations may take anywhere from an hour to several days, weeks, or months. The plaintiff's lawyer or the prosecutor makes the first presentation.

The presentations are conducted through examination, or questioning, of witnesses. The plaintiff's lawyer or the prosecutor calls the first witness to the witness stand. The judge reminds the witness about the seriousness of the trial and the importance of being truthful. The court clerk asks the witness to take an oath to tell the truth.

The lawyer then questions the witness about the facts of the case. When a lawyer questions a witness whom he or she has called to the stand, the questioning is called **direct examination**.

Illlustration 19-4   The lawyers for both sides begin a trial by making opening statements to the court.

Cross-Examination

After the plaintiff's lawyer or the prosecutor completes direct examination of the first witness, the defendant's lawyer has the opportunity to question that witness. This is called **cross-examination**. Generally, during cross-examination the lawyer may ask only about matters that were discussed in the direct examination.

The primary purpose of cross-examination is to **impeach** a witness—to cast doubt on the witness's testimony and convince the jury that the witness is unreliable. For example, if a lawyer can get the other side's witness to admit that he or she "stretched the truth" on even one small detail, the jury may be less willing to trust anything else the witness has said.

After the cross-examination, the plaintiff's lawyer or the prosecutor is permitted a redirect examination. The redirect examination is limited to issues that were discussed in the cross-examination. The lawyers may continue to take turns questioning the witness until both are satisfied that they have nothing further to ask that witness.

When both lawyers are finished questioning the first witness, the plaintiff's lawyer or the prosecutor may call other witnesses. The pattern of direct examination, cross-examination, and redirect examination is repeated for each witness. There is no limit to the number of witnesses a lawyer may call.

Once the plaintiff's lawyer or the prosecutor has questioned all of his or her witnesses, the lawyer **rests** (concludes his or her presentation). The defendant's lawyer then calls witnesses to the stand. Again, the pattern of direct examination and cross-examination is repeated for each witness. This time, however, the defendant's lawyer conducts the direct examination and the plaintiff's lawyer or the prosecutor conducts the cross-examination.

Objections

Both lawyers must follow strict **rules of evidence** in making their presentations. Among other things, these rules specify what kinds of questions the lawyers may ask witnesses. (You will read more about rules of evidence later in this chapter.)

If either lawyer appears to break a rule of evidence—for example, by asking the wrong kind of question—the other lawyer may interrupt by making an objection. An **objection** stops the questioning and brings the problem to the judge's attention. The objecting lawyer tells the judge what rule he or she thinks the first lawyer has broken. The lawyer accused of breaking the rule has a chance to defend the question he or she asked. The judge then decides whether to **overrule** (not permit) the objection or **sustain** (permit) it.

When a lawyer chooses to object to a question, he or she usually tries to make the objection before the witness has time to answer. Sometimes, however, the witness answers the question before the objection is made. If the judge sustains the objection, the objecting lawyer may ask the judge to **strike** (wipe out) the witness's answer. If the judge agrees to the request, the court reporter must remove the witness's answer from the transcript of the trial. The members of the jury are instructed to pretend that they never heard the witness's answer. They are told to disregard it when they are deciding the case.

It is each lawyer's responsibility to know the rules of evidence and make sure the other lawyer follows them. If either lawyer breaks a rule of evidence, the judge may ask the lawyer to rephrase his or her question. More often, however, the judge will remain silent unless the other lawyer objects.

Closing Statements

After both lawyers have completed their presentations, each lawyer has a chance to sum up his or her side of the case. These summaries are called **closing statements**. Usually the plaintiff's lawyer or the prosecutor goes first. The defendant's lawyer makes the second closing statement. Then, in some jurisdictions, the plaintiff's lawyer or the prosecutor is permitted to speak once more.

Each lawyer uses the closing statement to remind the jury of the evidence that supports his or her side. Each lawyer also draws attention to the weak points of the opponent's case. He or she may try to cast doubt on whether events could have happened the way the other side claims they did. Because closing statements are the last thing the jury will hear, they tend to be more forceful and emotional than opening statements.

REVIEW QUESTIONS

1. What does it mean to impeach a witness?
2. Explain the difference between overruling an objection and sustaining an objection.
3. What is a redirect examination?

RULES OF EVIDENCE

The rules of evidence dictate what information a jury will be allowed to hear. These rules are designed to exclude any evidence that may be irrelevant, incompetent, or untrustworthy. They help assure that the trial process will be fair to both parties.

Exhibits

In addition to witness testimony, a lawyer's presentation may include physical evidence such as weapons, written contracts, and medical reports. These kinds of items are called **exhibits**. There are strict rules about when and how a lawyer may use exhibits.

An exhibit can be introduced only through witness testimony. That is, before a lawyer can present an item as an exhibit, he or she must question a witness about it. For example, you recall the Golfing Gizmo case that opened this chapter. Let's say Fred Hauter's lawyer wanted to introduce the Gizmo as an exhibit. During Hauter's testimony, the lawyer might show Hauter the Gizmo and ask him what it is. Hauter could then testify that it is the Golfing Gizmo that caused his injuries. Once the witness has identified the item, the lawyer hands it to the court clerk, who marks it as an exhibit.

Relevance

All testimony and exhibits must be relevant (directly related) to the case. In a case involving a car accident, for example, evidence that it was raining or snowing on the day of the accident may be relevant. However, evidence that one driver had spent time in jail for shoplifting would probably not be relevant.

Certain types of evidence cannot be introduced even if they are relevant to the case. These include highly technical evidence that would take up too much of the court's time and evidence that is confusing or misleading.

For example, on November 21, 1972, a truck hit a car in Sand Creek, Oregon. The driver of the truck claimed that a Greyhound bus had cut him off and that he had collided with the car while trying to avoid the bus. He sued the Greyhound bus company for negligent driving.

Greyhound's lawyer knew that a police officer had given the truck driver a traffic ticket immediately after the accident. He wanted to present this ticket as evidence that the truck driver, not Greyhound, was at fault. The judge agreed that hearing about the ticket would give the jury a strong impression that the truck driver was at fault. That impression, however, would be wrong. A ticket, the judge said, is not proof of negligence—just as being arrested is not proof of guilt. He therefore refused to allow the ticket to be used as evidence.

There are other rules that may prevent relevant evidence from being used in court. Among the most important of these rules is the exclusionary rule. As you read in Chapter 3, the exclusionary rule says that if evidence is found or seized illegally, it cannot be used at a trial.

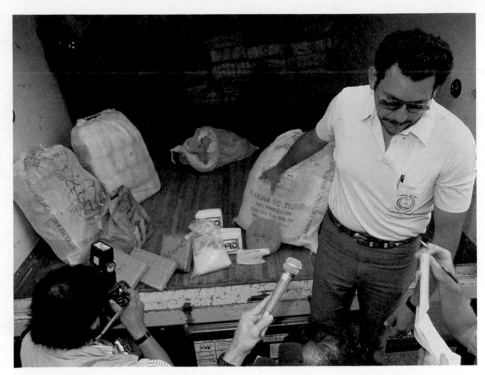

Illustration 19-5   According to the exclusionary rule, if evidence is found or seized illegally, it cannot be used at a trial.

Hearsay

Witnesses are supposed to testify only about events they have seen or heard. Occasionally, however, witnesses may talk about events that *other people* have seen or heard. For example, suppose a teacher sees Sean painting graffiti on the wall of the school building. The teacher tells the school principal what she saw. As a witness at Sean's trial, the principal says, "The teacher told me that Sean painted the graffiti."

According to the rules of evidence, the principal's testimony cannot be used to prove that Sean painted the graffiti. That sort of testimony is called **hearsay**—repeating someone else's out-of-court description of an event in order to prove that the event actually happened. In general, hearsay is not permitted in court.

In some cases, however, repeating what someone else said is not considered hearsay. A lawyer may ask a witness to repeat someone else's statement as long as the lawyer is not trying to prove that the statement is true. For example, one rainy night in Columbia, South Carolina, Nancy Carder borrowed Geraldine Thompson's car. While driving, she braked to avoid hitting a dog, but the car's tires were in such bad condition that she lost control and ran into a mailbox. Carder's passenger, Diane Player, was injured. Player sued Carder and Thompson.

Illustration 19-6   In general, courts will not permit a person to testify about events that some-one else told that person about.

South Carolina law does not allow people to drive a car if they know it has bad tires. The law requires that every car be inspected periodically to make sure it is safe to drive. Three weeks before the accident, Carder and Thompson had taken the car for such an inspection. At that time, the inspector had said that two tires on the car were dangerous and that the car would not pass the inspection.

At the trial, Player's lawyer proved that the car's tires were worn. The lawyer then asked Carder to repeat what the inspector had said about the tires. The judge refused to let Carder do so because her testimony would have been hearsay.

Player's lawyer appealed this ruling. He said that in asking Carder to repeat the inspector's statement, he was not trying to prove that the car was dangerous—he had already proved that. Instead, he was trying to prove that Carder *had reason to believe* that the car was dangerous. In other words, he was trying to prove that Carder had been negligent in ignoring the inspector's warning. The appeals court agreed that under these circumstances Carder should have been allowed to testify about what the inspector had said.

Questioning Witnesses

The laws of evidence specify the kinds of questions a lawyer may ask a witness. A lawyer may not, for example, ask a witness to speculate or give opinions. A lawyer may not repeat questions that the witness has already answered. All the lawyer's questions must be clear and must require only short answers.

Lawyers sometimes try to ask questions that suggest a particular answer, such as, "You were at the bank that day, weren't you?" Questions of this type are called **leading questions**. Leading questions are generally not permitted during a direct examination. There are some exceptions, however. A lawyer may use leading questions to remind a witness of something he or she has forgotten. A lawyer may also use leading questions with witnesses who have trouble expressing themselves—for example, children, shy or frightened people, and people who speak limited English.

For example, on July 24, 1979, John Louis Iron Shell assaulted a young girl on an Indian reservation in South Dakota. He was arrested and charged with assault with intent to rape. At his trial, the prosecutor called the young girl, Lucy, as a witness. He asked her what happened. She was reluctant to speak. He asked her, "What did the man do when he pushed you down, Lucy?" She still didn't answer. It was clear that she did not want to tell what was to her a painful story. The judge therefore permitted the prosecutor to ask leading questions such as "Did he put his hand on your neck?" and "When he pushed you down, did he hold you down?" Lucy could answer these questions with a simple yes or no.

Although leading questions are not usually allowed during direct examination, they are acceptable during cross-examination. In fact, most cross-examinations are conducted almost entirely through leading questions.

REVIEW QUESTIONS

1. What is the purpose of rules of evidence?
2. What is hearsay?
3. Under what circumstances may a lawyer ask a leading question?

VERDICT AND JUDGMENT

After a lawyer has called all of his or her witnesses, the other lawyer may ask the judge for a directed verdict. Like a summary judgment, a **directed verdict** is a ruling that there are no facts in dispute and that the case can be decided on legal issues alone. If the judge makes a directed verdict, the jury is dismissed and the trial is concluded. Although lawyers often request directed verdicts, judges rarely grant them. If the judge refuses to make a directed verdict, the case goes to the jury.

Instructing the Jury

Before a jury can decide a case, the judge must **charge** (instruct) the jurors. The judge begins by explaining the law that applies to the case. The judge may remind the jurors to consider only the evidence they have heard in court and to disregard any testimony that was stricken from the record.

Burden of Proof   The judge explains each party's **burden of proof**—that is, what each side is responsible for proving. Suppose Raymond is on trial for the murder of Julio. The prosecutor is responsible for proving the elements of the crime—that Raymond intended to kill Julio and that he did actually kill him. Raymond doesn't have to prove his innocence. However, if Raymond was responsible for Julio's death but has a defense, he is responsible for proving his defense. For example, if he says that he killed Julio in self-defense, he is responsible for proving that Julio was trying to kill him.

Standard of Proof   The judge must tell the jury which standard of proof applies to the case. The **standard of proof** defines how far the plaintiff's lawyer or the prosecutor must go in convincing the jury. As you read in Chapter 5, the standard of proof in a criminal trial is guilt "beyond a reasonable doubt." In other words, the jury can find the defendant guilty only if the prosecutor has left no reasonable doubt that the defendant committed a crime. Proving that the defendant probably committed a crime is not sufficient for a guilty verdict.

As you read in Chapter 7, the standard of proof in a civil trial is "a preponderance of the evidence." In other words, if the plaintiff's evidence is more convincing than the defendant's evidence, the jury must decide in favor of the plaintiff. In a civil case, therefore, "probably" is enough.

Deliberation

After listening to the judge's instructions, the jurors leave the courtroom to **deliberate**, or discuss the case. They select a **foreman** to lead the discussion and to announce the verdict. (In some jurisdictions, the judge selects the foreman.) The jurors gather in a private room called the **jury room**. The bailiff stands outside the room to make sure no one disturbs the jurors and to get them anything they need. Depending on the case, the jury may deliberate for a few minutes, a few hours, or several weeks.

There are almost no rules that tell a jury how to deliberate. Jurors may decide among themselves whether to vote orally or in writing, for example.

In criminal cases, most states require that a jury reach a unanimous decision. A unanimous decision may also be required in civil cases, though many states accept verdicts based on agreement of 10 of the 12 jurors.

If a jury can't reach a decision after a reasonable amount of time, the foreman may ask the bailiff to tell the judge that the jury is deadlocked. (A jury that can't reach a decision is sometimes called a **hung jury**.) If the judge believes that the jurors are still capable of reaching an agreement, he or she will order them back to the jury room to deliberate further. If the judge accepts that the jury is deadlocked, he or she will declare the trial to be a **mistrial**. The case may be tried again later with a new jury.

The Verdict

Once the jurors have agreed on a verdict, they let the bailiff know that they are ready to announce it. Everyone returns to the courtroom, and the judge asks the jury foreman to deliver the verdict. In a civil trial, the jury finds in favor of either the plaintiff or the defendant. In a criminal trial, the jury declares the

Illustration 19-7   In criminal trials, most states require a jury to reach a unanimous decision. A unanimous verdict may also be required in civil cases.

defendant guilty or not guilty. In most cases, the jurors are not required to give any information about how they reached their decision.

Judgment notwithstanding the Verdict

You already know that in certain cases one side or the other feels that no facts are in dispute. In those cases, a lawyer may ask the judge for a summary judgment (before the trial) or a directed verdict (after the case has been presented). Similarly, a lawyer for one party may feel that the jury's verdict does not reflect the true facts of the case. Under those circumstances, the lawyer may ask the judge to disregard the jury's decision.

You saw an example of such a case at the beginning of this chapter. In that case, the judge ruled in favor of the plaintiff even though the jury's verdict was for the defendant. This type of ruling is called a **judgment notwithstanding the verdict**. Like summary judgments and directed verdicts, judgments notwithstanding the verdict are very rarely granted.

Every trial ends with the judge's announcement of the judgment. In most cases, the judgment is a restatement of the jury's verdict. Once the trial is over, the only way a party can contest the judgment is to appeal to a higher court.

REVIEW QUESTIONS

1. When may a judge make a directed verdict?
2. Define *burden of proof* and *standard of proof*.
3. Who announces the verdict? Who announces the judgment?

Latest in the Law: Cameras in the Courtroom

The year was 1935. A German immigrant named Bruno Hauptmann was on trial for the kidnapping and murder of the young son of aviation hero Charles A. Lindbergh. The press had labeled the kidnapping the "crime of the century." The Hauptmann trial in Flemington, New Jersey, proved to be the trial of the century as well. It attracted hundreds of reporters and press photographers from all over the world. At that time, cameras were permitted in courtrooms. Dozens of photographers with shutters clicking and flashbulbs popping surrounded Hauptmann daily as he sat at the defense table.

The constant use of flashbulbs disrupted the courtroom, making it very difficult for the participants to concentrate on the trial. After that trial, cameras were barred from federal courtrooms for more than fifty years. State courts also prohibited cameras. Within the last ten years, however, many state courts have begun to allow both still and video cameras in their courtrooms. More recently, the federal court system has allowed limited use of cameras in some of its courts.

Recent Legislation

By May 1991, 44 states had enacted laws permitting cameras in the courtroom. The highest federal court—the U.S. Supreme Court—continues to bar cameras. However, on July 1, 1991, six federal district courts and two federal appeals courts began a three-year experiment permitting civil cases to be televised. Also in July of that year, a 24-hour cable channel, Courtroom Television Network, was launched to broadcast entire trials. These trials will be presented live and on tape to television viewers.

Of the 44 states that permit cameras in the courtroom, 26 require the approval of the trial judge. Ten require the consent of certain other parties to the trial—prosecuting and defense attorneys, defendants, and sometimes witnesses. Six states permit cameras to record only appeals court cases.

A recent survey of 245 judges who had presided over televised cases in the state of New York found that 91 percent of the judges either supported or had no objections to cameras in the courtroom. An even larger percentage of the judges stated that they felt that cameras did not affect a trial's fairness. Some defense attorneys, however, believe that cameras create false images of guilt because their clients are seen in handcuffs or being escorted by uniformed guards. Some defense attorneys also feel that short "sound bites"—15- or 30-second segments of film shown on the evening news—fail to convey to viewers the complex reality of a trial.

The Role of Videotapes in Trials

In addition to being used to record court proceedings, video cameras are being used to present evidence in trials. In recent years, some courts have allowed prosecutors to videotape the testimony of small children who were alleged to have been victims of child abuse. In this way, children are protected from the stress of the courtroom and from the trauma of facing the people they claim abused them. Videotaped confessions and videotapes of the erratic behavior of accused drunk drivers have also been admitted into evidence in some courts. In one case, the attorney for a female defendant was allowed to submit a videotape of the woman taken several months earlier. The tape, which showed her extensive physical injuries, was used to demonstrate that she had been battered by her husband.

With the overwhelming majority of states permitting cameras, it appears that cameras will remain in courtrooms from now on. It is not yet clear whether cameras distort the truth in the eyes of television viewers and newspaper readers. Cameras do, however, enable many thousands of people who have never been inside a courtroom to see the American justice system at work.

Chapter Review

Chapter Summary

■ A trial is conducted to settle questions of law and questions of fact. The process is similar for both criminal trials and civil trials.

■ Before a trial, the lawyers for both sides conduct discovery to learn as much as possible about the other side's case. The most common forms of discovery are depositions and interrogatories.

■ A judge may make a summary judgment if there are no questions of fact in a case.

■ Evidence in a trial is presented through questioning of witnesses. Witnesses who refuse to testify may be forced to do so by means of a subpoena.

■ Jurors are selected through the process of voir dire. The judge and lawyers question each potential juror. Those who seem biased may be challenged by the lawyers and dismissed by the judge.

■ Lawyers start the trial with opening statements. Then they examine witnesses through a series of examinations and cross-examinations. They finish with closing statements.

■ Courtroom rules of evidence dictate how lawyers may present evidence. If a lawyer breaks one of the rules, the other lawyer may make an objection. The judge then overrules or sustains the objection.

■ All evidence must be relevant and not confusing or misleading. Hearsay (using an out-of-court statement to prove the truth of that statement) is not permitted. Other out-of-court statements may be permitted.

■ Leading questions are usually not permitted, except during cross-examination.

■ After the testimony and closing statements are concluded, the judge tells the jurors what to keep in mind as they deliberate.

■ Once the jury has reached a verdict, the foreman announces the verdict and the judge announces the judgment.

Understanding Legal Terms

On a separate sheet of paper, match the terms below with the definitions that follow.

challenge	hearsay
charge	objection
cross-examination	strike
direct examination	subpoena
exhibit	voir dire

1. A court order requiring a person to appear in court or to deliver a document on a specific date
2. The process by which judges and lawyers question potential jurors for a trial
3. A request a lawyer makes to a judge asking that a prospective juror be dismissed
4. To instruct the jurors about points of law, done by the judge before the jury begins to decide a case
5. Questioning of a witness conducted by the lawyer who calls that person to the witness stand
6. Questioning of a witness conducted by the lawyer for the opposing side
7. A request made by one lawyer that the judge not allow the opposing lawyer to ask a certain question because it breaks a rule of evidence
8. To wipe out or remove a witness's answer from the court record
9. Witness testimony that repeats what someone else said in order to prove the truth of the statement
10. An item of physical evidence that is presented by a lawyer during a trial

Applying the Law

1. Yetta is injured when her new popcorn popper malfunctions. She sues the manufacturer for distributing an unsafe product. She believes that other people have been injured in the same way and that the manufacturer has complaints from these people on file. Before the trial begins, is there any way for Yetta to find out whether the manufacturer has records of other injuries? If so, what is it?
2. Katana is the plaintiff's lawyer in a contract dispute. After the third day of the trial, she becomes convinced that Mike, one of the jurors, is confused about the facts of the case. She sees him in the hallway of the court building and asks him if he has any questions about the case. How should Mike respond?
3. Alberto and Benito are neighbors. Every evening Benito parks his car in a way that blocks Alberto's driveway. Alberto goes to court and asks for an injunction that will force Benito to park somewhere else. At the trial, Benito wants to testify that Alberto is an alcoholic. Will the judge permit this testimony? Why or why not?
4. Barbara is on trial for prostitution. The prosecutor asks Barbara's roommate, Kim, to testify. When Kim testifies that Barbara is a prostitute, the lawyer asks how she knows. Kim says that a friend, Donna, told her. What is wrong with Kim's answer? What can Barbara's lawyer do about it?
5. Jaime, an immigrant, sues his landlord for discrimination. Jaime understands English but doesn't speak it very well. At the trial, Jaime's lawyer asks Jaime to explain what his landlord has done. Jaime has trouble answering the questions. The lawyer starts asking simpler, yes-or-no questions.

The opposing lawyer objects that the lawyer is leading the witness. Will the judge sustain or overrule the objection? Explain your answer.

6. The jurors in a rape trial have been deliberating for over a week. They have discussed the case many times but cannot agree on a verdict. Four jurors think the defendant is innocent, and eight think he is guilty. None will change their minds. What should they do?

Case Studies

1. While Margaret Green was using a pay phone on the front porch of a grocery store, she leaned against a column. The column was loose and gave way. Green fell and was injured. She sued the phone company. Green and the phone company agreed about what had happened. Their only disagreement was about whether the phone company should be held liable for her injuries. What could the parties do to avoid a trial?

2. Garnett Johnnie Jones was on trial for bank robbery. During the voir dire, the judge asked all the prospective jurors whether they or anyone in their families had been victims of a bank robbery. One man said that his daughter-in-law had been but that she had not been harmed and had never spoken with him about it. Why did the judge ask this question? What could happen to the prospective juror who answered the question?

3. John Rainford stood trial for the crime of assault with intent to commit rape. Rainford's young stepdaughter, who claimed to be the victim of his assault, testified at the trial. During the direct examination, the prosecutor questioned the girl about the details of the incident. She told the story of how her stepfather had attacked her. The defense attorney wanted to show the jurors why they should not believe the story she told. What could the defense attorney do?

Appendix A: The Constitution of the United States

(In the following copy of the Constitution, the spelling and capitalization of the original text have been used. Parts that have been changed by subsequent amendments to the Constitution are presented in italic type.)

We the People of the United States, in Order to form a more perfect Union, establish Justice, insure domestic Tranquility, provide for the common defence, promote the general Welfare, and secure the Blessings of Liberty to ourselves and our Posterity, do ordain and establish this Constitution for the United States of America.

ARTICLE I

SECTION 1. All legislative Powers herein granted shall be vested in a Congress of the United States, which shall consist of a Senate and House of Representatives.

SECTION 2. The House of Representatives shall be composed of Members chosen every second Year by the People of the several States, and the Electors in each State shall have the Qualifications requisite for Electors of the most numerous Branch of the State Legislature.

No Person shall be a Representative who shall not have attained to the Age of twenty five Years, and been seven Years a Citizen of the United States, and who shall not, when elected, be an Inhabitant of that State in which he shall be chosen.

Representatives and direct Taxes shall be apportioned among the several States which may be included within this Union, according to their respective Numbers, which shall be determined by adding to the whole Number of free Persons, including those bound to Service for a Term of Years, and excluding Indians not taxed, three fifths of all other Persons. The actual Enumeration shall be made within three Years after the first Meeting of the Congress of the United States, and within every subsequent Term of ten Years, in such Manner as they shall by Law direct. The Number of Representatives shall not exceed one for every thirty Thousand, but each State shall have at Least one Representative; and until such enumeration shall be made, the State of New Hampshire shall be entitled to chuse three, Massachusetts eight, Rhode Island and Providence Plantations one, Connecticut five, New York six, New Jersey four, Pennsylvania eight, Delaware one, Maryland six, Virginia ten, North Carolina five, South Carolina five, and Georgia three.

When vacancies happen in the Representation from any State, the Executive Authority thereof shall issue Writs of Election to fill such Vacancies.

The House of Representatives shall chuse their Speaker and other Officers; and shall have the sole Power of Impeachment.

SECTION 3. The Senate of the United States shall be composed of two Senators from each State, *chosen by the Legislature thereof*, for six Years; and each Senator shall have one Vote.

Immediately after they shall be assembled in Consequence of the first Election, they shall be divided as equally as may be into three Classes. The Seats of the Senators of the first Class shall be vacated at the Expiration of the second Year, of the second Class at the Expiration of the fourth Year, and of the third Class at the Expiration of the sixth Year, so that one third may be chosen every second Year; *and if Vacancies happen by Resignation, or otherwise, during the Recess of the Legislature of any State, the Executive thereof may make temporary Appointments until the next Meeting of the Legislature, which shall then fill such Vacancie*s.

No Person shall be a Senator who shall not have attained to the Age of thirty Years, and been nine Years a Citizen of the United States, and who shall not, when elected, be an Inhabitant of that State for which he shall be chosen.

The Vice President of the United States shall be President of the Senate, but shall have no Vote, unless they be equally divided.

The Senate shall chuse their other Officers, and also a President pro tempore, in the Absence of the Vice President, or when he shall exercise the Office of President of the United States.

The Senate shall have the sole Power to try all Impeachments. When sitting for that Purpose, they shall be on Oath or Affirmation. When the President of the United States is tried, the Chief Justice shall preside: And no Person shall be convicted without the Concurrence of two thirds of the Members present.

Judgment in Cases of Impeachment shall not extend further than to removal from Office, and disqualification to hold and enjoy any Office of honor, Trust or Profit under the United States: but the Party convicted shall nevertheless be liable and subject to Indictment, Trial, Judgment and Punishment, according to Law.

SECTION 4. The Times, Places and Manner of holding Elections for Senators and Representatives, shall be prescribed in each State by the Legislature thereof; but the Congress may at any time by Law make or alter such Regulations, except as to the Places of chusing Senators.

The Congress shall assemble at least once in every Year, and such Meeting shall *be on the first Monday in December*, unless they shall by Law appoint a different Day.

SECTION 5. Each House shall be the Judge of the Elections, Returns and Qualifications of its own Members, and a Majority of each shall constitute a Quorum to do Business; but a smaller Number may adjourn from day to day, and may be authorized to compel the Attendance of absent Members, in such Manner, and under such Penalties as each House may provide.

Each House may determine the Rules of its Proceedings, punish its Members for disorderly Behaviour, and, with the Concurrence of two thirds, expel a Member.

Each House shall keep a Journal of its Proceedings, and from time to time publish the same, excepting such Parts as may in their Judgment require Secrecy; and the Yeas and Nays of the Members of either House on any question shall, at the Desire of one fifth of those Present, be entered on the Journal.

Neither House, during the Session of Congress, shall, without the Consent of the other, adjourn for more than three days, nor to any other Place than that in which the two Houses shall be sitting.

SECTION 6. The Senators and Representatives shall receive a Compensation for their Services, to be ascertained by Law, and paid out of the Treasury of the United States. They shall in all Cases, except Treason, Felony and Breach of the Peace, be privileged from Arrest during their Attendance at the Session of their respective Houses, and in going to and returning from the same; and for any Speech or Debate in either House, they shall not be questioned in any other Place.

No Senator or Representative shall, during the Time for which he was elected, be appointed to any civil Office under the Authority of the United States, which shall have been created, or the Emoluments whereof shall have been encreased during such time; and no Person holding any Office under the United States, shall be a Member of either House during his Continuance in Office.

SECTION 7. All Bills for raising Revenue shall originate in the House of Representatives; but the Senate may propose or concur with Amendments as on other Bills.

Every Bill which shall have passed the House of Representatives and the Senate, shall, before it become a Law, be presented to the President of the United States; If he approve he shall sign it, but if not he shall return it, with his Objections to that House in which it shall have originated, who shall enter the Objections at large on their Journal, and proceed to reconsider it. If after such Reconsideration two thirds of that House shall agree to pass the Bill, it shall be sent, together with the Objections, to the other House, by which it shall likewise be reconsidered, and if approved by two thirds of that House, it shall become a Law. But in all such Cases the Votes of both Houses shall be determined by yeas and Nays, and the Names of the Persons voting for and against the Bill shall be entered on the Journal of each House respectively. If any Bill shall not be returned by the President within ten Days (Sundays excepted) after it shall have been presented to him, the Same shall be a Law, in like Manner as if he had signed it, unless the Congress by their Adjournment prevent its Return, in which Case it shall not be a Law.

Every Order, Resolution, or Vote to which the Concurrence of the Senate and House of Representatives may be necessary (except on a question of Adjournment) shall be presented to the President of the United States; and before the Same shall take Effect, shall be approved by him, or being disapproved by him, shall be repassed by two thirds of the Senate and House of Representatives, according to the Rules and Limitations prescribed in the Case of a Bill.

SECTION 8. The Congress shall have Power To lay and collect Taxes, Duties, Imposts and Excises, to pay the Debts and provide for the common Defence and general Welfare of the United States; but all Duties, Imposts and Excises shall be uniform throughout the United States;

To borrow Money on the credit of the United States;

To regulate Commerce with foreign Nations, and among the several States, and with the Indian tribes;

To establish an uniform Rule of Naturalization, and uniform Laws on the subject of Bankruptcies throughout the United States;

To coin Money, regulate the Value thereof, and of foreign Coin, and fix the Standard of Weights and Measures;

To provide for the Punishment of counterfeiting the Securities and current Coin of the United States;

To establish Post Offices and post Roads;

To promote the Progress of Science and useful Arts, by securing for limited Times to Authors and Inventors the exclusive Right to their respective Writings and Discoveries;

To constitute Tribunals inferior to the supreme Court;

To define and punish Piracies and Felonies committed on the high Seas, and Offences against the Law of Nations;

To declare War, grant Letters of Marque and Reprisal, and make Rules concerning Captures on Land and Water;

To raise and support Armies, but no Appropriation of Money to that Use shall be for a longer Term than two Years;

To provide and maintain a Navy;

To make Rules for the Government and Regulation of the land and naval Forces;

To provide for calling forth the Militia to execute the Laws of the Union, suppress Insurrections and repel Invasions;

To provide for organizing, arming, and disciplining, the Militia, and for governing such Part of them as may be employed in the Service of the United States, reserving to the States respectively, the Appointment of the Officers, and the Authority of training the Militia according to the discipline prescribed by Congress;

To exercise exclusive Legislation in all Cases whatsoever, over such District (not exceeding ten Miles square) as may, by Cession of particular States, and the Acceptance of Congress, become the Seat of the Government of the United States, and to exercise like Authority over all Places purchased by the Consent of the Legislature of the State in which the Same shall be, for the Erection of Forts, Magazines, Arsenals, dock-Yards, and other needful Buildings;—And

To make all Laws which shall be necessary and proper for carrying into Execution the foregoing Powers, and all other Powers vested by this Constitution in the Government of the United States, or in any Department or Officer thereof.

SECTION 9. The Migration or Importation of such Persons as any of the States now existing shall think proper to admit, shall not be prohibited by the Congress prior to the Year one thousand eight hundred and eight, but a Tax or duty may be imposed on such Importation, not exceeding ten dollars for each Person.

The Privilege of the Writ of Habeas Corpus shall not be suspended, unless when in Cases of Rebellion or Invasion the public Safety may require it.

No Bill of Attainder or ex post facto Law shall be passed.

No Capitation, or other direct, Tax shall be laid, unless in Proportion to the Census or Enumeration herein before directed to be taken.

No Tax or Duty shall be laid on Articles exported from any State.

No Preference shall be given by any Regulation of Commerce or Revenue to the Ports of one State over those of another: nor shall Vessels bound to, or from, one State, be obliged to enter, clear, or pay Duties in another.

No Money shall be drawn from the Treasury, but in Consequence of Appropriations made by Law; and a regular Statement and Account of the Receipts and Expenditures of all public Money shall be published from time to time.

No Title of Nobility shall be granted by the United States: And no Person holding any Office of Profit or Trust under them, shall, without the Consent of the Congress, accept of any present, Emolument, Office, or Title, of any kind whatever, from any King, Prince, or foreign State.

SECTION 10. No State shall enter into any Treaty, Alliance, or Confederation; grant Letters of Marque and Reprisal; coin Money; emit Bills of Credit; make any Thing but gold and silver Coin a Tender in Payment of Debts; pass any Bill of Attainder, ex post facto Law, or Law impairing the Obligation of Contracts, or grant any Title of Nobility.

No State shall, without the Consent of the Congress, lay any Imposts or Duties on Imports or Exports, except what may be absolutely necessary for executing its inspection Laws: and the net Produce of all Duties and Imposts, laid by any State on Imports or Exports, shall be for the Use of the Treasury of the United States; and all such Laws shall be subject to the Revision and Controul of the Congress.

No State shall, without the Consent of Congress, lay any Duty of Tonnage, keep Troops, or Ships of War in time of Peace, enter into any Agreement or Compact with another State, or with a foreign Power, or engage in War, unless actually invaded, or in such imminent Danger as will not admit of delay.

ARTICLE II

SECTION 1. The executive Power shall be vested in a President of the United States of America. He shall hold his Office during the Term of four Years, and, together with the Vice President, chosen for the same Term, be elected, as follows:

Each State shall appoint, in such Manner as the Legislature thereof may direct, a Number of Electors, equal to the whole Number of Senators and Representatives to which the State may be entitled in the Congress: but no Senator or Representative, or Person holding an Office of Trust or Profit under the United States, shall be appointed an Elector.

The Electors shall meet in their respective States, and vote by Ballot for two Persons, of whom one at least shall not be an inhabitant of the same State with themselves. And they shall make a List of all the Persons voted for, and of the Number of Votes for each; which List they shall sign and certify, and transmit sealed to the Seat of the Government of the United States, directed to the President of the Senate. The President of the Senate shall, in the Presence of the Senate and House of Representatives, open all the Certificates, and the Votes shall then be counted. The Person having the greatest Number of Votes shall be the President, if such Number be a Majority of the whole Number of Electors appointed; and if there be more than one who have such Majority, and have an equal Number of Votes, then the House of Representatives shall immediately chuse by Ballot one of them for President; and if no Person have a Majority, then from the five highest on the List the said House shall in like Manner chuse the President. But in chusing the President, the Votes shall be taken by States, the Representation from each State having one Vote; A quorum for this purpose shall consist of a Member or Members from two thirds of the States, and a Majority of all the States shall be necessary to a Choice. In every Case, after the Choice of the President, the Person having the greatest Number of Votes of the Electors shall be the Vice President. But if there should remain two or more who have equal Votes, the Senate shall chuse from them by Ballot the Vice President.

The Congress may determine the Time of chusing the Electors, and the Day on which they shall give their Votes; which Day shall be the same throughout the United States.

No Person except a natural born Citizen, or a Citizen of the United States, at the time of the Adoption of this Constitution, shall be eligible to the Office of President; neither shall any Person be eligible to that Office who shall not have attained to the Age of thirty five Years, and been fourteen Years a Resident within the United States.

In Case of the Removal of the President from Office, or of his Death, Resignation, or Inability to discharge the Powers and Duties of the said Office, the Same shall devolve on the Vice President, and the Congress may by Law provide for the Case of Removal, Death, Resignation or Inability, both of the President and Vice President, declaring what Officer shall then act as President, and such Officer shall act accordingly, until the Disability be removed, or a President shall be elected.

The President shall, at stated Times, receive for his Services, a Compensation, which shall neither be encreased nor diminished during the Period for which he shall have been elected, and he shall not receive within that Period any other Emolument from the United States, or any of them.

Before he enter on the Execution of his Office, he shall take the following Oath or Affirmation:—"I do solemnly swear (or affirm) that I will faithfully execute the Office of President of the United States, and will to the best of my Ability, preserve, protect and defend the Constitution of the United States."

SECTION 2. The President shall be Commander in Chief of the Army and Navy of the United States, and of the Militia of the several States, when called into the actual Service of the United States; he may require the Opinion, in writing, of the principal Officer in each of the executive Departments, upon any Subject relating to the Duties of their respective Offices, and he shall have Power to grant Reprieves and Pardons for Offences against the United States, except in Cases of Impeachment.

He shall have Power, by and with the Advice and Consent of the Senate, to make Treaties, provided two thirds of the Senators present concur; and he shall nominate, and by and with the Advice and Consent of the Senate, shall appoint Ambassadors, other public Ministers and Consuls, Judges of the supreme Court, and all other Officers of the United States, whose Appointments are not herein otherwise provided for, and which shall be established by Law: but the Congress may by Law vest the Appointment of such inferior Officers, as they think proper, in the President alone, in the Courts of Law, or in the Heads of Departments.

The President shall have Power to fill up all Vacancies that may happen during the Recess of the Senate, by granting Commissions which shall expire at the End of their next Session.

SECTION 3. He shall from time to time give to the Congress Information of the State of the Union, and recommend to their Consideration such Measures as he shall judge necessary and expedient; he may, on extraordinary Occasions, convene both Houses, or either of them, and in Case of Disagreement between them, with Respect to the Time of Adjournment, he may adjourn them to such Time as he shall think proper; he shall receive Ambassadors and other public Ministers; he shall take Care that the Laws be faithfully executed, and shall Commission all the Officers of the United States.

SECTION 4. The President, Vice President and all civil Officers of the United States, shall be removed from Office on Impeachment for, and Conviction of, Treason, Bribery, or other high Crimes and Misdemeanors.

ARTICLE III

SECTION 1. The judicial Power of the United States, shall be vested in one supreme Court, and in such inferior Courts as the Congress may from time to time ordain and establish. The Judges, both of the supreme and inferior Courts, shall hold their Offices during good Behaviour, and shall, at stated Times, receive for their Services, a Compensation, which shall not be diminished during their Continuance in Office.

SECTION 2. The judicial Power shall extend to all Cases, in Law and Equity, arising under this Constitution, the Laws of the United States, and Treaties made, or which shall be made, under their Authority;—to all Cases affecting Ambassadors, other public Ministers and Consuls;—to all Cases of admiralty and maritime Jurisdiction;—to Controversies to which the United

States shall be a Party;—to Controversies between two or more States;—*between a State and Citizens of another State*;—between Citizens of different States,—between Citizens of the same State claiming Lands under Grants of different States, *and between a State, or the Citizens thereof, and foreign States, Citizens or Subjects.*

In all Cases affecting Ambassadors, other public Ministers and Consuls, and those in which a State shall be Party, the supreme Court shall have original Jurisdiction. In all the other Cases before mentioned, the supreme Court shall have appellate Jurisdiction, both as to Law and Fact, with such Exceptions, and under such Regulations as the Congress shall make.

The Trial of all Crimes, except in Cases of Impeachment, shall be by Jury; and such Trial shall be held in the State where the said Crimes shall have been committed; but when not committed within any State, the Trial shall be at such Place or Places as the Congress may by Law have directed.

SECTION 3. Treason against the United States, shall consist only in levying War against them, or in adhering to their Enemies, giving them Aid and Comfort. No Person shall be convicted of Treason unless on the Testimony of two Witnesses to the same overt Act, or on Confession in open Court.

The Congress shall have Power to declare the Punishment of Treason, but no Attainder of Treason shall work Corruption of Blood, or Forfeiture except during the Life of the Person attainted.

ARTICLE IV

SECTION 1. Full Faith and Credit shall be given in each State to the public Acts, Records, and judicial Proceedings of every other State. And the Congress may by general Laws prescribe the Manner in which such Acts, Records and Proceedings shall be proved, and the Effect thereof.

SECTION 2. The Citizens of each State shall be entitled to all Privileges and Immunities of Citizens in the several States.

A Person charged in any State with Treason, Felony, or other Crime, who shall flee from Justice, and be found in another State, shall on Demand of the executive Authority of the State from which he fled, be delivered up, to be removed to the State having Jurisdiction of the Crime.

No Person held to Service or Labour in one State, under the Laws thereof, escaping into another, shall, in Consequence of any Law or Regulation therein, be discharged from such Service or Labour, but shall be delivered up on Claim of the Party to whom such Service or Labour may be due.

SECTION 3. New States may be admitted by the Congress into this Union; but no new State shall be formed or erected within the Jurisdiction of any other State; nor any State be formed by the Junction of two or more States, or Parts of States, without the Consent of the Legislatures of the States concerned as well as of the Congress.

The Congress shall have Power to dispose of and make all needful Rules and Regulations respecting the Territory or other Property belonging to the

United States; and nothing in this Constitution shall be so construed as to Prejudice any Claims of the United States, or of any particular State.

SECTION 4. The United States shall guarantee to every State in this Union a Republican Form of Government, and shall protect each of them against Invasion; and on Application of the Legislature, or of the Executive (when the Legislature cannot be convened) against domestic Violence.

ARTICLE V

The Congress, whenever two thirds of both Houses shall deem it necessary, shall propose Amendments to this Constitution, or, on the Application of the Legislatures of two thirds of the several States, shall call a Convention for proposing Amendments, which, in either Case, shall be valid to all Intents and Purposes, as Part of this Constitution, when ratified by the legislatures of three fourths of the several States, or by Conventions in three fourths thereof, as the one or the other Mode of Ratification may be proposed by the Congress; Provided *that no Amendment which may be made prior to the Year One thousand eight hundred and eight shall in any Manner affect the first and fourth Clauses in the Ninth Section of the first Article; and* that no State, without its Consent, shall be deprived of its equal Suffrage in the Senate.

ARTICLE VI

All Debts contracted and Engagements entered into, before the Adoption of this Constitution, shall be as valid against the United States under this Constitution, as under the Confederation.

This Constitution, and the Laws of the United States which shall be made in Pursuance thereof; and all Treaties made, or which shall be made, under the Authority of the United States, shall be the supreme Law of the Land; and the Judges in every State shall be bound thereby, any Thing in the Constitution or Laws of any State to the Contrary notwithstanding.

The Senators and Representatives before mentioned, and the Members of the several State Legislatures, and all executive and judicial Officers, both of the United States and of the several States, shall be bound by Oath or Affirmation, to support this Constitution; but no religious Test shall ever be required as a Qualification to any Office or public Trust under the United States.

ARTICLE VII

The Ratification of the Conventions of nine States, shall be sufficient for the Establishment of this Constitution between the States so ratifying the Same.

DONE in Convention by the Unanimous Consent of the States present the Seventeenth Day of September in the Year of our Lord one thousand seven hundred and Eighty seven and of the Independance of the United States of America the Twelfth. IN WITNESS whereof We have hereunto subscribed our Names.

Attest William Jackson
Secretary

Go Washington
Presidt and deputy from Virginia

DELAWARE
- Geo: Read
- Gunning Bedford jun.
- John Dickinson
- Richard Bassett
- Jaco: Broom

MARYLAND
- James McHenry
- Dan of St. Thos. Jenifer
- Danl. Carroll

VIRGINIA
- John Blair—
- James Madison Jr.

NORTH CAROLINA
- Wm. Blount
- Richd. Dobbs Spaight
- Hu Williamson

SOUTH CAROLINA
- J. Rutledge
- Charles Cotesworth Pinckney
- Charles Pinckney
- Pierce Butler

GEORGIA
- William Few
- Abr Baldwin

NEW HAMPSHIRE
- John Langdon
- Nicholas Gilman

MASSACHUSETTS
- Nathaniel Gorham
- Rufus King

CONNECTICUT
- Wm. Saml. Johnson
- Roger Sherman

NEW YORK
- Alexander Hamilton

NEW JERSEY
- Wil: Livingston
- David Brearley
- Wm. Paterson
- Jona: Dayton

PENNSYLVANIA
- B. Franklin
- Thomas Mifflin
- Robt. Morris
- Geo. Clymer
- Thos. FitzSimons
- Jared Ingersoll
- James Wilson
- Gouv Morris

Amendment I

Congress shall make no law respecting an establishment of religion, or prohibiting the free exercise thereof; or abridging the freedom of speech, or of the press; or the right of the people peaceably to assemble, and to petition the Government for a redress of grievances.

Amendment II

A well regulated Militia, being necessary to the security of a free State, the right of the people to keep and bear Arms, shall not be infringed.

Amendment III

No Soldier shall, in time of peace be quartered in any house, without the consent of the Owner, nor in time of war, but in a manner to be prescribed by law.

Amendment IV

The right of the people to be secure in their persons, houses, papers, and effects, against unreasonable searches and seizures, shall not be violated, and no Warrants shall issue, but upon probable cause, supported by Oath or affirmation, and particularly describing the place to be searched, and the persons or things to be seized.

Amendment V

No person shall be held to answer for a capital, or otherwise infamous crime, unless on a presentment or indictment of a Grand Jury, except in cases arising in the land or naval forces, or in the Militia, when in actual service in time of War or public danger; nor shall any person be subject for the same offence to be twice put in jeopardy of life or limb; nor shall be compelled in any criminal case to be a witness against himself, nor be deprived of life, liberty, or property, without due process of law; nor shall private property be taken for public use, without just compensation.

Amendment VI

In all criminal prosecutions, the accused shall enjoy the right to a speedy and public trial, by an impartial jury of the State and district wherein the crime shall have been committed, which district shall have been previously ascertained by law, and to be informed of the nature and cause of the accusation; to be confronted with the witnesses against him; to have compulsory process for obtaining Witnesses in his favor, and to have the assistance of counsel for his defence.

Amendment VII

In Suits at common law, where the value in controversy shall exceed twenty dollars, the right of trial by jury shall be preserved, and no fact tried by a jury, shall be otherwise re-examined in any Court of the United States, than according to the rules of the common law.

Amendment VIII

Excessive bail shall not be required, nor excessive fines imposed, nor cruel and unusual punishments inflicted.

Amendment IX

The enumeration in the Constitution, of certain rights, shall not be construed to deny or disparage others retained by the people.

Amendment X

The powers not delegated to the United States by the Constitution, nor prohibited by it to the States, are reserved to the States respectively, or to the people.

Amendment XI

The Judicial power of the United States shall not be construed to extend to any suit in law or equity, commenced or prosecuted against one of the United States by Citizens of another State, or by Citizens or Subjects of any Foreign State.

Amendment XII

The Electors shall meet in their respective states, and vote by ballot for President and Vice-President, one of whom, at least, shall not be an inhabitant of the same state with themselves; they shall name in their ballots the person voted for as President, and in distinct ballots the person voted for as Vice-President, and they shall make distinct lists of all persons voted for as President, and of all persons voted for as Vice-President, and of the number of votes for each, which lists they shall sign and certify, and transmit sealed to the seat of the government of the United States, directed to the President of the Senate;— The President of the Senate shall, in the presence of the Senate and House of Representatives, open all the certificates and the votes shall then be counted;— The person having the greatest number of votes for President, shall be the President, if such number be a majority of the whole number of Electors appointed; and if no person have such majority, then from the persons having the highest numbers not exceeding three on the list of those voted for as President, the House of Representatives shall choose immediately, by ballot, the President. But in choosing the President, the votes shall be taken by states, the representation from each state having one vote; a quorum for this purpose shall consist of a member or members from two-thirds of the states, and a majority of all the states shall be necessary to a choice. *And if the House of Representatives shall not choose a President whenever the right of choice shall devolve upon them, before the fourth day of March next following, then the Vice-President shall act as President, as in the case of the death or other constitutional disability of the President.*—The person having the greatest number of votes as Vice-President, shall be the Vice-President, if such number be a majority of the whole number of Electors appointed, and if no person have a majority, then from the two highest numbers on the list, the Senate shall choose the Vice-President; a quorum for the purpose shall consist of two-thirds of the whole number of Senators, and a majority of the whole number shall be necessary to a choice. But no person constitutionally ineligible to the office of President shall be eligible to that of Vice-President of the United States.

Amendment XIII

SECTION 1. Neither slavery nor involuntary servitude, except as a punishment for crime whereof the party shall have been duly convicted, shall exist within the United States, or any place subject to their jurisdiction.

SECTION 2. Congress shall have power to enforce this article by appropriate legislation.

Amendment XIV

SECTION 1. All persons born or naturalized in the United States, and subject to the jurisdiction thereof, are citizens of the United States and of the State wherein they reside. No State shall make or enforce any law which shall abridge the privileges or immunities of citizens of the United States; nor shall any State deprive any person of life, liberty, or property, without due process of law; nor deny to any person within its jurisdiction the equal protection of the laws.

SECTION 2. Representatives shall be apportioned among the several States according to their respective numbers, counting the whole number of persons in each State, excluding Indians not taxed. But when the right to vote at any election for the choice of electors for President and Vice President of the United States, Representatives in Congress, the Executive and Judicial officers of a State, or the members of the Legislature thereof, is denied to any of the male inhabitants of such State, being twenty-one years of age, and citizens of the United States, or in any way abridged, except for participation in rebellion, or other crime, the basis of representation therein shall be reduced in the proportion which the number of such male citizens shall bear to the whole number of male citizens twenty-one years of age in such State.

SECTION 3. No person shall be a Senator or Representative in Congress, or elector of President and Vice President, or hold any office, civil or military, under the United States, or under any State, who, having previously taken an oath, as a member of Congress, or as an officer of the United States, or as a member of any State legislature, or as an executive or judicial officer of any State, to support the Constitution of the United States, shall have engaged in insurrection or rebellion against the same, or given aid or comfort to the enemies thereof. But Congress may by a vote of two-thirds of each House, remove such disability.

SECTION 4. The validity of the public debt of the United States, authorized by law, including debts incurred for payment of pensions and bounties for services in suppressing insurrection or rebellion, shall not be questioned. But neither the United States nor any State shall assume or pay any debt or obligation incurred in aid of insurrection or rebellion against the United States, or any claim for the loss or emancipation of any slave; but all such debts, obligations and claims shall be held illegal and void.

SECTION 5. The Congress shall have power to enforce, by appropriate legislation, the provisions of this article.

Amendment XV

SECTION 1. The right of citizens of the United States to vote shall not be denied or abridged by the United States or by any State on account of race, color, or previous condition of servitude.

SECTION 2. The Congress shall have power to enforce this article by appropriate legislation.

Amendment XVI

The Congress shall have power to lay and collect taxes on incomes, from whatever source derived, without apportionment among the several States, and without regard to any census or enumeration.

Amendment XVII

The Senate of the United States shall be composed of two Senators from each State, elected by the people thereof, for six years; and each Senator shall have one vote. The electors in each State shall have the qualifications requisite for electors of the most numerous branch of the State legislatures.

When vacancies happen in the representation of any State in the Senate, the executive authority of such State shall issue writs of election to fill such vacancies: Provided, That the legislature of any State may empower the executive thereof to make temporary appointments until the people fill the vacancies by election as the legislature may direct.

This amendment shall not be so construed as to affect the election or term of any Senator chosen before it becomes valid as part of the Constitution.

Amendment XVIII

SECTION 1. *After one year from the ratification of this article the manufacture, sale, or transportation of intoxicating liquors within, the importation thereof into, or the exportation thereof from the United States and all territory subject to the jurisdiction thereof for beverage purposes is hereby prohibited.*

SECTION 2. *The Congress and the several States shall have concurrent power to enforce this article by appropriate legislation.*

SECTION 3. *This article shall be inoperative unless it shall have been ratified as an amendment to the Constitution by the legislatures of the several States, as provided in the Constitution, within seven years from the date of the submission hereof to the States by the Congress.*

Amendment XIX

The right of citizens of the United States to vote shall not be denied or abridged by the United States or by any State on account of sex.

Congress shall have power to enforce this article by appropriate legislation.

Amendment XX

SECTION 1. The terms of the President and Vice President shall end at noon on the 20th day of January, and the terms of Senators and Representatives at noon on the 3d day of January, of the years in which such terms would have ended if this article had not been ratified; and the terms of their successors shall then begin.

SECTION 2. The Congress shall assemble at least once in every year, and such meeting shall begin at noon on the 3d day of January, unless they shall by law appoint a different day.

SECTION 3. If, at the time fixed for the beginning of the term of the President, the President elect shall have died, the Vice President elect shall become President. If a President shall not have been chosen before the time fixed for the beginning of his term, or if the President elect shall have failed to qualify, then the Vice President elect shall act as President until a President shall have qualified; and the Congress may by law provide for the case wherein neither a President elect nor a Vice President elect shall have qualified, declaring who shall then act as President, or the manner in which one who is to act shall be selected, and such person shall act accordingly until a President or Vice President shall have qualified.

SECTION 4. The Congress may by law provide for the case of the death of any of the persons from whom the House of Representatives may choose a President whenever the right of choice shall have devolved upon them, and for the case of the death of any of the persons from whom the Senate may choose a Vice President whenever the right of choice shall have devolved upon them.

SECTION 5. Sections 1 and 2 shall take effect on the 15th day of October following the ratification of this article.

SECTION 6. This article shall be inoperative unless it shall have been ratified as an amendment to the Constitution by the legislatures of three-fourths of the several States within seven years from the date of its submission.

Amendment XXI

SECTION 1. The eighteenth article of amendment to the Constitution of the United States is hereby repealed.

SECTION 2. The transportation or importation into any State, Territory, or possession of the United States for delivery or use therein of intoxicating liquors, in violation of the laws thereof, is hereby prohibited.

SECTION 3. This article shall be inoperative unless it shall have been ratified as an amendment to the Constitution by conventions in the several States, as provided in the Constitution, within seven years from the date of the submission hereof to the States by the Congress.

Amendment XXII

SECTION 1. No person shall be elected to the office of the President more than twice, and no person who has held the office of President, or acted as President, for more than two years of a term to which some other person was elected President shall be elected to the office of the President more than once. But this Article shall not apply to any person holding the office of President when this Article was proposed by the Congress, and shall not prevent any person who may be holding the office of President, or acting as President, during the term within which this Article becomes operative from holding the office of President or acting as President during the remainder of such term.

SECTION 2. This article shall be inoperative unless it shall have been ratified as an amendment to the Constitution by the legislatures of three-fourths of the several States within seven years from the date of its submission to the States by the Congress.

Amendment XXIII

SECTION 1. The District constituting the seat of Government of the United States shall appoint in such manner as the Congress may direct:

A number of electors of President and Vice President equal to the whole number of Senators and Representatives in Congress to which the District would be entitled if it were a State, but in no event more than the least populous State; they shall be in addition to those appointed by the States, but they shall be considered, for the purposes of the election of President and Vice President, to be electors appointed by a State; and they shall meet in the District and perform such duties as provided by the twelfth article of amendment.

SECTION 2. The Congress shall have power to enforce this article by appropriate legislation.

Amendment XXIV

SECTION 1. The right of citizens of the United States to vote in any primary or other election for President or Vice President, for electors for President or Vice President, or for Senator or Representatives in Congress, shall not be denied or abridged by the United States or any State by reason of failure to pay any poll tax or other tax.

SECTION 2. The Congress shall have power to enforce this article by appropriate legislation.

Amendment XXV

SECTION 1. In case of the removal of the President from office or of his death or resignation, the Vice President shall become President.

SECTION 2. Whenever there is a vacancy in the office of the Vice President, the President shall nominate a Vice President who shall take office upon confirmation by a majority vote of both Houses of Congress.

SECTION 3. Whenever the President transmits to the President pro tempore of the Senate and the Speaker of the House of Representatives his written declaration that he is unable to discharge the powers and duties of his office, and until he transmits to them a written declaration to the contrary, such powers and duties shall be discharged by the Vice President as Acting President.

SECTION 4. Whenever the Vice President and a majority of either the principal officers of the executive departments or of such other body as Congress may by law provide, transmit to the President pro tempore of the Senate and the Speaker of the House of Representatives their written declaration that the President is unable to discharge the powers and duties of his office, the Vice President shall immediately assume the powers and duties of the office as Acting President.

Thereafter, when the President transmits to the President pro tempore of the Senate and the Speaker of the House of Representatives his written declaration that no inability exists, he shall resume the powers and duties of his office unless the Vice President and a majority of either the principal officers of the executive department or of such other body as Congress may by law provide, transmit within four days to the President pro tempore of the Senate and the Speaker of the House of Representatives their written declaration that the President is unable to discharge the powers and duties of his office. Thereupon Congress shall decide the issue, assembling within forty-eight hours for that purpose if not in session. If the Congress, within twenty-one days after receipt of the latter written declaration, or, if Congress is not in session, within twenty-one days after Congress is required to assemble, determines by two-thirds vote of both Houses that the President is unable to discharge the powers and duties of his office, the Vice President shall continue to discharge the same as Acting President; otherwise, the President shall resume the powers and duties of his office.

Amendment XXVI

SECTION 1. The right of citizens of the United States, who are eighteen years of age or older, to vote shall not be denied or abridged by the United States or by any State on account of age.

SECTION 2. The Congress shall have power to enforce this article by appropriate legislation.

Appendix B:
Selected
State-by-State
Legal
Information

Minimum Age for Specified Activities

| State or Jurisdiction | Age of Majority (a) | Minimum Age for Making a Will | Minimum Age for Buying (b) | | Minimum Age for Serving on a Jury | Minimum Age for Leaving School (c) |
			Liquor	Beer or Wine		
Alabama	19	19	21	21	19	16
Alaska	18	18	21	21	18	16
Arizona	18	18	21	21	18	16
Arkansas	18	18	21	21	18	17
California	18	18 (d)	21	21	18	16
Colorado	18	18	21	21	18	16
Connecticut	18	18	21	21	18	16
Delaware	18	18	21	21	18	16
Florida	18	18	21	21	18	16
Georgia	18	18	21	21	18	16
Hawaii	18	18	21	21	18	18
Idaho	18	18 (d)	21	21	18	16
Illinois	18	18	21	21	18	16
Indiana	18	18	21	21	18	16
Iowa	18	18	21	21	18	16
Kansas	18	18	21	21	18	16
Kentucky	18	18	21	21	18	16 (e)
Louisiana	18	16 (d)	21	21	18	17
Maine	18	18	21	21	18	17
Maryland	18	18	21	21	18	16
Massachusetts	18	18	21	21	18	16
Michigan	18	18	21	21	18	16
Minnesota	18	18	21	21	18	16 (f)
Mississippi	18	18	21	21	21	17
Missouri	18	18	21	21	21	16

Minimum Age for Specified Activities Continued

State or Jurisdiction	Age of Majority (a)	Minimum Age for Making a Will	Minimum Age for Buying (b)		Minimum Age for Serving on a Jury	Minimum Age for Leaving School(c)
			Liquor	Beer or Wine		
Montana	18	18	21	21	18	16 (g)
Nebraska	19	18	21	21	19	16
Nevada	18	18	21	21	18	17
New Hampshire	18	18	21	21	18	16
New Jersey	18	18	21	21	18	16
New Mexico	18	18	21	21	18	18
New York	(h)	18	21	21	18	16 (i)
North Carolina	18	18	21	21	18	16
North Dakota	18	18	21 (j)	21 (j)	18	16
Ohio	18	18	21	19	18	18
Oklahoma	18	18	21	21	18	18
Oregon	18	18	21	21	18	18
Pennsylvania	21	18	21	21	18	17
Rhode Island	18	18	21	21	18	16
South Carolina	18	18	21	21	18	17
South Dakota	18	18	21	21	18	16 (g)
Tennessee	18	18	21	21	18	17
Texas	18	18 (d)	21	21	18	17
Utah	18	18	21	21	18	18
Vermont	18	18	21	21	18	16
Virginia	18	18	21	21	18	18
Washington	18	18	21	21	18	18
West Virginia	18	18	21	21	18	16
Wisconsin	18	18	21	21	18	18
Wyoming	19	19	21	21	19	16
District of Columbia	18	18	21	21	18	17

(a) Generally, the age at which an individual has legal control over his or her own actions and business (e.g., the ability to contract) except as otherwise provided by statute. In many states, the age of majority is arrived at upon marriage if the minimum legal marrying age is lower than the prescribed age of majority.

(b) As of early 1986. Legislation enacted; may not yet be effective.

(c) Without graduating.

(d) Age may be lower for a minor who is living apart from his or her parents or legal guardians and managing his or her own financial affairs or who has contracted a lawful marriage.

(e) Signed parental approval prior to age 18.

(f) Age 18, year 2000.

(g) Or completion of eighth grade, whichever is earlier.

(h) As defined in general obligation (for purposes of contracting) and civil rights codes, 18 years.

(i) Age 17 in New York City and Buffalo.

(j) Two military bases permit 18-year-olds to purchase.

Source: Adapted with permission from The Council of State Governments, *The Book of the States*, 1990–1991 Edition, Vol. 28, p. 417.

Marriage Laws

| State | Age with parental consent | | Age without consent | | Physical exam & blood test for male and female | | | |
	Male	Female	Male	Female	Maximum period between exam and license	Scope of medical exam	Waiting period Before license	Waiting period After license
Alabama*	14a	14a	18	18	—	b	—	s
Alaska	16z	16z	18	18	—	b	3 da., w	—
Arizona	16z	16z	18	18	—	—	—	—
Arkansas	17c	16c	18	18	—	—	v	h
California	aa	aa	18	18	30 da., w	bb	—	s
Colorado*	16z	16z	18	18	—	bb	—	s
Connecticut	16z	16z	18	18	—	—	4 da., w	ttt
Delaware	18c	16c	18	18	—	—	—	e, s
Florida	16a, c	16a, c	18	18	—	b	3 da.	s
Georgia*	aa	aa	16	16	—	b	3 da., g	s*
Hawaii	16d	16d	18	18	—	b	—	—
Idaho*	16z	16z	18	18	—	bb	—	—
Illinois	16	16	18	18	30 da.	b, n	—	ee
Indiana	17c	17c	18	18	—	bb	72 hrs.	t
Iowa*	18z	18z	18	18	—	—	3 da., v	tt
Kansas*	18z	18z	18	18	—	—	3 da., w	—
Kentucky	18c, z	18c, z	18	18	—	—	—	—
Louisiana	18z	18z	18	18	10 da.	b	72 hrs., w	—
Maine	16z	16z	18	18	—	—	3 da., v, w	h
Maryland	16c, f	16c, f	18	18	—	—	48 hrs., w	ff
Massachusetts	16d	16	18	18	60 da.	bb	3 da., v	—
Michigan	16c, d	16c	18	18	30 da.	b	3 da., w	—
Minnesota	16z	16z	18	18	—	—	5 da., w	—
Mississippi	aa	aa	17gg	15gg	30 da.	b	3 da., w	ff
Missouri	15d, 18z	15d, 18z	18	18	—	—	—	—
Montana*	16	16	18	18	—	b	—	—
Nebraska	17	17	18	18	—	bb	—	ff
Nevada	16z	16z	18	18	—	—	—	—
New Hampshire	14j	13j	18	18	30 da.	b, l	3 da., v	h
New Jersey	16z, c	16z, c	18	18	30 da.	b	72 hrs., w	s

State	With consent (M)	With consent (F)	Without consent (M)	Without consent (F)				
New Mexico	16d	16d	18	18	30 da.	b	—	—
New York	14j	14j	18	18	—	nn	—	24 hrs., w, t
North Carolina	16c, g	16c, g	18	18	—	m	v	—
North Dakota	16	16	18	18	—	—	—	t
Ohio*	18c, z	16c, z	18	18	30 da.	b	5 da.	t, w
Oklahoma*	16c	16c	18	18	30 da., w	b	—	s
Oregon	17	17	18	18	—	—	3 da., w	—
Pennsylvania*	16d	16d	18	18	30 da.	b	3 da., w	t
Puerto Rico	18c, d, z	16c, d, z	21	21	—	b	—	—
Rhode Island*	18d	16d	18	18	—	bb	—	—
South Carolina*	16c	14c	18	18	—	—	1 da.	—
South Dakota	16c	16c	18	18	—	—	—	tt
Tennessee	16d	16d	18	18	—	—	3 da., cc	s
Texas*	14j, k	14j, k	18x	18x	—	—	—	s
Utah	14	14	18	18	30 da.	b	—	s
Vermont	16z	16z	18	18	30 da.	b	3 da., w	—
Virginia	16a, c	16a, c	18	18	—	b	—	t
Washington	17d	17d	18	18	—	bbb	3 da.	t
West Virginia	18c	18c	18	18	—	b	3 da., w	—
Wisconsin	16	16	18	18	—	b	5 da., w	s
Wyoming	16d	16d	18	18	—	bb	—	—
Dist. of Columbia*	16a	16a	18	18	30 da., w	b	3 da., w	—

* Indicates 1987 common-law marriage recognized; in many states, such marriages are only recognized if entered into many years before. (a) Parental consent not required if minor was previously married. (aa) No age limits. (b) Venereal diseases and Rubella (for female). In Colorado, Rubella for female under 45 and Rh type. (bbb) No medical exam required; however, applicants must file affidavit showing non-affliction of contagious venereal disease. (c) Younger parties may obtain license in case of pregnancy or birth of child. (cc) Unless parties are over 18 years of age. (d) Younger parties may obtain license in special circumstances. (e) Residents before expiration of 24-hour waiting period; non-residents formerly residents, before expiration of 96-hour waiting period; others 96 hours. (ee) License effective 1 day after issuance, valid for 60 days only (f) If parties are under 16 years of age, proof of age and the consent of parents in person is required. If a parent is ill, an affidavit by the incapacitated parent and a physician's affidavit to that effect required. (ff) License valid for 180 days only. (g) Unless parties are 18 years of age or more, or female is pregnant, or applicants are the parents of a living child born out of wedlock. (gg) Notice to parents necessary if parties are under 21. (h) License valid for 90 days only. (j) Parental consent and/or permission of judge required. (k) Below age of consent parties need parental consent and permission of judge. (l) With each certificate issued to couples, a list of family planning agencies and services available to them is provided. (m) Mental incompetence, infectious tuberculosis, venereal diseases and Rubella (certain counties only). (n) Venereal diseases; test for sickle cell anemia given at request of examining physician. (nn) Tests for sickle cell anemia may be required for certain applicants. Marriage prohibited unless it is established that procreation is not possible. (p) If one or both parties are below the age for marriage without parental consent (3 day waiting period). (s) License valid for 30 days only. (t) License valid for 60 days only. (tt) License valid for 20 days only. (ttt) License valid for 65 days. (v) Parties must file notice of intention to marry with local clerk. (w) Waiting period may be avoided. (x) Authorizes counties to provide for premarital counseling as a requisite to issuance of license to persons under 19 and persons previously divorced. (y) Marriages by proxy are valid. (yy) Proxy marriages are valid under certain conditions. (z) Younger parties may marry with parental consent and/or permission of judge. In Connecticut, judicial approval. (zz) With consent of court.

Reprinted by permission of Pharos Books, *The World Almanac and Book of Facts*, 1991 Edition, p. 826.

Source: Gary N. Skoloff, Skoloff & Wolfe, Livingston, N.J.: as of June 1, 1990.

Motor Vehicle Laws (as of 1991)

State or Jurisdiction	Minimum Age for Driver's License			Vehicle Inspection (a)	Child Restraints Mandatory for Passengers below Age — (b)	Mandatory Seat Belt Law (c)
	Regular	Learner's	Restrictive			
Alabama	16	15 (d)	14 (e)	(f)	5	*
Alaska	16	14 (g)	14 (g)	Spot	7	*
Arizona	18	15 + 7 mos. (d, g)	16 (g)	(h)	5	*
Arkansas	16	d	14 (g, i)	*	6	*
California	18	15 (i, j)	16 (j)	(h)	5 (k)	* (l)
Colorado	21	15 + 6 mos. (d, m)	16 (g)	(h)	4 (k)	*
Connecticut	18	(o)	16 (j)	(h)	4	*
Delaware	18	15 + 10 mos. (d, i, j)	16 (j)	*	5	. . .
Florida	16	(d)	15 (g)	(h)	6	*
Georgia	21	15	16 (g)	. . .	4	*
Hawaii	18	(d)	15 (g)	*	4	*
Idaho	16	(d)	14 (j)	. . .	4	*
Illinois	18	(d)	16 (g, j)	(h)	6	*
Indiana	18	15 (j, m)	16 + 1 mo. (g, j)	(h)	5	*
Iowa	18	14	16 (j)	Spot	6	*
Kansas	16	. . .	14 (i)	Spot	4	*
Kentucky	18	(d)	16 (g)	. . .	(k)	. . .
Louisiana	17	. . .	15 (p)	*	5	*
Maine	17	(d, i)	15 (j)	*	5	(l)
Maryland	18	15 + 9 mos. (d, i)	16 (g, j, p)	(q)	5	*
Massachusetts	18	16 (d)	16 + 6 mos. (g, p)	*	5	(l)
Michigan	18	(d)	16 (g, j, r)	Spot	4	*
Minnesota	19	(d)	16 (j)	Spot (f)	4 (l)	*
Mississippi	15	(d)	. . .	*	2	*
Missouri	16	. . .	15 (m)	*	4	*
Montana	18	(d)	15 (g, j)	. . .	4 (k)	*
Nebraska	16	15 (d, i)	(r)	. . .	4	. . .
Nevada	18	15 + 6 mos.	16 (j)	(q)	5	* (l)
New Hampshire	18	(n)	16 (j)	*	12	. . .
New Jersey	17	(i)	(r)	*	5	* (l)
New Mexico	16	15 (i)	15 (g, j)	. . .	11	*
New York	18	(d, i)	16 (g, p)	*	4	*
North Carolina	18	15 (i, j)	. . .	*	7	* (l)
North Dakota	16	(d)	14 (j)	Spot	16	. . .
Ohio	18 (s)	(i)	(r)	(h)	4 (k)	*
Oklahoma	16	(m)	15 + 6 mos. (j)	*	6	*
Oregon	16	15 (d)	(r)	Spot (h)	16	*
Pennsylvania	18	(d)	16 (g, p)	*	4	*

Rhode Island	18	(d)	16 (j)	*	14	. . .
South Carolina	16	15 (i)	15	*	6	*
South Dakota	16	14 (i)	14 (p)	. . .	5	. . .
Tennessee	16	15	. . .	(f)	4	*
Texas	18	15 (i, m)	16 (j, r)	*	4	*
Utah	16 (j)	(d)	. . .	*	8	*
Vermont	18	15 (i)	16 (i)	*	5	* (k)
Virginia	18	15 + 8 mos. (d, g, j)	16 (g, j)	*	4	*
Washington	18	15 (d, m)	16 (j)	(h)	5	*
West Virginia	18	(d)	16 (g)	*	9	. . .
Wisconsin	18	(d)	16 (j)	Spot	4	* (l)
Wyoming	18	15 (i)	16 (g)	. . .	3	*
District of Columbia	18	(d)	16 (g)	*	7	*

(a) Spot indicates a spot check (usually for reasonable cause) or a random roadside inspection for defective or missing equipment.

(b) The type of child restraint (safety seat or seat belt) required may be different depending on the age of the child.

(c) These states have enacted mandatory seat belt legislation. Unless otherwise specified, legislation covers the driver and front-seat passengers.

(d) Permit required. In Arkansas, for 30 days prior to taking a driving test. In Delaware, for up to two months prior to 16th birthday. In Michigan, for 30 days prior to application for first license. In Minnesota, not required if driver can pass road test. In Oregon, not required if applicant can already drive.

(e) Restricted to mopeds.

(f) Cities have the authority to maintain inspection stations. In Alabama, state troopers are also authorized to inspect at their discretion.

(g) Consent of guardian or parent required.

(h) Emission inspection. In Arizona, Colorado, Indiana, Connecticut, Florida, Colorado, Georgia, and Washington, mandatory annual emission inspections in certain counties. In California, biennial inspections are required in portions of counties that do not meet federal clean air standards. In Oregon, biennial inspections in Portland metro area and Jackson County. In Washington, also other checks (e.g., out-of-state purchases, salvaged).

(i) Driver must be accompanied by licensed operator. In California and Vermont (learner's permit), a licensed operator 25 years or older. In Kansas, may drive to school or work without licensed operator. In Maine, New York, Texas, Vermont (restrictive license), Virginia, and Wyoming, a licensed oeprator 18 years or older. In Maryland, a driver 21 years or older who is licensed to drive a vehicle of that class and licensed for three or more years. In Nebraska, a licensed operator 19 years old or older. In New Jersey, driver licensed for same classification as the learner's permit. In South Carolina, a licensed operator 21 years or older.

(j) Must have successfully completed approved driver education course.

(k) Ohter restrictions. In California, Colorado, Montana, and Ohio, age restriction or child under 40 pounds. In Kentucky, 40 inches high or under. In Vermont, seat belts are required only for children ages 5 through 12. In Arkansas, seat belts are required only in some cities.

(l) Covers other passengers in vehicle. In California, Washington, and District of Columbia, all passengers. In Minnesota, driver, front-seat passengers, and anyone under 11. In New Jersey, all passengers between 5 and 18 years as well as driver and all front-seat passengers over 18 years. In New York, all back-seat occupants under 10 years and over 3 years as well as all front-seat occupants. In Maine, mandatory for children ages 4–15. In Massachusetts, mandatory for children ages 5–12. In Wisconsin, all passengers.

(m) Must be enrolled in driver education course. In Colorado, if not in such course, must wait until 15 years + 9 mos.

(n) Required for motorcyclists only. In New Hampshire, unlicensed persons who are being taught to drive other vehicles must be accompanied by a licensed operator.

(o) Trucks, buses, and trailers only.

(p) Various restrictions to driving hours, especially at night.

(q) Mandatory inspection only under certain circumstances. In Maryland, on all used cars upon resale or transfer. In Nevada, emission inspection on used cars being registered to new owner or being registered for the first time and on all renewals in Clark and Washoe counties.

(r) License will be granted at a lower age under special conditions, such as proof of hardship.

(s) Probatory license issued to persons between ages 16 and 18 upon completion of approved driver education course.

Notes: Asterisk (*) means the state has a provision. Three dots (. . .) means the state has no provision.

Source: Adapted with permission from The Council of State Governments, *The Book of the States*, 1990–1991 Edition, using information from the American Automobile Association, *Digest of Motor Laws*, 1991.

Sanctions for a First-Offense Conviction for DWI/DUI When There Was No Accident or Injuries

State or Jurisdiction	Illegal BAC Level	License	Fine	Jail
Alabama*	0.10	S[1] 90 days	$250–$1,000	1 yr. max
Alaska*	0.10	R[2] 30 days. May be followed by limited license for 60 days.	$250–$5,000	72 hrs.–1 yr. + CS[3]
Arizona*	0.10	S 30 days. followed by restricted license for not less than 60 days.	$250–$1,000	24 hrs.–6 mos. 8–24 hrs. CS in addition to or instead of jail.
Arkansas*	0.10	S 90–120 days	$150–$1,000 CS possible for person unable to pay fine.	24 hrs.–1 yr. or CS
California*	0.08	S 6 mos. Under 21—S 1 yr. Under 18—R 1 yr. or until 18th birthday, whichever is longer.	$390–$1,000	96 hrs.–1 yr.
Colorado*	0.10	S 1 yr. Under 21—R 1 yr.	$300–$1,000	5 days–1 yr. + 48–96 hrs. CS
Connecticut	0.10	S 1 yr.	$500–$1,000	48 hrs.–6 mos. 100 hrs. CS instead of 48 hrs. jail possible.
Delaware	0.10	R 90 days–1 yr.	$200–$1,000	60 days–6 mos.
Florida*	0.10	R 180 days–1 yr.	$250–$550	Up to 6 mos. + 50 hrs. CS
Georgia	0.12	S 120 days–1 yr.	$300–$1,000	10 days–1 yr.
Hawaii*	0.10	S 30 days. Restricted license for additional 60 days.	$500–$1,000	48 hrs.–30 days 72 hrs. CS possible in addition to or instead of other penalties.
Idaho	0.10	S 180 days max.	$1,000 max.	6 mos. max.
Illinois	0.10	R 1 yr. Under 21—R 1 yr.	$1,000 max.	1 yr. max.
Indiana*	0.10	S 90 days–2 yrs. or S 30 days + 180 days' probationary license	$500 max.	Not more than 60 days
Iowa*	0.10	R 180 days	$500–$1,000 or CS 200 hrs. max. instead of fine.	Up to 1 year

Kansas*	0.10	<u>S 30 days</u> + 330 days' restriction	$200–$500	<u>48 hrs.</u>–6 mos. or CS 100 hrs.
Kentucky	0.10	<u>R 6 mos. or S 30 days + treatment program</u>	$200–$500	<u>48 hrs.</u>–30 days
Louisiana*	0.10	S 90 days; restrictive license may be issued. Drivers age 13–18 may face additional sanctions.	$125–$500	10 days–60 mos. CS alternative available
Maine*	0.08	<u>S 60</u>–90 days	<u>$300</u>–$1,000	<u>48 hrs.</u>–not more than 1 yr.
Maryland*	0.10	R 6 mos.	Up to $1,000	Up to 1 yr.
Massachusetts*	0.10	<u>S 45 days</u> (with alcohol education program). Otherwise, <u>R 1 yr.</u>	$100–$1,000	Up to 2 yrs. + CS up to 30 hrs.
Michigan*	0.10	S 6 mos.–2 yrs.	<u>$100</u>–$500	Up to 90 days + up to 12 days' CS
Minnesota*	0.10	R not less than 30 days	Not more than $700	Up to 90 days
Mississippi*	0.10	<u>S 30 days</u>–1 yr.	<u>$250</u>–$1,000	Not more than 24 hrs.
Missouri*	0.10	R 30 days + 60 days' restricted driving privileges. <u>Under 21—R 1 yr.</u>	$300–$500	15 days–6 mos.
Montana*	0.10	S 6 mos.	$100–$500	<u>24 hrs.</u>–60 days + CS
Nebraska*	0.10	R 60 days–6 mos.	$500	30 days
Nevada	0.10	<u>R 45</u>–90 days	$200–$1,000	<u>2 days</u>–6 mos. CS possible instead of jail.
New Hampshire*	0.10	<u>R 90 days</u>–2 yrs.	<u>$350</u>–$1,000	None
New Jersey*	0.10	<u>R 6 mos.</u>–1 yr.	$250–$400 + insurance surcharges	Not more than 30 days
New Mexico*	0.10	R 1 yr.	$300–$500	30–90 days
New York*	0.10	R 6 mos. <u>Under 21—R 1 yr.</u>	<u>$350</u>–$500	1 year max.
North Carolina*	0.10	R 1 yr.	Up to $100	24 hrs.–60 days + 24 hrs. CS
North Dakota*	0.10	<u>S 30</u>–91 days	<u>$250</u>–$500	30 days max.
Ohio	0.10	<u>S 15 days</u>–3 yrs. <u>Under 18—S until age 18 or completion of treatment program.</u>	<u>$200</u>–$1,000	<u>3 days</u>–6 mos.
Oklahoma*	0.10	<u>R 30</u>–90 days	$100–$300	10 days–1 yr. + CS

Oregon*	0.08	S 1 yr. Between 13–17—S 1 yr. or until age 17, whichever is longer.	Not more than $2,500	48 hrs.–1 yr. CS 80–250 hrs. as alternative to jail.
Pennsylvania*	0.10	S 12 mos.	$300–$5,000	48 hrs.–2 yrs. or CS
Rhode Island	0.10	S 3–6 mos.	$100–$300	Not more than 1 yr. + 10–60 hrs. CS
South Carolina*	0.10	S 6 mos.	$200	48 hrs.–30 days or CS min. of 48 hrs. instead of prison.
South Dakota	0.10	R 30 days–1 yr. Hardship license available.	$1,000	1 yr.
Tennessee*	0.10	R 1 yr. Hardship license available.	$250–$1,000	48 hrs.–11 mos., 29 days CS possible instead of or in addition to other penalties.
Texas*	0.10	90–365 days	$100–$2,000	72 hrs.–2 yrs. + CS
Utah*	0.08	S 90 days	Not more than $1,000	48 hrs.–6 mos. or 24–50 hrs. CS
Vermont*	0.10	S 90 days	Not more than $750	Not more than 1 yr.
Virginia*	0.10	R 6 mos. Under 18—R 1 yr. or until 18th birthday, whichever is longer.	Up to $1,000	12 mos.
Washington*	0.10	S 30 days–90 days Restrictive license may be required after this period.	$250–$1,000	24 hrs.–1 yr.
West Virginia*	0.10	R 90 days–6 mos.	$100–$500	1 day–6 mos.
Wisconsin*	0.10	S 6–9 mos.	$150–$300 and/or CS	None
Wyoming*	0.10	S 90 days	Up to $750	6 mos.
District of Columbia	0.10	R 6 mos.	Up to $300	Up to 90 days

1. S = license suspension.
2. R = license revocation.
3. CS = community service.

Note: States marked with an asterisk (*) also have alcohol treatment/education programs that may be required in addition to other sanctions. Underscored sanctions are mandatory, or required.

Source: U.S. Department of Transportation, National Highway Traffic Safety Administration, Digest of State Alcohol–Highway Safety Related Legislation, Ninth Edition, 1991.

Glossary

The numbers in parentheses after the definitions refer to the chapter in which the terms appear.

acceptance the act of agreeing to an offer, needed to make a legal contract (9)

accessory after the fact a person who knowingly helps a criminal after a crime has been committed, for example, by hiding the criminal or destroying evidence (4)

accomplice a person who helps complete a crime (4)

acquit to declare not guilty (3)

adjudication hearing the juvenile court equivalent of a criminal trial, during which a judge listens to testimony and decides whether a child is delinquent, in need of supervision, or abused or neglected (6)

adjudication inquiry the juvenile court equivalent of a criminal arraignment, during which a judge tells a child what the child is accused of and explains the child's constitutional rights (6)

administrator a person appointed by a probate court to settle all matters having to do with the estate of a person who has died without a will (13)

adoption a process by which a person who is not a child's biological parent becomes that child's legal parent (11)

adoptive parent a person who adopts a child (11)

advance directive a legal document that lets others know how a person wants to be treated if he or she becomes incompetent, the most common types being the durable power of attorney and the living will (13)

advertising substantiation proof that a seller's claims in an advertisement for a product are true (15)

affinity relationship through marriage (10)

affirmative action laws laws which give special treatment to groups that have historically been discriminated against; a constitutionally accepted way to overcome past discrimination (2)

affirmative disclosure a statement of a product's limitations that a seller may be required to include in an advertisement (15)

aftercare early release from a juvenile detention facility, similar to parole for an adult prisoner, during which a child is supervised by a juvenile probation officer (6)

age of majority the age at which a person gets all the rights and responsibilities of an adult; age 18 in most states (11)

alimony money paid by one spouse to support the other spouse as established by a separation agreement or divorce decree; also called spousal support or maintenance (12)

amendment a change or an addition to a law or constitution (1)

anatomical gift act a law that permits adults to donate their body or body parts upon their death (13)

annulment a declaration by a court that a marriage never existed (12)

answer in a civil lawsuit, the defendant's formal written response to the plaintiff's complaint (7)

antenuptial agreement a written agreement made before marriage that explains the rights and responsibilities of the husband and wife; also called a prenuptial agreement (10)

appellate jurisdiction the authority of a court to review cases appealed from a lower court (1)

arbitration the process of settling a dispute by having a neutral third party act as a judge and make a decision (7)

arbitrator a neutral third party who listens to both sides of an argument and makes a final decision (7)

arraignment a pretrial criminal court appearance during which a judge reads the charges against the defendant, reminds the defendant of his or her constitutional rights, and asks the defendant to state his or her plea to each charge (5)

arrest to take into custody (3)

arrest warrant a court order, signed by a judge, that authorizes the arrest of a particular person (3)

arson destroying or damaging someone's property by means of fire or explosives (4)

artificial insemination a reproductive process by which a woman's egg is fertilized by a man's sperm without sexual intercourse (11)

assault an act that makes a person fear that he or she will be a victim of battery (4, 8)

assign to give someone else the tenant's legal rights and duties under a rental agreement (16)

attempt the act of trying and failing to commit a crime (4)

attorney a lawyer who is representing a client in a legal matter (18)

attorney-client privilege a rule of confidentiality, or privacy, that prohibits a lawyer from discussing conversations he or she has had with a client (18)

audit an Internal Revenue Service review of a tax return and the records supporting the information on that return (17)

bail a sum of money that an accused criminal deposits with a court in exchange for being allowed to go free until the time of trial (3)

bailiff an officer of the courtroom whose job is to keep order (19)

bait and switch a sales practice of luring a buyer into a store by advertising a low-priced item that is not available and getting the buyer to take a higher-priced product instead (15)

balancing test a test a court may use when a law conflicts with the rights of an individual, in which the court weighs the interests of the government against the rights of the individual (2)

bankruptcy a legal procedure in which a court takes charge of the finances of a person who cannot pay his or her debts (15)

bar state agency that licenses lawyers and oversees the practice of law (18)

battery physical contact with someone against his or her will (4, 8)

beneficiary a person or organization that inherits money or property through a will (13)

benefits additional compensation beyond wages that is offered to an employee (14)

bigamy having two spouses at the same time (10)

Bill of Rights the first ten amendments to the U.S. Constitution, which list the basic rights guaranteed to all American citizens, including freedom of speech, freedom of religion, freedom of the press, and certain criminal rights (2)

bona fide occupational qualification a person's age, sex, or race, when it is considered a legitimate reason for hiring the person for a particular job, such as modeling, acting, or doing police undercover work (14)

booking a clerical procedure in which the police make a formal record of a person's arrest (5)

breach to fail to do something, as in failing to act with reasonable standards of care or failing to do what was agreed to in a contract (8, 9, 16)

brief a written statement that a lawyer presents to a court to explain and argue a client's case (1)

burden of proof what each side in a trial is responsible for proving (5, 19)

burglary entering someone's property with the intent to commit a crime (4)

capital punishment the death penalty (3, 5)

caveat emptor the rule that buyers have no protection when they purchase a product; the phrase means "let the buyer beware" in Latin (15)

cease and desist order an order from the Federal Trade Commission that requires sellers to stop an illegal practice (15)

challenge a request a lawyer makes to a judge asking that a prospective juror be dismissed from the jury (19)

challenge for cause a request by a lawyer during jury selection that a potential juror be dismissed for a specific reason such as the person's knowing one of the parties in the case (19)

charge to instruct jurors about points of law, done by the judge before the jury begins to deliberate (19)

checks and balances a system set up in the U.S. Constitution that gives each branch of the federal government ways of influencing what the other branches do, so that no branch becomes too powerful (1)

child abuse mistreatment of a child (11)

child labor laws laws restricting employers' rights in hiring people under age 18 (14)

child neglect failure of a parent to give his or her child proper care (11)

child support money paid by a noncustodial parent for the benefit of minor children (12)

child welfare laws laws designed to protect the well-being of children (11)

civil law the body of law that deals with all issues not covered by criminal law, including family matters, housing, business contracts, civil rights, and physical injuries (1, 7)

civil rights acts laws that protect individuals from unequal or unfair treatment (2)

clemency mercy or leniency granted to a person accused of a crime (1)

closing costs certain one–time costs that a person buying a house must pay; may include title search fees, a real estate agent's fees, and inspection fees; also called settlement costs (16)

closing statement a summary statement made by the

lawyer for each side in a trial (19)

codicil an amendment to a will (13)

cohabitation agreement a contract between an unmarried couple regarding their financial affairs (12)

collateral a valuable item that a person agrees to give a creditor if the person fails to pay money he or she owes (15)

collection agency a business that specializes in collecting debts for creditors (15)

collective bargaining the process by which unionized employees join together to negotiate with their employer (14)

common law a body of law based on judges' decisions (1)

common law marriage an agreement between a man and a woman to be married without a license or a ceremony (10)

community property system a property division system by which property acquired by either spouse as a result of that spouse's efforts during the marriage is automatically owned by both spouses equally; may affect the distribution of property in a divorce (12)

compensation in civil law, payment for a loss or injury (7)

complaint the first document filed in a civil lawsuit, in which the plaintiff explains his or her side of the story to the court and requests a specific remedy from the defendant (7)

concurrent jurisdiction authority to hear cases that is shared by federal and state courts (1)

concurring opinion a written explanation by one or more judges in a case who agree with the majority ruling, but for different reasons (1)

condominium an apartment in a multiunit building in which units are individually owned and responsibility for common areas is shared (16)

conflict of interest a situation in which a lawyer has opposing duties or desires in a case (18)

consanguinity blood relationship (10)

consent permission to do something; may be used as a defense to an intentional tort (8)

consent order a voluntary agreement by a merchant to stop an illegal sales practice (15)

consideration the legal term for "something of value" that is exchanged by the parties to a contract (9)

conspiracy the act of two or more people planning a crime (4)

constitution a legal document that explains the powers and limits of government and lists the freedoms and rights of the people (1)

constructive eviction an action by a landlord that prevents a tenant from having undisturbed use of a rental unit (16)

consumer a person who buys a product or service for personal use (15)

contest to oppose the validity of a will (13)

contingency fee a fee paid to a lawyer that is a percentage of the money the lawyer collects for a client in a lawsuit; allowed only in cases that involve money (18)

contract an agreement between two or more parties that is enforceable by a court (9)

contract of adhesion a contract in which one party makes all the rules and the other party is given the choice of accepting or not accepting (9, 15)

cooling-off period a three-day time period after a door-to-door sale is made during which a consumer may cancel the sale (15)

cooperative apartment an apartment in a building that is owned by a corporation in which all the building's residents own shares (16)

corrective advertising advertising in which a seller corrects misstatements made in earlier ads (15)

count each separate crime with which a defendant is charged (5)

counteroffer a response to an offer that is different from the original offer and cancels the original offer (9)

court clerk a judge's assistant who handles all court papers and watches over any physical evidence presented during a trial; also usually calls and swears in all witnesses and jurors (19)

court reporter a person who keeps a written record of what is said at a trial (19)

credit purchasing an item that the buyer pays for over a period of time; money that is lent (15)

credit bureau a company which collects information on consumers that is used by creditors to indicate whether a person is a good credit risk; sometimes called a consumer reporting agency (15)

credit card a card issued by stores and banks that allows a person to buy goods and services on credit (15)

credit history history of whether a person has bought things on credit before and whether payments were made on time (15)

credit limit a limit on how much a person can buy on a credit card; depends primarily on a person's income (15)

creditor a person or business that provides credit (15)

credit report a report that a creditor requests of a credit bureau in order to find out about a person's credit background (15)

criminal law the body of law that defines crimes and spells out punishments (1)

criminal procedure the process by which suspected criminals are identified, arrested, accused, and tried in court (5)

cross-examination questioning of a witness conducted by the lawyer for the opposing side (19)

damages money paid as compensation (7)

deadly force force that is likely to cause death or serious bodily injury (4)

debit card a card used by a buyer that allows the amount of a purchase to be deducted by computer from the buyer's bank account (15)

debtor a person who makes a purchase on credit (15)

defamation spoken or written lies that hurt a person's interests or reputation (2)

default to stop making payments on a loan (16)

defendant in a criminal proceeding, a person who has been charged in court with a crime; in a civil action, a person who is being sued (3, 5, 7)

defense an excuse or explanation for an action (8)

deliberate to discuss a case, as a jury does (19)

delinquent a child who commits an action that would be considered a crime if done by an adult (6)

dependent someone a person supports (17)

deposition sworn testimony given out of court by a witness or a party before a trial begins (19)

determinate sentence a fixed-length jail or prison term, such as 15 years (5)

deterrence a goal of punishment to teach a criminal a lesson so that he or she will be discouraged from breaking the law again (5)

detrimental reliance reliance on a promise that causes a person to suffer a loss; exception to the rule that promises can't be legally enforced (9)

direct descendant one's child or a descendant of one's child (13)

directed verdict a ruling made by a judge during a trial, stating that there are no facts in dispute and that the case can be decided on legal issues alone (19)

direct examination questioning of a witness conducted by the lawyer who calls that person to the witness stand (19)

disaffirm to cancel a contract, as by a minor (9)

disbarment permanent suspension of a lawyer from practicing law (18)

disclaimer a notice to a buyer that some warranties do not apply (15)

discovery the pretrial process by which the lawyer for each party gathers facts in order to find out about the other side's case (7, 19)

disinherit to purposely omit a child from one's will (13)

disposition a treatment plan for a child judged to be delinquent, in need of supervision, or neglected or abused (6)

dissenting opinion a written explanation of the views of one or more judges in a case who disagree with the decision of the majority of the judges in that case (1)

diversion the transfer of a child out of the juvenile justice system and into the care of another agency (6)

divorce a court order that legally ends a marriage (12)

DNA fingerprinting a blood test that can be used to determine whether a particular man is the father of a particular child; compares the man's and the child's DNA, or genetic code (11)

docket a list of cases to be tried or reviewed by a court of law (1)

doctrine of necessaries the rule that makes a husband or wife responsible for his or her spouse's debts (10)

domestic partnership a legal agreement in which two unmarried people affirm a close personal relationship; may give a couple some of the legal benefits received by a married couple (10)

door-to-door salesperson a sales representative who goes from house to house demonstrating and selling products (15)

double jeopardy being tried twice for the same crime (3)

dower rights the right of a wife to use one third of her deceased husband's land during her lifetime (10)

down payment the portion of the purchase price of an item bought on credit that must be paid initially, as the amount paid by a home buyer when a mortgage is obtained (16)

dram shop laws laws under which bartenders and bar owners have a duty to keep their customers from driving while intoxicated (8)

due process the set of legal procedures that the government must follow when punishing or taking away the property of an individual (2)

durable power of attorney a legal document in which one person appoints another person to speak on his or her behalf if he or she becomes incompetent (13)

duress the act of making another person commit a crime by threatening immediate harm; may be used as a defense to a criminal charge by the person who was threatened (4)

elective share the portion of a deceased spouse's estate to which the surviving spouse is legally entitled by state law (13)

emancipation the process by which a child becomes an adult, usually by reaching the legal age of majority (11)

embezzlement keeping property that one is legally allowed to use but that belongs to someone else (4)

employee-at-will an employee who does not have an individual written employment contract with an employer (14)

equitable distribution system a method of determining property division in a divorce that is used in most states, requiring the court to divide marital property fairly (12)

Establishment Clause part of the First Amendment to the U.S. Constitution which guarantees that Congress will not establish a national religion or pass laws that favor one religion over another (2)

estate all the money and property a person owns (13)

euthanasia the act of ending a person's life to relieve incurable or insufferable pain (13)

eviction a court order issued at the request of a landlord that forces a tenant off the landlord's property (16)

excise tax a tax imposed on the production, sale, and consumption of selected goods and services (17)

exclusionary rule the rule which prevents evidence that is found or seized illegally from being used in court in a criminal case (3)

exclusive jurisdiction authority held solely by a federal or state court to hear certain types of cases (1)

exclusive remedy compensation available to an injured person that, if taken, prevents that person from receiving other damages (14)

executor the person who is appointed in a will to take charge of the deceased person's estate (9, 13)

exhibit an item of physical evidence, such as weapons, written contracts, or medical reports, that is presented during a trial (19)

expert witness a person with special knowledge, training, or skills who may be asked to answer questions about technical matters at a trial (19)

express warranty a promise by a seller about a product (15)

extortion the use of threats to take away someone's property illegally; also called blackmail (4)

fair comment the right of the media to make a broad range of unmalicious statements of fact and opinion about people involved in public activities (8)

false imprisonment illegally keeping a person in a confined space against his or her will (8)

false pretenses using trickery or lies to acquire someone else's property (4)

federal supremacy a provision in the U.S. Constitution making federal law a higher authority than state law (1)

felony a crime for which the punishment may be imprisonment for a year or longer or death (4)

felony murder a murder that takes place during the commission of a felony (4)

fetal alcohol syndrome a medical condition of a child that may result when the child's mother drinks alcoholic beverages during pregnancy (11)

FHA-insured loan a mortgage loan, guaranteed by the Federal Housing Administration, that helps low-income people buy a first home (16)

fighting words speech used to insult someone with the intention of starting a fight (2)

first-degree murder killing that is premeditated, or thought about beforehand (4)

fixed-term lease a written rental agreement that specifies a definite rental term, such as one year (16)

flat fee a fixed price for a service (18)

foreclosure a procedure by which a bank or other lender takes a home away from a person who has defaulted on a mortgage loan (16)

foreman jury member selected to lead the deliberation and announce the verdict (19)

forgery making, altering, or signing a legal document with the intent to defraud (4)

foster care any placement of a child away from that child's family (11)

fraud the use of lies or dishonest statements for personal benefit (9)

Free Exercise Clause part of the First Amendment to the U.S. Constitution which guarantees that Congress will not pass laws that restrict an individual's practice of religion (2)

frisk a type of search in which the police pat down a suspected criminal to look for weapons; does not require a search warrant (3)

Full Faith and Credit Clause a clause of U.S. Constitution that requires states to honor each other's laws, records, and court decisions (1)

full warranty a promise by a seller to repair or replace any defective part of a product (15)

garnish to collect a portion of each paycheck a person earns until that person's debt is paid off (15)

general practitioner a lawyer who handles most routine legal matters (18)

good cause a sufficient legal reason (14)

Good Samaritan laws laws that protect from liability doctors and nurses who volunteer to help others in an emergency (8)

grand jury a randomly selected group of citizens who decide whether there is probable cause to bring to trial a person who has been charged with a crime (5)

grand jury hearing in criminal procedure, a type of probable cause hearing during which a jury hears evidence from the prosecutor and decides whether there is probable cause for a trial (5)

grounds the legal basis for a divorce or an annulment (12)

guardian ad litem a person appointed by a court to serve as a child's advocate in a legal matter (11)

hearsay witness testimony that repeats someone else's out-of-court description of an event in order to prove that the event actually happened (19)

heir an individual who takes or shares the estate of a person who has died (13)

holographic will a will that is written entirely by hand (13)

homicide the act of killing another person (4)

hourly fee a fee per hour of work (18)

housing codes laws that set minimum standards for residential properties, such as safe electrical wiring and a sanitary plumbing system (16)

hung jury a jury that cannot reach a decision; a deadlocked jury

impeach to formally accuse a public official of misconduct; to cast doubt on a witness's testimony during a trial (1, 19)

implied consent permission that is assumed to have been given because of the situation (8)

implied contract a contract between parties that is understood but not stated explicitly (9, 14)

implied warranty a seller's promise about a product that is not stated explicitly (15)

implied warranty of habitability the right of a tenant to expect that a rental property is livable, e.g., that it has heat and running water and does not have dangerous structural conditions (16)

incapacitation a goal of punishment to prevent a criminal from committing more crimes by locking the person in prison (5)

incarceration confinement to jail or prison (5)

income tax a tax paid by individuals and corporations on the money they make (17)

income tax return a formal statement, filed annually by taxpayers, telling the government how much a taxpayer earned and what deductions he or she qualified for and indicating the individual's tax liability (17)

incorrigible unlikely to respond to rehabilitative treatment (6)

independent contractor a person who is self-employed (14)

indeterminate term a jail or prison sentence that is stated as a range of time, such as five to ten years (5)

indictment the list of criminal charges against a defendant that a prosecutor presents to a grand jury (5)

informal probation release of a child from custody without a trial on the condition that the child report to a probation officer and follow certain rules (6)

information the list of criminal charges against a defendant that a prosecutor presents to a judge (5)

informed consent permission that is given after receiving complete information, as a patient's consent for medical treatment based on a knowledge and understanding of the treatment, the risks, and the likelihood that the treatment will work (8, 13)

inheritance money or property received by the heirs to an estate (13)

injunction a court order requiring a person or corporation to stop doing something (7)

intake interview the procedure conducted to decide whether formal charges should be brought against a juvenile (6)

intentional infliction of emotional distress an intentional tort in which one person causes another person extreme distress through outrageous conduct (8)

intentional tort a wrong done to another person on purpose (8)

interest money a person pays for the right to buy on credit or for the money a person has borrowed (15)

intermediate scrutiny the level of scrutiny, or review, a court uses, in which the court determines whether a law satisfies an important government interest and is substantially related to that interest; used mostly for laws that discriminate on the basis of sex (2)

Internal Revenue Service (IRS) the federal government agency that collects taxes and administers tax law (17)

interrogatories written questions submitted by the lawyer for one party in a lawsuit to the other party (19)

intestate dying without a will (13)

intestate succession laws that specify how property is to be divided when a person dies without a will (13)

invasion of privacy an intentional tort that involves an intrusion into someone's private life, such as spying, electronic monitoring, or reading someone's mail (8)

in vitro fertilization a reproductive process in which a woman's egg is removed from her body, fertilized by a man's sperm in a laboratory, and then placed in the woman's womb and carried through a normal pregnancy (11)

involuntary manslaughter a killing that happens accidentally, as a result of someone's gross negligence or reckless behavior (4)

joint legal custody a custody arrangement by which parents who live separately have equal rights and responsibilities regarding their child (12)

joint physical custody a custody arrangement by which a child whose parents live separately lives with each parent about half the time (12)

joint tenancy property ownership shared by two people; when one dies, the other becomes the sole owner (16)

joyriding borrowing a car without permission; a criminal act in some states (4)

judgment notwithstanding the verdict a judge's ruling to set aside a jury verdict (19)

judicial review the power of courts to rule whether a statute or other act of government is unconstitutional (1)

judicial separation a court-ordered or court-approved separation agreement that is given only when a couple have grounds; also called legal separation, decree of separate maintenance, or divorce from bed and board (12)

jurisdiction authority of a court to hear and decide a case (1)

jury a group of citizens, randomly selected from the community, who are responsible for listening to the testimony from both sides of a case during a trial and then deciding all questions of fact (19)

jury room a private room where jurors go to deliberate a case (19)

juvenile justice system a specialized court system for children and adolescents (6)

labor union a group of workers that engages in collective bargaining to make sure its members get fair wages and good working conditions (14)

landlord a property owner who leases or rents his or her property (16)

larceny taking someone else's property with the intent to keep it (4)

lawsuit the process of resolving a dispute in civil court; also called litigation (7)

lawyer referral service a service, run by state or local bar associations, that helps match lawyers with clients (18)

layoff letting employees go in order to reduce costs; usually meant to be temporary (14)

leading question a question, asked in court by a lawyer, that suggests a particular answer (19)

lease a written rental agreement between a landlord and a tenant (16)

legal aid society a nonprofit organization that offers free legal services to low-income people (18)

legal clinic an organization that offers low-cost legal services (18)

lemon laws laws that protect people who buy chronically defective cars (15)

liability insurance a contract with an insurance company by which the company agrees to pay the damages for which the insured party is held liable (8)

liable legally responsible (7)

libel written lies that hurt a person's interests or reputation (2)

limited warranty a promise by a seller to repair or replace only certain defective parts of a product (15)

liquidate to sell valuable items to raise cash (15)

liquidated damages the amount of money agreed upon in advance to be paid if either party breaches a contract (9)

litigation the process of resolving a dispute in civil court; a lawsuit (7)

living will a set of instructions describing the kind of medical care a person wants if he or she becomes incompetent (13)

majority opinion a written explanation of a court ruling, reflecting the view of the majority of judges in the case (1)

malice willful intent to hurt someone (8)

malicious mischief destroying or damaging someone's property, either intentionally or through reckless behavior; also called vandalism (4)

mediation the use of a neutral third party to help conflicting parties solve a problem (7)

mediator a neutral third party brought in to help negotiate a settlement between conflicting parties (7)

merchant a person who is in the regular business of selling (15)

minor a person who has not yet reached the age of legal adulthood (9)

Miranda warnings statements law enforcement officers must make to a person at the time of arrest explaining that person's rights, such as the right to remain silent and the right to have a lawyer present during questioning (3)

misdemeanor a crime for which the maximum penalty is less than a year in jail (4)

misrepresentation saying something that is untrue or exaggerated (8)

mistrial an unsuccessful trial, for example, because the jury can't reach a decision (3, 19)

mitigate to reduce, as the amount of damage caused by a breach of contract (9)

mobile home a house built in a factory and towed to a location selected by the owner; also called manufactured housing (16)

month-to-month lease an open-ended rental agreement that in most cases requires the tenant or landlord to give 30 days' notice of intent not to renew (16)

mortgage agreement an agreement by which a lender lends the buyer of a house money, which the buyer pays back with interest in monthly installments (16)

murder killing with the intent to kill or to cause serious bodily injury (4)

necessity doing something because of unavoidable circumstances or natural events; can be a defense in criminal or civil cases (4)

negative option plan a selling plan by which consumers agree to accept unordered products sent by mail (15)

negligence failure to act with reasonable standards of care (8)

negotiation an informal way of settling a dispute by working out an agreement through discussion (7)

no-fault divorce a type of divorce that does not require either spouse to prove fault on the part of the other spouse (12)

nominal damages a small amount of money a defendant in a civil case must pay for having been wrong; also known as damages in name only (7)

notice advance warning given by an employer or an employee who intends to end an employment agreement; warning given by a tenant or a landlord who intends to end a rental agreement (14, 16)

objection a request made by one lawyer during a court proceeding that the judge not allow the opposing lawyer to ask a certain question because it breaks a rule of evidence (19)

obscenity illegal words or pictures portraying sexual matter in an offensive manner (2)

offer a legally binding proposal, needed to make a contract (9)

opening statement a statement made by the lawyer for each side at the beginning of a trial, in which each lawyer outlines the case he or she intends to present (19)

opinion a court's explanation of the legal issues in a case and the precedent on which the explanation is based (1)

original jurisdiction authority of a court to hear a case first (1)

out-of-court settlement an out-of-court agreement reached by the plaintiff and the defendant that ends the dispute and stops the trial (7)

overrule a judge's decision to disagree with an objection made by a lawyer during a court proceeding (19)

overtime payments extra compensation an employer must pay nonsalaried employees who work more than 40 hours a week; required by law to be at least one and a half times an employee's normal hourly rate (14)

palimony support payments made by one member of an unmarried couple to the other member when the couple break up (12)

pardon power of the President and governors to release a person from criminal punishment (1)

parole a system that allows for the release of a prisoner before he or she has served the full sentence (5)

party in a civil case, the defendant and the plaintiff; in a criminal case, the defendant and the prosecutor (19)

paternity suit a lawsuit brought to determine whether a certain man should legally be considered the father of a child (11)

payroll tax payment made by employers and employees to finance government programs that benefit workers, such as social security and unemployment insurance (17)

pension plan a plan by which money is put away for a person's retirement (14)

peremptory challenge the right of a lawyer during jury selection to have a potential juror dismissed without having to give a reason (19)

personal autonomy the right of adults to make decisions about themselves, their bodies, and their property (13)

personal exemption the allowance each payer of income tax receives for himself or herself and for each dependent (17)

petition a document, filed with the juvenile court, that lists the charges against a child and states the facts that support the charges (6)

picket to march in protest; often used to make others aware of an employer's labor practices (14)

plaintiff in a civil action, the person who begins litigation (7)

plea bargain an agreement between a prosecutor and a defendant in a criminal case; the defendant pleads guilty and gives up the right to a trial in exchange for reduced charges or a lighter sentence (5)

polygamy having more than two spouses at the same time (10)

polygraph test a series of questions asked of a person who is hooked up to a machine that measures changes in the person's breathing, pulse, and blood pressure; done to determine whether the person is lying; also called a lie detector test (14)

precedent court decisions that are referred to when courts are making decisions in future similar cases (1)

preliminary hearing in criminal procedure, a type of probable cause hearing during which a judge hears evidence from the prosecutor and the defense attorney and decides whether there is probable cause for a trial (5)

premeditated thought about beforehand (4)

prenuptial agreement a written agreement made before marriage that explains the rights and responsibilities of the husband and wife; also called an antenuptial agreement (10)

preponderance of evidence the standard of proof in a civil trial; a situation in which the evidence only has to support the plaintiff's case better than it supports the defendant's case (7)

presentence report a document prepared by a probation officer that gives a judge information about a defendant's background, education, and behavior, as well as other matters (5)

pretermitted heir a child who is accidentally left out of his or her parent's will (13)

preventive law advance preparation that may help a person avoid a legal problem (18)

principal a person who actually commits a crime (4)

privilege protection from liability; for example, protection given to statements made in the public interest or in the interest of others (8)

probable cause the reasonable belief that a crime has been committed or that a certain person has committed a crime; needed in order to obtain a search warrant or an arrest warrant (3)

probable cause hearing in criminal procedure, a court hearing during which the prosecutor must show that there is reason to believe the defendant is guilty (5)

probate a procedure in which a court establishes a will's validity and distributes the deceased person's estate (13)

probate court a court that has jurisdiction over matters involving the property of people who die (13)

probation a criminal sentence that involves no jail or prison time but requires the criminal to follow certain rules for a fixed amount of time (5)

probation officer a social services professional who supervises criminal defendants and juveniles and helps with their rehabilitation (5)

products liability legal responsibility of manufacturers and sellers for injuries or damage caused by defects in their products (8, 15)

progressive tax a tax that takes a larger percentage of income from high-income people than it does from low-income people (17)

property tax a tax that is based on the value of a piece of land and the buildings on it (17)

proportional tax a tax that takes the same percentage of income from everyone regardless of income level (17)

prosecutor a lawyer who represents the government in a criminal case and whose job it is to prove the defendant guilty; also called the district attorney or the state's attorney (3, 5)

proxy an individual whom a person appoints to speak on his or her behalf (13)

public defender a lawyer assigned by a court to help low-income people who have been accused of crimes (3)

public housing government-owned houses or apartments that are available for rental by low-income families (16)

puffery exaggerated claims made by a seller about a product (15)

punitive damages money that a defendant in a civil case must pay as punishment for breaking a civil law (7)

rape the act of forcing a woman (or in some states any person) to have sexual intercourse or having intercourse with a woman without her consent (4)

ratify to approve or confirm, as a constitution or an amendment (1)

real estate agent an expert in finding, buying, and selling homes (16)

reasonable relationship test the level of scrutiny, or review, a court uses, in which the court determines whether a law satisfies a reasonable government interest and is reasonably related to that interest (2)

recall to ask consumers to return a product they have purchased, usually because the product has been found not to meet Consumer Product Safety Commission standards (15)

redlining a discriminatory practice in which mortgage lenders refuse to make loans to people who buy homes in certain neighborhoods (16)

referee a person who interviews a child who has been taken into custody in the juvenile justice system (6)

reformation a remedy in a civil case in which a court orders a change in a contract (7)

refund money the government returns to those who have overpaid their taxes (17)

regressive tax a tax that takes a larger percentage of income from low-income people than it does from high-income people (17)

rehabilitation a goal of punishment to help a criminal become a law-abiding member of society (5)

rehabilitative alimony alimony that is paid for a short period to give a spouse a chance to enter or reenter the work force and become self-supporting (12)

remedy in civil law, a way to make up for damage that has been done (7)

rent a sum of money paid by a tenant to a landlord for the right to live on the landlord's property (16)

rental agreement a contract giving a tenant the right to live temporarily on property owned by a landlord (16)

rent control laws laws that protect tenants by restricting landlords' right to raise the rent (16)

rent supplement money provided by the government to help low-income tenants afford to live in apartments owned by private landlords (16)

repossess in consumer law, the right of a creditor to take away something bought on credit if the buyer fails to pay the money owed; in housing law, the right of a landlord to require a tenant to move out if the tenant breaches the rental agreement (15, 16)

rescission a remedy in a civil case in which a contract is canceled (7)

rest to conclude a lawyer's presentation of his or her client's case during a trial (19)

restitution in criminal law, repayment by a criminal to his or her victim for items stolen or for damage done; in civil law, the return of a piece of property (5, 7)

retainer a partial payment made by a client to a lawyer before any work is done on the client's case (18)

retaliatory eviction an action by a landlord to remove a tenant from a rental property as revenge for the tenant's complaints (16)

retribution a goal of punishment to get back at a criminal for what he or she has done (5)

revoke to take back or cancel (9, 13)

right to quiet enjoyment the right of a tenant to live in a rented property without being disturbed (16)

robbery taking something from another person through the use of force or threats (4)

rules of evidence rules that lawyers must follow when presenting a case in court, which dictate what information the jury will be allowed to hear (19)

salary a fixed amount of money an employee earns (14)

sales tax money paid by a buyer when purchasing goods (17)

search warrant a court order that authorizes a search of a particular place for evidence in a crime; lists the items the police are looking for and the place where they intend to look for them (3)

second-degree murder killing that is intentional but not premeditated, or killing by outrageously reckless conduct (4)

secondhand smoke smoke from other people's cigarettes (14)

secured credit credit that requires a debtor to provide collateral (15)

security deposit money a tenant pays a landlord before moving into a property to cover damage by the tenant and to cover rent that may be owed (16)

self-incrimination statement a person makes while in custody or in court that may link that person with a crime (3)

separation agreement a contract between married people who are no longer living together; spells out the rights and responsibilities of the couple, including alimony payments and child support and custody arrangements (12)

separation of powers a feature of government that divides the powers and responsibilities of the executive, legislative, and judicial branches so that no branch has too much authority (1)

severance pay a sum of money an employer gives an employee who is fired or laid off (14)

shareholder a person who owns parts, or shares, in a corporation; also called a stockholder (16)

shoplifting taking an item from a store without paying for it or concealing something while in a store with the intent to steal it (4)

slander spoken lies that hurt someone's interests or reputation (2)

small claims court a court that handles disputes over small amounts of money, usually no more than $2,000, and that does not require lawyers (7)

social report a juvenile court report, similar to a presentence report in criminal court, that contains summaries of a child's prior court history, family situation, school record, and psychological profile (6)

solemnize to have a wedding ceremony before a civil or religious authority (10)

solicitation the act of persuading others to commit a crime (4)

specialist a lawyer who has expertise in a limited area of law, such as criminal law, personal injury, or real estate (18)

specific performance a court order requiring a person to do something, such as carry out a contract (7)

standard deduction a fixed amount of money a person can subtract from his or her total income when determining income tax payments (17)

standard of proof the extent to which the plaintiff's lawyer or the prosecutor must go in convincing the jury; in civil law, the standard of proof is a preponderance of evidence; in criminal law, the standard of proof is beyond a reasonable doubt (19)

status offense an act that can be considered wrong only when done by a child (6)

statute a law enacted by a legislative body (1)

statute of limitations a law that sets a time limit for taking legal action (18)

statutory rape the act of a man who has sexual intercourse with a girl under a certain age (usually 16) (4)

steering a discriminatory practice in which real estate agents direct buyers and renters of different races to different neighborhoods (16)

strict liability in criminal law, legal responsibility for committing a crime, even if there was no criminal intent; in civil law, legal responsibility for damage and injury caused by dangerous actions that do not involve negligence or bad intent (4, 8)

strict scrutiny the level of scrutiny, or review, a court uses, in which the court determines whether a law satisfies a compelling government interest and is necessary to meet that interest; used mostly for laws that discriminate on the basis of race or national origin (2)

strike in labor law, to refuse to work until certain employment conditions are changed; at a trial, to remove a witness's answer from the court record (14, 19)

sublet to retain certain tenant's rights under a rental agreement while allowing someone else to occupy that rental unit (16)

subpoena a court order requiring a person to appear in court or deliver a document to court on a specific date (19)

subversive speech illegal speech that represents a danger to national security, such as giving away national secrets during wartime (2)

sue in civil law, to take someone to court (7)

suffrage the right to vote (2)

summary judgment a decision made by a judge that there is no dispute about the facts of a case and that the case can be settled without a trial (19)

surrogate mothering a contractual agreement in which one woman carries and gives birth to a child for another woman (11)

suspended adjudication an order by a juvenile court judge that allows a child to go without restrictions as long as the child stays out of trouble (6)

suspended sentence a criminal sentence that is not carried out as long as the defendant commits no further crimes (5)

sustain a judge's decision to agree with an objection made by a lawyer during a court proceeding (19)

symbolic speech expression of opinions through actions rather than words, such as flag burning (2)

taking against the will taking an elective share; asking the probate court to set aside the will and give a surviving spouse his or her statutory share of the deceased spouse's estate (13)

taxable income after deductions and exemptions, the amount of money on which income taxes must be paid (17)

tax assessor a person who determines a property's value for tax purposes (17)

tax fraud intentional misrepresentation of income in order to avoid paying taxes (17)

tax liability the amount of tax a person must pay (17)

tax revenue the money governments collect to provide services and to pay for public expenses (17)

tax withholding federal and state income tax money withheld by an employer from an employee's paycheck (17)

tenancy in common an ownership agreement by which two people hold separate title to the same property; when one dies, the deceased person's title passes to his or her heirs (16)

tenant a person who rents property (16)

testator a person who writes a will (13)

theft deliberately taking or keeping property that belongs to someone else (4)

title legal ownership, as of a home or car (15, 16)

Title VII of the Civil Rights Act a federal law that forbids employers to consider a person's race, religion, national origin, or sex when making employment decisions (14)

tort any unreasonable action that hurts a person or does damage to a person's property (8)

transcript a court reporter's record of trial proceedings (19)

transfer tax a tax imposed when a person inherits or is given property (17)

trespassing entering someone's property without permission (4)

unconscionable grossly unfair, to the point of offending public standards (9, 10, 15)

unconstitutional conflicting with or interfering with rights guaranteed in the Constitution (1)

unemployment compensation a series of payments the government gives to workers who lose their jobs through no fault of their own (14)

Uniform Commercial Code (UCC) a set of laws establishing the rights and duties of people who buy and sell products (15)

union contract a contract negotiated between elected labor union representatives and an employer on behalf of all the members of the union (14)

unsecured credit credit that does not require the debtor to provide collateral (15)

use tax a tax imposed by a state on purchases made in another state or on goods that are rented or leased (17)

utilities services, such as heat, electricity, and water, provided to a property by a public service company and paid for by the property owner or tenant (16)

VA loan a mortgage loan offered to military veterans, which is guaranteed by the Department of Veterans Affairs (16)

vandalism the crime of destroying or damaging someone's property, either intentionally or through reckless behavior; also called malicious mischief (4)

vehicular homicide causing a death through negligent use of a motor vehicle (4)

veto the power of the President and governors to reject laws passed by the legislature (1)

voir dire a process by which the judge and the lawyers in a case select jurors for the trial (19)

voluntary manslaughter a killing committed in the "heat of passion," when a person is angry and upset and temporarily loses his or her sense of reason and self-control (4)

wages payment for work (14)

waive to give up, as a constitutional right (3)

warrant a court order, signed by a judge, that authorizes a search or an arrest (3)

warranty of fitness for a particular purpose an implied promise by a seller that the product being sold will work for a particular purpose (15)

warranty of merchantability an implied promise by a seller that the product being sold can be used for its ordinary purpose (15)

warranty of title an implied promise by a seller that he or she legally owns the property that is being sold (15)

withholding allowance a claim made by an employee that reduces the amount of income tax money that is taken out of each paycheck (17)

workers' compensation money that covers wages and medical expenses for an employee who is injured on the job (14)

wrongful act violation of the duty to act reasonably (8)

wrongful discharge illegal firing of an employee for reasons such as race, religion, national origin, sex, age (if over 40), joining a union, or protesting unfair treatment (14)

zoning laws local laws that restrict property use (16)

Index

A

Abortion:
 changing legal position on, 44
 privacy rights and, 37
 viewpoints on, 42
Abuse:
 child, 121, 223, 233–237
 drug and alcohol. *See* Alcohol
  abuse; Drug abuse
 sexual, 234
 spouse, 215–216
 of unborn children, 234
Acceptance, in contract law, 181–184
Access, computer, 81–82
Accessory after the fact, 76
Accomplice, 75–76
Accountants, 366, 368, 381
Accused persons, rights of. *See* Criminal justice process, rights of accused in
Acquaintance (date) rape, 79
Acquired immune deficiency syndrome (AIDS):
 discrimination and, 42
 marriage laws and, 209
Acquittal, 64
Act:
 criminal, 73–74
 failure to, in tort law, 165–167
 wrongful, 158
Action lines, 317
Adhesion, contracts of, 189, 309
Adjudication:
 hearing, 126
 inquiry, 126
 suspended, 128
Administrative agencies, 6
Administrative law, 6
Administrator, 266
Adoption, 226–228, 238
Adultery, as grounds for divorce, 247
Ad valorem tax, 360
Advance directive, 276
Adversarial system of justice, 119
Advertising:

corrective, 319
deceptive, 315
substantiation of, required by
 FTC, 319
Affinity, defined, 205
Affirmative action, 40
Affirmative disclosure, 319
Aftercare, in juvenile justice process,
 128
Age:
 for criminal versus juvenile justice, 122
 discrimination based on, 42, 289–290, 345
 of majority, 224
 required for drinking, 84, 441
 required for marriage, 205
 required for voting, 8
Age Discrimination in Employment
 Act of 1967, 42, 289
Agency:
 administrative, 6
 collection, 324–325
 government. *See* Government
Agent, real estate, 340–341
Aggravated:
 assault and battery, 78
 burglary, 82
 robbery, 81
Agreement. *See also* Contract(s)
 cohabitation, 253
 in contract law, 181–184
 employment, 293–296
 lawyer-client, 388
 lease, 331–335. *See also* Lease
 mortgage, 342
 prenuptial, 206–207
 rental, 331. *See also* Lease
 separation, 246
 sales, 308–314
 unconscionable, 207, 189, 309
AIDS. *See* Acquired immune deficiency syndrome (AIDS)
Airports, warrantless searches at, 57
Alcohol:
 driving under the influence of.

See Driving under the influence (DUI)
 minimum drinking age for, 84, 441
 sex discrimination in sale of, 40–41
 taxes on, 359
Alcohol abuse:
 dram shop laws and, 166, 168
 habitual, as divorce grounds, 247
 legal capacity and, 87, 269
 tests for, 85, 94, 299–300. *See also* Drug testing
 unborn children and, 234
 vehicular homicide and, 85, 94
 vehicular manslaughter and, 106
 warrantless searches and, 56
Alimony:
 on annulment, 245
 barkrupcy and, 252
 defined, 245
 on divorce, 251–253
 rehabilitative, 252
 tax returns and, 366
 unmarried couples and, 214, 252–253
Alterations of leased premises, 338
Amendments, 8, 10, 17. *See also* Bill of Rights; specific amendments passed after Civil War, 36, 39
American Civil Liberties Union
 (ACLU), 396
American flag:
 burning of, 34
 peace symbol taped to, 34
 pledge of allegiance to, 26, 31
American Nazi party, 36
American Revolution, 7, 27
Americans with Disabilities Act of
 1990, 42, 290
Amish religion, 31–32
Anatomical donations, 279–280
Anatomical gift acts, 279
Annulment, 244–245
Answer (in lawsuit), 140
Antenuptial agreement, 206–207

U

Photo Credits

Chapter 1   p. 2: Michal Bryant/Woodfin Camp & Associates, Inc.; p. 5: Don Smetzer/Tony Stone Worldwide; p. 8: Bob Doemmrich/STOCK, BOSTON; p. 11: Rick Reinhard/Impact Visuals; p. 18: The Supreme Court/© Nat. Geo. Society

Chapter 2   p. 25: UPI/BETTMAN; p. 27: Historical Pictures Services; p. 29: F.M. Kearney/Impact Visuals; p. 31: Bill Gillette/STOCK, BOSTON; p. 31: Thomas B. Hollyman/PHOTO Researchers, Inc.; p. 35: UPI/BETTMAN NEWSPHOTOS; p. 37: THE BETTMANN ARCHIVE; p. 41: Michal Heron/Woodfin Camp & Associates, Inc.; p. 42: Bob Daemmrich/STOCK, BOSTON

Chapter 3   p. 48: Teri Gilman/Tony Stone; p. 53: Richard Pasley/STOCK, BOSTON; p. 55: © Michael Jaeqqi; p. 57: David Young-Wolff/Photo Edit; p. 61: Paul Conklin/Photo Edit; p. 62: Mary Kate Denny/Photo Edit

Chapter 4   p. 72: Renee Lynn/PHOTO Researchers, Inc.; p. 74: Paul Conklin/Photo Edit; p. 78: Kenneth Jarecke/Woodfin Camp & Associates, Inc.; p. 80: Richard Hutchings/PHOTO Researchers, Inc.; p. 82: Deborah Davis/Photo Edit; p. 83: Jim Pickerell/Tony Stone Worldwide; p. 84: David Vita/Impact Visuals

Chapter 5   p. 93: Don Smetzer/Tony Stone Worldwide; p. 97: Brian Seed/Tony Stone Worldwide; p. 101: © John Livzey; p. 104: Jim Pickerell/Tony Stone Worldwide; p. 106: Wasyl Szkodzinsky/PHOTO Researchers, Inc.; p. 108: © John Livzey

Chapter 6   p. 116: Richard Hutchings/PHOTO Researchers, Inc.; p. 118: James L. Shaffer/Photo Edit; p. 121: Dorothy Littell/STOCK, BOSTON; p. 125: Blair Seitz/PHOTO Researchers, Inc.; p. 129: UPI/BETTMANN

Chapter 7   p. 136: © Mike Jaeggi; p. 139: Robert Brenner/Photo Edit; p. 143: Larry Mulvehill/Science Source/PHOTO Researchers, Inc.

Chapter 8   p. 156: Bohdan Hrynewych/STOCK, BOSTON; p. 158: Mike Jaeggi/Meyers Photo Art; p. 160: David Young-Wolff/Photo Edit; p. 162: Rafael Macia/PHOTO Researchers, Inc.; p. 166: Bob Daemmrich/STOCK, BOSTON; p. 170: Evan Johnson/Impact Visuals; p. 172: Elizabeth Zuckerman/Photo Edit

Chapter 9   p. 178: David Young-Wolff/Photo Edit; p. 185: Al Henderson/Tony Stone Worldwide; p. 189: Lawrence Migdale/PHOTO Researchers, Inc.; p. 195: © John Livzey

Chapter 10   p. 202: Myrleen Ferguson/Photo Edit; p. 210: Robert Goldwitz/PHOTO Researchers, Inc.; p. 212: Robert Brenner/Photo Edit; p. 213: James D. Wilson/Woodfin Camp & Associates, Inc.; p. 215: Bill Aron/Photo Edit

Chapter 11   p. 222: Myrleen Ferguson/Photo Edit; p. 225: Leif Skoogfors/Woodfin Camp & Associates, Inc.; p. 227: Myrleen Ferguson/Photo Edit; p. 229: Rich Gigli/Sygma; p. 231: Lawrence Midgale/STOCK, BOSTON; p. 234: David Young-Wolff/Photo Edit

Chapter 12   p. 242: Barbara Filet/Tony Stone Worldwide; p. 245: Jerry Howard/STOCK, BOSTON; p. 247: Will & Deni McIntyre/PHOTO Researchers, Inc.; p. 250: David Young-Wolff/Photo Edit; p. 251: David Young-Wolff/Photo Edit;p. 257: Rick Browne/STOCK, BOSTON

Chapter 13   p. 263: Owen Franken/STOCK, BOSTON; p. 269: Paul Conklin/Photo Edit; p. 272: Nathan Benn/Woodfin Camp & Associates, Inc.; p. 274: Joseph Nettis/STOCK, BOSTON

Chapter 14   p. 286: Max MacKenzie/Tony Stone Worldwide; p. 288: John Coletti/STOCK, BOSTON; p. 290: Laima Druskis/STOCK, BOSTON; p. 292: Tony Freeman/Photo Edit; p. 294: Donna Binder/Impact Visuals; p. 297: Michael Grecco/STOCK, BOSTON; p. 300: Miro Vintoniv/STOCK, BOSTON; p. 302: Cary Wolinsky/Tony Stone Worldwide

Chapter 15   p. 307: Rhoda Sidney/Photo Edit; p. 310: Brent Jones/STOCK, BOSTON; p. 314: Michael Newman/Photo Edit; p. 320: Robert Brenner/Photo Edit

Chapter 16   p. 330: Rafael Macia/PHOTO Researchers, Inc.; p. 334: John Lei/STOCK, BOSTON; p. 336: Tony Freeman/Photo Edit; p. 340: Wolinsky/STOCK, BOSTON; 343: John Feingersh/STOCK, BOSTON; p. 345: Blair Seitz/PHOTO Researchers, Inc.

Chapter 17   p. 351: David Woo/STOCK, BOSTON; p. 360: Blair Seitz/PHOTO Researchers, Inc.; p. 367: Michael Newman/Photo Edit; p. 369: © Mike Jaeggi

Chapter 18   p. 378: Tony Freeman/Photo Edit; p. 380: Alon Reininger/Woodfin Camp & Associates, Inc.; p. 383: Catherine Karnow/Woodfin Camp & Associates, Inc.; p. 384: John Running/STOCK, BOSTON; p. 385: Robert V. Eckert Jr./STOCK, BOSTON; p. 387: Mary Kate Denny/Photo Edit; p. 394: Thomas Bowman/Photo Edit; p. 396: Michael Newman/Photo Edit

Chapter 19   p. 402: Bob Daemmrich/STOCK, BOSTON; p. 404: © Mike Jaeggi; p. 406: John Neubauer/Photo Edit; p. 407: James L. Shaffer/Photo Edit; p. 410: Billy Barnes/STOCK, BOSTON; p. 413: Bob Daemmrich/STOCK, BOSTON; p. 414: Robert Brenner/Photo Edit; p. 417: © Jim Pickerell